The Directory of
RELIGIOUS ORGANIZATIONS
in the United States

The Directory of
RELIGIOUS ORGANIZATIONS
in the United States

Second Edition

A Consortium Book
McGrath Publishing Company
Falls Church, Virginia

Printed and bound in the United States of America

ISBN-0-8434-0757-3

INTRODUCTION

The second edition of THE DIRECTORY OF RELIGIOUS ORGANIZATIONS IN THE UNITED STATES describes 1,628 organizations active in the field of religion. The first edition of the DIRECTORY described 1,569 organizations, of which 328 were religious orders and 1,241 were general organizations. The second edition includes only general organizations.

The 1,628 general organizations in the second edition of the DIRECTORY, up from 1,241 in the first edition, represent an increase of 31 percent, which reflects the increasing size and complexity of religion in American life. The organizations include departments of national churches, professional associations, volunteer groups, government agencies, businesses, foundations and fraternal societies. The word organization is used to define all groups having in common a religious purpose that directs their widely varied works.

In defining general religious organizations, it is important to bear in mind that, while the DIRECTORY describes certain departments of national churches (as well as the Campaign for Human Development of the United States Catholic Conference) it does not describe religious bodies (such as the Catholic Church). Religious bodies are fully described, both historically and theologically, in THE ENCYCLOPEDIA OF AMERICAN RELIGIONS. Religious orders are described in THE DIRECTORY OF RELIGIOUS ORDERS IN THE UNITED STATES.

The DIRECTORY describes organizations that are secular as well as church affiliated and includes organizations from all denominations and sects, both major and minor. Small and obscure organizations as well as large and prominent ones are described. The DIRECTORY does not separate organizations by denomination, but church affiliation is indicated.

The DIRECTORY lists the 1,628 organizations in one alphabet. Within that list there are religious organizations that have many different purposes. Some of the most common purposes are:

Evangelical organizations: Such organizations proselytize within the United States or support such work. Many such organizations focus their work in distributing the printed scripture or in conducting radio campaigns.

Academic and Educational: Such organizations are learned societies and professional organizations in the fields of religious education, higher education and such disciplines as theology and church history.

Media: Such organizations publish books, magazines, or newspapers or produce radio and television programs.

Foreign Missionary Work: Such organizations proselytize outside of the United States or support the work of organizations that proselytize outside of the United States.

Spiritual Life: Such organizations have as their principal purpose the personal sanctification and spiritual enrichment of their members.

Social Justice: Such organizations address the social problems of our time on the national and international levels: sexism, racism, drug and alcohol abuse, health services and poverty.

There are as well many other types of organizations that support professional purposes, ecumenical goals and a variety of special ministries that amplify the pastoral aims of the American churches by ministry to special groups: students, prisoners, military personnel, the poor, and other groups toward whom the churches make special efforts. Many other organizations support the work of the churches by addressing questions of liturgical reform, fund raising, vocation development, retreats and revivals, and various other activities that lend special strength to regular parochial ministry.

Each organization in the DIRECTORY is described in thorough detail, including complete name, address, telephone number, name of the chief executive officer, membership and staff statistics, religious affiliations, and former names. The purpose and work of the organization are discussed in about 200 words and the specific activities, programs and projects of the organization are listed. These specific activities include such details as schools, colleges, seminaries, research centers and programs, hospitals and homes of the aged, orphanages, publications of books, magazines and newsletters, bookstores, radio and television stations or programs and meetings or conventions.

The information on each organization was derived from a questionnaire completed by that organization. Those organizations that did not complete a questionnaire, but relied on the information that they provided for the first edition of the DIRECTORY, are marked with an asterisk. The editors would like to express their gratitude to the organizations that patiently and carefully responded to the questionnaires. The editors will appreciate the comments and criticism of the readers, so that future editions of the DIRECTORY will be of increased utility.

RELIGIOUS ORGANIZATIONS

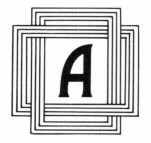

1. A J Holman Company

Nondenominational
James W. Clark, President
127 Ninth Avenue, North
Nashville, Tennessee 37234
(615) 251-2510

A J Holman is the oldest American Bible publisher, having begun in Philadelphia in 1801. The purpose of the company is to facilitate the bringing of men to God through the scriptures. To do that it publishes the Bible in five versions — King James, New American Standard, Revised Standard, Lamsa, and Beck — and in many editions from simple text to elaborate study Bibles and in bindings ranging from paper to the most expensive leathers.

Founding Date: 1801
Staff: 9

2. aaa Church Building Services, Inc.

Nondenominational
Charles R. Akers, AIA, President
CBS Building
Highway 32-E
Crawfordsville, Indiana 47933
(317) 362-2560

Church Buildings Services specializes in building services for churches and related institutions. Three main areas of service are available: Building Program Analysis, a feasibility study of growth potential, financial capability, and housing needs; Architectural/Engineering Services, normal services as defined by the AIA; Construction Management Services, the actual construction of the building.

Staff: 6
Former Name: Christian Building Services, Inc.

3. Abbey Press

Roman Catholic
Rupert Ostdick, OSB
29 Hill Drive
St. Meinrad, Indiana 47577
(812) 357-8011

The purpose of the Abbey Press is the enrichment of Christian family living through publications, recordings, greeting cards, and gift items. Abbey Press is part of St. Meinrad Archabbey, a religious and not-for-profit corporation which conducts Saint Meinrad College and Saint Meinrad School of Theology, training schools for the education of young men for the priesthood.

Staff: 275
Publications:

> *Marriage and Family Living,* a special interest, ecumenical monthly that is devoted to the enrichment of married life and family living

4. Abraham Lincoln Centre*

Unitarian Universalist Association
Othello R. Ellis, Executive Director
3858 South Cottage Grove Avenue
Chicago, Illinois 60653
(312) 373-6600

The Abraham Lincoln Centre strives "for the advancement of the physical, intellectual, social, civic, moral, cultural and religious interests of the community without restrictions as to age, sex, race, creed, color or economic circumstances." It provides high-priority social services, family and individual counseling, and group services (social development); recruits and trains professionals and volunteers in social work; operates a day-care center for pre-school children and a feeding program for two other day-care schools; provides special education for mentally retarded and disturbed school-age children; provides camping services through other resources and a program of health and physical education with emphasis upon physical fitness; operates a summer day camp; provides vocational counseling, job recruitment and placement, varied recreation programs, special interest groups of youth, adults, and senior citizens, and an arts program of music, dance, dramatics, and photography. The programs are supported by private funds, voluntary contributions, government contracts, and grants.

5. Academy of American Franciscan History

Roman Catholic
Alexander Wyse, OFM, Director
Post Office Box 34440
Washington, D.C. 20034
(301) 365-1763

The Academy of American Franciscan History is an institution for scholarly research into the history of the Order of Friars Minor (founded by St. Francis of Assisi in 1209) under the prism of its contribution to the development of the New World. The core group — presently seven resident members who constitute the community of the Friary of Our Lady of Guadalupe in Potomac, Maryland — is assisted by Associate Members (other Franciscan scholars in many parts of the world) and Corresponding Members (secular scholars from libraries, universities, and other centers of learning in scores of countries). The Academy aims to discover and publish (in the original and/or translation) the primary sources for the record of the Franciscan presence and action, and also to stimulate and foster creative studies on diverse aspects of the Franciscan contribution in all the countries of North, Central, and South America. Naturally, there is an emphasis on the missions in territories once subject to the Spanish Crown, outstanding examples of which are the missions in the Southwest and in Florida. From time to time, the Academy confers "The Serra Award of the Americas" for outstanding contributions to inter-American understanding and good-will.

Founding Date: 1944
Staff: 7
Membership: 250
Publications:
> *The Americas*, a quarterly review of inter-American cultural history

Meetings:
> Occasional conferences on the premises of the Academy

6. Academy of Homiletics

Nondenominational
Prof. Donald Macleod, Secretary
Princeton Theological Seminary
Post Office Box 101
Princeton, New Jersey 08540
(609) 921-8300

The American Academy of Homiletics is a learned society which meets annually for three days on the campus of Princeton Theological Seminary. The members are all teachers of homiletics (the art and science of preaching) in theological seminaries or schools throughout the United States and Canada. Scholarly papers are read, lectures are given, discussions of pedagogical methods are held, and bibliographical resources are shared.

Founding Date: 1966
Membership: 85 clerical
Former Name:
> (1978) American Academy of Homiletics

7. Academy of Parish Clergy

Interdenominational
Dr. Glen O. Peterman, Executive Vice-President
Post Office Box 86
Princeton, New Jersey 08540
(201) 369-3365

The Academy of Parish Clergy is a nationwide, interfaith organization of ministers, priests, and rabbis who are helping each other grow in the arts and skills of a congregation-based ministry. It focuses upon the congregation as the primary place of clergy growth and fosters the formation of local colleague groups for case study sharing. Academy members accept the discipline of 150 clock hours of continuing education each triennium, half of which is within and half beyond the congregation. The Academy provides counsel to members in designing the programs of growth which are suited to their needs, resources, and incomes. A computerized Data Bank enables the clergy to share their knowledge with each other and with the profession as a whole. The Academy is affiliated with the Association of Theological Schools and the Society for the Advancement of Continuing Education in Ministry.

Founding Date: 1969
Staff: 3
Membership: 500
Publications:
> *Sharing the Practice*, a bimonthly journal

Meetings:
> Annual convocation at various locations throughout the United States

8. Accent Publications, Inc.

Baptist
Dr. Robert L. Mosier
12100 West Sixth Avenue
Denver, Colorado 80215

Mailing Address
Post Office Box 15337
Denver, Colorado 80215
(303) 988-5300

The purpose of Accent Publications, Inc., is two-fold: first, it publishes Sunday School material and other Christian Education courses for use in churches; second, it publishes a line of inspirational paperback books dealing with a wide range of subjects.

Founding Date: 1946
Staff: 80 plus
Publications:
> *Success,* Magazine for Christian Educators, quarterly

Former Name: Baptist Publications, Inc.

9. Action International Ministries (AIM)

Interdenominational
Doug Nichols, International Director
10026 Main Street
Bothell, Washington 98011

Mailing Address:
Post Office Box 490
Bothell, Washington 98011
(206) 485-1967

The purpose of Action International Ministries is to help fulfill the Great Commission of Jesus Christ. Its ministries include evangelism, discipleship, and human development. Among the activities of AIM are: underprivileged children's camps, gospel ad-evangelism, film evangelism, relief, open air evangelism, summer intern programs, publications, literature ministry, film production, rehabilitation, etc.

Founding Date: 1975
Staff: 8
Membership: 35
Publications:
> *Action News*, quarterly

Meetings:
> Annual conference for missionaries of AIM, 1 in the Philippines, 1 in the United States

10. ACTS International

Nondenominational
Rev. Richard W. Innes, Executive Director
3928 Floral Avenue
Claremont, California 91711
(714) 593-5746

ACTS International is a Christian communications organization whose main objective is to share the gospel with every family in Australia and New Zealand. This is done chiefly through mail evangelism, radio ad-evangelism, and publishing literature for local churches to help them reach their communities with the gospel and Christian message. Seminars, counseling, cassettes, books, and Home Study Bible Courses support the major ministries, as do public church services. The United States office helps support the overseas work and is now making outreach literature available to home churches.

Staff: 20
Membership: 50 corporation members
Publications:
> *Encounter 80,* monthly
> Encounter leaflets for church distribution

Radio/TV Programs:
> One-minute radio spots are used in Australia

Meetings:
> Seminars on Communications and Personal Life Enrichment are conducted in Australia, 10 per year
> Public meetings, 25 per year

11. Adult Christian Education Foundation (ACEF)*

Interdenominational
Dr. Harley A. Swiggum, Executive Director
The Yahara Center
Post Office Box 8398
Madison, Wisconsin 53708
(608) 849-5933

The Adult Christian Education Foundation is sponsor of the Bethel Series used in denominations in the United States, Canada, and five foreign countries. The Bethel Series is not a Sunday morning Bible course, but a long range program that assists the church to involve more adults in the study of Scripture, develop lay leadership to carry on adult study, and present an overview study of the Bible that is essential to more meaningful Sunday school teaching, lay witnessing, and sermon listening. The local minister is responsible for a theological approach to lesson content. The program does not replace denominational materials, but strengthens the use of them. The new Yahara Center of the Foundation is a beautiful, 150-person conference facility for the ACEF program and is available for meetings of any other organization.

Founding Date: 1959

Staff: 65

Membership:

Involvement in 3,800 churches, 17 denominations, 65,000 trained teachers, and 740,000 students

Meetings:

Organized programs in the United States, Canada, Japan, Korea, Thailand, and Australia

12. Advent Christian Church, Woman's Home and Foreign Mission Society*

Advent Christian Church

Mrs. Jean P. Balser, Executive Secretary and Treasurer
Post Office Box 23152
Charlotte, North Carolina 28212
(704) 545-6161

The Woman's Home and Foreign Mission Society is the women's work of the Advent Christian Church. Its purpose is to engage and unite the efforts of the women of the denomination in sending the Gospel throughout the world. Further, it seeks to deepen spiritual life among believers in Christ, and, through organization, to render more efficient the work of the women of the churches.

Membership: 5,000 lay

Publications:

Advent Christian Missions, monthly

Meetings:

Biennial meeting

13. AFFIRMATION, Gay and Lesbian Mormons

The Church of Jesus Christ of Latter-day Saints

Paul Mortensen, General Secretary
Post Office Box 46022
Los Angeles, California 90046
(213) 851-1695

The purpose of AFFIRMATION is to bring together all gay and lesbian Mormons and interested friends for social interaction, education and dialogue, and spiritual development. The ultimate goal is towards understanding, tolerance, and eventual acceptance of gay persons as full, equal, and worthy members of the Church.

Founding Date: 1978

Staff: 25

Membership: 500

Publications:

General newsletter, monthly
Chapter newsletters, monthly

Meetings:

Annual general conference

14. Afghan Border Crusade (ABC)

Interdenominational

Bob Waymire, Chairman
1107 Mayette Avenue
San Jose, California 95125
(408) 448-2144

The Afghan Border Crusade is an evangelical, international, and interdenominational faith mission which aims to evangelize the Pathans and tribespeople in and around the frontier area of Pakistan, formerly the famous North West Frontier Province of India. It is thrusting laborers into this difficult harvest field as the Lord provides, and seeking to evangelize these people by means of itinerant and localized work and the establishment of churches. Literature, gospels, and Bibles are sold whenever possible, but where there are those too poor to buy, the literature is given free of charge. Book rooms, dispensaries, camps, conferences, evangelistic meetings, and Bible schools are also used to spread the Gospel light.

Founding Date: 1945

Staff: 5 in the United States

Membership: 14 field workers

Publications:
   Prayer Bulletin, quarterly
Meetings:
   3 board meetings per year
Former Name: ABC Mission

15. Africa Evangelical Fellowship

Nondenominational
Rev. Robert Fine, Executive Director
733 Bloomfield Avenue
Bloomfield, New Jersey 07003

Mailing Address
Post Office Box 1679
Bloomfield, New Jersey 07003
(201) 748-9281

Africa Evangelical Fellowship is a nondenominational, international evangelical sending agency. The prime objectives are to preach the Gospel, to establish believers in the faith, and to assist them to maturity in a fellowship of local churches in the field. Evangelism, aviation, literature, education, and radio and TV workshops help carry out these objectives. Dr. Andrew Murray, a pastor in Capetown, South Africa, and Spencer Walton, a lay preacher of England, founded the agency, originally called the Cape General Mission. When its outreach spread north of the Cape, it became the South Africa General Mission, with services for the Lord in seven central and southern African countries. In 1964 the name was changed to Africa Evangelical Fellowship with sending councils in England, Canada, the United States, Republic of South Africa, Australia, and New Zealand.

Founding Date: 1889
Staff: 40 in 5 home councils
Membership: 133 foreign missionaries
Publications:
   African Evangel, quarterly
   Family News, a quarterly prayer sheet
Radio/TV Programs:
   Radio and TV programs in Zambia
   Radio programs in Swaziland, South Africa, Botswana, Rhodesia, and Malawi
Meetings:
   Meetings of the council every 2 months
   Annual Weekend Family Conference in May at the Tuscarora Inn, Mount Bethel, Pennsylvania
   Annual banquet in October at the Wayne Manor, Wayne, New Jersey

Former Names:
   (1844) Cape General Mission
   (1964) South Africa General Mission

16. Africa Inland Mission (AIM)

Interdenominational
Rev. Peter Stam, Director
Post Office Box 178
Pearl River, New York 10965
(914) 735-4014

The Africa Inland Mission is an interdenominational, international organization of more than 800 missionaries working in Central and East Africa, the islands of the Indian Ocean, and the urban centers of the United States. Its objectives are to fulfill the mandate of the Greater Commission in Matthew 28:19-20 to preach the Gospel into all the world, to recruit missionary personnel and train them for missionary service, to plant churches that will outlast the missionary presence, to assist national churches in their growth and development, and to create a growing missionary spirit among the home constituency. The Mission has established more than 3,000 places of worship, dozens of secondary schools, two seminaries, 12 hospitals, 45 dispensaries, two orphanages, 12 bookstores, three printing presses, a radio studio, and three schools for missionary children in Africa.

Founding Date: 1895
Publications:
   Inland Africa, a quarterly informational journal on the activities of the Africa Inland Mission
   Kesho, a monthly magazine in Swahili for East African readers
   Today, a bimonthly magazine in English for East African readers
Staff: 75
Membership: 738 missionary members
Radio/TV Programs:
   Approximately 100 radio programs monthly over Voice of Kenya
   Occasional TV programs over Voice of Kenya
   Weekly missionary program for American audience
Meetings:
   Hundreds of missionary conferences, meetings, and seminars conducted throughout the year

17. Africa Inter-Mennonite Mission (AIMM)

Mennonite

James E. Bertsche, Executive Secretary
224 West High Street
Elkhart, Indiana 46514
(219) 294-3711

Africa Inter-Mennonite Mission is an agency which coordinates the missions outreach of several Mennonite groups into Africa. Since its founding in 1911, the services of some 230 missionaries have given birth to a church of over 35,000 baptized members and have helped meet many kinds of human needs. Mennonites have traditionally blended spiritual and social ministries. While maintaining its original purpose to preach the Gospel of Christ by word and deed to every creature and to build His church, AIMM pursues a strategy geared to the rapid socio-political changes on the continent. AIMM is now serving in Zaire, Botswana, Lesotho, and Upper Volta.

Founding Date: 1911

Staff: 60 ordained pastors in Zaire

Membership: 35,000

Publications:
  AIMM Messenger, quarterly
  Contact, newsletter, eight times a year

Radio/TV Programs:
  Religious programming in Tshiluba

Meetings:
  Biennial missionary retreats held in Zaire
  Annual retreats jointly sponsored with other Mennonite groups in Botswana, Lesotho, and Upper Volta

18. African Enterprise (AE)

Nondenominational

Keith Jesson, Executive Director
232 North Lake Avenue, Suite 200
Pasadena, California 91101
(213) 796-5830

African Enterprise raises financial and prayer support for teams of national evangelists working in East and South Africa. At the invitation of and in cooperation with local African churches, the teams hold clergy and lay training courses and evangelistic missions. Reconciliation is the primary goal of the AE evangelists. They teach the spiritual oneness in Christ that overcomes racial, cultural, denominational, and political barriers. An outgrowth of preaching the whole Gospel has been a lunch program in South Africa, where thousands of school children are given a daily hot meal and minor medical aid. A program in East Africa has provided sponsorship for hundreds of refugee college students, as well as relief and medical aid to thousands of war-ravaged Ugandans.

Founding Date: 1962

Staff: 52 staff members; 30 team evangelists

Publications:
  Outlook, a monthly newsletter

Radio/TV Programs:
  Radio programs in the United States, Lesotho, Swaziland, and East Africa.

Meetings:
  22 clergy conferences
  54 preaching missions
  2 conferences

19. African Methodist Episcopal Church, Department of Education*

African Methodist Episcopal Church

Dr. Sherman L. Greene, Jr., Executive Secretary
1461 Northgate Road, N.W.
Washington, D.C. 20012
(202) 723-6147

The Department of Education of the African Methodist Episcopal Church promotes development of curricular and extracurricular programs in institutions of higher education designed to fulfill the purpose and mission of the A M E Church; solicits and develops financial support of universities, colleges, and theological seminaries sponsored by the A M E Church; promotes and conducts Leadership Training Programs for ministers and laymen serving in the A M E Church; recruits students for A M E colleges and seminaries; and promotes Campus Christian Life Programs for A M E students in church-related, private, and tax supported institutions of higher education.

Membership: 8 lay; 9 clerical

Meetings:
  2 conferences and 6 other meetings per year

20. African Methodist Episcopal Zion Church, Department of Foreign Missions*

African Methodist Episcopal Zion Church
Bishop William A. Hilliard, Chairman
475 Riverside Drive, Room 1910
New York, New York 10027
(212) 749-2952

The Department of Foreign Missions promotes the cause of world missions in the African Methodist Episcopal Zion Church. It promotes the knowledge of Jesus Christ as the Divine Saviour to all people in all lands. It persuades them to become His disciples and, in turn, to form the Christian Churches for building the Kingdom of God.

Founding Date: 1875
Membership: 1,075 lay; 1,355 clerical
Publications:
    The Missionary Seer, monthly
Meetings:
    4 annual conferences
    4 seminars
    4 Christian education conventions and workshops

21. African Mission Services, Inc. (AMS)

Interdenominational
A.E.K. Brenner, President
1012 City Avenue
Philadelphia, Pennsylvania 19151
(215) 642-2255

African Mission Services, Inc., is a non-profit organization staffed by volunteers who provide assistance to missionaries, mission stations, and other evangelical ministries throughout Africa with whatever their needs may be and at little or no cost. Food, religious, pharmaceutical, and medical supplies, educational materials and maintenance parts, fuel, and vehicles are purchased in South Africa or in the United States and shipped to most African nations. Concerned Christians throughout the world support AMS with their prayers and their financial gifts. Some manufacturers and suppliers donate their products.

22. Agudath Israel of America

Jewish
Rabbi Morris Sherer, President
5 Beekman Street, Suite 910
New York, New York 10038
(212) 964-1620

Agudath Israel of America is a broadly-based Orthodox Jewish movement with chapters in communities throughout the United States and Canada. It sponsors a wide range of constructive projects in the fields of religion, education, children's welfare, and social action. The organization's leaders include the nation's most respected rabbinic scholars, and its constituents consist of a comprehensive coalition of Orthodox Jews from every walk of life.

Founding Date: 1921
Staff: 165
Membership: 80,000
Publications:
    The Jewish Observer, an English-language monthly on Jewish affairs
    Dos Yiddishe Vort, a Yiddish-language monthly on Jewish affairs
    Agudah News Reporter, a newsletter with review of events and activities in the Agudath Israel Movement
Meetings:
    World congress, every several years
    Annual conventions, held in Rye Town Hilton, Portchester, New York
    Annual dinner, held in New York Hilton
    Annual breakfast conference on Social Concerns, held in New York Hilton

23. Aid Association for Lutherans

Lutheran
Henry F. Scheig, President
4321 North Ballard Road
Appleton, Wisconsin 54919
(414) 734-5721

Aid Association for Lutherans is a fraternal benefit society providing life, health, and annuity insurance and ther fraternal, social, and educational benefits to $1.3 million of the nation's nine million Lutherans. Assets of $2.5 billion and life insurance in force of 14.5 billion place it as number 28 among the nation's 2,000 life insurers. Its members belong to 5,700 local branches. It provides many fraternal benefits in the areas of scholarships, support for Lutheran high schools, seminaries and colleges, special projects of national church bodies, supplemental funds for fund raising activities of its local branches, and many other programs. In 1981 it invested $27.5 million in various kinds of fraternal benefits and returned $117.2 million in surplus refunds to its members.

Founding Date: 1902

Staff: 2,600

Membership: 1.3 million

Publications:

> *Correspondent*
> *Branching Out*
> *Common Concerns*
> *Who's Who, Update*
> Ten newsletters

Meetings:

> Hundreds of thousands, including local meetings

24. AIM, Inc. (Assistance in Missions)

Nondenominational

Richard Calmquist, President
9003 Terhune Avenue
Sun Valley, California 91352
(213) 257-8969

The purpose of AIM, Inc., is to assist missionaries home on furlough by providing automobiles to meet their transportation needs. These are automobiles that have been donated by interested individuals; they are fixed up and made available to missionaries on a first-come, first-serve basis. Automobiles are available only from the Los Angeles headquarters. Upkeep and normal maintenance are the responsibility of the missionary while he is driving the car. AIM asks, but does not charge, $25 per month for the use of the car to cover its expenses.

Founding Date: 1960

Staff: 5

25. Alba House

Roman Catholic

Rev. Anselm J. Viano, SSP, Superior Publisher
2187 Victory Boulevard
Staten Island, New York 10314
(212) 761-0047

As a part of its world-wide mission (of the Society of Saint Paul which is established in 22 countries), Alba House at Staten Island is engaged in publication of books dealing with theology, scripture, religion-information, and Christian education. In recent years it has averaged about 16 new titles per year, although in the last two years this number of titles has somewhat declined. The staff at Alba House consists largely of members (brothers and priests) of the Society of Saint Paul who work without salary. In recent years, however, it has become necessary to augment its staff with salaried employees. The members are engaged in this mission in an effort to help spread the Good News, working for the glory of God and to bring peace to their fellow persons.

Staff: 3 lay; 15 clerical-religious

26. Alba House Communications

Roman Catholic

Rev. Edmund Lane, SSP, Director
Post Office Box 595
Canfield, Ohio 44406-0595
(216) 533-5503

Alba House Communications is a publisher and distributor of religious sound filmstrips, records, cassettes, 16mm films, and multi/media kits. New products of interest to the religious education market are published annually. Alba House Communications is operated by the Society of St. Paul as part of its communications ministry.

Staff: 30 lay; 10 clerical religious

Publications:

> 20 books (paperback); 29 cassette programs; 8 multi-media programs; 20 sound filmstrips; 15 lp records and cassettes; 3 16mm films; religious multi-media catalogues

27. The Alban Institute, Inc.

Interdenominational

Loren B. Mead, Executive Director
Mt. St. Alban
Washington, D.C. 20016
(202) 244-3588

The Alban Institute is an ecumenical organization for research and development in religious systems, focusing on the life and work of the local congregation. It operates through a small central office in

Washington, linked to a broad network of persons engaged in attempts to increase the effectiveness and substance of the local congregation. It seeks to gather and generate knowledge. The Institute is an open partnership of people who want to improve the quality of religious life and religious institutions. The Institute exists to provide two kinds of support: making information available — the Institute is a network linking people who are finding out how to do the job with those who need to know, making information available through publications (books, study guides, papers, and *Action Information*, its quarterly journal) and also through training events, referrals, and direct consultative and advisory services; and learning from experience. As an organization concerned for church research and development, the Alban Institute is in business to help congregations learn from looking at experience, their own and that of others. In some cases this means locating or supporting practical research efforts already under way; in other cases it means initiating new work. The Institute is a private, non-profit, tax-exempt, nondenominational corporation in the District of Columbia.

Founding Date: 1974

Staff: 16

Membership: 4,000 plus

Publications:
> A variety of books, monographs, and research reports.

28. The All-Church-Press, Inc.

Nondenominational
Lambuth Tomlinson, Publisher
1200 West Berry Street
Ft. Worth, Texas 76101
Mailing Address:
Post Office Box 1159
Fort Worth, Texas 76101
(817) 926-2411

The All-Church-Press is the nation's largest publisher of religious newspapers.

Founding Date: 1912

Publications:
> *Dallas World; Fort Worth Tribune; Houston Times; Memphis Mirror; Oklahoma City Star; Tulsa Herald; Wichita Light; Churchweek;* and *Register* system newspapers

Meetings:
> 3 seminars per year

29. Alleluia Press

Interdenominational
Dr. José M. de Vinck, Owner
672 Franklin Turnpike
Allendale, New Jersey 07401
Mailing Address:
Post Office Box 103
Allendale, New Jersey 07401
(201) 327-3513

Alleluia Press publishes books on theology, philosophy, and Byzantine liturgy and music. Specializing in works of first-rate scholarship and high typographical quality, the Press offers qualified authors complete editorial and design service for works published either at their expense or, if acceptable, as Alleluia Press books. The Press distributes throughout the English-speaking countries, as well as Germany, Italy, Holland, and Sweden. Most of the books are printed in Belgium for reasons of credit, quality, and economy.

Staff: 1

30. Alpha Sigma Nu

Roman Catholic
Richard J. Panlener, Executive Director
1324 West Wisconsin Avenue
Milwaukee, Wisconsin 53233
(414) 224-7542

Alpha Sigma Nu is the National Jesuit Honor Society. Its main purposes are to honor students of Jesuit colleges and universities who distinguish themselves in scholarship, loyalty, and service; to band together and encourage those so honored, both as students and as alumni, to understand, to appreciate, and to promote the ideals of Jesuit education; and to encourage establishment of active chapters in all Jesuit colleges and universities.

Founding Date: 1915

Staff: 2

Membership: 14,000

Publications:
> *Newsletter,* semiannually
> *Faculty Advisors Bulletin,* monthly during school year

Meetings:
> National triennial convention
> Meetings of local chapters in accordance with their local activities

31. Ambassadors for Christ, Inc. (AFC)

Interdenominational

Rev. Moses Chow, President
Post Office Box AFC
Paradise, Pennsylvania 17562
(717) 687-8564

The purpose of Ambassadors for Christ, Inc., is to introduce Chinese students in America to Jesus Christ as Savior and Lord. Its programs pursue campus evangelism, Christian nurture, and world challenge. AFC offers summer, family, and pastors' conferences, in addition to several training programs. The organization's ministry involves personal contact, literature thrusts, and group gatherings, and it offers its staff for preaching, counseling, and conducting workshops. CONTEMPO is a program of AFC which channels Christian Chinese graduates to ministries overseas.

Founding Date: 1963

Staff: 7

Publications:
> *Ambassadors Magazine,* bimonthly in Chinese
> *Communique,* biannually in English
> *Prayer and Praise,* quarterly in Chinese and English

Meetings:
> AFC Family Conference, annually, at Tuscarora Inn, Mt. Bethel, Pennsylvania
> Editor and Writer Training Camp, annually, at Paradise Farm, Paradise, Pennsylvania
> AFC Summer Camp, annually, at Paradise Farm, Paradise, Pennsylvania
> AFC Student Conference, annually, location varies
> Discipleship Training Seminar, annually, location varies

32. America Press, Inc.

Roman Catholic

Rev. Joseph A. O'Hare, SJ, President and Editor-in-Chief
106 West 56th Street
New York, New York 10019
(212) 581-4640

America Press, Inc., is a non-profit religious corporation directed by Jesuit priests. It publishes a weekly journal of opinion (*America*) and a monthly documentation magazine (*Catholic Mind*). It also runs the Catholic Book Club whose main activity is to provide, through a monthly newsletter, information on books of interest to its readers. Other associated activities are the John La Farge Institute, which sponsors several meetings each year on issues that have a religious or ethical dimension, and the John Courtney Murray Forum, which sponsors a yearly lecture on themes connected with ecumenical activity.

Staff: 11 clerical; 14 lay

Publications:
> *America,* a weekly journal of opinion edited by Jesuit priests
> *Catholic Mind,* a monthly of reprints of significant articles, speeches, and church documents

Meetings:
> The John La Farge Institute sponsors several meetings each year on issues that have a religious or ethical dimension. The meetings are conducted at 106 West 56th Street New York, New York 10019.

33. American Academy of Religion

Nondenominational

Charles E. Winquist, Executive Director
Department of Religious Studies
California State University
Chico, California 95929
(916) 895-5108

The American Academy of Religion is a society of college and university professors and others engaged in teaching and research in the field of religion. Its purpose is to stimulate scholarship, foster research, and promote learning in the complex of disciplines that constitute religion as a field of inquiry. The Academy is also a professional society keeping its membership informed of developing programs, newly-available materials, and opportunities for study grants and research funds. The Academy is affiliated with the Council on the Study of Religion and cooperates in the publication of its bulletin, a professional news magazine, and also in the publication of TOIL, a job registry in the field of religion.

Founding Date: 1909

Staff: 1

Membership: 4,200

Publications:
> Scholarly books, 100 titles in print
> *Journal of the AAR,* quarterly scholarly journal

Meetings:

   1 national meeting and 9 regional meetings annually

Former Name:

   National Association of Biblical Instructors

34. American Association for Jewish Education (AAJE)

Jewish

Arthur Brody, President
114 Fifth Avenue
New York, New York 10011
(212) 675-5656

The American Association for Jewish Education, founded in 1939, is the central national service agency for coordination, promotion, and research in American Jewish education. The AAJE seeks to promote higher standards of Jewish education to assist local communities and national agencies in organizing and operating Jewish education programs. It fosters the establishment of central communal agencies of Jewish education; conducts studies for central communal bodies; publishes pedagogic materials suitable for all types of Jewish schools across the ideological spectrum within the community; evaluates curricular materials and disseminates information about them to the educational community, both lay and professional; seeks to enhance the security and status of teachers and administrators; and stimulates lay interest in the field of Jewish education. Research projects are carried out through the National Curriculum Research Institute and the Department of Community Services, Information, and Studies.

Founding Date: 1939

Staff: 21

Membership:

   1,000, plus 51 local and 17 national organization affiliates in the United States and Canada

Publications:

   26 educational texts and units
   The Pedagogic Reporter
   Jewish Education News
   SAFRA

Meetings:

   Approximately 12 meetings per year are held in various sections of the country

35. American Association of Bible Colleges (AABC)

Nondenominational

John Mostert, Executive Director
Post Office Box 1523
Fayetteville, Arkansas 72701
(501) 521-8164

The American Association of Bible Colleges provides the following services in the field of undergraduate Biblical and church vocational education: accrediting Bible colleges; assisting schools in the achievement of objectives; establishing standards to improve educational quality; promoting Bible college interests; issuing a list of approved schools; providing a basis of selection for students, teachers, and other interested individuals; working to facilitate the educational mobility of Bible college students/graduates; and conducting research projects.

Founding Date: 1947

Staff: 4

Membership: 74 member institutions

Publications:

   AABC Newsletter, quarterly
   22 scholarly books

Meetings:

   1 meeting each year

Former Names:

   (1957) Accrediting Association of Bible Institutes and Bible Colleges
   (1973) Accrediting Association of Bible Colleges

36. American Association of Pastoral Counselors

Interdenominational

James W. Ewing, PhD, Executive Director
3000 Connecticut Avenue, N.W., Suite 300
Washington, D.C. 20008
(202) 387-0031

The American Association of Pastoral Counselors is a professional organization committed to setting standards and criteria for the training and practice of pastoral counseling and the sound operation of pastoral counseling centers; to the promotion of relationships with ecclesiastical and interprofessional groups; and to the encouraging of research. Its membership consists of clergy and religious professionals who, through academic and clinical training, have integrated religious resources and inspiration with the insights of the behavioral sciences. As specialists they practice an in-depth ministry of pastoral counseling and psychotherapy as an extension of their total pastoral function.

Staff: 6

Membership: 2,300

Publications:
Newsletter, quarterly
Journal of Pastoral Care, quarterly

Meetings:
Annual meeting/conventions
Regional meetings, 1-2 annually

37. American Baptist Assembly (ABA)

American Baptist Churches /USA

Dr. Roger W. Getz, Executive Director
Green Lake, Wisconsin 54941
(414) 294-3323

The American Baptist Assembly is a non-profit organization established in 1943. The Assembly is the National Training Center for the American Baptist Churches/USA, related to the Board of Educational Ministries. It is governed by a 22 member Board of Directors. In addition to the full summer schedule of American Baptist conferences, approximately 500 other religious, educational, and character-building agencies and local churches use the facilities for meetings and conferences throughout the year. Located on 1,100 acres of lush, green countryside, the Assembly has a wide variety of housing available including campgrounds, cabins, dormitories, an 81-room hotel, and many old estate homes. The Assembly operates year-round and features ski touring in winter and one of the country's finest golf courses. Other recreational facilities include a competition-sized indoor pool, boating, tennis, biking, fishing, and beautiful, nature-filled hiking trails. While primarily a conference ground, the ABA is open as a Christian resort center, and guests are always welcome.

Founding Date: 1943

Publications:
Newsletter, 3-4 times a year

Meetings:
About 500 conferences per year serving approximately 57,000 people, on the grounds of the American Baptist Assembly

38. American Baptist Association, Missionary Committee

American Baptist Association

Dr. D. S. Madden, Secretary-Treasurer
Post Office Box 1050
Texarkana, Texas 75504
(214) 792-2783

The Missionary Committee of the American Baptist Association is composed of one representative from each church of the American Baptist Association and a group of 25 men elected by the messengers of the Association. The 25 men act as an executive of the Association between sessions. The primary duty of the Missionary Committee is to review those recommended by the churches to the Association for endorsement as missionaries on salary by the Association.

Founding Date: 1924

Staff: 2

Membership: 25 standing; 1,000 total

Publications:
ABA Missions Bulletin, quarterly

Meetings:
Once each spring

39. American Baptist Churches/USA, American Baptist Foreign Mission Society

American Baptist Churches/USA

Rev. Chester J. Jump, Jr., Executive Director
Valley Forge, Pennsylvania 19481
(215) 768-2200

The American Baptist Foreign Mission Society, a/k/a International Ministries, is chartered "for the purpose of diffusing the knowledge of the religion of Jesus Christ, by means of missions, throughout the world." It requires the involvement of all Christians to respond to the totality of human need. Therefore, International Ministries carries on educational, agricultural, medical, and social ministries, with a major emphasis upon leadership training.

Founding Date: 1814

Membership:
203 United States missionaries
16,491 overseas national Christian leaders

Publications:
Moments With Mission, quarterly
Circle-ettes, quarterly

Missionary Newsletters, 200 per year
A Survey of Overseas Mission, annually
Insight, quarterly
Occasional promotional materials

Meetings:
Annual World Missions Conference, Green Lake, Wisconsin

Merger:
(1955) Women's American Baptist Foreign Mission Society

Former Names:
(1845) The General Convention of the Baptist Denomination in the United States for Foreign Missions
(1910) American Baptist Missionary Union

Also Known As:
American Baptist Churches/USA, International Ministries

40. American Baptist Churches/USA, The American Baptist Historical Society

American Baptist Churches/USA
Dr. William H. Brackney, Director
1106 South Goodman Street
Rochester, New York 14620
(716) 473-1740

The Historical Society is the offical archives of the American Baptist Churches/USA. The Society operates a highly specialized research library, devoted to Baptist life and thought, especially in the fields of history and theology. The library contains some 60,000 volumes and 250,000 pamphlets and annual reports. Its collections are a valuable source of information on social and cultural conditions in religious groups in England and America from 1640 to the present day.

Founding Date: 1853

Staff: 5

Membership:
Membership is composed of the members of the General Board of the American Baptist Churches/USA

Publications:
Foundations, quarterly
A Baptist Bibliography, 25 volumes

Meetings:
Biennial convention

41. American Baptist Churches/USA, American Baptist Home Mission Society and Women's American Baptist Home Mission Society

American Baptist Churches/USA
Dr. William K. Cober, Executive Director
Valley Forge, Pennsylvania 19483
(215) 768-2400

The American Baptist Home Missions and Women's American Baptist Home Missions Societies exist to proclaim the gospel of Jesus Christ in North America, to establish churches, and to minister to persons of special need. Activities include pastoral information systems; money-lending for church building; training workshops for pastors and lay people in evangelism; church renewal; ministry of the laity in the world; programs related to social responsibility of corporations; feminism; aging; racism; urban church life; ethnic ministries; refugee resettlement; chaplaincy; governmental relations; and the United Nations.

Founding Date: 1832

Staff: 56

Membership: 1,478,000

Meetings:
Numerous conferences, meetings, and workshops

42. American Baptist Churches/USA, American Baptist Homes and Hospitals Association

American Baptist Churches/USA
Kenneth L. George, Executive Director
Valley Forge, Pennsylvania 19481
(215) 768-2382

The American Baptist Homes and Hospitals Association is related to the American Baptist Churches/USA through the Board of National Ministries as one of the denomination's Associated Organizations as provided for in the denomination's constitution. The Association promotes fraternal and cooperative relationships among accredited and associate members. Its main objective is to engage its members in a program of fellowship bringing administrators, board members, professional staff personnel, and persons who support American Baptist health and social ministries to a sense of unity and strength in a common cause.

Staff: 1
Membership: 77
Publications:
  Perspective, quarterly

43. American Baptist Churches/USA, American Baptist Women

American Baptist Churches/USA
Dr. Doris Anne Younger, Executive Director
Valley Forge, Pennsylvania 19481
(215) 768-2284

American Baptist Women is a national organization composed of the 500,000 women members of the American Baptist Churches/USA. Its purpose is to unite all the women of the churches into a fellowship that will help each one to grow as a person in personal devotion to Jesus Christ as Lord and Savior and in commitment to the mission of His church, through worshipping, working, and witnessing in the home, the community, the nation, and the world. A lay board of managers promotes the world mission budget of the American Baptist Churches; material aid and world relief; leadership development, study, and action in matters of Christian social concern and international affairs; and a program which is actively involved in the life of the church, as well as the women's program.

Founding Date: 1951
Staff: 4
Membership: 500,000
Publications:
  1 program book yearly
  The American Baptist Woman, 3 times a year
Meetings:
  1 annual national conference at American Baptist Assembly, Green Lake, Wisconsin
Former Name:
  (1965) National Council of American Women

44. American Baptist Churches/USA, Board of Educational Ministries

American Baptist Churches/USA
William T. McKee, Executive Secretary
Valley Forge, Pennsylvania 19481
(215) 768-2000

The Board of Educational Ministries of the American Baptist Churches/USA coordinates a program of Christian higher education through 43 denominational schools, colleges, and theological seminaries; provides training for about 30,000 persons annually at the American Baptist Assembly, Green Lake, Wisconsin; and edits and publishes a wide variety of curriculum materials, books, and magazines.

Publications:
  Secret Place, a devotional
  The American Baptist, a news magazine
  Input, a professional newsletter
  Baptist Leader, for church education leaders
  Fe y Vida Hispanic
  3 curriculum series for church school
  books through Judson Press
  Soundings, a cassette service

45. The American Benedictine Academy

Roman Catholic
Rev. Colman G. Grabert, OSB, President
St. Meinrad Archabbey
St. Meinrad, Indiana 47577
(812) 375-6581

The American Benedictine Academy is a non-profit association whose purpose is to cultivate the Benedictine heritage and to promote that heritage within contemporary cultures. The Academy fulfills this purpose by sponsoring and promoting disciplinary and interdisciplinary collaboration among its members and by publicizing the results of their work.

Founding Date: 1947
Staff: 8
Membership: 170
Publications:
  The American Benedictine Academy Newsletter, biannually, in-house contact bulletin
  The American Benedictine Academy, Research Studies, series appears ad hoc
  A Directory of Benedictine Resource Personnel for North America, Volume 1
Meetings:
  The American Benedictine Academy Convention, biennially, usually in August

46. American Bible Society (ABS)*

Interdenominational
1865 Broadway
New York, New York 10023
(212) 581-7400

The American Bible Society continues to work towards the goal it set for itself when founded over a century and a half ago: that of making Scriptures available to every man, woman, and child who wants them, in his or her own language, and at a price each can afford. In pursuit of this aim, ABS translates, publishes, and distributes the Word without profit, and without note or comment. The Bible Society is at work in over 150 countries and territories, including the United States, and actively distributes in over 400 languages. Some Scriptures are for those with special needs such as the blind, those learning to read, and young people. It distributes well over 200 million Scriptures in any given year.

Founding Date: 1816

Staff: 450

Membership: 367,000

Publications:
> Scriptures in over 400 languages and numerous formats
> *American Bible Society Record,* magazine for donors, 10 months a year

Meetings:
> Annual meeting in New York City on the second Thursday in May

47. American Biblical Encyclopedia Society

Jewish
Rabbi Bernard Greenbaum, Executive Vice-President
24 West Maple Avenue
Monsey, New York 10952
(914) 352-4609

The purpose of the American Biblical Encyclopedia Society is to foster Biblical, Talmudical and Midrashic research. It publishes *Torah Shelemah* (Hebrew), a 34-volume encyclopedia on the Pentateuch. The Society also publishes the *English Encyclopedia of Biblical Interpretation* (9 volumes), and has published the *Annotated and Illustrated Israel Passover Haggadah; NOAM,* a study in contemporary Jewish Law (22 volumes); *Hatekufah HaGedolah; Yom Kippur War; Shma Yisroel; Kav HaTaarich-the Jewish Dateline,* complete with maps;

16 volumes of *Tzophnaat Paaneah,* the writings of Rabbi Yosef Rosen of Rogotchov, and other miscellaneous works.

Founding Date: 1930

Staff: 22

Meetings:
> Annual convention held in New York City in March

48. American Board of Examiners in Pastoral Counseling (ABEPC)

Nondenominational
Rt. Rev. Fonzy Joseph Broussard, PhD, DMin, President
23820 Arlington, #15
Torrance, California 90501

The American Board of Examiners in Pastoral Counseling has developed certification examinations for pastoral counseling personnel. The objectives of the certification program are to insure acceptable standards of practice and to maintain competence, responsibility, and accountability. The qualifying exams are of such quality that legal agencies governing the practice of pastoral counseling within each state could, at their discretion, grant a license without further examination to these candidates who pass the ABEPC examinations and who are holders of the diplomas of the Board. The ABEPC provides a broad representation of relevant members of the pastoral counseling community to qualify the candidates in three divisions: Diplomate, Fellow, Member. The ABEPC also issues specialty certificates by examination and gives approval of centers via site visits.

Founding Date: 1979

Staff: 10

Membership: 165

Publications:
> *Explorations,* quarterly

Meetings:
> Examinations are held in four areas annually

49. American Board of Missions to the Jews (ABMJ)

Nondenominational
Harold A. Sevener, President
Post Office Box 2000
Orangeburg, New York 10962
(914) 359-8535

The American Board of Missions to the Jews (Beth Sar Shallom) is an independent faith mission presenting the Gospel to Jewish people throughout the world. In doctrine it is evangelical; in practice it is progressive; in the management of funds it is conservative. While its missionaries and ministers are ordained by various church bodies and while they have liberty of independent convictions, they are unanimous in affirming doctrines fundamental to the faith. A staff of 122 workers labor in the major cities of the United States, Canada, Europe, Israel, and South America, witnessing, discipling, winning Jewish people to Christ, and involving them in a local church program. Ministries of the ABMJ include centers, literature, Bible conferences, TV specials, radio programs, media presentations of the Gospel, and campus and youth ministries.

Founding Date: 1894

Staff: 6 executives; 7 administrators

Membership: 92 missionaries; 17 clerical members

Publications:
> *The Chosen People,* 11 months per year
> *The End Times,* bimonthly radio publication
> *Shepherd of Israel,* quarterly missionary publication
> Tracts and books relating to Jewish evangelism
> Annual Jewish Art calendar

Radio/TV Programs:
> Radio program, *The Chosen People News Hour,* 15 minutes per day, 5 days per week throughout the United States
> Foreign language broadcasts in France and Israel

Meetings:
> Area prophetic conferences conducted at various locations throughout the United States and Canada with the cooperation of local evangelical churches
> Summer conferences at various campgrounds in the United States and Canada

50. American Catholic Correctional Chaplains Association

Roman Catholic

Rev. Dismas Beoff, OSB, Secretary
2900 East Boulevard
Cleveland, Ohio 44104
(216) 623-6170

The American Catholic Correctional Chaplains Association is the official organization of Roman Catholic clergy or religious and laymen who work in the correctional ministry (prisons, jails, juvenile centers, halfway houses, etc.). Its purposes are to unify and implement the church's corrective and rehabilitative efforts for the spiritual welfare of inmates under the correctional chaplain's care and to foster a Catholic approach to the problems in the correctional field in accord with the principles of Holy Scriptures, Catholic philosophy, and theology. It provides resource materials, issues certification, and offers training programs for correctional chaplains.

Founding Date: 1952

Staff: 4

Membership: 200

Publications:
> Manuals and pamphlets
> *Chaplett,* quarterly

Meetings:
> 1 annual
> 1 mid-winter
> 1 regional

51. American Catholic Historical Association

Roman Catholic

Rev. Robert Trisco, Executive Secretary
Mullen Library, Room 305
The Catholic University of America
Washington, D.C. 20064
(212) 635-5079

The Association pursues two main objectives. One is to promote a deeper and more widespread knowledge of the history of the Catholic Church, not only in terms of its internal development, but also of its external relations with the civil government and the influence of its members on the intellectual, cultural, political, and social progress of mankind. The other important aim is the advancement of historical scholarship in all fields among American Catholics and other members of the Association by rendering them various services, offering them opportunities to utilize their talents, and according them public recognition for their demonstrated merits. Through special committees, the American Catholic Historical Association promotes the study of the history of American Catholicism and the teaching of church history in secondary schools. It sponsors the editing and publication of historical documents; most recently, the papers of John Carroll, the first American bishop. The Association awards the John

Gilmary Shea Prize, the Howard R. Marraro Prize, and the Peter Guilday Prize annually.

Founding Date: 1919

Staff: 1

Membership: 1,100

Publications:
Catholic Historical Review, quarterly

Meetings:
One national meeting (December 28-30) in conjunction with the American Historical Association and other societies
One regional meeting, spring

52. American Catholic Philosophical Association

Roman Catholic
Catholic University of America
Washington, D.C. 20064
(202) 635-5518

The objectives of the American Catholic Philosophical Association are the promotion of philosophical scholarship and publication, the improvement of the teaching of philosophy, and communication with other individuals and groups of like interest.

Founding Date: 1926

Staff: 2

Membership: 1,400

Publications:
The New Scholasticism, quarterly
Proceedings of the ACPA, annually

Meetings:
One per year in April

53. American Church Union (ACU)

Episcopal
The Rt. Rev. Robert S. Morse, President
6013 Lawton Avenue
Oakland, California 94618
(415) 655-4951

The American Church Union is a national organization of Anglo-Catholics which traces its heritage back to the Oxford or Tractarian movement in the Church of England in the 19th century and beyond. The ACU is committed to the preservation of Catholic faith and order within the Anglican or Episcopalian

tradition, and to the propagation of the orthodox Catholic faith to the whole world.

Founding Date: 1938

Staff: 3

Membership: 1,670

Publications:
Scholarly and popular books, 40 titles in print
New Oxford Review, monthly

Meetings:
Annual council in fall

Former Name:
(1938) Catholic Congress Organization

54. American Commission on Ministerial Training

Nondenominational
Rt. Rev. Harry Edwin Smith, ThD, DMin
Educational Director
23820 Arlington, Suite 15
Torrance, California 90501
(213) 539-5565

The American Commission on Ministerial Training was established to promote as well as clarify what constitutes well-balanced, essential non-degree-granting ministerial programs. To this end the American Commission on Ministerial Training will approve (not accredit) non-degree-granting institutes or programs and continuing education courses when provided with complete information about the curriculum, faculty, length of time required to complete, and entrance requirements.

Founding Date: 1957

Staff: 5

Membership: 30

Publications:
Newsletter, monthly
Bulletins, as necessary

Meetings:
Yearly - Los Angeles

55. American Committee for Shaare Zedek Hospital in Jerusalem, Inc.

Jewish
Morris Talansky
Senior Executive Vice-President
49 West 45th Street
New York, New York 10036
(212) 354-880l

The American Committee for Shaare Zedek Hospital in Jerusalem, Inc., is the fund raising arm of the Shaare Zedek Medical Center, Jerusalem, Israel, in the United States. With nine regional offices, the American Committee organizes a full program of activities for the benefit of the Shaare Zedek Medical Center.

56. American Conference of Cantors (ACC)

Reform Judaism/Union of American Hebrew Congregations
838 Fifth Avenue
New York, New York 10021
(212) 249-0100

The American Conference of Cantors is the most recent affiliate of the UAHC. Its members receive their investiture as cantors at the graduation ceremonies of the Hebrew Union College-Jewish Institute of Religion, School of Sacred Music. The ACC, through its Joint Placement Commission, serves congregations seeking cantors and music directors. Its members serve on the faculty of the HUC-JIR, as well as on a variety of programs under the auspices of the UAHC and its other affiliates. Since its affiliation with the UAHC, the ACC has created an Associate Membership as well as a Guild of Temple Musicians, consisting of music directors and organists serving Reform congregations throughout the country.

57. The American Congregational Association

Nondenominational
Rev. Arnel M. Steece, President
14 Beacon Street
Boston, Massachusetts 02108
(617) 523-0470

The American Congregational Association was founded in Boston to care for and perpetuate a library of books, pamphlets, and manuscripts, and a collection of portraits and relics of the past; to promote friendly intercourse and cooperation among Congregational ministers and churches, and with other denominations; and to do whatever else that would serve to illustrate Congregational history and promote the general interests of the Congregational tradition. The Association is the Proprietor of the Congregational Library.

Founding Date: 1853
Staff: 7
Membership: 88
Publications:
> *Bulletin of the Congregational Library,* three times a year

Meetings:
> Annual convention in May

58. American Correctional Chaplains Association

Nondenominational
William Hanawalt, Secretary
Brevard Correctional Institution
Camp Road
Sharpes, Florida 32959
Mailing Address
Post Office Box 340
Sharpes, Florida 32959
(305) 632-6711

The purpose of the Association is to offer those engaged in the religious ministry, in correctional institutions, and in related agencies an opportunity for fellowship and a channel for the exchange of experience-gained ideas and information. Further, it provides its members with an opportunity to formulate standards and procedures for a more effective chaplaincy service and serves as a vehicle in which to cooperate with the American Correctional Association and its affiliated bodies.

Founding Date: 1885
Memberships: 253
Meetings:
> One annual meeting in August
> One mid-year meeting

59. American Council for Judaism

Jewish
Clarence L. Coleman, Jr., President
307 Fifth Avenue
New York, New York 10016
(212) 889-1313

The Council believes that Judaism is a religion of universal values, not a nationality or ethnic grouping. Since this is but one of several views of Judaism, it recognizes the right of others to present their views but insists that this not be done in the name of Jewry.

Such efforts are a disservice to Jewry, and the Council believes that they should be challenged. It publishes a monthly newsletter and a quarterly which treats these issues more comprehensively. Both publications are furnished without charge to individuals and institutions requesting them.

Founding Date: 1943

Membership: 20,000

Publications:
> *Special Interest Report,* monthly
> *Issues of the American Council for Judaism,* quarterly

60. American Council of the Ramabai Mukti Mission

Interdenominational

Rev. Donald Kitchen, Executive Secretary
Post Office Box 4912
Clinton, New Jersey 08809
(201) 735-8770

The Ramabai Mukti Mission is an international, inter-denominational mission of evangelical faith wholly dependent upon God. It is located in Kedgaon, Poona District, India, but has representative councils in the United States of America, Canada, England, Scotland, Ireland, The Netherlands, Australia, and New Zealand. The Mission was started as a school for high-caste widows in 1889 by Pandita Ramabai, one of India's great reformers for women. Today, the Pandita Ramabai Mukti Mission occupies 64 acres of food-providing land and consists of nurseries; homes for 19 families; homes for working girls and junior staff; homes of service (working women), of peace and love (elderly and retired), and of mercy (rescue cases); a home for the blind; and Sunset home for the infirm, mentally retarded, and crippled. Other departments include Bethel (married couples who work in the Mission or in their own business), a marriage committee (helps arrange marriages for the Mukti girls to Christian young men), educational facilities, industrial departments, the Mukti Church, and the Krishnabai Memorial Chapel. An evangelistic outreach program is carried out through teams of girls and young women in village classes on Sundays and through the week. The Supa Outstation nine miles away houses a small hospital and a kindergarten school. The Mission also runs Bible-centered clubs reaching out as a nation-wide girls' training program for the church of India.

Founding Date: 1889

Staff: 9

Publications:
> *Mukti Means Salvation,* bimonthly
> *India's Buds and Blossoms,* bimonthly
> A monthly prayer sheet

61. American Council on Schools and Colleges (ACSC)

Nondenominational

Rt. Rev. Harry Edwin Smith, ThD, DMin, President
3916 Sepulveda Boulevard, Suite 111
Torrance, California 90501
(213) 539-5565

Membership in the American Council on Schools and Colleges is available to religious institutes and cultural organizations whether they teach by resident courses or external or correspondence courses, or supervise individual research and administer tests for the purpose of evaluation or certification. Membership is also made available to publishers of religious educational material and study aids. The ACSC has established and will maintain helpful, friendly relations with federal, state, and local agencies that affect private religious schools and colleges.

Founding Date: 1927

Staff: 5

Membership: 75

Publications:
> Membership list, annually
> Newsletter, quarterly

Meetings:
> Next meeting May 1983—Los Angeles

Former Name:
> National Association of Colleges and Universities

62. American Ethical Union, National Women's Conference*

American Ethical Union

Rebecca Goldblum, President of Board
2 West 64th Street
New York, New York 10023
(212) 874-5200

The National Women's Conference, the women's organization of the American Ethical Union, is a humanistic religious and educational movement founded on the belief that the process of moral growth is the basis for spiritual life. The organization's interest is social legislation and those issues relating to separation of Church and State.

They initiate programs in education in areas such as family planning, and child-care problems; promote action on key issues, such as right of abortion; promote the program of the Ethical Culture Movement; and have United Nations representatives.

Membership:
    800 to 900 lay members in organized women's groups plus women in the general membership of the American Ethical Union

Publications:
    Newsletters; special reports

63. American Federation of Jewish Fighters, Camp Inmates and Nazi Victims, Inc.

Jewish

Solomon Zynstein, President
823 United Nations Plaza
New York, New York 10017
(212) 490-2525

The purpose of The American Federation of Jewish Fighters, Camp Inmates and Nazi Victims, Inc., is the furtherance of Holocaust studies through educational projects of its own or jointly with Jewish and non-Jewish organizations and institutions. It distributes material on the Holocaust by mobile exhibitions, booklets, films, and related material. The Federation is a roof organization for all Survivor Organizations and calls jointly with national and Jewish organizations for the observance of Yom Hashoah U'Hagvurah, the Holocaust and Rememberance Day, on the 27th day of Nisan. This is the day that is being observed uniformly by the Jewish communities throughout the world.

Founding Date: 1971
Staff: 2
Publications:
    Martyrdom and Resistance, bimonthly
    Annual Journal

64. American Friends Service Committee

Religious Society of Friends

Asia Bennett, Executive Secretary
1501 Cherry Street
Philadelphia, Pennsylvania 19102
(215) 241-7000

The American Friends Service Committee is an independent Quaker organization founded to provide conscientious objectors with an opportunity to aid civilian victims during World War I. Today, with international headquarters in Philadelphia, 10 regional offices across the United States, and 17 program operations overseas, it is chartered to carry on religious, charitable, social, philanthropic and relief work on behalf of the several branches and divisions of the Religious Society of Friends (Quakers) in America. The AFSC is established as a non-profit Corporation consisting of 161 Quakers, appointed by 24 Yearly Meetings of American Friends and also chosen at large. A Board of Directors drawn from the membership of the Corporation, governs the policies, programs and administration of the AFSC. Numerous program and administrative committees at home and abroad oversee the operations of the AFSC and consult with the more than 400 men and women who make up the staff of the committees. Hundreds of volunteers assist the work; thousands of contributors of many religious affiliations, or none, support it.

Founding Date: 1917
Publications:
    Quaker Service Bulletin, three times yearly
    AFSC Annual Report

65. American Jewish Alternatives to Zionism, Inc.

Jewish

Elmer Berger, President
133 East 73rd Street, Suite 404
New York, New York 10021
(212) 628-2727

American Jewish Alternatives to Zionism, Inc., is a District of Columbia non-profit organization. Its educational program applies Judaism's values of justice and common humanity to the Arab/Zionist/Israeli conflict in the Middle East and advocates a one-to-one human relationship between Jews and all Americans in the United States. In both areas of its concern, the organization rejects Zionism/Israel's "Jewish people" nationality attachment of all Jews to the State of Israel. These political-nationality claims distort constructive humanitarian programs and are inconsistent with American constitutional concepts of individual citizenship and separation of church and state. They are also a principal obstacle to Middle East peace. The organization members believe that their program helps advance peace in the Middle

East and prevents Zionist/Israel from succesfully achieving its legislated objective of reversing the integration of American Jews by capturing the Jewish community for its self-segregating "Jewish people" nationality attachment of Jews to the State of Israel.

Founding Date: 1969

Membership: 1,000

Publications:
> *Report,* 4-5 times a year
> Miscellaneous pamphlets addressed to same subject matter

Former Name: Jewish Alternatives to Zionism

66. American Jewish Committee

Jewish

Bertram H. Gold, Executive Vice-President
165 East 56th Street
New York, New York 10022
(212) 751-4000

The American Jewish Committee is the country's pioneer human relations organization. It combats bigotry, protects the civil and religious rights of Jews in the United States and elsewhere, and seeks improved human relations for all people.

Founding Date: 1906

Staff: 350

Membership: 40,000

Publications:
> *Commentary,* monthly
> *Present Tense,* quarterly

Radio/TV Programs:
> *Jewish Dimension,* weekly, WPIX, New York

Meetings:
> One annual meeting in May in New York

67. American Jewish Congress

Jewish

Henry Siegman, Executive Director
15 East 84th Street
New York, New York 10028
(212) 879-4500

The American Jewish Congress is a voluntary membership organization of American Jews dedicated to fostering the unity and creative survival of the Jewish people. As a public affairs and human rights agency,

it fights anti-Semitism and all forms of racism, works toward full equality in a free society for all Americans, encourages a positive sense of Jewish identity and helps Israel develop in freedom, security and peace. The Congress uses education, public relations efforts and legal action in the courts to further its goals.

Founding Date: 1918

Staff: 105

Membership: 28,000

Publications:
> *Congress Monthly,* 8 times per year
> *Judaism,* quarterly
> *Boycott Report,* monthly

Meetings:
> Approximately 150 annually, including national and regional meetings, conferences, conventions, etc. National meetings are usually held in New York City, where the national headquarters is located

68. American Jewish Historical Society (AJHS)

Jewish

Bernard Wax, Director
2 Thornton Road
Waltham, Massachusetts 02154
(617) 891-8110

The American Jewish Historical Society collects, catalogs, preserves, and displays materials relating to the Jewish experience in America. It also serves as a reference center on the history of the Jewish Americans and provides materials for display by other institutions. It sponsors an in-service training course for teachers in New York City, holds lectures, provides audio-visual materials on American Jewish history, promotes research on the relationship of America and the Holy Land, and maintains a film archive of Yiddish language motion pictures produced in America. A headquarters library is maintained on the campus of Brandeis University.

Founding Date: 1892

Staff: 9

Membership: 3,000 lay; 300 clerical

Publications:
> *American Jewish History,* quarterly
> *Newsletter of the American Jewish Historical Society,* occasionally
> Books

Meetings:
Annual convention

69. American Jewish Joint Distribution Committee (JDC)

Jewish

Ralph I. Goldman, Executive Vice-President
60 East 42nd Street
New York, New York 10017
(212) 687-6200

American Jewish Joint Distribution is "the Jewish radar, the distant early warning system of the Jewish people." It is quick to rush to a man-made or natural disaster to bring help to stricken Jewish communities. JDC's activities in other countries depend on local needs and conditions of the various segments of the Jewish population: the care of the elderly, poor, care of transmigrants, aid to Jewish education, aid to sick and handicapped, and religious programs. JDC constantly re-evaluates and reviews its budget and redirects its priorities to send help where it is needed most and to make sure that it achieves maximum results with its available resources.

Founding Date: 1914
Staff: 37
Former Name:
Joint Distribution Committee for Relief of Jewish War Suffers

70. American Jewish Press Association (AJPA)*

Jewish

c/o Jewish Exbonet
226 South 16th Street
Philadelphia, Pennsylvania 19102
(215) 893-5700

The American Jewish Press Association is a voluntary organization comprised of 82 major American Jewish community newspapers, printed in English, in the United States and Canada. In addition, several Jewish magazines, monthly publications, and wire services are associate members. The AJPA provides a forum for the editors and publishers of member newspapers to exchange views and ideas, as well as editorial material; to plan trips and study seminars to Israel and other areas; and to work toward the enhancement of journalistic and business standards for member newspapers.

Founding Date: 1943
Membership:
82 American Jewish newspapers and other media
Publications:
AJPA Bulletin
Periodic newsletter to members
Meetings:
2 mid-team meetings in November
Annual meeting in June

71. American Leprosy Missions, Inc. (ALM)

Nondenominational

Roger K. Ackley, President
1262 Broad Street
Bloomfield, New Jersey 07003

Mailing Address
AMISLEP
Bloomfield, New Jersey 07003
(201) 338-9197

The principal objective of American Leprosy Missions, Inc., is to witness to the Gospel of Christ — in all ways — to those with leprosy, without regard to race, nationality, creed or sex. Its witness includes, but is not limited to: medical treatment, social and physical rehabilitation, training of leprosy workers, public health programs, scientific research, public information about leprosy, and health education for patients and communities. Working with other organizations, ALM engages in a broad-based effort to eliminate leprosy from the world. ALM runs four research programs and provides contacts for the World Health Organization. ALM supports nearly 1,000 hospitals, clinics, and dispensaries in 20 countries, reaching over 100,000 men, women, and children.

Founding Date: 1906
Staff: 18
Membership: 44,000
Publications:
ALM Bulletin, field news, bimonthly
International Journal of Leprosy, quarterly
Meetings:
ALM sponsors two week-long international training seminars on leprosy held in conjunction with the U.S. Public Health Service Hospital in Carville, Louisiana
Former Name: (1950) American Mission to Lepers

72. The American Lutheran Church, Division for Life, and Mission in the Congregation*

American Lutheran Church
Paul A. Hanson, DD
422 South Fifth Street
Minneapolis, Minnesota 55415
(612) 338-3821

The Division for Life and Mission in the Congregation assists congregations with their work in the areas of worship, learning, witness, service, and parish management. Dialogue with congregations and/or persons and groups in congregations is primarily through publications and consultation.

Meetings:
 125

73. American Lutheran Church Women

Lutheran
Julie Stine, Director
422 South Fifth Street
Minneapolis, Minnesota 55415
(612) 330-3100

American Lutheran Church Women are united through a structural network which serves the spiritual, personal, and social needs of women and equips them in and through the Word of God for full participation in the life and mission of the American Lutheran Church. Main activities include monthly Bible study through circle groups, prayer fellowship, service projects, and miscellaneous education experiences for life and growth. Education and service opportunities give occasion for sharing, not only their faith, but the many other facets of life. The ALC Women is divided into 18 districts, 214 conferences, and nearly 5,000 local auxiliaries—the same divisions as the American and leader's manual, guides for officers, and education and stewardship resources to assist local officers in planning. A packet of resources is sent annually free of charge to each of about 4,800 local presidents.

Founding Date: 1960
Staff: 4 program and 3 support staff
Membership: Estimated at 300,000
Publications:
 Scope (published by Augsburg Publishing House)
Meetings:
 Triennial national conventions

74. American Lutheran Education Association (ALEA)

Lutheran
Dr. Donald A. Vetter
Wartburg College
Waverly, Iowa 50677
(319) 352-1200, ext/280

The purpose of the American Lutheran Education Association is to: work toward advocacy, promotion, and development of Lutheran elementary schools as an opportunity for the church in mission; support congregations involved in school ministry; provide services to its members; and serve as a forum for idea exchange to foster Christian commitment and professional competence.

Staff: 7 officers
Membership: 210 schools
Publications:
 Annual yearbook
 Periodic monographs
 Promotional materials
Meetings:
 Two large regional conventions per year (West coast, Midwest)
 Eight regional units in various locations once per year
 Retreats for principals and board members

75. American Lutheran Publicity Bureau

Inter-Lutheran
Rev. Glenn C. Stone, Executive Director
155 East 22nd Street
New York, New York 10010
(212) 254-4640

American Lutheran Publicity Bureau is an inter-Lutheran organization whose area of service and board membership includes the several Lutheran bodies in the United States and their constituencies. Its purpose is "to proclaim the Gospel of Jesus Christ according to the teachings of Holy Scripture and the confessions of the Lutheran Church; to make known the doctrines, practices, History and life of the Lutheran Church; to work for and support the movement toward unity among Lutherans; to promote and strengthen Lutheran cooperative mission and ministry; to facilitate exchange of ideas and information among Lutherans and all Christians."

Founding Date: 1914

Publications:
Lutheran Forum, quarterly
Forum Letter, monthly
Various tracts, pamphlets, and audio-visuals
Meetings:
Sponsors the annual Inter-Lutheran Forum held in New York City in the fall

76. American Messianic Fellowship

Interdenominational
Rev. William E. Currie, General Director
7448 North Damen Avenue
Chicago, Illinois 60645
(312) 743-3410

"The object of the American Messianic Fellowship shall be to promote the intellectual, social, and religious welfare of all nationalites." Its main activities include visitation in hospitals, homes, nursing homes; Bible Classes; distribution of literature; and speaking in churches.
Founding Date: 1887
Staff: 21
Publications:
AMF Monthly Magazine, monthly except August
Meetings:
Annual convention, first Thursday of November in Chicago, Illinois
Former Name: Chicago Hebrew Mission

77. American Ministerial Association

Interdenominational
Most Rev. Charles Virgil Hearn,
PhD, DMin, DD, President
2210 Wilshire Boulvard
Santa Monica, California 90403
(213) 394-0553

The American Ministerial Association prefers to be known not as a denomination but rather as an evangelistic and missionary movement; yet is has a familiar denominational organization, with home and foreign mission boards, a department of education, and a publishing commission. The President and a limited ecclesiastical authority vested in the national headquarters office guides the associational work in business, education, and benevolence. Its main work lies in the establishing of independent, nonsectarian local churches and missions. Regional offices are maintained throughout the United States and

Canada, and the ministers meet for mutual consultations and inspiration in conferences. A seminary is maintained in Denver, Colorado. Doctrine and teaching of the Association might be described as middle-of-the-road, embracing the customary Christian position "yet allowing its ministers to live the religious life unhampered by creedal obligations." The cosmopolitan complexion of its ministers and membership, including as it does representatives of many different schools of religious thought, naturally produces such an emphasis.
Founding Date: 1929
Staff: 3
Membership: 550
Publications:
Anchor, bimonthly
Meetings:
Meetings are held periodically
Former Name:
American Conference of Undenominational Ministers

78. American Missionary Fellowship

Interdenominational
Dr. E. Eugene Williams, General Director
672 Conestoga Road
Post Office Box 368
Villanova, Pennsylvania 19085
(215) 527-4439

American Missionary Fellowship works in urban and rural areas of the United States to share Jesus Christ with those not reached through other evangelical ministries. Through surveys the mission locates communities or specific groups not being reached with the Gospel and seeks to establish effective ministries in those places. Urban ministries currently include work in Washington, D.C., Philadelphia, and Los Angeles. Rural ministries span over 30 states with church planting, VBS, released time classes, and home Bible studies. During the 19th century, this organization was largely responsible for the growth of the Sunday school movement in the United States. Thousands of Sunday school missionaries followed the pioneers west starting Sunday schools in each new community along the way. While the organization has seen many changes over 160 years of ministry, it remains true to the original purpose of reaching Americans with the Gospel of Jesus Christ and forming them into a church body.
Founding Date: 1817

Staff: Home office staff — 23

Membership:

    Missionary Staff — 135 units, a unit includes husband and wife,

Publications:

    American Missionary Fellowship News, quarterly

Meetings:

    2 regional directors' conferences each year, one at Mission headquarters, one at another location

    4 regional conferences each year in various locations across the U.S.

    1 orientation seminar at mission headquarters

    Approximately 300 camps in various locations across the U.S.

Former Names:

    (1824) Sunday and Adult School Union

    (1974) American Sunday School Union

79. American Near East Refugee Aid (ANERA)

Nondenominational

Peter Gubser, President
1522 K Street, N.W., Suite 202
Washington, D.C. 20005
(202) 347-2558

The purpose of the American Near East Refugee Aid is to provide funds for social and economic development in the West Bank and Gaza and relief in Lebanon. ANERA works with indigenous organizations in the area; it does not conduct its own programs. The organization works with various cooperatives, municipalities, Arab Women's Unions, Red Crescent Societies, schools, and universities.

Founding Date: 1968

Staff: 10

Membership: 25,000 donors

Publications:

    Newsletter, quarterly

80. The American Protestant Correctional Chaplains' Association (APCCA)*

Nondenominational

South Carolina Department of Corrections
Post Office Box 11159
Columbia, South Carolina 29211

The American Protestant Correctional Chaplains' Association is a professional organization composed of Protestant clergy who are concurrent members of the American Correctional Chaplain's Association, an affiliate of the American Correctional Association. The objectives of the Association are to promote the professional identity of the chaplain; to interpret the role of the chaplain; to relate to correctional officials concerning chaplaincy and its responsibility to the treatment process; to encourage the chaplain to develop his skills through clinical pastoral education; to alert the chaplain to new trends in corrections through national and regional meetings; and to provide a certification procedure designed to upgrade the correctional chaplain's professional competence.

Membership: 300

Publications:

    APCCA Journal, quarterly

    APCCA Newsletter, quarterly

Meetings:

    1 annual meeting

    6 annual regional meetings

    1 annual mid-winter planning meeting

81. The American Protestant Hospital Association

Interdenominational

Charles D. Phillips, President
1701 East Woodfield Road, Suite 311
Schaumburg, Illinois 60195
(312) 843-2701

The purposes of the American Protestant Hospital Association are: to promote the public welfare through the development of all Protestant health and welfare institutions and their services including but not limited to hospitals, out-patient services, homes for the aged, and children's homes; to encourage and engage in professional education and scientific research in the administration of all health services, as well as aid in the education of the public with respect thereto; and to improve the quality and increase the distribution of all health services. The foregoing are exclusively for charitable, scientific, literary, or education purposes.

Founding Date: 1920

Staff: 7

Membership:

    250 institutional members

    1,500 personal members, College of Chaplains

Publications:
  The Bulletin, monthly
Meetings:
  Annual meeting concurrently with the Protestant
    Health and Welfare Assembly
  Board and committee meetings locally

82. American Sabbath Tract Society

Seventh Day Baptist Church

John D. Bevis, Editor
Post Office Box 868
510 Watchung Avenue
Plainfield, New Jersey 07061
(201) 561-8700

For over one 135 years, the American Sabbath Tract
Society has been the publishing arm of the Seventh
Day Baptist witness. Books, booklets, magazines,
and tracts have been a part of this ever-growing
ministry. The Society believes that one of the most
effective and yet least expensive ways of spreading
God's Word is through the printed page and is happy
to have a part in this work. It is also happy to assist
sister Seventh Day Baptist Conferences around the
world in their publication work and note that their
publication work now reaches some 25 countries.

Founding Date: 1843
Staff: 8
Membership:
  Members of Seventh Day Baptist Churches
Publications:
  The Sabbath Recorder, monthly denominational
    journal
  The Helping Hand, quarterly
  The Sabbath Visitor, monthly for children
  World Federation Newsletter, quarterly
Meetings:
  Annual convention, third Sunday of September in
    Plainfield, New Jersey

83. American Scripture Gift Mission, Inc.

Interdenominational

David B. Wylie, Executive Director
1211 Arch Street
Philadelphia, Pennsylvania 19107
(212) 561-3232

The American Scripture Gift Mission is an international, interdenominational service agency of independent tradition which publishes and distributes
Bibles and Scripture portions in over 600 languages.
The distribution of literature includes Bibles for the
elderly in retirement and nursing homes. The American Scripture Gift Mission was founded in 1915. Its
parent agency is the Scripture Gift Mission, whose
home office is in London.

Founding Date: 1915
Staff: 4
Publications:
  Newsletter, 3 times a year
Meetings:
  Annual convention

84. American Sephardi Federation, Inc. (ASF)

Jewish (Sephardi)

Gary Schaer, Executive Director
521 Fifth Avenue, Suite 1404
New York, New York 10017
(212) 697-1845

The American Sephardi Federation was founded in
1972 to educate Jews and non-Jews about Sephardi
history, customs, traditions, and to promote the
Sephardi-Jewish way of life. Sephardim, Jews who
trace their origins to the Middle East, North Africa,
the Balkans and the Iberian Peninsula, first arrived in
America in the 1600's and have maintained an ongoing presence in Jewish life and affairs in the United
States since that time. Although Sephardim number
only 200,000 in the United States, less than 3% of the
total Jewish population, they are a majority of
Israel's Jewish residents. Recognizing the above, the
A.S.F. has pledged itself to educating Ashkenazi
Jewry about Sephardim and the particular heritage
developed as a result of living in non-European countries (excepting Iberia and the Netherlands.)

Founding Date 1972
Membership: 45,000
Publications:
  Sephardi News Bulletin, monthly
  Sephardi World, semi-annually
  Sephardinews, press and information releases,
    50 per year
Meetings:
  Sephardi Scholars Conference, once a year
  General biennial convention
  Selected conferences, 4-5 per year

85. American Society for Reformation Research

Nondenominational
Gottfried Krodel, President
6477 San Bonita Avenue
St. Louis, Missouri 63105
(314) 727-6655

The American Society for Reformation Research fosters study, research, publication, and scholarly meetings centering on the sixteenth century reformation. An annual meeting is held in connection with meetings of the American Historical Association. An annual newletter is distributed to members, as well as two journals: the *Archive for Reformation History* and the *Literature-Review.* The *Archive* is international, associated especially with the German *Verein fur Reformationsgeschichte.*

Founding Date: 1947

Membership: 400

Publications:
    2 scholarly journals: *Archive for Reformation History,* and a *Literature-Review*
    Annual newsletter

Meetings:
    1 per year

86. American Society of Church History

Nondenominational
William B. Miller, Secretary
305 East Country Club Lane
Wallingford, Pennsylvania 19086
(215) 566-7126

The American Society of Church History seeks to advance and deepen historical knowledge of Christianity in all periods and places, in every aspect of its expression: institutional, religious, and intellectual, as well as its manifold interrelationships with nations, cultures, and other religions. The Society is an organization of men and women who share a common interest in the study of the historical record of the Christian church. Most members are professionals in teaching and writing church history, but the Society has always welcomed those with related interests and vocations. Its purpose is to encourage the gathering of historical materials, the formation of archives, the interchange of ideas, and the maintenance of high standards for research or for writing and teaching Christian history.

Founding Date: 1888

Membership: 1,500

Publications:
    Church History, quarterly

Meetings:
    2 per year

87. American Society of Missiology

Nondenominational
Dr. Wilbert R. Shenk, Secretary-Treasurer
Post Office Box 1092
Elkhart, Indiana 46515
(219) 294-7523

The American Society of Missiology was founded in 1973. Its purposes are: to promote the scholarly study of theological, historical, social, and practical questions relating to the missionary dimension of the Christian church; to relate studies in missiology to the other scholarly disciplines; to promote fellowship and cooperation among individuals and institutions engaged in activities and studies related to missiology; to facilitate mutual assistance and exchange of information among those thus engaged; and to encourage research and publication in the study of Christian missions.

Founding Date: 1973

Membership: 625

Publications:
    Missiology: An International Review, quarterly
    Monograph series of books

Meetings:
    1 annual meeting

88. American Temperance Society (ATS)

Seventh-day Adventist Church
Ernest H. J. Steed, Executive Director
6840 Eastern Avenue, N.W.
Washington, D.C. 20023
(202) 722-6729

The purpose of the American Temperance Society is twofold. On the one hand, the society aims to promulgate, through popular education, facts concerning benefits of true temperance, the evil effects of alcoholic beverages, tobacco, and narcotics. On the other hand, it aims to develop an enlightened public opinion which shall, by voice and pen and vote, demand of lawmakers the complete eradication of alcohol, tobacco, and narcotics. The ATS is nonpolitical and nonsectarian. Membership is open to all who make a commitment to nondrinking and nonsmoking, determining to support the aims of better living through personal example and testimony. Educational teaching aids such as films and literature are also available to the public. Two major community service projects are the Five-Day Plan to Stop Smoking and the Four DK Plan for Better Living without alcohol or drugs.

Founding Date: 1826

Staff: 19

Membership: 400,000

Publications:
> *Listen,* monthly
> *Smoke Signals,* monthly
> *The Winner,* 9 a year
> *Better Living*

Meetings:
> World Congress, quinquennial

89. American Theological Library Association, Inc.

Nondenominational

The Rev. David J. Wartluft, Executive Secretary
Lutheran Theological Seminary
7301 Germantown Avenue
Philadelphia, Pennsylvania 19119
(215) 248-4616, ext/36-37

The American Theological Library Association seeks to bring its members into closer working relationship with each other, to improve theological libraries, and to interpret the role of such libraries in theological education by developing and implementing standards of library service, promoting research and experimental projects, publishing literature, research tools and aids, and cooperating with organizations that have similar aims. To its institutional members ATLA provides the following: consultation services, periodicals exchange program, statistical dissemination, aids for accreditation self-study, and a common arena for interrelation among libraries. For individual members ATLA provides a personnel placement clearinghouse, aid in bibliographic systems, and opportunities for personal development. Present projects include continuing education, a national data base of bibliographic information for religious serials, a study of deterioration of library resources in religion, cooperative consultations, a microforms program, and indices of periodical literature and other multi-author works.

Founding Date: 1947

Staff: 1

Membership:
> 450 individuals
> 150 institutions

Publications:
> *Proceedings,* annually
> *Newsletter,* quarterly
> *Religion Index One: Periodical Literature,* biannually with biennial cumulations
> *Monograph Series* and *Bibliographic Series*

Meetings:
> 1 annual conference in June
> Occasional regional and special subject conferences

90. American Tract Society

Nondenominational

Dr. Stephen E. Slocum, Jr., President
1624 North First Street
Garland, Texas 75040
(214) 276-9408

The American Tract Society produces, publishes, and distributes Christian literature. Books, booklets, magazines, and leaflets are among the publications of the American Tract Society. In leaflets alone, volume now exceeds 30 million pieces annually and the impact has been felt around the world. For more than 100 years a special presentation of Bibles has been made to the Cadets at the West Point Military Academy. In addition, chaplains have widely distributed vast quantities of free literature to servicemen through seven major wars. Each year the Society gives more than $50,000 in literature to prisons, hospitals, and missionary organizations both in the United States and overseas. The Society is dependent upon Christian friends for the support of its work.

Founding Date: 1825

Staff: 20

Membership: 11,000

Publications:
> Christian leaflets

91. American Zionist Federation*

Jewish

Mrs. Faye Schenk, President
515 Park Avenue
New York, New York 10022
(212) 371-7750

The American Zionist Federation is an educational organization which serves as the spokesman of the entire Zionist Movement in the United States, embracing over one million members. It strives to educate the Jewish community in Jewish values, the meaning of Judaism, the relationship of the people of Israel to the land of Israel; and to deepen Jewish commitment to Israel. It also reaches out to the general American community on the subjects of Zionism and Israel, and engages in activities which will help interpret Israel and Zionism to that community.

Membership: 1,000,000

Publications:
Information and education magazines
Articles and program manuals

Radio/TV Programs:
Educational video tapes for cable TV

Meetings:
Approximately 20 to 30 annually

92. Americans for God, Inc.

Nondenominational
John C. Webb, Jr., President
Post Office Box 124
Gaithersburg, Maryland 20760
(301) 253-3496

Americans for God, Inc. was formed in response to the Supreme Court decision banning use of the Bible for devotional purposes in Maryland public schools. This limited ban has been stretched by Maryland public officials into a total ban on God and on Carroll's sacred trust, defined as "liberty to do our best for God and country," in public school textbooks. To alert Americans who are for God, the organization has accomplished the following: 1) Members of the Maryland Back to God Committee collected over 30,000 petition signatures for action on school prayer in 1969. The Committee helped convince the Maryland Legislature to pass a constitutional prayer amendment that did not ban God and prayer. Approved by voters in 1970, it is now part of the Maryland state constitution; 2) As a result of a four-year effort for an unprejudiced representation of American family values based on the Bible in sex education courses, the Board of Education published a pamphlet entitled "Religious Statements on Sexuality and Contraception." This pamphlet, which students must request, contains Catholic, Jewish, Protestant, and Fundamentalist Protestant view-

points; 3) The reprint of the official state history of "The Maryland Act of Religious Toleration — An Interpretation by Gerald W. Johnson" provides historical proof that Maryland legislators in 1649 were pioneers in the cause of separation of church and state; 4) Extensive publicity of the leadership of Marylander Charles Carroll of Carrollton helped inspire a state-wide student essay contest on Carroll sponsored by the Maryland Legislature.

Founding Date: 1968

Membership: Approximately 200

Publications:
America Back to God News, 1 periodically

Former Name:
(1969) Maryland Back to God Committee

93. Americans United

Nondenominational
R. G. Puckett, Executive Director
8120 Fenton Street
Silver Spring, Maryland 20910
(301) 589-3707

Americans United is a nonprofit, nonsectarian, nonpartisan educational organization founded in 1947. Its national headquarters is in Silver Spring, Maryland, minutes from Capitol Hill and The White House. Its single purpose is to maintain the American principle of separation of church and state by which the United States Constitution and the state constitutions guarantee religious liberty to all the people and churches of this republic. It is supported by the voluntary gifts of more than 40,000 members and subscribers to *Church and State,* its monthly magazine, and more than 4,000 churches, representing 31 denominations. It works with fraternal and civic groups concerned with preserving religious liberty in our nation. Americans United has 120 local chapters in cities across the nation, with metropolitan offices in St. Louis and Los Angeles.

Founding Date: 1947

Staff: 25

Membership: 40,000

Publications:
Church and State Review, monthly
A weekly press service to more than 650 newspapers all over the country

Meetings:
1 national conference

94. America's Keswick

Nondenominational
William A. Raws, General Director
Keswick Grove
Whiting, New Jersey 08759
(201) 350-1187

Part I of the Keswick ministries, The Keswick Colony of Mercy was established 83 years ago for the rehabilitation of alcoholics. There are 45 beds. Men are housed for 90 days at no charge and given a daily program of Bible study as a group, individual Bible study by the use of study books, six hour a day work therapy, and four general meetings a week in the chapel on the grounds. The organization's work is supported by interested people and churches concerned about the alcoholic. Part II of the Keswick ministries is the Keswick Bible Conference. A full conference ministry is conducted throughout the summer months with well-known Bible teachers. Special conferences and seminars are held at various times of the year for singles, couples, ministers and youth. During the winter months, month-end conferences are conducted and various church groups use the facilities for their retreats. The conference came into being during the prohibition era.

Founding Date: 1897
Publications:
   Clarion
Radio/TV Programs:
   Produces tapes for airing on Christian radio stations
Meetings:
   Summer conferences; several conferences and seminars throughout the year

95. AMG International*

Nondenominational
Spiros Zodhiates, President, Board of Trustees
6815 Shallowford Road
Chattanooga, Tennessee 37421
(615) 894-6062

AMG International is evangelistic in nature. It conducts radio broadcasts in many countries and languages, inserts gospel messages as paid advertisements, distributes scriptures and gospel literature, publishes books, operates bookstores, etc. In the field of relief, it sponsors orphanages, hospitals, leprosy units, day care centers, and feeding stations. In addition, it handles the distribution of clothing, food, and medicines.

Founding Date: 1942
Publications:
   300 books
   Five magazines
Radio/TV Programs:
   4 stations
   600 programs per week
Former Names:
   Advancing the Ministries of the Gospel
   (1953) America's Committee for the Evangelization of the Greeks
   (1974) American Mission to the Greeks

96. Anchor Bay Evangelistic Association, Inc.

Evangelistic
Dr. Roy John Turner, President
Base and Main Streets
New Baltimore, Michigan 48047
(313) 725-0821

Anchor Bay Evangelistic Association is a world-wide ministerial fellowship. It was founded in the city of New Baltimore, Michigan by Dr. Roy John Turner. The purpose of the fellowship is to license and ordain ministers, carry on works of charity, and establish churches and Christian workers in foreign fields. The Association also owns and operates Anchor Bay Bible Institute, which offers a three year ministerial course to prepare students to become evangelists, pastors, missionaries and Christian workers. There are missionaries located in 11 separate works in foreign fields.

Founding Date; 1940
Publications:
   Newsletter, monthly

97. The Anglican Society

Protestant Episcopal Church
Lloyd C. Minter, Treasurer
5916 Wayne Avenue
Philadelphia, Pennsylvania 19144
(215) 438-2205

The object of the Anglican Society is to promote and maintain Catholic Faith and Practice in accordance with the principles of the Book of Common Prayer.

Membership: 500
Publications:
   The Anglican, quarterly

98. Anthroposophical Society in America*

Nondenominational
211 Madison Avenue
New York, New York 10016
(212) 685-4618

The Anthroposophical Society in America promotes the Spiritual Science of Anthroposophy, through which man can obtain objective knowledge of spiritual realities. This involves inner development and training for a conscious approach to cognition as exacting as that required by natural science. The Society publishes a great variety of books which express its beliefs. It has organized activities and services in education, the arts, science, and medicine. Its members deliver lectures and conduct conferences.

Publications:
   Journal for Anthroposophy, semiannually
   Books, journals, bibliographies, lectures
Meetings:
   Annual conferences and lectures

99. Anti-Defamation League of B'nai B'rith (ADL)

Jewish
Maxwell E. Greenberg, National Chairman
823 United Nations Plaza
New York, New York 10017
(212) 490-2525

The Anti-Defamation League of B'nai B'brith is one of the nation's oldest human relations agencies. A recognized leader in its field, ADL is dedicated in purpose and program to translating this country's heritage of democratic ideals into a way of life for all Americans. Its history is an inspiring record of participation in democratic progress in the United States by a Jewish organization which knew from the very beginning that the security of all minority groups is intertwined with the security of democracy itself. ADL was founded in 1913 with a handful of stationery, two desks in a Chicago law office, and a group of determined volunteers who set as its goal "To stop the defamation of the Jewish people . . . to secure justice and fair treatment to all citizens alike." That was the beginning of what today is a global agency, headquartered in New York City, with 27 regional offices in this country, offices in Paris and Jerusalem, affiliated offices in Latin America, and a consultant in Rome.

Founding Date: 1913
Staff: 264
Publications:
   ADL Bulletin, monthly
   Facts
   Law
   Nuestro Encuentro
Meetings:
   Annual meeting of the members of the National Commission
   2 annual meetings of the National Executive Committee
Merger: (1965) Institute for Democratic Education

100. Apostleship of Prayer

Roman Catholic
Robert J. McAllister, SJ, National Director
114 East 13th Street
New York, New York 10003
(212) 673-9060

The Apostleship of Prayer is a worldwide association of Catholics who strive to make their ordinary, everyday lives apostolically effective. They do this by offering themselves and everything they do in union with Christ's Eucharistic Sacrifice. They also do this by saying and living the Daily Offering.

Founding Date: 1844
Staff: 5
Membership:
   5 million lay; 25,000 clerical
Publications:
   Newsletter to parishes
   Prayer cards, leaflets, pictures, etc.

101. Apostolic Christian Church Foundation

Apostolic Christian Church
Walter H. Meyer, General Secretary
Post Office Box 151
Tremont, Illinois 61568
(309) 925-3551

The Apostolic Christian Church Foundation was formed for the following purposes: to create and maintain funds for the purpose of spreading the gospel in the United States and in other countries; to provide the needed visitation by church workers in the churches and for isolated members and where possible to establish new churches; to provide exhortation and help in the churches as needed for the awakening and renewing of interest in the work of the Lord; to provide the necessary collaboration and assistance among the churches for the selection and preparation of bible school materials; to investigate the needs, to advise, and to assist in the procurement of church buildings and other needed facilities; to represent the Apostolic Christian Churches as a service organization regarding legal or governmental matters which may arise; to establish committees for the promotion of the purposes and objects of the corporation in different parts of the United States and other countries; and to solicit and disburse funds for the purpose of aiding the needy and the distressed in the United States and in other countries.

Founding Date: 1953

Publications:
> *Apostolic Christian Church Newsletter,* quarterly

Meetings:
> One camp in the West, one in the Midwest, and one in the East in the summer, one week each
> An annual meeting of the foundation
> Weekend retreats

102. Apostolic Christian Church of America, Apostolic Christian Mission Fund

Apostolic Christian Church of America
Ben C. Maibach, Jr., Bishop, Secretary-Treasurer
3420 North Sheridan Road
Peoria, Illinois 61606

Mailing Address
14726 Fox
Redford, Michigan 48239
(313) 531-3536

The purposes of the Apostolic Christian Mission Fund, as stated in its certificate of incorporation, are religious, charitable, and educational purposes for the worshiping of God and the spreading of the Christian religion, conducting of these activities as a non-profit organization according to the rules, regulations, customs, and practices of the Apostolic Christian Church of America as set forth by the Holy Scriptures. They seek to promote the cause of this

Christian religion in the interest of this Church; to conduct religious services, including Sunday Schools; to receive, hold, administer, disburse, and generally deal with gifts, bequests, endowments, and contributions of all kinds in furtherance of the religious and charitable purposes of this Corporation; to own, maintain, and sell real estate and buildings and do any and all things necessary or incidental thereto; to establish, erect, equip, maintain, manage, operate, and generally deal in convenient and comfortable homes for the aged and infirm, handicapped, or other unfortunate or displaced persons; and to accept and receive contributions and to make distribution of such funds as may be deemed advisable by the Trustees of the Corporation or their appropriate representatives.

Founding Date: 1835

Membership: 11,000

Publications:
> Hymnals: Gospel Hymns, Hymns of Zion and Zion's Harp
> Sunday School material
> Church history and directories
> *Silver Lining,* monthly news publication

Meetings:
> One brotherhood conference
> One meeting of ministers
> At least two meetings of bishops

103. Appalachian People's Service Organization, Inc. (APSO)

Episcopal
The Rev. R. Baldwin Lloyd
Post Office Box 1007
Blacksburg, Virginia 24060
(703) 552-3795

Appalachian People's Service Organization, Inc., is an independently constituted church organization sponsored by the Episcopal dioceses of the Appalachian region in cooperation with the Executive Council of the Episcopal Church. Its purpose is to serve the people of the mountain areas. Programs include: training of clergy and congregations for mission and ministry, support of grass roots community projects, development of new educational and communication programs, and special concern for youth groups.

Former Name:
> The Episcopal Church, Appalachian Ministries

104. Archconfraternity of Christian Mothers*

Roman Catholic
Father Bertin Roll, OFM Cap.
220 Thirty-seventh Street
Pittsburgh, Pennsylvania 15201
(412) 683-2400

The members of the Archconfraternity of Christian Mothers, and all Confraternities affiliated with it, are encouraged to provide the utmost in Christian home education for their children. They edify one another by fervent prayers and thus become the mainstay of spiritual life within their own families, and a fruitful source of belssings in the communities in which they live.

Publications:
The Christian Mother, quarterly
2 books
1 booklet

105. Arctic Broadcasting Association

Evangelical Covenant Church of America
Ralph V. Fondell, General Manager
Post Office Box 820
Nome, Alaska 99762
(907) 443-2213

Arctic Broadcasting Association, operating KICY-AM and KICY-FM, was established as an arm of the Evangelical Covenant Church in Alaska. Its purpose is to communicate the good news of forgiveness and salvation through faith in Jesus Christ, whether this communication be through the spoken word, music, or drama; to communicate the Word of God, the Bible; to nurture newly received spiritual life; and to provide a public service in the name of Jesus Christ. KICY recognizes the primacy of the written Word as the instrument of the Holy Spirit in instructing believers concerning the will and purposes of God, and in maturing their spiritual lives. Special emphasis is placed upon use of the Bible in the total ministry of the station. KICY seeks to provide programs of high quality, wholesome entertainment features, a variety of music, and political and public information programs geared to the needs of the local community and the greater listening audience. In its position as the Emergency Broadcast System (EBS) station for Northwestern Alaska, KICY serves the public as a vital outlet for civil defense information of local, regional, and national importance.

Publications:
KICY Call Letter, 3 times a year
Newsletter

106. Argus Communications

Interdenominational
Mr. Richard Leach, President and Publisher
7440 Natchez Avenue
Niles, Illinois 60648
(312) 647-7800

Argus Communications publishes book, filmstrip, film, and audiocassette and videocassette programs that appeal to an interfaith audience. These programs focus on topics such as scripture, prayer, personal growth, moral courage, and spirituality.

Radio/TV Programs:
Three TV video cassettes are available: *Free To Be Me, Families, Jesus as I Know Him*

107. Armenian Missionary Association of America, Inc. (AMAA)

United Church of Christ and two Churches affiliated with the United Presbyterian Churches in the United States of America
The Rev. G. H. Chopourian, PhD, Executive Director
140 Forest Avenue
Paramus, New Jersey 07652
(210) 265-2607

The Armenian Missionary Association was founded as a result of the Armenian genocide practiced by the Ottoman Empire. Its purpose was to serve Armenians who were dispersed over many parts of the Middle East and needed encouragement and brotherly concern. For half a century, the Association provided the necessary financial help to build churches, schools, and other institutions, and to raise the moral and spiritual level of the existing schools. Recently, the organization has moved into more aggressive services in evangelism, social service, and publication that also touch on the need in the United States. The Association administers Child Education Sponsorship Programs in five foreign countries. It also owns and administers, through a local Board of Managers, the Haigazian College in Beirut, Lebanon.

Founding Date: 1918
Staff: 6
Membership: 8,020

Publications:
> *The AMAA News,* bimonthly

Meetings:
> 1 annual meeting

108. Assemblies of God, Division of Christian Education

Assemblies of God

Hardy W. Steinberg, National Director
1445 Boonville Avenue
Springfield, Missouri 65802
(417) 862-2781

The Division of Christian Education, Assemblies of God, includes the Education Department and Church School Literature Department. The former has within its purview educational institutions from preschool through graduate school. Assemblies of God colleges (10) enroll 8,758. There are currently 935 Assemblies of God churches operating day schools. Total enrollment in day schools is 72,526. An 18-member Board of Education guides the work of the Education Department. The Church School Literature Department produces educational materials for the following levels: Baby and Toddler (birth to age two); Nursery (ages two, three); Beginner (ages four, five); Primary (grades one, two); Middler (grades three, four); Junior (grades 10-12); Young Adult; and Adult. Materials include teacher and student quarterlies, multi-media teaching packets, visual aids, take-home papers, and adult electives in paperback form. The department also produces vacation Bible school materials for the whole family each year.

Staff: 35

Publications:
> *Radiant Life,* Sunday school literature
> *The Assemblies of God Educator*

Meetings:
> Board of Education meets twice a year

109. Assemblies of God, Division of Church Ministries

Assemblies of God

Silas L. Gaither, National Director
1445 Boonville Avenue
Springfield, Missouri 65802
(417) 862-2781

The Division of Church Ministries includes the Sunday School, Music, Youth, Men's Ministries, and Women's Ministries Departments at the denomination's headquarters in Springfield, Missouri. The departments provide training, special services, and program materials for use by their counterparts in the 9,400 Assemblies of God congregations across the nation. World Ministries funding programs (Speed-the-Light, Boys & Girls Missionary Crusade, Light-for-the-Lost, Women's Ministries) coordinated by the departments exceed $9 million each year.

Publications:
> *Sunday School Counselor*
> *Light 'n Heavy,* youth
> *Youth Leader*
> *Woman's Touch*
> *CAM,* Campus Ambassadors Magazine—college youth
> *Missionette Memos,* leadership for girls
> *Motif,* Music in Ministry
> *High Adventure,* boys

110. Assemblies of God, Division of Communications

Assemblies of God

Rev. Leland Shultz, National Director
1445 Boonville Avenue
Springfield, Missouri 65802
(417) 862-2781

The departments of the Division of Communications include Radio-TV, *Pentecostal Evangel,* Audiovisual Services, *Advance* Magazine, and Office of Information. The radio program "Revivaltime" is heard almost 1,500 times each week. The *Pentecostal Evangel* is the official weekly publication of the Assemblies of God and has a current circulation in excess of 270,000. *Advance* Magazine is the church's journal for clergymen and has a current circulation of 22,000. Audiovisual Services provide rental films and cassette tapes to churches and members. The Office of Information provides news releases, multimedia programs, informational brochures, and other materials of an informational nature to the public inside and outside the denomination.

Publications:
> *Pentecostal Evangel,* weekly
> *Advance*

Radio/TV Programs:
> *Revivaltime,* a weekly radio broadcast sponsored by the Assemblies of God

111. Assemblies of God, Division of Foreign Missions*

Assemblies of God
J. Philip Hogan, National Director
1445 Boonville Avenue
Springfield, Missouri 65802
(417) 862-2781

The Division of Foreign Missions, Assemblies of God, seeks to bring the gospel to every man, woman, and child on the earth, and to prepare national pastors and local evangelists. To achieve these objectives, the Division has over 1,000 missionaries now in service and almost 150 foreign Bible Schools ranging from night classes to full college-level programs.

Membership: 1,000 Missionaries

112. Assemblies of God, Division of Home Missions

Assemblies of God
T. E. Gannon, National Director
1445 Boonville Avenue
Springfield, Missouri 65802
(417) 862-2781

The primary responsibility of the Division of Home Missions of the Assemblies of God is to act as an agency of the church in fulfilling its three missions. The essential function is the establishing of new churches through the auspices of the district councils. The work of the division includes three major departments: New Church Evangelism, Special Ministries, and Chaplaincy. The Special Ministries Department provides ministry among those people in the United States who need special help by reason of cultural, ethnic, or language barriers, handicaps, geographical or institutional isolation, drug addiction, or minority status. The Chaplaincy Department serves correctional and other institutions and military personnel.

Staff: 21

Publications:
> *Assemblies of God Home Missions,* bimonthly
> *At Ease,* bimonthly magazine for military personnel

Meetings:
> Annual conventions for gypsy and Jewish people
> Special Home Missions Institute for nearly 300 home missionaries and their companions

113. Assembly of Episcopal Hospitals and Chaplains (AEHC)

Episcopal
The Rev. C.K. Trewhella, Treasurer
1015 N.W. 22nd Avenue
Portland, Oregon 97210
(503) 229-7057

The Assembly of Episcopal Hospitals and Chaplains encourages the development of chaplaincy programs on the soundest professional level, using clergy trained in pastoral ministry skills. AEHC promotes the development of paid or volunteer chaplaincy programs in all hospitals. The Assembly reinforces the spiritual foundations on which all Episcopal hospitals were organized. The annual convention is an experience in personal and professional growth, with three days of outstanding speakers, workshops and seminars. For many this is the only opportunity to meet with fellow chaplains and administrators. AEHC has been involved in learning about Hospice, modifying the cancer personality and Wholistic Health Care from the early stages of their development.

Founding Date: 1951

Membership: 400-500

Publications:
> *Chaplair,* quarterly

Meetings:
> The annual convention of the Assembly meets at the same time and place as the Protestant Health and Welfare Assembly, of which AEHC is an affiliate. Four-day meetings are held in early March.

114. Associate Reformed Presbyterian Church, World Witness, Board of Foreign Missions

Associate Reformed Presbyterian
John E. Mariner, Executive Secretary
Associate Reformed Presbyterian Center
One Cleveland Street
Greenville, South Carolina 29601
(803) 232-8297

World Witness, the Board of Foreign Missions of the Associate Reformed Presbyterian Church, is organized to carry out the great commission of carrying the Gospel of Jesus Christ to the world. World Witness works through a variety of activities including direct evangelization, literature, adult literacy programs, public health, hospitals, radio, TV, Bible correspondence schools, camp programs, theological education by extension, church planting, education, dormitories, and crusades within the geographical boundaries of its work. The work of the Board is concentrated in the countries of Mexico and Pakistan.

Founding Date: 1839

Publications:
> *Prayer Warrior,* monthly

Radio/TV Programs:
> 2 radio programs in Mexico

Meetings:
> Approximately 12 each year

115. The Associated Church Press

Nondenominational
Donald F. Hetzler, Executive Secretary
321 James
Geneva, Illinois 60134
Mailing Address
Post Office Box 306
Geneva, Illinois 60134
(312) 232-1055

The purpose of the Associated Church Press is to promote acquaintance and fellowship, to foster helpfulness among editors and publishers of its member publications, and to stimulate higher standards of religious journalism in order to enable its member publications to render more useful service and to exert a more positive and constructive influence on contemporary civilization. The major program activities of the Associated Church Press are regional and national seminars, and annual covention, an annual "Adward of Merit" program for excellence in religious journalism, and a membership "Cluster" program in incipient stages.

Membership:
> 125 religious publications in the United States and Canada
> Twenty individual associate members

Publications:
> *Newslog,* bimonthly newsletter
> *ACP Directory,* annually

Meetings:
> Annual convention
> 2 regional seminars
> 1 national seminar

116. The Associated Missions

Interdenominational
Dr. Henry Campbell, President
756 Haddon Avenue
Collingswood, New Jersey 08108
(609) 858-0700

The Associated Missions exists as a worldwide umbrella for fundamental missionary agencies. It provides fellowship, information, and dissemination of data concerning the agencies' needs, programs, and projects. A primary distinctive of The Associated Missions is its separation from ecumenism and what is considered to be the compromise of the requirements of the Great Commission as found in Holy Writ. The Associated Missions also serves as the missionary arm of The International Council of Christian Churches. The Associated Missions was formed in 1948 with the founding of the International Council of Christian Churches (ICCC). Every missionary agency is autonomous and is not directed or dictated to by the overall Board of TAM. However, the agencies are required to subscribe to the Statement of Faith of The Associated Missions which is identical to that of the ICCC.

Founding Date: 1948

Membership: 65 affiliated agencies

Publications:
> Monthly newsletter

Meetings:
> Monthly meetings and regional meetings in various parts of the world

Former Name:
> (1952) Missions Commission of the International Council of Christian Churches

117. Association for Christian Schools*

Nondenominational
Dr. R. Vernon Colpitts, President
Post Office Box 35096
Houston, Texas 77035
(713) 666-3111

The Association for Christian Schools serves the purpose of encouraging and supporting the establishment of Christian Schools wherever possible. It embraces all denominations willing to participate knowing that the foundation principle of all that is done is that Jesus is Lord and Christ. The Association's most important activity is the annual Conference on Christian Schools held every spring at St.

Thomas' Episcopal School in Houston, Texas. This public gathering of pastors, teachers, and headmasters, together with interested Christian people from all over the country, proposes to stimulate a general recovery of Christian scholarship. There are also round table discussions of various stages of starting and running a school: preliminary planning and financing, curriculum and behavioral questions and answers, pitfalls to avoid in starting and running a Christian school, and the elements of administration.

Meetings:
    Annually in the spring

118. Association for Clinical Pastoral Education, Inc.

Nondenominational
Charles E. Hall, Jr., Executive Director
475 Riverside Drive, Suite 450
New York, New York 10027
(212) 870-2558

The Association for Clinical Pastoral Education promotes clinical pastoral education as a part of theological education and continuing education for the ministry; defines and promulgates standards for clinical pastoral education; accredits clinical pastoral education programs; certifies clinical pastoral education supervisors; and provides for the development of professional concerns of supervisors of clinical pastoral education and other members through publications, conferences, and research opportunities.

Founding Date: 1967
Staff: 5
Membership: 4,000
Publications:
    Journal of Pastoral Care, quarterly
Meetings:
    1 national conference
    9 regional conferences

119. Association for Jewish Studies

Jewish
Jane S. Gerber, President
Widener Library M
Harvard University
Cambridge, Massachusetts 02138
(617) 495-2985

The Association for Jewish Studies seeks to promote, maintain, and improve the teaching of Jewish Studies in American colleges and universities by sponsoring meetings and conferences, publishing a newsletter and other scholarly materials, setting standards for programs in Jewish Studies, aiding in the placement of teachers, coordinating research, and cooperating with other scholarly organizations.

Founding Date: 1969
Membership: 1,000
Publications:
    5 scholarly books
    2 scholarly periodicals
Meetings:
    1 per year

120. Association for Professional Education for Ministry

Nondenominational
Prof. Gaylord Noyce, President
409 Prospect Street
New Haven, Connecticut 06510
(203) 436-8454

The Association for Professional Education for Ministry was organized out of an interest in bringing together persons teaching in the various practical disciplines of theological education, and facilitating closer cooperation between these disciplines and others in the preparation of persons for ministry in the church. Its basic purpose is to integrate the classical biblical, historical, and theological disciplines of theological education by experience and theological reflection. Its ultimate goal is the "readiness for ministry" of the graduates of theological seminaries associated with the Association of Theological Schools of the United States and Canada (ATS).

Founding Date: 1950
Membership: 125
Publications:
    Biennial report
Meetings:
    Biennial convention
Former Name:
    (1970) Association of Seminary Professors in the Practical Fields

121. Association for the Development of Religious Information Systems (ADRIS)

Nondenominational

David O. Moberg, Coordinator
Department of Sociology and Anthropology
Marquette University
Milwaukee, Wisconsin 53233
Mailing Address
Dr. Richard F. Smith, Editor
Department of Theology, Fordham University
Bronx, New York 10458
(414) 224-6838

The Association for the Development of Religious Information Systems is a task-oriented professional association. Its goal is to promote coordination and cooperation among information services which are pertinent to religion by imparting relevant information, identifying needs, discussing mutual interests, exploring the feasibility of proposed projects, and stimulating cooperative ventures. The Association hopes that a clearinghouse of religious information sources eventually will emerge from ADRIS. In the meantime, its efforts are organized primarily around sharing information about resources that are designed to provide informational, educational, research, or administrative services relevant to religion. ADRIS' activities center around the quarterly *ADRIS Newsletter* and the *1971 International Directory of Religious Information Systems* which is currently undergoing revision.

Founding Date: 1971

Publications:
ADRIS Newsletter, quarterly

122. Association of Baptists for World Evangelism, Inc. (ABWE)

Baptist
Dr. Wendell W. Kempton, President
1720 Springdale Road
Cherry Hill, New Jersey 08034
(609) 424-4606

Founded as an independent Baptist faith mission, the Association of Baptists for World Evangelism, Inc., owes its origin to the urgent need to provide fundamental Baptist churches and individuals with a missionary agency which is true to the Word of God in doctrine and method. The purpose of this organization is to help fulfill the Lord's commission to evangelize the world with the gospel of individual salvation from sin through the blood of Christ. The objectives are to establish indigenous Baptist churches and to train national pastors and leaders. The more than 500 missionaries of the ABWE are working in the Philipines, Peru, Colombia, Brazil, Hong Kong,

Chile, Japan, Bangladesh, Papua New Guinea, Spain, Australia, Togo, Paraguay, United States of America, Gambia, Portugal, South Africa, Argentina, and Norway.

Founding Date: 1927

Membership: 515

Publications:
The Message, bimonthly, the official organ of the mission

Meetings:
Biennial conferences for missionaries in South America and the Philipines

123. Association of Camps Farthest Out, Inc. (CFO)

Nondenominational
Joyce A. Walker, Chief Administrative Officer
1569 Grand Avenue
St. Paul, Minnesota 55105
(612) 699-2183

The Association of Camps Farthest Out, Inc., is a non-profit nondenominational organization that brings together campers and leaders from many churches and traditions to participate through mind and spirit in the CFO camps and week-end retreats. The emphasis is on experience rather than doctrine. CFO believes there is an experience which supersedes the ability of the conscious mind to comprehend and categorize: a vital experience with the living God through Jesus Christ. It is this experience toward which the whole CFO program is directed. A traditional format is usually followed in the daily program. Balance is a key word: listening, participating, giving out, taking in. The days are filled with morning meditation, morning and evening talks, various creative experiences, and prayer groups and song services.

Membership:
CFO has no formal membership or membership fees. All who attend the camps and retreats become a part of CFO by their participation through mind and spirit. Between 10 and 12 thousand people of all ages attend the 63 camps held all over the United States and Canada each year.

Publications:
Fellowship Messenger, published in April, July, and October
Directory of Camps, published in January

Meetings:
> 63 camps and 19 retreats in 36 different states and four Canadian provinces will be held in 1980

124. Association of Catholic Colleges and Universities

Roman Catholic
Alice Gallin, OSU, Executive Director
One Dupont Circle, Suite 770
Washngton, DC 20036
(202) 293-5954

The Association of Catholic Colleges and Universities is a voluntary association of regionally accredited colleges and universities. Currently there are 214 institutional members. The Association also accepts individual members. The purpose of the Association is to facilitate exchange among Catholic institutions of higher education and to represent them with other national associations of higher education, church-related associations of institutions of higher education, the International Federation of Catholic Universities, and to various agencies of the Federal government. Special attention is paid to those areas of concern which have a particular relevance for institutions in their attempts to respond to the contemporary needs of church and society.

Founding Date: 1899
Staff: 3
Membership: 214
Publications:
> *Current Issues in Catholic Higher Education,* twice yearly magazine
> *Update,* bimonthly newsletter

Meetings:
> Annual meeting (Washington, D.C.) 1 per year

Former Name: Association of Catholic Colleges

125. Association of Chicago Priests

Roman Catholic
Rev. Thomas A. Libera, Chairman
1307 South Wabash, Room 204
Chicago, Illinois 60605
(312) 922-1638

The Association of Chicago Priests is an independent association of priests and permanent deacons interested in ministry in the Chicago area. Its purposes are to cooperate as an association with the Bishop in his pastoral role; to promote effective communication among priests; to promote dialogue on every level within the Christian community; and to seek common solutions to problems affecting the entire community. To promote these ends the following regular efforts are made: bimonthly publication of *Upturn* magazine; occasional study papers; a yearly plenary session for members; sponsorship of a yearly award night; and administration of the Bishop Michael Dempey Hunger Fund.

Founding Date: 1966
Staff: 2
Membership: 500
Publications:
> *Upturn,* bimonthly

Meetings:
> *Mardi Gras fundraiser* and award night in late February
> Membership Plenary Session in March

126. Association of Christian Television Stations (ACTS)*

Nondenominational
Dr. Lester Sumrall, President
Post Office Box 50250
Indianapolis, Indiana 46250
(317) 773-5030

The Association of Christian Television Stations comprises an increasing group of television stations in the United States which fellowship together and council together regarding the mass media. Its stations are all non-profit corporations. They function similarly to a local church, but on a larger scale. There are 13 stations which extend across the entire nation and exchange programs and information with one another.

Membership: 13
Radio/TV Programs:
> Each station produces many different types of programs each week

127. Association of Contemplative Sisters (ACS)

Roman Catholic
Sr. Annamae Dannes, OCD, President
Carmelite Monastery
3176 Fairmount Boulevard
Cleveland Heights, Ohio 44118
(216) 321-5658

The Association of Contemplative Sisters is an international non-profit organization for contemplative women of prayer. Its members represent a plurality of contemplative traditions in the United States and Canada. The Association's purposes are: to intensify and creatively develop our personal and communal life of prayer; to transform the dynamic energy of prayer into a new and positive force effective in society's formation of value systems; to encourage each member's personal growth; to stimulate free-flowing communication between our members and others; and to unite our contemplative women in a corporate effort which enriches all the People of God. Long range goals are: to help contemporary men and women understand the meaning of life through the member's own affirmation of the contemplative dimension of humankind; to encourage contemplative women to unite in the vision of their role and to express the primacy of prayer in a diversity of lifestyles; to foster the growth of each person in consciousness and freedom through our authentic living out of gospel values; and to enable each sister to participate in the decision-making process affecting her life through sharing in the functioning of the ACS and her own community.

Founding Date: 1969

Staff: 9

Membership: 400

Publications:

Contemplative Review, quarterly
ACS Newsletter, quarterly

Meetings:

Approximately 5 per year located in various regions: New York Metropolitan, Mideast, Midwest, New England, Eastern, and West

128. Association of Episcopal Colleges

Episcopal

The Rev. Dr. Frederic B. Burnham
815 Second Avenue
New York, New York 10017
(212) 986-0989

The Association of Episcopal Churches serves its member colleges by developing intercollegiate programs, fellowships, and scholarships between the nine colleges in order to strengthen their offering as Episcopal Church-related colleges. In addition, the Association helps the member colleges relate directly to the national, diocesan, and parish level Church for admissions and fund-raising purposes. It

sponsors intercollegiate chaplain seminars each year. It also provides a vehicle whereby lay men and women interested in value oriented, Church-related education may seek ways to contribute to Episcopal colleges.

Founding Date: 1962

Staff: 4

Membership: 9

Publications:

News of Episcopal Colleges, biannually

Meetings:

Annual meeting

129. Association of Jesuit Colleges and Universities (AJCU)

Roman Catholic

Rev. William McInnes, SJ, President
1717 Massachusetts Avenue, N.W., Suite 402
Washington, D.C. 20036
(202) 667-3889

The Association of Jesuit Colleges and Universities serves its members by representing them in developing public policy for higher education, in building communications systems between members, and in directing educational and training activities to broaden the vision of its constituents. Its 19 Conferences represent special interest groups within member institutions. The Conferences meet annually to exchange information and work on cooperative ventures. Workshops in international education, planning and research, and telecommunications help prepare members for the future.

Founding Date: 1970

Staff: 3

Membership: 28

Publications:

AJCU Higher Education Report, 10 issues a year
AJCU Directory, annually
Jesuit degree programs

Meetings:

19 conferences

Former Name: Jesuit Educational Association

130. Association of Jewish Book Publishers (AJBP)

Jewish

Sol Scharfstein, President
838 Fifth Avenue
New York, New York 10021

The Association of Jewish Book Publishers is a non-profit group. It supports book exhibits as well as the publication of Jewish books and the formation of Jewish divisions in public libraries, synagogues, and other communal institutions. The AJBP has attended the 1977, '79, and '81 Russian International Book Fairs where special Jewish book catalogues were distributed. The AJBP is currently preparing a comprehensive catalogue of Jewish books which it plans to distribute free of charge.

Founding Date: 1962

Membership: 30

Publications:
Jewish book catalogues, annually

Meetings:
Four meetings per year at 838 Fifth Avenue

131. Association of Jewish Chaplains of the Armed Forces

Jewish
Rabbi Gilbert Kollin, Administrator
15 East 26th Street
New York, New York 10010
(212) 532-4949

The Association is an organization composed of current and former military chaplains. Its primary function is to encourage its members to support the work of the Commission on Jewish Chaplaincy, the official ecclesiastical endorsing agency for Jewish chaplains. This is done informally by virtue of their membership in their respective groups. The Association sends representatives to communal functions and hosts occasional meetings to confer awards.

Membership: 800

Meetings:
1 annually

132. Association of Jewish Libraries

Jewish
Philip E. Miller, President
c/o National Foundation for Jewish Culture
122 East 42nd Street, Room 1512
New York, New York 10017

The Association of Jewish Libraries consists of two divisions: the Research and Special Library Division, representing university and research libraries and Jewish collections in larger libraries; and the Synagogue, School and Center Library Division, representing the bulk of the membership and serving the

smaller, more popular library. Goals of the AJL are: to promote librarianship and improve library services and professional standards in the field of Judaica; to serve as a center for the dissemination of Jewish library information and guidance; to promote publication of literature which will aid the Jewish library; to keep members abreast of the latest developments in Jewish librarianship. The AJL holds annual conventions featuring outstanding speakers, seminars, and problem clinics aimed at helping the Jewish librarian. The conventions also afford the opportunity to meet colleagues from around the United States and Canada and profit by their experience and knowledge. The SSC Division of the AJL makes an annual award to the author of an outstanding juvenile book in Judaica. It also offers an annual scholarship grant to a qualified library school student planning to enter the field of Judaica.

Founding Date: 1965

Membership: 625

Publications:
AJL Newsletter
AJL Bulletin, twice a year

Meetings:
Convention, once a year, 1983, Los Angeles

Mergers:
(1965) The Jewish Librarians Association and Jewish Library Association merged into the Association of Jewish Libraries

133. Association of Ladies of Charity of the United States (ALCUS)

Roman Catholic
Mrs. Alphonse J. Mayer, President
5339 North Santa Monica Boulevard
Whitefish Bay, Wisconsin 53217

The Association of Ladies of Charity of the United States is a worldwide association of dedicated women who, recognizing the pressing needs of the Church today, give personal service to the poor, the sick, the elderly, and the youth. In the spirit of Christ and St. Vincent de Paul, who made such personal assistance his life's concern, the Ladies work to help fill this pressing need of our day. It is not a secret association, but its members do not seek publicity or recognition of any sort. They work quietly and anonymously in the living shadow of Christ. ALCUS is not a social organization. It makes demands on its members that they give of themselves, their time, their devotion, their sacrifice and perseverance at all times. Personal fulfillment and spiritual growth are their compensations.

Founding Date: 1857 — Federation formed 1960

Membership: 200 associations; 40,000 women

Publications:
> *Servicette,* 5 times per year

Meetings:
> General Assembly, biennially
> Regionals, biennially

134. Association of Lutheran Secondary Schools

Lutheran

Rev. Frederick C. Hinz, President
60-02 Maspeth Avenue
Post Office Box 17
Maspeth, New York 11378
(212) 894-4000

The purpose of the Association of Lutheran Secondary Schools is to improve the quality of Christian Education in its member schools through the cooperative study of educational theory and practice. Its objectives are to identify the needs and implement the services that are desired by the Association; to explore and discuss in depth mutual problems in the field of secondary education; to study and improve curricular offerings in Lutheran secondary schools; to assist the Board of Parish Education in gathering and publishing information of value to the secondary schools and help them identify leadership potential for administrative positions in the Lutheran secondary schools; to provide information concerning staff needs to synodical institutions and Valparaiso University; to encourage regional conferences of teachers; and to assist faculty members in their dual roles as professional educators and ministers of Christian education and to this end provide them with suggestions and resource materials for inservice training.

Staff: 3

Membership: 100

Publications:
> *Lutheran Education,* 5 times a year

Meetings:
> Annual conference held in a different location each year

135. Association of Orthodox Jewish Scientists

Orthodox Jewish

Lester R. Kaufman, President
45 West 36th Street
New York, New York 10018
(212) 695-7525

The Association of Orthodox Jewish Scientists is a professional association which seeks to contribute to the development of science within the framework of Orthodox Jewish tradition. It obtains and disseminates information relating to the interface between traditional Jewish life and law and scientific developments on both an ideological and practical level. The Association has three major sections: Physical and Life Sciences, Medical Sciences, and Behavioral Sciences; and chapters throughout the country. Two main conventions are held each year and two journals *Intercom* and *Proceedings* are published.

Founding Date: 1947

Membership: 1350

Publications:
> *Intercom,* irregularly
> *Proceedings,* irregularly

Meetings:
> A mid-winter two-day conference sponsored by a community in the Metropolitan area
> A summer convention, annually

136. Association of Reform Zionists of America (ARZA)

Reform Judaism/Union of American Hebrew Congregations

838 Fifth Avenue
New York, New York 10021
(212) 249-0100

Association of Reform Zionists of America is the first UAHC affiliate to be organized on an ideological foundation. ARZA is a rapidly growing organization of UAHC congregational members who identify as Zionists under the banner of Reform Judaism. One of ARZA's primary goals is the achievement of full rights and recognition for Reform Judaism in the State of Israel and within the World Zionist Organization. On this front, ARZA scored the first major breakthrough in 80 years when the 29th Zionist Congress (1978) adopted its resolution endorsing Jewish pluralism. Within the American-Jewish community, ARZA seeks to build support for Israel, while raising consciousness of the religious, cultural, and ideological aspects of Israeli life. This is accomplished largely through a program which brings a variety of Israeli speakers to ARZA chapters. A catalogue of study materials is currently in preparation. ARZA's first National Assembly (September, 1978) ratified an ideological platform which is the first formulation of a Reform expression of Zionist commitment. ARZA also seeks to provide support for Reform activities and projects in Israel; a substantial portion of its annual budget is allocated for this purpose. ARZA is a full member of the World Zionist Organization and its regional affiliate, the American Zionist Federation.

137. Association of Romanian Catholics of America, Inc. (ARCA)*

Roman Catholic
General Assembly
4309 Olcott Avenue
East Chicago, Indiana 46312
(219) 398-3760

The Association of Romanian Catholics of America, with the help of inter-parish cooperation, seeks to promote and preserve the culture, traditions, and character of the Romanian Catholic Church among its adherents in America.

Membership: 4,000 lay; 15 clerical
Publications:
Spiritual, liturgical, and historical books
6 titles
monthly review
annual almanac
Meetings:
1 general meeting
2 special meetings annually

138. Association of Theological Schools (ATS)

Nondenominational
Leon Pacala, Executive Director
Post Office Box 130
Vandalia, Ohio 45377
(513) 898-4654

The primary purpose of the Association is to promote the improvement of theological education through conference and consultation, accrediting operations, consultation to various parts of the seminary community and other agencies related to theological education, educational events, fellowship programs for seminary personnel, publications, and research studies. A secondary purpose of the Association is to serve as an advocate for theological education to

agencies of government, philanthropic foundations, ecclesiastical bodies, the general public, and other parts of the post-secondary educational establishment. In addition the Association seeks to provide information regarding a theological education enterprise to the public, and as an international organization to recognize the existence and enable the achievement of desired national identity within the overall consensus of the Association.

Founding Date: 1918
Staff: 10
Membership: 200 member institutions
Publications:
Theological Education, semiannually
Directory, annually
Fact Book, annually
Meetings:
Biennial convention
Former Names:
(1936) Conference of Theological Seminaries of the United States and Canada
(1975) American Association of Theological Schools

139. Augsburg Publishing House

American Lutheran Church
Albert E. Anderson, Chief Executive Officer
426 South Fifth Street
Minneapolis, Minnesota 55415
(612) 330-3300

As the publishing unit of The American Lutheran Church, Augsburg Publishing House publishes books, curriculum, music, periodicals, worship materials, audiovisuals, and other resource materials for churches. These materials are distributed by mail, through its own stores, and through other suppliers. The objectives of Augsburg Publishing House are: to bring the Gospel to as many people as possible through the ministry of the printed word and other media; to provide and distribute materials necessary to assist congregations, pastors, and others in their worship and work; to make available literature, art, and music that will enrich the life of the church spiritually and culturally; and to publish material regarding the theology, life, work, history, and organization of the church.

Staff: 400
Publications:
Augsburg Media Messenger, quarterly, Reviews and information on current audiovisuals for church use

Book News Letter, bimonthly
Reviews and information on current books
designed for church, home, and personal use
Christ in Our Home, quarterly guide, daily devotions, issued in regular and large print editions
The *Lutheran Standard,* twice monthly except monthly in July, August, and December; official publication of The American Lutheran Church
Parish Teacher, monthly except July and August, for teachers and education leaders in parishes of The American Lutheran Church
ALCW Scope, monthly, for women of The American Lutheran Church

140. Ave Maria Press

Roman Catholic
Rev. John Reedy, CSC
Notre Dame, Indiana 46556
(219) 287-2831

Ave Maria Press is primarily a Catholic publishing house serving various and changing informational needs of the Church in the United States and abroad. Secondarily, it operates a printing service which economically serves its publishing activities as well as the printing needs of the University of Notre Dame, St. Mary's College, and the priests of the Congregation of Holy Cross. It fulfills its apostolic purpose by producing high quality books, publications, and audiovisual materials for pastoral, educational, spiritual, and general use by the entire Christian community.

Founding Date: 1865
Staff: 85
Publications:
129 books and booklets
46 cassettes
Spiritual Book News, 8 issues yearly

141. Baha'i Publishing Trust

Baha'i Faith
Wilmette, Illinois 60091
(312) 869-9039

Making Baha'i literature available to the believers is a central concern of the Baha'i Publishing Trust. The first translations of the writings of Baha'u'llah circulated from place to place in hand-typed copies. As early as 1902 a Publishing Society was formed in Chicago to consider ways of publishing and disseminating sacred Baha'i texts. Earlier efforts culminated in the creation of the present Baha'i Publishing Trust by the National Spiritual Assembly in 1955, which now distributes more than 300 titles through a national network of Baha'i librarians. Nine volumes of the writings of Baha'u'llah himself are among the titles distributed by the Publishing Trust. Complementing these are many volumes of authoritative interpretations of 'Abdu'l-Baha, son of Baha'u'llah, and by Shoghi Effendi, Guardian of the Baha'i Faith for 36 years following the death of 'Abdu'l-Baha in 1921. In recent years, dozens of books and pamphlets of exposition, commentary, analysis, and history have been published. An assortment of special materials and instructional media, such as films, film-strips, posters, audio-cassettes, video-cassettes, bumper stickers, postcards, and slide programs have been added to the lists. Providing materials for use by the blind has become an important service of the Publishing Trust. Basic texts have been published in braille and in audio-cassette form. Baha'i periodicals have braille and audio-cassette editions as well.

Founding Date: 1955

Publications:
> *World Order,* quarterly

142. Baha'i Faith, The North American Baha'i Office for Human Rights (NABOHR)

Baha'i Faith
Wilmette, Illinois 60091
(312) 869-9039

The North American Baha'i Office for Human Rights has four functions: the dissemination of information to combat racism and to develop action programs to this end. Baha'is observe Race Unity Day each year, the first Monday in June. Regional NABOHR conferences have been held as well as national conferences.

Founding Date: 1968

143. Baker Book House, Publishers

Protestant
Herman Baker, President
6030 East Fulton Road
Ada, Michigan 49301

Mailing Address
Post Office Box 6287
Grand Rapids, Michigan 49506
(616) 676-9185

Baker Book House, publishes aids for religious leaders, including religious reference works and textbooks for seminaries, Bible schools, and colleges; ministers, Sunday school workers, and lay leaders; and religious works of a more general nature to aid in promoting evangelical Christianity and a Scripture-based world and life view. The publishing house insists on high quality workmanship in the manufacture of its books. This includes the best of material for the purpose intended in order to make the books attractive as well as practical. Baker Book House accepts manuscripts solely upon the basis of merit. The company assumes all expense of publishing and promoting and the author is paid the standard royalty. The publishing house has nationwide sales representation. In addition, all Christian book stores in the country and major outlets abroad are on the Baker Book House mailing list.

144. Baptist Bible Fellowship Intl.

Baptist

Dr. David Cavin, President
Post Office Box 191
Springfield, Missouri 65801
(417) 862-5001

The Baptist Bible Fellowship, International, Missions Office is a clearing house and service center for 3,000 plus churches, 600 missionaries on 58 fields and nine colleges. We process and distribute the contributions sent in by the churches for the support of the missionaries and colleges. We counsel, train, correspond, report, assist in conferences, provide missions curriculum and process applications for missionary candidates. We act as a clearinghouse and distribution center for the disbursement of contributions as directed by the churches.

Staff: 21
Publications:
  Baptist Bible Tribune, weekly newspaper
Meetings:
  Graduation Fellowship, Baptist Bible College, third week of May
  Annual Fall Fellowship, different locations, third week of September
  Candidate orientation seminars, third week in April and fourth week in August
  Furlong Missionary Retreat, August 4-8, Sedalia, Colorado
  Mid-Winter Fellowship, third week in February, Jacksonville, Florida

145. Baptist Builders' Club (BBC)

General Association of Regular Baptist Churches
1300 North Meacham Road
Schaumburg, Illinois 60195

Since 1951, the Baptist Builders' Club has aided the General Association of Regular Baptist Churches in establishing new churches all across America. By being given the much-needed financial support they

require, the new congregations are better able to concentrate their efforts on programs of soul-winning, children's clubs, community outreach and spiritual growth. Financial aid to churches is disbursed under the careful direction of the Baptist Builders' Club board of administrators. To date, over $1,000,000 has been shared by the BBC with hundreds of Regular Baptist Churches.

146. Baptist Faith and Message Fellowship, Inc.

Southern Baptist Convention

Dr. William A. Powell, Sr., Executive Vice-President
Post Office Box 468
Buchanan, Georgia 30113
(404) 646-3856

The Baptist Faith and Message Fellowship was formed to inform the Southern Baptist people that the liberals within the Church deny the Bible as the infallible Word of God, and to encourage Southern Baptists to cooperate with the Fellowship in the effort to restore doctrinal integrity within the denomination. The Fellowship is working for the day when every teacher in the 72 denominational schools, the writers of the Sunday School literature, the leaders of the denominational programs, and the missionaries of the home mission and the foreign mission boards are personally and thoroughly committed to, The Lordship of Jesus, to the Verbal Inspiration of the entire Bible as the infallible Word of God, and to being and doing what the Bible teaches.

Founding Date: 1973
Publications:
  Southern Baptist Journal

147. Baptist General Conference, Board of World Missions

Baptist

Dr. Virgil A. Olson, Executive Secretary
1233 Central Street
Evanston, Illinois 60201
(612) 328-8500

The Board of World Missions is a denominational sending agency of Baptist tradition engaged in evangelism and church planting in 10 foreign countries. It is involved in theological education, medicine, broadcasting, literature, and support of national churches.

Staff: 61 lay; 43 clerical

Publications:
> *Mission in Action,* monthly
> A biweekly denominational paper

Radio/TV Programs:
> Several radio programs in 3 fields

148. Baptist Haiti Mission

Baptist
W. Glen Campbell, President
1537 Plainfield Avenue, N.E.
Grand Rapids, Michigan 49505
(616) 361-7046

The Baptist Haiti Mission establishes local churches and preaching stations in the rural area of Haiti. Almost every church also has a school for children. In addition to church related activities, the Mission operates a hospital, outpatient clinic, dispensary, and tuberculosis camp. The Mission's activities include: a public health program with a mobile clinic for rural villages; a summer Bible Institute for church leaders; teachers' seminars; youth and adult Bible conferences; a revolving loan fund to help erect church buildings; extensive relief and reconstruction programs for hurricanes and drought; agricultural development, animal husbandry, soil conservation by terracing; a reforestation program; and a self-help program with an outlet shop at Mission base.

Staff:
> 1 secretary-office manager at home office
> 7 missionary personnel on field assisted by several volunteers
> 9 members of the Board of directors

Publications:
> *Newsletter,* quarterly

Meetings:
> Youth and adult retreats on the field
> Pastors' conference in Haiti
> Bible school for pastors and workers

149. Baptist International Missions, Inc.

Independent Baptist
Dr. J. R. Faulkner, President
Post Office Box 9215
Chattanooga, Tennessee 37412
(615) 698-1523

Baptist International Missions is a nondenominational sending agency of fundamentalist and Baptist traditions engaged in evangelism, church planting, education, broadcasting, aviation, and ministry to servicemen.

Founding Date: 1960

Staff: 80

Membership: 925 missionaries

Publications:
> *World,* quarterly

150. Baptist Joint Committee on Public Affairs

Baptist
Dr. James E. Wood, Jr., Executive Director
200 Maryland Avenue, N.E.
Washington, D.C. 20002
(202) 544-4226

The Baptist Joint Committee on Public Affairs is authorized "to act in the field of public affairs whenever the interests or rights of the cooperating Conventions . . . or whenever Baptist principles are involved in, or are jeopardized through governmental action; to enunciate, commend, and defend the historic Baptist principle of religious freedom and the separation of church and state; to communicate and commend to the President, Congress, Courts, and Federal Government or state governments such declaration as Baptists adopt concerning public matters; to inform the Baptist constituencies of governmental movements and measures affecting . . . relations between church and state and the right application of Christianity to the life of the nation; to transmit . . . to the cooperating Conventions any findings that result from its investigations and research in the field of public affairs."

Founding Date: 1939

Staff: 10

Membership:
> 47 official representatives from 8 national Baptist bodies of the United States and Canada

Publications:
> 17 volumes of Religious Liberty Conference Background Study Papers
> *Report from the Capital,* magazine, 10 times a year
> Booklets, pamphlets, and staff reports periodically

Meetings:
> Religious Liberty Conferences
> Semi-annual convention

151. Baptist Life Association

Baptist

Nelson B. Rogers, President
8555 Main Street
Buffalo, New York 14221
(716) 633-4393

Baptist Life Association is a Christian fraternal insurance organization providing Life and Disability Income insurance to members of the Christian community in 28 states. Other activities of the Association include a Family Camping and Bible Conference Summer program, which provides recreation and Christian fellowship with accommodations and meals at nominal cost; college scholarships awarded in amounts from $800 to $2,000, and juvenile awards presented to all juvenile members at age 16. The Association provides the Over 85 Benefit which pays insurance premiums for members insured 25 years or more. Art and Photo contests are held alternate years with awards for all categories. Home Study Bible Courses are offered to the members through Moody Bible Institute with the cost completely subsidized for all successfully completing the courses, and a Branch Match Program encourages branch societies to engage in programs that will aid the local church, a mission project, or a worthwhile community action. The Association contributes up to $100 on approved programs with the branch society members raising 50% or more of the total funds needed. Tours to foreign countries are conducted periodically, and a World Relief Program provides members with an opportunity to contribute funds for the relief of distressed people.

Founding Date: 1883

Staff: 155

Membership: 13,465

Publications:
> *Baptist Life Association News,* quarterly

Meetings:
> Family Camping and Bible Conference held annually at LeToureau Camp, Canandaigua, New York
> Quadrennial Convention, location varies
> Sales Award Trip held annually, location varies

Former Name:
> (1934) German Baptist Life Association

152. Baptist Literature Board

Southern Baptist

M. O. Owens, Jr., President and Editor-in-Chief
202 Selig Drive
Atlanta, Georgia 30336
Mailing Address:
Post Office Box 44151
Atlanta, Georgia 30336
(404) 696-1212

Baptist Literature Board is involved in purchasing and editing Sunday school materials printed by other publishing companies. The Board also publishes a small quarterly newsletter sent to several thousand Southern Baptist pastors.

Publications:
> Newsletter, quarterly

153. Baptist Mid-Missions

Baptist

Allan E. Lewis, President
4205 Chester Avenue
Cleveland, Ohio 44103
(216) 432-2200

Baptist Mid-Missions began its work 60 years ago in French Equatorial Africa. It now has missionary outreach to 40 countries around the world. In addition to its evangelistic and church development programs, it operates 23 educational institutions, 12 youth camps, four hospitals, two dental clinics, four maternity clinics, an ophthalmology clinic, and printing presses in eight countries.

Founding Date: 1920

Staff: 35 members of the general council

Membership: 1,100 missionaries

Publications:
> *The Harvest,* quarterly

Radio/TV Programs:
> Daily TV religious program in Italy

Meetings:
> Triannual meetings, location varies

154. Baptist Missionary Association of America, Armed Forces Chaplaincy Committee

Baptist Missionary Association of America

Dr. William Charles Pruitt, Jr., Executive Director
Post Office Box 912
Jacksonville, Texas 75766

The Armed Forces Chaplaincy Committee approves members of the denomination who need endorsement to serve as chaplains in the Armed Services, the Civil Air Patrol, and the Veterans Administration. The executive director also aids in the placing of clergymen in hospitals that need chaplains.

155. Baptist Reformation Educational Ministries, Inc. (BREM)

Baptist

Jon Zens, Director-Editor
Post Office Box 40161
Nashville, Tennessee 37204
(615) 269-9600

The purpose of Baptist Reformation Educational Ministries, Inc., is to stimulate inquiry into the teachings of Scripture with regard to contemporary issues facing the churches; it attempts to do this through the quarterly publication of *Baptist Reformation Review* and, occasionally, through BREM Seminars held in various cities.

Staff:
> At present Jon Zens is the only formal organization member. There is an informal board of reference consisting of some seven men who assist in screening manuscripts and offering help in specific ways.

Publications:
> *Baptist Reformation Review,* quarterly

Meetings:
> Occasional BREM Seminars are held in various cities

156. Baptist Spanish Publishing House (BSPH)

Baptist

North Aldo Broda
7000 Alabama
El Paso, Texas 79914

Mailing Address:
Post Office Box 4255
El Paso, Texas 79914
(915) 566-9656

Baptist Spanish Publishing House is primarily a publisher and distributor of books, tracts, Bibles, New Testaments, magazines, and other church curriculum materials in Spanish. Its publications use one of the two labels: Casa Bautista de Publica-

ciones, for all church literature and many books; Editorial Mundo Hispano, for Bibles, some books, and specialty products. Thoroughly evangelical in viewpoint and practice, BSPH serves an ever-widening clientele from all denominations with materials for individuals, churches, and institutions. A limited line of church and theological materials in other languages (English, French, Dutch) is also offered for use outside the United States.

Publications:
> Approximately 700 titles
> 22 magazines for the educational program of the church
> 1 theological publication
> 4 general interest, Christian-oriented
> 1 student—all in Spanish

157. Baptist World Alliance

Baptist

Dr. Gerhard Claas, General Secretary
1628 Sixteenth Street, N.W.
Washington, D.C. 20009
(202) 265-5027

The Baptist World Alliance is a fellowship of 120 Baptist conventions and unions serving 34 million Baptists in 138 countries. The BWA Division of Evangelism and Education acts as a service unit to inspire, guide, and equip Baptists in every part of the world in training and winning people for Christ. Workshops on evangelism and Christian education are held at the request of Baptist conventions. Conferences on issues confronting theological education are sponsored to help future pastors become effective witnesses for Christ. Baptist mission secretaries of the various member bodies have met under the auspices of the BWA to exchange reports of their work and to share ideas for more effective mission strategies. The BWA speaks out on religious freedom and human rights. By negotiating with government officials, the Alliance has provided Bibles, helped to build and reopen churches, and helped to gain freedom for persons who have been imprisoned because of their faith. The BWA liaison at the United Nations keeps Baptists informed on the latest human rights issues and developments, and reports to the UN on matters of special concern. Study commissions provide a forum for Baptist scholars to come together and study relevant topics of mutual concern.

Founding Date: 1905

Staff: 15

Membership: 33 million

Publications:

Baptist World, a monthly international journal
Various brochures, leaflets, and program booklets are frequently printed.

Meetings:

World congress, every 5 years, next in 1985
Youth conference every 5 years, next in 1983
Men's conference, every 5 years, next in 1982

158. Beacon Press

Unitarian Universalist Association

MaryAnn Lash, Director
25 Beacon Street
Boston, Massachusetts 02108
(617) 742-2110

Beacon Press is a nonprofit publishing house
dedicated to responsible exploration of the human
condition through books. It publishes primarily in the
humanities, the social sciences, and liberal religion.
Beacon Press was a pioneer in the development of
the scholarly paperback for college use and is committed to a bold program of controversial social and
political publishing, assuring a forum for responsible
points of view often neglected by the commercial
press.

Founding Date: 1854

Staff: 14 employees

Publications:

Approximately 300 books

159. Beit Al Deen

Islamic

Post Office Box 29926
San Antonio, Texas 78229

Beit Al Deen is a newly established school that will
accommodate approximately 50 students to study
Islam in depth. Initially courses will be run for three
months. Subsequent courses will be of a longer duration. All students will be in residence.

Publications:

Will be publishing at some future date

Meetings:

Will be doing so at a future date

160. The Benevolent Fraternity of Unitarian Churches*

Unitarian Universalist

Rev. Dr. Virgil E. Murdock, Executive Director and
Minister-at-Large
110 Arlington Street
Boston, Massachusetts 02116
(617) 542-6233

The Benevolent Fraternity of Unitarian Churches is a
social service and social action agency, conducting
specialized ministries, community centers, and low
and moderate-income housing in the city of Boston.

Membership: 49 local churches

161. Bennington Religious Education Foundation

Interdenominational

Mrs. Clare Santway, Chairman
c/o St. Peter's Church
200 Pleasant Street
Bennington, Vermont 05201
(802) 442-8498

The Bennington Religious Education Foundation
exists to provide quality religious education in the
Bennington County area. Originally this was done by
developing programs on an ecumenical basis. More
recently, however, the Foundation has provided
financial support for programs initiated by others on
either an ecumenical or a denominational basis. In
March of each year the Foundation invites applications from churches, groups, and individuals. These
are studied by the members and the programs
accepted receive financial support. Funding is provided from the income of the Foundation.

Staff:

Each of the 7 founding churches is represented
by 2 members on the Board of the Foundation

162. Berean Mission, Inc.

Nondenominational

Rev. Joseph L. McCaskey, Interim General Director
3536 Russell Boulevard
St. Louis, Missouri 63104
(314) 773-0110

Berean Mission, Inc., is an independent, fundamental
faith mission with a strong biblical position and a

sound financial policy, sending out missionaries since 1938. BMI is not a church but, as part of the Body of Christ, is endeavoring to assist local churches in the propagation of the gospel to the ends of the earth, in the establishment of other local churches on the fields of ministry, and in the training of believers to serve the Lord. The mission is working in nine foreign countries and in the United States.

Founding Date: 1937

Staff: 20

Membership: 169

Publications:
> *Missiongrams,* quarterly

Meetings:
> Annual conference in July
> Annual banquet in February
> Seminars every other year; all held in St. Louis Missouri

163. Berry Street Conference

Unitarian Universalist Association
Rev. Greta W. Crosby, Scribe
First Unitarian Church
1501 Fairmont Street
Wichita, Kansas 67208

Founded by William Ellery Channing and his colleagues in 1820, this oldest continental organization for liberal ministers now meets annually at the time of the UUA General Assembly for the purpose of presenting the Berry Street "Lecture."

Founding Date: 1820

164. Bethany Fellowship, Inc.

Interdenominational
Rev. T. A. Hegre, President
6820 Auto Club Road
Minneapolis, Minnesota 55438
(612) 944-2121

Bethany Fellowship was founded by five families who were challenged by the command of Christ to go into all the world to preach the Gospel. Since that time, the home staff has grown to include over 50 families. The visible and practical results of this Fellowship include a missionary training institute which offers a four-year training course. At the present time, 230 students are in training. To support the work at home and the missionary commitments abroad, Bethany manufactures and sells camping trailers, solar panels, and electric grills, and has a large printing and publishing program. In 1962 a missionary society was formed. One hundred sixty-one missionaries are now serving in Brazil, the Bahamas, the Dominican Republic, Haiti, Honduras, Mexico, Puerto Rico, the Virgin Islands, Indonesia, and the Philippines. An additional 84 missionaries, graduates of the missionary training center serving with other missions, also receive support from the Fellowship. The Bethany Fellowship operates 25 places of worship, 13 schools, five seminaries, and 20 bookstores.

Founding Date: 1945

Staff: 115

Membership: 161 missionaries

Publications:
> In English: 300 book titles and *The Message of the Cross,* bimonthly official organ
> In Portuguese: 110 book titles, 21 children's titles, and *Mensagem da Cruz*
> In Spanish: 61 book titles, 41 children's titles, and *El Mensaje de la Cruz*

Meetings:
> 3 conferences per year are conducted at the international headquarters in Minneapolis
> Annual field conferences

165. Bethany Union for Young Women

Unitarian Universalist Association
Elsie Herrmann, President
256 Newbury Street
Boston, Massachusetts 02116
(617) 266-0240

Established by Universalists in 1889 as "a home away from home" for students and working girls, Bethany Union serves young women of all faiths, races, and nationalities who meet its standards of financial need and good character. As stated in its constitution, Bethany Union strives to offer a safe and reasonable place to live for all young women who qualify.

Founding Date: 1889

166. Bethesda Mission, Inc.

Grace Gospel Fellowship
Mr. Harry Rosbottom, Executive Director
3745 26th Avenue South
Minneapolis, Minnesota 55406
(612) 721-3929

Bethesda Mission, Inc., was founded by Pastor H. B. Prince. At its inception it was a function of Bethesda Evangelical Free Church of Minneapolis, but later it became an independent mission organization. The main activities of the Mission include evangelism, church planting, and training of nationals through Theological Education by Extension. The principal fields of missionary endeavor are Bolivia, Brazil, and the island of Curacao.

Founding Date: 1951

Staff: 2 home office staff

Membership:

> 25 full time missionaries in Bolivia, Brazil, and Curacao
> 2 short termers in Bolivia

Publications:

> *Praise and Prayer,* monthly

167. Bible Advocate Press

Church of God (Seventh Day)

LeRoy Dais, Manager
Post Office Box 33677
Denver, Colorado 80233
(303) 452-7973

The Bible Advocate Press is the publications agency of the Church of God (Seventh Day). The agency was established to publish and distribute the Gospel message for the salvation of the lost and for the edification of believers. Bible study is promoted through magazines, Sabbath School curriculum, and Gospel booklets and leaflets. The Press also publishes a worship hymnal, *Worship in Song,* and operates a Christian bookstore.

Founding Date: 1863

Publications:

> *Bible Advocate,* a monthly Bible study and inspirational magazine
> *Harvest Field Messenger,* a quarterly church news magazine
> *Sabbath School Lessons for Adults,* quarterly
> *Bible Study Helps for Senior Youth,* quarterly
> *Bible Study Helps for the Junior High Student,* quarterly

168. Bible Club Movement, Inc. (BCM)

Interdenominational

Mr. Oscar H. Hirt, General Director
237 Fairfield Avenue
Upper Darby, Pennsylvania 19082
352-7177 or 528-5437

Bible Club Movement began as a Bible teaching ministry with the firm conviction that it is the Word of God which changes lives. Their purpose is to present the Lord Jesus Christ as Saviour and as Lord of every day living to individuals of all ages and in all walks of life. The realization of this purpose is sought through Bible-centered teaching ministries, such as Bible Clubs; released time programs; correspondence courses; camping programs; retreats; and an active literature outreach. Today over 350 full-time missionaries and office staff, plus hundreds of volunteers, carry on this ministry in the United States, Canada, and 23 foreign countries. The workers and the funds are both given of God through prayer and trust.

Founding Date: 1936

Staff: 25

Membership: 323

Publications:

> *BCM Communicator,* every two months
> *Search,* magazine for boys and girls, each month except July and August

Meetings:

> Annual conference, once a year, in Pennsylvania
> Annual conference, once a year, in Montana
> European conference, every two years, in Europe

Mergers:

> Children's Temple
> Protestant Religious Education Service

169. The Bible for Today, Inc. (BFT)

Baptist (General Association of Regular Baptist Churches)

Rev. D. A. Waite, ThD, PhD, Director/President
900 Park Avenue
Collingswood, New Jersey 08108
(609) 854-4452

The leading purpose of The Bible for Today is to proclaim and defend the principles of the Bible through the dissemination of printed materials among its subscribers. The BFT presently carries over 780 titles that include books and mimeographed material published by both the BFT and others, as well as tapes and slide/tape presentations on various topics. The Catalog of Publications has a topical index pertaining to matters of the Bible and matters of today. The BFT motto is "First Century Christianity—For Problems of Today."

Staff: 6 office staff members

Membership:

No formal membership; about 6,000 active subscribers and about 6,000 inactive subscribers who receive samples occasionally

Publications:

The Bible For Today Newsreport, monthly

Radio/TV Programs:

The Bible For Today of the Air, twice a week, presently inactive

Meetings:

Home Bible Study Class weekly in the BFT offices

Seminars on special topics each summer at the BFT headquarters

Bible conferences and special speaking engagements in various churches and schools

170. The Bible for You, Inc.*

Nondenominational

Dr. Manford Gutzke, President
Post Office Box 15007
Atlanta, Georgia 30333

The Bible for You, Inc., aims to tell the world faithfully and plainly what the Bible says, and to explain simply and clearly what the Scriptures can mean to anybody willing to believe what is written.

Publications:

28 *Plain Talk Books*
10 study guides
63 booklets
700 cassettes

Radio/TV Programs:

More than 100 each week

171. Bible Literature International (BLI)

Nondenominational

John M. Falkenberg, President
Post Office Box 477
Columbus, Ohio 43216
(614) 267-3116

Bible Literature International is committed to the task of providing Bible literature, free of charge, to missionaries and nationals throughout the world. It supplies tracts, Bibles, New Testaments, Scripture portions, Bible correspondence courses, evangelical magazines, and a wide variety of other Christ-centered literature in more than 228 languages, serv-

ing missionaries from over 30 mission boards in 199 countries. BLI has no missionaries or other paid personnel on the mission fields. The printing is done overseas, and established missionaries and nationals carry out the distribution. The home office staff consists of 20 members, while 13 district representatives present BLI's ministry in churches across America. It is supported by donations from many Christians who represent a wide variety of churches and denominations. In 1979, 650 million pages were printed and literature was supplied to those serving in 73 nations.

Founding Date: 1923

Staff: 20

Membership: 13 district representatives

Publications:

Quiet Miracle, 8 issues per year
Monthly magazines for various mission boards overseas

Meetings:

4 per year

Former Name: (1967) Bible Meditation League

172. Bible Pathway Ministries

Nondenominational

John A. Hash, President & Editor
New Lascasas Road
Murfreesboro, Tennessee 37130

Mailing Address:
Post Office Box 1515
Murfreesboro, Tennessee 37130
(615) 896-4243

The primary objective of Bible Pathway Ministries is the publication of *Bible Pathway,* a Christ-centered devotional guide to encourage people to systematically read through the Bible in one year—reading only 15 minutes a day. Its purpose is to meet the need of people worldwide who have a hunger to read the Bible, and to create an awareness that "man does not live by bread alone, but by every word that proceedeth out of the mouth of God" (Matthew 4:4). *Bible Pathway* is a helpful tool to churches in getting their members to read through the Bible together. It is also shipped to missionaries and national Christian leaders in 146 countries of the world. An additional objective is the distribution of Bibles overseas.

Staff: 20

Publications:

Bible Pathway, a monthly devotional guide

173. Bible Translations on Tape, Inc. (BTT)

Nondenominational
W. Paul Smith, President
Post Office Box 2500
Cedar Hill, Texas 75104
(214) 299-5450

Bible Translations on Tape, Inc., assists Evangelical Missions in providing vernacular scriptures on cassettes for the world's non-educated. It supplies equipment, conducts seminars, and sends tape technologists to fields outside the United States. BTT is producing a spring-powered cassette player to reduce drastically the cost of batteries for cassette ministries.

Membership: 14

174. Bible Way Churches of Our Lord Jesus Christ Worldwide, Inc., Foreign Missions Board*

Apostolic
Bishop Smallwood E. Williams (Presiding Bishop)
1130 New Jersey Ave., N.W.
Washington, D.C. 20001
(202) 723-0505

The purpose of the Foreign Missions Board is to establish Bible Way Churches for carrying on religious, charitable, educational, and evangelistic work.

Membership: 200,300
Publications:
  Twenty Significant Sermons by Bishop S. E. Williams
  Bible Way News Voice
Radio/TV Programs:
  Weekly-worship programs
Meetings:
  1 conference; 1 convocation; 2 Diocese meetings

175. Bibles for the World (BFW)

Nondenominational
Dr. Rochunga Pudaite, President
1300 Crescent Street
Wheaton, Illinois 60187
Mailing Address:
Post Office Box 805
Wheaton, Illinois 60187
(312) 668-7733

The objective of Bibles for the World is to print, package, and mail a copy of the New Testament to everyone who is listed in the telephone books of the world. It seeks to utilize the best translations available in the various languages of the people to whom they are sent. As a non-profit organization, Bibles for the World solicits funds from dedicated Christians who wish to be missionaries "right from their own homes."

Founding Date: 1958
Staff: 300 national workers in India and Burma
Membership: 26 in the United States; 20,000 in India
Publications:
  Bibles for the World News
Meetings:
  1 "Enjoy the Bible" conference
Former Name: Partnership Mission, Inc.

176. Biblical Evangelism

An Independent Baptist Evangelistic Association
Dr. Robert L. Sumner, Director
11 Boulevard Motif
Brownsburg, Indiana 46112
(317) 852-3535

Biblical Evangelism is dedicated to the dissemination of the Gospel through the spoken and written word. It conducts evangelical crusades, both united and single church; holds seminars for pastors and church leaders on evangelism; publishes a monthly magazine; publishes evangelical literature in the United States; and finances the publishing of evangelical literature in the United States and other countries.

Staff: 14 clerical
Publications:
  The Biblical Evangelists, monthly
  17 evangelical religious titles, both popular and scholarly
Meetings:
  Approximately 250 per year

177. Biblical Films*

Rev. Stanley E. Hastillo, Producer-Distributor
120 West Granby Road
Granby, Connecticut 06035
(203) 653-3371

Biblical Films is the producer-distributor of one filmstrip, *A Life of Christ and the Holy Land.* The filmstrip and record of narration, (48 minutes) with 110 actual color photos of Holy Land places and scenes, has two parts. The record of narration gives a running biographical sketch or narrative of Christ's Life, Passion, and Resurrection, and ends with His Ascension and Final Command: "Go, Teach All Nations."

Staff: 1

178. Biblical Research Society*

Nondenominational
David L. Cooper, Jr., President
4005 Verdugo Road
Los Angeles, California 90065
(213) 257-8162

The objective of the ministry of the Biblical Research Society is: "to break down anti-Semitism and to disseminate facts and truths concerning God and Messiah." It observes the Biblical priority set forth by the Apostle Paul: ". . . to the Jew first, and also to the Greek" (Gentile) (Romans 1:16). The uniqueness of the Society's literary ministry relates to the fact that the vast knowledge of the Scriptures and collateral materials, gained during the lifetime of the founder, Dr. David L. Cooper, is being perpetually retained in printed form. The Society is worldwide in its scope, and has neither endowment nor pledges. It is dependent upon the Lord to move His people to sustain the work in answer to prayer.

Publications:
Messianic Series, 17 books, 8 booklets and tracts
Biblical Research Monthly, 8 times a year

179. Bill Glass Evangelistic Association

Interdenominational
Bill Glass, President and Evangelist
Post Office Box 356
Dallas, Texas 75221
(214) 291-7895

The main purpose of the Bill Glass Evangelistic Association is to spread the Gospel of Jesus Christ to the world by means of City- and Area-Wide Crusades in locations across the country and internationally, along with Total Person Weekend Crusades in prison institutions. The City- and Area-Wide Crusades are conducted in secular meeting places and are sponsored by the churches in a locality. Meetings are totally interracial and interdenominational in structure. They take place for eight consecutive nights, with special guests making appearances to give testimonies of faith in Jesus Christ. The prison meetings are conducted Friday through Sunday on given weekends. Format consists of top-name pro athletes making appearances, doing athletic "clinics," and giving testimonies of what Christ has meant in their lives. Then a very soft-sell Gospel message is presented by Glass. Teams of volunteer counselors trained in sharing the Gospel come at their own expense to talk with the inmates on a one-to-one basis.

Staff: 7
Membership:
33 members on the Board of Directors
71 members on the Advisory Board
Publications:
Goalposts, quarterly
Meetings:
City-wide crusades across the country
Total person weekends in prisons

180. Bishop's Helpers

Roman Catholic
Kathleen Toups, President
732 St. Louis Street
Lafayette, Louisana 70506
(318) 234-1434

The Bishop's Helpers is a diocesan secular institute whose members seek to serve God in their world through their particular professional skills. They work directly for the church or devote their leisure time to apostolic work such as the Legion of Mary or activities associated with religious education. Members make a promise of consecration to the single state, as well as promises of cooperation with the church and concern for the welfare of others.

Staff: 6 lay; 1 clerical

181. Black Methodists for Church Renewal, Inc.*

United Methodists
Mrs. Thelma D. Barnes, Executive Director
890 Beckwith Street, SW
Atlanta, Georgia 30314
(404) 758-8118

The purpose of Black Methodists for Church Renewal are: to empower Black Methodists for effective witness and service among pastors and lay persons in local churches, conferences and schools, and the larger community; to encourage and involve Black Methodists and others in the struggles for economic and social justice; to expose latent and overt forms of racism in all local, regional, and national agencies and institutions of The United Methodist Church; and to keep before the church crucial issues facing them by initiating action and supporting church agencies which realistically deal with the needs of black people.

Membership: 249,100 lay; 900 clerical

Publications:
Newsletter, monthly
Now, quarterly

Meetings:
1 national meeting
5 jurisdictional meetings
Several annual conference meetings

182. Bloch Publishing Company

Jewish

Charles E. Bloch, President
915 Broadway
New York, New York 10010
(212) 673-7910

Bloch publishes and distributes books of Jewish interest. It is a dealer and distributor of religious and ceremonial items: art works, prints, lithographs, Hebrew calendars, records, tapes, jewelry, and posters. The company operates one bookstore.

183. The Blue Army of Our Lady of Fatima, Inc.

Roman Catholic

The Most Rev. Jerome J. Hastrich, DD, President,
The Blue Army of Our Lady of Fatima National Organization.
National Center
Mountain View Road
Washington, New Jersey 07882
(201) 689-1700

The Blue Army of Our Lady of Fatima is an international organization of the faithful of the Roman Catholic Church. Its primary function is the dissemination and promotion of the Message of Fatima through various means. Blue Army members promise to pray the Rosary daily, wear the Scapular of Mt. Carmel, and offer up their daily duties in a spirit of penance as a reminder of their consecration to Our Lady. All members of the Blue Army pray for the conversion of Russia and for the reign of true peace as promised by Christ.

Founding Date: 1947

Publications:
Soul, bimonthly
Blue Army Leader, quarterly leadership magazine
Books; booklets; leaflets; and other items

Radio/TV Programs:
13 part *Prophecies of Fatima* TV series

Meetings:
Annual National Council meeting, held at National Center complex (Blue Army Shrine of the Immaculate Heart of Mary) in Washington, New Jersey

184. BMMF International, USA (Bible and Medical Missionary Fellowship

Interdenominational

T. Laurence Wynne, Director USA
241 Fairfield Avenue
Upper Darby, Pennsylvania 19082

Mailing Address:
Post Office Box 418
Upper Darby, Pennsylvania 19082
(215) 352-0581

Since 1852 the Bible and Medical Missionary Fellowship, now known as BMMF International (USA), has sought to share the gospel with the people of Asia through preaching, teaching, and healing. Interdenominational and international, BMMF stands for the historic Christian faith on the basis of the Bible, God's written Word, and is open to serve in partnership with all who love our Lord.

Founding Date: 1852

Staff: 3 full time staff

Membership: 36

Publications:
Goal, 3 times a year

Former Name:
(1979) Bible and Medical Missionary Fellowship

Merger:
(1976) United Fellowship for Christian Service

185. B'nai B'rith Hillel Foundations

Jewish

1640 Rhode Island Avenue, N.W.
Washington, D.C. 20036
(202) 857-6550

B'nai B'rith Hillel Foundations is the oldest and largest Jewish campus organization in the world devoted to the sponsorship of religious, educational, counseling, service, and social action programs for Jewish university students and faculty in the United States, Australia, Brazil, Canada, Colombia, Great Britain, Holland, Israel, Italy, Sweden, Switzerland, and Venezuela. Its network of over 300 full-time Foundations and part-time Counselorships and extension units is funded primarily by B'nai B'rith and Jewish federations and welfare funds, with supplementary support from parents, educational and family foundations, individual gifts, and voluntary student registration and activities fees.

Founding Date: 1923

Staff: 350 local groups

186. B'nai B'rith Women (BBW)

Jewish

Edna J. Wolf, Executive Director
1640 Rhode Island Avenue, N.W.
Washington, D.C. 20036
(202) 857-6689

B'nai B'rith Women is an international organization of over 150,000 members. In 1,100 chapters in the United States, Canada, and overseas, BBW members are actively pledged to serve. Since 1897, their commitment to the community has been increasingly relied upon for essential services. Wherever volunteers are needed, BBW members are involved, extending their effort into every sphere of community life. BBW members are volunteer workers in hospitals, centers for the mentally retarded, and in care for the elderly. The B'nai B'rith Women Children's Home in Israel, a modern residential treatment center for the rehabilitation of emotionally disturbed youngsters, is a permanent BBW project. B'nai B'rith Women provides educational programs that cover many of the complex human relations issues of our time, including women's rights and the changing role of women in our society. Other programs are designed to fight anti-Semitism, and to combat discrimination, prejudice, and bigotry. B'nai B'rith Women offers Jewish identification to every Jewish woman and provides her with a chance to enrich her knowledge of Judaism and to develop a deeper understanding of her heritage and its application to modern times.

Founding Date: 1897

Staff: 65

Membership: Over 150,000

Publications:
 Women's World, bimonthly

Meetings:
 Biennial convention
 Annual regional conferences

Former Name: (1957) Women's Supreme Council

187. B'nai B'rith Youth Organization

Jewish

Dr. Sidney Clearfield, International Director
1640 Rhode Island Avenue, N.W.
Washington, D.C. 20036
(202) 857-6634`

The B'nai B'rith Youth Organization helps Jewish teenagers achieve personal growth according to their individual capacities so that they may lead personally satisfying and socially useful lives in the Jewish community and in the larger community of which they are a part. This purpose is attained through membership and participation in democratically functioning groups under the guidance of professionally qualified staff. Specifically, the programs are geared to help members feel at home in the Jewish community, identify themselves with the common aspirations of the Jewish people with the state of Israel, and make contributions of distinctive Jewish values to the mosaic of their country's culture; to help members enhance their knowledge and appreciation of Jewish religion and culture; to afford members group life experiences which give them an understanding of, and loyalty to, their democratic heritage; to provide supervised leisure time activities in which youth make happy adjustments to real life situations by making friends, exploring and expressing individual interests, and developing skills; to provide learning experiences whereby youth develop devotion and competency in the fulfillment of family and community responsibilities.

Founding Date: 1924

Staff: 200

Membership: 35,000

Publications:

BBYO Judaism Pamphlet Series, a newspaper aimed at all members

A weekly newsletter for professional staff

A quarterly newsletter

A semiannual newsletter

Meetings:

1 national convention

1 national executive board meeting

1 national leadership conference

Approximately 500 local or regional conferences in various parts of the country

188. Bnei Akiva of North America

Jewish

Alan Green, National Executive President

25 West 26th Street

New York, New York 10010

(212) 889-5260

Named after Rabbi Akiva, famous talmudic sage, scholar, revolutionary leader and teacher of the Jewish people, Bnei Akiva educates its members toward religious labor Zionism, to be fulfilled in Israel through self-realization. A pioneering Zionist movement, it believes that the future of Am Yisrael is interwined with the destiny of Medinat Yisrael. Instilling in its members the ideal of chalutziut, Bnei Akiva endeavors to bring to Israel an aliya of American youth who are pioneering, idealistic, and committed to Torah Judaism. Bnei Akiva maintains camps in the United States and Canada that provide summer camping programs as well as month-long Leadership Training Seminars. It is affiliated with the world-wide religious youth movement of Bnei Akiva. In Israel, Bnei Akiva of North America conducts a one-year Scholarship Institute and summer programs.

Founding Date: 1934

Staff: 6

Membership: 6,000

Publications:

Zraim, an ideological and artistic magazine for high school age

Akivon, a monthly booklet for elementary school members featuring stories, essays, projects, games

Hamvaser, internal news bulletin of activities

Me-Ohalei Torah, research and creative thinking in Judaism

Pinkas Le Madrich, leadership source booklet

Meetings:

Annual national convention (September)

Winter retreat (December/January)

Regional meetings (April)

Former Name:

(1951) Hashomer Hadati, Benei Akiva

Merger: (1966) Bachard Organization

189. Bob Jones University Press, Inc.*

Dr. Bob Jones, President

Greenville, South Carolina 29614

(803) 242-5100

The purpose of Bob Jones University Press is to fulfill the Great Commission to "preach the Gospel to every creature" through print and recording media. It subscribes to the following creed: the inspiration of the Bible (both the Old and the New Testaments); the creation of man by the direct act of God; the incarnation and virgin birth of our Lord and Saviour, Jesus Christ; His identification as the Son of God; His vicarious atonement for the sins of mankind by the shedding of His blood on the cross; the resurrection of His body from the tomb; His power to save men from sin; the new birth through the regeneration by the Holy Spirit; and the gift of eternal life by the grace of God.

Publications:

FAITH for the Family, ten times per year

Textbooks and other teaching materials for Christian schools

General religious publications for bookstores, churches, etc.

190. Bookcraft, Inc.

The Church of Jesus Christ of Latter-Day Saints

Marvin W. Wallin, Owner-Manager

1848 West 2300 South

Salt Lake City, Utah 84119

(801) 972-6180

Bookcraft, Inc., is a wholesale publisher dealing with materials oriented to the Church of Jesus Christ of Latter-Day Saints.

191. Bookmates International, Inc.

Interdenominational

Helen Wessel, President

3905 Rolling Hills Road

St. Paul, Minnesota 55112

Mailing Address:
Post Office Box 9883
Fresno, California 93795
(209) 445-1840 or (714) 463-3441

Bookmates International is an independent, cooperative agency limited to book evangelism. It is a channel of communication through which book needs and sources of help are brought together to fill the Christian literature vacuum around the world. It works entirely through nationals, in cooperation with existing national or mission programs. Each project is aimed toward rapid independence upon the part of the nationals, and focuses on building up believers through good books, nurturing those newly won to Christ. Bookmates International is not a mission agency, but a service organization established as a catalyst, to help existing Christian book ministries and to stimulate others into existence. Its largest project is the Bookmates Seed Library program, whose aim is to place 25 free books in underprivileged churches in the United States and abroad.

Founding Date: 1969

Staff: 5 board members

Membership: No general membership

Publications:
4-6 newsletters a year; a few books

192. The Brandeis-Bardin Institute

Jewish
Dennis Prager, Director
Robert Bleiweiss, Executive Vice President
Brandeis, California 93064
(805) 526-1131 and (213) 348-7201

The Brandeis-Bardin Institute offers a unique opportunity for Jews to rediscover their Jewish identity. On 3,200 acres of secluded countryside in the Simi Valley of Southern California, thousands of Jews of all ages have explored the meaning and pertinence of their Jewishness with remarkable results. The Institute was founded by the late Dr. Shlomo Bardin at the urging and with the support of the late Supreme Court Justice, Louis D. Brandeis. The Justice was concerned with the flight of the young Jews from Judaism, a concern that many people share to this day. Such flight, he believed, caused maladjusted people, which was bad for both the individual and the United States. "It gradually became clear to me that to be good Americans, we must be better Jews," said Justice Brandeis. A start was made with college youth at Amherst, New Hampshire. Dr. Bardin moved

the Institute to its present location near Los Angeles in 1947, and he continued as its director and executive vice president to his death in May, 1976. Dr. Bardin's name was added to the Institute's in 1977. The Brandeis-Bardin Institute conducts three principal ongoing programs and a number of special activities. For college age youth there is the Summer training institute (BCI), for children in the Summer there is Camp Alonim and the House of the Book Association is for adults. The Brandeis-Bardin Institute is not affiliated with any organization or movement, religious or secular. Judaism is practiced. It is, in fact, celebrated but with attention to the demands of both tradition and modern life. Brandeis-Bardin seeks to demonstrate that living by Jewish law may constitute the most effective way to achieve universal moral ends, that living a Jewish life can provide joy, satisfaction and extraordinary quality, and that Judaism is a viable religious/moral option to the non-Jewish world as well as to the contemporary Jewish world.

Founding Date: 1941

Staff: 40

Membership:
1,100 House of the Book Association members
Approximately 6,000 BCI Alumni

Publications:
A quarterly newsletter

Meetings:
Approximately 12 introductory weekends per year
Approximately 12 member weekends per year
Two 4-week sessions of the BCI College Age Program
Three 3-week sessions of Camp Alonim (children 8-16)

Former Name:
Brandeis Camp Institute of the West
Brandeis Institute

193. Brazil Gospel Fellowship Mission*

Rev. Larry Lipka, Executive Secretary
121 North Glenwood
Springfield, Illinois 62702
Mailing Address
Post Office Box 355
Springfield, Illinois 62705

The Brazil Gospel Fellowship Mission establishes indigenous Churches for the preaching and teaching of the Word of God.

Founding Date: 1939

Membership: 40

Publications:

Brazil Gospel News, quarterly

Radio/TV Programs:

Evangelist and Bible teaching, 2 different programs

Meetings:

6 each year

194. The Brethren Church (Ashland, Ohio), Board of Christian Education

The Brethren Church

Charles G. Beekley, Director of Christian Education
524 College Avenue
Ashland, Ohio 44805
(419) 289-2748

The Board of Christian Education is responsible for the oversight of denominational programs relating to Sunday school, youth, camping, and leadership training. Educational materials are produced and disseminated denominationally. Resources are identified and made available through the national office.

Publications:

Historical, doctrinal, religious education books
2 newsletters

Meetings:

15 per year

195. The Brethren Church (Ashland, Ohio), Missionary Board

Brethren Church

M. Virgil Ingraham, General Secretary
524 College Avenue
Ashland, Ohio 44805
(419) 289-2195

The Missionary Board of the Brethren Church (Ashland, Ohio) directs missionary work in Argentina and Colombia, South America; Andhra Pradesh, India; and Penang, Malaysia. In addition, it is engaged in opening home mission churches in the United States. The Board sponsors a missionary couple in Nigeria, West Africa. A couple representing the Brethren Church is also in Nigeria, doing translation work for Wycliffe Translators.

Two missionary couples are presently serving as evangelists in Columbia. Also, two missionary couples serve on the Argentine field; one of these is working in a Bible Institute. All personnel are actively engaged in developing the Argentine Brethren Church. In cooperation with other evangelical groups, the Centro-Audio-Visual Evangelica de la Argentina prepares broadcasts for Spanish-speaking people for wide distribution. The Brethren Church established the Brethren Mission in India under the direction of two nationals. A national also directs the Brethren Church's work in Malaysia.

Membership: 16,279 lay; 180 clerical

Publications:

Brethren Evangelist
Insight

196. The Brethren Home Missions Council, Inc.

Fellowship of Grace Brethren Churches

Dr. Lester E. Pifer, Executive Secretary
1401 Kings Highway
Winona Lake, Indiana 46590

Mailing Address
Post Office Box 587
Winona Lake, Indiana 46590
(219) 267-5161

The Brethren Home Missions Council was incorporated under the law of the State of Indiana as a non-profit corporation. The purpose is to establish, maintain, or assist churches of the Grace Brethren faith in acceptable communities within the United States and Canada. The Brethren Home Missions Council is the church extension arm for the Fellowship of Grace Brethren Churches. In addition to church extension, special missions have been established for the Navajo Indians and other peoples in the United States. The Brethren Home Missions Council has added a department of Brethren Building Ministries, which is composed of architects and engineers, to prepare plans for church buildings and supervise church building programs. The Council has also branched out into Brethren church financing by incorporating the Brethren Investment Foundation with the same Board of Directors and officiary. Over one half of the 260 churches in the FGBC have been assisted in some way by the Brethren Home Missions Council. The major source of income for the operation of the BHMC comes from offerings given by the FGBC churches and designated for Brethren Home Missions.

Founding Date: 1939
Staff: 80
Membership: 12,000
Publications:
> *Communicator,* news of church extension
> *Desert Rain,* mission work among the Navajo Indians
> The BHMC subsidizes and contributes to the *Brethren Missionary Herald*

Meetings:
> 2 conferences each year for pastors and missionaries, locations vary

197. Brethren in Christ Church, Board For Missions

Brethren in Christ Church
J. Wilmer Heisey
Executive Secretary
500 South Angle Street, Route 1
Mount Joy, Pennsylvania 17552

Mailing Address
Post Office Box 27
Mount Joy, Pennsylvania 17552
(717) 653-8067

The purposes of the Board for Missions of the Brethren in Christ Church are to provide for mission services and ministries in foreign and North American special ministries; to assist in church planting and extension in North American regional conferences; and to develop and assist the peace position and program of the church. The Board has active mission/church programs in the United States, Canada, Nicaraqua, Venezuela, Zambia, Zimbabwe, Japan and India.

Staff: 4
Membership: 19 ministers; 12 lay
Publications:
> *Therefore,* monthly

Meetings:
> 10 to 30 per year

Also Known As: Brethren in Christ Missions

198. Brethren in Christ Church, Board for Schools and Colleges

Brethren in Christ Church
Wayne H. Schiedel, Chairman
Rural Route 6
Guelph, Ontario NIH 6J3, Canada
(519) 658-9972

The Board for Schools and Colleges supervises the educational program and seeks to determine the educational needs (all levels) of the Brethren in Christ Church. Although the Board does not administer any institution—the denomination's two institutions have their own boards of control—it does have charge of seminary training. And, although the denomination has no seminary of its own, it gives scholarship support to its seminarians who attend one of the seminaries recommended by the Board.

Membership: 3 ministers, 5 lay
Meetings:
> Seminarian retreat, annual or biennial, Campus of Messiah College, Grantham, Pennsylvania

199. Brethren in Christ Church, Board of Benevolence

Brethren in Christ Church
W. Dale Allison, Chairman
1050 South Locust Street
Elizabethtown, Pennsylvania 17022
(717) 367-2651

The purposes of the Board of Benevolence of the Brethren in Christ Church are to: provide supervison of all the beneficiary institutions of the Church; provide benevolent relief for the poor and needy when the local congregation cannot make provision; and provide necessary help, when needed, for retired missionaries, disabled ministers, evangelists, worthy widows, orphans, and invalids. The Board is also responsible to receive funds designed for charitable purposes, and to disperse these funds as temporal needs arise within the Church. The Church has a total membership of approximately 16,000 in the United States and Canada. It also has active Missions in the United States, Canada, Nicaragua, Venezuela, Zambia, Zimbabwe, Japan, and India.

Staff: 2
Membership: 4 ministers; 4 lay
Meetings:
> 2 per year

200. Brethren in Christ Church, Board of Christian Education

Brethren in Christ Church
Winifred Swalm, Executive Director
Duntroon, Ontario
L0M 1H0 Canada

Mailing Address:
301-305 North Elm Street
Nappanee, Indiana 46550
(219) 773-3164 or (705) 445-5892

In carrying out its purpose, the Board of Christian Education shall endeavor to provide for all important phases of Christian education as they relate to congregations, seeking to attain the following results: Christian decision, including Faith in Christ as personal Savior and commitment to the sanctified life; Christian growth including acceptance of church membership; and development of Christian relationships and participation in Christian Service.

Staff: 2

Membership: 9 ministers; 10 lay

Meetings:
French Lick Indiana Youth Retreat in December

201. Brethren in Christ Church, Ministerial Credentials Board

Brethren in Christ Church
Owen H. Alderfer, Chairman
c/o Messiah College
Grantham, Pennsylvania 17027
(717) 766-2511

The Ministerial Credentials Board examines Bible doctrines as accepted by the church, all ministers, members of church school religion department faculties, missionaries whose duties involve the teaching of doctrine of the Brethren in Christ Church, and other church servants as directed by General Conference. The Board provides the standards and requirements for ministerial ordination, facilitates with the Bishops the process of ordination, and issues ministerial credentials including the licensing stage. The Board, in cooperation with the Bishops, holds ministerial conferences and study sessions.

Membership: 7 all ministers

Publications:
Position papers on selected denominational themes, periodic

Meetings:
1 at Messiah College, Grantham Pennsylvania

202. Brethren in Christ Publication Board, Inc.

Brethren in Christ Church

Elwyn Hock, General Manager
301 North Elm Street
Nappanee, Indiana 46550
(219) 773-3164

The Brethren in Christ Publication Board operates under trade names as approved by the General Conference in the publishing of Church periodicals, dissemination of religious merchandise, and in other phases of work coming under its general stated purpose. The three current areas are: Evangel Press; Christian Light Book Stores, with 12 branches in the United States and Canada; and Denominational Papers.

Staff: 15

Membership: 3 ministers; 4 lay

Publications:
Evangelical Visitor, monthly denominational magazine
Printing Press production of books, pamphlets, papers, on demand
Therefore, Missions publication, monthly

203. Brethren/Mennonite Council for Gay Concerns

Brethren and Mennonite
Martin Rock, Coordinator
Post Office Box 24060
Washington, D.C. 20024

Brethren/Mennonite Council for Gay Concerns was founded to provide support for United States and Canadian Brethren and Mennonite gay men and lesbians, and their parents, spouses, relatives, and friends; to foster dialogue between gay and nongay people in the churches; and to provide accurate information about homosexuality from the social sciences, biblical studies, and theology.

Founding Date: 1976

Staff: 1

Membership:
No membership organization; any Brethren or Mennonite person can be placed on the mailing list free of charge

Publications:
Dialogue, quarterly
Occasional brochures

Meetings:
"Dialogue" sessions held in various locations across the countries when requested by church leadership or grassroots groups or congregations

204. Brethren Missionary Herald Co., Inc.

Fellowship of Grace Brethren Churches
Charles W. Turner
Executive Editor-General Manager
Post Office Box 544
Winona Lake, Indiana 46590
(219) 267-7158

The Brethren Missionary Herald Company is the publishing arm of the Fellowship of Grace Brethren Churches and its related missionary organizations. It operates a book store for the Church's college and seminary; writes, publishes, and distributes Sunday School curriculum and related literature; publishes a denominational magazine 12 times a year, and related newspapers and newsletters for various denominational organizations. It operates its own print shop for much of this work.

Publications:
> Religious, Bible study, and church history, 115 titles in print
> *Brethren Missionary Herald,* monthly
> 6 monthly, bimonthly or quarterly newspapers or newsletters

205. The Brethren Press

Church of the Brethren
Joel K. Thompson, Manager
1451 Dundee Avenue
Elgin, Illinois 60120
(312) 742-5100

The Brethren Press operates under the supervision of the General Services Commission of the Church of the Brethren General Board. The General Services Commission is the Board's primary resource for facilitating and supporting its total operations. It is responsible for interpreting the corporate witness of the church and encouraging moral and financial support of its program. The Brethren Press is responsible for the technical services related to the operation of the Church of the Brethren General Board. Currently these include such operations as: all phases of printing, photography, marketing, cataloging, stocking of merchandise, processing of orders, mailing operations of bookstores, and subscription management and development.

Publications:
> 114 religious titles in print
> *Messenger,* monthly
> 1 newsletter published 20 times a year

206. The Brethren Publishing Company

The Brethren Church
Ronald W. Waters
Executive Director and General Manager
524 College Avenue
Ashland, Ohio 44805
(419) 289-2611

The Brethren Publishing Company is the communications arm of the General Conference of Brethren Churches. It publishes a monthly magazine for the denomination as well as special interest periodicals for different divisions of the church. Some published books deal directly with the denomination. The Company also distributes Sunday School curriculum to the denomination and to area churches, operates a print shop, and administers a filmstrip rental library.

Publications:
> *The Brethren Evangelist,* monthly
> *The Woman's Outlook,* bimonthly
> *The Brethren Bible Class Quarterly,* a magazine for adults based on the Uniform (International) Lesson Series
> *Insight into Brethren Missions,* a newsletter about 6 times a year
> 6 titles in print related to Brethren Church history and doctrine

207. Brigham Young University Press

The Church of Jesus Christ of Latter-day Saints
Ernest L. Olson, Director of the Press
209 University Press Building
Provo, Utah 84602
(801) 378-2591

Brigham Young University Press is dedicated to publishing books and materials of enduring quality and excellence for scholarly, church, and general audiences. Brigham Young University Press books include creative and scholarly works, monographs, instruction materials, and multilith series. Noted particularly for its publishing in Western Americana, Mormon history, early childhood education, interior design, and outdoor recreation, BYU Press now produces approximately 25 new titles per year.

Staff: 22
Publications:
> Scholarly, religious, and general interest books, approximately 150 in print
> 2 periodicals: *Brigham Young University Studies* and *Family Perspective*

208. Brith Sholom

Jewish

Joshua Eilberg, Executive Director
3939 Conshohocken Avenue
Philadelphia, Pennsylvania 19131

Brith Shalom is a fraternal organization providing a common ground where men and women of all backgrounds can meet in a spirit of good fellowship to plan for their common welfare as Jews, as Americans, and as citizens of the world. It conducts the largest organized fraternal sports program in America; entertains thousands of servicemen and veterans, conducts religious services, and provides for their social needs and comforts; pursues an active program in defense of civil and religious liberties and combats anti-Semitism and racial bigotry through education and social action; serves as a vigilant watchman for the rights and fortunes of the Jewish people at home and abroad and supports Jewish educational and cultural activities; and offers a valuable insurance program. National Brith Sholom and its individual lodges provide many occasions for socializing. Some lodges provide blood banks, federal credit unions, and mortuary benefits. Brith Sholom has contributed significantly to the creation and the fulfillment of Israel. It also carries on an educational and public information program in support of the gallant people of Israel. Brith Sholom and its affiliated lodges have responded generously to worthy charitable causes — Jewish and non-Jewish — throughout the nation. Through the Brith Sholom Foundation, philanthropic arm of the organization, Brith Sholom sponsors a multi-million dollar apartment residence for elderly citizens in Philadelphia.

Founding Date: 1905

Staff: 4

Membership: 5,000

Meetings:
Annual convention

209. Buffalo Hebrew Christian Mission

Nondenominational
Rev. Karl Goldberg, Superintendent
28 Crestwood Avenue
Buffalo, New York 14216
Mailing Address
Post Office Box 1675
Buffalo, New York 14216
(716) 875-5260

The Buffalo Hebrew Christian Mission is an arm of evangelical, Bible-believing churches dedicated to evangelizing the Jewish people and to combating anti-Semitism. The organization's activities include disseminating Scriptures, writing and printing tracts, Bible studies in homes and at the Center, broadcasts and telephone ministry (dial-a-message), campus ministry, home and shop visitation, and counseling.

Staff: 6

Membership:
171 member churches
387 individual members

Publications:
Quarterly bulletin

Radio/TV Programs:
3 weekly radio broadcasts: Buffalo, Niagara Falls, Syracuse

Meetings:
In cooperation with churches

210. Bureau of Catholic Indian Missions

Roman Catholic
Msgr. Paul A. Lenz, Executive Director
2021 H Street, N.W.
Washington, D.C. 20006
(202) 331-8542

The Bureau of Catholic Indian Missions is engaged in collecting and distributing funds for the support of American Indian missions. The Bureau represents the missions in Government relations, especially in Washington, D.C. Activities are carried out throughout the United States wherever there are American Indian and Eskimo people.

Founding Date: 1874

Membership:
All Bishops, clergy, and interested laity in the United States

Publications:
A monthly newsletter

Meetings:
Annual meeting of associated directors

211. Byzantine Press

Eastern Orthodox/Byzantine Catholic

Marc Wilkinson, President
III-17 North 7th Street
Las Vegas, Nevada 89101
(702) 384-4200

Byzantine Press publishes religious books, principally liturgies and prayer books. These publications are only a portion of their general book publishing operation.

Founding Date: 1980

Staff: 25

212. California Yearly Meeting of Friends Church, Board of Missions

Friends Church

Lloyd McCann, Chairman of the Board
Post Office Box 1607
Whittier, California 90609
(213) 947-2883 or (714) 879-7242

The Board of Missions of California Yearly Meeting of Friends Church conducts mission work in the Kotzebue Sound area of Alaska, inner city work in Long Beach, California, and beginning work in Mexicali, Mexico. Its largest staff is working in Guatemala and Honduras, Central America. The Board's purpose is to win persons to Christ, and to establish new churches which will in turn reach others for Christ, nurture them in the Christian faith and equip them for ministry. To make this happen, the Board is involved in education, evangelism, camping, and humanitarian service. In Central America the Board has had medical services, agricultural projects and general education programs. But the major emphasis during the past several years has centered upon preparing others for ministry.

Founding Date: 1895

Staff:
26 members from among the constituent churches of California Yearly Meeting
20 field staff members

Membership:
5,074 members in the parent organization

Publications:
The California Friend, published 11 times a year

Radio/TV Programs:
Radio programs in Guatemala and in Kotzebue, Alaska

Meetings:
In connection with the conferences of the Yearly Meeting

213. The Calix Society

Roman Catholic

R. D. Dickinson, Director
7601 Wayzata Boulevard
Minneapolis, Minnesota 55426
(612) 546-0544

The Calix Society is an association of Catholic alcoholics who are maintaining their sobriety through affiliation with, and participation in, the Fellowship of Alcoholics Anonymous. The Society's first concern is to interest Catholics with an alcoholic problem in the virtue of total abstinence. The second stated purpose is to promote the spiritual development of the Society's members. The third objection strives for the sanctification of the whole personality of each member through meetings, celebrations of the Liturgy, reception of the Sacraments, personal prayer and meditation, and Retreats. The Society welcomes all alcoholics, even those who are not members of the Roman Catholic faith, and any others, who are concerned with the illness of alcoholism and wish to join in prayer for the Society's stated purposes.

Founding Date: 1947

Staff: 2

Membership:
1,500 lay members; 300 clerical members

Publications:
Chalice, monthly

Meetings:
1-2 monthly meetings for each unit
1 annual national convention

214. CAM International (Central American Mission)

Nondenominational
Albert T. Platt, ThD, President
8625 La Prada Drive
Dallas, Texas 75228
(214) 327-8206

CAM International was founded as The Central American Mission. Its aim is, under the direction of God, to bring the inhabitants of Spanish-speaking areas of the world to a saving knowledge of the love of God in Christ; to establish indigenous churches; and to assist already existing churches through its related service organizations (theological training centers, a publishing house, radio stations, clinics, and schools for missionaries' children).

Founding Date: 1890

Membership: 314

Publications:
> *CAM International Bulletin,* quarterly
> *Kids, It's For You,* annually
> *Prayer Guide Directory,* annually
> *Campo Prayer Shares,* monthly
> Numerous books and Sunday school materials in Spanish

Radio/TV Programs:
> Limited amount of programming aired on CAM'S radio station in Guatemala City
> Some TV productions
> Radio TGBA broadcasts in Barillas, Guatemala in seven Indian dialects

Meetings:
> Occasional summer conferences and weekend retreats at established conference centers
> Rallies, sacred concerts, and banquets conducted throughout the United States and Canada

Former Name: (1976) Central American Mission

215. Campaign for Human Development (CHD)

Roman Catholic
Rev. Martin A. Mottet, Executive Director
U.S. Catholic Conference
1312 Massachusetts Avenue, N.W.
Washington, D.C. 20005
(202) 659-6650

The Campaign for Human Development, founded by the American Catholic Bishops, is the Church's education/action program. The thrust of CHD is dual in nature: To raise funds through an annual collection in Catholic parishes to be allocated in the form of grants and loans to self-help projects that have been planned, developed, and directed by poor and low income persons; and to carry on a year-round educational effort directed toward Americans in general, and Catholics in particular, calling attention to the existence of poverty and injustice, and stimulating a response on the individual and/or collective levels. The general purpose of CHD can be summed up as "action on behalf of justice" which the Synod of 1971 stated was a "constitutive dimension of preaching the Gospel."

Founding Date: 1969

Staff:
> Each of the 160 plus Catholic dioceses has a local CHD Director, often assisted by a committee of clergy, religious and lay persons

Publications:
> *Newsletter,* quarterly

Radio/TV Programs:
> Public service spot announcements for radio and television produced semi-annually

Meetings:
> Frequent meetings, both on national and regional scope, location varies
> National Committee of 40 volunteers meets 3 times a year

216. Campus Crusade for Christ International

Interdenominational
William R. Bright, President
Arrowhead Springs
San Bernardino, California 92414
(714) 886-5224

Campus Crusade for Christ International is an interdenominational Christian organization. Staff members of many nationalities serve in 131 countries and protectorates around the world. The organization's emphases are discipleship, building Christians in their faith; and evangelism, carrying the faith to others. The Campus Crusade ministry was founded with the purpose of fulfilling "the Great Commission" of Jesus Christ to His disciples. College work has always been a major emphasis of the ministry, but there are more than 25 sub-ministries in all. Among the better known, in addition to the Campus Ministry, are Here's Life, America, Athletes in Action, The *Agape* Movement, and Here's Life, World. Campus

Crusade for Christ works primarily on a one-to-one basis. It has, however, been the sponsor of several large-scale events and common efforts, including EXPLO '72, in Dallas; EXPLO '74, in Seoul, South Korea; Here's Life, America (1975-77), and Here's Life, World. Here's Life, World, which refers to new life in Jesus Christ, takes in the movement to help provide every person on earth with the opportunity to say "yes" to Christ and grow in the Christian faith, and the fundraising effort that undergirds that movement. Working together with thousands of churches and other Christian organizations around the world, Campus Crusade has launched Here's Life movements in several hundred cities and towns outside the United States and in many rural areas since 1976-77.

Founding Date: 1951

Staff: Approximately 14,500

Publications:
> *Worldwide Challenge,* monthly
> *Collegiate Challenge,* annually
> *Athletes in Action,* quarterly

Radio/TV Programs:
> *Here's Life,* (radio program)

Meetings:
> Dozens of conferences and retreats each year

217. Canon Law Society of America

Roman Catholic

Rev. James H. Provost, Executive-Coordinator
Catholic University of America
Washington, D.C. 20064
(202) 269-3491

The purpose of the Canon Law Society of America is: to promote the pastoral ministry of the Church; to cooperate in the continuous revision and renewal of the universal law of the Church and with the National Conference of Catholic Bishops in proposing new legislation, resolving current legal questions, and implementing laws and structures which pertain to the vital life of the church; to encourage and participate in canonical research and study toward a constant renewal of Canon Law; to respond to the practical canonical needs of all the People of God in the respective capacities in which they serve and benefit from the Church; to facilitate the interchange of canonical ideas, practices, and decisions among canon lawyers and other members of the Society; to cooperate with individuals and organizations doing research in other Sacred Sciences for the promotion

of mutual interest; and to establish a dialogue and share ideas, proposals, and insights with other Canon Law societies in the world.

Founding Date: 1939

Staff: 1

Membership: 450 lay; 1,250 clerical

Publications:
> 15 publications

Meetings:
> 1 national meeting, annually
> 6 regional meetings annually

218. Cantors Assembly, Inc.

Hebrew

Samuel Rosenbaum, Executive Vice President
150 Fifth Avenue
New York, New York 10011
(212) 691-8020

The founding principles of the Cantors Assembly, to which the organization remains loyal, are to be concerned with the traditions of Jewish worship; to advance the influence and effectiveness of Conservative Judaism; to maintain the highest standards for Hazzanim and for their sacred calling; and to promote the welfare of its members. Of equal importance to the Cantors Assembly is the goal of enhancing and enlarging the treasured heritage which is Jewish liturgical music. With the passing of the great European Jewish communities of the past this task now becomes the shared responsibility and concern of Hazzanim, the guardians of this tradition, and of the broad American Jewish community.

Founding Date: 1947

Staff: 3

Membership: 350

Publications:
> *Journal of Synagogue Music,* twice yearly
> *Annual Convention Proceedings*

Meetings:
> Annual convention in the Catskill Mountains

219. Cardinal Mindszenty Foundation

Roman Catholic

Eleanor Schlafly, Executive Director
Post Office Box 11321
St. Louis, Missouri 63015
(314) 991-2939

The Cardinal Mindszenty Foundation provides educational materials dealing with the problems posed by atheistic Communism, its propaganda, tactics, strategy, and goals. Since its inception, the Foundation has used Pope Pius XI's encyclical *Divini Redemptoris* as its educational outline on the nature of Communism.

Founding Date: 1958

Membership: 5,000

Publications:

The Mindszenty Report, monthly

The Red Line, monthly

Radio/TV Programs:

1 weekly radio program entitled *Dangers of Apathy* (15 minutes), broadcast nationally by CBS

Meetings:

1 annual conference

220. Caritas

Roman Catholic

Ms. Barbara Bahlinger, Director
Post Office Box 308
Abita Springs, Louisiana 70420
(504) 892-4345

Caritas is an institute of Catholic laywomen who commit themselves by vows to a life of love for God, and the Church. Their commitment is to bring themselves and others to the fullness of their life in Christ by the continual discovery and development of that way of life that Jesus preached, manifesting the Kingdom, here and now. Laywomen of Caritas usually live in small groups, supported by one member's employment. They usually live in neighborhoods of the most invisible, powerless members of a society. Their purpose is to serve as a catalyst, a leaven, to enable themselves and others to be caring members of their community by intentionally responding to God in worship and in meeting the needs of their own community and of all mankind. They strive to serve as a bridge between peoples of different social classes, races, cultures, and religions. Caritas laywomen have lived and worked in the southern United States, Guatemala, and Kenya. Their parish and community activities have included religious education, community development, youth work, adult education, census-taking, para-liturgical worship and celebrations, summer religious day camps, retreats, parish workshops, intercultural seminars and travel-groups, and public performances. Their

Abita Springs headquarters is available for retreats and workshops.

Founding Date: 1950

Staff: 4

Membership: 4

Meetings:

Retreats—annual, in Louisiana (for members, some associates)

Four Spiritual Encounter weekends offered during the year

221. Carroll Center for the Blind

Nondenominational

Rachel Ethier Rosenbaum, Executive Director
770 Centre Street
Newton, Massachusetts 02158
(617) 929-6200

The Carroll Center for the Blind offers residential and commuter programs of diagnostic evaluation and personal adjustment rehabilitation training to congenitally and accidentally blind persons age 16 and up. The basic rehabilitation programs usually take about 16 weeks, are completely geared to the needs and goals of the individual, and are designed to equip the blind person to live independently in a sighted world. Other services include community rehabilitation programs (for age three and up), low vision services, volunteer services, public education and information, and professional training through seminars and supervision of student internships. The agency is supported by contractual arrangements with referring agencies and by donations from the public.

Founding Date: 1936

Staff: 38; 21 Board of Directors Members

Publications:

Aids and Appliances Review

Carroll Center News

Meetings:

Occasional workshops for clients in the field of blindness

Former Names:

Catholic Guild for all the Blind

(1974) Carroll Rehabilitation Center for the Visually Impaired

222. Carver Foreign Missions, Inc.

Interdenominational

Dr. W. D. Hungerpiller, Director
65 Haynes Street, S.W.
Atlanta, Georgia 30314

Mailing Address
Post Office Box 92091
Atlanta, Georgia 30314
(404) 525-9747

Carver Foreign Missions, Inc., was organized for the purpose of sending black missionaries to other countries with the Gospel. Its work is primarily concentrated in Liberia, West Africa. The organization operates two schools: The Monrovia Bible Institute, and Carver Mission Academy. Missionaries and nationals teach at both schools. The Monrovia Bible Institute offers both certificate and diploma programs. The Carver Mission Academy has pre-school instruction classes and grades one to nine. The purpose of these schools is to first reach the students with the word of God, and then to teach them academically and spiritually so that they might go forth and teach others. Adult literacy classes are also taught.

Founding Date: 1955

Staff:
9 general missionaries; 3 secretaries
1 director; 6 board members

Publications:
Prayer/Praise brochures, occasionally

Meetings:
1 missionary conference per year, usually in the spring, at the Carver Bible Institute and College in Atlanta

223. Cathedral Films, Inc.

Nondenominational

The Rev. Edward D. Eagle, President
Post Office Box 4029
Westlake Village, California 91359
(805) 495-7418

Cathedral Films produces and distributes a complete line of religious audio-visual materials, including 16mm films on the Life of Christ and the Life of Paul. Cathedral Films also produces and distributes an extensive line of religious filmstrips for use in Christian education.

Staff: 15

224. Catholic Alternatives

Roman Catholic

Joan Harriman, President
45 West 45th Street
New York, New York 10036
(212) 921-9111

Catholic Alternatives is an educational organization offering many alternatives regarding responsible human sexuality to Catholics and those of other faiths. It educates, counsels, and supports laypersons regarding decisions on sexuality. The organization establishes and develops alternatives regarding population concerns; it develops programs to elevate the status of women in society to responsible personhood so that their choice of whether or not to bear children will be a genuinely free choice. Catholic Alternatives conducts seminars and workshops regarding religion and reproduction. It develops, publishes, and disseminates educational materials and visual aids pertaining to human sexuality and population concerns; it supports individuals in their use and choice of contraceptive methods. The organization supports women in their choice to terminate a pregnancy in accordance with their medical, psychological, and economic capacities. Regarding involuntary, unplanned, and unwanted pregnancies, the intellectual perception of women demands ethical consideration. Catholic Alternatives supports women in their choice to have children within the context of quality-of-life for all humanity.

Membership: Not a membership organization

Publications:
What Is It
Questions & Answers
Film entitled *The Game*

Meetings:
Occasional conferences and meetings
Sexual Responsibility Workshops in Schools and Community Centers

225. The Catholic Biblical Association of America

Roman Catholic

Rev. Joseph Jensen, OSB, Executive Secretary
The Catholic University of America
620 Michigan Avenue, N.E.
Washington, D.C. 20064
(202) 635-5519

The Catholic Biblical Association of America was founded for the service of faith and science through the promotion of scholarly study of the Scriptures. One of its earliest projects, completed in 1941, was the revision of the *Challoner-Rheims New Testament*. A completely new critical translation of the entire Bible became the *New American Bible,* published in October, 1970. The CBA publishes *The Catholic Biblical Quarterly,* now in its 41st year, and more recently inaugurated *The Catholic Biblical Quarterly-Monograph Series.* The Association publishes a new periodical, *Old Testament Abstracts,* which began in the spring of 1978. Active membership in the CBA is open to those whose professional Scripture training is equivalent to the SSL degree of the Pontifical Biblical Institute or whose published writings indicate an equivalent competence. Associate membership is open to those who teach Scripture on the college or seminary level and to students in graduate Scripture programs.

Founding Date: 1936

Staff: 4

Membership:
661 active members, 286 associate members

Publications:
Scholarly books
2 magazines
Catholic Biblical Quarterly
Old Testament Abstracts
Catholic Biblical Quarterly Monograph Series

Meetings:
1 annual meeting; regional meetings

226. Catholic Campus Ministry Association

Roman Catholic
Sr. Margaret M. Ivers, IBVM, Executive Director
3700 West 103rd Street
Chicago, Illinois 60655
(312) 779-4095

The purposes of the Catholic Campus Ministry Association are: to provide a supportive community for its members; to be a strong and coordinated voice for the Church's ministry in higher education; to provide continuing education programs for its members; to provide liaison with other individuals and agencies of the Church interested in campus ministry, and the role of the Church in higher education; to advance ecumenical and inter-faith understanding and cooperation; to provide guidelines for, and assistance in, developing effective campus ministries. Programs and services of the institution include: a job bank; *Newsletter; Process;* speaker exchange; colleague consultation; scholarships; three annual, regionally based study weeks; and materials on theological and pastoral issues.

Founding Date: 1969

Membership:
600 clergy; 200 religious; 150 lay members

Publications:
Process, a professional journal
Newsletter, 9 issues a year

Meetings:
CCMA Study Weeks: Eastern — Miami, in January each year; Western — in April each year; Midwestern Regional Conference in October each year

Former Name:
(1969) National Newman Chaplains Association

227. Catholic Central Union of America (CCUA)

Roman Catholic
Harvey J. Johnson
Director, Central Bureau, CCUA
3835 Westminster Place
St. Louis, Missouri 63108
(314) 371-1653

The educational and charitable activities of the Catholic Central Union of America include: conferences, conventions, congresses, lectures, and publications. In addition, it gives aid to Catholic missionaries; maintains a day care center for children aged two to 13 years; and gives aid to needy persons through the Central Bureau, CCUA.

Founding Date: 1855

Staff: 7

Membership: 14,500

Publications:
Social Justice Review, bimonthly

Meetings:
1 national conference, location varies
1 regional conference, location varies

228. Catholic Church Extension Society

Roman Catholic
Rev. Edward J. Slattery, President
35 East Wacker Drive, Room 400
Chicago, Illinois 60601
(312) 236-7240

The Catholic Church Extension Society is a national funding organization serving the neediest missions in the United States and its protectorates. From its national office in Chicago, it provides the following services to missions under the care of diocesan and religious order priests, as recommended by the local bishop: chapel grants; monthly financial aid to needy home mission priests; support of seminarians studying for the home mission priesthood; campus ministry grants to support religious instruction at non-Catholic universities; mass stipends; church furnishings for missions; scholarships in religious education at Fordham University for future teachers in home mission areas; and emergency aid for specialized home mission needs.

Founding Date: 1905

Staff: 28 lay; 2 clerical

Publications:

Extension, 9 times a year

Meetings:

Annual Board of Governors Meeting

229. Catholic Commission on Intellectual and Cultural Affairs

Roman Catholic

Rev. William J. Rooney, Executive Director
620 Michigan Avenue, N.E.
Washington, D.C. 20064
(202) 635-5520

The Commission on Intellectual and Cultural Affairs was formed to bring together representative Catholic intellectual and cultural leaders from the various professions and scholarly fields for mutual reinforcement; for study and research on common problems of intellectual and cultural nature; and to promote collaboration with similar groups in other countries. The Commission holds one general meeting annually, as well as meetings of sub-groupings of members to encourage study and research on problems of interest to the members.

Founding Date: 1946

Staff: 248 lay members; 72 clerical

230. Catholic Committee of Appalachia (CCA)

Roman Catholic

Sr. Honor Murphy, OP, Executive Director
31-A South Third Avenue
Prestonburg, Kentucky 41653
(606) 886-8488

The Catholic Committee of Appalachia is committed to support its membership in personal growth for effective ministry and corporate action in all phases of Church mission to the people of Appalachia: reli-

gious education, evangelism, liturgy, new forms of pastoral ministry, new forms of lay apostolate, and active participation in the social concerns of the Church. It is also committed to renewed and ongoing dialogue with institutional Church, Catholic and ecumenical; it counsels and supports the Catholic delegates to the Commission on Religion in Appalachia (CORA), selects those delegates, raises appropriate annual contributions to CORA budget, and cooperates with CORA to implement its projects at the grass-roots level. The Committee works for, represents, and advocates the needs and interests of the people of Appalachia in all circles: the Federal Government, State and local Government, the United States Catholic Conference, and the National Conference of Catholic Bishops. It strives to promote action for justice and empowerment of people of Appalachia by taking public positions on issues that affect Appalachian people, by recognizing and encouraging local leadership, and by offering support to individual CCA members involved with justice issues.

Founding Date: 1972

Staff: 3 office staff

Membership:

500 active CCA members involved in
     Appalachian ministries
26 Catholic Bishops of Appalachia
26 Diocesan representatives

Publications:

Appalachian Catholic Bishops' Pastoral Letter
     entitled *This Land is Home to Me*
Patchquilt, monthly
Membership *Alerts* to proposed legislation,
     socio-economic issues, etc., published as
     needed

Meetings:

2 meetings of the general membership annually
Bimonthly meetings of the Executive Committee

231. Catholic Committee on Urban Ministry (CCUM)

Roman Catholic

Dr. Helen C. Volkomener, SP, Executive Director
1112 Memorial Library
Notre Dame, Indiana 46556
(219) 283-3293

The Catholic Committee on Urban Ministry (CCUM) is a national network of clergy, religious and laity, who are engaged in ministry for social justice in urban, suburban, and rural areas. They are in parishes, religious communities, neighborhood groups, and interfaith organizations in every diocese in the United States and in many places in Canada. Their work in a variety of programs of social ministry is founded on the belief that action for justice and participation in the transformation of the world are constitutive dimensions of the Gospel. Support for and cooperation with persons and groups laboring for justice, equal opportunity, and peace are the key to CCUM's purposes. CCUM holds a particular commitment to working for the development of an equitable national urban policy, as well as to assuring the investment of Church interest and resources in urban neighborhoods. Through national and state conferences, regional workshops, seminars, summer institutes, training programs, and personal contact with others in comparable ministries, CCUM provides encouragement and support as well as exchange of ideas, development of strategies, and the sharing of resources.

Founding Date: 1969

Staff: 8

Membership: 10,000 members, 47 Board members

Publications:
> *Connector,* 6 times a year

Meetings:
> Annual Fall Conference
> Summer Institutes at the University of Notre Dame and at Georgetown University in Washington, D.C.
> Topical regional meetings

232. Catholic Communications Northwest

Roman Catholic
Dr. Maury R. Sheridan, Executive Director
1511 3rd Avenue
Seattle, Washington 98101
(206) 622-0440

Catholic Communications Northwest is a regional clearinghouse for communications through the media serving the Catholic dioceses, religious orders, organizations, and agencies of Alaska, Idaho, Montana, Oregon, and Washington. CCN was established by Catholic Bishops and Major Superiors of the Northwest to assist the Church in taking an active approach to media communications; to provide accurate and comprehensive information on contemporary social and moral issues; and to facilitate the flow of that information between local and national agencies.

Founding Date: 1974

233. Catholic Daughters of the Americas

Roman Catholic
Miss Mary E. Murray, National Regent
10 West 71st Street
New York, New York 10023
(212) 877-3041

Catholic Daughters of the Americas is a national women's fraternal organization engaged in religious, charitable, and educational activities. It sponsors Junior Catholic Daughters of the Americas, a youth program for girls six to 18 years of age. Other areas of activity include Renewal, Apostolate, and Community. Members must be practicing Catholics, 18 years of age or over.

Founding Date: 1903

Staff: 17

Membership: 170,000 members

Publications:
> *Share,* 4 times a year

Meetings:
> National Biennial Convention

Former Name: (1979) Catholic Daughters of America

234. Catholic Digest*

Roman Catholic
Robert L. Fenton, Publisher
Chrysler Building
405 Lexington Avenue
New York, New York 10017
(212) 867-9766

Catholic Digest publishes, *Catholic Digest* magazine and operates Catholic Digest Book Club. It also operates a trade book division, Carillon Books.

Staff: 30

Publications:
> *Catholic Digest*

235. Catholic Foreign Mission Society of America

Roman Catholic

Rev. James Noonan, MM, Superior General
Maryknoll Missioners
Maryknoll, New York 10545
(914) 941-7590

Maryknoll, legally incorporated as the Catholic Foreign Mission Society of America, was established by the American Bishops to recruit, train, send and support American missioners in areas overseas approved by the Holy See. The Society was founded to provide American Catholics with representation in the foreign missions of the Church. Through Maryknoll, they are given an opportunity to participate either directly by going overseas, or indirectly by supporting Maryknoll's work. Since 1911, Maryknoll has grown into a worldwide organization with many thousands of Americans as loyal supporters. Today there are some 900 Maryknoll missioners working in 22 countries in Latin America, Africa, and Asia. In addition to staffing mission parishes and supporting the apostolic works of local churches, the missioners run hospitals, dispensaries, orphanages, student hostels, homes for the aged, and schools for the blind and deaf. In the sphere of Mission Education at home, the main purpose is to instill in the minds and hearts of men, women, and children in the United States a knowledge and understanding of the problems and aspirations of the people in mission countries, especially in the Third World. Maryknoll promotes Mission Education primarily through the *Maryknoll* magazine, as well as films, television and radio programs and news releases describing mission activities around the world. The Society also publishes Orbis Books which are written by distinguished authors on a variety of subjects, such as modern theology and the liberation and development of nations.

Founding Date: 1911

Staff:
Approximately 500 lay employees
5 priests on General Council

Membership:
Approximately 1,000 priests, brothers, lay members, and students

Publications:
Maryknoll, monthly
Orbis Books, publishing house
Revista Maryknoll, monthly, bilingual

Radio/TV Programs:
Maryknoll Hour
Numerous programs for NBC

Meetings:
10 lecture series per year
8 film series per year
2 Mission Institutes per year
Updating workshops at the Center for Mission Studies

236. Catholic Golden Age

Roman Catholic

Margaret Mealey, President
National Headquarters
Scranton, Pennsylvania 18503
(717) 342-3294

Catholic Golden Age is a national nonprofit association striving continually to enrich the lives of Catholics 50 years of age and over, and to unite millions into a cohesive national organization. The purposes of Catholic Golden Age, as stated in its Articles of Incorporation are: to study and discuss the meaning of a longer life and gerontology, with special emphasis on religious and spiritual aspects; to provide older persons with an instrumentality to better enable them to lead self-fulfilling lives, both in their human facet and their spiritual facet; to develop and coordinate a program of counseling on death and degenerative disease; to constructively emphasize the role of religious faith in the endeavors and activities of older people; to sponsor member-oriented religious worship with an emphasis on participation; to mobilize its members for apostolic and charitable work, especially with less fortunate senior citizens; and to aid the aged in their needs — social, physical, economic, intellectual, and spiritual.

Founding Date: 1974

Staff: 25

Membership: 700,000

Publications:
CGA World Magazine, bimonthly

237. The Catholic Health Association of the United States

Roman Catholic

John E. Curley, Jr., President
1438 South Grand Boulevard
St. Louis, Missouri 63104
(314) 773-0646

The mission of the Catholic Health Association is to assist health care organizations affiliated with the Catholic Church, through education and advocacy, in providing optimal health care services and programs, and to promote and conduct all other activities and purposes consistent with applicable federal and state laws, the Articles of Incorporation, and the Bylaws of the Association. The Association is an ecclesiastical community dedicated to and faithful to the healing mission of the Church. As such, its individual and corporate inspiration is Jesus and His Gospel message. Its mission is to witness in the power of the Spirit the abiding presence and healing ministry of Jesus. This is done by promoting the health of those who are sick or those who are infirm by age or disability; by respecting human dignity in the experience of sickness and death; and by fostering the physical, psychological, emotional, spiritual, and social well-being of people.

Founding Date: 1915

Staff: 65

Membership: 1,500 general members

Publications:
> *Hospital Progress,* monthly
> *Newsbriefs*
> *The CHA in Washington,* monthly
> Newsletters, books, brochures, pamphlets

Meetings:
> 1 annual meeting
> Variety of institutes around the country

Former Name: (1979) Catholic Hospital Association

238. The Catholic Knights of America

Roman Catholic
Fred F. Rottman, National President
3525 Hampton Avenue
St. Louis, Missouri 63139
(314) 351-1029

The Catholic Knights of America is a fraternal benefit society which provides life, hospitalization, and disability insurance for its members. It also assists the Church by sponsoring seminarians, promoting vocations, and contributing to the Catholic Communications Foundation. In addition, it provides sports programs, contests for its youth members, and many other social and charitable programs through its local units.

Founding Date: 1877

Membership: 18,758

Publications:
> History book of the Society entitled *Rounding Out a Century*
> *The CKA Journal,* monthly

Meetings:
> Triennial national convention

239. Catholic Knights of St. George

Roman Catholic
Joseph J. Miller, Supreme President
709 Brighton Road
Pittsburgh, Pennsylvania 15233
(412) 231-2979

The Catholic Knights of St. George is a fraternal benefit society organized to provide financial security for Catholic families through life and health insurance programs. Its fraternal programs include a home for the aged; retreats; camps for needy and disadvantaged children; and college scholarships. There are 296 local lodges.

Founding Date: 1881

Staff: 50

Membership: 67,000

Publications:
> *Knights of St. George,* 5 times a year

Meetings:
> District conferences and branch officer training seminars, in alternate years

240. Catholic League for Religious and Civil Rights

Roman Catholic
Rev. Vergil C. Blum, SJ, President
1100 West Wells Street
Milwaukee, Wisconsin 53233
(414) 289-0170

The Catholic League is a Catholic civil rights union and anti-defamation league. It is committed to serving the Catholic community in the same manner that the Anti-Defamation League and the American Civil Liberties Union serve their respective communities. Among the goals of the League are the defense or attainment of the following rights: the right of Catholics not to have their beliefs and values ridiculed or defamed; the right of Catholics and other parents to send their children to church-related schools without the denial of tax funds for tuition; the right to life of the unborn child, the aged and the handicapped; and the right of Catholics to express their religious and moral beliefs in the politcal arena. The League pursues these goals through education and litigation.

Founding Date: 1973

Staff: 8 professional staff

Membership: 30,000 national membership

Publications:
Newsletter, monthly

Meetings:
Annual convention

241. Catholic Library Association (CLA)

Roman Catholic

Matthew R. Wilt, Executive Director
461 West Lancaster Avenue
Haverford, Pennsylvania 19041
(215) 649-5250

The purpose of the Catholic Library Association is the betterment of librarians and of religious libraries, especially in terms of theology, philosophy, sociology, and ecumenism. It promotes discriminating taste in literature and other communication media; encourages the compilation, publication, and use of religious reference tools; and supports publications reflecting current religious trends. Further, the CLA promotes accepted standards of library services and professional librarianship; provides sponsorship and encouragement in the field of librarianship by means of scholarship funds and an active recruitment program; fosters interest in scientific research and technical developments relating to libraries and librarianship; and urges membership cooperation with all associations having mutual interests.

Founding Date: 1921

Staff: 10

Membership: 3,127 general members

Publications:
Catholic Library World
5 professional tools for librarians

Meetings:
1 Annual Convention in conjunction with National Catholic Educational Association: 1980—New Orleans, 1981—New York City, 1982—Chicago, and 1983—Washington, D.C.

242. Catholic Medical Mission Board (CMMB)

Roman Catholic

Rev. Joseph J. Walter, SJ, Director and President
10 West 17th Street
New York, New York 10011
(212) 242-7757

The Catholic Medical Mission Board has a double purpose: it gathers and ships medicines and medical supplies, and it recruits and assigns medical and paramedical personnel to overseas Missions and dispensaries. In 52 years, it has shipped more than 41 million pounds of supplies. During 1979, CMMB shipped more than 9 million dollars in medicines to 1,968 hospitals and dispensaries in 51 countries, and placed 55 medical volunteers in 12 countries.

Founding Date: 1928

Staff: 27 lay; 2 clerical

Publications:
Medical Mission News and *Professional Placement News Notes,* bimonthly

Meetings:
1 per year

243. Catholic Near East Welfare Association (CNEWA)

Roman Catholic

Rev. Msgr. John G. Nolan, National Secretary
1011 First Avenue
New York, New York 10022
(212) 826-1480

The Catholic Near East Welfare Association is a fund raising organization for the Churches of the Eastern Rite in the countries of the Middle East. The Pontifical Mission for Palestine is affiliated with the Association. CNEWA trains native priests and sisters; cares for orphans and the aging; builds and maintains churches, clinics, convents, and rectories; and supports clergy and religious.

Founding Date: 1926

Staff: 35

Publications:
Catholic Near East Magazine, quarterly

244. The Catholic Negro-American Mission Board*

Roman Catholic

Rev. Benjamin M. Horton, Director
335 Broadway, Room 1102
New York, New York 10013
(212) 226-6843

The Catholic Negro-American Mission Board serves as an agency to raise funds to help pay the salaries of brothers, nuns, and lay teachers involved in the education of black American youth, especially in the South.

Publications:
Educating In Faith, monthly

245. The Catholic News Publishing Company

Roman Catholic

Victor L. Ridder, KM, President and Publisher
80 West Broad Street
Mt. Vernon, New York 10552
(914) 664-8100

The Catholic News Publishing Company publishes an annual directory of all churches, schools and institutions in the metropolitan New York area; an annual directory of colleges throughout the country and commercial and specialized schools in the East; an annual guide to graduate schools in the East, South, and Midwest; an annual directory of religious communities throughout the country; and an annual directory of colleges and universities with a Catholic tradition and heritage.

246. Catholic Pamphlet and Book Society of the United States

Roman Catholic

Rev. Msgr. Paul T. Cronin, Secretary/Director
2171 Fillmore Avenue
Buffalo, New York 14214
(716) 837-5163

The Catholic Pamphlet and Book Society was founded as a non-profit organization of volunteer workers. It distributes Catholic pamphlets from parish pamphlet racks in all 300 churches of the Buffalo Diocese and about 1,500 outside the Diocese. The total number of pamphlets distributed in a year reaches 125,000. Each pamphlet rack is taken care of by a Pamphlet Supervisor, a member of the parish. The Society also operates one bookstore.

Founding Date: 1938
Staff:
About 300 Pamphlet Supervisors
3 clerical members
Meetings:
Meetings with the Bishop and his committee about 4 times a year

247. Catholic Peace Fellowship (CPF)

Roman Catholic

Thomas Cornell, National Secretary
339 Lafayette Street
New York, New York 10012
(212) 673-8990

The primary purpose of the Catholic Peace Fellowship is to initiate educational and action programs designed to acquaint Catholics with the evangelical, pacifist, nonviolent tradition of the pre-Constantinian Church to just war theories and to modern teachings and developments in secular and religious areas bearing on the morality of war and peace, and to bring these understandings into the wider area of ideas in the hope thereby to hasten the day when war and violence will be replaced by peaceful means of social change, defense, and reconciliation. The CPF works toward the development of a "theology of peace" as well as principles and techniques of nonviolent resistance to help meet the desperate needs and just demands of oppressed peoples here in the United States and abroad, and to meet the threats to our fragile biosphere by promiscuous consumption and continued reliance upon weapons of mass destruction for defense. The three major areas of concern are disarmament, the draft and militarism, and Central America. Services offered include publications, reprints, a literature list from which to order a modest selection of books, speaking tours of national and international spokespersons for non-violence, assistance in setting up workshops and seminars in local areas, assistance in developing nonviolent action projects in local areas, training programs in nonviolent direct action, assistance in developing local chapters of the Fellowship, and expert and immediately available legal and moral counseling for conscientious objectors, draft resisters, and others with draft problems.

Founding Date: 1964
Staff: 3
Membership: 2,500 active

Publications:

Bulletin, three times a year

Organizers News, three times a year

Peace Education Supplements and pamphlets

Meetings:

New England Regional Conference, Saturday after Easter

248. Catholic Press Association of the United States and Canada

Roman Catholic

James A. Doyle, Executive Director
119 North Park Avenue
Rockville Centre, New York 11570
(516) 766-3400

Catholic Press Association is a professional association for Catholic newspapers, magazines, book publishers, and their staff. It collects and disseminates information on postal rates, tax matters, and the like to its members; conducts conventions, regional conferences and seminars; publishes association bulletins and other publications; and represents members with Government agencies and other professional associations. It is a North American member of the International Federation of Church Press Associations and the International Catholic Union of the Press in Geneva, Switzerland.

Founding Date: 1911

Staff: 4

Membership: 260 publications; 240 individuals

Publications:

Catholic Press Directory

Catholic Journalist

Meetings:

8

249. Catholic Relief Services (CRS)

Roman Catholic

Most Rev. Edwin B. Broderick, Executive Director
1011 First Avenue
New York, New York 10022
(212) 838-4700

Catholic Relief Services is the official overseas aid and development agency of American Catholics. It was organized by the Catholic Bishops of the United States as a compassionate response to the victims of World War II. Since then it has quietly grown to be the largest private voluntary relief and development organization in the world. Catholic Relief Services provides overseas emergency and disaster relief, self-help development assistance, refugee aid, and care for the disabled and infirm. Although best known for its immediate assistance during natural and man-made disasters, the majority of its programs are aimed at the elimination of the root causes of poverty and hunger. Christian compassion motivates Catholic Relief Services' practical response to the needs of the poor. Its activities are a living expression of love of one human for another out of love for God. Catholic Relief Services helps 14 million people in 86 countries each year with a program valued at $340 million. It extends its assistance to all in need, regardless, of race, color, creed, or political affiliation. Catholic Relief Services is supported through the generosity of the people of the United States. Administrative support is provided by Catholics through an annual church collection. Operation Rice Bowl, a program of sacrificial sharing, and the Thanksgiving Clothing Collection provide additional support. The remainder comes from unsolicited donations, foundation grants, and contracts with the United States Government and the governments of the countries where CRS operates.

Founding Date: 1943

Staff: 1,000 employees worldwide

Membership: No membership

Publications:

Frequent press releases; Annual report

Brochure series; In-house newsletters

Newspaper features; Educational material

Radio/TV Programs:

Public Service Announcements are produced twice a year for distribution to radio and TV stations; films and filmstrips are available for loan

Former Names:

(1955) War Relief Services—National Catholic Welfare Conference

Catholic Relief Services—National Catholic Welfare Conference

Also Known As:

Bishop's Welfare, Emergency and Relief Fund

250. Catholic Theological Society of America (CTSA)

Roman Catholic

Thomas F. O'Meara, OP, President
Office of the Secretary
Saint Mary of the Lake Seminary
Mundelein, Illinois 60060
(312) 566-640I

The Catholic Theological Society of America promotes studies and research in theology, relates theological science to current problems, and fosters a more effective theological education by providing a forum for an exchange of views among theologians and with scholars in other disciplines. The Society seeks to assist those entrusted with a teaching ministry in the Church; to develop in the Christian people a more mature understanding of their faith; and to further the cause of unity among all men through a better appreciation of the role of religious faith in the life of man and society.

Founding Date: 1946

Membership: 1,200

Publications:

> *Proceedings,* annually (papers and report of the annual convention)
> A news report to the members in the *Bulletin* of the Council on the Study of Religion, quarterly
> Final reports of various research teams set up by the Society, occasionally

Meetings:

> 1 annual national convention held in different cities

251. Catholic Traditionalist Movement (CTM)

Roman Catholic
Rev. Dr. Gommar A. De Pauw, President
Catholic Traditionalist Center
210 Maple Avenue
Westbury, New York 11590
(516) 333-6470

The Catholic Traditionalist Movement, literally grown "from the grassroots" as early as 1964, was publicly launched on March 15, l965, and subsequently incorporated under the laws of the State of New York as a non-profit, educational organization "to provide the Catholic laity with all information necessary for the correct understanding and implementation of the Second Vatican Council's decisions in full conformity with the traditional doctrine and practices of the Roman Catholic Church." Since 1968 when, as a result of erroneous interpretations and implementations of the Second Vatican Council's decisions, the centuries-old Sacrifice of the Mass became threatened with extinction, the CTM has concentrated its efforts on maintaining the completely unchanged Latin Roman Catholic Mass, sometimes called the "Tridentine Mass" or "Mass of St. Pius V."

Founding Date: 1965

Publications:

> *Sounds of Truth and Tradition,* quarterly
> Cassettes of traditional Roman Catholic Latin Mass

Radio/TV Programs:

> Worldwide short-wave *Radio Mass* (traditional Roman Catholic Latin Mass), also broadcast over selected AM and FM radio stations in various tourist centers in the United States

Meetings:

> Conferences as per demand; regular Sunday and Holyday traditional Latin Masses at Headquarters' chapel

252. Catholic Viewpoint Publications

Roman Catholic
1205 Whitlock Avenue
Bronx, New York 10459
(212) DA9-3660

Catholic Viewpoint Publications publishes reasonably priced pamphlets, books, and charts which are in keeping with the concepts of the Catholic Church. Their purpose is to uplift the moral and social behavior of the people. All are written by clergy or lay people who are authors, lecturers, and professors at leading Catholic universities and colleges.

253. Catholic Views Broadcasts, Inc.

Roman Catholic
Rev. Kenneth Baker, SJ, President
86 Riverside Drive
New York, New York 10024
(212) 799-2600

Catholic Views Broadcasts, Inc., is an organization of outstanding priests and laymen who speak out on contemporary issues facing the nation and the world. Subjects such as abortion, narcotics, moral breakdown, and cults are part of the domestic issues programming. Such international topics as communism in Asia, and refugees and persecuted Christians in Lebanon and the Soviet Union are also covered. Weekly 15-minute public affairs segments are aired coast to coast.

Membership: No formal membership

Publications:
>*Key,* a monthly inspirational digest
>*A Different Voice,* a promotional flyer

Radio/TV Programs:
>*Views of the News,* a weekly 15-minute radio program dealing with today's vital issues

254. Catholic War Veterans, USA, Inc.*

Roman Catholic

National Commander
2 Massachusetts Avenue, N.W.
Washington, D.C. 20001
(202) 737-9600

The Catholic War Veterans, USA, is an organization dedicated to the protection of the American system of government. It joins hands with other veterans' organizations in programs that promote the welfare of all veterans and the betterment of society.

Membership: 60,000 lay, 1,000 clerical

Publications:
>The *Catholic War Veteran,* 6 times per year

Meetings:
>6 national board meetings
>1 national convention

255. Catholic Women for the ERA

Roman Catholic

Maggie Quinn, National Coordinator
2222 Kroger Building
1014 Vine Street
Cincinnati, Ohio 45202
(513) 621-9100

Catholic Women for the ERA (Equal Rights Amendment) is a national organization of Catholic women who believe that gaining full legal equality for women is an expression of their commitment to full human dignity for all persons. Members of the Catholic Women for the ERA are encouraged to support the ERA by writing to and lobbying the legislators of unratified states and by contacting established Catholic groups in ratified and unratified states and urging them to speak up for the Amendment. Members are kept informed of the status of the ERA.

Founding Date: 1974

Publications:
>Newsletter

256. Catholic Worker (CW)

Roman Catholic

Peggy Scherer, Managing Editor
36 East 1st Street
New York, New York 10003
(212) 254-1640

Catholic Worker is a Christian pacifist, anarchist movement encouraging communities among the poor. As part of the alternative social order, the CW operates houses of hospitality and farming communes. A monthly newspaper, *The Catholic Worker,* sets forth its philosophy of non-violence, voluntary poverty, decentralization, and communitarianism.

Founding Date: 1933

Publications:
>*The Catholic Worker,* monthly

257. Catholics United for Life (CUL)

Roman Catholic

Theo Stearns TOP, prioress
41095 Hwy 41
Coarsegold, California 93614

Mailing Address
Post Office Box 390
Coarsegold, California 93614
(209) 683-2633

Catholics United for Life is a Third Order Dominican Community of single and married people living under the Fundamental Rule of the Third Order Secular and with special statutes for community life approved by the Master of the Order in Rome. The members live a common life in the community which maintains a chapel with resident chaplain, Father Arthur Klyber, CSSR, St. Rose School for the community children, a pro-life, family life apostolate, and a printing operation. The apostolate of CUL is a non-profit educational organization with regular distribution of a newsletter to over 25,000 people, and distribution of pro-life, family-life, and religious literature in Spanish and English. CUL provides pro-life speakers and programs for schools, colleges, and universities and conferences. CUL has two NFP instructors and distributes and writes articles in defense of Humanae Vitae. An outreach program to pregnant women who are considering abortion offers medical services, food, clothes, and whatever aid is necessary to save the life of the child. CUL members pray the rosary outside abortion clinics and offer alternatives to women entering and in this way save a number of babies each week.

Founding Date: 1974

Staff: 16

Membership: 42

Publications:

    Catholics United for Life, newsletter published 5-6 times yearly

    Natural Family Planning

    A series of pamphlets on human life issues and religious life for families

258. Catholics United for the Faith, Inc.

Roman Catholic

Mrs. Madeline F. Stebbins, President

222 North Avenue

Post Office Box S

New Rochelle, New York 10801

(914) 235-9408

The apostolate of Catholics United for the Faith was established as a means by which the laity might give a due response to the gifts which they have received from the Holy Spirit through Baptism and Confirmation for the building up of the Church. The Council itself called for a strengthening of the apostolate "under its collective and organized form" saying that "only a well-knit combination of efforts can completely attain all the aims of the modern apostolate and give its fruits good protection" (Decree on the Apostolate of the Laity, #18). Catholics United for the Faith was established by the laity themselves, in accordance with the specific decrees of the Second Vatican Council, in order to do the work of the lay apostolate. In the words of the Second Vatican Council, the work of the lay apostolate is to assist the laity to be, "through the vigor of their Christian spirit, a leaven in the world" (Decree on the Apostolate of the Laity, #2).

Founding Date: 1968

Staff: 12

Membership: 13,500

Publications:

    Lay Witness, 11 issues each year

    The Pope, The Council, and the Mass, answers to the questions "traditionalists" have been asking

    Book Catalogue, once each year

Meetings:

    Lenten Retreat, Baltic, Conn., once each year

    Consecration to Sacred Heart of Jesus and Immaculate Heart of Mary, site to be determined each year

259. CBM International (Christian Blind Mission Int'l.)

Interdenominational

Magdalena Wiesinger, President

1506 East Roosevelt Road

Wheaton, Illinois 60187

Mailing Address

Post Office Box 175

Wheaton, Illinois 60187

(312) 690-0300

CBM International is a worldwide Christian ministry to the handicapped. It serves the blind, deaf-mute, and physically handicapped poor with spiritual guidance and practical help in programs that heal the sick, restore sight to curable blind, cleanse those suffering from leprosy, feed the hungry, train the blind and deaf in schools and workshops, and preach the Gospel.

Founding Date: 1908

Staff: 8 in the United States

Membership: 173 foreign; 2,067 national

Publications:

    Light, bimonthly

    Light for the World, report on the combined ministry, annually

Radio/TV Programs:

    TV — *What Color is the Wind*

260. Celebration Publications

Evangelical Protestant

William Lynn Gravestock

50224 Road 426

Oakhurst, California 93644

Mailing Address

Post Office Box 610

Oakhurst, California 93644

1-683-6284

The purpose of this organization is to teach through cartoon media the doctrine of the salvation of mankind through the doing and dying of the Lord Jesus Christ, The Saviour of the world. That "He was not willing that any should perish, but that all should come to repentance." (11.Peter 3:9) Therefore, from the Book of Romans in the New Testament which is the Great Treatise on salvation exclusively, we concluded and derived our name — for it is "catholic" in nature meaning universal and international — a knowledge of the saving, redeeming Grace of God revealed in and through Jesus Christ, that is.

Founding Date: 1979

Staff: 6

Membership: 500

Publications:
   Ben Trying, German Baptist, Sinai, John Bunyan

261. Center for Applied Research in the Apostolate (CARA)

Roman Catholic

Rev. Cassian J. Yuhaus, CP, President
3700 Oakview Terrace, N.E.
Washington, D.C. 20017

Mailing Address
Post Office Box 29150
Washington, D.C. 20017
(202) 832-2300

Center for Applied Research in the Apostolate is a non-profit organization, incorporated in the District of Columbia. It was conceived and established by representative leaders of every facet of the Church in the United States. It exists specifically to serve the postconciliar Church by supplying reliable scientific data on which meaningful action must be based. CARA's goal is to discover, promote, and apply modern techniques and scientific informational resources for practical use in a coordinated and effective approach to the Church's social and religious mission in the modern world, at home and overseas.

Founding Date: 1964

Staff: 17 professional, 9 others

Publications:
   CARA Seminary Directory (provides detailed information on all Roman Catholic seminaries in the United States, annually
   CARA Seminary Forum, quarterly bulletin dealing with seminary matters
   CARA Forum for Religious, quarterly bulletin for members of religious orders
   The CARA Report, occasional bulletin about CARA and its work

Meetings:
   About 15 a year: workshops for specialized clienteles related to CARA's mission

262. The Center for Pastoral Liturgy*

Roman Catholic

The Catholic University of America
Washington, D.C. 20064
(202) 635-5230

The Center for Pastoral Liturgy was established to bring the resources of the Catholic University of America to service the pastoral liturgical needs of the church in the United States.

Founding Date: 1975

Publications:
   Bulletin published in January, May, September
   Occasional brochures and leaflet essays

Meetings:
   18 institutes
   10 workshops in 20 cities across the United States

263. Center for the Scientific Study of Religion

Nondenominational

W. Widick Schroeder, Assistant Secretary/Treasurer
5757 South University Avenue
Chicago, Illinois 60637

The Center for the Scientific Study of Religion is a non-profit, interfaith, and interdisciplinary research center. Scholars associated with the Center undertake studies in the area of religion and society. The primary public activity of the Center is the publication of studies undertaken by people associated with the Center.

Staff: 6 Governing Members; 10 Associate Members

Publications:
   Studies in Religion and Society, edited by W. Alvin Pitcher, W. Widick Schroeder, and Gibson Winter

264. Center for the Study of Campus Ministry (CSCM)

Lutheran

The Rev. Phil Schroeder, Director
Valparaiso University
Valparaiso, Indiana 46383
(219) 464-5459

The Center for the Study of Campus Ministry is a multi-faceted program that aims to provide resources that will give increased direction and strength to professional ministry in a learning society. Its offices are located at Valparaiso University, but its main constituency and prime target area are the 250 Lutheran campus ministries and the 900 Lutheran contact congregations in the United States and Canada.

Founding Date: 1973

Staff: 1

Publications:

CSCM Yearbooks

Meetings:

Study conferences

Summer seminar (one week)

265. Center for the Study of World Religions*

Nondenominational

John B. Carman, Director

42 Francis Avenue

Cambridge, Massachusetts 02138

(617) 495-4495

The Center for the Study of World Religions, located at Harvard University, is the focus of an academic community engaged in the comparative study of religion. Administratively linked to Harvard Divinity School, its senior membership is drawn from those who are teaching in the various departments of the University. Most of the student members are doctoral candidates in Comparative Religion. The Center seeks to provide facilities for the pursuit of a coordinated understanding of the historical traditions and living faith of the diverse religious communities of mankind.

Meetings:

Wednesday Evening Colloquium, weekly

Annual conferences and celebrations

266. Center for Women and Religion (CWR)

Nondenominational

Barbara Waugh & Mary Cross, Directors

Graduate Theological Union

2465 Le Conte Avenue

Berkeley, California 94709

(415) 841-9811

Using the insights of women's experiences and a feminist perspective, the Center for Women and Religion seeks to: transform theological education; affirm and support equal and just participation of women within religious institutions; affirm and support ministry by CWR and by women beyond the traditional structure of the church and theological education; and develop its seminary and extra-seminary funding sources. For the organization, feminist perspective entails a search for justice which dispels oppression based on sexuality, race, class, age, and other particularities. CWR is engaged in that search and that struggle.

Membership:

There are no clear definitions of membership: all from the seminaries and surrounding community who wish to participate are welcome. The primary participants are women from the seminaries in the Graduate Theological Union.

Publications:

A quarterly *Newsletter*

Books, workshop resource materials, multi-media slides and tape programs, reports

Radio/TV Programs:

Irregularly

Meetings:

Frequent meetings and conferences at the Graduate Theological Union

267. Center of Concern

Interdenominational

William F. Ryan, SJ, Director

3700 13th Street, N.E.

Washington, D.C. 20017

(202) 635-2757

The Center of Concern is a flexible public interest group that seizes on selected issues as these become timely for consciousness-raising and influence toward justice in public policy and individual action. The process involves prior study of a potential area of involvement; frequently, staff members are consultants in planning for and participation in global conferences and seminars. Findings are then translated into action programs by the staff as priorities and capabilities permit. The Center has been attempting to keep four purposes directing all of its efforts. First, the voice of the third world should be heard in policy discussions in North America, whether in general calls for a New International Economic Order (NIEO), or in specific debates over energy, food, population, women's rights, unemployment, etc. Second, a positive effort should be made to link domestic and global issues, to show that a single problem of justice exists—who has power, and in whose interests it is used. Third, a radically open interdisciplinary approach should be used in evaluating global policy issues. And fourth, an effort should be made to integrate a commitment to social change with spiritual resources.

Membership: 10

Publications:
Center Focus, bimonthly
Several specialized memos

Meetings:
6 per year

268. Central Conference of American Rabbis* (CCAR)

Jewish

Rabbi Joseph B. Glaser, Executive Vice President
790 Madison Avenue, Suite 601
New York, New York 10021
(212) 734-7166

The Central Conference of American Rabbis is the professional rabbinical organization of Reform Judaism. Together with the Union of American Hebrew Congregations (the congregational arm) and the Hebrew Union College-Jewish Institute of Religion (its seminary, with branches in Cincinnati, New York, Los Angeles, and Jerusalem) the Central Conference serves the religious, educational, scholarly, and social needs of its membership. The Central Conference has 53 committees, delegations or representations in such areas as liturgy, continuing education, social action, Israel, worship, youth, Soviet Jewry, etc.

Membership: 1,200 rabbis

Publications:
2 prayerbooks, rabbi's manual, Haggadah, songster, and 5 scholarly titles
CCAR Journal, quarterly
Monthly newsletter
Annual Yearbook

Meetings:
Annual national convention and regional annual conclaves

269. Charismatic Renewal Services, Inc.*

Roman Catholic

237 North Michigan
South Bend, Indiana 46601
(219) 234-6021

Charismatic Renewal Services is a non-profit corporation established by the Catholic Charismatic Renewal Service Committee, the People of Praise, and the Word of God, serving the worldwide charismatic renewal. It publishes *New Covenant and Pastoral Renewal* magazines, Word of Life Books, teaching cassettes, and music from The Word of God, and sponsors a variety of conferences.

Publications:
New Covenant
Pastoral Renewal
10 books per year

Meetings:
Approximately 10 conferences a year

270. Charles Trombley Ministries, Inc.

Nondenominational

Charles Trombley, Director
500 North Elm Place
Broken Arrow, Oklahoma 74012
(918) 251-7290
(918) 455-7480

Charles Trombley Ministries, Inc., is a biblically oriented educational ministry with a foreign missionary emphasis. Through a five point program, teaching tapes, video programs, books, literature, radio, television and personal appearances are provided. The emphasis of this ministry is ecumenical and intra-church. It has been involved with the Charismatic Renewal since 1959. Through the personal ministry of Director Charles Trombley, crusades and seminars are conducted. On the foreign field these consist primarily of ministers retreats and teaching sessions. Recently the ministry has expanded construction of Christian Radio in Venda, South Africa.

Publications:
Sword of the Spirit

Radio/TV Programs:
15-minute radio program, daily
Half-hour television program, weekly

271. Child Evangelism Fellowship, Inc. (CEF)

Nondenominational

Mr. Alan George, Senior Vice-President
Post Office Box 348
Warrenton, Missouri 63383
(314) 456-4321

Child Evangelism Fellowship, Inc., is a worldwide organization engaged in evangelizing children to the Christian faith through weekday Bible clubs called Good News Clubs and Five-Day Clubs, plus many other facets of evangelism. Working closely with local churches, CEF provides teacher training classes and Christ-centered materials for training

Sunday school teachers. The staff of nearly 1,200 workers minister in 86 countries of the world. Full-time workers are trained at the CEF Institute at War-renton, Missouri.

Founding Date: 1937

Staff: Home Office — 80

Membership: 1,200

Publications:
> *Evangelizing Today's Child*
> *Fellowship News,* bimonthly
> Scores of visualized songs
> Bible lessons

Radio/TV Programs:
> Half-hour weekly TV children's program called *Treehouse Club*
> 15-minute weekly radio program called *Here's How,* for adults

Meetings:
> International Conference — every three years
> Regional Conferences (five) — every three years
> State Conferences — every three years

272. Children's Haven International, Inc.

Nondenominational
Lee and Shirley Mendoza, Directors
514 South Cage Boulevard
Pharr, Texas 78577
(512) 787-7378
(512) 781-1908

Children's Haven International was formed to give a home to needy Mexican children and to teach them to become responsible Christian citizens. The children come from poverty-stricken backgrounds and from homes in which they have no parents or only one parent who is unable to care for them. The children come at any age and stay until they go away to college, get a job and make it on their own, or until their parent is able to care for them. The home itself is on the outskirts of Reynosa, Mexico, although headquarters and office are in Texas. The organization is supported by donations from the United States and Canada. An additional children's home associated with a clinic is planned for LaCapilla, Hidalgo State, Mexico.

Founding Date: 1970

Membership:
> No formal membership; the home houses about 80 children

Publications:
> *Stepping Out,* 6 times a year

Meetings:
> Staff orientation and Board meetings
> Programs in churches and trailer parks by children's groups
> Tours by singing groups to churches in the United States and Canada each summer

273. Chinese Christian Mission (CCM)

Nondenominational
Rev. Mark Kor Cheng, General Secretary
951 Petaluma Boulevard South
Petaluma, California 94952
(707) 762-1314

The Chinese Christian Mission is an evangelical faith mission dedicated to preaching the Gospel of Jesus Christ to the Chinese all over the world. Its ministries include literature, preaching, training, audio-visual, and other inter-church projects.

Founding Date: 1961

Staff: 14

Publications:
> *Chinese Christian Today,* monthly in Chinese
> *Challenger,* monthly, in English
> Books on general topics (missions, eschatology, evolution, etc.)
> Book notices in Chinese
> Quarterly *Reports* to CCM supporters

Meetings:
> Internship Program to train young Christian workers every summer
> Seminar on Christian Home Help
> Speech engagements at mission conferences
> Seasonal retreats, and rallies

274. Chinese for Christ, Inc. (CFC)

Nondenominational
Rev. Calvin Chao, Executive Director
50 North Bunker Hill Avenue
Los Angeles, California 90012
Mailing Address
Post Office Box 29126
Los Angeles, California 90029
(213) 628-8078

The main purpose of Chinese for Christ, Inc., is to win the Chinese to Christ and through them to have missionary programs in the world. The emphasis has been on winning Chinese students who are in the United States from Taiwan and Mainland China, as well as American-born Chinese. They will exercise great influences on the nation and the world through their Christian testimonies. CFC has five churches in California and one each in Chicago and New York. There are student centers located in Los Angeles, Berkeley, and Chicago. The CFC Taiwan Branch runs a student center, school for the blind, and summer conferences. There are missionary representatives in the Philippines and Hong Kong. To promote cultural relations with the non-Christians, CFC operates a library and bookstore in Los Angeles.

Founding Date: 1959

Membership: 750 average attendance each week

Publications:
    Quarterly newsletters
    Periodic booklets and other literature in English and Chinese

Radio/TV Programs:
    2 radio broadcasts: Taiwan and Northern China

Meetings:
    Weekly meetings in 5 different locations at churches and student centers
    Approximately 2 retreats per year for each location
    1 annual retreat in Taiwan

275. CHOSEN, (Christian Hospitals Overseas Secure Equipment Needs)

United Presbyterian Church in the U.S.A.
Richard C. Love, Executive Director
3642 West 26th Street
Erie, Pennsylvania 16506
(814) 833-3023

CHOSEN is a non-profit Christian organization linking American resources to overseas needs and American Christians to human needs abroad. The volunteer service of Christians helps maintain CHOSEN's image as a high yield, low budget project. Purposes of the organization are: providing Christian lay people with a "hands on" project to demonstrate their concern for the medical needs of people in the third world countries; procuring donations of equipment and supplies for mission hospitals in the third world countries, repairing the equipment and preparing it for shipping; purchasing parts and appropriate manuals and instruction/installation sheets for equipment; arranging shipping of equipment to overseas destinations, usually with the cooperation of

Church World Service or Catholic Medical Mission Board; promoting training of overseas equipment maintenance staff who service hospital equipment; installing, repairing and instructing as to use of AMSCO hospital equipment.

Staff: 2

Membership: 29

Meetings:
    Monthly staff and production meetings
    Yearly corporation meeting

276. Christ Centered Ministries (OCCM)*

Dr. David Forbes Morgan
Post Office Box 824
Denver, Colorado 80201
(303) 832-1547

Christ Centered Ministries, or the Order of Christ Centered Ministers (OCCM), is an ecumenical Christian Community with a loose affiliation with Roman Catholics and Episcopalians. Daily office and the Eucharist are the chief elements of its worship. The community prays for Christian unity and devotes itself to both active and quasi-contemplative pursuits. At its study center, courses are offered in theology, studies in the Scriptures, and other subjects of religious interest.

Membership: 20 lay; 4 clerical

Publications:
    10 books on *Religion in Life*
    The Triad

Meetings:
    4 retreats per year

277. Christ for Everyone, Inc.*

Paul A. Stewart, Director
Post Office Box 200
Belmont, Michigan 49306
(616) 364-8721

Christ for Everyone maintains a half-hour daily radio broadcast heard across the United States and in Canada; publishes a bimonthly devotional booklet to provide help and inspiration for its readers; maintains correspondence with its radio listeners, offering them counseling and free literature to help solve their problems; sends out large print literature to benefit the visually handicapped and aged, and also supplies free AM/FM radios to qualifying blind persons to enable them to listen to religious programs; and maintains a daily prayer time.

Publications:

God's Message for You, bimonthly devotional booklet

Other religious, inspirational titles

Newsletters, occasionally

Radio/TV Programs:

Christ for Everyone, half-hour, 5 times a week

Problems, 5-minutes daily

Meetings:

5 per year

278. Christ For The Nations, Inc.

Interdenominational

Mrs. Gordon (Freda) Lindsay, President

Post Office Box 24910

Dallas, Texas 75224

(214) 376-1711

Christ For The Nations, Inc., is a missionary service organization that supports programs at home and abroad by providing foreign church construction money, literature, seminar training, and mass media assistance. The organization maintains a Bible Institute in Dallas and aids other Bible Schools abroad. Its purpose, as set forth by its founder, the late Gordon Lindsay, is to serve the Body of Christ wherever needs arise. In doctrine, the organization treasures the fundamental Christian truths and encourages the charismatic ministries of the Holy Spirit.

Founding Date; 1948

Publications:

Over 250 religious, instructional, and inspirational books printed in 58 languages, majority by Gordon Lindsay

Christ For The Nations, monthly

Prayer and Share, Appeal, quarterly

Alumni Newsletter

Radio/TV Programs:

Weekly 30-minute radio program

Meetings:

Annual Seminar, held in Dallas each year

Annual Retreat, held in Dallas each year

Writers Conference, held in Dallas each year

Approximately 15 to 20 banquets held throughout the United States during the year

Former Name: (1967) Voice of Healing

279. Christ for the Philippines

Baptist

Rev. Ruperto Alparaque

Post Office Box 6172

Grand Rapids, Michigan 49506

(616) 243-9459

Christ for the Philippines is a missionary radio outreach to the Philippines. Its goal is to saturate the Philippines with the gospel of Christ in spoken word, music, and literature, using radio as a primary media of communication.

Specific goals are: to obtain local commercial radio time in the Philippines for Christian broadcasts; to establish a recording studio in the Philippines to produce Christian broadcasts; to produce recorded music translated into the local dialect; to produce different types of programming, such as children's programs, and evangelistic drama in the language of the Filipino people; to produce Christian literature in the local dialect to offer to the radio listeners.

Founding Date: 1975

Staff: 9

Membership: 75

Publications:

The Bread Caster

Radio/TV Programs:

Radio programs in Ilonggo (one of the major dialects in the Philippines) broadcasted in 3 commercial stations in the Philippines

Meetings:

Annual Meeting in Grand Rapids, Michigan

280. Christ in Youth, Inc. (CIY)

Christian Church/Church of Christ

O. Ben Carroll, President

4633 East 3lst

Tulsa, Oklahoma 74101

Mailing address

Post Office Box 2170

Tulsa, Oklahoma 74101

(918) 749-4491

Christ in Youth was founded by Bob Stacey to provide youth with an understandable Christian witness. The organization has established four major areas of ministry: evangelism, counseling, training, and publishing. CIY's evangelists and teams serve in local and area-wide crusades, recording ministry, and special conferences held for both youth and adults.

Workers counsel youth and adults by mail, telephone, and in person at CIY offices. CIY offers Sponsor Training Seminars, Family Life Seminars, and Retreats, as well as "on campus" seminars in Bible Colleges, study guides, and training tapes, and publishes and distributes tracts, Bible study helps, sheet music, and records. CIY operates branches in Buffalo, New York; Cincinnati, Ohio; Grayson, Kentucky; Elizabeth City, North Carolina; Atlanta, Georgia; Dallas, Texas; Joplin, Missouri; San Diego, California; Canon City, Colorado; St. Louis, Missouri; and Lincoln, Illinois.

Founding Date: 1968

Staff: 75 staff members in the United States

Publications:
CIY News
Journal of Christian Ministry
Booklets, tracts, and youth program materials

Meetings:
Conferences in Michigan, Missouri, Oklahoma, and North Carolina
Hundreds of crusades, rallies, and seminars across the nation

281. Christian Aid Mission

Independent Fundamentalist
Robert V. Finley, President
Route Ten
Charlottesville, Virginia 22901
(804) 977-5650

Christian Aid is a foreign mission board with a three-fold purpose: it investigates indigenous, independent evangelistic ministries in "mission field" countries of the world and evaluates their work with regard to doctrinal position, spirituality, growth, productivity, fruitfulness, accomplishments, financial accountability, administration and management; it communicates to the Christian public in the United States and Canada accurate information concerning these overseas groups, and exhorts the churches to support indigenous ministries rather than colonial-type missionary operations; and it sends financial assistance to indigenous evangelistic ministries in poorer countries of the world in order that they may have the necessary resources to carry on their works of evangelism, church planting, training institutes, publication, broadcasting, medical clinics, and help for the poor.

Founding Date: 1953

Membership: Not a membership organization

Publications:
Christian Mission, quarterly

282. Christian Apologetics: Research and Information Service (CARIS)

Interdenominational
Robert Passantino, Director, California
James Valentine, Director, Midwest
Post Office Box 1783
Santa Ana, California 92702
Mailing Address
Post Office Box 1659
Milwaukee, Wisconsin 53201
(714) 957-0249

Christian Apologetics: Research and Information Service gathers, researches, analyzes, and disseminates information from an evangelical Christian persuasion on the various cults, occultic activities, religious movements, and non-Christian movements in the United States and around the world. This information is disseminated through publication, lectures, seminars, radio and television. Inquiries by phone or mail are encouraged and are answered personally.

Staff: 12

Membership: 2,000

Publications:
Quarterly journal
Quarterly newsletter
Books, booklets, cassettes, and tracts

Meetings:
Conduct lecture series throughout the year at churches and organizations by request
Host an annual conference for leaders of similar organizations
An annual spring-time conference open to the public held in Southern California
An annual seminar held in Milwaukee

283. Christian Arts, Inc. (CAI)

Nondenominational
Derek de Cambra, Artistic Director
1755 West End Avenue
New Hyde Park, New York 11040
(516) 328-2693

Christian Arts Inc. is a non-profit Christ-centered performing arts organization whose motto reads: "We put Christianity back into the arts and the arts back into Christianity." CAI accomplishes its purpose in presentations of the following programs: "I Am the Way," a sacred opera on the life of Jesus Christ; sacred concerts featuring outstanding artists who, as part of the concert program, give their Christian testimony; a Christian art festival, a display of graphic arts, sculpture, glass mosaics, special films, along with renowned artists and speakers; Operation Concern, variety entertainment with a Christian emphasis in hospitals, prisons, youth detention homes, old age homes, etc; lecture programs on "Religion in the Arts"; special ghetto projects bringing unique programs to the ghetto; and the Christian Artist Service, providing Christian artists for special programs. Putting Christ-love into action through actual involvement is one of the keynotes of CAI. This simply means serving the fellow man in the Christ Spirit, free of the restrictions sometimes imposed by man because of racial, social, economic, or religious background.

Founding Date: 1955

Staff:
9 staff and Board members
5 staff members of sacred opera "I Am the Way"

Publications:
Annual newsletter

Radio/TV Programs:
Programs for radio and television

Meetings:
Seminars on Christianity in the Arts
CAI artists participate in conferences, meetings, retreats, and other type religious/entertainment programs

284. Christian Association for Psychological Studies

Nondenominational
Dr. J. Harold Ellens, ThM, PhD, Executive Secretary
26705 Farmington Road
Farmington Hills, Michigan 48018
(313) 477-1350

The Christian Association for Psychological Studies enlists the fellowship of professionals in psychiatry, psychology, medicine, the ministry, sociology, social work, education, guidance, and related disciplines. It aims to help those professionals cooperate in the search for a better understanding of interpersonal relationships and to integrate a Christocentric frame of reference within these disciplines.

Founding Date: 1955

Membership: 1,500

Publications:
Scholarly professional books on psychological, social and theological sciences
The Bulletin, quarterly

Meetings:
Regional semi-annual, international annual convention
Lecture series by Executive Secretary

285. Christian Blind Mission International

Interdenominational
John Holcomb, United States Director
1506 East Roosevelt Road
Wheaton, Illinois 60187

Mailing Address
Post Office Box 175
Wheaton, Illinois 60187
(312) 690-0300

The Christian Blind Mission is an interdenominational fellowship of committed Christians dedicated to the service of the poor and the handicapped. It supports projects in developing countries of the world through eye clinics and hospitals, free dispensaries, optometric services, schools for the blind, support of orphans, emergency feeding of children, disaster relief, care of the multiply handicapped and leprosy patients, preaching, and pastoral care.

Membership:
No organizational membership. Supported solely by voluntary donations from individuals throughout Europe and North America.

Publications:
Light

286. Christian Board of Publication

Christian Church/Disciples
Dr. W. A. Welsh, President
Post Office Box 179
St. Louis, Missouri 63166
(314) 371-6900

The Christian Board of Publications is the national publishing and printing house of the Christian Church (Disciples of Christ). However, its services have not been limited to the one denomination, as it serves Protestant churches throughout the United States and Canada through active participation in the National Council of Churches of Christ in the United States and other ecumenical organizations. It publishes periodicals, curriculum materials, and books — many in cooperation with other denominational publishing houses — and distributes various items of merchandise for church use.

Founding Date: 1910

Staff: 225

Publications:

> Religious — approximately 150 titles presently in print
>
> *The Disciple* — a journal of the Christian Church (Disciples of Christ,) plus other church-Sunday school related magazines

287. Christian Booksellers Association (CBA)

Nondenominational

Mr. John T. Bass, Executive Vice-President
2620 Venetucci Boulevard
Colorado Springs, Colorado 80901

Mailing Address
Post Office Box 200
Colorado Springs, Colorado 80901
(303) 576-7880

Christian Booksellers Association is a service organization specifically designed to serve the Christian bookseller. Its purposes are: to encourage the widest and most effective distribution possible of Bibles, Christian books and literature, and church supplies; to provide a common forum between the members for the mutual exchange of ideas and suggestions relating to the trade; to strengthen the individual members of the Association and provide a means of discussing and solving the common problems and interests of the trade by such means as conferences, conventions, and any other media deemed desirable; to supply the members with merchandising suggestions and assistance of all types; to keep the members currently informed on all new ideas, developments, laws, and other matters of general interest; to otherwise promote the best interests and welfare of the trade through trade literature, news releases, and advertising on a national basis or otherwise; to work toward the establishment of generally accepted uniform policy standards for the trade; to provide a means of liaison and to promote cooperation between members of the trade and the publishers and suppliers; to encourage the establishment of new retail outlets where none previously existed; and to do any and all other acts and adopt other policies consistent with these purposes which will be of aid and assistance to the members of the

association, and which will further its fundamental purpose of being of service in the distribution of Christian literature and supplies.

Founding Date: 1950

Staff: 24

Membership:

> 3,000 Christian bookstores
> 600 publishers/suppliers

Publications:

> *The Industry,* monthly
> *ETC,* monthly
> *The Bookstore Journal,* 11 times a year
> *CBA Suppliers Directory,* annually
> *Current Christian Books,* annually

Meetings:

> Annual convention
> Regional conferences
> Advanced management seminars, employee seminars

288. Christian Business Men's Committee of USA*

Post Office Box 3380
Chattanooga, Tennessee 37404
(615) 698-4444

The purpose of the Christian Business Men's Committee is to present Jesus Christ as Savior and Lord to business and professional men; also, to develop Christian business and professional men to carry out the Great Commission.

289. Christian Camping International

Nondenominational

John W. Pearson, Executive Director
Post Office Box 400
Somonauk, Illinois 60552
(815) 786-8453

Christian Camping International organizes conventions, publications, group insurance programs, certification, training, and legislative activities for Christian camps and conferences, their directors and staff.

Founding Date: 1959

Membership: 4,000

Publications:

> *Journal of Christian Camping,* 6 issues a year

Meetings:

> 5 regional conventions in October in odd-numbered years

1 national convention in October in even numbered years
State conventions annually

290. Christian Children's Associates, Inc. (CCA)

Nondenominational
Jean Donaldson, President
Post Office Box 446
Toms River, New Jersey 08753
(201) 240-3003

Christian Children's Associates, Inc., is a nondenominational organization with the purpose of reaching boys and girls with the Gospel of Jesus Christ. The organization produces the *Adventure Club,* a 15-minute weekly children's radio program, and 30-minute weekly TV program heard in the continental United States, Alaska, Puerto Rico, and British West Indies. The format includes songs, quizzes, dramatized and visualized stories, and puppets. Children and youth earn free Bibles and Bible Story Books through correspondence courses. The CCA team also conducts rallies for children and youth.

Founding Date: 1973

Staff: 14

Membership: 17 clerical

Publications:
Newsletter, monthly
Records — stories and songs

Radio/TV Programs:
24 children's radio programs
12 cable TV children's programs

Meetings:
100 rallies — East to Midwest

291. Christian Church (Disciples of Christ) Council on Christian Unity

Christian Church (Disciples of Christ)
Paul A. Crow, Jr., President
222 South Downey
Indianapolis, Indiana 46219
Mailing Address
Post Office Box 1986
Indianapolis, Indiana 46206
(317) 353-1491

The Council on Christian Unity is the ecumenical office of the Christian Church (Disciples of Christ). Its executive staff represent the CC (DC) on the Consultation on Church Union (COCU), World Council of Churches, National Council of Churches, Disciples-Roman Catholic International Dialogue, and other world consultations on Christian unity and union. The Council, through its publications and through addresses, seminars, and staff writings, helps keep ministers and lay persons of the Christian Church (Disciples of Christ) aware of their church's long commitment to unity, and communicates with readers in many denominations.

Founding Date: 1910

Staff: 2

Membership:
All members of the Christian Church (Disciples of Christ)

Publications:
Mid-Stream: An Ecumenical Journal, quarterly
Inside the Oikoumene, bimonthly

292. Christian Church (Disciples of Christ), Division of Higher Education

Christian Church (Disciples of Christ)
Dr. D. Duane Cummins, President
119 North Jefferson
St. Louis, Missouri 63103
(314) 371-2050

The Division of Higher Education is an incorporated unit within the general structure of the Christian Church (Disciples of Christ). The Division functions as a service agency for three affiliated educational networks, colleges and universities, seminaries, and campus ministries and for the Church at large. Eighteen colleges and universities, 11 institutions engaged in ministerial education and over 300 campus ministries currently relate to the Christian Church (Disciples of Christ.) The Division serves as a resource center and clearinghouse for the flow of information between the Church and its affiliated networks. Services of the Division include a financial aid program for persons and projects in all three networks; a personnel referral service that assists in the movement of professors, administrators and campus ministers; a mailing program through which interpretative and promotional information is distributed to congregations; an annual statistical analysis of each network's financial stability; technical assistance in institutional funding; an intern experience for undergraduate ethnic minority students considering ministry as a vocational choice; and a biennial seminarians' conference bringing together Disciple seminary students for personal introduction to the Church's organizational life. The Division is governed by a Board of Directors with advice and counsel received from the Council of Colleges and Universities, the Council on Theological Education and the Council on Ministries in Higher Education.

Staff: 6 staff members; 24 directors

Publications:

Footnotes*, quarterly

Meetings:

14-16 per year in various locations but primarily in the St. Louis area

293. Christian Church (Disciples of Christ), Division of Homeland Ministries

Christian Church (Disciples of Christ)

Kenneth A. Kuntz, DD, President
Post Office Box 1986
Indianapolis, Indiana 46206
(317) 353-1491

The Division of Homeland Ministries is the Home Mission organization of the Christian Church (Disci ples of Christ). The Division has six departments: Christian Education, Church Men, Church Women, Church in Society, Evangelism and Membership, and Ministry. The Division carries liaison relationships with four Home Mission Centers: All Peoples, Los Angeles, California; Hazel Green Academy, Hazel Green, Kentucky; Inman Center, San Antonio, Texas; and Yakima Center, Yakima, Washington. The primary task of the Division is to provide resources in planning and programming for congregational life and work in cooperation with the Regions of the Church in the United States and Canada. The Division's current priorities are: Human Rights, Food For All, Renewing Congregational Life, and Witness. Among other work, the Division provides pastoral oversight and program support for 185 military and institutional chaplains, and helps undergird black clergy through educational programs, salary subsidies, scholarships, and emergency aid. A comprehensive strategy for evangelism in the 1980's is developed and working. The Division provides consultant services to congregations, as well as comprehensive guidance and resources for the congregation's educational, evangelistic, social action, youth, leader development, and lay programs.

Staff: 6 men, 6 women, 6 clergy

Publications:

Vanguard, a quarterly program resource journal

Meetings:

Conferences are conducted by the departments of Christian Education, Church Men, Church Women, Evangelism and Membership, Ministry, and Church in Society.

294. Christian Church (Disciples of Christ), Division of Overseas Ministries

Christian Church (Disciples of Christ)

Robert A. Thomas, President
Post Office Box 1986
Indianapolis, Indiana 46206
(317) 353-1491

The Division of Overseas Ministries is engaged in witness, service, and action on behalf of the Christian Church in its response to God's gifts in Christ, and provides a link for the Christian Church (Disciples of Christ) with various partner churches and church organizations around the world. The Division tries to find ways of working with them in a common mission and ministry. This has largely taken place overseas, but the Division of Overseas Ministry is beginning to find ways in which representatives from overseas churches can assist them in mission and ministry in the United States.

Founding Date: 1920

Staff:

There are 85 staff supported by the Division overseas, and another 20 supported by other organizations

Meetings:

3 Board Meetings per year

295. Christian Church (Disciples of Christ), International Christian Women's Fellowship (ICWF)

Christian Church (Disciples of Christ)

Mrs. Fran Craddock
222 South Downey Avenue
Indianapolis, Indiana 46219
(317) 353-1491

The purpose of the International Christian Women's Fellowship is to provide a channel by which women of the Christian Church (Disciples of Christ) of Canada and the United States may be joined in fellowship and find a means for effective participation in the Christian Church and in Christ's mission on earth. Participation includes holding positions of leadership in the Church by serving on policy-making boards and committees; providing opportunities for spiritual growth, enrichment, education and creative ministries for women; and developing a sense of personal responsibility for the mission of the Church.

Membership: 200,000 lay members

Publications:

Guideposts, semiannually

Meetings:

Advisory Committee — annually
ICWF Commission — biannually
Quadrennial Assembly

296. Christian Church (Disciples of Christ), The National Benevolent Association (NBA)

The Christian Church (Disciples of Christ)

William T. Gibble, President
115 North Jefferson
St. Louis, Missouri 63103
(314) 531-1470

The National Benevolent Association is the division of social and health services of The Christian Church (Disciples of Christ). A service delivery system providing care for children, youth, older adults, the ill, the physically handicapped and the mentally retarded, in 44 services centers, affiliated centers, centers currently under development, and community based programs. NBA provides services at the local level in the areas of housing for older adults, nursing homes, convalescent hospitals, emergency care centers for abused and battered children, residential treatment facilities for emotionally disturbed children, residential care for neglected dependent children, housing for physically handicapped, residential treatment, group homes and care for mentally retarded adults and children, schools and sheltered workshops for the mentally retarded, single parent programs, and a training center for clergy and lay leaders in ministry with the aging.

Staff: 44 facilities throughout the United States

Publications:

Family Talk, quarterly
20 newsletters from the various NBA facilities

Radio/TV Programs:

Radio programs produced by local facilities
In-house TV programming at facilities for older adults
Radio and TV spot announcements

Meetings:

General Staff Conference annually in March, St. Louis
Child Care Workers Retreat Conference annually in the fall in various locations
Age Care Conference annually at various locations
Participate fully in conferences and assemblies of the Christian Church

297. Christian Church of North America, Assistances, Benevolent Institutions and Lay Fellowships (ABIL)

Christian Church of North America

Rev. Carmine Reigle, Executive Director
Post Office Box 644
Niles, Ohio 44446
(216) 652-9386

The objectives of the Assistances, Benevolent Institutions and Lay Fellowships Department of the Christian Church of North America are to motivate Christian women to minister to the spiritual and economic needs of Christian and non-Christian children, elderly, etc.; to encourage the establishment and maintenance of orphanages, senior citizen homes, hospitals, and other beneficent institutions; to provide funds for those who have been deprived of lodging by disaster; to promote Christian fellowship among believers; to help provide for needy ministers, widows, etc.; and to encourage and comfort those who are victimized by developments which tend to shatter hope.

Founding Date: 1948

Staff: 3

Publications:

Pamphlets, leaflets, etc.

Former Name: Benevolence Department

298. Christian Church of North America, Department of Statistics, Public Relations and Finance

Christian Church of North America

Rev. Richard Tedesco
141-A, RD 1
Transfer, Pennsylvania 16154-9005
(412) 962-3501

The Department of Statistics, Public Relations and Finance of the Christian Church of North America has several purposes. It directs the Department of Finances; functions officially as National Treasurer of the General Council; maintains the archives, records, minutes, etc., of the General Council; represents the General Council in its relationships with other evangelical bodies, with government social agencies, and the like; functions as Corresponding and Recording Secretary; and maintains statistical records.

Founding Date: 1927

Staff: 4

Publications:
> Directory
> Yearly Convention Report

Radio/TV Programs:
> Audio Visual presentations

Former Names:
> General Secretary of The Christian Churches of the United States of America
> General Treasurer of the CCNA, Missionary Society of the CCNA

299. Christian Church of North America, Evangelism, Radio and TV Department

Christian Church of North America
Rev. David Fariner, Executive Director
4l Sherbrooke Road
Trenton, New York 08638
(609) 882-0677

The purposes of the Evangelism, Radio and TV Department of the Christian Church of North America are to evangelize at home and abroad via various media—radio, TV, evangelistic crusades, tent meetings, summer camps, etc.; to distribute religious literature (Bibles, Scripture portions, tracts); to encourage and promote interest and participation in various outreach programs; to evangelize English-speaking and foreign language groups (ethnic and racial diversity); and to encourage the development of community outreach programs.

Founding Date: 1948

Staff: 4

Publications:
> Newletter, irregularly

Radio/TV Programs:
> *The Voice of Hope,* in Italian
> Various church-sponsored programs in Italian/ English/etc.

Meetings:
> Camp Meetings—Malaga, New Jersey and Sharpsville, Pennsylvania
> Radio Rallies
> Evangelistic Crusades, United States and Overseas

300. Christian Church of North America, Faith and Order, Credentials, Unity and Standards Department (FOCUS)

Christian Church of North America
Rev. Guy Bongiovanni, Executive Director
3740 Longview Road
West Middlesex, Pennsylvania 16159
(412) 981-4766

The Faith and Order, Credentials, Unity and Standards Department of the Christian Church of North America certifies qualified ministers and missionaries; seeks ways and means of improving the caliber of ministers; helps define and maintain doctrinal positions, set the churches in order, and propagate "the faith once delivered unto saints"; administers discipline with a view to rehabilitation; and helps maintain unity within the Fellowship (ecclesiastical structure, church federation, etc.) while cherishing New Testament standards of morality and moral conduct.

Founding Date: 1948

Staff: 6

Publications:
> Official Directory of Churches and Credential Holders

Radio/TV Programs:
> In process of establishing an official English Broadcast

Meetings:
> Seminars conducted by the Department of FOCUS on various themes/subjects

Former Name:
Department of Faith and Order, Christian Church of North America

301. Christian Church of North America, Foreign and Home Missions Department

Christian Church of North America
Rev. Richard Tedesco, Executive Director
Box 141-A
Rural Delivery 1
Transfer, Pennsylvania 16154-9005
(412) 962-3501

The objectives of the Foreign and Home Missions Department of the Christian Church of North America are to establish mission stations; to support missionaries throughout the world; to train and send forth missionaries; to train and support indigenous mission fields; to establish schools and other institutional structures overseas; to administer mission funds for the propagation of the Gospel (dissemination of literature, Bibles, Scripture portions throughout the world; and to work in cooperation with WEF, WFMA, etc.

Founding Date: 1948
Staff: 5
Membership: Various mission outreaches
Publications:
>Newsletters, various newsletters Australia, Argentina, Northern Europe, Philippines, etc.
>International newsletter, semiannually
>Various pamphlets and booklets

Meetings:
>Missions convention, annually various east-coast cities
>Opportunities seminars, annually
>Mini-mission teams, various, South America, Philippines
>Missions rallies, various, Barbados, Africa, Europe, etc.

Former Name:
>Missionary Society of the C.C.N.A

302. Christian Church of North America, General Council

Christian Church of North America
Rev. Carmine Saginario, General Overseer and President
Post Office Box 124
Breezewood, Pennsylvania 15533

Mailing Address:
Headquarters, Box 141-A
Rural Delivery 1
Transfer, Pennsylvania 16154-9005
(412) 962-3501

The objective of the General Council, Christian Church of North America, is to evangelize and minister to men and women in the United States and abroad in a redemptive way; to train and educate youth for the ministry, missionary endeavor, and other areas of Christian enterprise; to propagate the Gospel of Jesus Christ by word and deed; to ordain and certify qualified ministers; to establish and support orphanages, homes for the aged, hospitals, and Bible schools and colleges; to cooperate with other "full Gospel" groups and evangelical groups; and to help bridge the gap between peoples of varying religious (Biblical) postures.

Founding Date: 1907
Staff: Executive Board, 12
Membership: 15,000
Publications:
>*Vista,* monthly
>*Il Faro,* monthly
>Newsletters, quarterly
>*Our Heritage,* 50th Anniversary Book
>Various booklets

Radio/TV Programs:
>*La Voce Della Speranza* (The Voice of Hope), Italian program
>Various other radio or TV programs (by local churches)

Meetings:
>Annual convention, various Eastcoast cities
>Annual youth conferences, northeast region
>Various retreats (youth/singles/married couples)
>Ministers retreats (several per year)

Former Name:
>Unorganized Christian Churches — USA
>Missionary Society of the Christian Church of North America

303. Christian Church of North America, Publications Department

Christian Church of North America
Rev. Frank Bongiovanni, Executive Director
561 South Transit Road
Lockport, New York 14094
(716) 433-3574

The purposes of the Publications Department of the Christian Church of North America are to provide instructional reading materials to their constituency; to help bridge the gap between CCNA and non-CCNA individuals; to promote the Gospel cause via the printed page; to cultivate a stronger bond among the churches; to help distribute Biblical literature; to publish periodicals, etc., for the benefit of all adherents; and to compile hymnals, chorus books, etc.

Founding Date: 1948

Staff: 4

Publications:

　　Vista, monthly
　　Il Faro, monthly
　　Our Heritage, 50th Anniversary Yearbook

304. Christian Church of North America, Youth-Education-Sunday School Department (YESS)

Christian Church of North America

Rev. James DeMola, Director
Post Office Box 157
Mullica Hill, New Jersey 08062
(609) 478-2759

The purposes of the Youth-Education-Sunday School Department of the Christian Church of North America are to encourage, train, and motivate youth to dedicate themselves to God in a manner vital to the spiritual, political, social, and economic welfare of mankind; to inculcate principles of responsible citizenship; to cultivate high and holy ideals; to provide a viable and visible alternative to anomie, moral relativism, and philosophic humanism; to provide a program of instruction for elementary, collegiate, and post-graduate students; to sift and refine Sunday School materials for religious instruction; to provide wholesome activities for youth; and to encourage spiritual, mental, psychological, and physical development and help preclude involvement in disruptive enterprises.

Founding Date: 1944

Staff: 3

Publications:

　　Christ Crusaders (Youth) publications
　　Bible Institute publications, quarterly
　　What We Believe (Articles of Faith)
　　Seminar pamphlets and booklets
　　Seminar tapes

Meetings:

　　Youth conference, annual; youth rallies, monthly; youth retreats, various district retreats; singles retreats; S.S. conferences; RBC School of Theology seminars; minister's seminars

Former Name:

　　Christian Youth Endeavor (CYE)
　　The Christian Standard Bearers

305. Christian Classics, Inc.

Roman Catholic

John J. McHale, Director
Post Office Box 30
Westminster, Maryland 21157
(301) 848-3065

Christian Classics publishes and sells religious books. It issues eight to ten new titles yearly and publishes occasional reprints of proven value. It also serves as a distributor of selected religious titles from here and abroad. In addition, with an inventory of over 100,000 books, Christian Classics provides an antiquarian book service.

Staff: 1 full-time and 5 part-time staff members

Publications:

　　See description above

306. Christian Concern Foundation & Kaleo Lodge

Interdenominational

Creath Davis, Executive Director
Post Office Box 8049
Dallas, Texas 75205
(214) 691-3535

Christian Concern Foundation is a fellowship of men and women across denominational lines who acknowledge Jesus Christ as Lord and Saviour of their lives and who are voluntarily joining themselves together for the purpose of expressing creatively the new life they have found in Him. This fellowship is committed to spiritual renewal within the organized church and not to withdrawal from it. Other areas of endeavor include Bible study classes, prayer therapy groups, personal counseling, lay witnessing, and lay-training seminars. Christian Concern could best be described as an effort to awaken men to the greatness of the Person and the Purpose of Jesus

Christ that they might become vitally related to Him and to each other. As an integral part of its ministry, the Christian Concern Foundation owns and operates the Kaleo Lodge located on Campbell Lake in East Texas. The Lodge is a place to which men and women seeking a deeper meaning to life are invited. It is designed for informal retreats which are held by Christian Concern on a regularly scheduled basis and conducted by the Executive Director and other Christian leaders. The retreats furnish an opportunity for couples, single adults, and college students to spend a weekend in an unstructured, comfortable atmosphere. The Lodge is also available on open weekends for Christian groups who wish to provide their own program.

Staff: 7 staff members, 11 directors

Membership:
> No membership but approximately 1,800 people participate annually in the retreats at Kaleo Lodge, Bible Studies, Seminars and Counseling

Publications:
> 4 newsletters annually

Meetings:
> 50 retreats annually at Kaleo Lodge

307. Christian Conference Office

Roman Catholic
Sister Isabel Bettwy, Director
The College of Steubenville
Steubenville, Ohio 43952
(614) 283-3771

The Christian Conference Office, a department of the College of Steubenville, is charged with the task of planning and executing conferences for specific groups of people: priests and deacons, religious women, young people, youth ministers, and business and professional people. The purpose of the conferences is to help persons come to a personal knowledge of Jesus Christ and to assist them in integrating their call to live a gospel life into their personal lives, their families, occupations, and even recreations.

Publications:
> 2 newsletters
> *Business-Professional,* monthly
> *Steubenville Conferences*

Meetings:
> Conferences — average 5 per year

308. Christian Crusade

Independent Evangelical

Dr. Billy James Hargis, President
6555 South Lewis Avenue
Tulsa, Oklahoma 74102

Mailing Address:
Post Office Box 977
Tulsa, Oklahoma 74102
(918) 494-6611

The Christian Crusade, and independent Christian evangelical organization, has lived up to its motto for more than 30 years of being "For Christ and Against Communism." It believes Communism is Satanic and dedicated to the destruction of Christianity. Founder and President Billy James Hargis preaches and heads a communications network of radio, television, newspaper, and book publishing interests dedicated to spreading the Gospel of Christ and opposing Communism throughout the world. Dr. Hargis makes annual speaking tours in America and several foreign countries, usually those threatened by Communism. He is a frequent guest on national television and radio network programs. The Church of the Christian Crusade conducts church services each Sunday at the Tulsa, Oklahoma headquarters for a local congregation and visitors to the ministry. Through its "Good Samaritan" missionary arm the ministry supports humanitarian work among American Indians in the Southwest and provides help for homeless and afflicted children in many foreign lands.

Founding Date: 1948

Staff: There is a permanent staff of about 25

Membership:
> Newspaper circulates to about 125,000 readers; Dr. Hargis' newsletters have gone to as many as 3 million supporters in one mailing

Publications:
> *The Christian Crusade Newspaper,* monthly
> *The Christian Life-Line Magazine,* quarterly
> Periodic newsletters to regular supporters

Radio/TV Programs:
> A daily 15-minute and Sunday 30-minute radio broadcast to a network of stations from Florida to California and from Mexico to Minnesota
> A one-hour weekly TV program and a one half-hour weekly TV program telecast over the PTL Network satellite

Meetings:

A series of annual "Homecoming" meetings are hosted each summer from 2-4 weekends at Dr. Hargis's farm in the Missouri Ozarks.

309. Christian Destiny, Inc.

Independent Protestant

Dr. David W. Breese, President
Christian Destiny, Inc.
Hillsboro, Kansas 67063

Mailing Address:
Post Office 100
Wheaton, Illinois 60187
(312) 469-7100 (Illinois)
(316) 947-3765 (Kansas)

Christian Destiny, Inc., was founded as an outgrowth of the evangelistic ministry of Rev. David Breese of Wheaton, Illinois. The many demands for printed copies and recordings of his sermons and lectures in churches and universities necessitated the development of an organization to distribute them on a global basis. Christian Destiny is a conservative evangelical organization holding a statement of faith similar to that distributed by the National Association of Evangelicals. It is committed to the proposition that the only destiny that individuals can know is in the message of historic Christianity.

Founding Date: 1963

Staff: Not a membership organization

Publications:

Destiny Newsletter
Destiny Bulletin
Numerous booklets

Radio/TV Programs:

A 30-minute weekly radio news update entitled *Dave Breese Reports*
A 30-minute weekly TV program

Meetings:

Evangelistic crusades, Bible conferences, seminars

310. Christian Education and Publications, Inc.

General Baptist

Riley M. Mathias, Executive Director
100 Stinson Drive
Poplar Bluff, Missouri 63901
(314) 785-7746

In the constitution of the General Association of General Baptists, the following purpose is stated for the Christian Education and Publications Board: "This board shall be responsible for the curriculum and the promotion of Christian Education, publications, leadership training, minister's home study, and camping. It also shall be responsible for the merchandising of the General Baptist educational materials. This board shall make evangelism, stewardship, missions, and related denominational objectives integral parts of the total Christian Education program of the local church." The Christian Education and Publications Board writes, edits, publishes and distributes the General Baptist Sunday School literature. Some materials are acquired through contracts with Scripture Press and Standard Publishing Houses. The board operates a printing press, three bookstores, and two youth camps. The board has a vital ministry in promotion of Christian Education among the General Baptist churches throughout the United States and on foreign fields. Some areas of service are: youth ministry, pastoral ministry, Sunday School leadership, leadership training, family service, church and denomination communication, retreats, seminars, and workshops.

Membership: 18 members

Publications:

Bible Class Sunday School, quarterly
Young Adult Sunday School, quarterly
Senior High Sunday School, quarterly
Senior High Teacher Sunday School, quarterly
General Baptist Messenger, a monthly magazine

Meetings:

Camp Brosend—5 months continuous retreats and conferences
Camp Allen—4 months continuous retreats and conferences
7 staff members conduct approximately 200 retreats, conferences, and speaking engagements per year
12 Christian Education consultants conduct approximately 200 Christian seminars per year

311. Christian Enterprises, Inc.

Interdenominational

James N. Birkitt, President
Post Office Box 272
Ashland, Virginia 23005
(804) 798-4711

Christian Enterprises, Inc. is a non-profit, tax-exempt, religious charitable organization chartered by the State of Virginia. It currently owns and operates WKDH 1430 AM Christian radio in Ashland, Virginia as well as The Christian Book Store and Church Supply. The organization is chartered to operate Christian retreat centers, develop Christian schools, publish Christian books and materials, and operate additional Christian broadcasting facilities. Christian Enterprises, Inc. is affiliated with National Religious Broadcasters, National Association of Broadcasters, and Christian Book Sellers Association.

Radio/TV Programs:
> Producers of "The Radio Bible Institute," a 15-minute daily teaching program hosted by the Rev. James N. Birkitt and the "Book and Record Corner," a daily book and record review radio program

312. Christian Evangelizers Association, Inc.

Nondenominational
Cecil Todd, Founder/Director
1200 North Main Street
Joplin, Missouri 64801
(417) 624-0749

The ministries of the Christian Evangelizers Association include: evangelistic crusades and rallies; church building; missionary work in India, Haiti, and Africa; national crusades such as "Clean Up TV," "Bible Reading Put Back Into Public Schools," and "Revive America"; national TV ministry; and radio in America and overseas.

Staff: 25

Membership: 60,000

Publications:
> *Revival Fires Magazine*

Radio/TV Programs:
> A 30-minute weekly radio program called "Revival Fires"

Meetings:
> Regular meetings

313. Christian Family Renewal

Nondenominational
Murray Norris, JD, PhD, President
1070 Brookhaven
Clovis, California 93612

Mailing Address:
Post Office Box 73
Clovis, California 93612
(209) 298-8794 or 291-4958

Christian Family Renewal was organized to show Christians how to win against moral evils attacking our families: abortion, pornography, satanism, homosexuality, a moral sex education, and humanism in the schools. The belief of the organization is that if Christians know others are winning against these evils, they will be more likely to win also; the motto is "you can win if you pray and act." The organization provides seminars on "How to be a winning parent," "Christian counseling," and "Christian political stewardship." It creates its own radio and TV material, produces and distributes a number of publications, and operates the National Pregnancy Hotline to help girls with troubled pregnancies.

Membership:
> No direct membership; the organization serves 200,000 clients — individuals and groups

Publications:
> Over 100 separate items including regular newspapers: *Right to Life News, Occult Observer, Sex Education,* and *Mental Health Report* (all in tabloid form)

Radio/TV Programs:
> Radio shows varying from 30 second spots to half-hour programs
> TV programs from telethons to 30 second spots by Pat Boone

Meetings:
> Seminars provided through Valley Christian University; teaching sessions in the United States and in Europe on demand

314. Christian Films

Nondenominational
Virgil C. Wemmer
415 West Imperial Highway
La Habra, California 90631

Mailing Address:
Post Office Box 2305
La Habra, California 90631
(213) 691-0967 and (714) 525-5670

Christian Films is a Christian film rental library.

Staff: 9

315. Christian Forum Reserch [SIC] Foundation

Sidney Reiners, president
1111 Fairgrounds Road
Grand Rapids, Minnesota 55744
(218) 326-1765

The Christian Forum Reserch Foundation is a non-profit, independent organization dedicated to the study of various aspects of Biblical study and religious activity. Our goal of most interest to the general public is the study of religious liberty problems in totalitarian nations, especially the problems of Seventh-day Adventists and other Sabbath-keeping Christians. We also aim to bring these problems to the attention of the general public, with the objective of securing a lessening of persecution, the extradition of those who are special targets of persecution, and supplying religious material to those who are unable to obtain it, either out of poverty or government interference. The foundation currently is joining the movement to free Rostislav Galesky, leader of the True and Free Seventh-day Adventists of Russia.

Founding Date: 1981
Staff: 1
Membership:
4 (Board of Directors, not currently membership-seeking)
Publications:
News releases at irregular times, as needed

316. Christian Heritage Center

Nondenominational
Dr. N. Burnett Magruder, Executive Vice President and Secretary
1941 Bishop Lane, Suite 205
Louisville, Kentucky 40218
Mailing Address:
205 Watterson City West
1941 Bishop Lane
Louisville, Kentucky 40218
(502) 452-1592

Christian Heritage Center is a movement to recover the faith of Early America—God's great Providence for His glory and man's good; for a government to protect its people from all enemies at home and abroad (The Constitutional Oath); to help members of the Body of Christ in Communist countries; to prepare Christians to face the coming storm in our country and to prevail; for pro-Constitution, pro-Family and pro-Right to Life; for all historic liberties under Law.

Founding Date: 1965
Staff: 3
Membership: 1,200
Publications:
Revival and Survival Bulletin, monthly
The Coming Storm, monthly
Radio/TV Programs:
Liberty Radio, daily 15 minutes

317. Christian Holiness Association (CHA)

Nondenominational
Rev. Darius Salter, Executive Director
7 Lawrence Avenue
Stanhope, New Jersey 07874
(201) 347-1272

The distinguishing characteristic of the Christian Holiness Association is its adherence to the Wesleyan-American theological position. All major religious bodies in America who identify with this interpretation are members of the Association. The Christian Holiness Association was founded as the National Camp Meeting Association for the Promotion of Holiness. Today there are more than 2,000 holiness camp meetings in America. It is to this root organization that several modern-day denominations and other fellowships trace their beginnings. In 1970, several holiness associations outside the United States affiliated with the NHA and the name was changed to the Christian Holiness Association. The purpose of CHA today is to give a united voice to the holiness movement and to develop cooperative ministries among the holiness denominations and organizations.

Founding Date: 1867
Staff: 2
Membership: 16 denominations; 5 million individuals
Publications:
5 books; 1 newsletter
Meetings:
6 per year
Former Name: (1971) National Holiness Association

318. Christian Homesteading School

Roman Catholic
Richard Fahey, Director
Rural Delivery 2
Oxford, New York 13820

The Christian Homesteading School was started as a Catholic community housed on 70 acres of land of the Homesteading Center in Oxford, New York. Its purpose is to better the world we live in by helping people to homestead, by opening their awareness of things that have always been around them, and assisting them in acquiring new skills and a fresh appreciation of life. The basic instructional programs offered to single persons and families include: Basic and Advanced Homesteading, Carving, Herbalism, Work Horse and Veterinary Weeks, Log Cabin Instruction, Trapping and Hunting, Home Childbirth, Home Schooling of Children, and Christian Customs. The community makes no profit and the small registration fees pay for materials used in the classes, advertising, postage, and literature. Programs are open to all, without regard to race or creed.

Founding Date: 1963
Staff: 4
Publications:
> *The Homesteading News,* approximately bimonthly

Meetings:
> 20 per year

319. Christian Information Service, Inc.

Evangelical
Rev. William T. Bray, President
117 West Wesley
Wheaton, Illinois 60187
(312) 668-8767

The Christian Information Service, Inc., is a non-profit religious mission organized under the laws of the State of Illinois and recognized by the United States Government (IRS) as non-profit charity and tax-exempt. The society was formed by William T. Bray to provide news and information to the secular media in Bangkok, Thailand. Since 1973, the mission of CIS has been carried on in the United States and has expanded to cover a variety of mass-media communications and development services. By charter, CIS has six purposes: to raise support for communications staff workers not normally supported by church budgets; to release and exchange news and information between Christian organizations and the secular media; to handle special communications campaigns and projects for need causes and Christian organizations; to develop a media consciousness and help the church make use of modern communication and marketing techniques; to inspire and train a Christian communication corps to serve the mass media needs of the church, and to provide a fellowship within which Christians in the media, arts, and marketing can encourage each other and promote common interests.

Founding Date: 1967
Membership: 500 active members
Publications:
> *Evangelical Marketing Report*, a newsletter for national broadcasters, fundraisers, manufacturers, promoters, and publishers
> *Outreach News,* a newsletter for local Christian book and supply stores, broadcasters, charities, and missions
> *President's Report,* a monthly call to action for members and friends of CIS
> *CIS Guide to Christian Periodicals,* an annual guide to over 1,500 religious magazines and newspapers published in the United States

Meetings:
> Numerous seminars and conferences throughout the year
> Wheaton Institute in Christian Development, held annually

320. Christian Legal Society

Nondenominational
Lynn Robert Buzzard, Executive Director
Post Office 2069
Oak Park, Illinois 60303
(312) 848-7735

The purposes of the Christian Legal Society are: to provide a means of sharing among Christians; to provide Christian witness to fellow attorneys within their areas of influence; to clarify and promote the concept of the Christian lawyer; to encourage and aid Christian students who are preparing for the legal profession; to provide a forum for the discussion of problems relating to Christianity and law; and to cooperate with bar associations and other organizations in asserting and maintaining high standards of legal ethics.

Founding Date: 1961

Staff: 12

Membership: 2,200

Publications:

The Christian Lawyer, a journal

Scholarly books — *Christian Teacher and The Law, Legal Guidelines for Christian Organizations, Christian Perspectives on Law and Justice, Law and Gospel*

A newsletter

Meetings:

3 national conferences

5 student conferences

Several regional meetings

321. Christian Life Missions

Interdenominational

Robert Walker, President
396 East Saint Charles Road
Wheaton, Illinois 60187
(312) 653-4200

Christian Life Missions was organized for the purpose of employing the latest in communication techniques to disseminate the Gospel of Jesus Christ, and to meet the suffering of people throughout the world in need of medicine, food, and spiritual encouragement. Christian Life Missions publishes two periodicals, Christian Life, a consumer publication, and Christian Bookseller, a publication to instruct and encourage those involved in the sale or distribution of Christian literature, books, Bibles, tapes, records, etc. The mission also publishes books through its book publishing division Creation House, and operates a correspondence school in writing techniques, Christian Writers Institute.

Founding Date: 1945

Staff: 24

Publications:

Christian Life, monthly
Christian Bookseller, monthly

Meetings:

Christian Writers Institute Conference and Workshop — held on Wheaton (Illinois) College campus — 1 per year

322. Christian Literature Communications Foundation

Nondenominational

Gary C. Wharton, Director
3040 Charlevoix S.E.
Grand Rapids, Michigan 49506
(616) 949-2250

The purpose of the Christian Literature Communications Foundation is to develop and/or support multimedia communications programs compatible with the Christian ethic. The emphasis, as the name suggests, is literature and its dissemination.

Publications:

Christian Communication News, quarterly

Meetings:

College and Careers Communications Conference

Christian Communications Educators Conference

International Booksellers Seminars.

323. Christian Literature Crusade

Nondenominational

Robert Gerry, North American and International Director
701 Pennsylvania Avenue
Fort Washington, Pennsylvania 19034
(215) 542-1242

The Christian Literature Crusade is a fellowship of men and women dedicated to the Lord Jesus Christ and to the specific goal of using the printed word to introduce people to Him and lead them on into the thrilling experience of living continually under His Lordship and leadership. The Crusade is not a book business, but a meaningful ministry with eternal goals and objectives. CLC is interdenominational, interracial, and international. More than 450 dedicated men and women make up the present Crusade fellowship, and serve in 45 countries sending the printed message into more than 150 countries. The Crusade operates 130 bookstores in 45 countries, four print shops, and 13 publication centers.

Founding Date: 1941

Staff: 454 lay members

Publications:

Floodtide Magazine, quarterly
International Viewpoint, bimonthly
Caribbean Challenge, published and printed in Jamaica monthly
Over 1,000 evangelical Christian books

324. Christian Literature International

Nondenominational
Dr. Gleason H. Ledyard
Post Office Box 777
Canby, Oregon 97013
(503) 266-9734

Christian Literature International is a nondenominational organization which publishes and distributes the *New Life* Testament (and related books) which uses a controlled vocabulary of 850 words. Distribution agencies are located in most countries where English is used as a second language. Some books have been, and are presently being translated into many other languages. Seminars are conducted to train poorly educated national pastors in systematic theology. In North America, the controlled vocabulary *New Life* publications (which can be read and understood by children in the second grade) are used extensively by new literates, the deaf, minority groups, immigrants, poor readers, and international students.

Founding Date: 1967
Staff: 6
Publications:
Religious books, 15 titles

325. Christian Medical Society (CMS)

Nondenominational
Joseph Bayly, General Director
1616 Gateway Boulevard
Richardson, Texas 75080

Mailing Address:
Post Office Box 689
Richardson, Texas 75080
(214) 783-8384

The Christian Medical Society is a professional organization of physicians and dentists, practicing, teaching, or conducting research, and medical and dental students. The members have banded together to serve Christ through their profession. CMS lives with the conviction that medicine is an avenue of ministry that offers unique opportunities. It helps its members wrestle with the increasing ethical problems in the profession, enhance the quality of care given to the whole person, and interact with other members of the healing professions who face common problems. CMS has a Christian commitment. That means that its members take the historic Christian faith quite seriously. They believe that the term

"Christian" is not synonymous with the word "gentleman." When a physician, dentist, or student joins the Society, he is committed to certain historic beliefs about the Scriptures and Jesus Christ, and these beliefs are a vital part of the life and work of CMS.

Founding Date: 1931
Staff: 30 full and part-time
Membership: 4,800
Publications:
Christian Medical Society Journal, quarterly
News and Reports, bimonthly
Radio/TV Programs:
Through the help of Moody Bible Institute's WMBI, the Society has a short public-service radio program, "For Better Health," which is aired on various stations throughout the country.
Meetings:
Approximately 15 weekend conferences throughout the country in the Fall and Spring
1 large annual business meeting each year in different locations
3 student leadership conferences (East coast, Ohio, California)
Occasional symposia
10-12 short-term medical group mission trips to the Caribbean

326. Christian Men, Inc. (CMI)

Interdenominational
Leonard L. Holloway, Administrative Director
Post Office Box 670
Kerrville, Texas 78028
(512) 896-2505

An interdenominational public charity, Christian Men, Inc. is primarily involved in lay ministries and services through retreats, lay theological education leadership service, and communications. Laity Lodge, a Center for Christian Learning in the Texas hill country, is a place for a majority of the organization's meetings. The major program emphasis is on biblical studies, behavioral relationships, and experiences in the Christian life. Lay theological education weekends are taken to communities in cooperation with the Council of Southwest Theological Seminaries. A LAICOM (laity communications) program consists of films, books, study guides, and cassette tapes that are produced specifically for thoughtful lay persons. The H. E. Butt Foundation, a private foundation, underwrites and provides facilities, staff salaries, and other support for CMI. The organization is developing new programs to encourage creativity as well as seminars for serious laity studies. The organization is also involved in the Laity Lodge Youth Camp, a private Christian youth camp program conducted during the summer months.

Membership:
> The organization does not have a membership. It is programmed and directed by a 6-member Board of Directors.

Publications:
> *Newsletter,* quarterly

Meetings:
> 34 retreats annually at the Laity Lodge Renewal Center
> 10 Lay Theological Education Study programs annually in the Southwest
> Meetings for specific purposes in the area of laity leadership or laity theological education

327. Christian Methodist Episcopal Church, General Board of Christian Education*

Christian Methodist Episcopal Church

Reverend William R. Johnson, Jr., General Secretary
1474 Humber Street
Memphis, Tennessee 38106
(901) 948-0839

The Board of Christian Education, Christian Methodist Episcopal Church, is responsible for developing and promoting church school curriculum materials, religious education conferences, pastor's institutes, leadership training, and educational programs for children, youth, and adults. The Board generally superintends the institutions of higher learning under the auspices of the CME Church, and their relationships with the denomination. This includes the recruitment, enlistment, and training of ministerial students, and the provision of scholarship aid.

Staff: 3

Publications:
> Religious and denominational books
> *Christian Education,* quarterly

Meetings:
> 25 to 30 per year

328. A Christian Ministry in the National Parks (ACMNP)

Interdenominational

Warren W. Ost, Director
222½ East 49th Street
New York, New York 10017
(212) 758-3450/3451

A Christian Ministry in the National Parks provides 66 different national parks, recreation areas, seashores, and monuments with student ministers, directors of Christian education and music. These people lead services of worship, Bible studies, and discussion groups. It is a Christian ecumenical outreach to people who live in or near the park and especially those who visit our national parks. The students are employed by either the National Park Service or the private concessionaires who operate lodges, inns, restaurants, stores, and the like in each park. The students' work with ACMNP is volunteer. This ministry is centered around the summer months, although the agency has approximately 26 people in 15 different areas during the colder months. Full-time positions are quite scarce in this program; therefore the Ministry recruits and sends students who are looking for part-time involvement.

Staff: 100 members of the National Program Board
Membership:
> Approximately 4,200 alumni and contributors
> Approximately 700 other contacts

Publications:
> Newsletter semiannually for the alumni and contributors

Meetings:
> 9 orientation conferences in the spring held in California, Minnesota, Illinois, Texas, Ohio, Missouri, New England, Georgia, and New Jersey

329. Christian Mission for the Deaf

Christian Brethren

Dr. Andrew Foster, General Director
Post Office Box 1254
Flint, Michigan 48501

Christian Mission for the Deaf was incorporated in Michigan as a non-profit organization aimed at helping deaf Africans. The Mission's immediate task is twofold: reaching widely scattered benighted souls; then penetrating their silence and often illiteracy with the Gospel of Jesus Christ. Every possible and legitimate method is necessary. The Mission therefore utilizes primary schools, where the Bible forms part of the curriculum, Christian centers, Sunday schools, Bible classes, Bible correspondence courses, camps, and a Bible institute for training indigenous Christian leaders. CMDA has pioneered schools for the deaf in Ghana, Nigeria, Ivory Coast, Togo, Chad, and, indirectly, Liberia. It has also trained workers from Uganda, Zambia, Kenya, Cameroon, Togo and Benin, as well as Ghana and Nigeria.

Founding Date: 1956

Staff: 7 General Council Members

Membership:
2 full-time North American missionaries
4 part-time office assistants
Scores of African colleagues

Publications:
Deaf Witness

330. Christian Missions in Many Lands, Inc. (CMML)

Nondenominational
Samuel E. Robinson, President
Post Office Box 13
Spring Lake, New Jersey 07762
(201) 449-8880

Christian Missions in Many Lands, Inc., was established to assist Christian assemblies of New Testament pattern in the United States and missionaries commended by them to full-time service for Christ. These missionaries have gone forth in faith in the living God "to the uttermost parts of the earth," for the purpose of preaching the gospel and teaching the doctrine of the risen Savior.

Founding Date: 1829

Publications:
Christian Missions in Many Lands, monthly

Meetings:
2 meetings a year in New Jersey

331. Christian Nationals' Evangelism Commission

Nondenominational
Rev. Allen B. Finley, President
1470 North Fourth Street
San Jose, California 95112
(408) 298-0965

The primary purpose of the Christian Nationals' Evangelism Commission is to spread the Gospel by assisting and encouraging citizens of various nations to reach their own people for Christ. Its projects include evangelism, church growth, leadership development, theological education by extension, literacy work, publishing houses, Christian day schools, and aid to Bible colleges and seminaries. There are also vital self-help projects in agriculture, medicine, and technical training. Christian Nationals' does not recruit and send missionaries in the traditional manner. Aid is given to established and locally supervised indigenous or national church ministries. Several thousand children are sponsored to enable them to attend school; almost two hundred Bible school and seminary students are assisted through a sponsorship program. On the basis of such partnership and cooperation, the Great Commission of Christ is carried out with mutual respect. The Commission operates or supports 34 schools, 10 Bible schools and seminaries, four clinics, three youth centers, and five bookstores. All institutions are overseas.

Founding Date: 1943

Staff: 50 international staff members

Membership: 1,100 nationals

Publications:
The World Report, monthly
Communique, annually
The Prayer and Praise, monthly
Books through publishing houses in various countries in different languages
Magazines in various languages overseas
Booklets, pamphlets, brochures

Radio/TV Programs:
Produced a series of 60 five-minute spots interviewing nationals concerning the ministries in their various countries that are broadcast in the United States and Canada. Nationals produce Christian radio broadcasts in Nigeria, India, Brazil, Mexico, Sri Lanka, Japan, and Argentina.

Meetings:
Hundreds of meetings throughout the year in 35 countries
Weekly church meetings, Bible studies, youth clubs, seminars for pastors, and lay training seminars, as well as evangelistic campaigns, camps, and retreats
Co-sponsor of a weekly family conference at Mt Hermon, California in July

Former Name:
(1950) China Native Evangelistic Crusade
(1961) Chinese National Evangelistic Crusade

332. Christian Pilots Association, Inc. (CPA)

Interdenominational

Howard Payne, Founder-President
802 North Foxdale
West Covina, California 91790
(213) 962-7591

The purpose of Christian Pilots Association (CPA) is to mobilize committed born-again pilots and airmen throughout the world who want to volunteer their flying skills and expertise in a wide variety of services broadly summed up in the motto: Flying for Jesus and Human Need. Members have from zero flying time to over thirty thousand hours, with twenty-one airlines represented by member captains. Occupations run a wide variety with members in most of the states and some other countries. An attempt continues to be made to organize members into associated wings (local bases of operation) as key leaders surface and are willing to commit their time, talents, and treasure to this ministry. Some men in CPA give themselves full-time in service to the challenge this association represents. Association activities include airlifts for the cause of Christ such as flying missionaries and preachers to various churches; involvement in times of national or international disaster; building orphanages; caring for children; feeding the poor; building hospitals; and providing doctors and dentists to remote areas of need. Members distribute Gospel literature, show films, preach, sing and give their personal testimony at various churches and fraternal organizations. Most members work in other professions and donate their weekends and vacation periods to the work of the Association. Many of the members pay for all of the costs they incur, but usually ask that those who use their services, and are able to do so, pay their fair share of the fuel and incidental expenses. Although most members are pilots, it is not a membership requirement. Doctors, contractors, preachers, and others who have special talents are encouraged to join the Association.

Founding Date:
   July 3, 1972 (IRS Determination letter of tax-exempt)
Staff: 2 office; 7 executive
Membership: 250 with 3000 interested pilots
Publications:
   Christian Pilot News, quarterly
Meetings:
   Christian Pilots Airshow being scheduled for June 1983

333. Christian Record Braille Foundation, Inc

Seventh-day Adventist

B. E. Jacobs, General Manager
4444 South 52nd Street
Lincoln, Nebraska 68506
(402) 488-0981

The purpose of Christian Record Braille Foundation is to enrich the lives of blind and visually and physically imparied persons, regardless of race, creed, economic status, or sex. The following services are provided: eleven magazines in braille, large print, and on flexible discs; a lending library (including Bibles) in braille, large print, cassettes, and on records; full-vision books—a combination of ink-print and braille for blind parent and sighted child; a bible correspondence school, and Bible study guides in braille, large print, records, or cassettes; National Camps for Blind Children. Thirty-eight camps were conducted during the 1979 season. Approximately 2,000 campers attend annually; representatives who personally visit blind people in their homes; scholarship program for carefully selected students; glaucoma screening clinics; and coordination of the translation of materials and signing for deaf persons. Christian Record Braille Foundation is supported by contributions from civic-minded individuals and organizations, wills, trusts, and annuities. No tax money or government aid is received.

Founding Date: 1899
Staff: 160
Publications:
   The Christian Record, monthly in Braille
   The Christian Record Talking Magazine, bimonthly
   Life and Health, monthly
   The Childrens Friend, monthly in Braille
   Young and Alive, monthly
   The Student, monthly
   Encounter, monthly
   First Aid Manual
   Bible Study guides

334. Christian Reformed Church, Board for Christian Reformed World Missions

Christian Reformed Church

Dr. Eugene Rubingh, Executive Secretary
2850 Kalamazoo Avenue S.E.
Grand Rapids, Michigan 49560
(616) 241-6568

The Christian Reformed World Missions dates from 1888. Work among the Navajo and Zuni Indians was initiated in 1896, followed in 1920 by a mission to China. Currently work is carried on in 18 countries by 275 missionaries sent by the 700 congregations of the Christian Reformed Churches of the United States and Canada. The work is based on the doctrine of the sovereignty of God over all the earth and hence seeks to witness to the establishment of His Kingdom worldwide. While church growth is given high priority in this enterprise, the rule of Christ over all of life is emphasized by a comprehensive mission program dedicated to demonstrating His salvation and significance in every area of life.

Founding Date: 1888

Staff: 268 missionaries

Publications:
> *World to Win,* CRWM's annual report to its constituency
> *Mission Courier,* newspaper typed in cooperation with 3 other CRC mission agencies
> *Heartbeat,* newsletter to pastors

Radio/TV Programs:
> "New Life For All," radio and TV programs in Nigeria
> Radio broadcasts in Japan and Taiwan

Meetings:
> Annual board meeting (February)
> Bimonthly executive committee meeting
> Bimonthly area meetings overseas

335. Christian Reformed Church, Board of Home Missions

Christian Reformed Church
Rev. John G. Van Ryn, Executive Secretary
2850 Kalamazoo, S.E.
Grand Rapids, Michigan 49560
(616) 241-1691

The Christian Reformed Church in North America, in obedience to the great commission, established the Christian Reformed Board of Home Missions and assigned it the responsibility of directing the home missions program of the denomination. The Board of Home Missions, hereafter referred to as the Board. Gives leadership to the denomination in its task of bringing the gospel to, and drawing the people of Canada and the United States into fellowship with, Christ and his church. The mandate of the Board has two aspects: the Board shall encourage and assist congregations and classes in their work of evangelism, and carry on mission activity in places or fields where the program is beyond the scope or resources of local congregations or a classis. The Board administers its work in accordance with the Word of God and in harmony with the regulations of the Church Order and the Home Missions Order.

Staff: 240 home missionaries

Publications:
> *Reach,* evangelism information to pastors
> *Our Home,* evangelistic community outreach
> *Home Mission News,* mission information to denomination

Meeting:
> Conferences and retreats arranged for Home Missions personnel
> Evangelism retreats and conferences held according to request of churches

336. Christian Reformed Church, Education Department of the Board of Publications

Christian Reformed Church
Dr. Harvey Smit, Director and Theological Editor
2850 Kalamazoo Avenue S.E.
Grand Rapids, Michigan 49560
(616) 241-1691

The purpose of the Education Department of the Board of Publications is to provide leadership, direction, materials, and training for church education efforts in the Christian Reformed Church and other denominations. Since 1972 the Committee has produced a unique church school curriculum reflecting the historical and theological position of the Reformed Faith. This curriculum, popularly known as the *Bible Way* curriculum, has become recognized in major denominations throughout the English speaking world where the reformed influence is strong, especially the United States, Canada, and Australia.

337. Christian Reformed World Relief Committee (CRWRC)

Christian Reformed Church
John De Haan, Executive Director
2850 Kalamazoo Avenue S.E.
Grand Rapids, Michigan 49560
(616) 241-1691

The Christian Reformed World Relief Committee was established to minister, in the name of Christ, to people distressed by the calamities of life, and to relieve suffering. Disaster relief throughout the world and development programs in 11 foreign countries, as well as in the United States and Canada, are its chief programs. In development work, CRWRC attempts to increase the ability of groups to identify and solve their major problems, and to identify and meet spiritual needs.

Founding Date: 1962

Staff:
44 board Members
60 North American staff (most serving overseas)

Publications:
Deacon Digest, monthly
CRWRC Newsletter, quarterly
Mission Courier, quarterly (in cooperation with other mission agencies)

Meetings:
Annual board meeting in Grand Rapids
Regional board conferences, two per year at convenient locations

338. Christian Research Institute, Inc.

Nondenominational
Dr. Walter R. Martin, Director
Post Office Box 500
San Juan Capistrano, California 92693
(714) 991-1280

The Christian Research Institute was founded to meet the threat to Christian Evangelism and established congregations posed by non-Christian religions and cults. Recognizing this problem for what it is, a massive threat to the missionary life of the whole Christian Church, the Christian Research Institute deals with this issue on a international basis. The Institute is headed by Professor Walter Martin, a recognized authority on cults, the occult, and non-Christian religions. The Institute supplies to mission agencies, schools, churches, and laymen up-to-date information concerning the history, doctrines, and methods of the major religious systems functioning in the United States and all major world mission fields. Christian Research Institute is a pioneer in the field of evangelizing the cults and the occult, and is building a team of missionaries and researchers who devote all of their time to actively evangelizing members of the cults and the occult

through personal witnessing, research, publications, and lecture series in interested churches and schools throughout the country.

Founding Date: 1960

Staff: 7

Membership: 7

Publications:
Forward
Fact Sheets, tracts on various cults
Books and tapes

Radio/TV Programs:
Bible Answer Man, a radio call-in, question and answer program, 2 hours a week
Dateline Eternity, a daily 30-minute expository on Bible, Christianity, and comparative religions

Meetings:
25-30 seminars a year conducted by Dr. Martin around the world

339. Christian Salvage Mission, Inc.

Interdenominational
Rev. David Brown, President
200 Free Street
Fowlerville, Michigan 48836
(517) 223-3193

The Christian Salvage Mission is a corporation, registered with the State of Michigan for the purpose of receiving and distributing Christian literature. It must function within these limits. It is not underwritten nor endowed, but is dependent upon the voluntary contributions of materials and money for its continued operation. While there is a shortage of certain materials such as commentaries, Bible dictionaries, certain theological books, and Christian fiction, the primary problem is a shortage of money for operating expenses and postage. Their literature is sent primarily overseas and only upon request. These materials go to missionaries, native pastors and evangelists, Sunday School teachers and individuals.

Founding Date: 1958

Staff: 13

Membership: 5,000 on the mailing list

Publications:
Newsletter, monthly

Meetings:
Presentations in local churches upon invitation

340. Christian Schools International (CSI)

Nondenominational
Dr. Michael T. Ruiter, Executive Director
3350 East Paris Avenue S.E.
Grand Rapids, Michigan 49508
(616) 957-1070

Christian Schools International is an international service organization providing help and leadership to its more than 350 member schools throughout North America. Individual Christian schools are limited in time, space, talent, and funds to attempt certain projects on their own. CSI coordinates and channels individual school efforts and resources into a common, unified, strong program. On behalf of its member schools and through its competent staff, CSI produces Christian curriculum materials in many subject areas — textbooks, teacher resource units, manuals, filmstrips, and tapes. Its staff of experts conducts workshops in major curriculum areas; administers Christian School Pension Plans and Trust Funds, Group Life and Health insurance programs, a tax-sheltered annuity plan, a program of student insurance, and more; presents a united voice in representing Christian schools at state/provincial and federal government levels and assists in the administration of government programs for the schools; provides promotional materials, workshops for school board members, salary studies, research, and surveys on operating costs, and, upon request, expert and confidential analyses of member school programs and operation; and publishes, in addition to texts and other materials, a monthly magazine, *Christian Home and School.*

Founding Date: 1920

Staff: 25

Membership: 370 member schools

Publications:
Christian Home & School, 10 times a year

Meetings:
An annual convention is held every August in various places in the United States and Canada

Former Name:
(1978) National Union of Christian Schools

341. Christian Service Agency

Nondenominational

Raymond F. Wilson, President
Post Office Box 1947
311 East Elk
Glendale, California 91205
(213) 246-2200

Christian Service Agency represents Christian or non-profit institutions in all areas of Media Communication. We produce Radio and Television programs. Serve as Media time and space buyers, design and produce brochures and other related promotional material for our clients — serve as direct mail consultants and secure mailing lists for client fund raising projects.

Staff: 8

Radio/TV Programs:
CSA produces 1 daily radio program and presently has 3 60-minute TV specials in distribution.

342. Christian Service Brigade, Inc.

Nondenominational
King J. Coffman, President
Post Office Box 150
Wheaton, Illinois 60187
(312) 665-0630

Christian Service Brigade serves evangelical churches by providing a program through which local laymen develop the social, physical, mental, and spiritual aspects of boys' lives. More specifically, the organization seeks to motivate and prepare Christian men to influence boys and young men to accept Jesus Christ as Savior and follow Him as they mature into Christian manhood. This program involves leadership education and direct counsel of church laymen and clerical staffs. This is accomplished through a combination of literature, staff contact conferences, seminars, and informal training. The activity program for boys involves weekly meetings, games, sports, crafts, Bible study, and service projects. There are specific group structures for boys in grades 1-12. The organization works cooperatively with its counterpart, Christian Service Brigade of Canada.

Founding Date: 1937

Staff: 45

Membership: 75,000

Publications:
Venture and Dash, magazines for boys
Brigade Leader, magazine for adult leaders

Meetings:
60 per year (regional)

343. Christian Services, Inc.

Interdenominational
Donald D. Moore, General Director
7000 Lanham Lane
Minneapolis, Minnesota 55435
(612) 944-2959

Christian Services assists missionaries and missionary organizations through the preparation and mailing of prayer letters. It also assists missionaries in the purchase of housing. Other ministries include both missionary and non-missionary-related services such as charitable aid and Christian music.

Founding Date: 1973

Publications:
Individual missionary and other news and prayer letters

Former Name:
Christian Services Fellowship, Inc.

344. Christian Singles

Interdenominational
Jean Smith, Director
Post Office Box 203-D
Union City, California 94587

Christian Singles is a pen pal club for Bible believing Christians in the United States and Canada, with a few participants in other countries as well. It offers Christians the opportunity to correspond with one another through letters and/or cassette tapes to share Christian fellowship. Pen pals are able to encourage and be encouraged, share joys, goals, problems, Christian experience, and the love of Christ with others of like faith. It offers single Christians an opportunity for fellowship with many more single Christians than would otherwise be possible. Christian Singles is NOT a dating service. The organization is interdenominational and open to all born again single Christians from Bible believing churches.

Staff: 2

Membership: Approximately 1,000 participants

345. Christian Spiritual Alliance*

Spiritualist
Roy Eugene Davis, Director
Rabun Road
Lakemont, Georgia 30552

Mailing Address:
Post Office Box 7
Lakemont, Georgia 30552
(404) 782-3931

The Christian Spiritual Alliance is a New Age brotherhood, free from hierarchical authority, whose members are encouraged to tread the path which leads to enlightenment of consciousness and true understanding. Its outreach ministry includes the conducting of retreats and seminars in cooperation with established organizations; mainly Unity School (churches) and Religious Science churches. The Center for Spiritual Awareness is the teaching department of the Christian Spiritual Alliance. The director of the center is Roy Eugene Davis, a personal disciple of Paramahansa Yogananda.

Membership: 5,000 lay; 10 clerical

Publications:
Self-help, metaphysical, inspirational books, 50 titles in print
Truth Journal
Orion
Numerous bulletins, flyers, and circulars

Radio/TV Programs:
Help Yourself to Life, an insirational 30-minute broadcast heard each Saturday over KLRO-FM, San Diego, and XEMO from San Diego, covering all of the West Coast

Meetings:
About 40 seminars and retreats where meditation and contemplation are taught and practiced

346. Christian Television Mission, Inc.

Nondenominational
Don W. Vernon, Executive Director
1918 South Ingram Mill Road
Springfield, Missouri 65804
(417) 881-6303

Christian Television Mission is a missionary ministry, existing for the sole purpose of preaching the Gospel of Jesus Christ to lost mankind. The Mission was organized as an outgrowth of a weekly television program by the Vernon Brothers Quartet over KOAM-TV, Pittsburg, Kansas. The resulting outreach of this ministry can be seen in its performance on television; in revivals and crusades; in establishing new churches; in its films being used by missionaries; in Faith Promise and church missionary rallies; and in foreign evangelistic tours.

Founding Date: 1950

Staff:

7

18 Board members

Membership:

Thousands of church and individual supporters

Publications:

Christians TV News, bimonthly except for July-August

Radio/TV Programs:

Produced a weekly television series entitled *Homestead USA* consisting of 78 programs

12 prime time and holiday specials

Meetings:

Vacation and Spiritual Encounter (Family Camp) at the School of the Ozarks at Point Lookout, Missouri, once a year

347. Christianica Center

Nondenominational
John Palmer Gabriel, Director
6 North Michigan Avenue
Chicago, Illinois 60607
(312) 782-4230

Christianica Center is involved in publishing to help people pray. The organization publishes books, records, and cassettes.

Founding Date: 1961

Staff: 4

Publications:

Books, records and cassettes

348. Christianity Today, Inc.

Nondenominational
Harold L. Myra, President & Publisher
465 Gundersen Drive
Carol Stream, Illinois 60187
(312) 260-6200

Christianity Today, Inc, founded the magazine *Christianity Today* to provide a forum for the expression of evangelical conviction in the realms of theology, evangelism, church life, cultural life, and society. Since its establishment, the magazine has brought a growing sense of spiritual unity to Bible-believing Christian laymen, ministers, and theologians in many different denominations. It has been active in promoting the defense of historic Christianity in the world of ideas as well as providing Christian believers with information, knowledge and the tools for Christian service.

Founding Date: 1956

Publications:

Christianity Today, semimonthly
Leadership: A Practical Journal for Church Leaders, quarterly

349. Christians in Action

Interdenominational
Lee Shelley, Director
Post Office Box 7271
Long Beach, California 90807
(213) 428-2022

Christians in Action is primarily a church planting organization. It has approximately 160 missionaries and candidates serving on five continents. International training schools operate in Long Beach, California; London, England; Guatemala City, Guatemala; and Okinawa, Japan. Curriculum includes only subjects needed for effective missionary service. Classroom instruction is coupled equally with supervised field experience in personal evangelism. Thus trainees are proven soul winners and disciple makers before appointment. A newly appointed missionary can be serving on the field only one year after enrollment as a student. Christians in Action also offers a short-term missionary service, as well as a summer missions program. Besides recruiting, training, appointing, and sending missionaries, Christians in Action has a major thrust in equipping laymen to be effective soul winners. One-week evangelism seminars are held each summer and six-week institutes three times a year. Action Night is held each week to offer soul winning training to laymen and churches. Many lay outreach programs have been started in the United States and abroad through this organization. "House to house" evangelism is part of the "20-20 vision" (Acts 20:20). Christians in Action is not sponsored by any denomination or group but draws support and personnel from a broad spectrum of churches. Both the organization and its individual missionaries are supported financially by faith through gifts of interested individuals and churches.

Founding Date: 1958

Staff: 18

Membership: 160 missionaries

Publications:
> *Christians in Action,* bimonthly

Radio/TV Programs:
> 15-minute radio broadcasts in Long Beach (KGER) 5 nights a week
> Saturday broadcast in Orange County (KYMS)

Meetings:
> Annual missions conference (2 weeks, open to the public)
> Annual missionary seminar (6 weeks, for furloughing missionaries)
> Weekly church meetings, action rallies, and Action Nights

Former Name:
> (1947) Missionary and Soul Winning Fellowship

350. Christmount Christian Assembly, Inc.

The Christian Church (Disciples of Christ)

Melba B. Banks, Executive Director
Route 1, Box 38-E
Black Mountain, North Carolina 28711
(704) 669-8977

Christmount is a conference center owned and operated by the Christian Church (Disciples of Christ). It is open to all denominations. The Assembly provides year-round accommodations of motel quality for meetings. In addition, a summer camp program is conducted in cabins. Camps include activities for youth of the denomination, deaf teenagers, disadvantaged youth, mentally retarded persons, and autistic persons. The camps are held during the summer months along with retreats by such groups as the Red Cross youth development program. In addition to Adult programs in music and Bible study, senior citizens programs and family retreats are offered. Other denominations use the facilities for their own programs upon proper application. Day meetings are scheduled for Church Women United, social agencies, andministers' groups; swimming and first aid classes are offered regularly.

Membership:
> Each member of the Christian Church (Disciples of Christ) is considered a member of the organization for Christmount

Publications:
> *The Christmount Voice,* monthly

Meetings:
> Approximately 100 per year

351. The Christopher Publishing House

Nondenominational

Thomas A. Christopher
53 Billings Road
North Quincy, Massachusetts 02171
(617) 328-3880

The Christopher Publishing House is a general book publisher (both hardcover and paperback). Over 30% of its publications are in the fields of philosophy and religion and 40% in the field of education. Its titles include the works of religious leaders representing nearly every denomination. The Christopher Publishing House operates its own bookstore.

Founding Date: 1910

Publications:
> 200 active titles — 70% religious and scholarly

352. The Christophers, Inc.

Roman Catholic

Rev. John T. Catoir, Director
12 East 48th Street
New York, New York 10017
(212) 759-4050

The goal of The Christophers is to motivate people to exercise leadership in the church, in their community and community organizations, in their neighborhoods, at work, and within the family so that the efforts of all will make for a better society consistent with Judeo-Christian principles. The organization publishes *Christopher News Notes* seven times a year and *Christopher World* twice yearly and distributes them free of charge. Separate newspaper columns, "Three Minutes a Day" and "Light One Candle," are syndicated to daily and weekly publications, respectively, and to magazines. The Christophers also produce a weekly television talk show entitled *Christopher Closeup* and a daily inspirational radio spot entitled *Christopher Thoughts for*

Today. The organization also publishes inspirational books twice yearly and distributes the "Christopher Appointment Calendar."

Founding Date: 1945

Staff: 50

Publications:
>*Christopher News Notes,* seven times a year
>*Eco Cristoforos,* Spanish, six times a year

Radio/TV Programs:
>TV: *Christopher Closeup*
>Radio: *Christopher Closeup* (¼-hour program)
>Radio: *The Christopher One-Minute Thoughts for Each Day* (one-minute spots)

353. Christ's Mission

Interdenominational

Rev. Royal L. Peck, Executive Director
275 State Street
Hackensack, New Jersey 07601

Mailing Address
Post Office Box 176
Hackensack, New Jersey 07602
(2101) 342-6202

Loving, serving, discipling and enlarging the Body of Christ at Home and abroad. Having identified a specific need, we are intent upon enlarging the Body of Christ in areas of the world that are inhabited by nominal Christians, unconverted and uncommitted to the Lordship of Jesus — especially to those centers of Europe and North America that are predominantly Roman Catholic in culture. We meet the need with a four-fold ministry: Church planting in areas where no evangelical church presently exists; producing sound, Biblical Literature, geared to produce growth; church education (strengthening the community of the local church in its effectiveness and witness to nominal Christians, both Protestant and Roman Catholic), and re-orientation and rehabilitation of former priests. Our church planting strategy is accomplished in collaboration with, and at the invitation of other Mission Societies, national associations, or local churches. The new church is affiliated with the inviting society, association or church. Its volunteers make a project commitment rather than lifetime commitment, and the ministry is done in teams of 20 to 30 workers collaborating to plant one local church.

Founding Date: 1883

Staff: 138

Publications:
>*The Planter,* bimonthly bulletin

Meetings:
>One conference held annually at Isola Del Gran Sasso, Italy

Former Name: Christ's Mission of New York

354. Church and Synagogue Library Association

Interdenominational

Dorothy J. Rodda, Executive Secretary
Post Office Box 1130
Bryn Mawr, Pennsylvania 19010
(215) 853-2870

The purpose of the Church and Synagogue Library Association is to aid and encourage the development of library service in churches and synagogues. To this end, a bimonthly bulletin is published, as well as a series of guides to congregational library practice, booklists, etc. An annual three-day conference with speakers and workshops for beginning and more advanced congregational librarians is held in different parts of the country. Local and regional chapters are encouraged and sponsored. Cooperation with other library and religious groups is emphasized.

Founding Date: 1967

Membership: 1,300

Publications:
>*Church and Synagogue Libraries*
>12 educational books and 1 slide set

Meetings:
>1 three-day conference per year in various cities throughout the United States
>Regional workshops and seminars sponsored by 15 chapters

355. The Church Center for the United Nations*

Interdenominational

777 United Nations Plaza
New York, New York 10017
(212) MU2-3633

The Church Center for the United Nations grew out of a desire to give United Nations delegates from other lands, many of whom were graduates of Christian mission schools, warm hospitality and practical help in a strange country. Most of all it grew out of a Christian passion to contribute to world peace and unity through education of its own people and witness to the international community. From the beginning the project was planned as an interdenominational venture: a place for meditation, prayer, study, dialogue and action. It provides settings for human contact across the usual bonds of culture, race, and nationality. The Church Center today is a vital hub of international, ecumenical, and inter-religious activity. The activity of the nearly 20 groups in the building includes the struggle for human rights, media work, a Montessori School for children from the international community, seminars, and conferences.

Meetings:
Seminars and conferences

356. Church Growth Book Club

Nondenominational
Roger Schrage, General Manager
1705 North Sierra Bonita Avenue
Pasadena, California 91104
(213) 798-0819

The Church Growth Book Club is a mail order distribution business selling books dealing with the Christian mission. Subjects include mission strategy, Church growth, theological education by extension, and specific area and case studies from around the world. Annual membership includes a subscription to the bimonthly *Church Growth Bulletin.* Most books are sold at 40% off the retail price. The books distributed are published by many well-known religious publishers.

Staff: 10
Membership:
Approximately 4,000 members of the club
Publications:
Church Growth Bulletin, bimonthly

357. Church Growth Services

Nondenominational
Marvin H. Walz, President
120 Callander Street
South Bend, Indiana 46614

Mailing Address
Post Office Box 2409
South Bend, Indiana 46680
(219) 291-4777

Church Growth Services is a privately owned corporation serving as church consultants in the areas

of ministry planning, financial guidance, and architectural design.

Founding Date: 1959
Staff: 20
Former Name:
Evangelical Church Building Corporation

358. Church Music Association of America

Roman Catholic
Rev. Msgr. Richard J. Schuler, President
548 Lafond Avenue
Saint Paul, Minnesota 55103
(612) 226-5103

The purpose of The Church Association of America is to maintain the highest artistic standards in church music and to preserve the treasury of sacred music, especially the Gregorian chant, while at the same time encouraging composers to write artistically fine music, especially for more active participation of the people, all according to the norms of the Second Vatican Council. To accomplish these ends the Association publishes a quarterly journal, the oldest continuously published music magazine in the United States. They also have had biennial conventions, but because of high travel and lodging costs, they have been temporarily postponed.

Founding Date: 1964
Membership: 1,000
Publications:
Sacred Music, quarterly
Merger:
Formed from a merger of the Society of Saint Cecilia of America and The Saint Gregory Society

359. Church of God (Anderson, Indiana), Board of Christian Education

Church of God (Anderson, Indiana)
Donald A. Courtney, Executive Secretary-Treasurer
1303 East 5th Street
Anderson, Indiana 46011

Mailing Address
Post Office Box 2458
Anderson, Indiana 46011
(317) 642-0257

The Board of Christian Education is responsible for developing program designs and resources to develop lay leadership for a variety of nurture and educational ministries for the local congregations of the Church of God. It also seeks to develop program designs and resources for specialized ministries in the areas of early childhood education, children's ministries, youth ministries, single adult ministries, older adult ministries, family life ministries, worship and the arts, camping, urban ministries, and campus ministries. The Board of Christian Education works cooperatively with the Publication Board of the Church of God in developing curriculum for the Sunday school and in cooperation with other communions' curriculum for vacation church school.

Staff:
>   15 members of the Board
>   5 members of the Board of Directors
>   10 staff employees

Publications:
>   *Christian Leadership,* 10 times a year
>   *About,* 6 times a year

Meetings:
>   Many varied meetings throughout the United States

360. Church of God (Anderson, Indiana), Board of Church Extension and Home Missions*

Church of God

M. J. Hartman, Chief Executive
Post Office Box 2069
Anderson, Indiana 46011
(317) 644-2555

The assignment of the Board of Church Extension and Home Missions is to extend the evangelistic outreach of the Church of God in the United States and Canada; to do home missions work among the disadvantaged and underprivileged; and to assist local congregations in building programs through counseling, planning, and financing.

Membership: 10 lay; 11 clerical
Publications:
>   *Focus,* quarterly

Meetings:
>   200 or more each year

361. Church of God (Anderson, Indiana), Mass Communications Board

Church of God (Anderson, Indiana)

Dr. Maurice Berquist, Executive Secretary/Treasurer
Post Office Box 2007
Anderson, Indiana 46011
(317) 642-0256

The primary function of the Mass Communications Board of the Church of God, Inc., is to produce and distribute radio and television programs for the Church of God (Anderson, Indiana). Its "Christian Brotherhood Hour-English," begun in 1947, is carried on nearly 400 radio stations, while "Christian Brotherhood Hour-Spanish" is carried on 63 stations. The Mass Communications Board also produces "Christian Brotherhood Hour-Portuguese."

Radio/TV Programs:
>   Christian Brotherhood Hour, carried on 400 radio stations; also in Spanish and Portuguese

362. Church of God (Anderson, Indiana), Men International

Church of God (Anderson, Indiana)

Donald C. Ritchey, President
536 Tiffin Avenue
Findlay, Ohio 45840
(419) 423-8960

The Church of God, Men International, is an organization of laymen and pastors who encourage participation in the overall mission of the church on the local, state, national, and international levels. Included among its projects are: conducting a Men's Congress and family retreat every two years in August; sponsoring church-wide Bible reading; conducting work shop seminars on Christian witnessing and stewardship; and developing devotional and layman Sunday programs to be used each fall.

Membership: 3,000 lay; 200 clerical
Publications:
>   4 newsletters a year to all members
Meetings:
>   10 meetings of local groups a year

363. Church of God (Anderson, Indiana), Missionary Board

Church of God (Anderson, Indiana)

Dr. Donald D. Johnson
Executive Secretary-Treasurer
Post Office Box 2498
Anderson, Indiana 46011
(317) 642-0258

The Missionary Board of the Church of God is incorporated under the laws of the State of Indiana. Its objects are religious, philanthropic, and educational, and designed to promote the gospel of Christ throughout the world. The Board is the agent of the General Assembly of the Church of God for organizing, supporting, and administering the program of world ministries and activities which are found in countries other than the United States and Canada. It is responsible to the General Assembly and gives reports of its proceedings every year for review and approval, It is subject to directions given by the General Assembly. The Board consists of 20 members, who are elected by the General Assembly. It meets for business purposes once each year. During the intervals between annual or called meetings, the administration of the Board's work is carried on by a Board of Directors. The Missionary Board is charged with the duty of raising funds for missionary purposes, working closely with the Division of World Service and the Budget Committee of the Executive Council. It is also charged with the responsibility for selecting and sending suitable persons to serve as missionaries, including teachers, doctors, nurses and other specialized personnel. In a general way, the Board coordinates the work of missionary personnel through its Board of Directors so as to produce harmonious and efficient operation.

Staff:
> 20 members of the Missionary Board
> 5 members of the Board of Directors
> 6 administrative staff members

Publications:
> *Church of God Missions,* missions magazine

Radio/TV Programs:
> "Christian Brotherhood Hour," a radio program in English and in Spanish for Latin America
> Other local programs

Meetings:
> As needed

364. Church of God (Anderson, Indiana), Women of the Church of God, Inc.

Church of God (Anderson, Indiana)
Nellie Snowden, Executive Secretary-Treasurer
Post Office Box 2328
Anderson, Indiana 46011
(317) 642-0255

The purpose of The Women of the Church of God is to cooperate with all recognized agencies of the Church of God which are affiliated with, recognized by, or subordinate to the General Assembly of the Church of God, in helping to promote missionary work in various fields; to encourage liberality and wisdom in the stewardship of prayer, of personality, and of possessions; to promote Christian understanding and fellowship; and to bring to bear on all human life the spirit and principles of Christ. The program of Women of the Church of God is made available to any woman of the Church of God.

Founding Date: 1932

Staff: 3

Membership: Approximately 40,000 lay members

Publications:
> Co-publishers of *Church of God Missions* with Board of Home Missions and Missionary Board, 11 issues a year

Meetings:
> Annually in June; Anderson, Indiana

Former Name:
> (1975) National Women's Missionary Society of the Church of God

365. Church of God (Cleveland, Tennessee), Department of General Education

Church of God (Cleveland, Tennessee)
Dr. Robert E. Fisher, Director
Keith at 25th Street, N.W.
Cleveland, Tennessee 37311
(615) 472-3361

The Department of General Education coordinates the total educational ministry of the Church. This includes a graduate school, four colleges in the United States, a college in Canada, ministerial training schools for the Spanish-speaking and the American Indian, and over 50 Bible schools and seminaries in other countries around the world. In an effort to provide training which is both scriptural and practical for the beginning minister who is unable to attend a Bible college, the department has developed the Ministerial Internship Program. An innovative "grass roots" educational ministry sponsored by the department is the Bible Institute for Ministerial and Lay Enrichment. For those students who wish to receive a college degree but are unable to attend school as a resident, the Church of God Continuing Education Program offers an accredited "in home" program of study leading to a bachelor's degree. The department is also involved in the development of Christian day schools, pastoral institutes, and family life seminars and retreats. Through the R. Leonard Carroll Loan Fund ministerial students are provided long-term, low-interest loans to complete their education.

Staff: 9

Publications:
> *Pulse,* quarterly
> *Pulse 2,* quarterly
> *Ministerial Internship Program Newsletter,* monthly December through May

Meetings:
> Education Leadership Retreat, annually
> Christian School Conference, annually
> International Conference of Educators, biennially

366. Church of God (Cleveland, Tennessee), Department of Evangelism and Home Missions

Church of God (Cleveland, Tennessee)
Raymond E. Crowley, Director
Keith at 25th Street, N.W.
Cleveland, Tennessee 37311
(615) 472-3361

The purpose of the Evangelism and Home Missions Department is to implement the evangelistic thrust of the church on a general, state, district, and local level, by developing and promoting a unified program which properly relates the message, method, motivation, and spirit of New Testament Evangelism. The ministries of the Department are: Architecture, Senior Adult Fellowships, Prison and Institutional, Ministers Placement, American Indians, Cross-Cultural, Big Brother Program, Major City Crusades, Impact Rallies, and Chair on Evangelism in Colleges. The Office of Lay Affairs is an adjunct to the Department and serves as a liaison between the laymen and ministry of the church.

367. Church of God (Cleveland, Tennessee), Ladies Auxiliary

Church of God (Cleveland, Tennessee)
Ruth J. McCane, Executive Secretary
Keith at 25th Street, N.W.
Cleveland, Tennessee 37311
(615) 472-3361

The goals of the Church of God Ladies Auxiliary are: to strengthen home and family life by encouraging young women in their roles as wives, mothers, and homemakers; to contribute to the spiritual life of the Church by the formation of prayer partnerships and prayer groups, sustained Bible reading and study programs, and by stimulating regular church attendance; to encourage an active and regular program of home and hospital visitation; and to reach the unsaved and unchurched, and bring them to the fellowship of the Church. In addition to helping support local churches, the Ladies Auxiliary gives financial assistance to its Church's world and home missions programs, and provides funds for orphanages. The organization holds to the "Unto the least of these my brethren" precept, and practices it wherever the need exists. Members of the Auxiliary share in community projects, serve as counselors and guides for the Young Ladies Auxiliary (YLA) and the Joy Belles (Junior Girls' Club), and promote child evangelism through "Kids Klubs."

Founding Date: 1929

Staff:
> 5 staff members
> 9 Board of Directors members

Publications:
> *Willing Worker*
> *Rapporter,* magazine for teen girls
> *Woman Power Newsletter* to State Ladies Auxiliary Presidents
> *Heartbeat Newsletter* to District Directresses

Meetings:
> Frequent meetings, the number and location varies

Former Name: (1970) Ladies' Willing Workers Board

368. Church of God (Cleveland, Tennessee), Publishing House

Church of God (Cleveland, Tennessee)
Dr. Oliver C. McCane, General Director
1080 Montgomery Avenue
Cleveland, Tennessee 37311
(615) 476-4512

The purpose of the Church of God Publishing House is to serve the printed needs of the Church of God, the Pentecostal, Evangelical and Protestant world; and to minister through the printed page by printing and publishing literature for Sunday schools, source books for ministers and workers, music for choirs, and other products for churches around the world. These purposes are accomplished through maintaining a staff of qualified writers and editors who are constantly creating curriculum and periodicals; Tennessee Music and Printing Company (a subsidiary of the Church of God Publishing House) that creates convention and choral arrangements in songbooks, sheet music, tapes, etc; a trade division, Pathway Press; and retail outlets, Pathway Bookstores. The General Editorial and Publications Board is a vital part of the Department and serves in the roll of policy making for the publishing entity of the Church of God.

Founding Date: 1910

Staff: 18

Membership: 185

Publications:
> *Evangel,* bimonthly
> *Leadership,* quarterly
> *Lighted Pathway,* monthly
> *Pathway Ministries,* quarterly

Meetings:
> Teacher Enrichment Seminars (major cities), twice monthly
> Pathway Bookstore Managers Meetings (various cities, yearly

369. Church of God (Cleveland, Tennessee), Stewardship Department

Church of God (Cleveland, Tennessee)
Al Taylor, Director
Keith at 25th Street, N.W.
Cleveland, Tennessee 37311

Mailing Address
Post Office Box 2430
Cleveland, Tennessee 37311
(615) 472-3361

The Department of Stewardship serves the Church of God through conferences and seminars designed to help laity and clergy in the management of possessions according to the guidelines of scripture. The individual and his family receive estate planning information and assistance enabling them to protect the family's interests and accomplish spiritual objectives as well. Annual campaigns are designed to teach God's principles of economics in each local church. This educational emphasis provides the knowledge and inspiration to conform to God's plan. Such conformity is stewardship. Scriptural stewardship results in more of God's blessings upon the faithful steward, his family, and his church.

Founding Date: 1980

Publications:
> *Tax Economics of Charitable Giving*
> *Venture in Faith*
> *This Grace Also*

Meetings:
> Pastors' National Conference on Stewardship, Cleveland, Tennessee (1 per year)
> Saturday Seminars, various cities (4 per year)

370. Church of God (Cleveland, Tennessee), World Missions

Church of God (Cleveland, Tennessee)
Dr. Robert White, Executive Director
Keith at 25th Street, N.W.
Cleveland, Tennessee 37311
(615) 472-3361

The Church of God missionaries are ministering today in nearly 100 countries with 108 territorial overseers, leading more than 8,600 congregations and 600,000 members outside the United States in an all-out effort to win their people to Jesus Christ. Its 52 Bible Schools, located in strategic centers, train national preachers and workers.

Founding Date: 1886

Publications:
> *Sow,* bimonthly
> *Missionline,* bimonthly
> *Communicator,* a newsletter to missionaries, bimonthly

Meetings:
> Annual conferences in each of the superintendent areas and countries
> Retreat for the whole territory

371. Church of God (Cleveland, Tennessee), Youth and Christian Education Department

Church of God (Cleveland, Tennessee)
R. Lamar Vest, General Director of Youth and Christian Education Church of God Department of Youth and Christian Education
Keith at 25th Street, N.W.
Cleveland, Tennessee 37311
(615) 472-3361

The Youth and Education Department is a service and resource agency with multiple responsibilities for advancing the many facets of the total Christian education program in the local church. The work of youth and Christian education in the church centers in five functions; reach, teach, win, train, and send out. The consummate results are evangelism and nurture. Some of the major agencies serviced by the department are: Sunday school, Family Training Hour, local church and regional youth ministries, Church Training Course, youth camps, STEP (Summer Training and Evangelism Partners), and YWEA (Youth World Evangelism Action). In addition to a strong national ministry, the department is constantly looked to for advice and council by youth and Christian education workers of other countries. Special leadership workshops and Christian education conventions are conducted throughout the United States and in many countries around the world.

Staff: General 14, State 48, District 750

Publications:

> *Youth and Christian Education LEADERSHIP,* (in cooperation with Pathway Press), a magazine of training and resource for local church leaders, quarterly
>
> *Touch,* a monthly contact with state leadership
>
> *Focus,* a quarterly contact with district leadership

372. Church of God, Seventh Day (Denver, Colorado), Media Outreach Agency

Church of God (Seventh Day)
John Roina, Director of Media Outreach
Post Office Box 33677
Denver, Colorado 80233
(303) 452-7973

The Media Outreach Agency has the purpose of encouraging church growth and discipleship by providing outreach tools and training. The agency produces evangelistic radio spots, booklets, print ads, and followup materials. Church growth training workshops are conducted for districts and local churches. Media services and promotion assistance is provided to all organizational levels of the Church of God (Seventh Day).

Staff:

> The Staff of the General Conference office numbers 20 full-time employees
>
> The staff of the Media Outreach Agency numbers 2 full-time employees

Membership:

> The general membership of the Church of God (Seventh Day) numbers 7,000

Publications:

> *The Bible Advocate* is a monthly magazine published by our publishing house, The Bible Advocate Press

Radio/TV Programs:

> The Media Outreach Agency of the Church of God (Seventh Day) produces a series of one minute radio spots targeted to unchurched/ unsaved people. These are aired by local churches or districts wishing to sponsor a radio outreach.

Meetings:

> The General Conference of the Church of God (Seventh Day) convenes biennially
>
> On alternate biennial years there are district level conferences. Each district sponsors its own retreats.
>
> The Media Outreach Agency often conducts workshops at conference meetings

373. Church of God, Seventh Day (Denver, Colorado), Missions Abroad Agency*

Church of God (Seventh Day)
Robert Coulter, Director
Post Office Box 2370
Denver, Colorado 80201
(303) 452-7973

Missions Abroad directs the missionary program of the Church of God (Seventh Day) in ten countries around the world. It serves the needs of the Church's missionary endeavors by supplying funds, materials, and equipment for its missions. Missions Abroad serves a membership exceeding 8,000 in 10 countries. It supports missionaries in Colombia and Ecuador. The remainder of its missionary activities are directed toward the support of nationals. The objective of this agency is to establish missions through which the teaching of the Church of God (Seventh Day) may be made known.

Membership: More than 8,000

Meetings:

> One Agency meeting annually
>
> Weekly meetings in the local congregation

374. Church of God, Seventh Day (Denver, Colorado), National Women's Association*

Church of God (Seventh Day)

Mrs. Sandra Lawson, Director
Post Office Box 2370
Denver, Colorado 80201
(303) 452-7973

The National Women's Association is an auxiliary organization of the Church of God (Seventh Day) which encourages the development of local chapters of women whose purpose is to assist in the missions of the church. It publishes a quarterly magazine, *Wand* (Women's Association News Digest) and sponsors an organization for children, ages 9-12, called *Seekers.*

Publications:
   Wand, quarterly
Meetings:
   Biennial meetings
   Monthly meetings in its local chapters

375. Church of God, Seventh Day (Denver, Colorado), Radio Outreach Agency*

Church of God (Seventh Day)
Robert Coulter
Chairman of the United Missions Board
Post Office Box 2525
Denver, Colorado 80201
(303) 452-7973

The Radio Outreach Agency of the Church of God (Seventh Day) produces a radio broadcast called *Faith for Our Time.* It is aired over 26 stations throughout the United States more than 50 times weekly. It also conducts the Searchlight Bible Correspondence School, a free correspondence Bible course offered to anyone interested in further Bible study.

Radio/TV Programs:
   Bible Study broadcasts of 5, 25, and 30 minutes in length

376. Church of God General Conference, Department of Outreach and Church Development

Church of God General Conference
Rev. Warren Sorenson, Director
131 North Third Street
Oregon, Illinois 61061

Mailing Address
Post Office Box 100
Oregon, Illinois 61061
(815) 732-7991

The Church of God General Conference Department of Outreach and Church Development exists for the purpose of assisting local churches in their evangelistic outreach, their growth, and the development of their Sunday School and youth programs. This organization also is involved in helping to establish new churches, and it oversees the foreign mission efforts of the Church of God General Conference. Specific duties of the organization include: surveying fields for establishment of new churches; selecting and developing missionary personnel; developing a planned program for establishing new churches; maintaining liaison with mission churches and workers at home and abroad; developing programs for use of mass media in evangelism; planning programs of financial support; administering pastoral aid and special church aid programs; providing on-site counseling and consultation to churches; establishing growth and attendance goals and recording results; planning and administering youth programs, including camps and retreats; providing youth literature; and training youth workers.

Founding Date: 1978
Staff: 4
Membership:
   5,000 members in Church of God General Conference Churches
Publications:
   Challenge, for young people ages 12-22, every other month
Meetings:
   Christian Workers Seminar, Gatlinburg, Tennessee, one per year
   Berean Youth Conference, Milford, Indiana, one per year
Mergers:
   Evangelism and Missions Board and Sunday School Board were merged into this department

377. Church of God General Conference Publishing Department

Church of God General Conference
Rev. Russell Magaw
Editor and Director of Publications
131 North 3rd Street
Oregon, Illinois 61061

Mailing Address
Post Office Box 100
Oregon, Illinois 61061
(815) 732-7991

The Church of God General Conference Publishing Department exists for the purpose of publishing educational materials for use in the Church of God General Conference member churches. It oversees the writing, editing, and printing of a complete line of Sunday School quarterlies, Bible study materials, Bible school material, a Christian Journal called *The Restitution Herald,* and a house organ called *The Progress Journal.*

Founding Date: 1921

Staff: 9

Membership:
    Serves 5,000 members of the Church of God
       General Conference

Publications:
    Truth Seekers Beginners Quarterly
    Sunday School material, quarterly
    The Restitution Herald, 10 times per year
    The Progress Journal, 10 times per year
    Challenge Magazine, 6 times per year

378. Church of God in Christ Publishing Board* (Church of God in Christ, Inc.)

Roy L. H. Winbush, President
272 South Main Street
Memphis, Tennessee 38101

Mailing Address
Post Office Box 2017
Memphis, Tennessee 38101
(901) 527-0328

The Church of God in Christ Publishing Board is responsible for the production and distribution of books, tracts, newsletters, periodicals, curriculum materials, and supplies used in its churches and church schools. The Publishing House prints, publishes, and produces all Sunday School Literature, Training Union (YPWW) Literature, Prayer and Bible Band Literature, Home and Foreign Mission Literature, general departmental literature (pamphlets, brochures, etc.), and general Pastoral and Teaching Aids for its constituency.

Publications:
    Books, authorized autobiographies, biographies
    Official Discipline Manual
    The Whole Truth, Church history newspaper

church schools. The Publishing House prints, publishes, and produces all Sunday School Literature, Training Union (YPWW) Literature, Prayer and Bible Band Literature, general departmental literature (pamphlets, brochures, etc.), and general Pastoral and Teaching Aids for its constituency.

Publications:
    Books, authorized autobiographies, biographies
    Official Discipline Manual
    Church history Newspaper The Whole Truth

Meetings:
    Five per year

379. The Church of Jesus Christ of Latter-day Saints, Church Educational System

The Church of Jesus Christ of Latter-day Saints
Henry B. Eyring, Commissioner of Education
50 East North Temple
Salt Lake City, Utah 84150
(801) 531-2161

The Church's educational system operates in the United States and in more than 50 other countries. Where public and private schools provide non-religious education for most Church members, this system emphasizes religious instruction. Its activities include weekly religion classes for high school and college students; elementary, secondary, and post-secondary schools in a number of foreign countries; a scholarship program in Latin America and the Pacific; a literacy program in several foreign lands; and the operation of several institutions of higher learning and adult education programs.

380. The Church of Jesus Christ of Latter-day Saints, Curriculum Department

The Church of Jesus Christ of Latter-day Saints
Elder M. Russell Ballard, Executive Director
50 East North Temple
Salt Lake City, Utah 84150

The Curriculum Department of the Church of Jesus Christ of Latter-day Saints includes the divisions of Church Magazines; Publications Coordination; Copyrights and Permissions Office; Curriculum Planning and Development (including Graphic Design and Editing); and Audio-visual Materials. Its responsibilities include determining, in cooperating with other originating Church organizations, both English and non-English curriculum needs of individuals and families, publishing three English-language magazines, and, using much of the material in those magazines, producing 16 other non-English magazines in various parts of the world.

381. The Church of Jesus Christ of Latter-day Saints, The Development Office (TDO)

The Church of Jesus Christ of Latter-day Saints
Post Office Box 7188
University Station
Provo, Utah 84602
(801) 378-4444

The purpose of the Development Office of The Church of Jesus Christ of Latter-day Saints is to develop philanthropic financial support for Church programs in education, social and health services, and missionary and genealogy work.

382. The Church of Jesus Christ of Latter-day Saints, Distribution Center

The Church of Jesus Christ of Latter-day Saints
Neil Kooyman, Manager
1999 West 1700 South
Salt Lake City, Utah 84104

The Distribution Center of the Church of Jesus Christ of Latter-day Saints receives, warehouses, and ships Church curriculum materials, furniture, and equipment to Church units or individuals. It operates a self-service store where items may be purchased by customers.

383. The Church of Jesus Christ of Latter-day Saints, Genealogical Department

The Church of Jesus Christ of Latter-day Saints
Royden G. Derrick, Executive Director
50 East North Temple Street
Salt Lake City, Utah 84117
(801) 531-2331

Under the direction of its Genealogical Department, the Church of Jesus Christ of Latter-day Saints and

its members have gathered millions of volumes of birth, marriage, death, and other records. Today hundreds of millions of microfilmed records are available for research through the Department. The genealogical library is one of the largest in the world, and is located at Church headquarters in Salt Lake City. Copies of the records are stored in a spacious vault carved out of a solid granite mountain in a canyon near Salt Lake City. This massive cavern permanently safeguards these valuable records from natural disaster and preserves them under ideal storage conditions. To appreciate the Church's emphasis on genealogy, it is necessary to understand the importance of the family in the lives of Latter-day Saints. Mormons who obey the teachings of Christ may enter into a marriage covenant that not only lasts until death, but continues eternally. These eternal marriages are solemnized in the temples of the Church. In addition, the Church teaches that those who have died without a true knowledge of the gospel of Jesus Christ may be baptized by proxy as a first step in their exaltation. Proxy temple work, including baptism and marriage, opens the way for people who have died without a full knowledge of the gospel to accept the gospel's saving principles and to participate in its necessary ordinances. The living gather vital statistics on their ancestors so that the dead can have all the blessings of the gospel.

Founding Date: 1894
Staff: 550 plus

384. The Church of Jesus Christ of Latter-day Saints, Historical Department

The Church of Jesus Christ of Latter-day Saints
Donald T. Schmidt, Director
50 East North Temple
Salt Lake City, Utah 84150

The Historical Department of the Church of Jesus Christ of Latter-day Saints maintains Church history and records in accordance with the Scriptures and directions of the First Presidency, including creation, preservation, and use of Church-related records, paintings, and artifacts; plans and operates the Church Museum of History and Art; maintains a program for historic sites and meetinghouse libraries; carries out such projects as the First Presidency may direct and authorize; and provides approved services to the General Authorities, Church members, and the public.

385. The Church of Jesus Christ of Latter-day Saints, International Mission

The Church of Jesus Christ of Latter-day Saints
Elder Carlos E. Asay, President
50 East North Temple, 12th Floor
Salt Lake City, Utah 84150

The International Mission, Church of Jesus Christ of Latter-day Saints, cares for members of the Church who live in areas outside the boundaries of established stakes and missions. It shares the responsibility of taking the Gospel to all nations. This includes some responsibility for opening up and supervising the work in new areas, and preparing those areas and nations for the establishment of missions.

386. The Church of Jesus Christ of Latter-day Saints, LDS Social Services

Church of Jesus Christ of Latter-day Saints
Harold C. Brown, Commissioner
50 East North Temple
Salt Lake City, Utah 84150
(801) 531-2848

The LDS Social Services Department was established by the Church of Jesus Christ of Latter-day Saints to be a resource to the ecclesiastical leaders of the Church in providing services to members, especially services performed by licensed agencies. These services include adoption, foster care, unwed parent services, and placement of Indian students in foster homes for the school year for their educational and personal growth and leadership opportunities. LDS Social Services also exists as a resource to the ecclesiastical leaders in assisting members with difficult individual, marriage, and family problems. LDS Social Services is a Utah corporation operating as a foreign corporation in other states of the United States and in some foreign countries. Scattered across the United States and giving service to all 50 states are 31 licensed agencies, and 11 sub-offices of these agencies. There are eight international offices in England, New Zealand, Japan and Korea, Australia and Canada.

Founding Date: 1969
Meetings:
    Annual training and educational seminars for personnel

387. The Church of Jesus Christ of Latter-day Saints, Missionary Department

The Church of Jesus Christ of Latter-day Saints
Elder Carlos E. Asay, Executive Director
50 East North Temple, 12th Floor
Salt Lake City, Utah 84150

The Missionary Department of the Church of Jesus Christ of Latter-day Saints administers the worldwide missionary program of the Church, Functions of the Department include providing proselytizing programs and materials, processing missionary recommendations, coordinating missionary preparation and training efforts, coordinating visitors' centers, assisting with mission finances, and handling personal missionary matters.

388. The Church of Jesus Christ of Latter-day Saints, Missionary Training Center

The Church of Jesus Christ of Latter-day Saints
Joe J. Christensen, President
2005 North 900 East
Provo, Utah 84601

The Missionary Training Center of the Church of Jesus Christ of Latter-day Saints provides training for newly-called missionaries in English and approximately 24 other languages. Missionaries going to English-speaking missions attend for three weeks, and those going to non-English-speaking missions attend for eight weeks.

389. The Church of Jesus Christ of Latter-day Saints, Office of General Counsel

The Church of Jesus Christ of Latter-day Saints
Wilford W. Kirton, Jr., General Counsel
330 South Third East
Salt Lake City, Utah 84111

The Office of General Counsel, Church of Jesus Christ of Latter-day Saints, handles the legal problems of the Church, including corporate legal problems, tax problems, property acquisitions, sales, Church building projects, and Church investments, together with advising each of the Church departments and the General Authorities on matters of law.

390. The Church of Jesus Christ of Latter-day Saints, Personnel Department

The Church of Jesus Christ of Latter-day Saints
50 East North Temple, 14th Floor
Salt Lake City, Utah 84150

The Personnel Department of the Church of Jesus Christ of Latter-day Saints, is responsible for providing a devoted and productive work force to serve the Church worldwide and to see that the needs of the Church and its employees are mutually understood and met. Functions of the Department include employment, salary administration, employee benefits, personnel development and training, and international personnel services.

391. The Church of Jesus Christ of Latter-day Saints, Presiding Bishopric

The Church of Jesus Christ of Latter-day Saints
Bishop Victor L. Brown, Presiding Bishop
50 East North Temple, 18th Floor
Salt Lake City, Utah 84150

The Presiding Bishopric, Church of Jesus Christ of Latter-day Saints, has responsibility for the temporal affairs of the Church. Those operations under its direction are: Administrative Services, Finanace and Records Department, Information Systems Department, Investments Department, Materials Management Department, Physical Facilities Department; Presiding Bishopric International Office, the Development Office, and Welfare Services Department.

392. The Church of Jesus Christ of Latter-day Saints, Priesthood Department

The Church of Jesus Christ of Latter-day Saints
Elder Dean L. Larsen, Executive Director
50 East North Temple
Salt Lake City, Utah 84150

The Priesthood Department of the Church of Jesus Christ of Latter-day Saints has several divisions. The Melchizedek Priesthood General Committee reviews materials and programs and prepares and recommends material and programs for the Melchizedek Priesthood Quorum Administration and Training, Family Home Evening, Home Teaching, Programs for Single Adults, and Melchizedek Priesthood Curriculum. The Military Relations Committee is responsible for fostering the welfare of members of the Church in military service. And the Activities Committee serves to foster cultural arts, recreation, and athletic activities through existing Church organizations; coordinate, develop, and implement cultural arts and physical activities that cross organizational lines; and to develop resources and guidelines for cultural arts and physical activities.

393. The Church of Jesus Christ of Latter-day Saints, The Primary

The Church of Jesus Christ of Latter-day Saints
Dwan J. Young, President
50 East North Temple
Salt Lake City, Utah 84150
(801) 531-2391

The Primary helps parents to teach their children between the ages of three and twelve the principles of the gospel. Each Sunday children meet to receive religious instruction and to enjoy social interaction. The Primary also sponsors an early scouting program for boys and a similar program for girls. This division depends from the Priesthood department.

Founding Date: 1878

394. The Church of Jesus Christ of Latter-day Saints, Public Communication Department

The Church of Jesus Christ of Latter-day Saints
50 East North Temple, 25th Floor
Salt Lake City, Utah 84150

The Public Communications Department of the Church of Jesus Christ of Latter-day Saints assists in bringing the Church out of obscurity and developing its image through the various media. It also works with the Missionary Department in paving the way for its work. The Department has three divisions: Public Affairs; Media Programming; and Administration and International Operations.

395. The Church of Jesus Christ of Latter-day Saints, Relief Society

The Church of Jesus Christ of Latter-day Saints
Barbara B. Smith, President
76 North Main Street
Salt Lake City, Utah 84150
(801) 531-2636

More than 1.5 million women worldwide hold membership in the Relief Society of the Church of Jesus Christ of Latter-day Saints, which is one of the oldest and largest women's organizations in the world. The Relief Society was established to help the sick, the poor, and others in need of compassionate service. During its weekly meetings, the society also provides instruction on a variety of topics, including theology, social relations, literature, fine arts, cultures of other countries, homemaking, and mother education. The society also has "visiting teachers." Each woman in the Church is visited at least once a month by two of these visiting teachers, who are assigned to assist with temporal and spiritual needs.

Founding Date: 1842

Former Name: Female Relief Society of Nauvoo

396. The Church of Jesus Christ of Latter-day Saints, Sunday School

The Church of Jesus Christ of Latter-day Saints
Hugh W. Pinnock, President
50 East North Temple
Salt Lake City, Utah 84150
(801) 531-2282

Members of the Church of Jesus Christ of Latter-day Saints 12 years of age and older attend Sunday School, which provides religious training for each age group. Sunday School classes are held in all wards and branches throughout the world. The purpose of Sunday School is to teach the Gospel of Jesus Christ; to build faith; and to strengthen families.

Founding Date: 1872

Former Name: Deseret Sunday School Union

397. The Church of Jesus Christ of Latter-day Saints, Welfare Services Department

The Church of Jesus Christ of Latter-day Saints
R. Quinn Gardner, Managing Director
50 East North Temple
Salt Lake City, Utah 84150
(801) 531-3281

Welfare Services of the Church of Jesus Christ of Latter-day Saints exists to assist the poor, the needy, and the distressed of the Church. Its resources include fast offerings by Church members; an employment system; bishop's storehouses of commodities produced by Church members; social services; a chain of thrift stores; and missionaries.

Founding Date: 1936

398. The Church of Jesus Christ of Latter-day Saints, The Young Men

The Church of Jesus Christ of Latter-day Saints
Robert L. Backman
50 East North Temple
Salt Lake City, Utah 84150
(801) 531-2132

Social and cultural activities for the boys of the Church are provided primarily by the Young Men organization. Boys from 12 through 18 years of age meet in age-group classes on Sundays for religious study. They also meet several times during the month to participate in social, cultural, and recreational activities that are designed to build faith, character, and physical fitness. All members are given the opportunity to develop their talents in speech, music, drama, dance, sports, and leadership. The Young Men program includes the largest Church-sponsored Boy Scout program in the world in proportion to Church membership.

Founding Date: 1875

Former Name:
Young Men's Mutual Improvement Association

399. The Church of Jesus Christ of Latter-day Saints, The Young Women

The Church of Jesus Christ of Latter-day Saints
Elaine A. Cannon
50 East North Temple
Salt Lake City, Utah 84150
(801) 531-2141

Social and cultural activities for the young women of the Church are provided primarily by the Young Women organization. Young women from 12 through 18 years of age meet in age-group classes on Sundays for religious study. They also participate in activities designed to build faith, character, and physical fitness. All members are given the opportunity to develop their talents in speech, music, drama, dance, sports, and leadership. The goal of this organization is to help young women work toward exaltation.

Founding Date: 1869

Former Names:
Retrenchment Association
Young Ladies' Mutual Improvement Association

400. Church of the Brethren, World Ministries Commission

Church of the Brethren
Ruby Rhoades, Executive Secretary
1451 Dundee Avenue
Elgin, Illinois 60120
(312) 742-5100

The primary function of the World Ministries Commission is to assist the Church of the Brethren in its corporate participation in God's reconciling activity in the world. To do this, it enlists participation in specific efforts aimed at peace and justice, joins in partnership to establish and strengthen the Christian fellowship for mission and ministry. and participates with churches and other agencies to improve the conditions of persons in health, education, and general welfare.

Founding Date: 1884

Staff: 9

Merger:
(1969) Foregn Missions Commission, Brethren Service Commission

401. Church of the Larger Fellowship, Inc. (CLF)

Unitarian Universalist
Rev. George N. Marshall
25 Beacon Street
Boston, Massachusetts 02108
(617) 742-2100

The Church of the Larger Fellowship offers a member-at-large ministry to the Association for persons who cannot participate in local churches or fellowships. The purpose of this church is to provide a spiritual home for isolated Unitarian Universalists and their families, and to transfer the allegiance of its members to local Unitarian Universalist churches whenever possible. Its program is aimed at the individual, seeking to help him or her fulfill the experiences of the liberal way of life. It has pioneered in developing new resources for expanding individual and family religious experience. The Church provides a continuous ministry, including pamphlet distribution, a lending library, a program for the religious instruction of children in member families (with the

guidance of a special Religious Education Committee), and the monthly distribution of sermons and news bulletins. The CLF also prepares other materials for family use and conducts a youth program. The Church of the Larger Fellowship carries out the original purpose of the American Unitarian Association, which was founded "to publish and distribute books and tracts inculcating correct views of religion . . . "

Founding Date: 1944

Staff: 30

Membership: 3,500

Publications:
Monthly news bulletins with sermons, CLF Book Club & Lending Library of Sermon Cassettes

Other Programs:
Independent study programs for adults and a program of religious education in which parents teach religion to their children.

402. Church of the Lutheran Brethren of America, Board of Education

Church of the Lutheran Brethren of America
Rev. C. Lloyd Bjornlie, President
815 West Vernon
Fergus Falls, Minnesota 56537
Mailing Address
Post Office Box 317
Fergus Falls, Minnesota 56537
(218) 739-3373

Lutheran Brethren Schools are three linked institutions administered by the Board of Education of the Church of the Lutheran Brethren. Lutheran Brethren Seminary is a three-year, post-baccalaureate program of theology, preparing pastors for ministry in churches affiliated with the Church of the Lutheran Brethren. Graduates meeting the requirements receive the Master of Divinity degree. A diploma is also offered for older, non-college graduates who complete essentially the same program. A two-year degree (the Master of Arts in Religion) is offered for college graduates seeking the logical training for lay ministries. Lutheran Brethren Bible College is a two-year, junior-college-level Bible institute program leading to the Associate of Arts in Bible degree. The object of this program is to prepare laypersons for para-professional ministries in the church. It also serves as means for personal spiritual growth and finding the Lord's will for one's life. Hillcrest Lutheran Academy, the third linked institution of

Lutheran Brethren Schools, is a three-year senior high school, largely college preparatory with the strong emphasis in music and athletics. Its purpose is to reach spiritually those who have not committed their lives to the Lord and to ground all students in the Word and knowledge of the Christian faith. Together with a strong academic program, it seeks to graduate thoughtful Christian young people with a high school diploma who are prepared to serve the Lord in an effective life's vocation.

Founding Date: 1903

Staff: 36

Membership: 200

Publications:
> *Alumnus,* quarterly

Meetings:
> World Mission Conference, campus, end of January, annually
> Home Mission Conference, campus, March, annually
> Homecoming, campus, October, annually

Former Name: (1948) Lutheran Bible School

403. Church of the Lutheran Brethren of America, Board of World Missions

Church of the Lutheran Brethren of America

Rev. Robert Overgaard, Director
1007 Westside Drive
Fergus Falls, Minnesota 56537

Mailing Address
Post Office Box 655
Fergus Falls, Minnesota 56537
(218) 736-5666

The Board of World Missions of the Church of the Lutheran Brethren has for purpose to so live and preach the Gospel that associations of churches will be founded among peoples served, thus establishing an ongoing Christian church. Ministries include church planting, education, leadership training, medical ministries, and various radio ministries. Countries now being served are Cameroon, Chad, Japan, and Taiwan.

Staff: 41

Publications:
> Denominational paper, prayer letters

Radio/TV Programs:
> Japan: *Dial of Hope*
> Africa: *Radio Voice of the Gospel* (participating)

Also Known As: Lutheran Brethren World Missions

404. Church of the Lutheran Brethren of America, Lutheran Brethren Home Missions

Church of the Lutheran Brethren of America

Rev. Harland Helland, Director of Home Missions
1007 Westside Drive
Fergus Falls, Minnesota 56537

Mailing Address
Post Office Box 655
Fergus Falls, Minnesota 56537
(218) 736-5666

The work of Lutheran Brethren Home Missions is church planting. The department places great emphasis on church revitalization and lay involvement. Its current program goals are: to broaden the evangelistic vision of the synod in reaching souls with the gospel message; to stimulate and encourage pastors and laity to develop and exercise the gifts of ministry that God has given them; and to encourage congregations to think and plan for church growth.

Staff: 2

Publications:
> *Mission to America Newsletter*

Meetings:
> Two board meetings per year

405. Church of the Lutheran Brethren of America, Women's Missionary Fellowship

Church of the Lutheran Brethren

Mrs. Adeline Mathison, President
1007 Westside Drive
Fergus Falls, Minnesota 56537

Mailing Address
Post Office Box 655
Fergus Falls, Minnesota 56537
(218) 736-5666

The purposes of the Women's Missionary Fellowship are: to awaken and deepen interest in and love for the Kingdom of God at home and abroad, thus sharing in the great missionary enterprise of the Christian Church through the dissemination of information concerning missions in general and the missions of the Lutheran Brethren in particular, and by supporting financially the missionary activities of the Lutheran Brethren Church through its regularly established Boards; to unite all the women of the Lutheran Brethren Church into the deeper fellowship of consecrated service and cooperation for the missions, the charities, and the Christian Education program of the church; and to organize mission societies and children's mission groups wherever possible. The activities of the Women's Missionary Fellowship include Bible Studies, monthly Inspirational Meetings, various sewing projects for Missions such as baby clothes, lap robes, and bandages, and serving food and furnishing housing for church related programs. The organization is subdivided into six districts: Eastern, Central, Western, Pacific Northwest, Pacific Southwest, and Canadian District.

Staff: No paid officers

Membership:
> 90 local member organizations ranging in membership from 15 to 125 each

Publications:
> Women's page in the bimonthly Church magazine *Faith and Fellowship*
> A newsletter, *District Echoes* published by the Pacific Northwest District of the Fellowship bimonthly

Meetings:
> National Annual Convention, usually held in Fergus Falls, Minnesota
> 2-3 district meetings a year
> District retreats (usually 1 per district per year)

406. Church of the Nazarene, Communications Division

Church of the Nazarene
M. A. (Bud) Lunn
6401 The Paseo
Kansas City, Missouri 64131
(816) 333-7000

The purpose of the Communications Division, Church of the Nazarene, is to advance the cause of Christian Holiness by awakening and strengthening interest throughout the church in the value and proper use of contemporary media resources.

407. Church of the Nazarene, Division of Christian Life and Sunday School

Church of the Nazarene
Phil Riley, Division Director
6401 The Paseo
Kansas City, Missouri 64131
(816) 333-7000

The Division of Christian Life and Sunday School, Church of the Nazarene, seeks to advance the cause of Christian holiness through Christian Life and Sunday School, to articulate the philosophy of Christian education, to enhance the role of the Sunday School, to strengthen other training in the church, and to emphasize the importance of ministry to home and family as a task of the church.

408. Church of the Nazarene, Division of Church Growth

Church of the Nazarene
Bill Sullivan, Division Director
6401 The Paseo
Kansas City, Missouri 64131
(816) 333-7000

The purpose of the Division of Church Growth, Church of the Nazarene, is to advance the cause of Christian holiness in the United States and Canada through the implementation of concepts and principles of church growth in the areas of public, personal, and program evangelism, church renewal, discipling and conserving, pastoral ministries, new churches, new districts, language, cultural and urban missions, and the development of church buildings that help evangelize.

409. Church of the Nazarene, Division of Finance

Church of the Nazarene
Thane Minor, Division Director
6401 The Paseo
Kansas City, Missouri 64131
(816) 333-7000

The objective of the Division of Finance, Church of the Nazarene, is to facilitate the cause of Christian Holiness through responsible budget planning, operation, and review, and to give oversight and direction to those services and programs of the General Church which deal primarily with financial matters.

410. Church of the Nazarene, Division of World Mission

Church of the Nazarene
L. Guy Nees, Division Director
6401 The Paseo
Kansas City, Missouri 64131

Among the goals of the Division of World Mission, Church of the Nazarene, are: the establishment of churches; the recruitment and processing of candidates for missionary service; the administration of the "mission policy" and "national church policy"; the financial administration of the Division; and the responsibility of establishing and maintaining a balanced missionary program, i.e., outreach, medical, and educational.

411. Church of the Nazarene, Nazarene Chaplaincy Services

Church of the Nazarene
Dr. Earl C. Wolf, Director
6401 The Paseo
Kansas City, Missouri 64131
(816) 333-7000

Nazarene Chaplaincy Services is a function of Pastoral Ministries in the Division of Church Growth. It aids ministers who seek to serve as military chaplains. Specifically, it supplies information on chaplaincy requirements, and helps prospective chaplains process their applications for ecclesiastical approval or endorsement. It also aids ministers who seek to serve in chaplaincy ministries in hospitals, or in correctional institutions. Through the Division of Church Growth (Rev. Bill Sullivan, Director) the Church of the Nazarene fosters and strengthens the ties between the church and all those serving in the armed forces. It sponsors annual military personnel retreats in Europe and the Far East.

Founding Date: 1940
Meetings:
Advisory Committee, on call

412. Church of the Nazarene, Nazarene Publishing House Board

Church of the Nazarene
M. A. (Bud) Lunn, President
6401 The Paseo
Kansas City, Missouri 64131

The Nazarene Publishing House Board is responsible for the efficient operation of the Nazarene Publishing House, which is the printing and merchandising agency of the Church of the Nazarene.

413. Church of the Nazarene, Service Personnel Ministries

Church of the Nazarene
Rev. Harold Ivan Smith, Director
6401 The Paseo
Kansas City, Missouri 64131
(816) 333-7000

Service Personnel Ministries of the Church of the Nazarene serves enlisted military personnel and their families. It works to strengthen the ties between enlisted personnel and the local churches where they hold their membership. It provides a *Directory of Nazarene Churches Near Military Bases* and other literature designed for military families.

414. Church of the United Brethren in Christ, Inc., Board of Missions

United Brethren in Christ
Duane A. Reahm, Bishop Overseas District
302 Lake Street
Huntington, Indiana 46750
(219) 356-2312

The Board of Missions of the Church of the United Brethren in Christ is the body delegated by the General Conference to direct the foreign mission program of the church and to assist in selected home mission endeavors. It has as its purpose to share in the proclamation of God's Word, to bring people to Christ, to build them up in Christ, and to send them forth to work for Christ. To this end the Board, jointly with others, sponsors a Bible College. It also sponsors 30 elementary schools and two high schools. It maintains one hospital, one high school, an elementary school, and a Bible Institute. The Board also fully supports a doctor serving in India. It assists in the support of personnel with Wycliffe Bible Translators, OMS International, Trans World Radio, and Mission to Europe's Millions.

Founding Date: 1853
Staff: 14 members of the Board
Publications:
Mission Impact, monthly
Radio/TV Programs:
Radio broadcast in LaCeibs, Honduras
Mende programs aired over ELWA in Monrovia, Liberia
Meetings:
Meetings in each country except India

Former Names:
> Domestic Frontier and Foreign Mission Society
> Parent Board of Missions

415. Church Periodical Club*

Episcopal

815 Second Avenue
New York, New York 10017

The Church Periodical Club supplies free literature to people around the world. It works through individuals, parishes, and dioceses, and is the only Episcopal agency devoted to providing this service. Its financial support comes from contributions. All printed material — religious, educational, medical, technical, and recreational — needed for the church's larger mission is supplied. Braille for the blind; translations of the prayer book; hymnals; large print literature for the visually handicapped; devotional literature for prayer groups; church school materials, text books, and reference works for use on reservations, in ghettos, in campus and community centers; inspirational, recreational reading for servicemen, shut-ins, and missionaries; materials needed to train nurses, doctors, technicians, and indigenous clergy — all are provided.

Founding Date: 1888

416. Church Women United (CWU)

Interdenominational

Dr. Thelma C. Adair, President
475 Riverside Drive, Room 812
New York, New York 10115
(212) 870-2347

Church Women United in the United States is a national movement through which Protestant, Roman Catholic, Orthodox and other Christian women express the ecumenical dimensions of their faith, working in a visible fellowship to witness to their faith in Jesus Christ, and enabled by the Holy Spirit to go out together into every neighborhood and nation as instruments of reconciling love. It is open to all Christian women who wish to show their unity through fellowship, study, and cooperative action. It is national in scope with approximately 2,000 local units and units in every state and the greater Washington area. The movement has many international relationships. Church women in the local communities worship together in three nationwide days of Celebration: World Day of Prayer, the first Friday in March; May Fellowship Day, the first Friday in May; and World Community Day, the first Friday in November. Church Women United members participate locally in community service and advocacy programs. Intercontinental Grants for Mission are made for programs of concern to women in the United States and globally.

Founding Date: 1941

Staff: 30

Publications:
> *The Church Woman,* bimonthly
> *Lead Time,* bimonthly newsletter for state, local and national leadership

Meetings:
> Annual meeting of the Common Council
> Quadrennial Ecumenical Assembly, July 19-24, 1984
> Regional assemblies
> State and local meetings

Former Names:
> (1950) United Council of Church Women
> (1966) Department of United Church Women of the National Council of Churches
> (1969) Church Women United in the U.S.A.

417. Church World Service (CWS)

National Council of Churches of Christ in the USA

Dr. Paul McCleary, Executive Director
475 Riverside Drive
New York, New York 10027
(212) 870-2257

Church World Service (CWS) is a unit of the Division of Overseas Ministries of the National Council of Churches of Christ in the United States. As such, it is the collective expression of 31 Protestant and Orthodox communions representing over 31 million persons in the United States. CWS works in development assistance, disaster response, and assistance to refugees and displaced persons, and works with overseas social organizations, usually church related, in more than 70 countries. United States public policy advocacy and constituency education are carried on as complementary and integral components of overseas activities. CWS channels human, material, and financial resources to overseas colleague agencies in support of their task of helping the poor and oppressed fulfill their own basic needs.

Founding Date: 1946

Staff:
120
A committee (equivalent to a Board of Directors) of 53 persons overseeing policy and finances

Membership:
31 member churches representing 31 million Protestant and Orthodox church members

Publications:
CWS Update, quarterly; *Hunger Fact Sheet,* 3 times a year; Annual Report; *One Great Hour of Sharing* materials, annually; *Services News,* 5 times a year; promotional and educational materials such as films, filmstrips, posters, books, brochures, slide sets, displays, and fact sheets

Radio/TV Programs:
6 TV spots per year on the general theme of world hunger awareness
12 radio spots per year

Meetings:
Five meetings a year

418. Churches of Christ in Christian Union, Foreign Missions Department

Churches of Christ in Christian Union
Carl E. Waggoner
General Missionary Superintendent
459 East Ohio Street
Circleville, Ohio 43113

Mailing Address
Post Office Box 30
Circleville, Ohio 43113
(614) 474-8856

The Missions Department is the missionary arm of the Churches of Christ in Christian Union, a conservative evangelical church in the Wesleyan tradition. It is a sending agency for overseas staff in autonomous fields and in conjunction with other agencies in areas where it maintains no facilities of its own. Currently the Missions Department has 54 overseas missionaries on staff, serving in Mexico, Honduras, three islands in the West Indies, Papua, New Guinea, Korea, and Kenya. In addition, the agency has people working with Indian evangelism in Arizona. The agency's missionaries are active in evangelism, church planting, Bible translation, literacy programs, medical services, schools, and ministerial training. The work in Korea features extensive contact with college and university youth.

Founding Date: 1909

Staff:
10 members of the home executive and administrative staff
Approximately 100 overseas staff members

Membership:
Approximately 6,000 general overseas membership

Publications:
Missionary Tidings, monthly informational and promotional publication

Radio/TV Programs:
Spanish language radio broadcasts in Mexico

Meetings:
Numerous

419. Citizens for Educational Freedom

Interdenominational
Sister Renee Oliver, OSU, Associate Director
Washington Building, Suite 854
15th Street and New York Avenue, N.W.
Washington, D.C. 20005
(202) 638-6423

Citizens for Educational Freedom is an organization working for parents' rights to educate their children according to their own moral, religious, and cultural values without added financial burden. CEF believes that a tuition tax credit and/or voucher system would help to make freedom of choice in education a right of all parents and not just the privilege of the wealthy. CEF lobbies Congress for tuition tax credit legislation and disseminates literature to educate parents concerning their basic human rights.

Founding Date: 1959

420. Claretian Publications

Roman Catholic
Rev. Mark J. Brummel, CMF
221 West Madison
Chicago, Illinois 60606
(312) 236-7782

Claretian Publications is the publishing arm of the Congregation of Sons of the Immaculate Heart of Mary (Claretian Fathers and Brothers). The goal of Claretian Publications is to recognize and conduct dialogue on the concerns and issues affecting the average Catholic. This editorial policy covers many issues, including: changes in the Catholic Church, moral problems, politics, prayer, Scripture, marriage and family relationships, and sex. The flagship publication, *U.S. Catholic,* is known as the most-quoted Catholic magazine in the country. It has a reputation for open-mindedness and progressive editorial policy. The Claretian Publications staff feel that their publications touch the pulse of the American Catholic Church. The ultimate goal of Claretian Publications is to express the worthwhile values of the Catholic Christian tradition and to explore their importance and relevance for contemporary American life.

Publications:
> *U.S. Catholic,* monthly; *Bringing Religion Home,* monthly; *Generation,* a monthly newsletter for Catholics 55 years and over; *Context,* a 4-page newsletter on the interaction of religion and culture; Claretian Paperbacks and Pamphlets; Guadalupe Books/Pamphlets (in Spanish); Fides/Claretian Books

421. Clergy and Laity Concerned (CALC)

Interdenominational
Barbara Lupo, M. M. and John Collins, Co-directors
198 Broadway
New York, New York 10038
(212) 964-6730

Clergy and Laity Concerned is a grass-root interfaith peace and justice organization with a nationwide network of chapters and action groups. Founded in 1965, it mobilized the opposition to the VietNam war. Today, it continues to assist the American people in the interface of their religious/ethical values with the policies and practices of the United States Government and corporations at home and abroad. The educational and organizational work done by CALC is inspired by a vision of society where resources, both human and technical, are used to meet the real needs of people rather than the special interests of a particular group. CALC concentrates on four program areas: Human Rights; The Politics of Food; Human Security: Peace and Jobs (Nuclear Issues); The Legacies of VietNam. CALC is funded by membership dues, individual contributors, and by grants from various religious denominations and several foundations.

Founding Date: 1965
Staff: 12

Membership:
> Membership-at-large: 7,000
> Contributors: 25,000

Publications:
> *CALC Report,* 8 times a year; it contains articles on current issues, theological comments, news from the CALC network, action suggestions, etc.

Meetings:
> Occasionally — when a need arises

Former Names:
> National Emergency Committee of Clergy Concerned About Vietnam
> Clergy and Laymen Concerned About Vietnam
> Clergy and Laymen Concerned

422. Coalition for Human Needs*

Episcopal
Rt. Rev. Richard B. Martin
815 Second Avenue
New York, New York 10017
(212) 867-8400

Coalition for Human Needs is an agency within the Church In Society program of the Episcopal Church. This Coalition is the main grant-making program for minority community action groups and has the flexibility to deal with issues which are not directly accessible through ethnic groupings. The program has as its stated objectives: to address new and emerging needs relating to social justice or minority concerns in church or community based programs; to co-ordinate the work of the various ethnic programs, and programs dealing with issues and with groups having special needs so that maximum mutual support, effectiveness, and comprehensiveness can be achieved; and to make grants in furtherance of the social ministry and social justice concerns of this Church within the guidelines of the General Convention and the Executive Council.

423. Coalition 14*

Episcopal
The Rev. Samuel Van Culin
815 Second Avenue
New York, New York 10017
(212) 867-8400

Coalition 14 is an agency of the National and World Mission program of the Episcopal Church. It consists of 14 dioceses which have voluntarily joined together to share resources and skills to achieve their common goals. Member bodies of the Coalition disclose all revenues openly and allocate funds mutually. They frequently share staff and services. The Diocese of Alaska joined the Coalition in 1976.

Membership: 14

424. Coalition on Women and Religion

Nondenominational
Jessie Kinnear, President
4759 15th Avenue N.E.
Seattle, Washington 98105
(206) 525-1213

The Coalition on Women and Religion is a non-profit corporation dedicated to claiming, exploring, and expanding the spirituality of women. It is an interfaith group engaged in action to further the cause of equality for all people, and a mutual support group helping women feel less alone in the pursuit of their rights. Publishing is one part of the organization's purpose. The Coalition communicates not only with women and men who have resigned from their religious denominations but with all possible established religious denominations. The Coalition is a unit of the Church Council of Greater Seattle, with a seat on the Board of Directors, and accomplishes most of its work through that organization. Before incorporating, the organization embarked upon projects on its own, such as the establishment of the Seattle Shelter for Battered Women (New Beginnings). As a member of Washington Women United, the Coalition engages in appropriate political activity and works to support the passage of the Equal Rights Amendment to the Constitution.

Founding Date: 1973

Membership:
　About 500, scattered throughout the United States, several abroad.

Publications:
　The Flame, monthly
　Books on Women and Religion: *The Woman's Bible, Study Guide to the Woman's Bible, The Word For Us, Flame Cartoons,* and a Mini-Poster

Radio/TV Programs:
　Several TV programs done in the past on request by local television stations

Meetings:
　Regular meetings twice a month
　Conferences and retreats periodically

425. CODEL, Inc. (Coordination in Development)

Interdenominational
Rev. Boyd Lowry, Executive Director
79 Madison Avenue
New York, New York 10016
(212) 685-2030

CODEL, Inc., is a consortium of 41 church-related organizations incorporated for work in developing countries. It is a development agency which brings together in a united Christian action a variety of Catholic and Protestant mission sending and service societies. CODEL provides consultative and fundraising services to its member organizations. The selection of joint projects for CODEL Project Fund support marks its collaborative style. CODEL's goal is to bring dignity to people who lack the resources to achieve the level of development to which, under God, they are entitled. The organization accomplishes this goal by supporting projects which meet certain criteria basic to effective self-help: they are community-based at "grass roots," they provide fullest possible local level ownership and participation, and they have significant ecumenical backing. CODEL's members work with Churches and their organizations overseas in the field of development in over 70 countries. They maintain field representatives in all the countries, many highly skilled in particular disciplines. Agriculture, vocational training, health and nutrition, and communication are some specialties available as needed in CODEL-sponsored programs. Funding for CODEL-supported projects is secured from the member agencies' own resources, government grants, and from other organizations, foundations, and corporations.

Founding Date: 1969

Staff: 14

Membership: 36

Publications:
　CODEL News, 6 times a year
　Comprehensive Projects Review, biannually
　Annual Report

Meetings:
　Projects committee meeting, 3 times a year
　Executive committee meeting, 3 times a year
　Board of Governors meeting, 2 times a year

426. The College of Chaplains

Interdenominational

Rev. Kermit W. Smith, Executive Director
1701 East Woodfield Road, Suite 311
Schaumburg, Illinois 60195
(312) 843-2701

The College of Chaplains is the official name for the personal (rather than the institutional) membership of the American Protestant Hospital Association. The Association's goals are: to advocate the spiritual dimension of health and illness in health care programming; to support the philosophy and demonstrate the dignity of the person and promote a Christ-like quality of caring for the individual; to foster and demonstrate the dignity of the person through all education and research programs; to assist in the establishment of chaplaincy services in all health care institutions; to provide a unified voice on issues of vital concern to health and welfare institutions supporting the Protestant principle; to secure, maintain, and enhance the support of churches for Protestant health and welfare institutions; to motivate youth to work in Christian health and welfare careers; to support a national structure for chaplaincy; to foster quality and efficiency in all elements of Christian-related health care; to interpret to the public the purposes and needs of Protestant-affiliated and other health and welfare institutions; to engage in dialogue and cooperate with other health and welfare organizations; to encourage awareness in member institutions of persons lacking adequate health care and to cooperate in the development of resources to provide adequate care; to stimulate stewardship by greater cost effectiveness; and to demonstrate Christian responsibility through education and job opportunities for minority persons in health care institutions.

Founding Date: 1946

Staff: 3

Membership: 1,500

Publications:
   The Tie, bimonthly

Meetings:
   Annual meeting concurrently with the Protestant Health and Welfare Assembly

Former Name:
   (1968) Chaplains Association of the American Protestant Hospital Association

427. College Theology Society (CTS)

Roman Catholic

Vera Chester, CSJ, President
221 North Grand Boulevard
St. Louis, Missouri 63103
(314) 658-2865

The College Theology Society is a professional organization of college and university professors of religion in the United States and Canada. The purpose of the Society is to improve the quality of the teaching of religion. It does so by stimulating and sharing scholarly research; by developing programs of Theology and Religious Studies which meet student needs and interests while being genuinely intellectual in content; by exploring, evaluating, and encouraging effective ways of teaching which are interdisciplinary and ecumenical; and by trying to determine the place of religious studies in the total college curriculum. It has a pastoral concern in relating faith to life and in purifying and deepening the life of faith.

Founding Date: 1954

Membership: 729

Publications:
   Scholarly
   CTS Proceedings, 9 in print
   Horizons, biannually

Meetings:
   National annual convention
   Regional meetings once or twice a year

428. Commission for Catholic Missions among the Colored People and the Indians

Roman Catholic

Monsignor Paul A. Lenz, Executive Director
2021 H Street, N.W.
Washington, D.C. 20006
(202) 331-8542

The Commission was organized by the Third Plenary Council of Baltimore as trustee of funds collected in churches for support of the Black and Indian mission work in the United States.

Membership:
   All United States Catholic Bishops and Churches

Publications:
   The Quarterly, quarterly

Meetings:
   Annual meetings of the directors

429. Commission on Religion in Appalachia, Inc. (CORA)

Interdenominational
Rev. John B. McBride, Regional Coordinator
864 Weisgarber Road N.W.
Knoxville, Tennessee 37919
(615) 584-6133

The Commission on Religion in Appalachia (CORA) was organized by 17 communions and other church bodies to deal with the religious, moral, and spiritual implications inherent in the economic, social, and cultural conditions in the Appalachian region. As the Commission seeks to develop a united approach to fulfilling the Church's mission in Appalachia, the purpose is achieved by: consultation, providing a consultative body for the sharing of information, concern, and funding, primarily among the religious but also social, economic, educational, and governmental agencies serving the Appalachian region; research, study, and education, expanding understanding of the conditions of the Appalachian region and to give guidance to appropriate programs of the Churches and Church bodies; coordination, providing a means of discovering suitable areas of staff and program coordination, recognizing that there is a place for both denominational and interdenominational programs in Appalachia; and projects, engaging in works which fulfill the Church's mission.

Founding Date: 1965

Staff:
   4 leadership staff
   3 support staff members

Membership:
   19 Christian Denominations
   10 State Councils
   Related agencies

Publications:
   CORAspondent, a quarterly newsletter

Meetings:
   2 commission meetings per year
   3 Board meetings per year
   2 meetings per program area per year

430. Committee for the Furtherance of Torah Observance

Jewish
Rabbi Bernard Levy, President
1430 57th Street
Brooklyn, New York 11219
(212) 851-6428

The Committee for the Furtherance of Torah Observance, a professional organization composed of rabbis, inspects food processing plants to determine whether or not to certify foods as kosher.

431. Committee on Christian Literature for Women and Children in Mission Fields

Nondenominational
Dr. Marion Van Horne, Executive Officer
475 Riverside Drive, Room 670
New York, New York 10027
(212) 870-2383

The purpose of the Committee on Christian Literature for Women and Children in Mission Fields is to supply educational materials for women and children in mission fields overseas.

432. Committee on Women's Concerns

Presbyterian Church, United States
Carole Goodspeed, Executive Staff
341 Ponce de Leon Avenue, N.E.
Atlanta, Georgia 30308
(404) 873-1531

Among the responsibilities of the Committee on Women's Concerns are: to develop a national strategy for expressing concerns of women; to identify major issues involving women; and to develop increased responsiveness in the church to the resources of women for the mission of the church. The functions of the Committee include the following: representing the concerns of women; helping people understand the changing role of women in church and society; encouraging women to prepare for positions of leadership; helping women recognize and accept responsibility in serving the church and the world; and seeking further opportunities for women to use their abilities in the life and work of the church. The Committee on Women's Concerns maintains a data bank on PCUS women leaders; encourages formation of presbytery advocacy groups on women's concerns; sponsors advocacy for women's events; promotes ratification of the Equal Rights Amendment; recommends to the General Assembly on women's issues; works with the Religious Committee for ERA; works ecumenically wherever possible; and works for inclusion of more women in decision making positions. The Committee believes in the human dignity and freedom of all persons and recognizes oppression on the basis of race, sex or class as interrelated. The Committee seeks to replace old patterns of authority with new models of relationships that will permit persons to contribute to the ministry of the church in society all the talents God has given them.

Staff: 22 volunteer members

Publications:
Matrix, 3 times a year

Meetings:
1 fall conference to support advocacy for women
1-2 regional conferences
Pre-Assembly Briefing for women at the General Assembly

433. Community for Creative Non-Violence (CCNV)

Nondenominational
1345 Euclid Street N.W.
Washington, D.C. 20009
(202) 667-6407

The Community for Creative Non-Violence began as an expression of both faith and moral outrage. A few concerned Christians faced a war and the question of what to do about it. They were also faced with questions of justice and human rights and what to do about them as well. The Community's daily life and work revolves around the two drop-in centers they maintain, where those who are on the streets can find a place to sit down, get a fresh change of clothes, have a cup of tea, and enjoy some conversation. One of the centers is specifically aimed at the unique needs of older homeless people. Thousands of people each month are served a hot meal, and use the laundry, showers, clothing room, and other services, provided by a staff which, by and large, first

entered the centers as guests. The tiny buildings house a refuge of huge proportions. The Community has a spiritual foundation, expressed in a variety of ways. While predominantly Christian, the religious makeup of CCNV is richly varied. They have merged from an assortment of backgrounds, commonly denoted by the past tense: a research chemist, a truck driver, a city planner, a veteran, a mathematician, a secretary, an ex-convict, a college student, a housewife, living and struggling together. They have come together to serve directly and through resistance, to stretch the meaning of their faith, to turn beliefs into daily acts. CCNV also coordinates Corpus Christi: a campaign to change the name of the USS Corpus Christi nuclear submarine.

Founding Date: 1970

Membership:
30-40 all are full-time live-in volunteers, acting as staff

Publications:
A Forced March to Nowhere, a 100-page report on homelessness as a national priority and problem, for the House District Committee, September 1980, $5.

434. Community for Religious Research and Education, The CRRE Collective (CRRE)

Post Office Box 9164
Berkeley, California 94709
(415) 548-2785

CRRE publishes the quarterly journal *Radical Religion,* which investigates the relationships between religion and progressive social change from a socialist and ecumenical perspective. It also conducts contracted research and maintains a data bank on topics related to the journal's concerns. In addition, CRRE has begun a program of publishing books which relate its perspective to established fields of scholarly investigation; the first title is *The Bible and Liberation.*

Membership: 12

Publications:
Radical Religion, quarterly

Meetings:
10 each year

435. Compassion International, Inc.

Nondenominational
W. H. Erickson, President
3955 Cragwood Drive
Colorado Springs, Colorado 80933
Mailing Address
Post Office Box 7000
Colorado Springs, Colorado 80933
(303) 594-9900

Compassion International is a ministry of Christian love to children emphasis is *child development.* That is a much broader task than merely helping children survive present poverty. Compassion helps children develop physically, mentally and spiritually through a variety of ministries in over 30 countries. These ministries include Child Sponsorship; Community Action; and Relief and Rehabilitation. The organizations now has over 1,100 sponsorships projects in 31 countries and cares for nearly 60,000 needy children.

Founding Date: 1952
Staff: 80 at United States headquarters, 74 overseas
Publications:
>   *Compassion,* bimonthly

Radio/TV Programs:
>   Compassion produces television specials to be aired on TV stations
>   In 1981 the special was Children: The World's Most Valuable Resource, host was Dean Jones

Meetings:
>   1 international conference each year

436. The Concerned Group, Inc., dba Concerned Communications

Nondenominational
R. L. Potter, II, President
146, 154, and 200 Traffic Way
Arroyo Grande, California 93420
Mailing Address
Post Office Box 700
Arroyo Grande, California 93420
(805) 489-4848

The purposes of the Concerned Group, Inc., are publishing, marketing, fund raising, and design services specializing in the fields of health, religion, and education. It is a full-service agency with in-house editors, creative directors, art directors, and typesetting services. The organization also produces children's publications designed for public, private, and parochial school systems.

Founding Date: 1973
Staff: 14
Publications:
>   *Planet Earth,* children's newspaper, monthly, September through June
>   *Bodywise,* children's health education magazine, semimonthly, September through June
>   *Orion,* children's Christian/character building magazine, semimonthly

Radio/TV Programs:
>   Scripts and production on assignment from clients

437. Concordant Publishing Concern

Nondenominational
Dean H. Hough, President
15570 West Knochaven Road
Canyon Country, California 91351
(805) 252-2112

The principal goal of Concordant Publishing Concern is to present as accurate an English translation of the Sacred Scriptures as possible. The Concordant Version of the New Testament and the work presently being done on the Old Testament attempt to combine literal consistency with readability. Although it is not a word-for-word translation, every effort is made to use an English word for only one original Greek or Hebrew term. Also, through the use of special typefaces and signs and symbols, the publisher seeks to provide for the Bible student the opportunity to trace out the literal wording of the manuscripts.

Membership: 5 members of the Board of Directors
Publications:
>   Scholarly books—12 titles
>   Devotional books—2 titles
>   Scripture study magazine entitled *Unsearchable Riches*

438. Concordia Historical Institute

Lutheran Church—Missouri Synod
Dr. Aug. R. Suelflow, Director
801 DeMun Avenue
St. Louis, Missouri 63105
(314) 721-5934

The Concordia Historical Institute is the Department of Archives and History of The Lutheran Church—

Missouri Synod. Its general purposes are: to promote interest in the history of the Lutheran Church of America, particularly of The Lutheran Church — Missouri Synod; to serve as a general advisory and correlating agency for the historical interests within The Lutheran Church — Missouri Synod; to collect and preserve articles of historical value for the Lutheran Church of America; and to stimulate historical research and publish its results. The Institute's archival, historical library and museum collections include documents and manuscripts; books, pamphlets and periodicals; microfilm; photographs and pictures; and museum artifacts, all relating to the development of Lutheranism in America. These collections are made available to researchers and other interested persons for personal research in Institute facilities or by loan of materials, research by Institute staff, photoduplications and publication.

Founding Date: 1847

Staff: 9

Membership:

1,500 divided between individuals and libraries. In addition, there are 38 regional depositories, one in each of the North American districts of The Lutheran Church — Missouri Synod (addresses and locations are available upon request).

Publications:

Quarterly journal
Concordia Historical Institute Quarterly
Newsletters, *Historical Footnotes* and *The Regional Archivist*

Meetings:

Biennial membership conventions
Biennial conference on Archives and History

Former Name: (1911) Concordia Historical Society

439. Concordia Publishing House (CPH)*

Lutheran Church — Missouri Synod
Ralph L. Reinke, LittD, President
3558 South Jefferson Avenue
St. Louis, Missouri 63118
(314) 664-7000

Concordia Publishing House is the official publishing house of the Lutheran Church — Missouri Synod. Concordia Publishing House has, for over 100 years, had as its mission the development, production, marketing, and distribution of products that communicate, foster, and support the Christian faith for use by members of the Lutheran Church-Missouri Synod, other Christians, and the public in general. Concordia publishes books, periodicals, curriculum, worship bulletins, works of religious art, and sacred music. It also offers a wide range of Christian gifts. In addition, CPH provides a service for the custom design of church furniture and fixtures.

Founding Date: 1869

Publications:

Scholarly, adult fiction and non-fiction, children's fiction and non-fiction texts, approximately 700 titles presently in print
10 periodicals including 2 adult general 2 teacher, 1 church musician, 1 children's devotional

440. Concordia Tract Mission

Lutheran
Mr. Emil W. Benz, Director
3558 South Jefferson Avenue
St. Louis, Missouri 63166

Mailing Address:
Post Office Box 201
St. Louis, Missouri 63166
(314) 664-7000, extension 280

Concordia Tract Mission has as its general purpose the sharing of the "Good News" of salvation in Jesus Christ with individuals, congregations, and the whole world, through tracts and literature. To attain this purpose, tracts are being sent to 38 countries in 29 languages. Other Christian literature is also being distributed. Materials reach people through missionaries, chaplains, native pastors, evangelists, and other denominational church groups.

Founding Date: 1958

Staff: 4

Publications:

Worldwide Evangelist, quarterly
Tracts

441. The Conference of Jewish Communal Service (CJCS)

Jewish
Matthew Penn, Executive Director
15 East 26th Street
New York, New York 10010
(212) 683-8056

The Conference of Jewish Communal Service serves as the broad forum for all professional philosophies which have currency in the field of community service. It is the meeting place for all who have a new experience to test, who have a new idea to propose, who wish to question or to reaffirm an old concept. The Conference furnishes the stage, the participants, and the audience for the critical examination and review of all that is old or new, tried or untried, in the professional direction of Jewish communal service. CJCS, as the only broadly based professional organization in Jewish communal life, has done this since 1899. Agencies and practitioners in the following fields are part of CJCS: Care of the Aged, Child Care, Community Organization, Community Relations, Family Service, Group Work, Health Service, Immigration Service, Jewish Culture, Jewish Education, Synagogue Administration, and Vocational Service. Each of these groups has a national organization for the advancement of its own special field of interest and the promotion of its own type of service, which works in close cooperation with CJCS.

Membership: 3,000 individuals and 320 agencies

Publications:
Journal of Jewish Communal Service, quarterly

Meetings:
Annual conference held in May/June

Former Name:
National Conference of Jewish Communal Service

national voice communicating the corporate views of the major superiors of men on vital and contemporary issues. Approximately 4,500 American religious missionary priests and brothers, under the direction of CMSM members, are actively engaged in educational, charitable, and social work in more than 90 countries around the world. CMSM has as its purpose to CALL religious superiors and through them all religious to the identification and clarification of their proper role in the Church and in the world; to ENABLE religious superiors and through them all religious to fulfill their proper role in the Church and in the world; and to effect a corporate IMPACT and influence in the Church and the world through its President, National Assembly, and other Conference instrumentalities. In responding to the expectations of the Church and of the world, the Conference sees the role of religious today as that of prophecy through which beliefs are put to the test.

Founding Date: 1956

Staff: 5

Membership: 264 (major superiors)

Publications:
CMSM News, bimonthly
CMSM Information and *CMSM Documentation* occasionally

Meetings:
Annual National Assemblies
Semi-annual regional meetings (6 regions across the nation)

442. Conference of Major Superiors of Men (CMSM)

Roman Catholic
Rev. Alan McCoy, OFM, President
1302 18th Street, N.W.
Suite 601
Washington, D.C. 20036
(202) 223-4164

The Conference of Major Superiors of Men is an association of major religious superiors (supervisors) of the various Roman Catholic religious orders of men. The Conference promotes the welfare of more than 30,000 priests, brothers, and candidates in the United States. It furnishes its members with information and services on matters of importance to religious life; it provides a forum for an exchange of views and ideas on the use of personnel and resources for common goals; and it serves as a

443. Conference of Presidents of Major American Jewish Organizations

Jewish
Yehuda Hallman, Executive Director
515 Park Avenue
New York, New York 10022
(212) 752-1616

The Conference of Presidents of Major American Jewish Organizations is composed of 34 national Jewish secular and religious organizations. Their memberships represent the overwhelming majority of the Jewish community in the United States, making it the most all-embracing coalition of the world's largest Jewish community. Its purpose is to protect and enhance the security and dignity of Jews abroad. Toward this end, it meets with leading American and world figures and gives voice to the security and dignity of Jews abroad, particularly the people of

Israel and the beleaguered Jewish communities in the Soviet Union and Arab lands.

Founding Date: 1954

Staff: 4

Membership: 34 member organizations

Publications:
> *Middle East Memo*
> *Annual Report*

444. Conference on Christianity and Literature (CCL)

Nondenominational

John Timmerman, Editor
Christianity and Literature
Department of English
Calvin College
Grand Rapids, Michigan 49506
(616) 949-4000, extension 264

Conference on Christianity and Literature is an interdisciplinary society allied with the Modern Language Association. It is dedicated to exploring the relationships between Christianity and literature. It now has a thousand active members from a variety of religious traditions and academic institutions. Focusing on the interplay of literature and faith, CCL encourages fellowship among its members; conference discussions; and selective publication. For 10 years, CCL has been sponsoring various seminars on religion and literature at the annual meeting of MLA and at many regional conferences. Its quarterly, *Christianity and Literature*, is indexed in the PMLA Annual Bibliography. The Society presents a citation each year to the winner of the CCL Book of the Year Award for a work which "has contributed most to the dialogue between literature and the Christian faith." CCL also sponsors annually a student writing contest for essays, poems, and stories which discuss or reflect Christian themes in life or literature.

Organized: 1956

Membership: 1,000

Publications:
> *Christianity and Literature,* quarterly, published at Calvin College, Grand Rapids, Michigan

Meetings:
> 1 national meeting
> 8 regional conferences each year

445. The Conference on Faith and History (CFH)

Nondenominational

Richard V. Pierard, Secretary-Treasurer
Department of History
Indiana State University
Terre Haute, Indiana 47809
(812) 232-6311 ext. 2305/2761

The Conference on Faith and History is an organization of Christians who are interested in the study of history. Members include both professional historians and those in other walks of life who have an orientation toward historical concerns. Among the objectives of the Conferences on Faith and History are the following: to encourage Christian scholars to explore the relationship of their faith to historical studies; to provide a forum for discussion of philosophies of history, and to survey current scholarship and foster research in the general area of faith and history; to establish more effective means of interaction between historians associated with religiously oriented and non-sectarian institutions of higher learning; and to arrange for discussion and exchange of ideas among evangelicals from all walks of life who are interested in the study of faith and history.

Founding Date: 1967

Membership: 500

Publications:
> *Fides et Historia,* semiannually
> *Newsletter,* semiannually

Meetings:
> Host sessions at the annual meeting of the American Historical Association
> Sponsor a fall meeting every other year

446. Conference on Jewish Social Studies*

Jewish

Jeannette M. Baron, President
250 West 57th Street, Room 904
New York, New York 10019
(212) 247-4718

The Conference on Jewish Social Studies is a nonpartisan association of scholars and laymen devoted to the idea that sound policies and intelligent action in Jewish affairs must be based on the most accurate and reliable information obtainable. Therefore, the Conference is organized to promote, by means of scientific research, a better understanding of the position of the Jews in the modern world. These studies are directed by recognized specialists, and their results and published in the quarterly journal *Jewish Social Studies*, and in separate volumes. Published material is made available to Jewish and other agencies, as well as to the public at large.

Membership: 1,500 individuals and libraries

Publications:

Jewish Social Studies, quarterly
Scholarly books

Meetings:

Annual conference meetings

447. Conference on the Religious Life in the Americas

Anglican

Connor Lynn, OHC, Superior-Chairman
Office of the Superior
4245 West Washington Boulevard
Chicago, Illinois 60624
(312) 722-7989

The Conference on the Religious Life is an association of religious orders of men and women. Its purpose is to coordinate the interests and experience of the various communities with the stated aim of setting before the church a united voice. It meets every third year for discussion and fellowship. There is an advisory council which meets annually. The Conference also strives for the continuing education of the church about the place and function of religious orders.

Membership: 22 religious orders

Meetings:

A general meetings every three years
Annual meetings of the Advisory Council

448. Confraternity Home Study Service

Roman Catholic

Rev. Jerome D. Fortenberry, CM, Director
3473 South Grand Avenue
St. Louis, Missouri 63118
(314) 664-8669

Confraternity Home Study Service offers mail courses in the Roman Catholic faith to Catholics and

non-Catholics. There is no charge for the material or the instruction. At present there are two courses: "The Kingdom of Jesus," a basic study of the moral and dogmatic teachings of the Catholic Church; and "Search of the Sriptures," a study of the development of Catholicism as found in the Acts of the Apostles. The Confraternity also operates the Knights of Columbus Religious Information Bureau. The Bureau distributes pamphets and other material throughout Missouri and advertises eight times a year in 130 local Missouri papers and 7 editions of the TV-Guide Magazines.

Membership:

Approximately 10-12 thousand persons take the the courses by mail each year

Radio/TV Programs:

Sponsors *Overview,* a weekly news broadcast heard on 20 Missouri radio stations; also sponsors a weekly religious news program with the Missouri Council of Churches

449. Conservative Baptist Home Mission Society

Conservative Baptist

Rev. Jack Estep, General Director
25 West 560 Geneva Road
Wheaton, Illinois 60187

Mailing Address
Post Office Box 828
Wheaton, Illinois 60187
(312) 653-4900

The purpose of the Conservative Baptist Home Mission Society is to preach the Gospel of Jesus Christ and start new churches in North and Central America, the West Indies, and United States possessions. This activity involves evangelism and church planting in both urban and suburban communities. Other activities include a church-related ministry among students on American college campuses, ministry to military personnel and American Indians, a radio station in Honduras, elementary and secondary schools in Central America, and the training of both lay and pastoral leaders through resident and extension schools.

Founding Date: 1950

Membership:

225 appointed ministers
1,100 supporting churches

Publications:

The Challenge, 6 times a year

Action Line, 2 times a year
New Churches Now-Letter, 8 times a year
Prayer Focus, 4 times a year

Radio/TV Programs:
1 radio station in Honduras

Meetings:
1 Annual meeting
4 regional meetings

450. Conservative Mennonite Conference, Rosedale Mennonite Missions (RMM)

Mennonite
David I. Miller, President
9920 Rosedale
Milford Center Road
Irwin, Ohio 43029
(614) 857-1366

Rosedale Mennonite Missions (RMM) is the mission organization of Conservative Mennonite Conference. The Conference was organized by a group of Amish Mennonite leaders. The present membership is about 7,000, with churches in 18 states of the United States. RMM believes pure Christianity is true, Jesus is the only way to salvation, and the church is enabled by the Holy Spirit. Its doctrinal position is Evangelical and Anabaptist. The Mennonite Confession of Faith (1963) is accepted as a statement of position. RMM is active in spiritual ministries: to win individuals to a saving faith in Jesus Christ; to provide a circle for fellowship, edification, and witness; and to work toward indigenous churches and leadership. Community development is sponsored to relieve human suffering and to encourage understanding and use of local resources for health and well-being. Mission outreach has extended to locations in Costa Rica, Nicaragua, Colombia, Germany, and the United States.

Founding Date: 1910

Staff:
7-person controlling board with direct responsibility to Conservative Mennonite Conference which consists of about 200 pastoral leaders

Membership:
Representing a constituency of about 7,500

Publications:
Brotherhood Beacon, mission-related materials
Focus, an occasional mimeographed release consisting largely of material from the field

Meetings:
Participate in the annual sessions of Conservative Mennonite Conference in August and in the ministers' meeting held in February

Former Name:
(1954) Mission Board of Conservative Amish Mennonite Conference

451. Consortium Perfectae Caritatis

Roman Catholic
Sr. Mary Elise, SND, Executive Director
13000 Auburn Road
Chardon, Ohio 44024
(216) 286-7101

Consortium Perfectae Caritatis, translated as an association of perfect charity, is a fellowship of women religious. Consortium implies united effort; perfectae caritatis is the goal toward which the effort is directed. The Consortium has headquarters in Washington, D.C. It is directed by an Administrative Council headed by the Executive Director. A bishop serves as Spiritual Advisor; a priest serves as Theological Consultant and another as Coordinator. The Consortium is a voluntary association of like-minded religious communities whose leadership is agreed on a common course of action in regard to religious life. Its aim is to present to the people of God the witness of authentic life lived by women dedicated to the interior life in a permanent commitment to a corporate apostolate. The members subscribe to a fundamental code which emphasizes basic principles of religious life as set forth in Conciliar Documents and in subsequent directives from the Holy See. The major activity of the fellowship is the semiannual general assembly sponsored by the consortium. The assemblies have convened in major cities of the United States. Conferences given during these meetings are presented by carefully chosen speakers recognized for their orthodoxy, eruditon, and professional competence as well as their expressed loyalty to the Holy See. Conferences are recorded by professional technicians and cassettes are later made available.

Founding Date: 1971

Membership: 750

Publications:
Newsletter, quarterly
Proceedings, including copies of all the addresses delivered during the general assemblies held during the respective year

Meetings:
General Assembly, semiannually

452. Consultation on Church Union

Interdenominational
Dr. Gerald F. Moede, General Secretary
228 Alexander Street
Princeton, New Jersey 08540
(609) 921-7866

Consultation on Church Union is an organization dedicated to uniting Protestantism. Its member denominations are the African Methodist Episcopal Church, African Methodist Episcopal Zion Church, Christian Church (Disciples of Christ), Christian Methodist Episcopal Church, Episcopal Church, National Council of Community Churches, Presbyterian Church in the United States, United Church of Christ, United Methodist Church, and United Presbyterian Church in the United States of America.

Founding Date: 1982

Staff: 7

Membership: 10 Protestant denominations

Publications:
Historical and liturgical guides

453. CONTACT Teleministries USA Inc. (CTUSA)

Nondenominational
Robert E. Larson, Jr. Executive Director
900 South Arlington Avenue, Room 125
Harrisburg, Pennsylvania 17109
(717) 652-3410

CONTACT Teleministries USA is an ecumenical agency promoting and assisting the development of telephone counseling/crises intervention centers as lay Christian ministries. The agency also serves as an accrediting body for these ministries. It is a member of LIFE LINE International, an international association of similar ministries in 11 countries. Each accredited CONTACT center in the United States of America offers 24-hour a day telephone counseling, providing a listening ear, information and referral, crisis intervention, and suicide prevention services.

Founding Date: 1968

Staff: 175 employed staff members

Membership:
14,000 volunteers
100 CONTACT ministries in 30 states

Publications:
CONTACT Paper, quarterly
CONTACT Communique, bimonthly
CONTACT Helplines, bimonthly

Meetings:
Annual Conference at various locations nationwide
Triennial International Conventions in different countries

Former Name:
(1971) National Council for Telephone Ministries

454. Convergence, Inc.

Roman Catholic
Joseph Cunneen, President
West Nyack, New York 10994
(914) 358-4898

Convergence, Inc., is an organization whose purpose is to encourage interdisciplinary, international and ecumenical cooperation through publications, lectures, and meetings.

Staff: Editorial staff

Membership: Approximately 12 corporate members

Publications:
Cross Currents, a quarterly journal to explore the implications of Christianity for our times

455. The Conversion Center, Inc.*

Independent Fundamental Churches of America
Rev. H. Gregory Adams, Director
18 West Eagle Road
Havertown, Pennsylvania 19083
(215) 446-6700

The purpose of The Conversion Center is to promote the gospel of Jesus Christ; to foster, promote, and encourage understanding and good will among members of all religious faiths, and to discourage the use of violence, boycotts, and sanctions by adherents of one religion against adherents of another. The organization accomplishes these goals by holding religious meetings and conferences; by radio and television broadcasting; by the imprinting of Gospel messages on records and transcriptions; by producing and distributing Gospel motion pictures; by printing and publishing religious literature; by employing and contributing to the support of missionaries; and by conducting such other activities as promote this purpose. This corporation places particular emphasis on the evangelization and conversion of adherents of the Roman Catholic faith, providing spiritual, temporal, and financial assistance, especially to their converted clergy.

Membership:
> 18 clerical
> 54 staff and missionaries

Publications:
> *The Gospel Catholic,* 6 times a year

Radio/TV Programs:
> Question and answer type, 7 days a week, 4 stations

Meetings:
> 52 meetings a year
> Special conferences throughout the year on various subjects

456. Convert Movement Our Apostolate (CMOA)

Roman Catholic

Rev. Msgr. Erwin A. Juraschek, National and International Director
Our Lady of Grace Rectory
430 Avenue West
Brooklyn, New York 11223
(212) 371-1000

Convert Movement Our Apostolate was founded for the purpose of bridging the gap between clergy and separated or non-Christian brethren by encouraging the laity to make use of their individual talents in bringing souls to Christ and Christ to souls; and by training laity, under the supervision of the hierarchy, to tutor non-Catholics, non-Christians, uninformed Catholics, and the unchurched on the teachings of the Faith on a parish level, one-to-one basis. Cassettes, slides, and brochures are part of the training program used throughout the United States parishes and mission countries. The program consists of in-service training and a workshop on techniques in convert work.

Founding Date: 1945

Staff: 14 members of the Executive Staff

Membership:
> 10 volunteers
> General membership throughout the United States of America and in the mission countries includes pastors, tutors, and chaplains assigned to the program within each parish

Publications:
> *CMOA Bulletin,* quarterly

Former Name: Convert Makers of America

457. Corpus (Corps of Reserve Priests United for Service)

Roman Catholic

Frank J. McGrath, EdD, Facilitator
Post Office Box 2649
Chicago, Illinois 60690
(312) 764-3399

Corpus was founded by four married priests of the Chicago Archdiocese as a response to Pope Paul's Holy Year call for reconciliation. They suggested there could be no better example set for the Holy Year than the restoration of harmonious relations between the bishops of the Church and their married priests. The founders believed that many married priests remain committed to their priesthood and are eager to utilize their abilities in service to the Church in a manner consistent with their present life styles. The response to their statement on the part of the resigned priests verified their thesis — by June 1976 Corpus had acquired over 600 subscribers and the organization presently has over 1,000 resigned priests as members. Corpus argues that the Church needs the services of its married priests and, further, that the married priests are willing to serve. The organization sends appropriate reprints and survey reports to bishops and encourages meetings of celibate and married priests. Newsletters report on various ministries of married priests and openness on the part of a few bishops, hoping to encourage others to do likewise. In promoting their cause, Corpus plans no protests, no demonstrations, no public celebrations, no demanding ultimatums. It does plan collection and documentation of statistics and relevant information and hopes to maintain contact with married priests and concerned bishops; it hopes to encourage models of ministry by married priests and to alert the laity about the availability of married priests to serve their needs. The approach of Corpus is seen as being direct, respectful, and honest, but also firm, forceful, and political.

Founding Date: 1974

Membership:
> 1,050 resigned priests
> 900 associated ordained priest members
> 210 "Friends" of Corpus

Publications:

Newsletter, about 6 times a year

Reprints of various relevant articles

Survey relative to the utilization of married priests about every other year

458. Council for American Indian Ministry (CAIM)

United Church of Christ

Henry Good Bear, Board Chairperson
122 West Franklin Avenue
Minneapolis, Minnesota 55404
(612) 870-3679

The Council for American Indian Ministry is a National Agency of the United Church of Christ. The historic Indian congregations of the UCC, leadership training for pastors and lay leaders of the Indian congregations, Urban Indian Ministry, and Treaty Rights and Indian Concerns are CAIM's priorities.

Staff: 13 Board members, 2 staff members

Publications:

CAIM News, quarterly

Meetings:

Meetings and workshops on local levels at different locations

459. Council of Jewish Federations (CJF)

Jewish

Robert I. Hiller, Executive Vice-President
575 Lexington Avenue
New York, New York 10022
(212) 751-1311

The Council of Jewish Federations is composed of 194 Jewish Federations, Welfare Funds, and Community Councils. It represents some 800 communities, embracing over 95% of the Jewish population of the United States and Canada who, together, spend one-half billion dollars annually for local, national, and oversees services. CJF provides national and regional services to associated Jewish community organizations aiding in fund raising, community organization, health and welfare planning, personnel recruitment, and public relations. It serves as the central instrument of its member Federations, doing jointly on their behalf what each would otherwise do

separately; taking joint action on common purposes; and helping to strengthen their work and impact.

Founding Date: 1932

Staff: 78

Membership: 194 Jewish Federations

Publications:

Newsletter, 2-3 times a year

50 general and technical reports, directories, yearbooks, and bulletins

Meetings:

Annual General Assembly in November

Former Name:

(1978) Council of Jewish Federations and Welfare Funds

Merger:

National Council of Jewish Federations and Welfare Funds and Bureau of Jewish Social Research

460. Council of Theological Seminaries

United Presbyterian Church in the USA

John H. Galbreath, Director
475 Riverside Drive
New York, New York 10115
(212) 870-2825

The Council of Theological Seminaries relates to seven United Presbyterian Seminaries which provide theological education in preparing competent professional ministers for the church; advance theological scholarship; offer a variety of opportunities for continuing education; and maintain theological faculties' expertise for the whole church for dealing with the world in light of the Gospel of Jesus Christ. The Council provides unity amid diversity among the seminaries of the UPCUSA, by which the entire enterprise of theological education relates to the whole church, and offers means for communication, coordination, support, long-range planning, and evaluating under safeguards which assure the priority of theological considerations.

Membership: 14 lay; 33 clerical

Meetings:

Annually

461. Council on Religion and International Affairs (CRIA)

Nondenominational

Dr. Robert J. Myers, President
Merrill House
170 East 64th Street
New York, New York 10021
(212) 838-4120 or 838-4121

The Council on Religion and International Affairs is an independent, nonpartisan, nonsectarian and tax-exempt organization established by Andrew Carnegie. The Council seeks to apply the insights of ethics and religion to international affairs, including the formulation of foreign policy. Its members believe that the *ethical* implications of policy decisions ought to be weighed along with political, economical, and security considerations. Therefore, the Council works to promote a better understanding of the values and conditions which make for peaceful relations among nations and consequently a better life for people everywhere. The inter-relationship of religion and foreign policy is a unifying theme of the work of CRIA.

Founding Date: 1914

Staff:

15 staff members; 5 officers
28 trustees; 5 honorary trustees

Publications:

Worldview Magazine, monthly
Studies in Ethics and Foreign Policy, yearly

Meetings:

Bi-weekly CRIA Conversations at the Merrill House
Yearly CRIA Distinguished Lecture Programs at various public auditoriums
Carnegie's Center Leadership Program at Fort Hill, Long Island
Biannual conferences

Former Name: Church Peace Union

462. Council on the Study of Religion (CRS)

Nondenominational

Walter Capps, President
University of California
Santa Barbara, California 93106

The Council on the Study of Religion is dedicated to advancing the discipline of Religious Studies through publications of various kinds, through research projects, and through providing a variety of services to its constituent societies. Constituent societies of the Council are as follows: American Academy of Religion; American Society of Church History; American Society of Missiology; Association of Professors and Researchers in Religious Education; College Theology Society; Catholic Biblical Association of America; Catholic Theological Society of America, Institute on Religion in an Age of Science; North American Academy of Religion; Society of Biblical Literature; Society of Christian Ethics; and the Society for the Scientific Study of Religion. The Council on graduate studies in Religion is an affiliate member.

Founding Date: 1969

Membership: 13,500, 12 organizations

Publications:

CRS *Bulletin,* 5 times yearly
Religious Studies Review, a quarterly review of publications in the field of religion and related disciplines
TOIL (Teaching Opportunities Information Listing), the job registry of the Council, 5 times yearly
The Council on the Study of Religion Directory of Departments and Programs of Religious Studies in North America, every 3 years

463. Covenant Press

Evangelical Covenant Church of America

Rev. James R. Hawkinson
Executive Secretary of Publications
5101 North Francisco Avenue
Chicago, Illinois 60625
(312) 784-3000

Covenant Press is the publishing and distributing arm of the Evangelical Covenant Churches of America, a Protestant evangelical church with roots in the State Lutheran Church of Sweden, as influenced by late 19th century Pietism and the revival movement. It is charged with specific responsibilities for editing and publishing *The Covenant Companion* (denominational) and other periodicals of a devotional and theological nature. The Press operates one bookstore.

Publications:

The Covenant Companion, twice monthly
The Covenant Quarterly, a theological journal

The Covenant Home Altar, a daily devotional guide

Approximately 25 religious books in print

Radio/TV Programs:

Video cassettes

464. Coventry House, Inc.

Presbyterian

Arthur L. Kay, Director

Lewis Hill Road

Coventry, Connecticut 06238

Mail Office

Post Office Box 505

Coventry, Connecticut 06238

(203) 742-7391

Coventry House, located on 60 acres in rural Connecticut, has been established for the following purposes: to stress the importance of interpersonal relationships in the communication of the Gospel; to provide an extended family facility for troubled young adults who are goal-oriented in the area of improving their self-worth and ability to relate to others; to provide a small-group facility for seminars, conferences, and retreats conducted by Coventry House staff or by outside groups; and to provide individual, family, and marriage pastoral counseling.

Meetings:

6 conferences a year on Interpersonal Relationships at the Coventry House

Occasional seminars on Interpersonal Relationships in the Northeast United States

465. The Co-Workers of Mother Teresa in America, Inc.

Roman Catholic

Mrs. Warren L. Kump, Chairman

4243 Glenwood Avenue

Minneapolis, Minnesota 55422

The Co-Workers of Mother Teresa are people who choose a particular way of life that calls for seeing God in every human being. It is not an "organization" in the ordinary sense of the word, but rather a family whose members seek to come closer to God through prayer and loving service to their fellow man. The Co-Workers seek to maintain deep family love and loyalty in the home; and to serve the lonely, the ill, the poor, and the unwanted.

Founding Date: 1969

Publications:

The Co-Worker, 3 times yearly

466. Creation House (Division of Christian Life, Inc.)

Nondenominational

Robert Walker, President

396 East Saint Charles Road

Carol Stream, Illinois 60187

653-1472

Creation House is a publisher of Evangelical and fundamental Christian Literature. Titles include fiction and non-fiction for children and adults.

Staff: 24

Publications:

Books

467. Creation-Life Publishers

Nondenominational

George Hillestad, President

Post Office Box 15666

San Diego, California 92115

(714) 449-9420

Creation-Life Publishers and its Master Books Division strive to produce books that are timely, scientifically and historically accurate, and true to God's Word. They provide the answers needed for the creation/evolution controversy and sound replies to the radical theories being thrust upon society today.

Founding Date: 1974

Staff: 8

Publications:

Books, general and religious titles

468. Creation Social Science and Humanities Society (CSSHS)

Nondenominational

Dr. Paul D. Ackerman, President

4726 East 25th

Wichita, Kansas 67220

Mailing Address

1429 North Holyoke

Wichita, Kansas 67208

(316) 683-3610

The Creation Social Science and Humanities Society (CSSHS) was incorporated in Wichita, Kansas. The

CSSHS is educational, and promotes and disseminates information on the implications of the Biblical creation model of origins for the social sciences and humanities, with emphasis on the development of these disciplines in accordance with the rapidly emerging and increasingly well-established natural scientific models of Biblical creation. The CSSHS publishes a *Quarterly Journal* directed toward teachers and students of the social sciences and humanities, especially in institutions of higher learning. The CSSHS may also publish books, monographs, and other writings, and sponsor speakers, seminars, and research projects related to its educational purpose.

Founding Date: 1977

Publications:
　Quarterly Journal
　Books and monographs

469. CREED (Christian Rescue Effort for the Christian Emancipation of Dissidents)

Dr. Ernest Gordon, President
310 South Lee Street
Alexandria, Virginia 22314

Mailing Address
Post Office Box 8007
Washington, D.C. 20024
(703) 549-3093

CREED is a community of concerned Christians dedicated to the ministry and mission of freedom. Its objectives are: to educate and involve the American people and their elected representatives in Congress regarding the plight of people persecuted and imprisoned for living and expressing their faith; to serve as a link between the private and public sectors in order to inform and to initiate beneficial action; to communicate with persecuted Christians and to plead their cause on the basis of the UN Declaration of Human Rights, 1948, the Helsinki Accords of 1975, and the UN Declaration on Religious Persecution of November, 1981; to coordinate with ethnic/religious groups, and to cooperate in common ventures; to insure the security of its sources and those it seeks to serve; to educate people in the nature of the biblical doctrine of freedom and its implications for moral responsibility; to inform people in countries of religious oppression that people in the United States care for them, and are working in their behalf. CREED's broadcasts have been made via the Voice of America, Radio Free Europe, and the BBC. Letters

of support have been distributed in over seven languages; and to provide assistance to refugees who come to this country.

Founding Date: 1980

Meetings:
　2 conferences per year, Washington, D.C.

470. Crusade for Family Prayer, Inc.*

Roman Catholic
Rev. Patrick Peyton, CSC
773 Madison Avenue
Albany, New York 12208
(518) 462-6458

The purpose of Crusade for Family Prayer is to promote daily family prayer and the family rosary through the organization of diocesan and local Family Rosary and Family Prayer Crusades.

471. CRUX Publications

Roman Catholic
Thomas A. Clemente, President
75 Chaplain Street (Business Office)
800 North Pearl Street (Editorial Office)
Albany, New York 12204
(518) 465-4591 (Business Office)
(518) 434-2616 (Editorial Office)

CRUX Publications publishes two newsletters, *CRUX of the News* and *The Crux of Prayer.* Both offer reports of current events, biweekly reports on current topics, a Resource section referring to seminars, workshops, books, AV material, and innovative ideas helpful in improving the work of Priests, Sisters, Deacons, and lay people in their particular Church apostolate. CRUX also publishes a weekly advertising supplement, *CRUX Exchange,* which accepts paid listing and display ads. In addition, CRUX publishes paperback books and audio cassettes.

Staff: 8 lay; 1 religious

Publications:
　CRUX of the News, weekly
　The Crux of Prayer, monthly

472. Cultural Integration Fellowship*

Mrs. Bina Chaudhuri
3494 21st Street
San Francisco, California 94110
(415) 648-6777

The purposes of the Cultural Integration Fellowship are: to build bridges of understanding between East and West, between Asia-Africa and Europe-America, by removing Western misconceptions of the spirit of Eastern Culture and Eastern misconceptions of the spirit of Western culture; to identify with precision the universal and humanistic values common to the great religions and cultures of the world; to lay the foundation for one universal conceptual language by translating the seemingly conflicting philosophical notions of different cultures into universally intelligible phenomenological and pragmatic terms; and to develop fundamental principles and techniques which can be applied in daily life with a view to bringing the deeper potentials of man to full flowering.

Membership: 250

Publications:

Books

473. Cumberland Presbyterian Church, Board of Missions

Cumberland Presbyterian Church

Rev. Joe Matlock, Executive Director
Post Office Box 40149
Memphis, Tennessee 38104
(901) 274-7513

The Board of Missions is an agency of the General Assembly of the Cumberland Presbyterian Church. It is responsible for mission concerns and activities in the continental United States as well as mission fields in Colombia, Japan, Hong Kong, and Macao. The work on the overseas field includes educational institutions, evangelistic programs, social services, and church extension. The work in the United States includes programs related to two minority groups, the Choctaw Indians and the Hispanics, as well as church extension (church development), women's work, evangelism, and education for mission activities.

Founding Date: 1880

Staff:

8 administrative staff members
6 overseas missionary families

Publications:

The Missionary Messenger, monthly

Meetings:

Annual Cumberland Presbyterian Women's Convention held at various locations

474. Daughters of Isabella

Roman Catholic

Mrs. Martine Ward, International Regent
375 Whitney Avenue
New Haven, Connecticut 06511
(203) 865-2570

The Daughters of Isabella is an international Catholic lay organization for all Catholic women over the age of 16. Each state and subordinate circle plans its own projects and takes on its own charitable activities. They include sponsoring scholarships, building churches and schools, working at homes for the aged and hospitals. In addition to money given to charity, many service hours each week are given to the needy, the aged, the handicapped, and others in need. The object of the Daughters of Isabella is to unite all Catholic women in a fraternal, beneficial, social society in order to promote friendships and to establish a bond of unit and truth that will be of mutual interest in times of trouble and distress. Devotion to Catholic interests predominates. The mission of the society is to preserve the memory and worth of a brilliant woman, Queen Isabella of Castile, to work for her canonization, and to have the Congress of the United States declare April 22nd, her birthday, in her honor.

Founding Date: 1897

Membership:
113,000 members in the United States and Canada

Publications:
Quarterly newsletter to the society's 825 circles

Meetings:
Biennial conventions

Former Name:
(1963) Daughters of Isabella, National Circle

475. Daughters of St. Paul Publishing Company

Roman Catholic

Sr. Mary Domenica, Provincial
50 St. Paul's Avenue
Boston, Massachusetts 02130
(617) 522-8911 or 522-0875

The Daughters of St. Paul are an international congregation of religious women blending contemplation with action. Their mission is evangelization with the media of communication—press, films, radio and TV. Through an intense spiritual life they strive to become living Gospels and to be able to say with St. Paul, "Christ lives in me." In carrying out their work, Daughters of St. Paul use the modern means of communication, especially the press, to spread the Word of God. The sisters write, illustrate, print, bind, and diffuse their own inspiring literature—books, magazines, pamphlets, and leaflets—among people of all faiths and races, and for every age level.

Founding Date: 1915

Membership: 2,500

Publications:
The Family; Strain Forward; and *My Friend (for children),* monthly
Books and pamphlets including catechisms, books of formation, lives of saints, Papal documents, theology, prayer books
Cassettes, records, filmstrip, and slide programs

Radio/TV Programs:
Religious radio programs on 23 stations across the country

476. David C. Cook Publishing Company, Inc.

Nondenominational

Dr. David C. Cook III, Chairman of the Board
850 North Grove Avenue
Elgin, Illinois 60120
(312) 741-2400

David C. Cook Publishing Company, Inc., is the largest of the independent publishers of evangelical church school materials, primarily for Protestant churches. Within the last 10 years, the Company has also developed a non-curriculum publishing division which has produced books and other Christian education materials totalling approximately 650 items. Other areas of diversification include a secular products division and a child care division. The stated purpose of the Company is to aid, promote, and contribute to the advancement of Christian education and instruction in churches, Sunday schools, and elsewhere; to encourage the acceptance of Jesus Christ as our leader and personal Savior and to aid, promote, and contribute to the teaching and putting into practice of His two great precepts — the love of God and of each other. There are 20 full-time curriculum representatives in the United States and Canada and five part-time consultants, as well as six full-time bookstore representatives. The Company's main offices and plant are in Elgin, Illinois with a distribution center in LaHabra, California and a Canadian subsidiary in Weston, Ontario. While the Company is a profit-making organization, it is wholly owned by the non-profit David C. Cook Foundation, which has a world-wide missionary and Christian education ministry.

Founding Date: 1875

Publications:
> *Christian Education Trends,* a monthly newsletter for pastors
> *Cook Report,* a monthly letter to Christian Booksellers Association members
> Religious children's and adult books (fiction and non-fiction), 300 titles
> Christian education books, 85 titles
> Complete line of dated Christian Education Curriculum (nursery-adult), 35 publications issued quarterly

477. Davis Evangelistic Association, Inc.

Protestant-Pentecostal
Dorothy Davis, President
Post Office Box 226
Houston, Texas 77001
(713) 861-9041

The Davis Evangelistic Association, Inc., is dedicated to spreading the Gospel of the Lord Jesus Christ through publications, missionary outreach, radio, television, magazine publications, book publications, field ministry in churches, auditoriums, and tent evangelism. Thousands of books (Dorothy Davis has written 16 booklets), go into the prisons absolutely free along with cassette tapes, some tape recorders, and literature. Hundreds of personal letters and birthday cards also go to the inmates across America. The Association is approximately 16 years old and during this period thousands have been reached through field evangelism and the printed page. Dorothy Davis has preached on many radio stations throughout the country in past years. She and Brother Davis have gone into prisons and ministered to the needs behind the walls, although most of their personal appearances have been to the free-world congregation. At the present time, the ministry sends monthly checks to three missionary outreaches.

Staff: 3

Publications:
> *His Miracle Power,* monthly
> *The Prisoner's Page,* monthly

Meetings:
> Evangelistic meetings held all over the country frequently

478. Daystar Communications, Inc.

Nondenominational
Dr. Stephen Talituala, Executive Director
392 East Third Street
Eugene, Oregon 97440
Mailing Address
Post Office Box 10123
Eugene, Oregon 97440
(503) 342-6712

Daystar Communications is dedicated to assisting churches and missions, particularly in Africa and

Asia, in their search for effective ways of presenting the message of Christ. Daystar's staff is a group of specialists in research, development, evaluation, and training, who are committed to world evangelism. Daystar provides a consultation service for those involved in Christian outreach that utilizes contemporary techniques of analysis, measurement, and evaluation. Daystar also offers training for church leaders and missionaries in the most effective use of resources to meet the needs of their communities. The training program for Daystar operates under the name of the International Institute of Christian Communications (IICC) and is designed specifically to provide the culturally-oriented training needed by Christian workers.

Founding Date: 1970

Staff:

Approximately 45 staff members at the International Headquarters in Nairobi, Kenya

Publications:

Daystar Reports

Radio/TV Programs:

Periodical broadcasts for Radio Voice of Kenya

Meetings:

Staff retreats

479. De Rance, Inc.

Roman Catholic

Harry G. John, President
7700 West Blue Mound Road
Milwaukee, Wisconsin 53213
(414) 475-7700

De Rance, Inc., is a private foundation. Its purpose is to aid religious, charitable and educational organizations in this country and throughout the world, with emphasis on Roman Catholic church support. Aid is provided for educational and other programs for Native American people, and for similar programs in Latin America, Africa and Asia. No grants are made to individuals or for endowment funds. Institutions must be qualified by the IRS.

Founding Date: 1946

Staff: 16 full-time; 5 part-time

Meetings:

Occasionally

480. Deaf Missions

Nondenominational

Duane King, Director
RR 2, Post Office Box 26
Council Bluffs, Iowa 51501
(712) 322-5493

The main purpose of Deaf Missions is to bring Christ to deaf people through: the preparation and distribution of Bible visuals for the deaf; training of Christian workers for the deaf; and personal Christian work with the deaf people. Activities include preparing, collecting, cataloging, and distributing movies in sign language, captioned slides, overhead transparencies, video tapes, and printed literature; establishing and teaching sign language classes at Bible Colleges; providing church services for the deaf locally and establishing churches at remote locations; planning, hosting, and leading workshops for the deaf and about the deaf. Although the organization is nondenominational, it is supported primarily by Christian Churches and Churches of Christ.

Staff: 7 full-time; 3 part-time staff members

Publications:

Christian News for the Deaf, monthly
Daily Devotions for the Deaf, monthly

Radio/TV Programs:

Video tapes for training purposes
Video programming in preparation

Meetings:

Annual Workshops on Deaf Evangelism
Annual Christian Leadership Clinic for the Deaf
Annual Bible Camp for the Deaf

481. Defenders of the Christian Faith, Inc. (DCF)

Nondenominational

Dr. Hart R. Armstrong, President
Post Office Box 886
Wichita, Kansas 67201
(316) 267-1084 or 267-2875

Defenders of the Christian Faith is a non-membership charitable religious corporation originally established to "defend the Christian Faith" against such dangers as the theory of evolution, liberal Christian teaching, socialism and communism. It publishes the *Defender* magazine, a religious monthly founded in 1926, as well as books, pamphlets, and tracts. The Organization assists national ministers overseas, and has sponsored Spanish-speaking churches in New York, New Jersey, and Chicago, as well as in Puerto Rico and Cuba. It maintains Defenders Fellowship, a service ministry for ministers and churches, and carries on the Defenders Seminary to provide religious educational study through external independent courses. It has assisted educational and religious work among the deaf, carries on a ministry to the retarded and handicapped by hiring and training them, and conducts an organized Bible or missionary tour to the Holy Land or missionary countries each year. It holds an organizational meeting, and an annual Bible Conference.

Founding Date: 1925

Staff: 20 to 25

Membership: Mailing list of 150,000

Publications:
 The Defender, monthly

Radio/TV Programs:
 We operate Radio Station KDSA-FM at 91.1 on the FM dial
 We have in the past (and expect again in the future) to do radio broadcasting on a national scale and also TV programming in the Kansas and surrounding states area

Meetings:
 Annual Bible Conference on the last week-end of July each year at our headquarters in Wichita

482. Delta Epsilon Sigma

Catholic

Dr. William A. Uricchio, President
Carlow College
Pittsburgh, Pennsylvania 15213

Mailing Address
Dr. Charles M. Hepburn
National Secretary-Treasurer
College of Great Falls
Great Falls, Montana 59405
(406) 761-8210, Ext. 502

Delta Epsilon Sigma is the national scholastic honor society for Catholic colleges and universities. Its purposes are to recognize academic accomplishments, foster scholarly activities, and encourage a sense of intellectual community among its members.

Founding Date: 1939

Membership: 25,000

Publications:
 Delta Epsilon Sigma Journal, quarterly

Meetings:
 National conclave at least once every 10 years

483. The Delta Ministry* (DM)

National Council of Churches

Owen H. Brooks, Executive Director
830 Nelson Street
Greenville, Mississippi 38701

Mailing Address
Post Office Box 457
Greenville, Mississippi 38701
(601) 334-4587

The Delta Ministry was organized by the Commission on Religion and Race of the National Council of Churches to be a ministry to the poor and oppressed in the State of Mississippi. Its purpose is to seek reconciliation in church, community, and nation with the fulfillment of human rights for all men. DM monitors federal and state regulations that affect the lives of people; has helped build and maintain a model system for health delivery to low income people in the Mississippi Delta; has assisted programs for pre-school children and high school age youth; continues to support broadly-based community organizations throughout the state; and provides emergency services to individuals and families in dire immediate need.

Founding Date: 1964

Membership: 5 lay; 1 clerical

Publications:
 Delta Ministry Reports, bimonthly
 Quarterly reports

484. Deseret Management Corporation

The Church of Jesus Christ of Latter-day Saints

36 South State Street, #1626
Salt Lake City, Utah 84111

Deseret Management Corporation provides centralized ownership, supervision, coordinated management, and control of certain corporate organizations owned or controlled by the Church of Jesus Christ of Latter-day Saints.

485. Deseret Mutual Benefit Association

The Church of Jesus Christ of Latter-day Saints
10 South Main Street
Salt Lake City, Utah 84101

The Deseret Mutual Benefit Association is a non-profit insurance company founded to service the employee insurance and retirement benefit needs of the Church of Jesus Christ of Latter-day Saints and its related organization's benefit program.

486. Dignity, Inc.

Roman Catholic
Frank P. Scheuren, President
1500 Massachusetts Avenue, Suite 11
Washington, D.C. 20005
(202) 861-0017

Dignity is organized to unite all gay Catholics, to develop leadership and to be an instrument through which the gay Catholic may be heard by the Church and society. Their four areas of concern are: Spiritual Development, Education, Social Involvement, and Social Events. Members of Dignity strive to promote the cause of the gay community by working for the development of the Church's sexual theology and for the acceptance of gays as full and equal members of the one Christ; working for justice and social acceptance through education and legal reform; and reinforcing the self-acceptance and sense of dignity of gays and aiding them in becoming more active members of the Church and society.

Founding Date: 1969

Staff: 1

Membership: 4,000

Publications:
> *Dignity,* monthly
> *Disturbed Peace,* paperback by Brian McNaught
> *Theological Pastoral Resources,* collection of articles on homosexuality from a pastoral perspective

Meetings:
> Convention every two years, next convention: Seattle, Washington, Labor Day Weekend, 1983

487. Dimension Books, Inc.

Roman Catholic
Thomas P. Coffey, President
One Summit Street
Rockaway, New Jersey 07866
Mailing Address
Post Office Box 811
Denville, New Jersey 07834-0811
(201) 627-4334

Dimension Books, Inc., publishes Catholic books by many distinguished and popular authors who deal with the challenges and new developments in Catholic life and faith today. It also distributes its publications to bookstores.

Founding Date: 1963

Publications:
> 261 books in print
> 572 published since 1963

488. Disciples of Christ Historical Society

Christian Church (Disciples of Christ)
Roland K. Huff, President
1101 Nineteenth Avenue South
Nashville, Tennessee 37212
(615) 327-1444

The Disciples of Christ Historical Society was established to preserve the heritage, past and present, of the Christian Church (Disciples of Christ), the Christian Churches related to the North American Christian Convention, and Churches of Christ. The Historical Society serves as common ground for these three church bodies having their roots in the Christian Church Movement in the early 1800's; and provides resources for research, study, and dialogue. The Society seeks to locate, secure for preservation, and process for research books, periodicals, pamphlets, manuscripts, personal papers, and other historical materials related to this Movement and the reformation-restoration-unity leaders. The Society works closely with individuals, congregations, and church organizations in preserving current materials of historic value. The Society offers guidance and counsel in the development of effective record management programs.

Founding Date: 1941

Staff: 3 professional staff members

Membership: 1,200
Publications:
  Discipliana, quarterly
Meetings:
  Forrest F. Reed Lectures every 3-4 years

489. Disciples Peace Fellowship (DPF)

Christian Church (Disciples of Christ)
Ian J. McCrae, Executive Secretary
222 South Downey Avenue
Indianapolis, Indiana 46206

Mailing Address
Post Office Box 1986
Indianapolis, Indiana 46206
(317) 353-1491

The Disciples Peace Fellowship carries on an education and action program for its membership and attempts to influence a nonviolent way of life within the total church and community. It conducts national and regional workshops on peace and justice issues. DPF raises money and lobbies for specific legislative causes in keeping with its purpose. Through its *News Notes,* gatherings during general assemblies and regional sessions, it serves as a fellowship for members of the Christian Church (Disciples of Christ).

Founding Date: 1935
Staff: 2
Membership: 1,100
Publications:
  News Notes, six times a year
Meetings:
  Biennial National Meeting

490. The Disciplined Order of Christ

Nondenominational
Mrs. Sylvia Zimmer, Executive Director
643 Indian Trail
Ashland, Ohio 44805
(414) 289-8487

The Disciplined Order of Christ was founded by a group of 120 clergy and laity meeting at Albion College in Michigan, under the leadership of the late Albert Edward Day. It is a small group movement seeking to respond to an inner need for spiritual insight and growth, ethical sensitivity, and social concern, through daily individual devotional study, prayer, and meditation; participation in small-group sharing; attendance at summer regional retreats; and active participation in the program of some local church. Emphasis is placed on an "octave" of personal disciplines: obedience, simplicity, humility, frugality, generosity, truthfulness, purity, and charity.

Founding Date: 1945
Membership: Approximately 1,500 members
Publications:
  New Life News, 5-6 times a year
Meetings:
  At least one major retreat a year in each of the six regions: Northeast, Southeast, North Central, South Central, Midwest, and Western

491. Don Bosco Films Multimedia

Roman Catholic
Rev. Joseph Perozzi, SDB, President
148 Main Street
Post Office Box T
New Rochelle, New York 10802
(914) 632-6562

Don Bosco Films Multimedia is a producer and distributor of Audio Visual material for Catholic Schools and Churches, distributor of 16mm film from major companies, and publisher of religious books and pamphlets.

Staff: 8 executive officers

492. Dorrance and Company

Nondenominational
Sylvia T. Bronner, Vice President
35 Cricket Terrace
Ardmore, Pennsylvania 19003
(215) 642-8303

Dorrance and Company is the oldest and foremost subsidy book publisher in America. Through the years, over 4,000 books of all types have been published. Interests include books with information, ideas, or insights that will add to reader enjoyment wisdom, and awareness. It believes everyone should be concerned with the revitalization of America's spirit and vision, as reflected by the effort and quality put into their work.

Founding Date: 1920

Publications:

> Books—600 titles in print: religious, scholarly, poetry, and fiction

493. Drama of Truth

Roman Catholic

Post Office Box 255
Harrison, New York 10528

Drama of Truth is an organization dedicated to broadcasting the *Church's Forgotten Alternative.* It is an alliance for truth on television and radio, and offers a number of series and special programs for local broadcast.

494. Eagles, Inc.

Interdenominational
Rev. Stephen J. Brock, Director
2131 North Main Street
Dayton, Ohio 45405
(513) 275-1320

Eagles, Inc., is an ecumenical education center for Christian growth. It exists to equip people to grow, develop, and live a Christian lifestyle in the context of a Christian community. Eagles' services include: courses on a variety of subjects focused on the Christian lifestyle, including meditation and prayer, dreams, journal keeping, personal growth for Christians, and women and Scripture; growth groups for individuals wishing to explore various aspects of their personal lives in a Christian context; consultation with congregations seeking help in the areas of Christian education, spiritual disciplines, creative worship, retreat ministries and community building; leadership for Sunday schools and congregational retreats; and individual counseling. Eagles is governed by a board of directors comprised of clergy and laity interested in education for Christian growth. It maintains a ministerial team and is further undergirded by a host of volunteers who give their time and energy in support of its ministry.

Publications:
Flightpath Newsletter, bimonthly
Meetings:
Varied in number, as to need and request

495. Eastern European Mission

Nondenominational
Walter E. Zurfluh, President
232 North Lake Avenue
Pasadena, California 91101
(213) 796-5425

Eastern European Mission is an interdenominational evangelical missionary society which sponsors a ministry of evangelism, Bible teaching, literature publication and distribution, radio broadcasting, and relief in Europe. Its present fields are in Bulgaria, Greece, the Netherlands, Poland, the Soviet Union, West Germany, and Yugoslavia. The Mission is the oldest independent American missionary society ministering in eastern Europe today.

Founding Date: 1927
Staff:
12 members of the Board of Trustees
4 headquarters staff members
25 workers and staff on field
Publications:
Gospel Call, bimonthly
Radio/TV Programs:
5 half-hour Russian radio broadcasts weekly produced in Stockholm, Sweden
3 weekly radio broadcasts in Polish produced in Warsaw, Poland
Meetings:
Occasional participation in conferences arranged by churches

496. Eastern Orthodox Books*

The Russian Orthodox Church Outside Russia
Vladimir Anderson
Post Office Box 302
Willits, California 95490
(707) 459-5424

Eastern Orthodox Books publishes books in the fields of spiritual writings, lives of saints, and the doctrine of the Orthodox Church. A series of booklets on similar subjects is also published. The books have been selected to provide the potential convert to the Orthodox Church, as well as the English speaking

Orthodox, with both the doctrinal basis of the Orthodox Faith and some of the treasury of Orthodox spirituality.

Membership: 8 lay

Publications:
    40 books in print

497. Ecumedia News Service

Interdenominational

L. Franklin Devine, Director
475 Riverside Drive, Suite 850
New York, New York 10115
(212) 870-2255

Ecumedia News Service is an interfaith broadcast news agency which supplies radio news stories to religious and secular radio news producers. Ecumedia's reports are heard on 1,600 United States radio stations. Lodged within the Communication Commission of the National Council of Churches, Ecumedia is an editorially-independent radio news service covering the broad-spectrum of American religion in a non-evangelizing, non-proselytizing way. Representatives of nineteen religious organizations make up Ecumedia's board.

Staff: 18 agencies

Radio/TV Programs:
    Produce a bi-weekly 30-minute Audio Feed tape of stories, features, commentary, and actuality covering the world of religion. The stories are designed for incorporation into subscriber's newscasts and magazine-format radio programs.

498. Ecumenical Fellowship of St. James of Jerusalem

Interdenominational

Rev. Enoch Jones, Jr., MDiv, ACSW
Executive Secretary, Extension Base Chapter #1
Post Office Box 2693, Terminal Annex
Los Angeles, California 90051
(415) 681-4088 (San Francisco Center)

The Ecumenical Fellowship of St. James of Jerusalem is an organized activity which promotes the maintenance of Christianity in the Holy Land. Its members' objectives are: to pray daily; to bind together in Catholic love, whether in the home parish or away; to endeavor to lead back into the fold those who have strayed; and to realize that the Church is the Body of Christ, "beginning at Jerusalem" (St.

Luke 24:47), based on "be ye DOERS of the word" (St. James 1:22). This Fellowship of activity finds organized efforts in many groups, especially through the Jerusalem and the Middle East Church Association which publishes *Bible Lands* quarterly. A prayer group within the Fellowship is the Ekklesia Nika Guild.

Publications:
    Bible Lands, quarterly

Meetings:
    At least 4 conferences and 1 general meeting yearly

Former Name: Fellowship of St. James of Jerusalem

499. The Ecumenical Institute*

Rev. Joseph Wesley Mathews, Dean
3444 Congress Parkway
Chicago, Illinois 60624
(312) 769-6363

The Ecumenical Institute is a non-profit organization with centers in 104 cities and a twenty-year history of community and church renewal. Its Impact, Research, Demonstration, and Training Programs are supported by individuals, corporations, foundations, and government agencies. The work of the Ecumenical Institute is carried out by an international, self-supporting staff and by thousands of individuals who are concerned about the future of the entire world. Religious, intellectual, and social methods are offered in The Academy, an 8-week construct for clergy and laymen, and in The International Training Institute, a 3-week construct for global churchmen.

Founding Date: 1956

Publications:
    The I.E. Newsletter

500. Ecumenical Research Academy (ERA)*

Nondenominational

Rev. J. Rodman Williams, PhD, Director
10 Freedman Way
Anaheim, California 92806
(714) 776-8965

The Ecumenical Research Academy was established to provide in-depth research into many areas of the Christian faith. It serves primarily as a study and research center for the contemporary charismatic movement. Scholars from the widest spectrum of Christian denominations probe into Biblical, historical and theological aspects of this movement as well as many of its psychological and sociological dimensions. Other areas such as drug abuse and alcoholism, Christian healing and medicine, spiritual dimensions in human behavior, and church renewal are also the concern of ERA scholars.

Membership: 4 lay; 8 clerical

Publications:
The Journal of Charismatic Theology

501. Ecumenical Women's Center

Interdenominational

Connie J. Takamine, Chair, Board of Directors
1653 West School Street
Chicago, Illinois 60657
(312) 348-4970

The Ecumenical Women's Center is a community of women committed to ministries with women in the church and in society, through reflection, education, and action. The members represent a wide spectrum of religious traditions and perspectives but are united in the struggle for justice for all women. They believe that as long as any person is oppressed, all persons suffer a loss of freedom; as long as any woman is prevented from developing her full potential, all women are impoverished. Recognizing that ministry with women must encompass a wide range of activities, the Ecumenical Women's Center provides a setting for growth and involvement in social justice issues and in spiritual and faith issues. The members engage in a continuing dialogue about the questions that concern them as women seeking recognition of the worth and dignity of all persons. The Center presently has the following four program areas: Life of Women in the Church, Women in Professional Ministry, Women in Prison, and Violence Against Women. In each of these areas the Center is involved in advocacy, education, and direct service.

Founding Date: 1972

Staff:
4 staff members
15 members of the Board of Directors
1 consultant

Membership:
300 supporting members
200 additional mailing list

Publications:
Because We Are One People, a non-sexist hymnal
Woman-Soul Flowing, a women's meditation book
Sing a Womansong, a feminist songbook
Monthly newsletter, calendar, conference information, job listings, book reviews, resources

Meetings:
Conferences, workshops, and seminars on the listed program areas

502. The Educational Center*

Episcopal
Rev. Elsom Eldridge
6357 Clayton Road
St. Louis, Missouri 63117
(314) 721-7604

The Educational Center is a small endowed institution engaged in research, consultation, and design in religious education. The Center believes that the primary task of religious education is to provide a context within which each individual may move toward his own fullness of life. Rather than imposing a set of external concepts and standards, it designs materials which expose the student to both traditional and contemporary understandings so that he may find his own meaning and values. Courses designed in this fashion are available for all age groups, pre-school through adult level. These materials are not sold separately and may be used only by those organizations under contract to the Center. The use of Center materials predicates a specific teacher training program. Centerpoint is an ongoing program for adults who: feel the need for a continuing framework for their own personal growth; feel that a psychological, as well as a theological, framework is valuable for them; have an acquaintance with, and enthusiasm for, Jungian psychology; and would like to continue moving inward within the context of others doing the same. A year's Centerpoint program consists of 18 two-hour sessions and is available to anyone (not just those under contract) who is interested. The Center is affiliated with the Episcopal Church, but increasingly serves other denominations and ecumenical groups, as well as secular groups.

Membership: 100 churches; 1,600 individuals

Publications:
Centerline

Meetings:
50 throughout the country

503. 8th Day Center for Justice

Roman Catholic
22 East Van Buren
Chicago, Illinois 60605
(312) 427-4351

8th Day Center was founded as a joint effort by six Roman Catholic religious congregations to actualize the Scriptural mandate to work for justice. The name 8th Day Center was chosen to acknowledge that creation is still in process. Today 10 congregations sponsor the Center. They provide staff and funds. Three congregations are Friends of the Center. Friends are groups and individuals who make a substantial financial contribution. The Center focuses its activities in a variety of issue areas. These include: hunger and food policy; women's issues; human rights including immigration questions; peace and disarmament; employment and family security; and the Nestle Boycott. The Center utilizes a variety of strategies to influence political, economic and social systems. These strategies include: corporate responsibility; legislative action; educational outreach; monitoring; advocacy; and direct action. In selecting issues, the Center focuses on those that relate to the poor and oppressed, involve action as well as education, link Third and First World concerns, and have local, national, and international ramifications. 8th Day Center's goal is to bring about a more just society by working to change the structures and systems that oppress. Any effort to build a more human world, that reflects the Gospel value of solidarity, must address the systemic roots of injustice.

Founding Date: 1974
Staff: 13
Publications:
> *LAS Bulletin,* monthly
> *8th Day Report,* six times a year
> Calendar, monthly; resource book; issue packets

504. Electronic Paperbacks (The Merton Tapes)

Roman Catholic
Norman Kramer, Editor and Publisher
31 Roaring Brook Road
Chappaqua, New York 10514

Mailing Address
Post Office Box 2
Chappaqua, New York 10514
(914) 238-8661

Electronic Paperbacks is an organization operated by Norman and Joann Kramer, Catholic laypersons, and devoted exclusively to the editing and publishing of tapes recorded by Thomas Merton at the Abbey of Gethsemani, under the direction of both the Abbey of Gethsemani and the trustees of the Merton Legacy Trust. These are the only tapes by Merton currently available for purchase by the general public. There are two series of cassette tapes now available: *Life and Prayer (Series I),* consisting of 12 cassettes, and *The Mystic Life Series,* consisting of 11 cassettes. A third series, *Life and Prayer (Series II),* also consisting of 12 cassettes, is now in preparation. When completed, a total of 35 cassettes by Merton will be available. These are all talks which Merton gave as novice conferences while novice-master and later, to the community at large after becoming a hermit. They were taped by him at various times from 1962 to 1968, the year of his death.

Founding Date: 1972
Staff: 2
Publications:
> Cassette tape recording by Thomas Merton in three series, a total of 35 titles, grouped in three series—*Life and Prayer (Series I and II)* and *The Mystic Life* series. The price is $8.95 per cassette, plus $1 per order for postage and handling.

505. Elim Fellowship

Pentecostal
Carlton Spencer, General Chairman
Post Office Box 15A
Lima, New York 14485
(716) 582-2790

Elim Fellowship is an association of churches, ministers, and missionaries seeking to serve the whole Body of Christ. It is of Pentecostal conviction and Charismatic orientation providing credentials, counsel, and direction to individuals and local churches. Elim Fellowship provides leadership seminars at home and abroad and serves as a transdenominational agency sending missionaries and personnel to work among national movements. The purpose of the Elim Fellowship may be defined as follows: to establish and maintain churches and missions at home and abroad; to assist through fellowship and financial support indigenous movements in various nations of the world, in contrast to building distinctively Elim assemblies or missions; to license and ordain candidates for the work of the gospel ministry; and to provide on the home front a vehicle of fellowship for ministers and churches without an accompanying sectarian spirit.

Founding Date: 1933

Staff: 14

Membership: 300 clerical

Publications:
> *Bell Tower,* bimonthly
> *Elim Circle,* monthly

Meetings:
> Annual Meeting of Members, Ministers' Seminar, Camp Meeting, Womens' Outreach Fellowship Convention — all held at Lima, New York
> 20 youth camps held at various locations

Former Name: Elim Missionary Assemblies

506. Encounter Ministries, Inc.

National Association of Evangelicals
Dr. Stephen F. Olford, Executive Director
Wheaton, Illinois 60187
(312) 690-7676

Encounter Ministries is a Christian organization dedicated to sharing the Good News of Jesus Christ. A registered, non-profit corporation, Encounter Ministries became part of the National Association of Evangelicals in 1979 to further the work of Christ's kingdom and to strengthen the local church. Basically, the outreach is represented through radio, television, cassettes, literature, preaching, and pastors' seminars.

Founding Date: 1960

Staff: 20 Board members; 6 staff members

Publications:
> *Encounter,* 5 times a year

Radio/TV Programs:
> A weekly half-hour radio program called *Encounter*
> A daily 5-minute radio program aired Monday-Friday called *Encounter with Truth*
> A half-hour weekly telecast called *Encounter* on cable TV systems

Meetings:
> Pastors' seminars in connection with the National Association of Evangelicals; location and number varies from year to year

Former Name: (1960) Encounter-TV

507. Episcopal Actors Guild of America, Inc.

Episcopal
Lon C. Clark, Executive Secretary
1 East 29th Street
New York, New York 10016
(212) 685-2927

The purpose of the Episcopal Actors Guild is the banding together of people of the theatre with the Church to promote social interchange and to provide for their general welfare, including help for the sick, needy, and indigent members of the theatrical profession of all religious faiths.

Founding Date: 1923

Staff: 560 lay; 40 clerical

508. The Episcopal Book Club (EBC)

Episcopal
Rev. H. L. Foland, DD
Hillspeak
Eureka Springs, Arkansas 72632
(501) 253-9701

The Episcopal Book Club operates in much the same manner as any other book club, with certain exceptions: it does not publish books, but acquires them in wholesale quantities from established publishers; and it issues only four books a year (bonus and dividend books are not offered because the profit is used to further the work of the club). Its books are selected on the basis of their literary value as well as their doctrinal content.

Founding Date: 1953

Membership: 4,000

Publications:
> *The Anglican Digest,* quarterly

509. The Episcopal Church, Appalachian Ministries

Protestant Episcopal Church
Mr. Woodrow Carter
815 Second Avenue
New York, New York 10017
(212) 867-8400

Appalachian Ministries is an agency of the Church in Society program of the Episcopal Church. It supports the Episcopal Dioceses in the Appalachian region in their efforts to work collaboratively with other denominations and community groups to meet the needs of exploited people in that area. Its programs include: training of church congregations for mission and ministry; support of grass roots community projects; development of new educational and communication programs; and special concern for youth groups.

510. The Episcopal Church, Board for Theological Education

Protestant Episcopal Church

Dr. Fredrica Thompsett
815 Second Avenue
New York, New York 10017
(212) 867-8400

The Board for Theological Education, an office of the Education for Ministry program of the Episcopal Church, has as its purpose to study the needs and trends of education for Holy Orders in the Episcopal Church; to assist and advise the seminaries and theological schools in the training of persons for Holy Orders; to develop criteria for the selection of future clergy; and to assist in the development of programs of lay theological education. The Board, which is aided by funding from other sources, administers grants in continuing education for clergy, and sponsors special consultations, programs, and studies.

511. The Episcopal Church, Church in Community

Protestant Episcopal Church

Mr. Howard Quander
815 Second Avenue
New York, New York 10017
(212) 867-8400

Church in Community, a part of the Church in Society program of the Episcopal Church, is divided into three programs: Housing Support is made available to those dioceses, parishes, and Church-related, non-profit housing corporations engaged in development and/or rehabilitation of housing. This support includes dissemination of housing information, development of national housing applications for federal funding, and advocacy of individual funding

applications; Urban Ministries provide conferences, training, and resources to strengthen parishes and dioceses in their work in the cities and better coordinate with ethnic, social mission, and evangelism programs; and New Forms Social Ministries assists dioceses and parishes to renew their witness to the Gospel as it relates to personal and social needs of their community, such as treatment for alcoholism and drug abuse, better health care, etc.

512. The Episcopal Church, Ethnic Ministry Programs

Protestant Episcopal Church

815 Second Avenue
New York, New York 10017
(212) 867-8400

The purpose of the Ethnic Ministry Programs, a part of the Church in Society program of the Episcopal Church, is to represent and serve as advocates for black, Hispanic, Indian, Eskimo, and Asian peoples on the national, diocesan, and local levels of the Church; and to provide input into the decision-making process, programmatic development, and the total life of the Episcopal Church.

513. The Episcopal Church, Evangelism

Protestant Episcopal Church

The Rev. A. Wayne Schwab
815 Second Avenue
New York, New York 10017
(212) 867-8400

The office of Evangelism is an agency of the Education for Ministry program of the Episcopal Church. It works through five regional evangelism coordinators to enable members of the Church to witness more effectively to Christ in their total life work. Each coordinator provides two full working weeks annually. There are also two meetings each year of the Task Force on Evangelism. A bimonthly *Evangelism Newsletter* and other resource materials are sent to 1,000 laity and clergy, who form a nationwide network to promote evangelism. Information and evaluation of all the various effective forms of evangelism is kept current. Each year pilot parish programs test new approaches to evangelism. Regular field reports are made of innovative programs. Cassettes and radio/television spots on evangelism are produced through the communication office and Church agencies such as the Episcopal Radio/Television Foundation in Atlanta. Two supplements are planned each year to "Resources for Evangelism and Renewal."

Publications:

Evangelism Newsletter, bimonthly

514. The Episcopal Church, Historical Society

Protestant Episcopal Church
The Rt. Rev. Scott Field Bailey, President
606 Rathervue Place
Austin, Texas 78705

Mailing Address
Post Office Box 2247
Austin, Texas 78768
(512) 472-6816

The Historical Society of the Episcopal Church is charged with the preservation of the archives and records of the Episcopal Church and as historiographer is responsible for the promotion of historical studies in Episcopal Church history. It publishes a quarterly journal and, working in conjunction with diocesan archivists, seeks to encourage church historical interest among members of the denomination.

Founding Date: 1910
Membership: 1,248
Publications:

The Historical Magazine of the Protestant Episcopal Church, quarterly

Former Name: (1975) Church Historical Society

515. The Episcopal Church, Lay Ministry

Protestant Episcopal Church
Mr. Barry Menuez
815 Second Avenue
New York, New York 10017
(212) 867-8400

The purpose of the office of Lay Ministry, an agency of the Education for Ministry program of the Episcopal Church, is to work for the renewal of lay involvement and leadership. It supports the development of lay ministries, especially at the parish and diocesan level, and gives emphasis to lay theological educa-

tion. The office is assisted by a regional network of lay assemblies. Resource materials such as "The 99 Percenter" are sponsored. Limited funds are provided for the development and evaluation of experimental programs. Assistance is given to the career development and placement of lay professional workers. The staff administers the United Thanks Offering Scholarship Funds for graduate study for women, and provides services for the triennial meeting of the women of the Church, Episcopal Church Women and their diocesan and provincial boards, and the Task Force on Women.

516. The Episcopal Church, Ministry in Higher Education

Protestant Episcopal Church
The Rev. James J. McNamee
815 Second Avenue
New York, New York 10017
(212) 867-8400

Ministry in Higher Education is a support network for university chaplains, faculty, administration, and students in the Episcopal Church. It sponsors continuing education, conferences, and retreats. The Ministry in Higher Education also seeks to help start new ministries and support other educational ministries. Its programs are: Youth Work, with an emphasis on developing effective adult leadership of youth programs on local and regional levels; providing various resources to support youth ministry; developing youth teams in two or three dioceses as a model which might be followed nationally; supporting selected summer projects for young people both in the United States and overseas; and developing new forms of ministry for young people ages 18-25, especially those who are not attending college; Higher Education, with an emphasis on strengthening the lay ministry by the further involvement of students and faculty; strengthening the ordained ministry, especially through college chaplains and clergy of college-related congregations; strengthening the support structures in higher education through the support of key ecumenical boards and diocesan boards with responsibility for college work; and creating an awareness of the Gospel imperatives at this level about such problems as hunger.

Membership: 1,200
Publications:

Connexion
Plumbline
Higher Education News

Meetings:
16 regional meetings
1 national annual meeting

517. The Episcopal Church, The Office of the Presiding Bishop's Suffragen for the Armed Forces

Protestant Episcopal Church

The Rt. Rev. Charles L. Burgreen Bishop for the Armed Forces
Episcopal Church Center
815 Second Avenue
New York, New York 10017
(212) 867-8400

The Office of The Presiding Bishop's Suffragen for the Armed Forces is an agency of the Education for Ministry program of the Episcopal Church. It serves as the endorsing agent for the Armed Forces, the Veterans Administration, and the Federal Bureau of Prisons. It provides pastoral care for the Episcopal Chaplains on Active Duty and, to a lesser extent, to Reserve Chaplains. It coordinates with the various Diocesan Armed Forces Committee to insure liaison with and pastoral care for Episcopal Church Members serving in the military services. It operates a training program for and licensing of lay readers. It conducts a series of professional development seminars and conferences to provide continuing education for clergy and lay people. It serves as an advisory office for other forms of institutional chaplaincies in the Episcopal Church.

Publications:
The Episcopal Chaplain, quarterly
Devotional Guide and *Intercession Prayer List,* quarterly

Meetings:
4 major meetings per year in: Washington, DC, Santa Barbara, California, Tokyo, Japan, and Berchtesgaden, Germany

518. The Episcopal Church, Religious Education

Protestant Episcopal Church

The Rev. David Perry, Coordinator
815 Second Avenue
New York, New York 10017
(212) 867-8400

Religious Education, an office of the Education for Ministry program of the Episcopal Church, exists to assist provinces, dioceses, and congregations in developing educational ministries which will enable the Christian community to grow in the quality of its life and witness to Jesus Christ. There are two major program goals: to develop educational leadership at all levels of Church life, and to provide programs, services, and resources for congregational use. Special attention is given to the development of new models of religious education for adults. Emphasis is given to the development of processes and resources to help individuals and groups reach an informed awareness of the implications of Christian faith in contemporary society. Ongoing consultations are held on Adult Education and on the study of Christian education in the seminaries.

519. The Episcopal Church, Social and Economic Justice

Protestant Episcopal Church

The Rev. Everett Francis
815 Second Avenue
New York, New York 10017
(212) 867-8400

Social and Economic Justice is a part of the Church in Society program of the Episcopal Church. Its four programs are: Criminal Justice—support for groups working for prison reform, a new approach to juvenile justice and model projects; Social Responsibility in Investments—support for the continuing involvement of the Church as a socially responsible institutional investor. Most funds for this purpose support inter-faith projects doing research and analysis and distributing proxy materials; Hunger Program—support for the growing concern of the Church in underlying causes of the hunger crisis. Over the past two years, provincial and diocesan committees have been developing educational programs and encouraging private and governmental efforts to deal with this crisis on a long-term basis. A Hunger Task Force consisting of three or four provincial presidents and representation from all nine provinces, is charged with general oversight of this work; Interfaith Coalitions—support for national organizations furthering the programs or policy concerns of this Church. Some of these groups, such as IMPACT, are ecumenical or inter-faith, others, such as the Leadership Conference on Civil Rights, and American Committee on Africa, are broad based coalitions.

520. The Episcopal Church, Specialized Ministries

Protestant Episcopal Church
Mr. Woodrow Carter
815 Second Avenue
New York, New York 10017
(212) 867-8400

Specialized Ministries is an agency of the Church in Society program of the Episcopal Church. It provides support for programs for people with special needs, the aging, the blind, and the deaf. This work is done through agencies such as the Episcopal Society for the Ministry to the Aging, the Episcopal Guild for the Blind, and the Episcopal Conference for the Deaf.

521. The Episcopal Church, Youth and Young Adult Ministries

Protestant Episcopal Church
Ms. Elizabeth L. Crawford, Coordinator
815 Second Avenue
New York, New York 10017
(212) 867-8400

The Youth and Young Adult Ministries Office, part of the Education for Mission and Ministry program of the Episcopal Church, coordinates Youth (junior/senior high school) and Young Adult (18-35) Ministries throughout the Episcopal Church. Its programs are: the National Youth Ministry Leadership Network for training and resourcing diocesan leaders in Junior and Senior High Ministries; administration of the Episcopal God and Country Program of the Boy Scouts of America; administration of the National Episcopal Register for Conscientious Objectors; Episcopal Young Adult Ministries Network which sponsors seminary internships in Young Adult Ministries, Young Adult Ministries Leadership Seminars, Regional Young Adult Conferences, and the newsletter *Sound the Call;* cooperative programming with other Christian Churches in Youth and Young Adult Ministries, e.g., Young Christians for Global Justice, Joint Educational Development (JED) Youth Staff Team, International Christian Youth Exchange (ICYE), and National Council of Churches (NCC) Young Adult Ministry Project.

Publications:
Sound the Call, quarterly
Meetings:
Varies annually

522. Episcopal Commission for Black Ministries

Protestant Episcopal Church
Rev. Franklin D. Turner, Staff Officer
815 Second Avenue
New York, New York 10017
(212) 867-8400

The Episcopal Commission for Black Ministries was created: to work with black Episcopalians and various other black groups in the church, such as the Union of Black Episcopalians, Absalom Jones Theological Institute, Organization of Black Seminarians, and the black colleges; to make the church more responsive to the needs of its black communicants; to assist black Episcopalians in their efforts for self-determination and development as an effective voice in the larger church; and to enable black Episcopalians to contribute to the entire church their valuable and unique gifts.

Founding Date: 1973

523. Episcopal Conference of the Deaf (ECD)

Protestant Episcopal Church
Rev. Arthur Steidemann, Executive Secretary
429 Somerset Avenue
St. Louis, Missouri 63119
(314) 961-1805

The Episcopal Conference of the Deaf is the Episcopal Church's officially recognized organization of church workers and church members. It acts as a central clearing house for all aspects of Christian work among the deaf. It encourages the establishment of missions; promotes recruitment, placement, and training of qualified workers; and assists in the expansion, growth, and perpetuation of these objectives, via seed-money grants, consultant services, and coordination of efforts. National in scope, the ECD seeks to serve those in deaf ministry on a National, Diocesan, and Parochial level.

Founding Date: 1880
Membership: 825 lay; 27 clerical
Publications:
The Deaf Episcopalian, bimonthly
The ECD Times, quarterly
The Language of Signs (sign language instruction book)
The Church's Ministry with Deaf People and Their Families (information brochure)

The Language of Signs (8mm instructional films)
The ECD Hymnal (hymnal with hymns translated into language for ease in signing)

Meetings:
Annual convention (location varies from year to year)
Board of Directors meetings (3 per year)
Clergy Conference (annually)
Occasional workshops

Former Name:
Conference of Church Workers Among the Deaf

524. Episcopal Guild for the Blind

Episcopal
Rev. Harry J. Sutcliffe, DD
157 Montague Street
Brooklyn, New York 11201
(212) 625-4886

The Episcopal Guild for the Blind provides the teaching and devotional literature of the Church to visually impaired and sightless persons through Braille, large type, and cassette recordings. The Guild maintains a small cassette reader service through which clients and readers are brought together on the basis of similar interests, and cassettes circulate back and forth containing the material the client desires to be read. The Guild provides pastoral and casework counseling to blind persons, their families, and friends to assist them in coping with the many and varied problems related to blindness. The Guild acts as an information center to provide relevant information regarding matters pertinent to blindness, such as appropriate resources and facilities (private and public); and assists blind persons, their families, and friends, when requested, in making application to the appropriate facility. Where expedient and necessary, the Guild acts as liaison and interpreter between client and a given agency to assist in the on going rehabilitation process.

Founding Date: 1959
Staff: 2 part-time

525. Episcopal Peace Fellowship (EFP)

Episcopal
John Gesell, Chairperson
Room 252, Hearst Hall
Wisconsin and Woodley, N.W.
Washington, D.C. 20016
(202) 363-5532

The Episcopal Peace Fellowship maintains a couseling program for veterans, those concerned about the draft, and those in current military service. It seeks to awaken the Episcopal Church and all people to the need to work actively for peace and justice and towards that end sends out a newsletter, arranges the sharing of peace and justice concerns, materials, etc., and makes available to local congregations program ideas and materials. It also works cooperatively with other peace organizations.

Founding Date: 1939

Staff: 1

Membership: 2,500 lay; 500 clerical

Publications:
1 newsletter
Occasional special papers

Former Name: Episcopal Pacifist Fellowship

526. Episcopal Radio-TV Foundation, Inc.

Protestant Episcopal Church
Dr. Caroline Rakestraw, Executive Director
3379 Peachtree Road, N.E.
Atlanta, Georgia 30326
(404) 233-5419

The Episcopal Radio-TV Foundation's mission is two-pronged: to produce, distribute, and promote radio and TV programs designed for the mass audience; and to produce, distribute, and promote audio cassettes designed for personal in-home and group in-church use. In television the Foundation is best known for the television program *The Lion, the Witch and the Wardrobe,* which was shown on the CBS network and which won an Emmy and a Chris Award. In radio, the Foundation is identified with the annual Episcopal Series of the Protestant Hour, now in its 35th year.

Founding Date: 1954
Staff: 3
Membership:
35 members of the Board of Trustees (bishops, priests, and lay persons elected from across the country)
Publications:
Newsletter, approximately 4 times a year
Meetings:
Occasional meetings

527. European Evangelistic Society (EES)

Christian Church/Disciples of Christ
W. L. Thompson, Executive Director
Post Office Box 268
Aurora, Illinois 60507
(312) 896-4333

The purpose of the European Evangelistic Society is to investigate Christian origins in order to understand how the Gospel produced the Church, what form or forms the Church (in earliest times) assumed, and what its essential nature was. This research is undertaken at the Institute for the Study of Christian Origins in Tuebingen, Germany, and functions alongside the theological faculties of that university. The Society also fosters the generation and maturing of Christian communities, rising out of and sustained by the Gospel.

Staff: 2 in the United States; 6 overseas

Membership:
30 members who make up the Society's directors

Publications:
European Evangelist, bimonthly

528. The Evangelical Alliance Mission (TEAM)

Protestant
Rev. Richard Winchell, General Director
Post Office Box 969
Wheaton, Illinois 60187
(312) 653-5300

The purpose of The Evangelical Alliance Mission is to preach the Gospel of Jesus Christ and establish churches which are evangelical and fundamental in doctrine in 24 world areas. Those areas include the following: Austria, Chad, Colombia, France, Italy, Irian Jaya, Japan, Korea, Netherlands Antilles, North India, Pakistan, Peru, Portugal, South Africa, Southeastern Europe, Spain, Sri Lanka, Taiwan, Trinidad, United Arab Emirates, Venezuela, West Indonesia, Western India, and Zimbabwe. Evangelism and church development are furthered through preaching, Bible classes, visitation, medical ministries, radio, films, camps, children's activities, student work, literature, primary and secondary schools, Bible institutes, Bible colleges, seminaries, and theological education by extension.

Founding Date: 1890

Staff: 75

Membership: 996 active missionaries

Publications:
Horizons, official organ, 6 times a year
Wherever, magazine for young adults, 3 times a year
11 magazines published overseas
Books

Radio/TV Programs:
3 radio stations
5 recording studios
552 broadcast hours per week

Meetings:
Many each year in various locations in North America
198 overseas conferences

529. Evangelical and Reformed Historical Society

United Church of Christ
Dr. Herbert B. Anstaett, Executiuve Secretary
Lancaster Theological Seminary
555 West James Street
Lancaster, Pennsylvania 17603
(717) 393-0654

Most of the work of the Evangelical and Reformed Historical Society is archival; preserving records of the German Reformed Church (later known as the Reformed Church in the United States), the Evangelical Synod of North America, the Evangelical and Reformed Church, and the United Church of Christ. It possesses a large manuscript collection of colonial and 19th century German Reformed pastors, as well as many church records maintained by the pastors and congregations. The Society's archives, which are made available to researchers, are located at the Lancaster Theological Seminary in Pennsylvania and at the Eden Theological Seminary in St. Louis. The Society holds annual meetings at which historical papers are read.

Founding Date: 1863

Membership: 1,400

Publications:
News from the Evangelical and Reformed Historical Society, 3 times a year
Occasional pamphlets of historical interest

Meetings:
1 annual meeting

Former Name
(1965) Historical Society of the Evangelical and Reformed Church

530. Evangelical Baptist Missions, Inc.

Baptist

David L. Marshall, General Director
426 South U.S. Highway 31
Kokomo, Indiana 46901

Mailing Address
Post Office Box 2225
Kokomo, Indiana 46901
Cable: Mission Kokomo
(317) 453-4488

The purpose of the Evangelical Baptist Missions is to take part in the evangelizing of the world in fulfillment of the Great Commission. The Mission serves independent Baptist churches in sending out missionaries to preach the Gospel, and assists churches and individuals in supporting missionaries and mission work. It provides a home base which is cognizant of laws and regulations governing missionary activities at home and abroad. It also stimulates missionary interest in churches and schools and renders assistance to missionaries and churches in every possible way, consistent with Biblical principles. The Mission's aims are: evangelization of all nations; baptizing believers; training believers in the Word of God; and establishing indigenous Baptist Churches.

Founding Date: 1929

Staff: 7

Membership:
130 missionaries in 13 countries
25 Board members

Publications:
The Evangelical Baptist, quarterly

Radio/TV Programs:
Evangelistic radio programming in Niger
Films in the language of people overseas and geared to their culture

Former Names:
(1946) Africa Christian Mission
(1957) Christian Missions, Inc.

531. The Evangelical Covenant Church of America, Board of Christian Education

The Evangelical Covenant Church

Rev. David S. Noreen, Executive Secretary
5101 North Francisco Avenue
Chicago, Illinois 60625
(312) 784-3000

The Board of Christian Education serves as the coordinating agency for the educational ministry of the Evangelical Covenant Church of America. It is organized under three management groups: Field Services, Educational Planning and Special Events, Resources and Publications. Within these divisions a network of field consultants serve the churches; a variety of national workships are scheduled each year speaking to the needs of all age levels; a national resource center is maintained in Chicago, and several publications seek to give help to the local church in its programs.

Publications:
Update, a Christian education newsletter
Christian Education Resources, study books

Radio/TV Programs:
Affiliated with Covenant Press Video, Communication Division of The Evangelical Covenant Church of America

Meetings:
Approximately 20 per year

532. The Evangelical Covenant Church of America, Board of World Mission

The Evangelical Covenant Church of America

Rev. Raymond L. Dahlberg, Executive Secretary
5101 North Francisco Avenue
Chicago, Illinois 60625
(312) 784-3000

The Evangelical Covenant Church of America, through its Department of World Mission, conducts missionary work in seven countries: Zaire, Japan, Taiwan, Thailand, Colombia, Ecuador, and Mexico. The missionaries work closely with local and national churches in their evangelistic and church planting ministries. An extensive educational and medical work has developed along with the evangelism outreach. Christian education, both elementary and secondary, as well as Bible school and seminary work, is an integral part of the work on almost every field.

Founding Date: 1885

Publications:
Praise the Lord, a missionary newsletter

Meetings:
15-20 per year

Former Name:
(1885) Swedish Evangelical Mission Covenant Church
Evangelical Mission Covenant Church

533. Evangelical Foreign Mission Association (EFMA)

Interdenominational
Dr. Wade T. Coggins, Executive Director
1430 K Street, N.W.
Washington, D.C. 20005
(202) 628-7911

The Evangelical Foreign Mission Association operates as a voluntary association of denominational and nondenominational foreign mission agencies. The membership is composed of 80 agencies, with more than 9,000 missionaries serving in approximately 130 mission fields. The Association provides its members with opportunities for spiritual fellowship and mutual encouragement through conferences, consultations, conventions, and retreats. It operates a travel agency, Universal Travel Service, which serves the general public, but specializes in travel arrangements for missionaries and other Christians. EFMA serves its members in many practical areas, such as passport and visa service, counseling on tax matters, providing the basis for a financial advisory service on world monetary conditions, and other related services.

Founding Date: 1945

Staff: 6

Membership: 80 organizations

Meetings:
2 per year

534. Evangelical Free Church of America, Church Ministries Department

Evangelical Free Church of America
Rev. R. Dean Smith, Executive Director
1515 East 66th Street
Minneapolis, Minnesota 55423
(612) 866-3343

The Church Ministries Department is an administrative and service department of the Evangelical Free Church of America. The Department is accountable to the Church Ministries Board which is elected by the delegates to the Annual National Conference of the Denomination. The Board is divided into six commissions which reflect the concerns and responsibilities of the Department. These are: Christian Education, Youth, Church Growth, Discipleship, Church Planting/Evangelism, Urban Ministries, and Camping.

Publications:
Connect, a newsletter for Christian education directors
The Planter, a newsletter for church planters
The Evangel, an evangelism newsletter
The Urban Forum Quarterly

535. Evangelical Free Church of America, Communication Department

Evangelical Free Church of America
Edwin L. Groenhoff, Executive Director of Communication
1515 East 66th Street
Minneapolis, Minnesota 55423
(612) 866-3343

The Department of Communication of the Evangelical Free Church of America is the printing, publishing, and distributing arm of the denomination. Through its press, it seeks to print and publish books, brochures, and magazines which promote the Christian message. Through its related bookstores, it seeks to distribute Christian literature to the denomination as well as the larger Christian community.

Founding Date: 1958

Staff: 30

Publications:
The Evangelical Beacon, semimonthly

536. Evangelical Free Church of America, Overseas Mission Department

Evangelical Free Church of America
Robert C. Dillon, Executive Director of Overseas Missions
1515 East 66th Street
Minneapolis, Minnesota 55423
(612) 866-3343

The Overseas Mission Department of the Evangelical Free Church of America is a religious and philanthropic organization with the primary goal of planting and nurturing churches in the 10 areas of the world where its missionaries are working. Reaching people with an evangelical Christian message of salvation is a basis for the above goal. The geographical areas of activity are Zaire, Venezuela, Hong Kong, Japan, Philippines, Malaysia, Singapore, Germany, Peru, and Belgium. Medical ministries including a

65-bed hospital in Hong Kong, a 165-bed hospital and numerous dispensaries in Zaire, educational institutions, orphanages, and numerous other projects of help and self help assistance. An annual budget of $3,500,000 is contributed by its North American constituency numbering 80,000 members.

Founding Date: 1887

Staff: 9 home staff; 209 overseas staff

Membership: 80,000

Publications:
> *The Evangelical Beacon,* a denominational periodical

Radio/TV Programs:
> Radio and TV programs of an evangelistic nature produced in Venezuela, Japan, and the Philippines; frequency varies from daily to once weekly

Meetings:
> Conferences, meetings, and retreats conducted on all the fields of activity

537. The Evangelical Free Church of America, Stewardship Department

Evangelical Free Church of America
Rev. Darrel D. Stark, Director of Stewardship
1515 East 66th Street
Minneapolis, Minnesota 55423
(612) 866-3343

The Stewardship Department of The Evangelical Free Church of America has a ministry in assisting congregations and individuals in the matters of wills, investments, and various other areas of estate planning, while at the same time seeking to promote a spiritual approach to the Christian's stewardship of all that he is and has.

Founding Date: 1966

Staff: 6

538. Evangelical Friends Church, Eastern Region, Friends Foreign Missionary Society

Evangelical Friends Church
Charles Robinson, President
1201 30th Street, N.W.
Canton, Ohio 44709
(216) 493-1660

The Friends Foreign Missionary Society has the following purpose: to make the Lord Jesus Christ known to all men as their divine Savior, to persuade them to become His disciples, and to gather those disciples into the Christian churches which shall, under God, be self-propagating, self-supporting, and self-governing. The Society seeks to realize this aim through a ministry of preaching, teaching, and healing. The Society works with national Christians in the fields in which it serves to evangelize and gather into groups for fellowship and Christian growth. It also works in the medical field, through the Christian Hospital in central India and clinics held in surrounding villages. It works in education through primary schools and cooperates with other missions in the Union Biblical Seminary in India. The Society serves in India, Taiwan, the Philippines, and Hong Kong. It also serves with four other Friends groups (organized in the Evangelical Friends Mission) in Mexico City.

Founding Date: 1884

Staff: 13

Membership: 8,532

Publications:
> *Missionary News & Prayer Requests,* monthly

Meetings:
> Friends Men In Mission annual meeting
> Women's Retreat annual meeting
> Yearly Meeting of the denomination, location varies

Former Name: Ohio Yearly Meeting of Friends

539. Evangelical Ministries, Inc.

Interdenominational
William J. Peterson, Executive Director
1716 Spruce Street
Philadelphia, Pennsylvania 19103
(215) 546-3696

Founded by the late Dr. Donald Grey Barnhouse, Evangelical Ministries, Inc., uses the mass media to communicate God's Word to modern man. The agency seeks to teach God's Word, to help people apply it to the issues of the day, and to help them incorporate it in their work and witness in the church and in the world. Through radio, the Evangelical Ministries stress systematic Bible teaching; this is also done by means of Bible Studies Magazine and by the Bible Studies cassette ministry. Through literature, the agency stresses the application and incorporation of God's Word to life and practice.

Founding Date: 1949

Staff: 20

Publications:

Eternity, monthly
Youth Letter, monthly
Bible Newsletter, monthly
Bible Studies, monthly
Evangelical Newsletter, biweekly

Radio/TV Programs:

The Bible Study Hour
Dr. Barnhouse and the Bible

540. Evangelical Missions Information Service (EMIS)

Interdenominational

Dr. Vergil Gerber, Executive Director
Post Office Box 794
Wheaton, Illinois 60187
(312) 653-2158

Evangelical Missions Information Service (EMIS) is a missions information arm of the Evangelical Foreign Missions Association (EFMA) and the Interdenominational Foreign Mission Association (IFMA), representing 130 theologically conservative mission agencies with more than 19,000 missionaries around the world. Its purpose is to provide succinct, well-packaged, relevant information on the global mission scene to mission executives, missionaries, mission professors, missions-minded pastors, mission-concerned laymen, church and school libraries, and overseas church leaders. It does this through publications, conferences, and consultations in North America, and church growth workshops overseas.

Founding Date: 1964

Membership: 130 agencies; 19,000 missionaries

Publications:

Missionary News Service, bimonthly
Evangelical Missions Quarterly; Africa, Asia, Europe, Latin America, Muslim World, Chinese World
Pulses, EMISsary, issued periodically as information becomes available on trends, developments, etc. in missions in these areas

Meetings:

Church Growth Workshops, 8-10 per year

541. Evangelical Press Association (EPA)

Evangelical

Gary Warner, Executive Secretary
Post Office Box 4550
Overland Park, Kansas 66204
(913) 381-2017

Evangelical Press Association seeks to promote the cause of evangelical Christianity and to enhance the influence of Christian journalism by: providing Christian fellowship among members of the Association; rendering practical assistance; stimulating mutual helpfulness among members; encouraging high ethical and technical standards in the field of Christian journalism; and suggesting concerted and timely emphasis on important issues. EPA publishes a weekly news service which is circulated internationally among editors, news broadcasters, pastors, teachers, writers and others in need of up-to-date, accurate news coverage of religious and moral activities. It is issued on a subscription basis — even to members — at rates which vary according to usage. Free copies and subscription information are sent upon request.

Staff: 2

Membership:

25 individual members

Publications:

About 250 publications

Meetings:

Annual convention/membership meeting each May

542. Evangelical Teacher Training Association (ETTA)

Interdenominational

Paul E. Loth, EdD, President
110 Bridge Street
Wheaton, Illinois 60187

Mailing Address

Post Office Box 327
Wheaton, Illinois 60187
(312) 668-6400

The Evangelical Teacher Training Association was organized by representatives from five Christian educational institutions who were convinced of the need for an association of Christian schools of higher education. One hundred ninety-five seminaries, colleges, and Bible institutes now comprise its membership. The Association, a not-for-profit organization, encourages cooperation among evangelical Christian educational institutions; it is deeply concerned with the advancement of every phase of Christian education; develops and distributes leadership training courses used in educational institutions and local churches; and encourages the use of textbooks of approved orthodoxy. Over 54,000 college and seminary graduates have been awarded ETTA diplomas and almost two million persons have studied ETTA courses. Twenty-five denominations use the courses as their official leadership training programs, and churches of over 30 other denominations use the courses to train their leadership. Courses are translated into eight languages and are being taught by missionaries in various parts of the world.

Founding Date: 1930

Staff: 10

Membership: 200

Publications:
    Leadership training textbooks (14 titles)
    Instructor's guides (14)
    Self-study books (3)
    Teacher Training Profile, quarterly

Meetings:
    Biennial Corporation Meeting
    Quarterly Board Meetings

543. Evangelical Theological Society (ETS)

Nondenominational

Dr. Simon J. Kistemaker
National Secretary-Treasurer
5422 Clinton Boulevard
Jackson, Mississippi 39209
(601) 924-5910

The purpose of the Evangelical Theological Society is to foster conservative Biblical scholarship by providing a medium for the oral exchange and written expression of thought and research in the general field of the theological disciplines as centered in the Scriptures. Membership in the Society is on an individual rather than an institutional basis. Every member must subscribe in writing annually to the Doctrinal Basis. The ThM degree or its theological equivalent is ordinarily required for membership in the Society. In exceptional instances men may be eligible for membership who lack the ThM degree or its theological equivalent, provided that they have made significant contributions in the realm of theology. The Society holds national meetings each year. Other meetings, including those of a regional nature, are held as desired with the concurrence of the executive committee.

Founding Date: 1949

Membership:
    1,403 members plus
    539 who subscribe to the *Journal* only

Publications:
    Journal of the Evangelical Theological Society,
        quarterly
    Some monographs

Meetings:
    1 national meeting at various locations each year
    7 regional meetings: Eastern, South Eastern, North Western, Mid-Western, South Western, Far West, and Canada

544. Evangelicals Concerned, Inc. (EC)

Evangelical

Dr. Ralph Blair, President
30 East 60th Street, Suite 803
New York, New York 10022
(212) 688-0628

Evangelicals Concerned is a national ministry of both homosexual and heterosexual evangelicals dedicated to helping homosexuals and their families and churches better understand homosexuality and to providing support for Christian growth and discipleship among homosexual Christians.

Founding Date: 1976

Membership:
    There is no official membership in national organization, local chapters have membership

Publications:
    Record, a quarterly newsletter
    Review, a quarterly book review

Meetings:
    At various times and locations

545. **Evangelism Center International (ECI)**

Interdenominational
L. Joe Bass, President/Founder
5189 Verdugo Way
Camarillo, California 93010
(805) 987-7881

Evangelism Center International has a four-dimensional work which is administered through its four divisions: Underground Evangelism, International Christian Aid, United Evangelism to the Chinese, and East/West News Service. Each division works to meet the needs of Christians and refugees repressed by communist-controlled regimes. Human needs in other unique situations throughout the world also receive assistance through ECI ministries. Underground Evangelism is the parent division—it began as a mission to communist lands. Bibles, Christian literature, ministry supplies, and assistance for the families of imprisoned Christians are provided to national workers inside the various countries. These workers then distribute the items within their country. International Christian Aid meets refugees as they flee areas of communist insurgence. Camps exist in Pakistan, Somalia, Portugal, Thailand, the Philippines, and Uganda. Food, clothing, medical aid, religious materials, and other needed assistance are provided. United Evangelism to the Chinese works with Chinese house churches to supply needed Bible and Christian literature on the Mainland. Other needs of the various churches are also met as they develop. East/West News Service collects information and data about religious rights and the church in communist-controlled areas of the world. EWNS then disseminates this information to the media, churches, and human rights groups.

Founding Date: 1960
Staff: 1,612 worldwide
Membership: 22 offices
Publications:
   Underground Evangelism Magazine, monthly in
     7 languages
   ICA News, bimonthly
   Target China, monthly
   East/West News Service, biweekly
Radio/TV Programs:
   More than 4,000 quarter-hours from stations in
     Europe and Asia in Ukrainian, Russian,
     Romanian, Bulgarian, German, Spanish,
     Vietnamese, and Hungarian

   UE has produced two television specials
   ICA six specials aired in the United States
Meetings:
   National meetings in 15 countries annually
   National conventions
Former Name: Underground Evangelism

546. **Evangelism Explosion III International (EE III)**

Interdenominational
Dr. D. James Kennedy, President and Founder
560 East McNab Road
Pompano Beach, Florida 33060
Mailing Address
Post Office Box 23820
Fort Lauderdale, Florida 33307
(305) 781-7710

Evangelism Explosion III International seeks to obey the Great Commission of Jesus Christ by enabling pastors to become even more effective in equipping laymen to equip other laymen in a continuing process of personal evangelism. This is accomplished in 17-week cycles of discipleship training in the local church. Each week's classroom lecture is followed by on-the-job training. The Gospel is presented in a clear, concise manner based on a five-point outline designed for consistency. Now effectively used in thousands of churches of all the major denominations across the United States and many other nations, this ministry grew out of Coral Ridge Presbyterian Church in Fort Lauderdale, Florida, where it has been continually practiced for almost 20 years. Six-day leadership training clinics are held in model churches which are healthy, growing churches with a generally well-balanced ministry and an effective Evangelism Explosion ministry so that pastors and key laymen can see the total impact of EE III in perspective. They are then encouraged to develop this discipleship training in their own church and relate through a process of certification to the international ministry. Laymen are discipled through a process of leadership training to be teachers in the local church and, in some cases, to assist as clinic teachers. Missionary trainers may participate in leadership clinics in all parts of the United States and countries around the world.

Staff:
   24 full-time staff members

14 part-time teaching staff (pastors of local churches)

Membership:

Thousands of pastors carry on the EE III ministry in their own churches

Publications:

EE III International Update, monthly

Radio/TV Programs:

A 6-8 minute segment included in Coral Ridge Ministries TV program, broadcast weekly over 15 UHF or VHF stations

5 cable stations

2 cable networks

Meetings:

Numerous 6-day leadership clinics conducted in local churches of various denominations across the United States and around the world

547. Evangelism to Communist Lands (ECL)

Nondenominational

Paul Popov, International President
Post Office Box 303
Glendale, California 91209
(213) 956-7500 or (800) 423-DOOR

Evangelism to Communist Lands focuses on the problems of people, particularly Christians, who face oppression and/or persecution for their religious beliefs or practices. Their main historic thrust has been printing and distributing Bibles and Christian Literature for Christians behind the Iron Curtain. A subsidiary, Christian Rescue Committee, has worked on more immediate humanitarian problems in countries such as Pakistan, El Salvador, and Poland. Another subsidiary, Door of Hope International, monitors human rights activities in communist lands and helps keep the American public informed.

Founding Date: 1972

Staff: 35

Publications:

Door Of Hope, monthly

Radio/TV Programs:

Let Our People Go

548. Evangelistic Faith Missions

Nondenominational

Dr. Victor Glenn, Director
Post Office Box 609
Bedford, Indiana 47421
(812) 275-7531

Evangelistic Faith Missions has representatives in nine foreign countries, as well as in Alaska and among the American Indians in Arizona. The organization operates Bible Schools for training national ministers in four countries; it does medical work in Honduras, is working among the Eritrean refugees in Sudan, and runs an orphanage and elementary and high schools in Ethiopia. The Missions' primary purpose is to win the lost to Christ, and it is using every method possible to reach that goal. As a result, the Missions' work is educational, medical, and above all spiritual. A Church magazine is published on each mission field with correspondence courses offered in Korea and Central America. Books are published in Arabic, Korean, and Spanish.

Founding Date: 1905

Membership:

32 missionaries on the field, on furlough, and under appointment

Publications:

Missionary Herald

Radio/TV Programs:

Dr. Victor Glenn, the Director of the Mission, has radio broadcasts on 50 radio stations in America and 7 overseas stations

There are radio ministries in 5 foreign countries

Meetings:

Conferences conducted on various mission fields

549. Evangelization Society

Nondenominational

Ralph T. Kemper, General Director
RD #1, Post Office Box 391
Gibsonia, Pennsylvania 15044
(412) 935-1304

The Evangelization Society began its missionary work in Central Africa among cannibalistic tribes in the Belgian Congo, now the Republic of Zaire. The Society began by forming an alphabet and teaching a language. Schools and churches were formed and spread into a large area. Today there are over 200 churches and many schools in the Society. Its headquarters are at Shabunda, Kivu Province.

Founding Date: 1922

Publications:

Newsletter, occasionally

550. "Evangelize China" Fellowship, Inc. (ECF)

Nondenominational

Dr. Paul C. C. Szeto, General Director
490 East Walnut Street, #14
Pasadena, California 91101
(213) 793-0153

"Evangelize China" Fellowship, Inc., was founded by Dr. Andrew Gib in Shanghai, China. ECF is an indigenous missionary society, training people from the local area to win their own people to the Lord Jesus Christ. Since 1949, it has been extended to many countries in Southeast Asia, spreading the Gospel among Chinese and other nationals in Taiwan, Hong Kong, Macau, Thailand, Singapore, Malasia and Indonesia, as well as the Chinese who settled in Canada and America. ECF has founded 50 churches and mission centers, two Bible colleges, a score of Christian schools and two orphanages. The ECF Council of Reference includes Billy Graham, Dick Hillis, Barry Moore, David Morken, Alan Redpath, Paul Rees, Oswald Smith, and J. Edwin Orr, as Chairman. ECF has representatives in Canada, New Zealand, Australia, British Isles, South Africa, West Germany, and Switzerland. The International Headquarters are in Pasadena.

Founding Date: 1947

Staff: 200

Publications:

Evangelize China Fellowship News, quarterly

Radio/TV Programs:

Sponsor radio programs for children in China

Meetings:

Help churches conduct evangelistic meetings, Church Growth Seminars and Workshops, Youth Conferences

551. The Evergreen Conference, Inc.

Protestant Episcopal Church in the United States

Dr. Thomas Matthews, President
Post Office Box 366
Evergreen, Colorado 80439
(303) 674-3525

The Evergreen Conference has been lending its property to summer conferences in the fields of Church Music and Religious Education every year since about 1922. During the winter months, some of its facilities are occupied by a Montessori School. The Conference also makes its facilities available to other denominational groups on a rental basis when not in use by its own programs. Financial support comes from fees charged and from generous contributions on the part of the constituency.

Publications:

The Needle, periodically

552. Ewing W. Mays Mission for the Handicapped

Nondenominational

Ewing W. Mays, President
Post Office Drawer 821
Heber Springs, Arkansas 72543
(501) 362-3183

The purpose of the Ewing W. Mays Mission is to provide spiritual and physical guidance to individuals both handicapped and non-handicapped. This is accomplished through a hospital tours visitation program, scholarships for needy individuals, and employment opportunities for the handicapped. The Mission presently employs sixteen handicapped individuals in the graphic arts field. It is recognized by both the Veterans Administration and the State of Arkansas Department of Human Services as a qualified vocational education center. Through these programs handicapped individuals became gainfully employed and productive members of the society.

Membership: About 200,000 supporters

Publications:

A quarterly newsletter

553. Ex-Mormons for Jesus Ministries

Nondenominational

Mrs. Melaine N. Layton, Co-Director
Post Office Box 312
Wheeling, Illinois 60090
(312) 541-1598

Ex-Mormons for Jesus is a fellowship of Born-Again Christians, most of whom are former Mormons. The fellowship began with three members, but is growing rapidly in numbers and ministry throughout the United States and abroad. The fellowship's purposes are: to evangelize Mormons; to provide opportunities for teaching and fellowship for those who have been freed from Mormonism through the acceptance of Jesus Christ as their Lord and Savior; and to educate other Christians about the doctrines of Mormonism, most of which are in diametric opposition to God's Written Word, the Bible, and God's Living Word, The Lord Jesus Christ.

Founding Date: 1976

Publications:

Books, tracts, tapes, and newsletters to be used as aids in witnessing to the Mormon people about the errors of Mormonism, and the truth of the Lord Jesus Christ as found in the Bible

Meetings:

Regular meetings are held about once a month by the California and Washington chapters of the fellowship

554. Exponent II, Inc.

Church of Jesus Christ of Latter-day Saints
Carrel Sheldon, President of Board of Directors
144 Pleasant Street
Arlington, Massachusetts 02174

Mailing Address:
Post Office Box 37
Arlington, Massachusetts 02174
(617) 641-0086

The purpose of Exponent II Inc. is to publish *Exponent II*, a quarterly newspaper concerning the interests, accomplishments, and activities of Mormon women and to promote the study of all aspects of the lives of Mormon women.

Founding Date: 1974

Staff: 50

Publications:

Exponent II, quarterly

Meetings:

Two retreats annually for staff only
Exponent II Inc. also sponsors the annual Exponent Day Dinner, in early June, in commemoration of the founding of the *Woman's Exponent*, the first women's newspaper published west of the Mississippi (1872-1914). The dinner is now in its tenth year.

555. Faith Alive

Episcopal
Fred C. Gore, President & Executive Director
373 West Market Street
York, Pennsylvania 17405

Mailing Address:
Post Office Box 1987
York, Pennsylvania 17405
(717) 848-2137

Faith Alive assists and encourages congregations to hold Faith Alive weekends, during which Christian witnesses are invited to share their faith with the congregation for the purposes of awakening or quickening new Christian reality within the body of the Church.

Membership: 16 lay members; 8 clerical members
Publications:
    Good News, monthly
Meetings:
    150 per year

556. Faith and Life Press

Mennonite
Ben Sprunger, Chairman
718 Main Street
Newton, Kansas 67114

Mailing Address
Post Office Box 347
Newton, Kansas 67114
(316) 283-5100

Faith and Life Press is the publisher for the General Conference Mennonite Church. It is owned and operated under the direction of the Department of Faith and Life Press of the Commission on Educa-tion of the above named conference. The general pur-pose is to prepare and publish curriculum materials, study items, and other books from the Anabap-tist/Mennonite perspective.

Founding Date: 1939
Staff: 6
Membership: 5
Publications:
    Various books and curriculum items
Meetings:
    With Commission on Education and General Conference Mennonite Church
Former Name: Mennonite Publication Office

557. Faith for Today*

Seventh-day Adventist Church
Seventh-day Adventist Radio, Television and Film Center Board of Trustees
6840 Eastern Avenue, N.W.
Washington, D.C. 20012

Faith for Today offers its public service program to reach the secular man with the Good News of Salva-tion through the media of television. It mainly uses a dramatic format to present its message, but has also produced historical documentaries. Faith for Today operates a correspondence school for children, youth, and adults which is free for those wishing to study the Bible. Its evangelistic association provides personnel, both evangelists and musicians, to fill invitations for gospel meetings in various areas of North America.

Founding Date: 1950
Membership: 48 lay; 10 clerical

Publications:
   Telenotes, bimonthly Bible correspondence school lessons

Radio/TV Programs:
   1 half hour drama-type religious telecast
   Produce religious documentaries and spot ministry

558. Family Life Broadcasting System, Inc. (FLR)

Nondenominational
Warren J. Bolthouse, Founder and President
505 Wildwood Street
Jackson, Michigan 49201
Mailing Address
Post Office Box 1128
Jackson, Michigan 49204
(517) 782-8205

Family Life Radio consists of five radio outlets broadcasting religious programs of scripture, sermons, and music on a non-commercial, listener-supported basis. The organization considers itself a complement to the local church, focusing on the needs of the family, reinforcing and supporting the work of the pastor, and being a positive influence and encouragement to the listening audience. Long-range plans call for the establishment of 14 similar stations across the country.

Founding Date: 1966

Staff: 60 plus, full and part-time staff members

Membership:
   Those who participate in the support of the ministry financially are called "Team Members" and currently total some 22,000 plus individuals, businesses, churches, and other Christian ministries

Publications:
   FLR Team Contact, a newsletter mailed four times a year to 20,000 supportors and twice to additional 33,000

Radio/TV Programs:
   5 radio stations with an average of 600 hours of programming each week

Meetings:
   A series of concerts held annually in March and April in or near cities with FLR radio stations

559. Family Rosary, Inc*

Roman Catholic
Rev. Patrick Peyton, CSC
773 Madison Avenue
Albany, New York 12208
(518) 462-6458

The purpose of this organization is to promote daily family prayer and the family rosary through the organization of diocesan and local Family Rosary and Family Prayer Crusades. In addition, Family Rosary sponsors the Families For Prayer program which is a five-week, family-centered parish renewal program to promote the unity, spirituality, vocation, and mission of the family through daily family prayer.

560. Family Theater, Inc.*

Roman Catholic
Rev. Patrick J. Peyton, CSC
7201 Sunset Boulevard
Hollywood, California 90046
(213) 874-6633

The Family Prayer Office in Albany, New York, sponsors family prayer campaigns on the local level in foreign countries. In these countries the Crusade includes the showing of Family Theater's *Life of Christ* films outdoors among the poor together with outdoor rallies when Father Peyton addresses the crowds and appeals for family prayer. A family that prays together is a family that communicates. This constant communication between husband and wife, parents and children, creates a strong bond of love and understanding and makes for a happy home.

Membership: 10 lay; 13 clerical

Publications:
   4 prayer books

Radio/TV Programs:
   TV and radio spots on prayer
   Half-hour seasonal TV programs
   5 minute TV films on the Psalms

561. Far East Broadcasting Company, Inc. (FEBC)

Nondenominational
Dr. Robert H. Bowman, President
15700 East Imperial Highway
La Mirada, California 90638

Mailing Address:
Post Office Box 1
La Mirada, California 90637
(213) 947-4651

The Far East Broadcasting Company, Inc., is an international Christian missionary radio organization headquartered in La Mirada, California. Its basic purpose is the proclamation of the Gospel of the Lord Jesus Christ, primarily by means of radio. FEBC Radio International is involved principally in the area of radio station ownership and operation. Related activities include printing, follow-up correspondence and personal contact with listeners, research, disaster relief, and closed-circuit television production in Thailand, and on local TV stations. FEBC Radio International broadcasts to Asia, the Middle and Near East, East and South Africa, and Latin America over its 28 transmitters, in 82 languages and dialects, with approximately 300 programming hours daily. The average letter response per month is about 30,000. In addition to Christian programming (evangelistic, Bible teaching, and so forth), other types of programs include music, news, health, public service, cultural, and educational programs. The transmitting sites are located in the Philippines, Korea, San Francisco, Saipan, and the Seychelles Islands. There are FEBC-owned studios and/or offices in La Mirada, Japan, Hong Kong, Thailand, Burma, Singapore, Indonesia, India, Australia, Canada, England, and New Zealand. In addition to the FEBC-owned production studios, there are approximately 50 other organizations that have built cooperative studios and that produce regularly for the Far East Broadcasting Company.

Founding Date: 1945

Staff:
> Approximately 650 staff members in various countries

Publications:
> *The Broadcaster Magazine,* quarterly
> *Newsletter,* monthly

Radio/TV Programs:
> 5-minute and 10-minute programs entitled *FEBC Radio International* aired over 62 stations, 5 days a week
> Approximately 300 transmitter hours daily broadcast on FEBC's own transmitters all over the world

Meetings:
> 2 public conferences a year
> Annual Directors Conference
> Quarterly Board of Directors meeting
> Occasional headquarters staff retreat

562. Far Eastern Gospel Crusade (FEGC)

Interdenominational
Frank M. Severn, General Director
Post Office Box 513
Farmington, Michigan 48024
(313) 477-4210

The Far Eastern Gospel Crusade is an interdenominational, evangelical mission serving both in North America and overseas. It has as its primary goal to evangelize and develop indigenous churches which will remain as lasting effective witnesses in areas where the church does not now exist. FEGC missionaries serve in Japan, Taiwan, Republic of the Philippines, and Alaska. It has sending posts in the United States, Canada, Australia, and Germany. In supporting its primary objective, Far Eastern Gospel Crusade is involved in the training of Christian leadership, the provision of centers of Christian education, medical work, radio work, and the distribution of gospel literature. FEGC embraces the historic fundamental doctrines of the church and serves as an interdenominational and inter-church agency for the fullest cooperation in missionary effort of evangelical Christians.

Founding Date: 1947

Staff: 24 North American staff members

Membership: 262 active members

Publications:
> *In My Corner of the World,* monthly prayer publication
> *World,* a quarterly newspaper reporting on news-stories of the mission activity in Alaska, Philippines, Japan, and Taiwan
> *Forward,* a monthly student newsletter
> FEGC Annual Report

Radio/TV Programs:
> The Mission operates radio station KCAM in Glennallen, Alaska, and is developing a new station in Petersburg, Southeast Alaska

Meetings:
> Annual Conference at the Spring Arbor College campus in Spring Arbor, Michigan, during the first week of August

563. Federation of Diocesan Liturgical Commissions (FDLC)

Roman Catholic

Rev. Carl A. Last, Administrator
1307 South Wabash Avenue
Suite 222
Chicago, Illinois 60605
(312) 663-1187

Federation of Diocesan Liturgical Commissions (FDLC) is a body of members from Diocesan Liturgical Commissions whose purpose is to promote the liturgy as the heart of Christian life, especially in the parish community. As a professional organization, the Federation is committed to assisting the American hierarchy and individual bishops in their responsibility of positive leadership in liturgical education and development. The Federation's task is: to foster and coordinate the work of liturgical commissions as they respond to the needs and utilize the resources of their people; to commission, gather, and dispense informational materials which will aid individual commissions in carrying out educational and promotional programs in their respective dioceses; to cooperate with the Bishop's Committee on the Liturgy (BCL) and its Secretariat in the sponsorship of national meetings of Diocesan Liturgical Commissions; to serve the BCL in an advisory capacity especially on matters to be proposed to the National Conference of Catholic Bishops (NCCB); to bring results of pastoral experience to the BCL; to encourage and facilitate the legitimate adaptation of liturgical rites and ceremonies to the American culture as envisioned by the Constitution on the Sacred Liturgy; to be a medium through which diocesan commissions can contribute responsibly and effectively to articulating the voice of priests, religious, and laity in the development of liturgy.

Membership:
> Diocesan Liturgical Commissions of over 160 Roman Catholic Dioceses in the United States

Publications:
> *FDLC Newsletter,* bimonthly

Meetings:
> Yearly national meeting of membership at various sites in the United States

564. Fellowship for Spiritual Understanding (FSU)

Nondenominational
Dr. Marcus Bach, Director
2516 Via Tejon, #307
Palos Verdes Estates, California 90274

Mailing Address
Post Office Box 816
Palos Verdes Estates, California 90274
(714) 373-2669

The Fellowship for Spiritual Understanding is a unique system of interpersonal understanding to help contemporary individuals find meaning, fulfillment, and a totally balanced, integrative daily life within a rapidly changing world environment. FSU believes that we understand people best when we understand what they believe, and we best understand what they believe when we put ourselves into their place. FSU is a research center for the interpretation of spiritual, social, philosophical, and scientific discoveries and trends as these relate constructively to the life of our time. FSU publishes a monthly newsletter, *Outreach*, designed to achieve the above objectives. FSU is an unseen Fellowship, reflected by a sort of fifth-dimensional feeling shared by all who have experienced an awakened consciousness.

Founding Date: 1966

Staff: 5

Membership: 4,500

Publications:
> *Outreach,* monthly, provides perceptive, sympathetic interpretations of most religious and cultures in the world

Former Name:
> Foundation for Spiritual Understanding

565. Fellowship of Baptists for Home Missions

Baptist
Rev. Austin Plew, President
Post Office Box 455
Elyria, Ohio 44036
(216) 365-7308

Fellowship of Baptists for Home Missions is a faith mission board whose purpose is to start new Baptist churches in the United States. There are approximately 300 missionaries located across the country with about 150-185 new projects being started all the time. Some of the new churches are financed through an investment loan department that is a part of the organization.

Staff:
> 4 administration members
> 12 home office staff members

Membership:
>300 missionaries
>2 area representatives

Publications:
>Newsletter, quarterly

Meetings:
>Candidate School for new missionaries each year in Elyria, Ohio (2 weeks)

566. Fellowship of Catholic Scholars

Roman Catholic

James Hitchcock, President
c/o Institute for Advanced Catholic Doctrine
St. John's University
Jamaica, New York 11439
(212) 969-8000

Fellowship of Catholic Scholars is an organization of scholars and teachers who are Roman Catholic and accept the fullness of Catholic teaching. Members place their scholarship at the service of the Church and use it in the development and penetration of the authentic Catholic tradition. The group exists to encourage such research and to make its fruits known to the larger world inside and outside the Church. Ordinarily, the membership is restricted to those who subscribe to the purposes and goals of the organization and who hold terminal degrees in their chosen fields. Exceptions to the latter requirement can be made in the case of those who have demonstrated scholarly competence in other ways.

Membership: 500

Publications:
>*Newsletter,* 6 times a year
>The proceedings of the annual convention are published in a single volume

Meetings:
>Annual convention at various locations, usually in early spring

567. Fellowship of Christian Assemblies

Interdenominational

7704 24th Avenue, N.W.
Seattle, Washington 98117

Fellowship of Christian Assemblies is an unincorporated fellowship of independent churches. Members gather at regional fellowship meetings and also at an annual National Convention. The Fellowship publishes a periodical and cooperates in various programs, such as foreign missions endeavors, Bible Schools, and Christian Camps.

Membership:
>150-200 churches in the United States and Canada

Publications:
>*Conviction,* monthly

Meetings:
>Regional or area Fellowship meetings are conducted on a monthly basis, while national Conventions are held once a year

568. Fellowship of Christian Athletics

Nondenominational

John Erickson, National President
8701 Leeds Road
Kansas City, Missouri 64129
(816) 921-0909

The Fellowship of Christian Athletes is a movement to present to athletes and coaches, and all whom they influence, the challenge and adventure of receiving Jesus Christ as Savior and Lord, serving Him in their relationships and in the fellowship of the church. FCA is a national, year-round ministry which focuses on junior and senior high Huddle groups, college Fellowship groups, adult Chapters, national summer conferences, coaches activities, and church involvement. FCA applies muscle and action to the Christian faith. It strives to strengthen the moral, mental, and spiritual fiber of the athletes and coaches of America. It is a fellowship through which ordinary people help each other become better persons and better examples of what God can do with a yielded life.

Founding Date: 1954

Staff: 150

Membership: 25,000

Publications:
>*The Christian Athlete,* five times a year
>*The Widening Circle,* three times a year
>Various brochures, films, cassette tapes, filmstrips, etc.

Meetings:
>Over 30 conferences are hosted each summer from coast to coast on college campuses for athletes and coaches

569. Fellowship of Christians in the Arts, Media and Entertainment (FCAME)

Nondenominational

Rev. Robert Rieth, National Executive Director
12936 Northeast 131st Street
Kirkland, Washington 98033
(206) 821-4852

Fellowship of Christians in the Arts, Media and Entertainment is a missionary ministry whose primary objective is to share the message of salvation, giving individuals in leadership positions the opportunity to personally accept Jesus Christ as their Savior. Christians working in the arts, media and entertainment make up FCAME. They have come together to encourage one another spiritually in the context of our chosen professions; to help each other see how Christ can bring genuine dimensions to careers, focusing on the verse, "Every good and perfect gift is from above, coming down from the Father . . . " (James 1:17); and to find ways in which those most creative and highest forms of expression can produce fruit in member's respective fields.

Founding Date: 1969

Staff: 2

Publications:
Limelight, hoping to be published quarterly

570. The Fellowship of Concerned Churchmen (FCC)

Anglican Catholic

Captian W.R. Swindells, Treasurer
Post Office Box 252
Eureka Springs, Arkansas 72632
(501) 253-9800

The purposes of the Fellowship of Concerned Churchmen are: to provide a forum for the expression of traditional Anglicanism, as embodied in the 1928 Book of Common Prayer and its predecessors, through a program of sound Christian education based upon the teachings of our Lord and His apostles and of the early Church Fathers as embodied in the proceedings and findings of the seven Ecumenical Councils; to encourage the perpetuation of the doctrine, discipline, and worship of the Church in accordance with Anglican tradition; to serve as a bridge for those who espouse these

views but remain in the established Episcopal Church, and those who have left the Church.

Founding Date: 1973

Membership: 3,500 readers and supporters

Publications:
News Exchange, monthly

Meetings:
Annual meeting in different locations

571. Fellowship of Contemplative Prayer*

Anglican

The Rev. Dr. R. L. Stinson, Honorary National Secretary of American Branch
Post Office Box 75
Mount Vernon, Virginia 22121
(703) 780-3081

The Fellowship of Contemplative Prayer was founded in England by Rev. R.G. Coulson. Its rule of life includes daily practice of contemplative prayer based on the reality of God in His Word. The Fellowship has branches in England, Ireland, and the United States. New members are received, and others renew their memberships, each year at an annual retreat. The retreats, conducted by experienced members, are "silent," and of three or four days duration.

Founding Date: 1946

Membership: 150 lay; 200 clerical

Meetings:
Regional retreats (3 or 4 per year) and 1 annual retreat

572. Fellowship of Grace Brethren Churches, Christian Education Department

Fellowship of Grace Brethren Churches

Pastor Knute Larson, Executive Director
1003 Presidential Drive
Winona Lake, Indiana 46590

Mailing Address
Post Office Box 365
Winona Lake, Indiana 46590
(219) 267-6622

The motto of the Christian Education Department is "Hoping to help in Christian education, youth and church growth." The Department endeavors to do this by being a service/resource center for Christian education material and information for the churches in the Fellowship of Grace Brethren Churches. Its aim is to encourage and assist all phases of Christian education according to the tenets of the Brethren Church. Assistance is provided on the local, district, and national levels through workshops, seminars, church visits, district representatives, publications, correspondence, and telephone contact.

Staff: 12 staff members, 15 board members

Membership: 39,605 lay, 548 clerical

Publications:

Ac'cent Magazine for youth

Inside Track, pastoral resource packet

Brethren Pro-Teens, youth sponsors resource packet

CE Youth Programs, monthly

SMM Leaders Helps

Ohhh, for pastors' wives

Hmmm, for pastors

Bzzz, for church secretaries

Meetings:

1 annual national Christian Education Convention

1 annual youth conference

Various local/district seminars

1 annual Board Meeting

1 meeting of Board Executive Committee

573. Fellowship of Grace Brethren Churches, Foreign Missionary Society

Fellowship of Grace Brethren Churches

Rev. John W. Zielasko, General Director

Post Office Box 588

Winona Lake, Indiana 46590

(219) 267-5161

The Foreign Missionary Society of the Brethren Church, although incorporated as a separate organization, is an official arm of the Fellowship of Grace Brethren Churches. The Society exists to provide the machinery, the funds, the personnel, and the experience necessary to cross cultural and linguistic boundaries in order to preach the Gospel effectively. Missionaries in the various fields are authorized to organize field councils to direct the work locally, subject to the approval of the board of trustees. A field superintendent is appointed for each field. It is the basic policy of the board to assist the missionaries

to carry out the evangelization of a given area of population, establish the believers in the faith, and instruct them in organizing truly indigenous churches. In the Central African Republic, where there are now more than 400 congregations, the Society also maintians several institutions in cooperation with the African church, such as a junior high school of theology, printshop, and literature ministry, a medical program, a hospital, and 16 dispensaries carried on under the direction of two doctors assisted by a corps of registered nurses and locally trained nurses.

Founding Date: 1900

Staff: 12 home staff

Membership:

105 missionaries in 9 countries

8,954 corporation members

Publications:

Missionary section of *The Brethren Missionary Herald*

Echoes

Meetings:

Each field conducts district and national conferences.

574. Fellowship of Independent Missions

Independent Fundamental Churches of America

Philip E. Weiss, President

1342 East Lincoln Highway

Langhorne, Pennsylvania 19047

Mailing Address

Post Office Box 72

Fairless Hills, Pennsylvania 19030

(215) 752-1170

The purposes of the Fellowship of Independent Missions are: to foster the preaching of the Gospel of Jesus Christ by independent missions and missionaries; to unite such missions and missionaries in a common bond; to plant churches and disciple of believers; and to establish elementary and secondary Christian schools, Bible Institutes, and seminaries.

Founding Date: 1950

Staff: 3

Membership: 80

Merger:

Morocco Evangelical Fellowship which merged with Sahara Desert Mission to become Fellowship of Independent Missions in 1959

575. The Fellowship of Missions (FOM)

Nondenominational

William J. Hopewell, Jr., DD, President
4205 Chester Avenue
Cleveland, Ohio 44103
(216) 432-2200

The Fellowship of Missions' purposes are: to encourage and coordinate the strength of such Mission Boards and Agencies as are committed to the propagation and defense of the pure Gospel to the ends of the earth; to further the testimony of separation from all apostasy and perversion of the Truth as revealed in God's Word, the Bible; to aid and encourage the formation of Bible-believing Missionary or Church Fellowships in as many countries as possible; to take whatever steps necessary to assure the availability of reliable Bible Translations in every language area, and to cooperate with such Bible societies, publishers, or other agencies as are committed to this purpose; and to serve the interest of its fellowshipping bodies in all possible ways. In fulfilling this last purpose, the FOM acts as an accrediting agency for the FOM constitutents and serves their interests, when needed, in matters pertaining to the relation of missions to governments. When requested, the FOM serves in the same capacity for individual missionaries or groups whom they may be in a position to help. It furnishes information as to where supplies and transportation can be secured, and, as possible and desirable, provides direct aid in these areas; arranges mission seminars, special study groups, linguistic or language institutes and similar services as needed; and furnishes to the FOM constituency periodic bulletins or information pertinent to its missionary interests.

Founding Date: 1969

Membership:

Membership is composed of mission agencies of which there are 14
Number of missionaries represented by these agencies is approximately 2,800

Publications:

Focus on Missions, an occasional news supplement for missionaries, appearing generally 3 times per year

576. Fellowship of Reconciliation (FOR)

Nondenominational

Richard Baggett Deats, Executive Secretary
Post Office Box 271
Nyack, New York 10960
(914) 358-4601

The Fellowship of Reconciliation is America's largest pacifist membership organization. Members represent all religious traditions. The organization has opposed war and militarism consistently since its founding. In pursuit of its aim of peaceful resolution of conflicts and the establishment of justice among all peoples, FOR offers a literature service, publishes a monthly magazine, and carries on a vigorous national and international program in such areas as disarmament, the Middle East conflict, and capital punishment. Membership is on the basis of agreement with its Statement of Purpose which includes the words: "They (members) refuse to participate personally in any way, or to give any sanction they can withhold from physical, psychological, or moral preparation for war."

Founding Date: 1915

Staff: 27

Membership:

26,800 lay members
4,500 clerical

Publications:

Fellowship, monthly

Meetings:

Biennial conference
Regular work-camps in areas of need, such as with the Red Wind School and Community in California

Absorbed:

(1976) Committee on New Alternatives in the Middle East

577. Fellowship of Religious Humanists (FRH)

Nondenominational

Dr. J. Harold Hadley, Executive Director
105 West North College Street
Yellow Springs, Ohio 45387
(513) 767-1324

The Fellowship of Religious Humanists is made up of Humanists from several liberal religious traditions who have joined together to form an educational agency dedicated to supporting and spreading the Humanist view among religious liberals. The

Fellowship serves as a coordinating and materials-producing agency and as the outreach-contact agent to college students, to students entering the liberal ministry, to Humanist professionals in philosophy, psychology, and the social sciences, and to newcomers in liberal denominations. The Fellowship presents national speakers of note at the Unitarian Universalist Association General Assembly and at its own annual meeting each fall, and plans Seminars for Humanists in many parts of the continent. The Fellowship of Religious Humanists is affiliated with the Unitarian Universalist Association, the American Ethical Union, the American Humanist Association, and the International Humanist and Ethical Union.

Founding Date: 1963

Staff: 2

Membership: 350 lay members; 50 clerical

Publications:
> *Religious Humanism,* quarterly
> *The Communicators,* bimonthly
> Pamphlets and other materials

Meetings:
> 1 meeting at the UU General Assembly
> 1 annual meeting

578. Fellowship of United Methodists in Worship, Music and other Arts*

United Methodist Church
Thomas C. Jones, Executive Secretary
Post Office Box 840
Nashville, Tennessee 37202
(615) 327-2700

The basic function of the Fellowship of United Methodists in Worship, Music and other Arts is to upgrade the program of local church worships, music, and the other arts through resourcing, training enterprises on the local church, district, conference, jurisdictional, and national level. A national convocation is held at different geographic locations on the odd years and five jurisdictional meetings are held on the even years. Music in the church finds its place in the worship life and so worship is a key to study. The use of drama, dance, and the visual arts is also encouraged by the Fellowship.

Membership: 1,600 lay; 300 clerical

Publications:
> Monthly newsletter

Meetings:
> 50-75 per year

Former Name:
> Fellowship of United Methodist Musicians

579. Fides/Claretian Books

Roman Catholic
221 West Madison
Chicago, Illinois 60606
(312) 236-7782

Fides/Claretian Books concentrates on domestic social issues as opposed to third-world and worldwide social justice concerns. These issues are only relevant to the Fides/Claretian focus in so far as they deal with Christian social-justice activity grounded in the Church. Biblically, the focus flows from the Beatitudes and the Corporal Works of Mercy; spiritually, from a developing personal and communal prayer life. Fides/Claretian social-justice books lean heavily on the concrete, especially "people" examples, as opposed to the ethereal, utopian vision. They ask involved people where they get their motivation and present them as role models. This down-to-earth approach helps readers to understand the essence of social justice/injustice in our society and doesn't cloud the issue with outer-worldly idealism, or worse, lead readers into melancholy and despair. Finally, Fides/Claretian books show how action social justice is sporadic and subject to "do-gooder burn-out" if it does not flow naturally from the inner prayer lives of the people involved. Therefore, F/C books must have an explicit and identifiable religious dimension.

Former Name: Fides Publishers, Inc.

580. Firm Foundation

Churches of Christ
G.H.P. Showalter, President
Post Office Box 610
Austin, Texas 78767
(512) 452-7651

Firm Foundation serves as a publishing arm for Churches of Christ, and, secondarily, for the public in general. It does all kinds of printing, including Sunday School literature, books, bulletins, and newsletters. Its basic aim is to promote evangelism and mission work among Churches of Christ.

Membership: 14 staff members

Publications:

A weekly magazine, Bible Class literature, books of all kinds, Church newsletters, etc.

581. First Catholic Slovak Union of the United States and Canada (FCSU)

Roman Catholic
Stephen F. Ungvarsky, Executive Secretary
3289 East 55th Street
Cleveland, Ohio 44127
(216) 341-3355

First Catholic Slovak Union of the United States and Canada is a fraternal life insurance society that provides life insurance, charitable donations, and scholarships. It operates its own museum and archives and a summer camp for children; its other activities and sponsorships include bowling and golfing tournaments, anniversaries, testimonials, church and parochial school donations, education of seminarians to priesthood, civic and cultural promotions, financial flood relief donations, and disaster-indigent donations.

Founding Date: 1890

Staff: 65

Membership: 90,000 lay members

Publications:

Jednota, weekly
Prayer books, magazines, periodicals

Meetings:

Numerous conventions and lodge meetings

Also Known As:

Porva Katolicka Slovenska Jednota

582. Focolare Movement (Work of Mary)

Roman Catholic
Miss Sharry Silvi, National Director, Women's Branch
Rev. Sebastian Grimaldi, National Director, Men's Branch
Post Office Box 496
New York, New York 10021
(212) 249-8283

Focolare is an international lay movement of more than two million persons whose aim is to "work for the realization of Christ's final prayer for unity of all men" and to spread the Gospel in the world through their own lives. The Movement began in Trent, Italy.

Chiara Lubich is the foundress and President. Although most Focolare members are Catholic, it encompasses large numbers of non-Catholics and promotes various ecumenical activities. In addition, many priests and religious take part in the Movement. At its heart are some 3,000 fully dedicated laymen in over 30 countries who live in small communities called Women's Focolare Centers and Men's Focolare Centers. ("Focolare" is from the Italian word for "hearth.") In the United States and Canada, "sympathizers" of the Movement number about 34,000; there are six resident centers in New York, four in Chicago, two in Boston, two in Los Angeles, one in San Antonio, and two in Toronto, Canada. Teen-age members are organized under the name "Gen Movement," standing for New Generation. The international Movement, with headquarters in Rome, Italy, is building an "Ideal City" at Loppiano, near Florence, Italy, with an international university at its center; lay apostles trained there will return to their home dioceses "to contribute toward a stronger and more profound Christian unity." Other cities are under construction in South America and Africa.

Founding Date: 1943

Membership:

34,000 in the United States

Publications:

By the New City Press, the publishing house of the Focolare Movement: 11 books on spirituality, 8 on experiences, 4 on other topics
Living City, monthly
Gen 2 and *Gen 3,* monthly for youth

Meetings:

3 national summer conventions (Mariapolis)
Local weekly and monthly meetings and weekends of formation

583. Food for the ·Hungry International (FHI)

Nondenominational
Larry Ward, President
7729 East Greenway Road
Scottsdale, Arizona 85260

Mailing Address
Post Office Box E
Scottsdale, Arizona 85252
(602) 998-3100

Food for the Hungry International is a non-profit charitable organization that was founded to offer both disaster relief and long-range self-help assistance. It seeks to work at the lowest possible overhead and channels its help to the hungry on a person-to-person basis. The organization is committed to three basic objectives: (1) information about the needs of the developing nations via publications, films, radio, and television; (2) relief moving swiftly when disaster strikes. This involves stockpiling of massive amounts of food in strategic areas worldwide for instant airlift and also pre-crisis negotiations in the developing countries; (3) development assistance helping people help themselves, mainly through the use of small-scale technology utilizing renewable energy sources and helping in rehabilitation and reconstruction. During its short history, Food for the Hungry has played a major role in relief efforts in Bangladesh, Nicaragua, Guatemala, and Africa. It has helped the Vietnamese "boat people" and thousands of refugees now in camps in Thailand. It has also given major assistance to areas of "chronic disaster" such as India and Haiti. Since its founding, Food for the Hungry has provided over fifteen million dollars in the form of food or funds to help needy people around the world.

Founding Date: 1971

Staff: 35

Membership: Not a membership organization

Publications:
    Newsletter published occasionally

Radio/TV Programs:
    One-hour TV special on world hunger and the
    work of FHI

584. Fortress Press, Fortress Church Supply Stores

Lutheran Church in America
The Rev. Robert W. Endruschat, General Manager
2900 Queen Lane
Philadelphia, Pennsylvania 19129
(800) 523-3824

Fortress Press and Fortress Church Supply Stores is the publishing arm of the Lutheran Church in America (Division of Board of Publication). It manufactures, produces, supplies, and sells religious and church goods, garments, vestments, and books. It operates 18 religious and church supply stores located throughout the United States and Canada. It manufactures and sells Friar Tuck clergy

shirts, imports religious articles and vestments, and publishes religious and theological books under the imprint of Fortress Press. As the Division of Board of Publication, it publishes curriculum and hymnals for Lutheran Church in America.

Publications:
    Curriculum and hymnals

585. Forward in Faith

Church of God
Carl Richardson, Director
Keith at 25th, N.W.
Cleveland, Tennessee 37311
(615) 472-3361

Forward in Faith is the radio/television function of the Church of God (Cleveland, Tennessee). The purpose of the radio and television department is to demonstrate concern for people in every community. One of the most effective means of reaching large numbers of people is through mass media. The weekly radio program *Forward in Faith* is heard over more than 400 stations in the United States and in many foreign countries. Radio and TV minute messages are a new format for ministry and are aired nationally. Prime-time, nation-wide TV specials are produced to reach literally millions of people. Through a cassette ministry, people are having church almost anywhere. Tapes are provided to prisoners, hospitals, the blind, and to many military outposts. Three full-length motion pictures are shown to hurting families across the nation. These films are entitled, "Future of the Family." Personal evangelism leads Director Carl Richardson into area-wide crusades in major cities like Miami, Florida and Washington, D.C. Foreign crusades are conducted in places like India and Puerto Rico. Plans are being made for a crusade in South Africa. Faith Productions Recording Studio is the newest vehicle for reaching people. It features ultra-modern recording facilities.

Founding Date: 1959

Staff: 22

Publications:
    Vision, quarterly
    Approximately 15 books and pamphlets,
    annually

Radio/TV Programs:
    Radio programs, weekly
    TV programs, occasionally

586. Forward Movement Publications

Episcopal

Rev. Dr. Charles H. Long, Director and Editor
412 Sycamore Street
Cincinnati Ohio 45202
(513) 721-6659

Forward Movement Publications publishes books and booklets for all occasions, in church and out — for pastoral aids, confirmation instruction, church information and teaching, group study, devotional help, inspiration and guidance, personal problems, evangelism, and witness. For almost everyone, sick or well, Christian or non-Christian, male or female, young or old, there is a suitable FM title.

Founding Date: 1934

Staff: 15

Publications:

Forward Day by Day, quarterly, daily guide to devotions and bible study — regular, large print, braille, and cassette editons

The Review of Books and Religion, 10 times a year

Anglican Cycle of Prayer, (annual) paperback

200 other paperbacks, booklets and tracts in print

587. Foundation for Biblical Research

Nondenominational

Ernest L. Martin, President
1000 East Walnut
Pasadena, California 91106
(213) 793-1144

The Foundation for Biblical Research advocates the following philosophical stand: to educate the general public through biblical research and analyses, without stated or implied dogmatism, and without demanding doctrinal conformity to the concepts of any organization or individual, and to promote the exercise of philosophical freedom in areas of personal belief.

Staff: 5

Membership: 5,000 members and associates

Publications:

The Commentator, a monthly newsletter
12 expositions on research subjects a year
2 lectures on cassette tape each month
An average of 2 booklets each year
Books

Meetings:

2 meetings a month in Arcata, California
Periodic tours throughout the United States, Canada, England, and the Middle East

588. The Foundation for Biblical Research and Preservation of Primitive Christianity*

Nondenominational

The Board of Trustees
Post Office Box 373
Charlestown, New Hampshire 03603
(603) 826-7751

The purposes of The Foundation are: to collect and preserve materials of an historical nature concerning the first three hundred years of early Christianity; to provide scholarly aids in the study and research of Biblical materials; to provide a museum and libraries in which opportunities are open for study and research; to aid students in the procuring of an education through scholarships and loans; and to provide cultural development for the community and the area.

Meetings:

25 per year

589. Foundation for Christian Living (FCL)

Nondenominational

Ruth Stafford Peale, Editor
Pawling, New York 12654
(914) 855-5000

The Foundation for Christian Living is engeged in carrying the Christian message to people everywhere who are struggling with the problems and difficulties of daily living. The Foundation is a non-profit organization which has been publishing and distributing practical Christian literature since 1940. More then 2,000,000 attractively printed sermons and other inspirational material is sent every month to over 700,000 people in all 50 states and 120 countries. Each year, through the generous help of friends and supporters, the Foundation is able to mail more than 3,000,000 pocket-size inspirational booklets to people requesting them, as well as to hospitals, prisons, nursing homes, the Salvation Army and the Armed Forces — entirely without charge. Thousands of letters pour into the Foundation from people who seek help, advice, prayers, and consolation. Each letter is answered with a helpful free booklet and other spiritual literature, or by a personal letter from a staff member. Foundation workers gather each morning at 9:50 to pray by name for those who ask for prayer support. Other ways which the Foundation seeks to widen the scope of its Christian services are through sending tape cassettes of messages by Dr. Norman Vincent Peale to the blind, hospitals, nursing homes, and other institutions; through the newspaper column "There's an Answer!"; through radio and television; through tours and fellowship gatherings with spiritual emphases; and through its School of Practical Christianity which is conducted for ministers and their wives. The Foundation sponsors a 24-hour global Prayer Partnership every Good Friday linking Christians around the world.

590. Foundation for Religion and Mental Health, Inc. (FRMH)

Nondenominational

The Rev. Robert C. Hamlyn, President
30 South State Road
Briarcliff Manor, New York 10510
(914) 762-1666

The Foundation for Religion and Mental Health was born out of the desire of people to achieve more effective lives. The Foundation administers 50 centers and offices in New York, New Jersey, and Connecticut. They are staffed by trained and qualified counselors who provide help to individuals, couples, families, and groups. An affiliate of the Institutes of Religion and Health, the Foundation is a non-profit tax-exempt corporation operating under the laws of the states of New York, Connecticut, and New Jersey. In cooperation with members of the clergy and of other helping professions, the Foundation provides professional counseling services on an interfaith basis. It draws on the expertise of psychiatrists, psychologists, social workers, and physicians as well as of pastoral counselors. The pastoral counseling staff has been carefully screened and selected for competence in psychotherapy. All pastoral counselors must meet extensive academic and professional standards and are qualified according to their standing in the American Association of Pastoral Counselors. The Foundation administers two training institutes: one in Individual and Pastoral Counseling, the other in Transactional Analysis.

Founding Date: 1968
Staff:
33 AAPC staff members
72 consultant staff
54 corporate members
Meetings:
Trustee meetings, staff conferences, seminars, and workshops as requested

591. Franciscan Apostolate of the Way of the Cross*

Roman Catholic

Rev. Cassian J. Kirk, OFM, Director
Saint Bonaventure Friary
174 Ramsey Street
Paterson, New Jersey 07501
(201) 684-0690

The Franciscan Apostolate of the Way of the Cross was organized to promote devotion to the passion and death of Christ. The organization has no membership in the traditional sense, no dues, and accepts only free-will offerings. A Station of the Cross Crucifix is sent or given to persons upon request. Its purpose is exclusively spiritual and is designed specifically for shut-ins and those who are unable to make the Way of the Cross in church.

592. Franciscan Communications (FC)

Interdenominational

Rev. Anthony Scannell, Capuchin Franciscan, President
1229 South Santee Street
Los Angeles, California 90015
(213) 748-8331

Franciscan Communications is dedicated to creating public service messages and contemporary audio-visual materials for moral enrichment and values education. In the spirit of St. Francis, it tries to be "an instrument of peace." FC provides public service messages, 30 and 60-second TeleSPOTS and AudioSPOTS, which are released to 750 television and 3,500 radio stations without cost to the stations. FC produces TeleKETICS films—short, open-ended, provocative films for value education and enrichment in schools, churches, and other organizations. Its other multi-media materials include filmstrips, slides, records, sound collages, posters, and audiotapes. They are released singly or combined in media kits to interpret and communicate the Good News of the Gospel. The Center also publishes the GOOD NEWS homily service which provides contemporary preaching materials to ministers throughout the English-speaking world.

Staff:
> 59 staff members, including Franciscan friars, women religious, and members of other religious communities

Publications:
> *Center Focus,* a quarterly publication for friends and benefactors
> *Good News,* homily service
> *Good Word,* a weekly bulletin insert for parish use
> *Family Booklets,* a series of inexpensive booklets for home use

593. Franciscan Herald Press

Roman Catholic

Rev. Mark Hegener, OFM, President and Managing Director
1434 West 51st Street
Chicago, Illinois 60609
(312) 254-4455

The Franciscan Herald Press is a not-for-profit corporation engaged in the publishing and disseminating of books, pamphlets, and literature on the Roman Catholic faith and the Franciscan Order for the benefit of its members. It also operates the Herald Book Club.

Founding Date: 1921

Staff: 9

Publications:
> 500 religious and scholarly books
> *Franciscan Herald,* monthly magazine for members of the Third Order
> Franciscan Herald Press publishes appoximately 30 titles a year

594. The Franciscan Institute

Roman Catholic

Rev. Conrad L. Harkins, OFM, Director
St. Bonaventure University
St. Bonaventure, New York 14778
(716) 375-2105

The Franciscan Institute is a center for learning, research, and publication related to the Franciscan

movement, principally its spirituality, theology, philosophy, and history. A major project of the Institute is the Latin critical edition of *William of Ockham's Philosophical and Theological Works*, which has been described as one of the most important projects in America in the area of medieval scholarship. Most noteworthy among its other publications are the series devoted to texts, philosophy, theology, and spirituality; the scholarly annual, *Franciscan Studies*; and a monthly of Franciscan Spirituality, *The Cord.* As a graduate department of St. Bonaventure University, it offers a program in Franciscan Studies leading to the M.A. degree. Through its library and resource people, it is a principal American center for Franciscan Research.

Membership: 7 lay; 19 clerical

Publications:
> 58 scholarly books
> 19 popular books
> 1 scholarly magazine
> 1 popular magazine

Meetings:
> 2 series of conferences per year
> 20 retreats (by arrangement with individual priest)

595. Franciscan Tertiary Province of the Sacrd Heart, Inc.

Roman Catholic

Rev. Mark Hegener, OFM, President
1458 West 51st Street
Chicago, Illinois 60609
(312) 254-4455

The main purposes of the Franciscan Tertiary Province of the Sacred Heart are to organize, promote, build, establish, operate, and maintain educational and charitable endeavors and institutions; to provide housing and related facilities and services for elderly families and persons on a non-profit basis; to secure unity of purpose, or direction, and of action among the Third Order fraternities under the jurisdiction of the Friars Minor of the Province of the Sacred Heart. Mayslake Village, a complex of 630 apartments for the elderly in Du Page County, Illinois, and Chariton Apartments in St. Louis, Missouri, were sponsored by this organization.

Membership: 10,000

596. Franciscan Vocation Conference

Roman Catholic
Brother Conrad Rebmann, OFM, President
10290 Mill Road
Cincinnati, Ohio 45231
(513) 825-1082

The Franciscan Vocation Conference is an organization of all the Franciscan (OFM) Vocation Directors of the United States and Canada. Its purpose is to render Franciscan friars conscious of their duty to educate and instruct the People of God in the area of Church-related vocations and to specifically promote cooperative efforts to promote Franciscan vocations within the Franciscan family.

Staff: 3

Membership: 20

Meetings:
1 conference per year, next one in February, 1983 in New Orleans, Louisiana

Former Name: Seraphic Society for Vocations

597. The Fransisters*

Nondenominational
Fransister Laurel, Chief Executive
2168 South Lafayette Street
Denver, Colorado 80210

The purpose of the Order of Fransisters is to help people become aware of their inner potentialities, to find peace and live a joyous life, free from most problems, and to feel that their living has made a beneficial contribution to the whole of humanity. Fransisters are ecumenical in that they embrace all religions which identify with a spiritual ideal of love, unselfish service and are based on kindness and reverence for all life. The only "dogma" is to follow the prayer attributed to St. Francis, "Lord, make me an instrument — ."

598. The Fraternity of Jesus*

Nondenominational
c/o Rev. Royce Hughes, Director
Post Office Box 214
Houston, Texas 77001

The Fraternity of Jesus is an association of celibate men, both clergy and laymen, who dedicate themselves to God and the service of others in some personal apostolate and are bound together by a common ideal. The Fraternity conducts a study program at the University of St. Thomas in Rome for the training of members.

Membership: 24 lay; 2 clerical

599. Free Anglican Church in America (Iona Conference), Centers for Human Relations

Free Anglican Church in America (Iona Conference)
Most Rev. Brian Glenn Turkington, STD, DMin, President
23820 Arlington #15
Torrance, California 90501
(213) 539-5565

The Centers for Human Relations are pastoral counseling facilities of the Free Anglican Church in America (IC) which are devoted to integrating mind, body, and spirit, by working with individuals, couples and families. They seek to be guided by the Holy Spirit in this work in an attempt to let God bring about the required healing in each person. It is apparent that a society can be no more healthy than its citizens' spiritual and mental health. They believe that the Judeo-Christian teachings of the Bible form the basic tenets for developing a healthy environment. Consequently, they dedicate their service to the gospel message of Jesus Christ; forgiveness, reconciliation, and inner healing. The Centers are dedicated to healing individual and family systems so they will become wholly functioning units of society, based on these spiritual truths. Further, to help individuals gain greater self-esteem and awareness of God's love in their personal lives, they offer a variety of counseling services directed toward individual needs.

Founding Date: 1981

Membership: 20 centers

Meetings:
An annual convention of the Free Anglican Church in America (IC)

600. Free Anglican Church in America (Iona Conference), Office of the Bishop Primus

Free Anglican Church in America (Iona Conference)
Most Rev. Brian Glenn Turkington, STD, DMin, DD, Bishop Primus
38 Currier Place
Cheshire, Connecticut 06410
(203) 272-9376

The Free Anglican Church in America (IC) has at its head the Bishop Primus. The responsibility of the Bishop Primus is in the following areas: spiritual direction, continuity of the precepts of the denomination, and working in conjunction with the Council of Bishops in terms of lay development, requirements for ordination, etc. The Council of Bishops is made up of the following: Suffragen Bishop, Metropolitan Bishops, Director of Education, and the Archbishops throughout the country. The Council of Bishops holds an annual convocation where policy and direction is established. All decisions are in consort with the Council of Bishops.

Founding Date: 1980

Staff: 5

Publications:

The Shield of St. Andrew, monthly

Meetings:

Annual convocation in June, New York City 1983

601. Free Anglican Church in America (Iona Conference), Office of Education

Free Anglican Church in America (Iona Conference)

Rt. Rev. Harry Edwin Smith, ThD, DMin, Director
23820 Arlington, #15
Torrance, California 90501
(213) 539-5565

The Office of Education reviews and sets the educational requirements for its ministry; designs its Bible School curriculum; provides supervision for its outreach program, Centers for Human Relations, and the denominations publications, such as the Celtic Cross.

Founding Date: 1980

Staff: 5

Publications:

Celtic Cross, monthly

602. Free Methodist Church of North America, Department of Christian Education

Free Methodist Church of North America

Dr. Catherine M. Stonehouse
General Director of Christian Education
Department of Christian Education
901 College Avenue
Winona Lake, Indiana 46590
(219) 267-7656

The mission of the general Department of Christian Education is to equip conference and local Christian Education leaders to fulfill the mission of the church through Christian Education. This is done by providing leadership. Denominational staff members assess the needs of the constituency, and keep abreast of trends and project plans for the future. The Department also provides resources for Christian Education. Curriculum materials for Sunday School and midweek activities for all age levels are developed and regularly refined. Training materials and opportunities are also provided by the Department. Regular communication pieces keep churches informed regarding programs, resources, training opportunities, and plans for the future.

Founding Date: 1967

Staff: 18

Publications:

Aldersgate Graded Curriculum
Light and Life Uniform Curriculum
New Horizons Bible Studies
Youth Ministries Resource
Christian Youth Crusader program materials

603. The Free Methodist Church of North America, Department of Evangelistic Outreach*

Free Methodist Church of North America

Rev. Robert F. Andrews, General Director
901 College Avenue
Winona Lake, Indiana 46590
(219) 267-7161

The international radio broadcast of the Free Methodist Church is produced under the Department of Evangelistic Outreach. This broadcast is called *The Light and Life Hour.* Mr. Andrews is speaker and director for the broadcast. The department is also involved in church extension through loans and grants, as well as counseling and spiritual guidance. Under the department is Volunteer In Action, organized for the purpose of directing volunteer teams and individuals who go out in various ministries witnessing for Christ in homes and public meetings; conducting vacation bible schools; assisting needy churches in painting and fixing up facilities; and working with summer camp programs. VIA involves teams in the United States, Canada, and the United Kingdom.

Founding Date: 1943

Publications:

Transmitter, bimonthly

The Light and Life Hour, a 30-minute radio broadcast in 10 languages

Meetings:
Annual conference
Continental Urban Exchange

604. Free Methodist Church of North America, Department of Higher Education and the Ministry

Free Methodist
Dr. Lawrence R. Schoenhals, General Secretary
901 College Avenue
Winona Lake, Indiana 46590
(219) 267-7161

Soon after its founding, the Free Methodist Church encouraged the establishment of schools, first at academy level and later at college and graduate levels. All were non-sectarian, co-educational, and open to students regardless of color. They continue to be unashamedly evangelical and doctrinally conservative in commitment. The educational tradition of Free Methodism is to be traced through general and liberal channels rather than through restricted vocational and technical channels. The goal then as now was to integrate general learning and Christian culture. Preparation for the ministry became a later objective.

Founding Date: 1860
Membership: Not a membership organization
Meetings:
1 graduate student seminar
Annual seminars and workshops in various professional areas

605. Free Methodist Church of North America, Division of Planned Giving

Free Methodist Church of North America
Rev. David M. Samuelson, Director
9th and Chestnut Streets
Winona Lake, Indiana 46590
(219) 267-7656

The Division of Planned Giving is a service ministry of the Free Methodist Church of North America, annual conferences, and affiliated Free Methodist

institutions. It provides information and assistance in the areas of stewardship, estate planning, and creative giving. The service is professional, confidential, and provided without cost to the individual. This ministry was authorized by the General Conference in 1974, is operated under the direct supervision of the denominational Investment Committee, and is coordinated by Dr. Stanley B. Thompson, Director of Planned Giving, Winona Lake, Indiana. Personal service is provided by a team of six representatives in the Northeast, Midwest, Central Plains, Southwest and Northwest regions of the country.

Founding Date: 1975
Staff: 4

606. Free Methodist Church of North America, Light and Life Men International (LLMI)

Free Methodist Church of North America
Tom Black, President and Acting Executive Director
Winona Lake, Indiana 46590
(219) 267-7656

Light and Life Men is a worldwide fellowship of men dedicated to discipling others for evangelism and service. The movement was founded by a small group of concerned Free Methodist men who wanted to see a bold new thrust of evangelism in the world. It has pioneered in a new evangelistic awakening in Free Methodism through the development of home Bible study evangelism, and more recently, discipleship cells. LLMI fellowships now function in Canada, the United States, the Dominican Republic, South Africa, the Philippines, and other countries. Its programs include Christian Witness Crusades, Decision to Discipleship, and Continental Urban Exchange.

Founding Date: 1947
Staff: 2
Membership: 3,000
Publications:
Light and Life Line, 6 to 8 times per year
Meetings:
Men's retreats and occasional other conferences or seminars are held in the various districts (conferences) of the Free Methodist Church. These are usually held either in the spring or the fall.
Former Name: Light and Life Men's Fellowship

607. Free Methodist Church of North America, Women's Missionary Fellowship International (WMFI)

Free Methodist Church of North America
Evelyn L. Mottweiler, President
901 College Avenue
Winona Lake, Indiana 46590
(219) 267-5982

The Women's Missionary Fellowship International of the Free Methodist Church is involved in home Bible studies; prayer circles; fund raising for overseas missions; and Christian Youth in Missions groups. The goals of WMFI are to: grow spiritually through Bible study and prayer; win and disciple others for Christ; support the church's world missions program through personal involvement; develop strong leadership on the conference and local level; plan for an increase in membership; and provide instruction in missions and Christian stewardship for our children and youth.

Founding Date: 1894
Staff: 4
Membership: 35,000
Publications:
    Missionary Tidings, 10 issues per year
Meetings:
    1 worldwide conference every 5 years
Former Name: Woman's Missionary Society

608. Free Methodist Urban Fellowship (FMUF)

Free Methodist Church of North America
Howard·A. Snyder, President
4918 North Whipple Street
Chicago, Illinois 60625
(312) 588-0682

The Free Methodist Urban Fellowship has as its purpose "to promote, support, and encourage Free Methodist urban ministries through communication, information exchange, opportunities for fellowship, and assistance in fund raising, proposal writing, and other suitable means." It is governed by a coordinating council which includes representatives of Light and Life Men International and the Women's Missionary Fellowship International (auxiliary organizations of the Free Methodist Church).

Founding Date: 1981

Staff: 1 part-time
Membership: 120
Publications:
    CUE-TIPS, approximately four times per year
    Occasional papers on urban ministry questions
Meetings:
    Continental Urban Exchange (CUE) urban ministry conference, held annually in the spring in a major city

609. Free Methodist World Fellowship

Free Methodist Church of North America
Bishop W. Dale Cryderman, President
901 College Avenue
Winona Lake, Indiana 46590
(219) 267-6287

The Free Methodist World Fellowship was established in recognition of the fact that the overseas church had matured to a level where it deserved more autonomy in its own affairs. Through the World Fellowship, lay and ministerial leaders of various countries are brought together in area fellowships to exchange ideas and to train the leadership of the church. These area fellowships are held once every five years in Latin America, Asia-Egypt, Central Africa, and Southern Africa. Every five years, just prior to the North American General Conference, the World Fellowship has its conference with representatives from every country served by the Free Methodist Church. Benefits have been mutual. The mother church has learned much and the overseas church has been strengthened by working together towards common goals.

Founding Date: 1962
Meetings:
    Quinquennial conference

610. Free Will Baptist Press Foundation, Inc.

Original Free Will Baptist
Walter Reynolds, Manager
811 North Lee Street
Ayden, North Carolina 28513
(919) 746-6128

The Free Will Baptist Press Foundation, Inc., has as its purpose to perpetuate the Gospel through the printed page. Dedicated to Christian service, the Foundation strives toward the realization of its objectives by printing a weekly magazine, Sunday school and league literature for adults, young adults, and children, annual daily vacation Bible school materials for all ages, and instructional program books for church auxiliaries, including the women's auxiliary of the church and youth groups. In addition to locally processed denominational publications, the Foundation, through its bookstores at Ayden, New Bern, Smithfield, Wilson, and Kinston (all in North Carolina) offers a variety of pastoral and Sunday school teacher helps, inspirational books, Bibles, and supplementary materials. The Foundation offers everything in the way of religious merchandise: church furniture, communion services, church steeples, baptismal pools, choir and clerical robes, music, and many other useful and needed items.

Founding Date: 1873

Publications:

The Free Will Baptist, weekly

611. Freedom of Faith: A Christian Committee for Religious Rights (FOF)

Interdenominational

John Hays-Greene, Executive Director
170 East 64th Street
New York, New York 10021
(212) 838-4120

Freedom of Faith (FOF) is an ecumenical organization of Christians working for religious freedom. As a Christian organization, it seeks to draw its strength from the symbols and resources of the Christian tradition. At the same time, its concern extends to believers of all faiths. FOF is politically and ideologically impartial, and asserts the right of all persons to be free from interference by government or others in: determining their faith by conscience; freely associating and organizing with others for religious purposes; expressing their religious beliefs in worship, teaching, and practice; and pursuing the implications of their beliefs in the social and political community. As Christians, the members of FOF feel that their sense of the value of the individual person is rooted in the Biblical truth that each person bears the image and destiny of God's creating and redeeming love. Further, the members believe that the effort to repress religious faith betrays a basic disdain for the civic virtues of justice, tolerance, compassion, and charity; that contempt for God and faith leads to

contempt for man. In working for religious freedom, FOF desires to cooperate with all who work for human rights and the dignity of man.

Founding Date: 1978

Staff: 1

Membership:

310 general membership
34 members of the Board of Directors and Endorsements

Publications:

Alert, a monthly newsletter highlighting violations of religious freedom from around the world

Monthly case sheets for concern and action on these cases of the violation of religious freedom

Occasional special country reports

612. Friendly Contact Associates (FCA)

Nondenominational

The Rev. James Cope Crosson, National Director
15 Myrtle Drive
Umatilla, Florida 32784

Mailing Address
Rt. 2, Post Office Box 1001
Umatilla, Florida 32784
(904) 357-9723

Friendly Contact Associates is engaged in research and study of the following: parapsychology; survival; reincarnation and mental, physical, and spiritual health; metaphysics.

Founding Date: 1965

Staff: 5

Membership: 375 national members

Publications:

A monthly news bulletin

Meetings:

Monthly meetings

613. Friends Africa Gospel Mission (FAGM)

Religious Society of Friends

Alfred Miller, Field Superintendent
c/o Mid-America Yearly Meeting of Friends
2018 Maple
Wichita, Kansas 67213
(316) 267-0391

The purpose and activities of the Friends Africa Gospel Mission include assisting an indeginous Friends Church of Burundi to provide educational, medical, vocational, and literary services for the humanitarian and spiritual welfare of the people and providing United States personnel to assist nationals with technical skills necessary for the function of the programs.

Founding Date: 1934

614. Friends Committee on National Legislation (FCNL)

Religious Society of Friends
Edward Snyder, Executive Secretary
245 Second Street, N.E.
Washington, D.C. 20002
(202) 547-6000

The Friends Committee on National Legislation is active in Washington, D.C., formally and officially lobbying members of Congress and the Administration on issues of peace, world order, and human justices which grows from historic Quaker faith and testimonies. FCNL's support comes from individuals who are in agreement with its policies.

Founding Date: 1943
Staff: 19
Membership: Circulation 8,000
Publications:
A newsletter, 11 times annually, informing constituency of legislative information
Meetings:
1 conference annually

615. Friends Council on Education (FCE)

Religious Society of Friends (Quakers)
Adelbert Mason, Executive Director
1507 Cherry Street
Philadelphia, Pennsylvania 19102
(215) 563-2752

It was the wish of its founders that the Friends Council on Education act as an integrating force in Quaker education in an advisory and consultative capacity, and that it stimulate members of the Society of Friends to take a greater interest in education. Some of its major functions are: to exercise leadership in drawing Friends educational institutions together in unity of aim and spirit and, where desirable and feasible, into cooperative endeavor; to aid Friends in

being a constructive force in education, through encouraging the association of Quaker educators with each other and with their colleagues in the larger educational responsibilities of Friends schools in the areas of personal development and human relations, and of the spiritual message of the Society of Friends; to aid Friends schools in recruiting high calibre staff members and in developing and training these persons.

Founding Date: 1931
Staff:
6 staff members
42 appointed members
7 members-at-large, plus representatives from different Friends Yearly Meetings throughout the country
Publications:
Quaker Educational Graffiti, quarterly
Occasional publications on matters pertaining to Quaker education
Meetings:
About 10 meetings per year at different locations, though mostly in the Philadelphia area

616. Friends for Lesbian and Gay Concerns (Philadelphia, Pennsylvania)

Religious Society of Friends
Eric Kristensen/Rachael Alexander, Clerks
c/o Friends General Conference
1520 Race Street
Philadelphia, Pennsylvania 19102

The Friends for Lesbian and Gay Concerns works within the Society of Friends as a support group and has local chapters in most major cities in the East. It extends pastoral care through its local and conference activities. While its business structure and annual mid-winter conference are inclusive of both men and women, regional groups and smaller conferences are often exclusively for men or women. The members of the organization have evidenced a desire to reach out into the Gay and Lesbian communities with what they feel is a significantly different religious alternative from those offered by other religious denominations.

Membership: 420
Publications:
Newletter, 5-6 times a year
Meetings:
Lesbian Conference, East coast in the spring
Lesbian Conference, West coast in the fall

Men's Conference, East coast in the fall
Men's and Women's Conference, Midwinter in the East
Small group meetings in Chicago, Boston, New York, Philadelphia, and Washington

617. Friends for Lesbian and Gay Concerns (Sumneytown, Pennsylvania)

Quaker
Post Office Box 222
Sumneytown, Pennsylvania 18084

The Friends for Lesbian and Gay Concerns has about four gatherings a year in different locations. They are times of worship and mutual support. Members are active in social concerns on an individual basis.

Membership: 425

Publications:
Newsletter, about 4 times a year

Meetings:
About 4 a year

618. Friends for Missions, Inc.

Interdenominational
Mary Ellen Goodwin, Executive Director
514 Lynnhaven Drive, S.W.
Terrace Apartment
Atlanta, Georgia 30310
Mailing Address
Post Office Box 10942
Atlanta, Georgia 30310
(404) 758-8410

The purpose of Friends for Missions is to help alleviate some of the suffering among God's Little Ones in the Republic of Haiti. Their program is divided into four categories, spiritual, nutritional, medical and educational. The goals of Friends for Missions are: to stimulate interest in missions, particularly foreign missions; to disseminate information regarding the needs of persons engaged in the foreign missions ministry and those whom they are serving; to be a source and channel of funds and other needed supplies to native pastors and mission projects serving people on the field; to encourage persons to go as firsthand observers that they might return with a greater understanding and deeper insight to inform, challenge, and inspire others; and to provide opportunities for employment among the

natives so that they may be able to help themselves and provide for their families.

Founding Date: 1968

Staff: 3 in National Office; 20 in Haiti

Membership: 2,300 on mailing list

Publications:
Extended Hand Newsletter, quarterly
Annual Report

Meetings:
Annual Meeting and Board Meeting, once a year
Regional Board Meetings and Luncheons held 4 times a year

619. Friends Historical Association (FHA)

Quaker
John M. Moore, President
(for business matters)
Haverford College Library
Haverford, Pennsylvania 19041
(for editorial matters)
Friends Historical Library
Swarthmore College
Swarthmore, Pennsylvania 19081
(215) 649-9600 (Haverford)
(215) 447-7496 (Swarthmore)

The Friends Historical Association encourages the study of the history of the Religious Society of Friends (Quakers). There is a sister organization in London, England, called the Friends Historical Society. The organization publishes a journal, *Quaker History,* formerly called the Bulletin of the Friends Historical Association, now in its 69th year. The Association holds two public meetings annually and supports the publication of material related to Quaker history.

Founding Date: 1873

Membership:
765 members, including approximately 100 library subscribers to *Quaker History*

Publications:
Quaker History, twice a year

Meetings:
2 public meetings annually
Occasional conferences held by a chapter of the Friends Historical Association called Conference of Quaker Historians and Archivists

Absorbed:
(1923) Friends' Historical Society of Philadelphia

620. Friends of Israel Gospel Ministry, Inc. (FIGM)

Interdenominational

Marvin J. Rosenthal, International Director
475 White Horse Pike
West Collingswood, New Jersey 08107

Mailing Address
Post Office Box 123
West Collingswood, New Jersey 08107
(609) 854-1120 or (215) 922-3030

The Friends of Israel Gospel Ministry, Inc., is an interdenominational, conservative, evangelical faith mission. It was founded for the purpose of reaching Jews throughout Europe during the time of the Hitler atrocities. The Friends of Israel are currently ministering in eight countries where there are vast numbers of Jews residing. Major emphasis is placed upon proclaiming the need for personal salvation, through faith in the Lord Jesus Christ to the Jew and also to the Gentiles. This task is accomplished through field evangelists, missionaries, and office staff. The mission publishes a large body of quality books and literature. It also conducts a film ministry, a camp and campus ministry, a growing home Bible study ministry, a relief program, and seminars on the "How To's of Jewish Evangelism."

Founding Date: 1938

Staff: 75

Publications:
Israel My Glory, bimonthly

Meetings:
1 Annual Public Conference

Former Name:
(1973) Friends of Israel Missionary and Relief Society

621. Friends of the Lusitanian Church

Episcopal Church U.S.A.

Rev. Cannon Edmund W. Olifiers, Jr.
Bishops' Commisary in the United States
Lindenhurst, New York 11757

Mailing Address
Post Office Box 165
Lindenhurst, New York 11757
(516) 957-2666

The purpose of the Friends of the Lusitanian Church is to stimulate interest, prayer, and financial support among the American Episcopalians and others for the Christian evangelism of Portugal through the work and program of the minority and relatively poor Episcopal Church in Portugal, known locally as the "Lusitanian Church," its ancient name. The "Friends" seek to aid the enterprise of this Portuguese Christian community through capital grants, programmatic seed money, and other forms of assistance. Brochures, publications, and a slide-show are available.

Staff: 4 officers

Membership: Approximately 450 supporters

Publications:
O Novo Despertar, in Portuguese
Spanish and Portuguese Church News

622. Friends of Turkey

Nondenominational

Post Office Box 3098
Grand Junction, Colorado 81502
(303) 241-0682

Friends of Turkey is an evangelical ministry organized to encourage, support, and engage in Christian evangelism among the peoples of Turkey and other lands; provide food or clothing for relief of the poor or distressed; support or assist missionaries and other Christian workers; provide informational services; encourage prayer for the Turks and other peoples of the world; and receive contributions for these purposes.

Founding Date: 1970

Staff: 9

Membership: 4,500

Publications:
FOT Newsletter, bimonthly

Former Name:
(1980) Friends of Turkey and Postal Evangelism, Inc.

623. Friends World Committee for Consultation, Section of the Americas

Religious Society of Friends

Herbert M. Hadley, Executive Secretary
1506 Race Street
Philadelphia, Pennsylvania 19102
(215) 563-0757

Friends World Committee for Consultation, Section of the Americas endeavors to: encourage and strengthen the spiritual life within the Society of

Friends through promotion of inter-visitation, study, conferences and a wide sharing of experience on the deepest spiritual level; help Friends to gain better understanding of the world-wide character of the Society of Friends and its vocation in the world today; promote consultation among Friends of all cultures, countries and languages. The Committee seeks to bring the different groups of Friends into intimate touch with one another on the basis of their common Quaker heritage, with a view to sharing experience and coming to some measure of agreement in regard to their attitude to modern world problems; to keep under review the Quaker contribution in world affairs, and to facilitate both the examination and presentation of Quaker thinking and concern.

Membership: 190

Publications:

Newsletter, 3 times a year
Friends World News, semiannually

Meetings:

Executive Committee (60 members), 2 times a year
Occasional regional or topical conferences

624. **Friendship House (FH)**

Roman Catholic
Hal Wand, Director
1746 West Division
Chicago, Illinois 60622
(312) 227-5066

Friendship House was founded by the Baroness Catherine De Hueck Doherty, who now lives in Canada and directs a group of Madonna Houses. FH orignially had houses in New York City; Washington, D.C.; Shreveport, Louisiana; and Portland, Oregon. The only remaining house is in Chicago, Illinois. FH started a civil rights program before there was any such activity. It received recognition from President L. B. Johnson. Today it is a Christian, non-violent, inter-cultural group working for social justice.

Founding Date: 1938

Staff: 20

Membership: 1,400 in the U.S. and abroad

Publications:

Community, quarterly

Meetings:

Spirituality and Justice Conference, monthly
Retreat, quarterly
Peace & Justice Meeting, weekly

625. **The Friendship Ministry**

Nondenominational
Dorothy C. Haskin, President
2216 West Burbank Boulevard
Burbank, California 91506
(213) 848-7996

The Friendship Ministry sends food, Christian literature, and Bibles to more than 90 groups of needy Christians in eight third world countries. Also, The Friendship Ministry sponsors children, Bible women and evangelists in these countries. The Friendship Ministry is a comparatively small organization headed by Dorothy C. Haskin, who is guided by a reputable board. The groups aided vary from a widow living alone to a home for more than 200 children. It is not a relief organization per se, but assists selected groups of needy Christians. The Friendship Ministry has no denominational basis.

Founding Date: 1970

Staff: 4

Membership: 20 volunteers

Publications:

Friendship, quarterly
Newsletter, monthly

626. **The Friendship Press, Inc.**

Nondenominational
Ward L. Kaiser, Executive Director
475 Riverside Drive, Room 772
New York, New York 10115
(212) 870-2495

Friendship Press publishes programs of mission education for use in 27 denominations. These publications include books, maps, plays, filmstrips, recordings, cassettes, pictures, games, and other educational materials for use in religious education. Its material is planned by a board of 100 educational professionals representing the denominations and is distributed through denominational bookstores and agencies and secular bookstores.

Membership:

100 primarily representing denominational boards and agencies in education, home and overseas mission, women's work, audio-visual productions and social action

Publications:

Popular religious education books of various kinds but especially on the mission of the church for use by average person in the church— not primarily for scholars

Meetings:
> A dozen conferences each summer on the mission of the church using the Friendship Press materials

Radio/TV Programs:
> *The Joyful Sound,* radio program, weekly

Meetings:
> 35 seminars per year

627. Friendship Reflections, Inc.

Nondenominational

Paul A. Stewart, Executive Director
3862 Plainfield Avenue, N.E.
Grand Rapids, Michigan 49505
(616) 364-8722

The principal purpose of Friendship Reflections, Inc., is to minister the Gospel of Jesus Christ; to promote spiritual, educational, charitable and benevolent work of the Christian faith. It is heard weekly on radio and supplies Christian books and literature.

Membership: No members, just secretarial staff

Publications:
> *Uplift,* monthly

Radio/TV Programs:
> Weekly

628. Fuller Evangelistic Association

Nondenominational

Carl F. George and David E. Hubbard,
Vice-Presidents
44 South Mentor Avenue
Pasadena, California 91102

Mailing Address

Post Office Box 989
Pasadena, California 91102
(213) 449-0425

The Fuller Evangelistic Association continues the ministry of Charles E. Fuller by raising support for evangelistic and humanitarian missionary projects and by providing consultation, training, and research to churches, districts, denominations, and para-church organizations in the area of church growth.

Founding Date: 1943

Membership: 26

Publications:
> *Today's Christian,* monthly

629. Gabriel Richard Institute

Roman Catholic

Rev. Thomas J. Bresnahan, Director
2315 Orleans Street
Detroit, Michigan 48207
(313) 965-5891

The Gabriel Richard Institute, a non-profit organization, began with the purpose of offering a training course in leadership fundamentals for the Christian Community. The Institute derives its inspiration from "The Christophers." It believes that *each* person can do something personally and individually to help change the world for the better; and that training in leadership fundamentals makes a person more effective in apostolic pursuits. The Course is composed of 10 interlocking sessions. The focus is on leadership skills and attitudes such as : self-confidence, speaking skills, effective human relations practices, and Christian purpose. It is open to any adult and to persons of all faiths. Instruction teams are made up of highly skilled men and women who volunteer their services after personally experiencing the benefits of the Course. Proceeds above actual course costs are used for scholarships and to promote the Course worldwide.

Founding Date: 1949
Membership: 799 lay; 10 clerical
Publications:
   Christopher Leadership Course
Meetings:
   Annual conference
Former Name:
   (1960) Christopher Career Guidance School

630. Gay people [sic] in Christian Science

Christian Science

15 Christopher Street
New York, New York 10014
(212) 889-8046 or 961-1282 or 242-9078

Gay people in Christian Science is an ad hoc group of Gay and non-Gay Christian Scientists working within the Christian Science movement to: make known the wholesomeness and normality of same-sex love relationships based on the First Commandment and the Golden Rule; end the present unfair treatment of Lesbians and Gay men by those in positions of authority within the Christian Science Organization; make the healing light of Christian Science widely available within the Gay community to heal false fears, guilt feelings and other related problems; and promote the return of the Christian Science movement to the pursuit of spirituality, unfettered by such bankrupt prejudices as racism, sexism, and heterosexism.

Publications:
   Announcements, issued periodically
Meetings:
   Occasional, open to the public

631. General Association of General Baptists, Foreign Mission Board

Baptist

Charles L. Carr, Executive Director
Samuel S. Ramdial, Director of Missions Education
100 Stinson Drive
Poplar Bluff, Missouri 63901
Mailing Address
Post Office Box 537
Poplar Bluff, Missouri 63901
(314) 785-7975

The General Baptist Foreign Mission Board conducts the mission program for the General Baptist denomination. The Board began with missions in the Mariana Islands. Its efforts are directed toward establishing churches, training leaders, and contributing to the spiritual and physical welfare of the people in whose areas it serves. Working through the national church, with a minimum investment in overseas missionaries, the Board seeks to plant churches which are guided and nurtured by national leadership. Evangelism and Christian instruction are strongly emphasized. The Board is a member of the Evangelical Foreign Missions Association, North American Baptist Fellowship, and Baptist World Alliance.

Founding Date: 1911

Publications:

Capsule, monthly

632. General Association of General Baptists, General Board

General Baptist

Glen O. Spence, Executive Secretary
100 Stinson Drive
Poplar Bluff, Missouri 63901
(314) 785-7746

The General Board of the General Association of General Baptists consists of 17 members, employing officers and employees as needed, including a Denominational Executive Secretary and Stewardship Director. The Denominational Executive Secretary is the principal administrative officer of the General Board. He is responsible for securing, tabulating and publishing statistical reports relating to the work of the Association. He acts as co-ordinator of the various agencies. The General Board acts for the General Association when it is not in session, studies the affairs of the boards and other agencies of the Association, and recommends a comprehensive unified budget. The General Board is the trust, fiscal, and executive agency of the General Association in all its affairs not specifically committed to some other board or agency.

Staff: 14

Membership: 17

Meetings:

1 pastors conference a year, location varies
1 General Association meeting a year, location varies
Stewardship Seminars, number and location varies

633. General Association of General Baptists, Home Mission Board, Inc.

General Baptist

Dr. Leland Duncan, Executive Director
100 Stinson Drive
Poplar Bluff, Missouri 63901

Mailing Address
Post Office Box 537
Poplar Bluff, Missouri 63901
(314) 785-7746

The General Baptist Home Mission Board is directly responsible for developing, initiating, promoting and supervising programs which will contribute to the expansion of the cause of Christ through the General Baptist Denomination in the United States. The Board strives to enhance the total ministry of the General Association of General Baptists in its task of leading persons to salvation in Christ Jesus, teaching them His plan of redemption for all mankind and enlisting them to an active participation through the local church.

Publications:

Broadcaster, monthly

634. General Association of General Baptists, Women's Mission Board

General Baptist

Brenda J. Kennedy, Executive Director
100 Stinson Drive
Poplar Bluff, Missouri 63901
(314) 785-7746

The Women's Mission Board is engaged in fund raising to supplement the incomes of the foreign and home mission programs, as well as the denomination's college. Individual groups help to sustain mission emphasis in the local churches, participate in community missions and provide mission teaching to small children and teenage girls. The Board furnishes financial backing for a paramedic ministry in the Philippines and other special projects. The office and Executive Director are responsible to 18 women chosen from various geographical areas. This group sponsors a Missionary Conference each year.

Membership: 7,000

Publications:

Study books for local missionary societies
Newsletter by subscription

Meetings:

Women's Missionary Conference
National Guild Girls Rally

635. General Baptist Press*

General Association of General Baptists
Riley M. Mathias
Post Office Box 790
Poplar Bluff, Missouri 63901
(314) 785-3031

The General Baptist Press began publishing the *General Baptist Messenger* 90 years ago. Its purpose is now stated as follows: "This board shall be responsible for the curriculum and the promotion of Christian education, publications, leadership training, minister's home study, and camping. It shall be responsible for the merchandising of General Baptist education materials. This board shall make evangelism, stewardship, missions and related denominational objectives integral parts of the total Christian education program of the local church."

636. General Commission on Chaplains and Armed Forces Personnel

Nondenominational
The Rev. Edward I. Swanson, Director
5100 Wisconsin Avenue, N.W.
Washington, D.C. 20016
(202) 686-1857

The General Commission on Chaplains and Armed Forces Personnel is the nation's oldest and largest Protestant interchurch agency concerned with religious ministries to people in the armed forces and in Veterans Administration health care facilities. By its constitution, it is committed to three basic functions. It serves as an Interchurch Forum, through which the churches keep informed about chaplains' ministries and the concerns of people in the armed forces, share with each other, and present a united front in dealing with agencies of the government; a Service Agency, developing and producing materials and programs for the use of churches and their chaplains. The Commission maintains a comprehensive guidebook and consultation service on the ecclesiastical endorsement of chaplains to assist denominational officials. For those denominations which need the additional service, the Commission also administers the processing of their clergy into various chaplaincy positions; an Information and Education Service, monitoring developments and trends in the military and veteran communities as well as the churches, and maintaining a regular flow of information in both directions. To a large extent, this is done through the

Commission's publications. Most of the Commission's financial support comes from the church bodies that own it. They are asked to contribute according to a fair-share scale, based on the number of chaplains each has on active duty. Direct contributions from individuals and local congregations assist greatly in expanding the Commission's services.

Founding Date: 1917

Staff: 4

Membership:
    36 member denominations
    5 associate denominations

Publications:
    Chaplaincy, successor to *The Chaplain,* a professional journal for clergy in military and V.A. ministries, quarterly
    Chaplaincy Letter, a monthly newsletter reporting current developments within the chaplaincies, the Congress, and the Churches

Meetings:
    2 meetings a year, in March and October

Former Names:
    (1947) Committee on Army and Navy Chaplains
    (1951) General Commissions on Chaplains

637. General Conference Mennonite Church, Commission on Education

General Conference Mennonite Church
722 Main Street
Newton, Kansas 67114

Mailing Address
Post Office Box 347
Newton, Kansas 67114
(316) 283-5100

The Commission on Education is responsible for programs of Christian education and for the preparation and publication of curriculum, periodicals, and literature for the church, home, and wider community. The Commission has a separate department of higher education, with appropriate staff, to provide an overall conference view of, and concern for, formalized parochial and post-high school education. Included are the 5 Mennonite colleges, the conference seminary, services to students at public colleges and universities, vocational-technical schools and extension programs for adults.

Staff: 18

Membership: 20

Publications:
Pamphlets and books related to the Church Sunday School curriculum
Periodicals for children, youth

Meetings:
1 annual meeting
1 mid-year conference

638. General Conference Mennonite Church, Commission on Home Ministries

General Conference Mennonite Church
E. Stanley Bohn, Executive Secretary
72 Main Street
Newton, Kansas 67114
Mailing Address
Post Office Box 347
Newton, Kansas 67114
(316) 283-5100

The Commission on Home Ministries administers mission and service programs in North America including Indian Ministries, Chinese and Hispanic language work, and 25 voluntary service units. It provides resources for congregational mission, church planting, and peace witness. The commission also assists in the production of television and radio programs.

Staff: 10

Membership: 15 commission members

Publications:
Congregational Goals Discovery Plan
A New Look at Church Growth
You and Your Options
ACTS Paper, (Articles About Churches for Churches), 6 times a year
God and Caesar, quarterly publication on war tax/militarism education
From Swords to Plowshares, quarterly publication on farm issues
House Church Newsletter, bimonthly
MVS (Mennonite Voluntary Service Connection), quarterly

Radio/TV Programs:
A number of special productions and TV and radio spots

Meetings:
10 reference council meetings
4 Executive Committee and commission meetings

639. General Conference Mennonite Church, Commission on Overseas Mission (COM)

General Conference Mennonite Church
722 Main
Newton, Kansas 67114
Mailing Address
Post Office Box 347
Newton, Kansas 67114
(316) 283-5100

The General Conference Mennonite Church began missionary work in 1900 in India. Today there are missionaries located in 14 countries: Zaire, Lesotho, Botswana, and Upper Volta in Africa; Mexico, Colombia, Brazil, Uruguay, Paraguay, and Bolivia in Latin America; India, Japan, Taiwan, and Hong Kong in Asia. The Commission on Overseas Mission is involved in programs of evangelism, church planting, leadership training, Christian education, literature and radio ministries, technical and agricultural development projects, and medical work. At present there are 140 missionaries serving in these countries.

Founding Date: 1900

Membership: 145 missionaries

640. General Conference Mennonite Church, Women in Mission (WM)

General Conference Mennonite Church
Joan Wiebe, Coordinator
Post Office Box 347
Newton, Kansas 67114
(316) 283-5100

The purpose of Women in Mission is to help its 10,000 members in approximately 440 groups become effectively involved in the total mission of the church. Bible study, prayer, and fellowship are blended with a desire to meet the physical, spiritual, educational, and emotional needs of those near and far. Women in Mission members believe that people committed to Christ and his work can be empowered for ministering in this difficult age.

Founding Date: 1917

Staff: 3

Membership: 10,000

Publications:
Window to Mission, six times a year

Former Name:
(1974) Women's Missionary Association

641. The Genesis Project

Interdenominational
Richard C. Beeson, President and Chief Executive Officer
5201 Leesburg Pike, Suite 800
Falls Church, Virginia 22041
(703) 998-0800

The Genesis Project is a company of people committed to putting the Bible back into the center of twentieth-century life using contemporary media. To achieve this The Genesis Project produces The New Media Bible, a visual translation of Scripture onto the medium of the twentieth century, film. Accompanying these 15- to 20-minute films is a complete teaching program for churches, schools, and institutions. Each film program includes a magazine of background information, *Bibletimes;* filmstrips of maps, illustrations, artifacts, and sacred sites; teacher's guides and guidebooks; student notebooks; posters; and songbooks. The Genesis Project also offers a home slide and study program to aid parents and families in religious education. The Genesis Project is an interdenominational company and maintains theological neutrality. Particular doctrinal or denominational interpretations of Scripture are left to the teachers.

Publications:
Films, Filmstrips, magazines, study guides, guidebooks, notebooks, posters, home slide programs

Meetings:
Educational seminars several times a year throughout the country

642. Geneva Point Center

National Council of the Churches of Christ in the United States
Rev. Harry Widman
Star Route 62, Box 469
Centre Harbor, New Hampshire 03226
(603) 253-4366

Geneva Point Center, also known as "Winni," is an ecumenical conference center owned by the Division of Education and Ministry of the National Council of the Churches of Christ in the United States. For more than 60 years the center has been of service to men, women, and children. People of every race, national origin, religion, handicap, and economic and social level meet and share the spirit encompassing

"Winni" with its sense of faith, freedom, and fellowship.

Founding Date: 1919
Staff:
Year round/full time 6
Spring, summer, fall: up to an additional 50
Former Name: Geneva Point Camp

643. GIA Publications, Inc. (Gregorian Institute of America)

Nondenominational
Edward Harris, President
7404 South Mason Avenue
Chicago, Illinois 60638
(312) 496-3800

The Gregorian Institute of America publishes church music including anthems, motets, psalms, masses, folk, vocal solos, instrumentals, and piano arrangements. A choral subscription service is available for parishes and summer workshops on liturgical music are conducted.

Meetings:
Summer workshops on liturgical music

644. The Gideons International

Nondenominational
R. Don Efird, President
2900 Lebanon Road
Nashville, Tennessee 37214
(615) 883-8533

The Gideons are laymen from various evangelical denominations, Christian business and professional men with a vital testimony for the Lord. Each Gideon is an active member of some local church and The Gideons as an association work in cooperation with all evangelical churches and denominations. The primary objective of The Gideons is to win others for Christ, and an effective means to this end has been a wide distribution of the Word of God. Gideons seek to spread the Bible and encourage its use as widely as possible. Bibles are placed in the rooms of hotels and motels, New Testaments with Psalms and Proverbs are given out at induction centers to men and women of the armed forces and, with the approval of school authorities, bright red New Testaments are distributed to elementary and high schools in the

United States. A Large Print New Testament with Psalms, light and easy for a patient to read in bed, is placed by hospital beds. Used Bibles removed from hotels and motels are distributed by Gideons to those incarcerated in jails and given to rescue missions. A copy of the Bible is placed in every airplane of most larger airlines throughout the world. Gideon Bibles are also placed in ships and trains.

Founding Date: 1899

Publications:
Bibles
The Gideon Magazine, monthly

645. Global Orphanages, Inc.

Interdenominational, Protestant
A.E.K. Brenner, President
1012 City Avenue
Philadelphia, Pennsylvania 19151
(215) 642-2255

The main purpose of Global Orphanages, Inc., is to provide financial assistance to established orphanages in the United States and developing countries by locating sponsors for individual orphans and/or orphanages. Activities in the United States are conducted by volunteers only.

Founding Date: 1951

646. Gnostic Aquarian Society*

World Esoteric Assembly
Carl L. Weschcke, President
213 East 4th Street
St. Paul, Minnesota 55101
(612) 291-1970

Gnostic Aquarian Society is a general membership organization bringing together participants from all the occult disciplines at a serious level of interchange and research. The Society is dedicated to the concept that we have entered a New Age calling for a coming together of the occult sciences with the more generally respected physical and psychological sciences to achieve a new synthesis to meet the challenges to the physical environment; to the need for individual relationship and personal expression of the religious experience; and for the need of group magical work. An annual Festival of the Occult Sciences is sponsored at the Fall Equinox to give impetus to this movement and to celebrate the growing

awareness and acceptance of the responsibility for such New Age work.

Membership: 600 lay; 25 clerical

Publications:
Gnostica, monthly

Meetings:
3 conferences per year

647. Go Ye Books

Christian Church and Church of Christ
Miles Baker, Manager
147 Avenida Cota
San Clemente, California 92672
(714) 496-6699 or 492-1333

The objective of Go Ye Books is to distribute the books and booklets written by Mark G. Maxey, missionary to Japan since 1950. His books and other writings are used by missionaries and their forwarding agents, by those who are considering going into a mission field as missionaries, by friends and supporters of the Maxey Family and The Kyushu Christian mission, as school mission textbooks, for soul winning among Japanese, and by those with an interest in missionaries in general and Japan in particular.

Staff: 2

Publications:
Linkletter, a monthly newsletter by the Mark G. Maxey missionary family

648. Good News

United Methodist
James V. Heidinger II, Executive Secretary/Editor
308 East Main Street
Wilmore, Kentucky 40390
(606) 858-4661

Good News is a magazine serving evangelical United Methodists as a voice and a conscience, and a movement advocating full Biblical authority, Wesleyan theology, and personal experience of Christ as the primary means of renewal for individuals, for society, and for the United Methodist Church. The goals of Good News are: to unite evangelical Methodists; to help them make the most effective witness for Christ within our denomination; to sound the alarm about un-Scriptural trends; to proclaim Scriptural truths; to discuss vital issues; to enter into dialog with other theological viewpoints; to seek a proportionate and fair voice for evangelicals in denominational affairs; to provide much-needed fellowship for evangelicals within the church; and to deepen appreciation for the dynamic Wesleyan heritage of Christian experience, transformed life, and Biblical authority.

Founding Date: 1967

Staff: 12 full-time, 3 part-time

Publications:

Good News, bimonthly

Candle, newsletter for women, published as funds permit

Catalyst, newsletter for United Methodist ministers and seminarians, quarterly

Evangelical Missions Council newsletter, quarterly sent to those interested in missions

Meetings:

Annual convocation, held in various large cities, each summer

Legal Name:

Forum for Scriptural Christianity within the United Methodist Church, Inc.

649. Good News Mission

Nondenominational

W. L. Simmer, President
R. A. Sauer, Executive Assistant
1036 South Highland Street
Arlington, Virginia 22204
(703) 979-2200

The Good News Mission is a ministry to prisoners, ex-offenders, and their families. It has 72 chaplains serving in federal, state, county, and city prisons and jails as well as juvenile detention centers, and its ministry extends from the tip of Long Island to Hawaii and from the Canadian border to Florida, and foreign countries as far away as India. The organization serves over 120 institutions on a regular basis plus many others on an intermittent basis. It is by far, the largest supplier of jail and prison chaplains in the United States and, by their estimate, in the world. The Good News Mission ministers to a daily average of 33,592 and an annual average of 520,810 men, women, and children. Its 72 chaplains are augmented by a staff of 5,000 volunteers, approximately half of whom donate time to this work on a regular weekly basis. In addition to those behind bars, the Mission maintains an active ministry to their families on the outside. It also operates a division of opportunity houses which serve as discipleship centers for the

recently released, assisting them in the transition from prison to freedom and seeking to build them into strong Christians who can take their places of service in local churches and other ministries as the Lord may lead. Each of the chaplains maintains a very busy schedule — they average over 60 hours a week on the job — conducting daily, all-day programs in their jails. In addition to services, the Mission offers individual counseling, Bible studies, Bible correspondence courses with an enrollment of well over 30,000, and numerous other programs.

Founding Date: 1961

Staff: 72 chaplains; 12 staff

Membership: 5,000 volunteers

Publications:

Update, monthly

136 Bible correspondence course lessons

Numerous tracts, brochures, and other publications

Meetings:

Correctional Chaplaincy Course, Mission Headquarters each January (the only training program for the correctional chaplain anywhere)

650. Good News Publishers

Interdenominational

Mrs. Clyde H. Dennis, President
9825 West Roosevelt Road
Westchester, Illinois 60153
(312) 345-7474

Good News Publishers is committed to bearing witness to Jesus Christ, the Incarnate Son of God, through publishing literature excellent in design and content that clearly and effectively reflects historic, biblical truth. Good News is committed to serving the Church of Jesus Christ on an interdenomination and international basis.

Founding Date: 1938

Staff: 22

Publications:

Books; booklets; tracts and devotional magazine

651. Good News Unlimited

Nondenominational

Calvin W. Edwards, Administrator
1212 High Street, Suite 201
Auburn, California 95603

Mailing Address
Post Office Box GN
Auburn, Califorinia 95603
(916) 823-9690

Good News Unlimited is committed to the preaching and teaching of the New Testament gospel of Jesus Christ. It is especially concerned with communicating the message of the cross of Christ and its liberating power. The specific ministries of Good News Unlimited include a national radio program featuring Dr. Desmond Ford — a half-hour weekly broadcast. It also publishes a variety of materials, including a monthly *Bulletin,* and produces cassettes. It is active in holding public seminars and congresses.

Founding Date: 1980

Staff: 7

Publications:
   The Good News Unlimited Bulletin, monthly
   Syllabi for congresses

Radio/TV Programs:
   Good News Unlimited, one half hour, weekly radio broadcast

Meetings:
   8-10 per year

652. Gordon Press, Publishers

Nondenominational

Raoul Gordon, President and Editor
Post Office Box 459
Bowling Green Station
New York, New York 10004

Gordon Press and its affiliate Krishna Press publish books and monographs on the history and philosophy of religion. The Press now has on it back list over 400 titles on the history and philosophy of the Roman Catholic Church, and the history of Protestantism and Islam, and has recently reissued in four volumes the *Complete Works of Jakob Boehme* that have been out of print for 300 years. Gordon Press publishes both scholarly reprints and originals, including doctoral dissertations, in the area of religious knowledge and history. It is especially interested in books and manuscripts on Jakob Boehme, John Huss, John Calvin, Buddhism, Confucianism, Taoism, Shintoism, Theosophy, Rudolf Steiner, Martin Luther, Billy Graham, Judaism, Early Church Fathers, Women in Religion, Mysticism, Islam,

African and Asian Religions, the Historical Jesus, Religious Archaeology, Religion as Applied to Social Problems, John Haynes Holmes, Christian History, etc. The Gordon Press affiliate Krishna Press publishes works on the religions of India, China, and Japan.

653. Gospel Advance Mission, Inc.

Interdenominational

Rev. Don E. White
Post Office Box 339
Salida, Colorado 81201
(303) 539-4079

Gospel Advance Mission, Inc., is an interdenominational service agency of evangelical tradition engaged in missionary and national worker recruiting, and education and training, including Bible correspondence courses. Summer and short-term United States missionary orientation and training is available at United States headquarters.

Founding Date: 1964

Publications:
   Newsletter, monthly

Radio/TV Programs:
   A 15-minute radio program once weekly

Meetings:
   Numerous: the headquarters is located on 240 acres of conference grounds with a private airport and camping facilities

654. Gospel Advocate Company*

Church of Christ

B. C. Goodpasture
Post Office Box 150
Nashville, Tennessee 37202
(615) 254-8781

Gospel Advocate Company is the publisher of Gospel Advocate Sunday School literature, Vacation Bible School materials, religious books, tracts, Bible foundations, and other materials for the Church of Christ.

655. The Gospel Association for the Blind, Inc. (GAB)

Nondenominational

Dr. Ralph Montanus, Director
Rev. Ralph Montanus, Jr., President
4705 North Federal Highway
Boca Raton, Florida 33431
(305) 395-0022

The main purpose of the Gospel Association for the Blind is carried out by Dr. Ralph Montanus who ministers to the world's darkest mission field through Braille, Talking Books, records, Christian camping, counseling, radio ministry, and fellowship meetings for the blind. In addition to ministry to the blind, the Gospel Association for the Blind reaches the deaf-blind and deaf-blind mutes with the Gospel through the sense of touch. The Association has a radio program called *That They Might See* which reaches many of the major cities in the United States and Canada.

Founding Date: 1947

Staff: 20

Membership:
> Approximately 100 churches and 3,000 individual members

Publications:
> *Jottings,* a monthly bulletin for sighted missionary partners and churches
> *The Gospel Messenger,* a monthly Braille magazine for blind adults
> *The Braille Pilot,* a quarterly Braille magazine for blind children

Radio/TV Programs:
> A radio program on 35 stations every Sunday

Meetings:
> Monthly Fellowship Meetings for the Blind in Boco Raton, Florida
> Annual Bible Conference and Camping Session for the Blind held each year in Jaffrey Center, New Hampshire at the end of July

656. Gospel Crusade, Inc.

Christian, Interdenominational, Charismatic

Gerald Derstine, President and Director
Upper Manatee River Road
Bradenton, Florida 33508

Mailing Address
Route 2, Post Office Box 279
Bradenton, Florida 33508
(813) 747-6481

The purpose of Gospel Crusade, Inc., is to proclaim the glorious Gospel message of the Kingdom of God around the world and to strengthen individuals, marriages, familes, churches, communities and nations in godly living, recognizing that the family unit is God's basis for all of societal living, and that righteousness exalts a nation, but sin is a reproach to any people. This multi-faceted ministry reaches multitudes annually via: televised Bible teachings (commercial networks, cable systems, satellite transmissions, and video cassettes); year-round Bible conference centers in Florida and Minnesota; 10-week Institute of Ministry training sessions offered four times each year (also available by correspondence through cassette tapes); a pastoral training school; world-wide distribution of Bible teachings via audio and video cassette tapes, books and printed tracts; a ministerial fellowship of over 800 credential-holders and 24 affiliated churches in the United States; overseas outreaches in Haiti, Jamaica, Honduras, the Philippines, and Israel, including support of missionaries and establishment of over 300 churches; vital interaction with numerous other Christian organizations, churches, and fellowships throughout the United States and Canada; and the western Florida Consulate for the International Christian Embassy in Jerusalem.

Founding Date: 1953

Staff: 92

Membership:
> Local church, 500 plus
> Ministers, 812 world-wide

Publications:
> *Blessings,* 6 issues per year
> Books authored by Gerald Derstine including *The Kingdom of God is at Hand; Destined to Mature; Lively Living, God, How Practical Can You Get?; Following the Fire; God Speaks Today; To Receive the Holy Spirit,* and *Woman's Place in the Church*
> Various ministry tracts

Radio/TV Programs:
> *Gerald Derstine Shares, Kingdom Living,* radio and T.V.

Meetings:
> Bradenton Florida Christian Retreat Conference Center, continual year 'round.
> Strawberry Lake, Minnesota, Christian Retreat Conference

657. Gospel Films, Inc.*

Nondenominational
Billy Zeoli, President
Post Office Box 455
Muskegon, Michigan 49443
(616) 773-3361

Gospel Films has dedicated itself to unleashing God's good news on film. Its films are available for showing in churches, schools, hospitals, military bases, prisons, evangelistic crusades, and television. Gospel Films' distribution centers are maintained in 49 population areas in the United States, with distribution in 160 countries outside of North America. Films are released in more than 40 languages to workers in more than 325 missionary organizations. Gospel Films' productions have been aired on television in more than 50 countries. Its motivation is to communicate the Gospel to millions of people through dedicated use of the film media.

Staff: 22 in home office

658. Gospel Furthering Fellowship*

Representative Council
Lot C II, Malvern Courts
Malvern, Pennsylvania 19355
(215) 644-2162

The goals of the Gospel Furthering Fellowship are to establish local, independent New Testament churches, and to train national pastors to serve in them. When the members of the Fellowship determine that a new congregation is capable of standing alone, they leave and enter a new area to begin anew.

Membership: 9
Publications:
    Newsletter, monthly

659. Gospel Light Publications

Nondenominational
William T. Greig, Jr., President
110 West Broadway
Glendale, California 91204
(213) 247-2330

Gospel Light Publications is a Christian enterprise dedicated to the task of preparing Christian education materials in a total Bible teaching plan to help Sunday Schools around the world achieve these goals: teach the Bible, God's inspired Word; present Jesus Christ as Saviour and Lord; relate the Bible to students' lives; train and inspire teachers; build the Church. Gospel Light publishes Sunday School curriculum, *Family Life Magazine,* and Christian paperback books. It also operates teacher training seminars and clinics.

Membership: 105
Publications:
    Family Life Today, monthly

660. Gospel Literature International (GLINT)

National Association of Evangelicals
Rev. Paul R. Fretz, Executive Director
Post Office Box 6688
Ventura, California 93006
(805) 644-3929

Gospel Literature International gives the free use of the copyrighted Gospel Light Sunday School lessons to overseas churches and missions for translation and publication into national languages. Where useful, art work is provided along with technical help. Funds for translation are provided when available. Gospel Literature International is therefore a missionary literature assistance organization and not a sending society, as workers are already present overseas. Funds are received from interested friends, Sunday School groups, and churches to assist in the translation work. Work is currently being carried on in approximately 90 languages.

Founding Date: 1961
Staff: 3
Publications:
    GLINT Focus, yearly
    Donor Letter, fund raiser and current needs on
        the mission field, monthly
Former Name:
    (1971) Gospel Light International

661. Gospel Literature Services

General Association of Regular Baptist Churches
1300 North Meacham Road
Schaumburg, Illinois 60195
(312) 843-1600

Gospel Literature Services is the international literature ministry of the Regular Baptist Press. Its function is to assist Regular Baptist Missionaries in funding their on-the-field printing needs or in providing specific gospel literature for the missionary. A literature Advisory Committee helps the director in evaluating all literature requests and all literature grants.

Founding Date: 1973

662. Gospel Mission of South America, Inc.

Interdenominational
Rev. Hudson Shedd, DD
1730 S.W. 22nd Avenue
Fort Lauderdale, Florida 33312

Mailing Address:
1401 S.W. 21st Avenue
Fort Lauderdale, Florida 33312
(305) 587-2975 or (305) 792-9555

The Gospel Mission of South America is involved in reaching not only Indians living in the country areas of Chile, but also people living in the urban areas in Chile, Argentina, and Uruguay. Its aim is a strong national church with dedicated pastors and capable leadership. The Mission is involved in Bible Institutes, radio ministry, Bible correspondence courses, and other means of evangelism and spiritual growth. These activities have created an immense need for more dedicated men and women who will go, who will pray, and who will give to maintain and enlarge the work. Supplication, Service, Sacrifice—these are needed that the message of redemption might be presented in the power of the Holy Spirit.

Founding Date: 1923

Staff: 5

Membership: 65

Publications:
> *Gospel Mission of South America,* quarterly

Radio/TV Programs:
> On the field we produce a TV program once a week and have several radio programs both in Chile and Uruguay

Former Name:
> (1973) Soldiers and Sailors Gospel Mission

663. Gospel Missionary Union (GMU)

Nondenominational
Dick L. Darr, President
10000 North Oak
Kansas City, Missouri 64155
(816) 734-8500

The purpose of the Gospel Missionary Union, as a missionary agency, identified and closely involved with sending and receiving churches in the cause of world evangelization, is to make disciples and to build Christ's church among the peoples of the world to whom God directs us: planting and developing responsible and God-honoring local churches; equipping and mobilizing them for growth, reproduction, and missionary outreach; and through them manifesting Christ's compassion and concern for the whole man and his community. Many types of outreach ministries are used to help reach these primary objectives, including such training programs as Bible Schools, short term institutes, TEE programs and correspondence courses. These ministries are supported by literature programs which include print shops, bookstores and bookmobiles; radio outreach through the Union's own radio stations and programs on other Christian and commercial stations; film and cassette ministries; aviation; youth work; camp efforts, and medical work in hospitals, clinics and dispensaries.

Founding Date: 1892

Staff: 35

Membership: 429 missionaries

Publications:
> *The Gospel Message,* quarterly
> *Communicate,* a monthly news sheet published from Malaga, Spain
> *Monthly Prayer* and *Praise Sheet;* monthly

Radio/TV Programs:
> *Public Service Missionary News* radio program, a 5-minute weekly over 50 stations in the United States
> 2 programs weekly in the Republic of Mali
> 11 weekly broadcasts in Spain
> 193 weekly broadcasts in Italy
> 8 programs in Ecuador

Meetings:
> Family Conference at GMU headquarters
> Annual Conferences held on all the fields of work

Former Name: (1901) World's Gospel Union

Merger: (1975) Evangelical Union of South America

664. Gospel Publishing House

Assemblies of God

William G. Eastlake, National Director
Division of Publication
1445 Boonville Avenue
Springfield, Missouri 65802
(417) 862-2781

Gospel Publishing House is the publishing arm of the General Council of the Assemblies of God. Its purposes are: to publish and distribute the *Pentecostal Evangel,* the denominations's official organ; to publish curricular material and other church school literature; and to produce other Gospel periodicals and publications. It serves as an agency of the church in a three-fold mission of evangelism, worship, and Christian growth. Gospel Publishing House produces an average of 17 tons of Gospel literature each day. It serves some 17,000 customers and distributes 50 million pieces of church school literature each year.

Membership:
320 employees in the Gospel Publishing House alone
Approximately 800 total number of employees

Publications:
Pentecostal Evangel, weekly

665. Gospel Recordings, Inc.

Nondenominational

Larry D. Allmon, General Director
122 Glendale Boulevard
Los Angeles, California 90026
(213) 624-7461

Founded by Joy Ridderhof, Gospel Recordings, Inc., makes recordings on the foreign fields of evangelistic Bible messages and local songs for transferring to records and cassettes. They are then distributed free of charge to missionaries, local pastors, and evangelists.

Founding Date: 1939

Staff: 71

Publications:
Sounds, quarterly

Meetings:
1 annual conference at Alpine Conference Grounds, Blue Jay, California

666. Gospel Revivals, Inc.

Nondenominational

W. C. Moore, President
Post Office Box 3457
Terminal Annex
Los Angeles, California 90051
(213) 790-2128

Gospel Revivals, Inc., publishes Christian literature aimed at promoting revivals of Christianity everywhere: calling God's people to a holy life and exhorting them to live in readiness for the coming again of the Lord Jesus Christ: encouraging love toward all who love the Lord Jesus Christ: and encouraging people to live by Biblical precepts and standards.

Staff: 14

Publications:
Herald of His Coming, monthly
6 non-periodicals

667. Gospel Services, Inc.

Church of Christ

Jule L. Miller, President
Post Office Box 12302
Houston, Texas 77017
(713) 472-5594

Gospel Services Inc., publishes religious filmstrips and slides together with scripts and recordings (records and cassettes).

Staff: 13

Publications:
Church Idea Packet, published every once in a while

668. Gospel Tract Society, Inc.

Nondenominational

Lester L. Buttram, President
1105 South Fuller Street
Independence, Missouri 64050
(816) 461-6086

The purpose of the Gospel Tract Society, Inc., is to print and distribute the Word of God in tract form for the evangelization of non-Christians and the edification of believers. The Society operates 37 churches and 11 schools in the country of Haiti. It conducts other benevolent actions in that country including feeding and clothing many needy people in the rural areas.

Staff: 18

Membership: 150,000

Publications:
The Gospel Tract Harvester, monthly
Over 500 titles of Gospel tracts a year

Meetings:
2 missionary conferences per year at the headquarters church in Port au Prince, Haiti

669. Grace Mission, Inc.

Grace Gospel Fellowship
Daniel C. Bultema, President
2125 Martindale, S.W.
Grand Rapids, Michigan 45909
(616) 241-5666

Grace Mission, Inc., conducts missionary work in Zaire, Africa. Its work includes three Bible institutes, evangelism, a hospital, leper work, a mobile medical clinic, a maternity and family planning clinic, agricultural help, a secondary school, 120 primary schools with 10,000 students, a Bible translation ministry, youth ministries, and 129 national churches with national pastors supported by the nationals. In Puerto Rico, Grace Mission owns a 1,000 watt missionary station, camp and conference ministry, and two indigenous churches. It is also engaged in evangelism work in India where it has 13 national churches with national pastors as well as literature and Christian film ministries. In addition, Grace Mission works among the Mormons in the United States and overseas. Grace Publications, Inc., is an auxiliary enterprise of Grace Mission, operating its own presses and printing literature for both the home and foreign fields. Closely associated with this phase of the work is Grace Line Bible Lessons, supplying dispensationally oriented Sunday School material.

Founding Date: 1939

Staff: 11

Membership: 15,000

Publications:
Outreach, bimonthly
Mission Memo, bimonthly
Missionary and Bible Study books and pamphlets
Tracts and prayer letters

Radio/TV Programs:
Radio programs in Puerto Rico

Meetings:
3 mission seminars annually in key areas of the country
3 annual Friendship Missionary Banquets in key areas of the country
Grace Mission Board Meetings 4 times a year
Executive Committee Meeting 6 times a year

670. The Grail

Roman Catholic
Mary A. Kane, President
Grailville
Loveland, Ohio 45140
(513) 683-2340

The Grail is an international movement of lay women engaged in religious search, social liberation, and collaboration through professional work, education, the arts, etc. Its activities include: alternative models of education for women; work for positive social change in local communities in educational and other social structures; and seminars on issues relating to women, religion and culture, liberation, ecology, etc. Grailville is a residential/commuter center for continuing education in these areas. Other centers are located at Cornwall-on-the-Hudson, New York, and San Jose, California. It is also known as the International Grail Movement.

Membership: 250

Publications:
Newsletter

Meetings:
50 conferences per year

671. Grand Council Young Men's Institute

Roman Catholic
R. A. Bettencourt, Grand Secretary
50 Oak Street
San Francisco, California 94102
(415) 621-4948

The Grand Council Young Men's Institute is a fraternal order of Catholic men organized in San Francisco. The motto of the order, is PRO DEO — PRO PATRIA (for God — for Country). The order is especially active in promoting laymen's retreats, Catholic press, essay contests, the Pro-Life Movement, Special Olympics, Aid to the Handicapped, and involvement in community affairs. The primary purpose of the order is to educate its members so they will be able to live a truly Christian life by growing in grace and wisdom.

Membership: 5,000

Publications:
Institute Journal, bimonthly

672. Grand Old Gospel Fellowship, Inc.

Independent Fundamental—Bible-Believing

Dr. B. Sam Hart, President
610 East Mount Pleasant Avenue
Philadelphia, Pennsylvania 19119
(215) 242-5550

Grand Old Gospel Fellowship is a missionary organization broadcasting the Gospel throughout the United States and foreign countries by means of a radio program, *Grand Old Gospel Hour.* Other ministries include: crusades, literature, Hart Boy's Home in Jamaica, and the establishment of New Testament churches.

673. Graymoor Ecumenical Institute

Roman Catholic

Charles V. LaFontaine, SA, Co-Director
Kenneth G. Stofft, SA, Co-Director
Atonement Friars
Graymoor/Garrison, New York 10524
(914) 424-3671

The Graymoor Ecumenical Institute is the principal ecumenical agency sponsored, conducted, and staffed by the Franciscan Friars of the Atonement in the United States. It is assisted by a Board of Consultors. The primary goals of the Graymoor Ecumenical Institute are the following: to provide a forum for ecumenical and interreligious conversation and dialogue; to sponsor and encourage prayer for Christian unity during the annual Week of Prayer for Christian Unity (January 18-25) and throughout the year in the United States; and to explore and foster the pastoral dimensions of ecumenism within the Christian communities in North America.

Founding Date: 1967

Publications:
Ecumenical Trends, monthly, containing ecumenical articles, documentation, resources, and news

Meetings:
Ordinarily, 2 annual conferences at the headquarters in Garrison, New York
The co-directors of the Institute participate in various capacities in retreats, days of renewal and consultations either at the headquarters or elsewhere in the United States

674. Great Commission Crusades, Inc.

Interdenominational

Rev. Edward E. Hayes, President
Post Office Box 55
Intercession City, Florida 33848
(305) 348-5206

The first mission established by the Great Commission Crusades was Haiti Inland Mission, which published the first New Testament, Psalms, and Genesis in Creole in cooperation with the Haitian Bible Society in 1951 and 1955. Haiti Inland Mission was turned over to the Free Methodist Church in 1964 and has continued its interchurch work as Great Commission Crusades since then. The mission promotes ten crusades: (1) the Bible for all; (2) youth enlistment; (3) Bible training centers; (4) evangelistic campaigns; (5) bookstores and libraries; (6) correspondence courses; (7) literacy; (8) Christian publications; (9) cooperatives; (10) neighbors' service.

Founding Date: 1949

Staff: 12

Membership: 50

Publications:
Christian Action, quarterly
L'Action Chretienne, monthly, published in Haiti

Meetings:
2 meetings annually in Haiti

Former Name: (1966) Haiti Inland Mission

675. Great Commission Publications*

Presbyterian

Rev. Robley J. Johnston, Executive Director
7401 Old York Road
Philadelphia, Pennsylvania 19126
(215) 635-6510

Great Commission Publications publishes curriculum materials (Grades 1-12) for use in Sunday Schools. It also publishes a hymnal, church bulletins, booklets, pamphlets, and books for use in Christian education programs. It provides educational support services in the areas of training and consultation. The emphasis of the support services is to better equip church leaders and teachers to carry on the tasks of Christian education.

Staff: 14

Publications:

Sunday school curriculum materials, Grades 1-12 and adult

Hymnal; Church bulletins; booklets and books useful in the educational ministry of the Church

Meetings:

Approximately 6 seminars per year

676. Greater Europe Mission

Nondenominational

Rev. Don Brugmann, Executive Director
Post Office Box 668
Wheaton, Illinois 60187
(312) 462-8050

Greater Europe Mission was organized initially as the European Bible Institute. In 1952, the functions broadened beyond the initial Bible Institute and the name Greater Europe Mission was adopted. Since that time, the work has expanded to 13 countries, and includes nine Bible institutes, one seminary, extension and correspondence course work, and evangelistic and church planting activities. The Mission's motto is "Training Europeans to Evangelize Greater Europe." The stress of the organization is in the training of nationals to provide leadership for their own work. The organization is nondenominational and therefore assists churches of many denominations throughout Europe.

Founding Date: 1949

Staff: About 30 North American staff members

Membership:

Approximately 250 missionaries and individuals appointed to missionary service

Publications:

Greater Europe Report, 6 times a year
Brochures regarding various aspects of the work and countries of service, occasionally

Meetings:

About 65 promotional dinners throughout the United States and Canada annually

Conferences and individual meetings in churches

Former Name: (1952) European Bible Institute

677. Greek Catholic Union of the USA (GCU)

Byzantine Catholic

Mr. George Batyko, National President
Miss Ann Lucas, National Secretary-Treasurer
502 East Eighth Avenue
Munhall, Pennsylvania 15120
(412) 462-9800

The Greek Catholic Union of the U.S.A. provides the following benefits for its members: (1) Life Insurance Plans for both adult and young members at low cost; (2) Fraternal Aid and Assistance to members who are victims of floods, hurricanes, mine disasters, and other calamities; (3) Support of Church Institutions through GCU lodges striving to preserve the rich traditions of the Christian East through annual contributions to the Byzantine Catholic Seminary and grants to religious orders and other significant Church-related programs; (4) Communications—all members receive the official newspaper, a weekly tabloid presenting reports on local and district levels, as well as a monthly children's supplement, and an attractive and informative yearbook; (5) Athletic Activities, including national bowling and golf tournaments held annually, offering both sporting and social opportunities for the entire family; tennis and swimming have been added in recent years; (6) Education and Culture in the form of GCU annual scholarship awards to members enrolled in accredited colleges and universities and sponsorship of study and research in the culture of its founding members.

Founding Date: 1892

Membership: 50,000

Publications:

Greek Catholic Union Messenger, biweekly
Annual *Yearbook (Kalendar)*

Meetings:

Monthly meetings at 400 local lodges and 11 regional districts
National Convention every 4 years
Board of Directors Meeting semi-annually

678. Greek Orthodox Archdiocese of North and South America, Missions Program

Greek Orthodox

His Excellency, Metropolitan Silas
of New Jersey, Chairman
10 East 79th Street
New York, New York 10021
(212) 628-2500

The Greek Orthodox Program provides scholarships for Orthodox students from Africa, South America, Alaska, and the Orient who are preparing themselves for the holy priesthood of the Orthodox Church or are being trained for church-affiliated work; supports the efforts of missionaries in the above areas; sends financial support to the churches and church institutions in those areas; and conducts drives to raise money for special projects, such as the World Hunger Drive and relief for victims of nature's calamities.

Membership: 1,000 laymen; 500 clergymen
Meetings:
> Several meetings per year held either at Hellenic College, 50 Goddard Avenue, Brookline, Massachusetts, or at the Archdiocese premises

Former Name: Foreign Mission Department

679. Greek Orthodox Ladies Philoptochos

Greek Orthodox Archdiocese of North and South America

Mrs. Katherine Pappas, National President
8 East 79th Street
New York, New York 10021
(212) 628-2500

The purpose of Greek Orthodox Ladies Philoptochos of the Greek Archdiocese of North and South America is to fulfill all the philanthropic, charitable, and eleemosynary objectives of their Church, which includes aid to those in need of guidance and referral in every community, in the areas of public services, old age assistance, scholastic and educational institutions, as well as those in need of emergency financial assistance. The National Philoptochos Office represents the foremost Greek Orthodox ladies philanthropic organization of the Greek Archdiocese of North and South America. Philoptochos is a primary mainstay organization in parishes throughout the Archdiocese. The national office represents approximately 475 chapters throughout North and South America, and works directly with the national board district and diocese officers and individual chapters in the fulfillment of their obligations in this united effort.

Membership: 475 chapters, 75,000 lay
Meetings:
> National meetings, quarterly

680. The Guild of Catholic Lawyers, Inc.*

Roman Catholic

James E. Foley, President
The Empire State Building
350 Fifth Avenue
New York, New York 10001
(212) 695-8150

The Guild of Catholic Lawyers sponsors quarterly forums on matters affecting the Church and the legal profession. It also sponsors a red Mass at St. Patrick's Cathedral in September of each year. Throughout the year, it takes positions on matters affecting the Church, the community, the legal profession, and morality.

Membership: 450 lay; 10 clerical

681. The Guild of Saint Ives

Episcopal

The Rev. Canon Walter D. Dennis
The Cathedral Church of St. John the Divine
1047 Amsterdam Avenue
New York, New York 10025
(212) 678-6901

Through the Guild of Saint Ives lawyers and priests study legal issues of topical importance to the Church and provide some legal help for Episcopalians lacking other resources.

Membership: 27
Publications:
> *A Report on Churches and Taxation*
> *Churches and Taxation Revisited*

682. Hadassah, The Women's Zionist Organization of Americas, Inc., and Hadassah Medical Relief Association (HWZOA)

Jewish

Aline Kaplan, Executive Director
50 West 58th Street
New York, New York 10019
(212) 355-7900

The Hadassah Medical Relief Association is sponsored by Hadassah, The Women's Zionist Organization of America, to carry out its program of practical work in Israel. It built and maintains the Hadassah-Hebrew University Medical Center (at Kiryat Hadassah, Jerusalem) which includes the Medical School, Moshe Sharett Institute of Oncology, Henrietta Szold School of Nursing, and the School of Dentistry, the Hadassah University Hospital, Mount Scopus, which includes Guggenheim Rehabilitation Medicine Pavilion, and School of Occupational Therapy. The Association supports family community health centers and provides special services to other hospitals and to municipal mother-and-child clinics in Jerusalem. It provides maintenance and education for young newcomers to Israel and culturally deprived Israeli youth through Youth Aliyah, of which Hadassah is the major organizational contributor. It operates a comprehensive, coeducational high school, the Hadassah Community College, and the Vocational Guidance Institute in Jerusalem; participates in a program of Jewish National Fund land purchase and reclamation; in the United States it carries on adult and youth education programs and sponsors Hashachar, a coeducational youth organization for ages 9-25.

Founding Date: 1912
Staff: 150
Membership: 370,000 members; 1,600 local groups

Publications:
Update, biweekly
Hadassah Magazine, 10 issues per year
Hadassah Headlines, bimonthly
Hadassah Medical Organization manual
Also publishes study guides and educational materials

Meetings:
Annual convention held in various locations in August or September

683. Haggai Institute for Advanced Leadership Training

Nondenominational/Christian

Dr. John Haggai, President
Post Office Box 13
Atlanta, Georgia 30301
(404) 325-2580

The Haggai Institute holds intensive training sessions in Singapore on the "how" of evangelism. Prominent Christian leaders from Third World countries are brought together for a concentrated study course in effectively reaching their own people with the Gospel. Upon completion of the course, the leaders are prepared to train other leaders in their home areas, so that they, too, will proclaim the message of Jesus Christ more effectively. The Gospel is presented in a culturally relevant manner which the people can understand. They respond favorably because it is presented by their own respected leaders. The Haggai Institute's faculty members are from Third World nations and the Institute concentrates heavily on training leaders from Third World nations, many from countries where Western missionaries can no longer go.

Founding Date: 1962

Membership:

Over 1,000 alumni from Haggai Institute training sessions in Singapore

Publications:

Straight from the Shoulder, quarterly

The New Door, a monthly Bible reading devotional guide

Meetings:

3 World Seminars throughout the year

Former Names:

Haggai Evangelistic Association

Evangelism International, Inc.

684. Handclasp International, Inc.

Nondenominational

Maurice Henrich, President

3310 West Harvard, #12

Santa Ana, California 92702

Mailing Address

Post Office Box 1496

Santa Ana, California 92702

(714) 549-1859

Handclasp International is a Christian-oriented organization, incorporated as a charitable organization. It operates a pharmaceutical warehouse, licensed by the California State Board of Pharmacy. At this warehouse donated supplies are processed and shipped to Christian hospitals, nurses, and doctors outside the United States. Mexico, Haiti, India, and the Philippines are some of the countries where the supplies have been shipped. The work at the warehouse is carried on entirely by volunteers. No salaries are paid. Officials also donate their time.

Founding Date: 1970

Membership: No membership

Publications:

Newsletters, periodically

685. Harold Institute*

Winifred K. Babcock, President

Post Office Box 11024

Winston-Salem, North Carolina 27106

(312) 271-7137

The purpose of Harold Institute is to bring to the attention of scholars and the public the work of Preston Harold, anonymous and deceased author of

The Shining Stranger, with Introductions by Gerald Heard and Winifred Babcock; and *The Single Reality,* with Introduction and Summary by Oliver L. Reiser, and *Preface for the Physical Scientist* by Robert M. L. Baker, Jr. (Dodd, Meade and Co., New York, 1967, 1971). Harold's work constitutes a monumental synthesis of religion, psychology, the sciences, economics, and the arts, presenting them in harmonious relationship. He presents new insights which reconcile the world's religions in a way that preserves the integrity of each faith.

Publications:

Books of Preston Harold, and related works by other authors, 6 in print

Meetings:

Conducts seminars, 2 or 3 a year

Cassette tape courses available

686. Hashomer Hatza'ir

Jewish

David Lutzker-Mazkir, National Secretary

150 Fifth Avenue

New York, New York 10011

(212) 929-4955

Hashomer Hatza'ir is a world-wide Zionist youth organization with branches in over 16 countries. The movement is more than a half century old, having originated in Eastern Europe. Its orientation is toward active Zionism, socialism, and a proud Jewish identity and awareness. The organization is non-religious and works constantly toward knowledge and respect of the Jewish heritage. Hashomer Hatza'ir sees the kibbutz — a communal, socio-economic community — as the practical interpretation of its socialist ideals. It has founded a kibbutz federation in Israel that today consists of 77 kibbutzim and is the largest of the three major kibbutz federations that comprise the Kibbutz Movement. In North America its branches are found on both the east and west coasts, and stretch from Los Angeles to Montreal and Toronto. Activities are conducted year round on a weekly basis, the highlights being a six-week summer camp, a one week winter camp and several weekend activities. These range from fun and social activities to nature hikes and intellectual-educational programs. The movement is run by youth, for youth, with the assistance of adult advisors who come from Israel. Hashomer Hatza'ir strives to be not only a social means for spending time, but a way of life altogether.

Founding Date: 1913

Membership: 1,000 members in North America

Publications:

Youth and Nation, quarterly

La Madrich, The Young Guard, L'Yidiatcha, Tarbuton, all internal publications

Meetings:

Leadership meetings twice a year

Chapter leaders meetings 4-5 times a year

4 summer camps

Regional outings and activities 3 times a year

Weekly Chapter meetings

Former Name:

Hashomer Hatzair Zionist Youth Organization

687. Hear O Israel, Inc.

Nondenominational

R. W. Weeks, Director

1710 15th Avenue South

Birmingham, Alabama 35202

Mailing Address

Post Office Box 2784

Birmingham, Alabama 35202

(202) 933-6922

Hear O Israel is dedicated to bringing the Gospel to God's chosen people, the Jews. It attempts to promote better understanding between Christians and Jews. Since God loves Israel "with an everlasting love," and since Paul expressed this also when he wrote, "my heart's desire and prayer to God for Israel is, that they might be saved," it follows that all Christians should show a similar love. The organization uses various means to reach Jewish people for Christ: a radio program directed specifically to the presentation of the Gospel to the Jewish people; visitation program in homes, hospitals, nursing homes, and business establishments in the South; literature program and mailing program. The members of Hear O Israel also speak in churches presenting to God's people the need of giving the Gospel to the Jews and the need for prayer and interest in this work.

Staff: 2

Publications:

Bimonthly newsletter

Radio/TV Programs:

Radio program each Sunday on WQEZ FM 96

Meetings:

5 or more speaking engagements a year in churches and at mission conferences in seven states in the South

688. Hebrew Christian Fellowship*

Rev. William J. Randolph

1033 Twining Road

Dresher, Pennsylvania 19025

Mailing Address

Post Office Box 777

Dresher, Pennsylvania 19025

(215) 887-3447

The Hebrew Christian Fellowship is seeking to acquire, under the guidance of the Spirit of God, a "family" of missionaries and volunteer personal workers who share the burden of giving the good news of the gospel to Israel. The goal of the Fellowship is to challenge individual Christians and churches to our Scriptural indebtedness to the Jewish people, encouraging them to help get the good news of the atoning death of Messiah before God's ancient people. This is done by door-to-door visitation, visitation of Jewish shops and stores, select mailings, tract distribution, witnessing to Jewish students on university campuses, Bible study classes, and taped telephone messages which provide contacts for follow-up. Extensive letter writing and lengthy telephone conversations also provide opportunity for a continuing ministry. Radio broadcasts over Christian stations to Jews behind the Iron Curtain are followed up by correspondence, clothes when needed, and Christian study books and Bibles in their own languages.

Membership: 13 plus volunteer help

Publications:

The Fellowship Bulletin, quarterly

Meetings:

Weekly classes

Board meetings as necessary

689. Hebrew Culture Foundation*

Prof. Milton Konvitz, Chairman

515 Park Avenue

New York, New York 10022

(212) 752-0600

The major objective of the Hebrew Culture Foundation is to encourage colleges and universities to introduce the study of Modern Hebrew and Hebrew Literature in the curriculum. The Foundation offers incentive grants to universities which make application.

Membership: 10

Meetings:
> One or two per year to consider applications for grants

690. Herald Book Club

Roman Catholic
Rev. Mark Hegener, OFM
1434 West 51st Street
Chicago, Illinois 60609
(312) 254-4455

Herald Book Club is an activity of the Franciscan Herald Press, a not-for-profit organization owned and operated by the Franciscan Province of the Sacred Heart with headquarters in St. Louis and Chicago. The book club offers one selection a month with various alternates and sends out a monthly bulletin to the members called *Herald Book Club News.*

Founding Date: 1957
Staff: 3
Membership: 800
Publications:
> *News* of Herald Book Club

691. Herald Publishing House

Reorganized Church of Jesus Christ of Latter-day Saints
Paul A. Wellington, Editorial Director
Drawer HH
3225 South Noland Road
Independence, Missouri 64055
(816) 252-5010

Herald Publishing House is the printer and publisher of all Church-related material for the Reorganized Church of Jesus Christ of Latter-day Saints. It also prints books by and for Church members, which are sent out to a book club comprised mostly of Church members. It prints most of the curriculum material used by the Reorganized Church of Jesus Christ of Latter-day Saints. Herald Publishing House also does commercial printing, has a trade division, and operates three bookstores.

Publications:
> Approximately 100
> 1 monthly general interest church magazine
> 1 monthly witnessing magazine

692. Heralds of Hope, Inc.

Nondenominational
J. Otis Yoder, President
Post Office Box 3
Breezewood, Pennsylvania 15533
(717) 485-4021

Heralds of Hope, Inc., was organized as a non-profit corporation to preach the Gospel of light and truth in Jesus to this confused and deceived world. This purpose is carried out by radio programming and literature. The first radio program, *The Voice of Hope,* is a 30-minute release of a capella music, interpretative Bible reading and expository preaching, aired only in the United States and reaching several population centers. *Hope for Today* is a 15-minute program of Bible exposition only, introduced with a few measures of orchestration, now aired on three Trans World Radio superpower stations reaching most of Asia, Africa, and the Middle East in English, and Northern Africa and the Middle East in Arabic. Both the English and Arabic programs are released from Radio ELWA, Monrovia, Liberia. Bible distribution has become a major offer on these programs and is the basis of a greatly increased response to the radio releases, especially in Africa. *Hope for Today* is also being used in the United States now on four stations, with fair response.

Founding Date: 1967
Staff:
> 5 members of the Board of Directors
> 11 full-time employees
> Some volunteers

Publications:
> *Hope Horizons and Prayer Card,* monthly
> *Bible Study Magazine,* quarterly
> Radio program messages printed in small booklets
> Calendars

Meetings:
> Yearly radio rallies called *Convocations of Hope* in the areas of listener concentration

693. Here's Life Publishers, Inc.

Interdenominational
David L. Orris, General Manager
2700 Little Mountain Drive
San Bernardino, California 92402
Mailing Address
Post Office Box 1576
San Bernardino, California 92402
(714) 886-7981

Here's Life Publishers is a for-profit publisher specializing in publication of Christian books. The product line includes books, tracts, tapes, booklets, pamphlets, magazines, and Bible studies. Approximately 50% of sales are to the Christian bookstore trade (bookstores, distributors, and rack jobbers). Approximately 30% of sales are to Campus Crusade for Christ staff and ministries. Approximately 10% is sold to other markets (churches, organizations, and individuals). Here's Life Publishers utilizes a large number of manufacturers to produce its products. No manufacturing is done in-house. The company is an affiliate of Evangelical Christian Publishers Association and is currently working cooperatively with the Association in developing industry trends, market profiles, customer profiles, and long-range forecasting of customer needs.

Staff:

> 6 members of the Board of Directors
> 23 staff members

Publications:

> *Athletes in Action*

694. Hermano Pablo Ministries

Interdenominational
Rev. Paul Finkenbinder, President
Post Office Box 100
Costa Mesa, California 92627
(714) 645-0676

Hermano Pablo Ministries produces Christian radio and television programs for Latin America. Over 500 radio stations are broadcasting these programs daily, and a TV Station in Quito, Ecuador, is showing the Ministries' 5-minute Christian television program. Hermano Pablo Ministries also travels through all of Latin America holding crusades.

Founding Date: 1955

Publications:

> Newsletter to friends of Hermano Pablo

Radio/TV Programs:

> Twenty-four 5-minute radio programs every four weeks

Meetings:

> Crusades in Latin America

Former Name: (1971) Latin America Radio Evangelism

695. High Flight Foundation

Nondenominational
James B. Irwin, Founder and President
202 East Chey Mountain Boulevard
Colorado Springs, Colorado 80901

Mailing Address
Post Office Box 1387
Colorado Springs, Colorado 80901
(303) 576-7700

High Flight Foundation is an interdenominational Christian foundation dedicated to resolving man's two greatest enigmas—his relationship to God and his relationship with his fellow man through the person of Jesus Christ. This purpose is fulfilled through speaking engagements, community-wide crusades, retreats, distribution of Christian publications, training activities related to sharing the Christian faith, radio and television programming, high school educational programs, two space museum facilities (one mobile, one at headquarters) with the theme *From Outer Space to Inner Space,* and an overseas witness program extending to 39 countries

Founding Date: 1972

Staff: 5

Membership: 2,500 lay members

Publications:

> *Apogee,* quarterly
> *The Highest Flight,* an edition of the living New Testament
> *To Rule the Night,* Colonel Irwin's autobiography
> *The Moon is Not Enough,* Mrs. Mary Irwin
> *An Astronaut's Flight Through Life,* Colonel Irwin's testimony tract

Radio/TV Programs:

> Several films, *High Flight, Project Uplift,* space education film

Meetings:

> Accepts invitations to share in conferences, retreats, meetings, etc.

696. High School Evangelism Fellowship, Inc.

Nondenominational
Rev. A. Brandt Reed, International Director
80 North Washington Avenue
Bergenfield, New Jersey 07621

Mailing Address
Post Office Box 780
Tenafly, New Jersey 07670
(201) 387-1750

The purpose of The High School Evangelism Fellowship is the evangelization of high school students and the Scriptural training of Christian students in the principles of Christian living and witnessing. The organization sponsors Hi-B.A. Clubs which meet weekly in homes under the leadership of full-time trained leaders.

Founding Date: 1944

Staff: 22

697. Hindustan Bible Institute

Nondenominational Protestant

Len Shockey, American Director
Post Office Box 2815
Terminal Annex
Los Angeles, California 90051
(213) 533-6097

The Hindustan Bible Institute is a four-year Bible college whose primary purpose is to train Indian young people for the work of the ministry. The college is located in Madras, South India. The Institute has several related ministries such as: orphanage work, with six orphans homes located in various parts of South India providing for over 250 children; radio work—the Institute broadcasts each week over two radio stations with inspirational messages in three different languages of South India; literature work—the Institute prints over two million pieces of religious literature each year in 12 different Indian languages; medical work—the Institute has two medical vans completely equipped and staffed with a doctor and nurse who go to six different medical stations and two out-patient clinics. The Hindustan Bible Institute is involved in many different ways in bringing the *Good News* of Jesus Christ to the land of India.

Founding Date: 1950

Staff:
17 members on the American Board of Directors
3 part-time office staff

Publications:
Voice of India, a monthly devotional and informative magazine

Radio/TV Programs:
The Voice of India radio program produced in Southern California

Meetings:
Several meetings per year, location and number vary from year to year

698. Historical Committee of the Mennonite Church*

Mennonite Church

1700 South Main Street
Goshen, Indiana 46526
(219) 533-3161, Ext. 327

The Historical Committee, composed of six members, promotes historical studies, conducts historical research on behalf of the church, administers the Archives of the Mennonite Church, serves as the "memory" of the brotherhood, reminding congregations of their vital Christian heritage.

Staff: 3

Membership: 6

Publications:
Mennonite Historical Bulletin, an eight-page quarterly

Meetings:
Semi-annually

699. The Historical Foundation of the Presbyterian and Reformed Churches in the United States

Presbyterian Church in the United States

Jerrold L. Brooks, Executive Director
Post Office Box 847
Montreat, North Carolina 28757
(704) 669-7061

The Historical Foundation is the archives for the Presbyterian Church in the United States (Southern) and the Associate Reformed Presbyterian Church. It is chartered to collect, preserve, and promote the use of materials for the study of the history of the Presbyterian and Reformed Churches of the world, but especially the Southern United States.

Staff: 10 full-time; 2 part-time

Membership: 3,000 members

Publications:

The Historical Foundation News

Meetings:

Seminar for Local Church History, annual

700. Holy Childhood Association

Roman Catholic

Rev. Francis W. Wright, CSSp, National Director
800 Allegheny Avenue
Pittsburgh, Pennsylvania 15233
(412) 323-0400

The Holy Childhood Association is the official children's mission-aid society of the Catholic Church. It provides assistance to mission children in over 90 countries. The United States National office furnishes mission education programs and materials to pupils in Catholic elementary schools and religious education (CCD) classes. The purpose of the Holy Childhood Association is to cultivate the relationship between children of different countries. Emphasis is placed on expressing concern for young people in Third World countries, together with a respect for other cultures. This children-to-children concept has reflected a unique dimension of the Holy Childhood since its foundation.

Founding Date: 1843

Staff: 14

Membership: 7,000,000 children in the United States

Publications:

Newsletter, quarterly

Meetings:

One national conference, location varies from year to year

Also Known As:

Pontifical Association of Holy Childhood

701. Holy Land Christian Mission

Nondenominational

R. Joseph Gripkey, President
2000 East Red Bridge
Kansas City, Missouri 64131
(816) 942-2000

The Holy Land Christian Mission is a non-profit, charitable organization that operates an 18-building complex, including a hospital, orphans' home, school, church and support facilities ministering to the physical and spiritual needs of crippled children, 237 orphans, 525 widows, and needy families in the Bethlehem area. Under the umbrella of this miniature city, the Mission provides outreach programs at the grassroots level. It operates eight child care centers, a Widow's Aid program, Mothers In-Home Teaching program (preschool activities mutually beneficial to mother and child), and a Foster Home program. At Christmas and Easter time a food basket distribution program is carried out to help the poor people of the area. Financial aid is also given to refugee families. The Mission's Mount of David Crippled Children's Hospital, the only free orthopedic hospital in the Middle East, publishes research findings in this area. Its satellite physiotherapy clinics provide post-operative therapy. The Mission is a member of the Advisory Committee on Voluntary Foreign Aid and a charter member of the Evangelical Council for Financial Accountability.

Founding Date: 1936

Staff: 50 staff members at Kansas City Headquarters

Publications:

Holy Land Pictorial News, an in-house religious periodical with 11 issues a year
Bookmarks, prayer calendars, small pamphlets
Cultural, religious and historical slide presentations about the Holy Land

Former Name:

(1936) Society of Christian Approach to the Jews

Mergers:

(1970) Holyland Christian Approach
(1974) Holy Land Mission

702. Home of Onesiphorus

Interdenominational

George Hedberg, President
3939 North Hamlin Avenue
Chicago, Illinois 60618
(312) 478-4092

The Home of Onesiphorus was founded in China by Rev. and Mrs. L. M. Anglin. The organization is named after Onesiphorus, mentioned in II Tim. 1: 16-18. It provides loving care for orphan, refugee, and physically handicapped children in Beirut, Lebanon; Ramallah, Israel; Kowloon, Hong Kong; and Tatung, Taiwan. The Home of Onesiphorus operates without denominational affiliation or emphasis, and is wholly dependent upon the freewill gifts and offerings of interested friends for its financial support. It is a member of the Interdenominational Foreign Missions Association.

Founding Date: 1916

Publications:
> *Onesiphorus Harvester,* 2-3 times a year

Meetings:
> Deputation meetings

703. Hope Aglow Ministries, Inc.

Nondenominational

Rev. Edward H. Martin, President
Post Office Box 3057
Lynchburg, Virginia 24503
(804) 845-6437

Hope Aglow Ministries is an evangelistic, fundamental, and independent organization which conducts a world-wide program of prison evangelism. Since its founding, thousands of prison inmates have enrolled in its Bible correspondence school. Personal evangelism work is carried on by Hope Aglow Volunteer Chaplains. The organization also offers counseling to the families of inmates. Its Gospel Literature ministry includes the widespread distribution of Rev. Martin's own testimony booklet, *The Man Who Broke Rocks.* It has been produced as a 60-minute 16mm film, *39 Stripes,* and a tape loan library has been started.

Founding Date: 1966

Publications:
> Newsletters

704. Horizon Publishers and Distributors, Inc.

Nondenominational

Duane S. Crowther, President
50 South 500 West
Bountiful, Utah 84010

Mailing Address
Post Office Box 490
Bountiful, Utah 84010
(801) 295-9451

Horizon Publishers publishes books on food storage, preparedness, and outdoor survival. Another segment of the business publishes books geared for a Mormon Church audience. Horizon also manufac-

tures bible cases and other vinyl products. Catalogues and price information are furnished on request.

Founding Date: 1971

Staff: 45

705. The Hymn Society of America, Inc.

Nondenominational

W. Thomas Smith, Executive Director
National Headquarters
Wittenberg University
Springfield, Ohio 45501
(513) 327-6308

The Hymn Society of America is a national voluntary organization founded to promote the production of new hymns and tunes relevant to the needs of contemporary society and people; to increase interest in and raise the standards of hymns and hymn tunes; and to encourage the best uses of texts and tunes by congregations. Members and friends are invited to consult the valuable source material in the Society's archives and library. A major project is the preparation of material to appear as a *Dictionary of American Hymnology.* The Society renders a wide service through correspondence with individuals and organizations. This includes providing factual information in the field of hymnology and counseling with regard to all aspects of hymnic activity. The Society includes in its program and service nationwide observances of notable hymnic activity.

Founding Date: 1922

Staff: 2

Membership: 3,200

Publications:
> *The Hymn,* quarterly, containing scholarly articles on hymnology
> *The Stanza,* semiannually

Meetings:
> One national convocation
> Many regional workshops

706. Ikonographics, Inc.

Roman Catholic
Robert Stack, Vice-President and General Manager
807 East Gray Street
Louisville, Kentucky 40204

Mailing Address
Post Office Box 4454
Louisville, Kentucky 40204
(502) 583-3506

Ikonographics, Inc., produces and distributes religious educational films, video, filmstrips, and audio programs to schools and churches in the English-speaking world. They also offer full creative services on contract to institutions and organizations, and operate an industrial division called Creative Media Productions which produces materials for business and industry.

Founding Date: 1974
Staff: 8
Radio/TV Programs:
    Films, filmstrips, audio and video cassettes

707. Immanuel Bible Foundation

Nondenominational
H. W. Studer, Director
1301 South Fell Avenue
Normal, Illinois 61761
(309) 829-3745

The purpose of the Immanuel Bible Foundation is to promote the teaching and use of the Holy Bible as a constant guide and a never-failing light in our everyday lives, and thus to make better Christian American citizens. It provides Sacred Music to create better Christian attitudes and to encourage coopera-tion of all faiths toward a common Christian good, regardless of denomination, race, or creed. It is an "undenominational Christian Service Center." The Foundation operates a Church Music Lending Library, serving up to 200 smaller churches which have a limited music budget. It hosts a complimentary breakfast for laymen and ministers during Holy Week. In conjunction with Illinois Wesleyan University it underwrites the cost of a Music Clinic (with nationally known leaders) for choir directors and church organists. Through the Lilly Endowment in Ecumenical Prayer seminars are held in various cities throughout the United States under the direction of the Foundation's president. Local churches use the facilities for retreats, women's meetings, board meetings, and seminars. Grants are made locally and not to individuals.

708. Impact

Interdenominational
Robert Odean, National Director
100 Maryland Avenue, N.E.
Washington, D.C. 20002
(202) 544-8636

Impact is an interfaith network which provides information on legislation and an opportunity for citizen action. Impact addresses a broad spectrum of issues pertaining to social justice and international peace, reflecting the concerns of sponsoring Protestant, Roman Catholic, and Jewish groups. It functions on both the national and local levels.

Publications:
    Prepare, a study report
    Action, legislative alerts
    Update, monthly

709. IMPACT for Today's World*

Associated Churches
Kenneth Westby and George H. Kemnitz
National Co-Directors
The Times Building
Westminister, Maryland 21157
(301) 848-2304

IMPACT for Today's World produces a monthly magazine and other literature on Biblical, doctrinal, and practical Christian living topics. It also provides a weekly radio ministry, a Bible study course, and a sermon cassette tape program serving the scattered members of Christ's spiritual church. IMPACT for Today's World is a ministry dedicated to Biblical understanding and Christian development; to expounding the plain and balanced teachings of God's Word, and to helping people of today's world apply the spiritual principles of scripture so that each individual might mature into the fullness of God's likeness and contribute his maximum service to the ever-increasing needs of today's world.

Publications:
IMPACT for Today's World, monthly
Newsletter, question series, Impact Bible Course
Other Biblical and Christian living literature
Radio/TV Programs:
Weekly 15-minute radio programs
Meetings:
Monthly ministers' meetings and seminars

710. The Independent Board for Presbyterian Foreign Missions (IBPFM)

Bible Presbyterian Church
Rev. Lynn Gray Gordon, DD
President and General Secretary
246 West Walnut Lane
Philadelphia, Pennsylvania 19144
(215) 438-0511

The Independent Board for Presbyterian Foreign Missions is a fundamental, Bible-believing foreign mission board dedicated to the task of promoting foreign mission activities in many countries of the world, except the United States of America. All missionaries serving under the IBPFM must be born-again Christians with a desire to win souls to Christ. One of the primary tasks on each foreign field is the training of nationals as pastors and church leaders. IBPFM is a member of the Associated Missions

(TAM) of the International Council of Christian Churches.
Founding Date: 1933
Staff: 10
Membership: 30 board members; 41 missionaries
Publications:
Biblical Missions, 10 times a year

711. Inner Light Foundation (ILF)*

Nondenominational
Betty Bethards
Post Office Box 761
Novato, California 94947
(415) 897-5581

Inner Light Foundation is a non-profit, nondenominational organization working to help all people develop an awareness of their unity with God, or Universal Consciousness. It teaches a simple method of concentration and meditation. Through lectures, workshops, publications, and media appearances, the ILF staff provides insight into spiritual truths and guidance for everyday living. The Foundation continuously expands its programs through ongoing research with educators, scientists, and spiritual leaders. Through a synthesis of ancient teachings and current scientific information, the ILF teaches techniques designed to help improve daily life. Lectures and workshops include such topics as improving interpersonal relationships, sex and psychic energy, death and reincarnation, healing, developing intuitional ability, loving yourself and others, partnerships, marriage and family, and mankind's future.

Publications:
12 titles in print
Meetings:
Monthly lectures

712. Institute for Advanced Pastoral Studies

Interdenominational
Dr. John E. Biersdorf, Director
29129 Southfield Road
Southfield, Michigan 48076
(313) 569-1616

The Institute for Advanced Pastoral Studies is the oldest independent, ecumenical continuing theological education facility in the nation. The Institute's vision of education for ministry is to connect the inner spiritual depth and maturity of the minister with the new knowledge and skills needed to minister effectively in an ever-changing society. The intention at the Institute is to build and deepen a Christian practice, rooted in a Christian heritage, enriched and challenged by the best in other religions and the frontiers of social science, and relevant to the personal and social needs of our time. The Institute offers a comprehensive educational program for varying educational backgrounds, levels of commitments, and areas of interest. This program includes Experiential Seminars, Congregational Renewal and Spiritual Counseling: Doctor of Ministry Program, a Church Resourcing Program, and Haelan, a series of publications on the state of the art in worship, prayer and meditation practice. The Institute has developed, over its history, a method of experiential education especially designed for the learning needs of clergy and lay leaders. Each seminar design includes: the sharing of ideas, concepts, and theory, skill practice and experience appropriate to seminar content, and application of this experience, practice, and learning to the ministry settings of participants. The Institute believes in peer learning, where all participate in teaching and learning, and that learning takes place in community where there is an atmosphere encouraging trust and openness for self-disclosure. They believe that effective learning is a process in which the whole person participates. Seminars are structured to invite persons to engage body, mind, and spirit in intensive study, personal interaction and creative play in the learning process. Everything done at the Institute is grounded in the practice of worship, prayer, and meditation.

Founding Date: 1957

Staff: 8

Membership: 100

Publications:
>   Catalogue, once yearly
>   *Haelan,* semiannually
>   Assorted newsletters, periodically

Meetings:
>   20 to 25 seminars yearly, at the Center in Southfield

713. Institute for American Church Growth

Interdenominational

Dr. Win Arn, Director
150 South Los Robles, #600
Pasadena, California 91101
(213) 449-4400

The Institute for American Church Growth was established to provide resources, conduct research, and disseminate practical insights on church growth directly to pastors and local church leaders. To achieve this purpose the Institute continues to be a pioneer in providing practical resources to church leadership. From its inception, the Institute has centered its church-enabling ministry in four specific areas: support of pastors and professional staff in church growth leadership training; help in motivating, training, and equipping laity to play effective parts in the Great Commission through their local church; support of regional conferences, districts, and judicatories concerned with disseminating church growth insights on a broader basis; serving as a reference and consultation resource for the church-at-large in its growth efforts.

Founding Date: 1972

Staff: 16

Publications:
>   *Church Growth: America,* bimonthly
>   *Church Growth Resource News,* quarterly
>   Various books in the field of church growth

Meetings:
>   Advanced Church Growth Seminar, Pasadena, Dallas, twice a year
>   Church Growth Specialty Workshops, held in 16 different cities
>   Basic Church Growth Seminar, held in sponsoring church

714. Institute for Bio/Social Services

Nondenominational

Rt. Rev. Fonzy Joseph Broussard, PhD, DMin, Director
4009 Pacific Coast Highway, Suite 462
Torrance, California 90505
(213) 539-5565

The Institute for Bio/Social Services trains the pastoral counselor in biofeedback and hypnosis. The certificate program is approved by the American Commission on Ministerial Training.

Founding Date: 1979

Staff: 4

Publications:
>   Manuals for Biofeedback and Hypnosis

715. Institute for Christian Studies*

Episcopal

The Rev. C. Christopher Epting, Director
130 North Magnolia Avenue
Orlando, Florida 32801
(305) 849-0680

The Institute for Christian Studies offers a two-year program of courses, equipping a student academically either for the permanent diaconate in the Episcopal Church or for various types of lay ministry. Periodically, five or six-week seminars are offered through the Institute for the people of the Diocese of central Florida. The Institute for Christian Studies' Counseling Center offers, in the context of Christian concern, expert counseling for the improvement and management of difficult life situations. Courses offered include: marriage and family counseling, adolescent problems, prayer counseling and spiritual direction, group therapy, and training and supervision for parish clergy in counseling skills.

Membership: 90 lay; 12 clerical
Meetings:
   15 per year

716. Institute for Creation Research (ICR)

Nondenominational

Dr. Henry Morris, Director
2716 Madison Avenue
San Diego, California 92116
(714) 440-2443

The Institute for Creation Research answers inquiries; provides literature-searching services; conducts courses, seminars, summer institutes, workshops, lectures, debates, and weekly radio broadcasts; distributes publications; and makes referrals to other sources of information. Services are free, except for some publications and summer institutes, seminars, and workshops, and are available to anyone.

Founding Date: 1970
Membership: Not a membership organization
Publications:
   Acts and Facts, monthly
   Books, cassettes of weekly radio broadcasts
Radio/TV Programs:
   A 15-minute weekly radio program with a Bible/Science theme entitled, *Science, Scripture, and Salvation*

Meetings:
   Summer Institutes (5 in 1980)
Former Name:
   (1973) Creation-Science Research Center

717. Institute for Ecumenical and Cultural Research

Interdenominational

Dr. Robert S. Bilheimer, Executive Director
Post Office Box 6188
Collegeville, Minnesota 56321
(612) 363-3366

The Institute for Ecumenical and Cultural Research is an incorporated agency located on the grounds of St. John's (Benedictine) Abbey and University in Collegeville, Minnesota. The purpose of the Institute is to encourage study and research concerning Protestant-Catholic-Orthodox unity, and the relation of Christianity to society and to other religious traditions. The goals of the Institute are to stimulate attention to, and to facilitate study of ecumenically important themes. The Institute offers free living and study facilities to residential scholars who apply for admission and are accepted, and organizes invitational study-consultations.

Founding Date: 1967
Staff: 3

718. The Institute for Religious and Social Studies

Interdenominational

Jessica Feingold, Director
3080 Broadway
New York, New York 10027
(212) 749-8000

The Institute for Religious and Social Studies is a scholarly and scientific fellowship of clergymen and other religious teachers who desire authoritative information regarding some of the basic issues now confronting spiritually minded men. The purpose of the Institute is to develop a keener awareness of the unique contributions which the various religious traditions have made to the advancement of civilization and can make toward solution of the perplexities of our day.

Membership: 300 clerical members

Meetings:

Occasional meetings

719. Institute for the Study of American Religion (ISAR)

Nondenominational

Director J. Gordon Melton, PhD
Post Office Box 1311
Evanston, Illinois 60201
(312) 271-3419

The Institute for the Study of American Religion is a research facility devoted to the study of small and minority religious bodies of the United States and Canada. It houses a 25,000 volume library of archival and primary research materials and provides for publication of materials.

Founding Date: 1969

Staff: 1

Publications:

Irregular monographs, mostly of a bibliographical nature

720. Institute of Carmelite Studies

Roman Catholic

Rev. Dr. John Sullivan, OCD
2131 Lincoln Road, N.E.
Washington, D.C. 20002
(202) 832-6622

The Institute of Carmelite Studies is an organization under the jurisdiction of the Provincial Council of the Washington Province of the Discalced Carmelites. The goal of the Institute is to promote Carmelite studies. In carrying out this goal, the Institute has several objectives: to establish a nucleus of Carmelite scholars who will engage in research and writing on Carmelite studies in their fields; to encourage and cooperate with the scientific research of Carmelite studies carried on outside the Discalced Carmelite Order by individuals or groups; to acquire and preserve Carmelite publications for the purposes of research and study; to discover, assemble, and publish documents relative to Carmelite subjects; to prepare for publication both the translations of Carmelite classics and original Carmelite studies; and to conduct conferences, seminars, and institutes in Carmelite studies.

Staff: 10

Meetings:

Meetings on an ad hoc basis with no regular schedule or location

721. Institute of Church Renewal (ICR)*

Ben C. Johnson, Director
1870 Tucker Industrial Road
Tucker, Georgia 30084
(404) 934-0830

The Institute of Church Renewal creates quality programs and resources which respond to the needs of today's churchmen. ICR conceives, tests, and releases to churches and denominations effective methods of renewing the church in our day. The Institute developed the Lay Witness Mission, an approach to renewal which has already been used in more than 40 denominations in every state and several foreign countries. In addition to the Lay Witness Mission, thousands of churches have scheduled 10 additional programs of ICR.

Staff: 21

Publications:

Books for use in specific ICR programs
Newsletter, bimonthly

722. Institute of Formative Spirituality

Roman Catholic

Susan A. Muto, Director
Duquesne University
Pittsburgh, Pennsylvania 15282
(414) 434-6026

The Institute of Formative Spirituality, the only Institute of its kind in the world, offers a unique combination of academic programs and apostolic activities to serve the entire church, clergy, religious, and laity. The Institute sponsors a master's program in ongoing formation; a master's program in formative spirituality for appointed formation leaders; and a doctoral program in this field. These programs are accredited by the Graduate School of Duquesne University. The program in formative spirituality is for people appointed by their dioceses or religious communities to a leading position in the formation of others or as teachers on the college, seminary, high school or parish level. The Institute also makes available a non-degree program in spiritual self-formation. This program aims to foster one's own ongoing formation by allowing leisure time for personal-spiritual growth. During the fall and spring semesters, mini-courses are offered by a highly qualified staff of visiting professors. To name a few of the courses offered: Prayer, Contemplation and Mysticism in the Great Traditions of the Church; Centering Prayer; Spirituality and Affirmative Living; and Practical Guidelines for Spiritual Direction. A Spring Lenten Series is offered — featuring lectures designed to increase your understanding and experience of the Christian spiritual life. A day-long public forum on Spiritual Formation and Reflective Living, featuring talks and discussions by outstanding visiting lecturers is sponsored by the Institute periodically. The faculty, along with some of its doctoral students, gives nationwide and international conferences, weekend conferences, retreats and days of recollection.

Founding Date: 1963

Publications:
>   *Studies in Formative Spirituality,* triannually
>   *Envoy,* bimonthly

Meetings:
>   16 per year throughout Pittsburgh area

Former Name: Institute of Man

723. The Institute of Jesuit Sources and the American Assistancy Seminar on Jesuit Spirituality (IJS)

Roman Catholic
Rev. George E. Ganss, SJ, Director of the IJS
Chairman of the Assistancy Seminary
Fusz Memorial
St. Louis University
3700 West Pine Boulevard
St. Louis, Missouri 63108
(314) 652-5737

The Institute of Jesuit Sources consists of a group of Jesuits in St. Louis, Missouri, assisted by collaborators in many English-speaking provinces of the Society. The chief aim of the Institute is to make the sources of Jesuit thought more readily available to the scholarly world in English-speaking countries, especially by publishing English translations of important books written in other languages by or about Jesuits. The Director of the Institute of Jesuit

Sources is also the Chairman of the American Assistancy Seminar on Jesuit Spirituality and the Editor of its series of booklets, *Studies in the Spirituality of Jesuits.* Approximately five of these appear each year.

Staff: 4 staff members of the IJS

Membership: 10 members of the Seminar

Publications:
>   Scholarly books published by the IJS
>   Periodical booklets by the Seminar

724. Institute of Society, Ethics and the Life Sciences; The Hastings Center (ISELS)

Nondenominational
Daniel Callahan, PhD, Director
360 Broadway
Hastings-on-Hudson, New York 10706
(914) 478-0500

The Institute of Society, Ethics and the Life Sciences addresses itself to the ethical questions raised by the advances of the biomedical revolution. It seeks to raise the level of competence and research in this area; aims to assist universities, and medical and professional schools in the development of programs designed to make consideration of ethical problems an integral part of the education process. It also strives to bring the importance of ethical and social problems in the life sciences to the attention of professional and policy-making bodies and to assist them, when requested, by supplying technical advice and by making available the results of analysis, study, and research. The work of the Institute is carried out by non-resident fellows and a small resident professional staff at the Hastings Center.

Founding Date: 1969

Staff: 25

Membership: 9,500

Publications:
>   *The Hastings Center Report,* bimonthly
>   *IRB, A Review of Human Subjects Research,*
>   10 times a year

Meetings:
>   20 research conferences a year held at the Center and open to participants in the research projects only

1 annual conference on bioethics open to the public
1 annual conference on applied ethics open to the public

725. Institute of The Heart of Jesus

Roman Catholic
Rev. David Scheider
Rev. John Lorenz
607 High Street
Des Moines, Iowa 50309
Mailing Address
Post Office Box 4692
Des Moines, Iowa 50306
(216) 747-4085

The Institute of the Heart of Jesus is a secular institute for diocesan priests which is presently experimenting with lay membership. The institute is strictly for personal spiritual growth and has no programs or activities except for prayer meetings and an annual retreat.

Founding Date: 1791 (restored 1918)
Membership: 1,400
Meetings:
    Annual retreat

726. Institute of Women Today

Nondenominational
Sister Margaret Ellen Traxler, Director
1307 South Wabash, Suite 202
Chicago, Illinois 60605
(312) 374-3197

Organized by a Roman Catholic Nun and a Jewish social scientist, the Institute endeavors to bring church-related women into the women's movement in order to have faith principles reflected in the women's struggle for equality. The Institute sponsors research in the field of women's studies. It conducts workshops over the country, using the disciplines of law, psychology, theology, and history to achieve the goals of searching for the religious and historical roots of women's liberation. Thirty such workshops have already been held. The Institute provides legal services to women in prison. The program package consists of four major thrusts: extensive interviews between lawyers and prison residents, between education staff and education specialists, and

between residents and psychologists; in-depth Progoff workshops for keeping diaries and journals; a survey course for women in prison on the basics of law fundamentals and legal rights; and vocation courses such as welding for job rehabilitation.

Founding Date: 1974

727. Institute on Religion in an Age of Science

Interdenominational
Dr. Karl E. Peters, Treasurer
Rollins College
Winter Park, Florida 32789
(305) 646-2139

The Institute on Religion in an Age of Science is established to promote creative efforts leading to the formulation, in the light of contemporary knowledge, of effective doctrines and practices for human welfare; to formulate dynamic and positive relationships between the concepts developed by science and the goals and hopes of man expressed through religion; and to state human values in such universal and valid terms that they may be understood by all men whatever their cultural background and experience, in such a way as to provide a basis for worldwide cooperation.

Founding Date: 1954
Staff: 6
Membership: 200
Publications:
    Zygon: Journal of Religion and Science, quarterly
    IRAS Newsletter, occasionally
Meetings:
    Annual conference, Star Island, New Hampshire
    One or two other conferences in conjunction with the American Association for the Advancement of Science or the American Academy of Religion

728. Institute on Religious Life

Roman Catholic
Rev. James E. Downey, OSB
Coordinator, National Office
4200 North Austin Avenue
Chicago, Illinois 60634
(312) 545-1946

The Institute on Religious Life was established at the

opening of the Holy Year in 1974. Its foundation is a direct result of a growing concern among bishops, priests, men and women religious and the laity regarding the spiritual crisis in the modern world and its consequent effect on religious communities and their apostolic work. The Institute is a national service organization established to foster a more effective understanding and implementation of the teachings of the Magisterium of the Church on religious life. This is accomplished by prayer and sacrifice, by study and research, by education and information, by advice and consultation, and by publicity and communication. Because of its unique composition involving bishops, priests, religious and the laity, the Institute is able to bring together a wide spectrum of dedicated personnel to accomplish its purposes. Religious and lay men and women cooperate in promoting retreats, seminars, data research and analysis. They seek to provide consultative services for religious groups and individuals in such crucial areas as a) vocation promotion, b) spiritual development, c) legal counsel, d) renewal and adaptation through provincial and general chapters and e) continuing education in the sacred sciences and in the spiritual life. There is now a Religious Life Center in Chicago which aids and facilitates these services.

Founding Date: 1974

Publications:
> One documentary: *Consecrated Life,* biannually
> One newsletter: *Religious Life,* monthly

Meetings:
> Conferences (Classes), 18 per academic year

729. Integrity, Inc.: Gay Episcopalians and Their Friends

Episcopalian
John C. Lawrence, President
Post Office Box 891
Oak Park, Illinois 60303
(617) 825-3368 or (312) 386-1470

Integrity has two major purposes. The first is to function as a support and advocacy group for gay Episcopalians and their friends. The second is to serve as a positive force for change in attitudes and behavior, through educational endeavors within the Episcopal Church. The objective is to achieve full and equal participation in the life of the Church for gay men and lesbians. There are support groups through chapters in about 40 major cities throughout the United States and Canada. Most chapters meet regularly and pro-

vide worship services, stimulating programs and discussion groups, and social events. Many chapters engage in educational outreach activities within the parish/diocesan framework in which they exist. Integrity also publishes *Forum,* a national literary journal for the gay Christian. The National organization also engages in outreach activities and represents gay Episcopalians' interests at the General Convention of the Church and in exchanges with a variety of Commissions and Committees of the Church. It also attempts to provide support and pastoral assistance to those who contact the Organization with problems or concerns. If it cannot help directly, it tries to make referrals through a network of supportive clergy and lay people who are available for counseling and other assistance.

Membership: 1,200

Publications:
> *Integrity Forum,* bimonthly
> Position papers on various topics
> Information brochures

Meetings:
> National Convention annually
> Retreats

730. Intercristo (The International Christian Organization, Inc.)

Interdenominational
C. Richard Staub, Executive Director
19303 Fremont Avenue North
Seattle, Washington 98133

Mailing Address
Post Office Box 33487
Seattle, Washington 98133
(206) 546-7330 (outside Washington (800) 426-1343)

Intercristo's purpose is to assist North American Christians in making informed vocational choices and to assist Christian organizations in recruiting personnel. This purpose is achieved through two services: Intermatch, providing the individual with information about specific opportunities in Christian organizations matching his/her stated vocational interests; and Intersearch, providing Christian organizations with information about individuals who qualify for their current personnel openings. Since 1970, 75,000 people have received personally-matched job listings, and currently more than 750 Christian organizations list over 28,000 work openings in 200 plus vocational categories worldwide.

Founding Date: 1967

Staff: 10

Radio/TV Programs:

> 10-, 30- and 60-second public service announcements for (Christian) radio stations

Merger:

> With CRISTA Ministries of Seattle, Washington, 1980

731. Interdenominational Foreign Mission Association of North America, Inc. (IFMA)

Interdenominational

Edwin L. Frizen, Jr., Executive Director
Post Office Box 395
Wheaton, Illinois 60187
(312) 682-9270

The Interdenominational Foreign Mission Association (IFMA) is an association of 49 foreign mission agencies without denominational affiliation, and representing more than 9,000 missionaries in over 115 countries. The IFMA is incorporated in the United States and Canada. It was founded for the purpose of strengthening the effectiveness and outreach of faith missions. As stated in the constitution, its purpose is "to further spiritual fellowship and intercessory prayer; to promote mutual helpfulness and conferences concerning missionary principles and practice; to make possible a united testimony concerning the existing need for a speedy and complete evangelization of the world; and to establish a united voice." Membership in the IFMA is an indication that the societies have met the requirements and standards of the Association, and are recommended for prayer and financial support, as well as for missionary service by conservative evangelical Christians. Member missions are governed by responsible councils or directorates; exercise control over missionaries; publish audited financial statements annually; approve each other on the field and at home in ethical practices; adhere to a strong conservative evangelical doctrinal position; and are engaged in taking the gospel of the Lord Jesus Christ to all people everywhere.

Founding Date: 1917

Staff: 3

Membership: 50 member organizations

Publications:

> *IFMA News,* quarterly
> *Evangelical Missions Quarterly,* published through a subsidiary

Meetings:

> 1 annual Association meeting
> 2-3 workshops and seminars of subsidiary organizations and committees

732. Interfaith Forum on Religion, Art and Architecture (IFRAA)

Interdenominational

Judith A. Miller, Executive Vice President
1777 Church Street, N.W.
Washington, D.C. 20036
(202) 387-8333

The Interfaith Forum on Religion, Art and Architecture, an affiliate of the AIA, represents the efforts of architects, clergy, craftspersons, and artists to improve the aesthetic and functional design of religious buildings. IFRAA is a professional organization in the field of architecture, the arts, and religion. Every aspect of building design for religious use is of primary interest. IFRAA is a nonprofit, educational organization. It provides a means through which all those interested in better design for religious use can collect their knowledge and experience for distribution. The four basic aims are: to promote excellence of design in architecture for religious use and in the allied arts; to develop greater understanding of the role of religion today and of current demands of religion on architecture and the allied arts; to assist architects without experience in the design of buildings for worship to a better understanding of fundamentals; and to encourage the study of architecture and of the allied arts for religious use.

Founding Date: 1939

Staff: 1 full-time, 1 part-time

Membership: 600

Publications:

> *Faith and Forum,* twice yearly
> *The In Between,* supplement to *Faith and Forum,* twice yearly
> Newsletter, 3-4 times per year

Meetings:

> 1 National Conference annually, location varies
> 2-3 Regional Conferences each year throughout the country

Merger:

> IFRAA was born following the merger of:
> Guild for Religious Architecture

American Society for Church Architecture
Commission on Church Planning and Architecture

733. Intermedia

Protestant

Rev. David W. Briddell, Director
475 Riverside Drive
New York, New York 10027
(212) 870-2376

Intermedia works in more than 30 countries around the world. Its major task is helping literacy and literature programs, audio-visual production centers, radio and TV programming and operations, publishing houses and bookstores, workshops and training centers. An important link in Intermedia's relationship to more than 200 communication programs is the World Association for Christian Communication. It provides technical training and project grants for Christian broadcasting and publishing programs which annually produce and distribute more than 600 new titles, plus thousands of copies of booklets, magazines, films, and hymnals. In the United States Intermedia engages in promotion and fund raising and prepares educational materials for use in church groups.

Founding Date: 1970

Publications:
Word at Work, quarterly
Two newsletters containing program information on overseas projects are published annually

Meetings:
2 Governing Committee meetings per year

Merger:
Committee on World Literacy and Christian Literature and Radio Visual Education and Mass Communications Committee

734. International Alliance of Catholic Churches

Old Catholic

The Most Reverend George W.S. Brister, DD
Post Office Box 60235
Oklahoma City, Oklahoma 73146
(405) 525-2527

The International Alliance of Catholic Churches is a gathering together of the scattered Catholic Churches not aligned with the Roman Catholic Church, the Orthodox Churches, and others such as the Episcopal — Anglican. The 30 or more non-Roman Catholic Churches possessing licit apostolic successions who feel the need for unity are within this organization. Membership is by application and is open to all non-Roman Catholic churches with valid apostolic successions. The organization is in its formative stages and no dues or assessments are applicable. This organization is not an ecclesiastical synod, but rather an umbrella for those Catholic churches without a clear denominational alliance.

Founding Date: 1979

Staff: 5

Membership: 35

Publications:
The Lamp, quarterly

735. International Anglican and Eastern Orthodox Church Association (IAEOCA)

Interdenominational

Most Rev. Brian Glenn Turkington, STD, DMin, DD, President
38 Currier Place
Cheshire, Connecticut 06410
(203) 272-9376

Membership in the International Anglican and Eastern Orthodox Church Association is open to all communicant members of the Anglican and Eastern Orthodox Churches, Churches in full communion with them, and Churches that wish to be communicants.

Founding Date: 1968

Staff: 2

Membership: 45

Publications:
The Way, monthly

Meetings:
Every two years in Hartford, Connecticut

736. International Association of Hillel Directors

Jewish

Rabbi Richard A. Morkef, President
80 Brown Street
Providence, Rhode Island 02906
(401) 863-2344

The Association is a professional organization concerned with all matters pertaining to the professional well-being of Directors and Associate and Assistant Directors at B'nai B'rith Hillel Foundations, and otherwise employed full-time Jewish campus professionals.

Founding Date: 1949

Membership: 90 plus

Publications:
Occasional newsletters and reports to membership

Meetings:
One general meeting; several regional meetings per year

Former Name:
(1972) National Association of Hillel Directors

737. International Association of Women Ministers*

Nondenominational
Rev. Constance Bradshaw, General Secretary
143 Locust Street
Manchester, Kentucky 40962

The purpose of the International Association of Women Ministers is to develop an enabling fellowship among women ministers; to promote equal ecclesiastical rights for women; to urge women to qualify themselves for increased efficiency in Christian service; and to encourage consecrated and capable women to take up the work of the ministry.

Membership:
56 sustaining, fraternal and student
350 women ministers

Publications:
The Woman's Pulpit, quarterly

Meetings:
General Conference once a year

738. International Catholic Deaf Association, Inc., (ICDA)

Roman Catholic
Mr. John G. O'Brien, President
814 Thayer Avenue
Silver Spring, Maryland 20910
(301) 588-4009 (TTY and voice)

The International Catholic Deaf Association is an organization of Catholic deaf people in the United States, Canada, and other countries. Local chapters, currently numbering 117, are affiliated with the international body, but govern and manage their own activities in accordance with the Constitution and By-Laws of the international association. All officers, except Chaplains, are deaf persons. Purposes of the ICDA are: to promote the development and share the responsibility of church work in the local diocese with all Catholic deaf people; to aid local Chapter chaplains and to provide missionaries to work among the Catholic deaf; to provide good spiritual, social, and recreational programs for deaf persons; to foster more Catholic schools and religious education programs for deaf children; to sponsor a Mission Fund whose finances are used to enable missionaries, priests, Sisters, and others to promote the Catholic Church and its teachings among the deaf; to cooperate with other organizations — deaf or hearing — to improve the living standards of all the deaf by helping to pass beneficial legislation, by educating persons in business and industry as to the capability of deaf persons as employees, and by cooperation with various government and private agencies to promote public awareness of deaf people.

Founding Date: 1949

Membership: 2,700 lay; 100 clerical

Publications:
The Deaf Catholic, the official journal, quarterly
Home Office Newsletter, monthly
ICDA Chaplains' News Notes, occasionally
Individual Chapters' newsletters published monthly on local level

Meetings:
International Convention held annually at a site voted by the delegates, second week in July
Regional conferences held in New England, New York State, Midwest, and Far West

739. International Center for Learning (ICL)

Interdenominational
Lowell E. Brown, Executive Director
2300 Knoll Drive
Ventura, California 93003

The International Center for Learning is a division of Gospel Light Publications, an evangelical publishing house serving churches and denominations. ICL is the training division, offering interdenominational teacher training seminars in 200 cities throughout the United States and Canada. Over 250,000 teachers, pastors, and administrators have participated in these seminars during the past nine years. ICL also produces training-related products to assist church administrators and teachers, including age-level concept books, planning guides, handbooks, Media Kits, a Christian Educator's manual, and filmstrips. This year, ICL introduced a new film rental program. The 13 available films come with leader's guides and viewer response sheets developed for age-level teacher training.

Founding Date: 1933

Publications:
 20 age-level concept books
 8 age-level planning guides and handbooks
 9 general books in Christian education
 4 Media Kits (CE resources for teacher training)
 9 filmstrips/cassettes

Meetings:
 2 Vocational Staff Conferences per year, one is held on the West Coast, the other in Midwest

740. International Christian Leprosy Mission, Inc., (ICLM)

Nondenominational

Mrs. Hattie A. Metcalf
General Director, United States
6917 Southwest Oak Street
Portland, Oregon 97223

Mailing Address
Post Office Box 23353
Portland, Oregon 97223
(503) 244-5935

The International Christian Leprosy Mission was established to help people who have leprosy and to assist in the care of their children, ministering to them medically and bringing to them the Gospel of the Lord Jesus Christ. In the Philippines, the ICLM sponsors a home for children whose parents have leprosy and are not able to care for them. Some of the children have been in the Home since babyhood and have matured and are now self-supporting. The children are all healthy and attend regular school. They are under the supervision of Dr. Maria Dellota, a physician, and Pastor Catalino Maquera, the Director of The Philippine Children's Mission Home. He watches over the grounds and trains the children to help with projects about the premises. The children's fathers or mothers are in the government Leprosariums in The Philippines. The children attend Sunday School and Church on the grounds in their Chapel and have vacation Bible Schools during vacation times. Bible instruction is a part of their training. They have sponsors who contribute to their support monthly. In the country of India, a new clinic is being completed under the direction of Dr. B. Paramanandam and his son. This new building will allow them to treat more leprosy patients who come for medical help. The ICLM has sent funds to construct the clinic. It will add to the service given the leprosy patients in the area of Gajuwaka, Visakapatnam, India.

Founding Date: 1943

Publications:
 Global Missions, 3 times a year

741. International Conference of Jewish Communal Service

Jewish

Ms. Miriam R. Ephraim, Secretary General
15 East 26th Street
New York, New York 10010
(212) 683-8056-7

The International Conference of Jewish Communal Service conducts quadrennial conferences in Jerusalem, Israel, which bring together professional workers from Jewish communities all over the world to review common concerns and enhance their services by exchanging experiences. The International Conference grew out of a sensitive awareness of the Jewish community as an organic unit without geographic boundaries. In 1965-66 steps were taken with the support of the National Conference of Jewish Communal Service to give concrete expression to a need felt among Jewish communal workers to strengthen their understanding of each others' problems and services and to establish ongoing communication with each other. The Ministry of Social Welfare in Israel, the Central British Fund, the European Council of Jewish Community Services, the Federation of Australian Jewish Welfare Agencies, the South African Jewish Board of Deputies, and colleagues in several Latin American countries responded enthusiastically to a proposal for the organization of such an international body. The first Conference was held in Jerusalem in August, 1967, immediately after the Six Day War. Subsequent Conferences have taken place in Israel in 1971, 1975, and 1978. Working Parties to plan these Conferences have taken place in Israel, London, Paris, and recently in Madrid to plan the 1981 Conference. Proceedings of these Conferences and background papers issued in advance have been published by the International Conference of Jewish Communal Service with the support of such organizations as the Memorial Foundation for Jewish Culture. The headquarters of the International Conference is located in New York City. The Board of Directors, elected after each quadrennial Conference, functions between Conferences to make policy decisions, promote financial support and develop programs and participation for each world-wide Conference.

Founding Date: 1965

Publications:
Conference Proceedings
Newsletter

742. International Evangelism Crusades (IEC)

Protestant
Dr. Frank E. Stranges, International President
7970 Woodman Avenue, Suite 207
Van Nuys, California 91402
(213) 781-7704

International Evangelism Crusades is dedicated to spreading the Gospel and acting as a service organization to other denominations and Christian Fellowships throughout the world to ordain and license ministers, provide schooling and other education through its sister education entities and to help those in need.

Membership:
Ministers, pastors, missionaries, 1,300
Membership, 32,774
Churches, 284

Publications:
The New Age, bimonthly

Radio/TV Programs:
2 TV programs in New York City
2 radio programs in New York City
2 radio programs in Albuquerque, New Mexico
1 radio program in Los Angeles

Meetings:
1 annual meeting

743. International Federation of Catholic Alumnae (IFCA)*

Roman Catholic
Miss Emilie B. Prose, President
Business Headquarters
416 Administration Building
The Catholic University of America
Washington, D.C. 20064
(202) 526-5916

International Federation of Catholic Alumnae, founded in New York City by Alumnae of St. Joseph College, Emmitsburg, Maryland, and Daughters of Charity of St. Vincent dePaul, with permission of Cardinal Gibbons, Archbishop of Baltimore, has as its purpose to consolidate and involve individuals and groups, the alumnae and alumni of Catholic secondary schools, schools of nursing, colleges, and universities, as well as individual Catholic graduates of other schools of secondary or higher education, as volunteers in programs of education and community service geared to the needs of the Church and of contemporary society, and to provide leadership for these programs.

Founding Date: 1914

Membership: 3,000-10,000 lay, clerical religious

Publications:
IFCA Bulletin, quarterly

Meetings:
Special meetings as necessary during the year
One Regional Conference each year
Conventions, biennially

744. International Fellowship of Evangelical Students (IFES)

Interdenominational
Brian Rust, North American Representative
Post Office Box 270
Madison, Wisconsin 53701
(608) 257-0263

The International Fellowship of Evangelical Students is a united body of 49 member movements representing 75 nations of the world. Helping each other sustain an ongoing witness to students, these movements are also pioneering in more than 20 countries not having the resources to develop their own witness to students. Inter-Varsity Christian Fellowship is one such member movement. Yearly, IVCF-

USA prays for, sends people to, and financially supports various aspects of the IFES work.

Staff: 50

Membership: 1,000

Publications:

In Touch, a newspaper

IFES Review, a staff "helps" magazine/journal

Certeza, a Latin American Evangelical student magazine

Meetings:

Annual International Student Conferences at Schloss Mittersill, Austria

745. International Films, Inc.

Nondenominational

Mr. C. Ray Carlson, President
1530 East Elizabeth Street
Pasadena, California 91104

Mailing Address
Post Office Box 40400
Pasadena, California 91104
(213) 797-0062

International Films, Inc., is a nondenominational, international specialized service agency of evangelical tradition, producing films particularly oriented to youth evangelism. Its films are intended for specific use in that area where they are produced. International Films, Inc., is a Member Agency of and is located on the campus of the United States Center for World Mission.

Founding Date: 1963

Staff: 5

Meetings:

Communication seminars, annually

Affiliates:

International Films, Inc.—UK, 235 Shaftsbury, London WC2H-8EL, and GIFTS, C-47 Eucress Building, Wadala East, Bombay 400-037

746. International Gospel League (IGL)

Interdenominational

Dr. Howard T. Lewis, President
854 East Washington Boulevard
Pasadena, California 91104
(213) 798-0551

The International Gospel League supports over 750 evangelists, pastors, hospital chaplains, doctors, nurses, teachers, and Bible women. The League's ministry includes evangelism (over 200 churches have been established); medical services (through hospitals, medical centers, and roadside and village clinics); malnutrition wards; leprosy research; day schools (with nearly 6,000 pupils worldwide); vocational training; seminaries; orphanages; radio evangelism; literature distribution; and village evangelism in every country where IGL is represented. The primary purpose is to bring people to know Christ as Savior through every means possible.

Founding Date; 1906

Membership: 17,500 lay; 15 clerical

Publications:

International Gospel News, monthly

747. International Institute

Nondenominational

Richard E. Wager, General Director
Post Office Box 99
Park Ridge, Illinois 60068
(312) 823-1852

International Institute offers approved grade school education for children who cannot attend school. It provides a workable, planned, and thorough home instruction course which includes teacher and student textbooks and workbooks, supplies, explicit day-by-day and hour-by-hour instructions, helps, and assignments that are carefully planned for the inexperienced home teacher. It is updated yearly. Advisement by professional teachers is available, and includes testing, checking over student work, and grading. Supplies and advisement are optional. Course and texts can be kept and reused for other members of the family, and there are large family and missionary discounts. A Bible course and supplementary subjects are included in each course. Many recognize the advantages of keeping the family together and of the tutor relationship, which is one of education's finest tools. Thousands of students have benefitted and are readily accepted in stateside schools.

Founding Date: 1960

Staff: 6

Membership: 10,000 students

748. International Liaison, Inc., United States Catholic Coordinating Center for Lay Volunteer Ministries

Roman Catholic

Mr. Matthew R. Paratore
1234 Massachusetts Avenue, N.W.
Washington, D.C. 20005
(202) 638-4197

The International Liaison, Inc., is the United States Catholic Coordinating Center for Lay Volunteer Ministries. It is an affiliate of the United States Catholic Conference. The specific purpose for which the International Liaison was founded is to coordinate and facilitate the efforts of lay volunteer mission organizations by communicating to the laity the urgency of their role in the mission of the Church, and by maintaining constant contact with the United States dioceses and religious communities to ascertain their needs for lay expertise in mission areas of the United States and of dioceses all over the world. The work of the National Office includes consultation, promotion, recruiting and referral of candidates for service programs. Every year doctors, nurses, dentists, teachers, mechanics, carpenters, engineers, agronomists, secretaries, community developers, and many other dedicated persons from all walks of life, share their professional expertise, their education and talents, and their Christian Faith with others who are in need. The International Liaison is not a receiving or a sending agency, but serves as a center of reference, a switchboard operation between various programs and agencies, and the personnel they endeavor to employ. The nature of the work is within the context of the Christian mission, specifically Catholic, with interdenominational ties.

Founding Date: 1963
Staff: 3 full-time; 3 part-time
Membership: 94 General Coalition members
Publications:
> *The Response,* annual directory describing opportunities for lay volunteer mission work in the United States and overseas
> *Newsletter,* quarterly, news of Coalition membership and news of interest to lay volunteers and to those working in church-related programs
> *Worldreach,* quarterly, compilation of articles and documents of interest to the International Liaison Coalition membership

Radio/TV Programs:
> Film *If We Could Share,* award-winning 15-minute 16mm color film on lay volunteer ministries, 1976

Meetings:
> General Assembly, annual 3 day conference in a different city each year

Former Name:
> (1975) International Liaison for Volunteer Service

Affiliate: United States Catholic Conference

749. International Lutheran Laymen's League (ILLL)*

The Lutheran Church—Missouri Synod

B.F. Jutzi
2185 Hampton Avenue
St. Louis, Missouri 63139
(314) 647-4900

The main projects of the Lutheran Laymen's League are in the mass media ministries of radio, television, and the printed page. The International LLL sponsors The Lutheran Hour, a worldwide broadcast heard on more than 1,100 stations in the United States and Canada, and some 800 broadcasts in 45 languages to 125 lands. The International LLL also sponsors the television dramatic series, *This Is The Life.* The League carries out a Gospel outreach through a program called *Preaching Through the Press.* This program offers special booklets to readers through advertisements in national magazines, newspaper supplements, and weekly news journals. Other ministries include cassette tapes, devotional booklets, and evangelism material.

750. International Lutheran Women's Missionary League (LWML)

Lutheran Church—Missouri Synod

Mrs. Howard E. Mueller
Headquarters Office Manager
3558 South Jefferson Avenue
Saint Louis, Missouri 63118
(314) 664-7000 Ext. 313

The Lutheran Women's Missionary League is the women's auxiliary of the Lutheran Church—Missouri Synod. Its objectives are Mission Education, Mission

Inspiration, and Mission Service. To accomplish these objectives, the organization provides program and resource materials for its districts and societies, such as an annual Bible study, wallet-size mini-Bible studies, program planning resources, programs and devotions, a quarterly magazine and other inspirational and educational resources. An active program of service to the church and community is encouraged. The LWML raises all of its funds through voluntary offerings collected in "Mite Boxes." These monies are given to specific mission projects, funded and/or approved by the Lutheran Church—Missouri Synod.

Founding Date: 1942

Staff: 3

Membership:

Approximately 200,000 in 43 districts in the United States and Canada

Publications:

Lutheran Women's Quarterly, quarterly

Meetings:

International conventions, biennial

District conventions, annual or biennial

Former Name:

(1976) Lutheran Women's Missionary League

751. International Metaphysical Association, Inc. (IMA)

Christian Science

Ethel Schroeder, President

20 East 68th Street

New York, New York 10021

(212) 249-2628

The purpose of the International Metaphysical Association is to advance the idea of divine metaphysics and its science as presented in the Bible and in *Science and Health with Key to the Scriptures* and other writings by Mary Baker Eddy. The IMA is a non-profit association, incorporated under the laws of the State of New Jersey. It was formed to facilitate the receipt and disbursement of funds for the furtherance of the purpose set forth above. Its work will be a contribution to all current activity in this field, and its function is to stimulate and not compete. Its aims are to fulfull the purpose set forth through any or all of the following media: publication of pamphlets and books; advertising of pamphlets, books, lectures, and classes; radio lec-

tures and announcements; television lectures and announcements; public lectures, classes and summer schools; scholarships for special schools and workshops; teaching and lecture tours; and recordings.

Founding Date: 1954

752. International Missions, Inc., (IM)

Nondenominational

Rev. Bill Tarter, President

Post Office Box 323

Wayne, New Jersey 07470

(201) 696-4804

International Missions, Inc., is a nondenominational sending agency of fundamentalist tradition establishing churches among Asian peoples world-wide and engaged in evangelism, education, literature, broadcasting, and re-translation. Current mission fields include: Hong Kong, India, Japan, the Philippines, Kenya, Surinam, Iran, Pakistan, Turkey, Holland, and Great Britain.

Founding Date: 1930

Staff: 10

Membership: 185

Publications:

Eastern Challenge, quarterly

Praise and Prayer, monthly prayer calendar

Radio/TV Programs:

3 radio programs per week—Bible lessons

Meetings:

Annual meeting in each mission field

Former Name: (1950) India Mission

753. International New Thought Alliance (INTA)

Nondenominational

Dr. Blaine C. Mays, President

7314 East Stetson Drive

Scottsdale Arizona 85251

(602) 945-0744

International New Thought Alliance is a free and open alliance of truth-motivated individuals and organizations who desire to unfold and practice a positive lifestyle of spiritual maturity and who are dedicated to the universal propagation of these principles as described in the Declaration of Principles. INTA is an alliance uniting individuals and organizations with common determination to bring out the best in individuals through an understanding of these eternal verities. The International New Thought Alliance is a year-round working organization, democratic in structure, and serves as the means through which metaphysical schools, churches, and centers of like mind can work together. Its purposes are: to teach people to come into a conscious realization of the divinity within and the unity of God and man, so that out of the sublimity of their souls they can say, "I and the Father are one."; to provide, at the annual congress and interim conferences, opportunities for exchange of ideas, viewpoints, and inspiration covering the whole spectrum of spiritual principles and laws and their application to daily life; to publicize its ideas in all mediums available such as the present quarterly magazine, *New Thought,* radio, TV, books, literature, press, schools, etc.; to encourage newly-formed centers with interest and attention and assist whenever and wherever possible; to invite and encourage the training of leaders and ministers, and to raise all teaching to an accredited academic level; to encourage the teaching of New Thought at all levels, paying more attention to the children, youth, and young adults; and to maintain a flow of materials into the archives of the New Thought movement.

Founding Date: 1917

Staff: 4

Membership: 2,700

Publications:
> *New Thought Quarterly*

Meetings:
> INTA annual congress meets in July and rotates geographically: 1983, Detroit, Michigan; 1984, Las Vegas, Nevada; 1985, Calgary, Canada; 1986, Houston, Texas; 1987, Portland, Oregon

754. International Organization for Masoretic Studies

Nondenominational
Prof. Harry M. Orlinsky, President
1 West 4th Street
New York, New York 10012
(212) 674-5300

The purpose of the International Organization for Masoretic Studies is to convene congresses in the United States and abroad where papers can be delivered and discussed on the numerous and varied aspects of the history and transmission of the Hebrew text of the Old Testament, especially since the Hebrew Bible was canonized around 100 A.D. The congresses are usually scheduled in conjunction with meetings of the Society of Biblical Literature United States, International Organization for the Study of the Old Testament (Europe), and the World Congress for Jewish Studies (Israel). The organization encourages and promotes the publication of articles and books in its area of specialization.

Publications:
> *Masoretic Studies,* volumes 1-5 to date

Meetings:
> Annual conferences

755. International Pentecostal Church of Christ, Global Missions Department

International Pentecostal Church of Christ
Dr. James B. Keiller, Global Missions Director
892 Berne Street, S.E.
Atlanta, Georgia 30316
Mailing Address
Post Office Box 18145
Atlanta, Georgia 30316
(404) 627-2681

The general purpose of the International Pentecostal Church of Christ is to advance the teaching of the Gospel of Jesus Christ and to institute, maintain, operate, and conduct Christ-centered institutions of higher learning; to cause to be published and distributed denominational periodicals and general literature; and to maintain and promote the work of Christian instruction and evangelism at home and around the world. There are both home and foreign missionary works. There are approximately 90 churches in the United States and 350 churches in foreign countries, as well as Bible colleges, etc., both at home and abroad.

Founding Date: 1914

Membership: 500 ministers; 45 missionaries

Publications:
> *Bridegroom's Messenger,* official church organ

Meetings:
> 1 annual conference
> 1 camp meeting
> Several youth camps

Former Name:
> International Pentecostal Assemblies World Missions Department

756. International Pentecostal Holiness Church, Armed Forces Department*

International Pentecostal Holiness Church

Post Office Box 12069
Oklahoma City, Oklahoma 73112
(405) 787-7110

The Armed Forces Department of the International Pentecostal Holiness Church is responsible for keeping in touch with all the church's military personnel by providing them with Christian literature of various types, keeping them informed of the Pentecostal Holiness Church nearest their camp, and encouraging them to attend one of the churches. There are five active chaplains, and it is the goal of this Department to meet the spiritual needs of all servicemen, both at home and abroad. This is done through revivals and spiritual retreats at military bases around the world.

757. International Pentecostal Holiness Church, Department of Education

International Pentecostal Holiness Church

7300 Northwest 39th Expressway
Oklahoma City, Oklahoma 73008
(405) 787-7110

The Department of Education of the International Pentecostal Holiness Church encourages young people to receive their education in a Christian school where the Bible is taught and its doctrines and ethics respected. Listed among the institutions supported by the Department of Education of the Pentecostal Holiness Church are: Emmanuel College, Franklin Springs, Georgia; Oklahoma City Southwestern College, Oklahoma City, Oklahoma; Holmes Theological Seminary, Greenville, South Carolina; and Berea Bible Institute, McAllen, Texas.

758. International Pentecostal Holiness Church, Department of Evangelism*

International Pentecostal Holiness Church

Leon Stewart, Director
7300 Northwest 39th Expressway
Oklahoma City, Oklahoma 73008
(405) 787-7110

The Department of Evangelism of the International Pentecostal Holiness Church is committed to fulfilling the Great Commission of Jesus to His followers. Its philosophy is that soul-winning should become a way of life with every born-again Christian. The Church helps people to become soul-winners through evangelism training schools; the bimonthly magazine, *Witness;* tracts; cassette tapes; child evangelism; and the Pioneer Outreach Club. The denomination is also involved in evangelism conferences, a national radio broadcast called *The Pentecostal Witness,* organizing new churches, and presenting Jesus to the American Indian.

Publications:
   Witness

Radio/TV Programs:
   The Pentecostal Witness

759. International Pentecostal Holiness Church, Department of Publications (Advocate Press)

International Pentecostal Holiness Church

Mr. Charles E. Bradshaw, General Administrator
Franklin Springs, Georgia 30639

The Advocate Press is the editorial, printing, and distribution arm of the Department of Publications of the International Pentecostal Holiness Church. It has been in operation for over 50 years, meeting the printing needs of the church and its people. Periodicals published by the Advocate Press include: *The Advocate,* a semi-monthly journal of the Pentecostal Holiness Church; *Reach,* a monthly magazine for youth; *Tips,* a quarterly magazine for Sunday School workers; and the *Helping Hand,* a monthly magazine for women. In addition, over 1,250,000 pieces of Sunday School literature are produced each year by Advocate Press, and all literature is distributed through Advocate Press bookstores across the nation.

Also Known As: Advocate Press

760. International Pentecostal Holiness Church, Women's Auxiliary

International Pentecostal Holiness Church

7300 Northwest 39th Expressway
Oklahoma City, Oklahoma 73008
(405) 787-7110

The International Pentecostal Holiness Church's Women's Auxiliary is dedicated to motivating women to spiritual commitment; this begins by maintaining a Christian atmosphere and Bible standards in the home. Ministries of the Auxiliary include projects to improve or beautify the local Church; hospitality services to pastors, evangelists, and missionaries; soul-winning and church enlistment visitation; ministry of united prayer and intercession; Bible and literature distribution; ministries to the sick, shut-in, bereaved; and visits and practical ministries to penal institutions, hospitals, rest homes, and sanatoriums. Missionaries, church schools, and church benevolent homes all share in the broad outreach of the Women's Auxiliary. The auxiliary is open to every woman who desires membership and actively participates in the program.

761. International Pentecostal Holiness Church, Inc., World Missions Department

Pentecostal Holiness Church, Inc.

Rev. B. E. Underwood, Vice Chairman of the Board of the International Pentecostal Holiness Church and Director of the World Missions Department
7300 Northwest 39th Expressway
Bethany, Oklahoma 73008

Mailing Address
Post Office Box 12609
Oklahoma City, Oklahoma 73157
(405) 787-7110 Ext. 220

The primary purpose of the World Missions Department of the Pentecostal Holiness Church is to fulfill the Great Commission of the Lord Jesus Christ. This involves: the proclamation of salvation to sinners, the truth that all believers are to be sanctified and baptized in the Holy Spirit; the sending of missionaries whose aim is to plant churches that will become self-supporting, self-governing and self-propagating; and the establishment of the Pentecostal Holiness Church witnessing to the people of other countries and cultures through the teaching of the Word of God, which is the basis for their doctrine and their pattern of conduct and living.

Founding Date: 1913

Staff: 8

Membership: Overseas, 157,241

Publications:
   Worldorama, monthly

Meetings:
   World Missions Training Seminar, once every year

762. International Pentecostal Press Association

Pentecostal

Dr. O. W. Polen, Secretary/Treasurer
1080 Montgomery Avenue
Cleveland, Tennessee 37311
(615) 476-4512 Ext. 214

International Pentecostal Press Association is a fellowship of Christians who are actively engaged in the journalistic profession. The purposes of this organization are to encourage acquaintance and cooperation among members; to gather and disseminate information on the Pentecostal movement; to promote excellence in the journalistic professions; to work in harmony with the World Pentecostal Conference; and to bring glory to God in all its concerns and actions. Projected functions of the Association include the following: to gather news of the Pentecostal movement worldwide, including news of books and articles about Pentecostal history, practice, and doctrine, and to disseminate it regularly; to establish and maintain a central library of member publications; to prepare, maintain, and publish among members every three years and prior to the general meeting a directory of members and member publications; to sponsor regular international and regional seminars for Pentecostal editors and writers; to syndicate to member and non-member publications major articles on Pentecostal history, practice, and doctrine; to organize a meaningful world-wide system of competition to promote excellence among members and member publications; to establish and award journalism scholarships for qualified Pentecostal young people; to create a writers' institute for correspondence study; and to fund, award, and supervise research fellowships for preparing works on Pentecostal history, practice, and doctrine.

Publications:
   Pentecost: International Report, quarterly

Meetings:
   General Meeting every three years to coincide with the World Pentecostal Conference

763. International Philosda Club

Seventh-day Adventist

G. Garland Day, President
410 Circle Avenue
Takoma Park, Maryland 20912

Mailing Address
Lorene Soderstrom, Membership Secretary
5261 Sonora Way
Carmichael, California 95608
(301) 891-2110

The purpose of Philosda is to provide Christian fellowship in both spiritual and secular contexts, spiritual growth, and a witnessing opportunity for unmarried Seventh-day Adventist adults. Philosda is a growing organization with chapters nationwide and representatives in neighboring countries. Membership in Philosda provides service through Christian fellowship, utilization of talents, and meaningful social activities. Privileges of members include discounts on club activities, insurance coverage, voting privileges, and receiving the two official publications of *Philosda*, the monthly *Bulletin* and the Club Membership Directory. The growing number of single SDA adults constitutes a vast and largely untapped resource of talent and dedication for the mission of the church. Through Philosda this talent is becoming available to the church through group effort. By means of retreats, Sabbath Schools, missionary projects, camping trips, social functions, and other activities, Philosda endeavors to challenge and provide fellowship for members and friends. Philosda also offers a counseling program for children of separation and divorce.

Founding Date: 1963
Staff: 14
Membership: 1,500
Publications:
> *IPC Bulletin,* monthly
> *IPC Membership Directory,* annually

Meetings:
> Three 10 day camp meetings each year in the East, Midwest, and West
> Weekend retreats, held at Easter, Memorial Day, Thanksgiving, and New Years

764. International Prison Ministry*

Nondenominational

Chaplain Ray, Chief Executive
Post Office Box 63
Dallas, Texas 75221
(214) 494-2302

The International Prison Ministry is a non-profit, religious, church organization which reaches out to provide spiritual help to prisoners throughout the English speaking world. This outreach is accom-plished via radio broadcasts; distribution of Bibles, study guides, and concordances; a personal ministry of answering prisoners' letters and questions; Bible Study Books, Soul-winning Books, and Life Changing Books sent free to prisoners; Cassette Bible Study outfits; large, full-color murals for display in dining rooms and chapels of prisons at Easter and Christmas; and free greeting cards distributed to in-mates for their personal use at Christmas and Mother's Day.

Publications:
> *Prison Evangelism,* bimonthly

765. International Religious Liberty Association

Dr. B. B. Beach, Secretary-general
6840 Eastern Avenue, N.W.
Washington, D.C. 20012
(202) 722-6681

The International Religious Liberty Association is an organization that promotes and defends religious liberty in all parts of the world. It supports religious liberty as a natural and inalienable right which includes freedom of conscience and freedom to profess, to practice, and to propagate religious beliefs. This liberty includes the right to change religion. In the exercise of religious liberty, every person has the duty to respect the religious liberty rights of others.

Founding Date: 1946
Staff: 13
Publications:
> *Conscience and Liberty,* biannually
Meetings:
> Last world conference held in 1977; next scheduled 1984

766. International Society of Bible Collectors

Nondenominational

Arnold D. Ehlert, President
1262 Camillo Way
El Cajon, California 92021

Mailing Address
Post Office Box 2485
El Cajon, California 92021
(714) 440-5871

International Society of Bible Collectors is an association of Bible collectors and those interested in Bible translations and versions.

Founding Date: 1964

Staff: 1

Membership:
129 personal; 84 libraries and institutions

Publications:
The Bible Collector, quarterly

767. International Society of Christian Endeavor (ISCE)

Interdenominational
Charles W. Barner, General Secretary
David G. Jackson, Executive Secretary
1221 East Broad Street
Columbus, Ohio 43216

Mailing Address
Post Office Box 1110
Columbus, Ohio 43216
(614) 258-9545

The International Society of Christian Endeavor brings together in conventions and conferences young people from different churches, denominations, nations, and races. Local churches determine the theology, program, activities, and relationships of the society. It serves as a vital instrument of Christian education in the local church. Activities are planned for and by young people with adult counsel. Expressional Bible-based meetings are held regularly. ISCE is a training program aimed at developing leadership abilities in young people. Emphasis is placed on the prayer life and on the stewardship of time, talent, and treasure of each individual. Commitment to Christ is the basic aim, as expressed in the first line of the pledge, "Trusting in the Lord Jesus Christ for strength. . . "

Founding Date: 1881

Membership: 1,000,000

Publications:
The Christian Endeavor World, quarterly

Meetings:
International conventions held in odd-numbered years
Board of Trustees' meetings annually in October
State and County Conventions held annually

Former Name:
(1927) United Society of Christian Endeavor

768. International Students, Inc. (ISI)*

Nondenominational
Hal Guffey, President
Post Office Box C
Colorado Springs, Colorado 80901
(303) 576-2700

The goals of International Students, Inc., are to demonstrate Christian friendship and Christian love; to win the international student to Christ; to train him to be a lifetime Christian witness; and to help and encourage him to spread the gospel of Jesus Christ among his own people. ISI staffers help the international student in hundreds of ways. They meet his plane, help him find living quarters and a job, take him on tours of the surrounding environment, establish contact with Christian families near his university, draw him into worship services, and ultimately lead him into a commitment to Jesus Christ.

Staff: 10

769. International Temperance Association (ITA)

Seventh-day Adventist
Dr. M. Hardinge, President
6840 Eastern Avenue, N.W.
Washington, D.C. 20012
(202) 722-6729

The International Temperance Association speaks authoritatively to the problems of alcohol, tobacco, and drugs, and sets the pace for prevention through positive alternatives. It recognizes the importance of creating a lifestyle that gives attention to proper nutrition, the forming of regular habits for life betterment, and the developing of confidence and trust in divine power as effective means toward prevention. National societies of ITA endeavor to highlight the positive alternatives to everyone either within or without the church, and take a decided approach in conducting projects that limit alcohol and tobacco advertising, and encourage individual choices built on scientific evidence. These projects include the Five-Day Plan to Stop Smoking, a community service in which more than 14 million people have participated, a plan for personal guidance called Home Help for Alcohol, Tobacco, or Drug Problems, and the Four-Dimensional Key to Better Living, which is the answer to alcoholism and drug use. Helping convey the ITA message are full-color 16mm feature films, super 8mm films and filmstrips, plus booklets, magazines, teaching aids, posters, and other organizational materials.

770. Interreligious Foundation for Community Organization (IFCO)

Interdenominational

Lucius Walker, Jr., Executive Director
348 Convent Avenue
New York, New York 10031
(212) 926-5757

The Interreligious Foundation for Community Organization is a church and community agency whose mission is to help forward the struggle of oppressed people for justice and self-determination. IFCO is a coalition of national religious agencies who have an historic concern for justice and liberation, and minority community groups who organize to fight against the injustices which society inflicts upon them. In carrying out its mission, IFCO works in the following program areas: community organization support and advocacy; the National Organizers Conference; human rights; Relief for Africans in Need (RAIN); education and training; and Native American concerns. The work of IFCO is in the spirit of a continuing commitment to its family, "some of whom are living, many of whom are dead, and most of whom are yet unborn."

Founding Date: 1966

Publications:
IFCO News, quarterly
IFCO Annual Report

771. Inter-Varsity Christian Fellowship*

Nondenominational

John W. Alexander
233 Langdon Street
Madison, Wisconsin 53703
(608) 257-0263

Inter-Varsity Christian Fellowship is a living, witnessing, praying, studying, and singing fellowship of students and faculty at hundreds of United States universities, colleges, and schools of nursing. Its major objectives are: to lead others to a personal faith in Christ as Lord and Saviour; to help Christians grow toward maturity as disciples of Christ by study of the

Bible, by prayer, and by Christian fellowship; and to present the call of God to the world mission of the Church, i.e., to help students and faculty to discover God's role for them.

Staff: 400

Publications:
250 books and booklets
HIS Magazine; The Branch, The Nurses Lamp plus periodicals

772. Inter-Varsity Press

Nondenominational

James F. Nyquist, Director
Post Office Box F
Downers Grove, Illinois 60515
(312) 964-5700

Inter-Varsity Press is the book publishing division of Inter-Varsity Christian Fellowship of the United States of America, an interdenominational student movement active on campuses at hundreds of universities, colleges and schools of nursing. The purpose of Inter-Varsity Press is to provide quality Christian literature for the academic community and those with academic interests.

Publications:
300 in print, 40 new titles each year— religious, scholarly, art
His Magazine for Christian college students, published monthly October through June

773. The Invisible Ministry

Church of the Trinity

Friend A. Stuart Otto, Director
Post Office Box 37
San Marcos, California 92069
(714) 746-9430

The Invisible Ministry is a corporate entity which includes the following departments: Church of the Trinity, Trinity Healing Prayer, Trinity School of Theology, the Dominion Press, the Committee for Elimination of Death, and the Chapel of the Eternal Word. All of these are housed in a single location known as Trinity Center. Most of its outreach is conducted by mail and telephone, in 64 countries, and in all 50 states of the United States.

Founding Date: 1963

Staff: 9 clerical

Publications:

Metaphysical theology, inspirational, about one dozen titles presently in print, plus about 50 others distributed, but not published by the press

Master Thoughts, weekly; *Tidings,* bimonthly

Life Lines, quarterly; *Theologia 21,* quarterly

Annual report

774. The Islamic Center*

Islam

Dr. Muhammad Abdul Rauf

2551 Massachusetts Avenue, N.W.

Washington, D.C. 20008

(202) 332-3451

The objective of the Islamic Center is to make Islam better known through the publication of genuine literature and by other means, and to serve the Muslim community at large, particularly those in the greater Washington area. The Islamic Center sponsors cultural, educational, religious, and charitable activities.

Membership: 15,000

Publications:

15 books, quarterly bulletin

Meetings:

Numerous

775. Israel's Evangelistic Missions, Inc.

Jewish

Dr. Ben David Lew, Director

14001 West 11 Mile Road

Oak Park, Michigan 48237

(313) 543-1252

The purpose of Israel's Evangelistic Missions is to obey the command of Christ to "go and teach" and propagate the Gospel of Jesus Christ, the good news that Christ died and rose again, to be the Saviour of "whosoever will" accept Him. The Scriptures repeatedly teach that God has a plan for this world and all peoples. The organization holds meetings, both at the Mission headquarters and across the country in Prophetic Conferences with Dr. Lew. It publishes a monthly magazine and produces radio and television programs, teaches classes in Hebrew and Bible Prophecy. No offerings are taken at the meetings; it is not a church, but a Mission, and its work is by faith.

Publications:

Hope of Israel, monthly

Radio/TV Programs:

TV program on Channel 62 every Sunday at 8:30 to 9:00 p.m.

Radio program six days a week on KLXL FM

Meetings:

Jewish Prophetic Conferences conducted in churches

Annual Mission Passover Dinner

776. Jack Van Impe Ministries

Baptist

Post Office Box J
Royal Oak, Michigan 48068
(313) 435-3322

The purpose of the Jack Van Impe Ministries is the proclamation of the Gospel of the Lord Jesus Christ through weekly international radio programs in translated languages, nationwide television programs (weekly and specials), evangelistic rallies, recordings and publications.

Staff: 85

Publications:

Perhaps Today, bimonthly prophetic news magazine.

Radio/TV Programs:

International radio programming on weekly basis in 83 languages

Weekly half-hour TV program, *Jack Van Impe Presents*

Hour long specials from crusade sites annually

Meetings:

Approximately 20 evangelistic crusades and rallies per year

777. Japan Evangelical Mission (JEM)

Nondenominational

Ben Ichikawa, Acting General Director
9047 Burke Avenue North
Seattle, Washington 98l03
(206) 522-1514

The Japan Evangelical Mission is a nondenominational Protestant missionary sending agency of evangelical and conservative tradition engaged in radio evangelism, church planting, Bible and Christian literature distribution, camps and conferences, Bible and theological training of national young people for the pastoral and other church ministries, leadership development, the teaching of English and child evangelism in Japan and Brazil.

Founding Date: 1951

Staff:

65 full-time members in North America, Japan, and Brazil

Publications:

JEMS magazine, 5 times a year

Meetings:

Business meetings regularly in Japan and Brazil

Family Conference every summer for national churches in Japan

778. Japan Evangelistic Band, Inc.

Interdenominational

Rev. Tudor J. Jones, North American Home Director
2237 Manhattan Avenue
Hermosa Beach, California 90254
(213) 376-5867

The Japan Evangelistic Band was founded by Barclay F. Buxton and Paget Wilks. The organization has a Bible School located in Kobe, Japan. Japanese young people at the school are instructed in the Bible and equipped to go out to teach their young people. Some of the graduates go out in a church planting ministry, some work as Bible Men or Women helping a missionary in tent campaigns and other evangelical efforts to reach the rural countryside with the Gospel of the Lord Jesus Christ. In Kobe the organization has a 'mission hall' in the heart of the theatre district. Students from the Bible School and other leaders conduct nightly evangelistic services.

Founding Date: 1903

Publications:
Newsletter and a missionary magazine

Radio/TV Programs:
A ministry in Japan using Scripture-based messages with invitations to phone to given locations

Meetings:
3 annual conferences and meetings in Japan

779. Japan International Christian University Foundation

Nondenominational

Miss Ruth Miller, Executive Director
475 Riverside Drive, Room 720
New York, New York 10027
(212) 870-2893

The Japan International Christian University Foundation is a non-profit organization incorporated in New York to assist in the founding and development of International Christian University in Japan (ICU). The Foundation works to raise funds for ICU in the United States and Canada; to provide information about this University to individuals and groups in North America; and to serve as an office of the University in contacts with prospective American students and faculty, and in other appropriate areas.

Founding Date: 1949

Staff:
60 Members of the Board of Directors
6 staff members

Publications:
Newsletter, quarterly

Meetings:
One annual meeting in New York City
Approximately 15 meetings of various Foundation committees annually, held in New York

780. Japan — North American Commission on Cooperative Mission (JNAC)

Interdenominational

Dr. Robert W. Northup, Executive Secretary
475 Riverside Drive, Room 618
New York, New York 10027
(212) 870-2021

The Commission was founded as Interboard Committee for Christian work in Japan. Its 10 members include North American churches, boards and agencies; the United Church of Christ in Japan/the Council of Cooperation (Japan Christian Social Work League; Christian Schools Council) and the Korean Christian Church in Japan. It appoints missionaries to Japan for a wide range of activities under invitation and direction from Japan. The purpose of the Commission is to engage in mutual mission in both Japan and North America. It conducts research; sponsors projects in Japan and North America; and shares its working papers for policy and mission study.

Founding Date: 1947

Staff: 10

Former Name:
(1973) Interboard Committee for Christian Education

Obsorbed: Okinawa Interboard Committee

781. Japanese Evangelical Missionary Society (JEMS)

Rev. Sam Tonomura, Executive Director
112 North San Pedro Street, Suite 317
Los Angeles, California 90012
(213) 629-1089

The purpose and activities of the Japanese Evangelical Missionary Society are to: send missionaries, both short and long-term, and support national workers to propagate the Christian Gospel in totality in Jesus Christ to the Japanese, especially in Japan and Brazil; publish journals in English and Japanese, reporting its activities as well as local church news; sponsor Christian projects, including concerts, at home and abroad; provide personnel and ministries (such as campus and music ministries) to supplement the work of the local congregations; sponsor Christian conferences, retreats, and seminars; and receive voluntary contributions to carry out these ministries.

Founding Date: 1950

Staff: 6

Publications:
JEMS Journal, in English and Japanese, bimonthly

Meetings:
JEMS Mount Hermon Christian Family Conference, Mount Hermon, California, annually

Tahquitz Pines Winter Retreat, Idyllwild,
California, annually
TRI-C Conference, Lake Hughes, California,
annually
Women's Retreat, Lake Hughes
Northern and Southern California Young Adults
Retreat, Watsonville and Lake Hughes

782. Jesuit Foreign Missions

Roman Catholic
Rev. William J. Raftery, SJ, Director
314 Dartmouth Street
Boston, Massachusetts 02116
(617) 536-7224

Jesuit Foreign Missions (of New England) is an
adjunct of the Provincial Offices for the New England
Province of the Society of Jesus. The purpose of the
Mission Office is to help in the financial support of
the foreign mission activities. This is done by:
direct mail appeals at specified times of the year; a
monthly donor organization; offerings for Masses
and other spiritual benefits; gifts received for missions in general or for specific missions and/or missionaries; legacies received; mission appeals in
parishes under the auspices of the Society for the
Propagation of the Faith. Funds received are used to
support programs on the Missions, men on the Missions, medical costs of Missionaries, care for the
elderly and retired Missionaries; and in general any
needs of men and missions.

Membership: 83
Publications:
The Jesuit, quarterly
Meetings:
Annual meeting of Jesuit Mission Offices and
Jesuit Seminary Guild Offices of the United
States usually held in May, location varies

783. Jesuit Philosophical Association

Roman Catholic
Rev. C. R. Bukala, SJ, Secretary-Treasurer
John Carroll University
Cleveland, Ohio 44118
(215) 879-7751

The Jesuit Philosophical Association is composed of
priests and scholastics of the Society of Jesus
(Jesuits) in the United States and Canada who share

a common interest in promoting research, teaching,
dialogue, and value-awareness in the area of
philosophy. The primary means for achieving their
goal is an annual meeting at which seminars and
discussions of scholarly papers are held. The one-
day meeting occurs on the Friday after Easter and is
immediately followed by the convention of the
American Catholic Philosophical Association. The
major papers for the annual meeting, as well as the
Presidential address of the previous year, are
published prior to the meeting and are sent to the
Jesuit membership, most of whom teach or study at
colleges and universities in the United States and
Canada.

Founding Date: 1935
Membership: 121 Jesuits
Publications:
Annual Proceedings (mailed to members one
month before the annual convention)
Meetings:
An annual convention in the city where
American Catholic Philosophical Association
holds its annual convention

784. Jesuit Secondary Education Association (JSEA)

Roman Catholic
Rev. Vincent J. Duminuco, SJ, President
1717 Massachusetts Avenue, N.W.
Washington, D.C. 20036
(202) 667-3888

The Jesuit Secondary Education Association is a service organization which coordinates the activities of
its 47 Jesuit high schools in the United States with
affiliated schools in Canada, and every continent in
the world. JSEA serves its schools with projects,
workshops, and news bulletins that focus on their
special emphasis as Jesuit schools. JSEA operates
through a full-time president and four commissions.
The Commission on Religious Education has eight
members; the Commission on Research and Development has three permanent full-time members, and
seven part-time members; and the Commission of
Assistant to the Provincials for Education coordinates the activities of the individual provinces with
the national effort. The Commission on Planning and
Development is composed of the 47 presidents of the
schools.

Founding Date: 1970
Membership: 1,700 lay teachers; 900 Jesuits

Publications:
>   *News Bulletin,* monthly
>   *Directory,* annually
>   Occasional monographs

Meetings:
>   2 meetings of the Board of Directors annually
>   2 meetings of each JSEA Commission annually
>   Location varies with each meeting

Former Name: Jesuit Educational Association

785. Jesuit Volunteer Corps: Northwest (JVC)

Roman Catholic

Laurence Gooley, SJ, Director
Post Office Box 3928
Portland, Oregon 97208
(503) 228-2457

The Jesuit Volunteer Corps is a Christian service organization under the auspices of the Society of Jesus. Jesuit volunteers are primarily college graduates, and work with people, mainly poor and minorities, in an effort to secure the physical and spiritual needs basic to their peace and dignity. The Corps also seeks the spiritual development of its members, fostering among them and among those they serve, true Christian community. Members volunteer for at least one year, are placed in areas all over the Northwest and Alaska, and work mainly with Eskimos, Indians, Chicanos, blacks and disadvantaged whites. Volunteers work in schools, health clinics, hospices, hospitals, youth recreation programs, day care programs, group homes, emergency shelters, legal clinics and mental health clinics.

Founding Date: 1956

Membership:
>   JVC: Northwest — 130 members, 7 staff
>   JVC: East, South, Midwest and California/Southwest combined have 160 members

Publications:
>   *Focus,* bimonthly

Meetings:
>   General Orientation for new volunteers in Spokane, Washington in August
>   Each volunteer region (Alaska, Montana, Washington/Oregon) meets twice a year for retreats and workshops

786. Jewish Academy of Arts and Sciences, Inc., (JAAS)

Jewish

Dr. Leo Jung, Rabbi, President
c/o Secretary, Dr. Hirsch Lazaar Silverman
123 Gregory Avenue
West Orange, New Jersey 07052
(201) 731-1137

Founded as an honor society of Jews who have attained distinction in the arts, sciences, and professions, The Jewish Academy of Arts and Sciences has enjoyed the leadership of noted scholars, including Dr. Henry Keller, Professor Morris Raphael Cohen, Dr. Chaim Tchernowitz, and Rabbi Dr. Leo Jung. The objectives of the Academy have been to encourage and promote the advancement of the arts, sciences, and all ancillary departments of knowledge; to encourage and stimulate the interchange of views on all branches of scholarship and learning, with particular emphasis on those bearing on Jewish life and thought; to cultivate and maintain friendly intercourse among its members and fellows; to use research, publication, discussion, and appropriate activities, including lectures and convocations, to enhance sound and constructive advancement of knowledge; and to establish and maintain professional relations with other academies, societies, and institutions of learning throughout the world.

Founding Date: 1927

Staff: 12

Membership: 49 Fellows; 145 members

Publications:
>   *Annals,* periodically, of scholarly papers articles, essays

Meetings:
>   2 convocations annually, in New York City, in Fall and Spring of each year

787. Jewish Educators Assembly of America (JEA)

Jewish

Dr. Herbert L. Tepper, Administrator
155 5th Avenue
New York, New York 10010
(212) 533-7800 Ext. 132

The Jewish Educators Assembly of America is comprised of educational and supervisory personnel serving Jewish educational institutions. The purpose of the Jewish Educators Assembly is: to advance the development of Jewish education in the congregation on all levels and in consonance with the philosophy of the Conservative Movement; to cooperate with the United Synagogue Commission on Jewish Education as the policy making body of the educational enterprise; to join in cooperative effort with other Jewish educational institutions and organizations; to establish and maintain professional standards for Jewish educators; to serve as a forum for the exchange of ideas; and to promote the values of Jewish education as a basis for the creative continuity of the Jewish people. The Assembly sponsors conferences and seminars, and maintains a placement service and a speakers bureau. Its committees represent the following areas: Ethics; Placement; Research; Scholarship; and Welfare.

Founding Date: 1951

Membership: 302

Publications:
    Observer, quarterly
    Yearbooks

Meetings:
    Annual convention
    4 meetings each year

788. Jewish Foundation for Education of Women

Nondenominational

Florence Wallach, Executive Director
120 West 57th Street
New York, New York 10019
(212) 265-2565

One hundred years ago the Jewish Foundation for Education of Women pioneered in supporting career training for women as the key to economic productivity and personal fulfillment. Today the Foundation provides scholarship assistance on a non-sectarian basis to women with valid educational programs at a broad range of undergraduate, graduate, professional, and vocational schools. Scholarship selections are based on an individual's motivation and determination as much as on a high level of academic achievement; but in all cases, need for financial assistance must be demonstrated. The Jewish Foundation for Education of Women is one of the few major sources of scholarship assistance not linked

to an educational institution, nor subject to the restraints of government programs.

Founding Date: 1880

Staff: 3

Membership: 29

789. Jewish Historical Society of New York, Inc.

Jewish

Steven W. Siegel, Executive Secretary
8 West 70th Street
New York, New York 10023
(212) 873-0300

The Jewish Historical Society of New York promotes interest and encourages research in American Jewish history and in Jewish history of the metropolitan New York area. It provides a variety of educational programs, including lectures, panel discussions, walking tours, and publications, and offers reference service on questions on American and New York Jewish history and Jewish family history.

Membership: 450

Publications:
    Monthly newsletter for members

Meetings:
    Monthly meetings for members

790. Jewish Peace Fellowship (JPF)

Jewish

Naomi Goodman, President
Post Office Box 271
Nyack, New York 10960
(914) 358-4601

The Jewish Peace Fellowship unites those who believe that Jewish ideals and experience provide inspiration for a nonviolent philosophy of life. Stimulated by elements in traditional and contemporary Judaism which stress the sanctity of human life, the JPF promotes respect for people and confidence in their essential decency. It endeavors to incorporate these attitudes in the personal relations of its members and friends. In striving to eliminate the causes of war, the JPF is also concerned with the advancement of freedom and justice for all. The JPF has supported the right to conscientious objection since its founding and has provided draft counseling during three wars and peace time conscription. Affiliated with the Fellowship of Reconciliation and through it with persons of many religious and humanitarian convictions and disciplines, the JPF is grounded in faith of Judaism, whereby love and non-violence are worked out in study and action. Thus, peace is put into perspective — not as apart from justice or the need for elemental human decency — but as the means no less than the end of life. The historic commitment to peaceableness is seen as ingrained in the Jewish tradition, beginning with the Decalogue of Moses, flowering under Isaiah, Jeremiah, and the other prophets, and perfected by the Talmudic sages.

Founding Date: 1941

Membership:
   1,200 members
   1,800 supporters and friends

Publications:
   Shalom, quarterly
   Occasional booklets and pamphlets as need prescribes

Meetings:
   Monthly meetings of the Executive Committee and local chapters
   Occasional public meetings

791. The Jewish Publication Society of America

Jewish

Muriel M. Berman, President
117 South 17th Street
Philadelphia, Pennsylvania 19103
(215) 564-5925

The Jewish Publication Society is a non-profit educational institution devoted to the advancement of Jewish culture and scholarship. Since its founding, nearly eight million volumes, divided among some 800 titles, have been published and distributed throughout the world, mainly in the United States. The goal of the Society is to provide significant, worthwhile, and informative books of Jewish content in the English language, so that the Jewish religion, history, literature, and culture will be understood and read and known. As the prime publisher of Jewish books of quality in the English-speaking world, over the years JPS has issued a body of works for all tastes and requirements. Its many titles include biographies, histories, novels, art books, holiday anthologies, books for young readers, religious and philo-

sophical studies, translations of scholarly and popular classics — and, of course, the famous JPS Bible.

Founding Date: 1888

Staff: 20

Membership: 15,000

Publications:

792. Jewish Reconstructionist Foundation

Jewish

Rabbi Ludwig Nadelmann, President
432 Park Avenue, South
New York, New York 10016
(212) 889-9080

The Jewish Reconstructionist Movement represents an attempt to assure physical and spiritual Jewish survival by suggesting how Jewish life can be lived to the maximum within the setting of a modern democratic state. Reconstructionism defines Judaism as an evolving religious civilization. It is committed to the interpretation of Jewish religion in the key of religious naturalism, viewing religion as the outgrowth of the experiences of the Jewish people in their search for the divine in life. The Reconstructionist Foundation, with headquarters in New York City, is the coordinating and policy planning body for Reconstructionist Judaism which encompasses: the Federation of Reconstructionist Congregations and Havurot (Fellowships); the Reconstructionist Rabbinical College, located in Philadelphia, Pennsylvania; the *Reconstructionist* Magazine, published monthly in New York City; the reconstructionist Press, with more than 50 titles in the field of Litrugy, Education, Jewish thought and Theology; and a Women's Organization.

Founding Date: 1940

Membership: 24,000 in 40 congregations

Publications:
   Reconstructionist, monthly
   Newsletter, three times annually

Radio/TV Programs:
   Occasional

Meetings:
   Annual convention
   Regional conferences
   Congregational institutes
   Academic meetings
   Study missions to Israel

793. Jewish Science Society of Jewish Science (SJS)

Jewish

Harry M. Hauptman, Executive Director
825 Round Swamp Road
Old Bethpage, New York 11804

Mailing Address
Post Office Box 114
Old Bethpage, New York 11804
(516) 249-6262

It is the aim of Jewish Science Society of Jewish Science to apply the teachings of the Jewish faith to daily experience, so as to eliminate worry and fear and tendencies to illness among its adherents, and to establish a state of perfect health, happiness, and optimism through unflinching faith in the Divine Help.

Founding Date: 1922

Publications:
The Jewish Science Interpreter, 8 times a year

794. Jewish Student Press Service (JSPS)

Jewish

Nina Wacholder, Administrative Director
Ora Kiel, Editor
15 East 26th Street, Suite 1350
New York, New York 10010
(212) 679-1411

The Jewish Student Press Service (JSPS) is the advisory and distribution center for Jewish student newspapers. JSPS works to develop and support high quality Jewish student publications through conferences, internship programs, and regional workshops. JSPS publishes *Jewish Press Features,* a monthly packet of in-depth articles on all aspects of Jewish life in Israel and the Diaspora. The packet includes features directly from JSPS' Israel Bureau as well as from correspondents around the world. Subscribers, including Jewish student publications, Anglo-Jewish community papers, libraries, Hillels, federations, and individuals, receive reprint rights to JSPS' award-winning articles.

Founding Date: 1970

Membership: 55 student papers

Publications:
Jewish Press Features, monthly from September through May, along with special issues

JSPS is also the distribution center for Jewish student publications — subscribers may receive copies of virtually every Jewish student publication in North America

Meetings:
National Editors Conference annually
Israel Editors Conference biannually
Regional journalism workshops and conferences occasionally

795. Jewish Teachers Association (JTA)

Jewish

Dr. Michael Leinwand, President
45 East 33rd Street
New York, New York 10016
(212) 684-0556

The purpose of the Jewish Teachers Association is to promote the religious, social, and moral welfare of children and teachers in the public and private schools of America.

Founding Date: 1924

Membership:
20,000 general members throughout the United States

Publications:
Morim, 3 times a year

Meetings:
One annual convention
Annual dinner-dance

796. The Jewish Theological Seminary of America

Jewish, Conservative

Dr. Gerson D. Cohen, Chancellor
3080 Broadway
New York, New York 10027
(212) 678-8000

Founded to train rabbis for American congregations, the Jewish Theological Seminary of America today embraces two undergraduate schools, Seminary College of Jewish Studies and Seminary College of Jewish Music; two professional schools, Rabbinical School and Cantors Institute; and a Graduate School. Students in the professional schools take all of their courses at the Seminary; most already hold bachelor's degrees. Students in the colleges and graduate school pursue Judaica studies at the Seminary and take supplementary liberal arts courses at other accredited colleges. As the academic center of the Conservative movement in American Judaism, the Seminary conducts educational outreach programs for various youth groups and other affiliates. The Seminary operates The Jewish Museum in New York, and has campuses in Los Angeles (University of Judaism) and Jerusalem (American Student Center at Neve Schechter).

Founding Date: 1886

Staff: 120

Publications:

> Seminary *Bulletin,* 7 times a year
> Seminary *Progress,* quarterly
> Midreshet Series (books), 1 or 2 per year

Radio/TV Programs:

> *Eternal Light Radio,* weekly on NBC network
> *Directions,* television, 12 per year on ABC-TV network
> *Eternal Light,* television, 4 per year, on NBC-TV network

797. Jews for Jesus

Nondenominational

Moishe Rosen
60 Haight Street
San Francisco, California 94102
(415) 864-2600

Jews for Jesus is a group of Jewish people who have come to believe that Jesus is the Messiah of Israel. They believe that both the Jewish Bible and the New Testament are true, and are committed to communicating the message of Jesus in a way that Jewish people can understand. Being Christians does not prevent individuals from being Jews. Members of Jews for Jesus are intent on maintaining their Jewish identity and continuing as part of the Jewish community. They are eager to preserve their customs and traditions. Being Jewish is part of the spiritual experience as well. It enhances understanding of Jesus, the Bible, and what God expects of man. Jews for Jesus has no membership, but estimates of how many Jews believe in Jesus range from 30,000 to

100,000. Branches and volunteer outposts are located in major cities with large Jewish populations. These branches have weekly and monthly gatherings, as well as yearly regional conferences of Jewish believers in Jesus. The organization produces and distributes millions of "broadside" Gospel tracts each year. A broadside uses contemporary language, humorous illustrations such as, "Christmas is a Jewish Holiday" and "If being born hasn't given you much satisfaction, try being born again!" Though lighthearted, each pamphlet contains a serious statement about Christ. They also produce literature to answer questions in more detail, as well as publishing *Issues: A Messianic Jewish Perspective,* a periodical that is sent free to Jewish people who want to learn more of Jesus. Jews for Jesus also sponsors a scholarship program to assist qualified Jewish Christians in their Bible education. One of the most unique aspects of the Jews for Jesus ministry is Mobile Evangelism. The group has spearheaded the development of Jewish Gospel Music, communicating the message of Christ with a very Jewish flavor. Their outreach utilizes the mass media as well, in the form of full-page evangelistic advertisements in newspapers and spots on commercial radio stations to explain how a Jew can believe in Christ. Jewish evangelism seminars are geared to teach Christians about Jewish sensitivities, how to initiate a witness, and what the Scriptures have to say about Jewish evangelism. Jews for Jesus is not affiliated with any one denomination or association, but is supported by individual Christians who see a need for a specialized ministry such as this. The organization does not believe it is their work to persuade. They feel their job is to present what they have found to be true. They believe that God Himself will show those people who really want to know that Jesus is indeed the Messiah of Israel.

Founding Date: 1973

Staff: 100

Publications:

> *Jews for Jesus,* monthly
> *Issues: A Messianic Jewish Perspective,* bimonthly
> Eight Albums, By the Liberated Wailing Wall, Israelight, and Eric Van Camp

Meetings:

> The Jews for Jesus Ingatherings (East Coast-Fall; West Coast-Spring; Midwest-fall)

Former Name: Hineni Ministries

798. Johannes Greber Memorial Foundation

Nondenominational

Fred H. Haffner, President
139 Hillside Avenue
Teaneck, New Jersey 07666
(201) 836-2191

The Johannes Greber Memorial Foundation was established to publish and distribute the books authored by Pastor Johannes Greber: *Communication with the Spirit World of God* and *The New Testament.*

Founding Date: 1944

799. The John Carroll Society

Roman Catholic

Ralph H. Brown, President
5617 32nd Street, N.W.
Washington, D.C. 20015
(202) 363-2751

The John Carroll Society was founded under the patronage of the Blessed Virgin Mary as a society of Catholic professional and business men. Women were admitted to membership in 1974. Its three major objectives are: (1) giving honor to God and His Blessed Mother; (2) the personal sanctification and instruction of its members; (3) dedication to the goals of the lay apostolate as enunciated by the Holy Father and the Ordinary of the Archdiocese of Washington. The Society holds four meetings a year, combining corporate Mass and Communion with a social event. At each of these meetings, a speaker of prominence is invited to address the membership on a topic of current interest. The Society annually sponsors the Red Mass (Votive Mass of the Holy Spirit) at the opening of the Supreme Court's Fall term, to pray for guidance of those in the legal profession. It contributes funds to the TV Mass for Shut-Ins and presents a burse to the Archbishop of Washington for a needy charity in the Archdiocese. Despite these charitable gifts, the Society is not involved in fundraising. Its purposes are spiritual and intellectual, focused on enabling its members to become better Catholics and better Americans for the benefit of God and country, loyal to the name and the ideals of the great patriot and churchman for whom it was named.

Founding Date: 1951
Staff: 1
Membership: Approximately 410
Publications:
Newsletter, bimonthly
Meetings:
4 meetings a year

800. John Knox Press

Presbyterian

Richard A. Ray, Managing Director and Editor
341 Ponce deLeon Avenue, N.E.
Atlanta, Georgia 30365
(404) 873-1531

The specific purpose of John Knox Press, as given by the General Assembly of the Presbyterian Church in the United States, is "to stimulate and encourage Biblical scholarship and Christian thought and living through the publication of books." John Knox Press publishes educational and mission-study books, textbooks, and books for popular lay reading, as well as church leadership resources. Subjects include Bible, theology, ethics, and history. Other books, made necessary by the work of the denomination are produced and distributed directly to the PCUS churches. Religious books for wholesale distribution to bookstores around the world are produced as well.
Staff:
14. It uses other staff of the denomination for accounting, data processing, and other services

801. John Milton Society for the Blind (JMSB)

Interdenominational

Rev. Chenoweth J. Watson, General Secretary
29 West 34th Street
New York, New York 10001
(212) 736-4162

The John Milton Society for the Blind exists to serve the spiritual needs of blind and visually handicapped people. This is done through the publishing of Christian books and magazines in Braille, Talking Book and Large Type form; by financial support of some 25 Church-related schools and agencies for the blind

257

overseas; by giving limited monthly financial assistance to selected overseas students who are in the United States preparing to teach in schools for the blind in their homeland.

Founding Date: 1928

Publications:

The Society produces and distributes a number of books and magazines in Braille, on records and in large type form, to thousands of readers who are unable to read ordinary print

Meetings:

3 meetings a year

Former Name: John Milton Society

802. John XXIII Center

Roman Catholic

Father Keith Hosey
407 West McDonald Street
Hartford City, Indiana 47348
(317) 348-4008

John XXIII Center is a Diocesan Retreat House that holds weekend retreats for a number of groups: Parish Renewal, Marriage Encounter, Singles, Prayer Retreats, College Age Retreats, and Growth Workshops. The Center programs events for groups that wish to plan for a special group encounter. Each event works toward building some community, celebrating a prayer liturgy, and creating a space for persons to be affirmed and to grow. The spirit of John XXIII Center is that of hospitality. Each person is encouraged to be at home, to receive affirmation and to give it to others, and to be part of the weekend hospitality by helping with domestic chores.

Meetings:

Approximately 40 retreats per year

803. Joint Strategy and Action Committee (JSAC)

Nondenominational

The Rev. John DeBoer, Executive Director
475 Riverside Drive, Room 1700-A
New York, New York 10027
(212) 870-3105

Joint Strategy and Action Committee is a consortium of "home mission boards" of several denominations which seek to collaborate in various areas of mission. It operates through task forces, including Asian

American Ministries, Church Development, Criminal Justice, Hispanic American Ministries, Housing, Indian Ministries, Metro Mission, New Communities, Non-Metro Mission and Voluntary Services, which attempt to develop common goals and strategies.

Founding Date: 1965

Publications:

Grapevine, 10 times a year
Various pamphlets and manuals

Meetings:

About 10 meetings per year

804. Jubilee, Inc.*

Nondenominational

John Alexander, President
Post Office Box 12236
Philadelphia, Pennsylvania 19144
(215) 849-2178

Jubilee, Inc., is dedicated to the cause of promoting social justice and Christian discipleship. Although emphasis is placed on the sin of oppression of blacks in the United States, its other areas of concern are: economic exploitation in the third world; militarism; sexism; and human rights.

Publications:

The Other Side

Former Name: The Other Side, Inc.

805. Judah L. Magnes Memorial Museum, Jewish Museum of the West

Jewish

Seymour Fromer, Director
Marvin Weinreb, MD, President
2911 Russell Street
Berkeley, California 94705
(415) 849-2710

The Judah L. Magnes Memorial Museum collects and preserves artistic, historical, and literary materials illustrating Jewish life and cultural contributions throughout history. The Museum is also a repository for historical documents and landmarks of Western Jewry. The Museum takes its name and inspiration from Judah L. Magnes, founder of the Hebrew University in Jerusalem, the American Civil Liberties Union, the American Jewish Committee and Hadassah. The Magnes Museum displays material of regional, national, and international significance. It conducts and encourages extensive historical research and operates the Western Jewish History Center and Jesse Coleman Library, which seek to document and study the influence of the Jewish population on the development, character, and culture of the Far West. Essential to research and education are the Museum's Goldstein Library of Judaica, which contains 6,000 books and periodicals in English, Yiddish, and Hebrew, and the Museum's publishing program, which has already produced volumes on Jewish life in California, San Francisco, and Europe. The Museum also serves the public by conducting tours of its exhibitions, by displaying its materials in other institutions, and by loaning its displays to distant areas.

Founding Date: 1962

Staff: 6 museum staff members

Membership:
1,300 museum members; 300 Women's Guild

Publications:
Catalogues
Books of general Judaic themes (approximately 4 publications each year)

Radio/TV Programs:
Produced several video tapes of oral history and biographies of Jews in the West

Meetings:
Annual meeting of the Women's Guild
6-8 opening receptions in honor of the artists of the Museum's exhibitions each year

806. The Judaica Press, Inc.

Jewish

Jack Goldman, President
521 Fifth Avenue
New York, New York 10017
(212) 260-0520

The Judaica Press publishes classical Hebrew books with English translation and commentaries. There are presently about 30 titles in print.

807. Judson Press

American Baptist Churches USA

Frank T. Hoadley, Director
Valley Forge, Pennsylvania 19481
(215) 768-2000

Judson Press publishes religious books, generally nondenominational in flavor, which are distributed by religious and general bookstores throughout the country. Its particular emphasis is on books for Christian education and Bible study. Judson Press also publishes some children's books. Presently it has 360 titles in print.

808. Jungle Aviation and Radio Service (JAARS)

Interdenominational

Martin Huyett, Executive Director
JAARS Road off Davis Road
Waxhaw, North Carolina 28173

Mailing Address
Post Office Box 248
Waxhaw, North Carolina 28173
704) 843-2185

Wycliffe's Jungle Aviation and Radio Service (JAARS) was organized to help Bible translators get in and out of the tribal villages where they were working. Cameron Townsend, "Uncle Cam," the founder of Wycliffe Bible Translators, was concerned about the danger and difficulty the translator/linguists were facing as they travelled through jungle swamps, crossed perilous rivers, and traversed steep mountain trails to reach isolated groups. It was especially difficult if they were in their village and had need to get back for emergency medical attention, so JAARS came into being. Not only does JAARS transport translators, it also provides radio communications between tribal locations and the linguistic study center in that country. JAARS airlifts supplies and mail, provides construction and computer services, and stands ready to give immediate assistance in times of emergency. JAARS also serves the national governments, when it's requested, thereby building relationships with countries and showing them the love of Christ.

Founding Date: 1947

Staff: 90

Membership: 902

Publications:
Beyond, monthly

Meetings:
Aviation Conference, JAARS Center, Waxhaw, one annually
Computer Conference, JAARS Center, Waxhaw, one biannually

Also Known As:
Wycliffe's Jungle Aviation and Radio Service

809. JW Ministry (Jehovah's Witnesses)

Nondenominational
Floyd Erwin
Post Office Box 4248
Gadsden, Alabama 35904
(205) 547-6324

The purpose of JW Ministry is to provide resource information on available materials dealing with the Jehovah's Witnesses' religious beliefs.

Founding Date: 1975
Staff: 1
Membership: 1

810. JWB (Jewish Welfare Board)

Jewish
Arthur Rotman, Executive Vice President
15 East 26th Street
New York, New York 10010
(212) 532-4949

The JWB is the key service agency for Jewish Community Centers and Jewish military personnel. It renders community planning assistance, building advice, personnel recruitment and training, administrative and management consultation, programming assistance, and central purchasing service. It also provides religious, cultural, recreational and social services to Jewish families, hospitalized veterans, and others.

Founding Date: 1917
Staff: 49
Membership: 1,000,000
Publications:
> Program and administrative manuals, approximately 400 titles
> *The JWB Circle*
> *Zarkor*
> *Program Directory of Performing Artists*

Meetings:
> National conventions every two years
> Board of Directors meeting 3 times a year
> JWB also sponsors a number of conferences, institutes, seminars, etc.

Former Name: (1977) National Jewish Welfare Board
Absorbed:
> (1921) Council of Young Men's Hebrew and Kindred Association

811. JWB, Commission on Jewish Chaplaincy

Jewish
Rabbi Gilbert Kollin, Director
15 East 26th Street
New York, New York 10010
(212) 532-4949

The JWB Commission on Jewish Chaplaincy recruits, endorses, and provides ecclesiastical oversight for Jewish chaplains in the armed forces, Veterans Administration, and other Federal hospitals. It represents Jewish concerns in the several endorsing agents' conferences concerned with the above chaplaincies. It acts as an advocate for the spiritual needs of Jewish military personnel and dependents, and hospitalized veterans in relation to both government agencies and the Jewish community. It recruits part-time civilian chaplains and approves and runs training workshops for Jewish military lay leaders.

Membership:
> The Commission consists of 21 members and is composed of three 7-member delegations: Central Conference of American Rabbis, Rabbinical Assembly of America, Rabbinical Council of America

Publications:
> *The Jewish Chaplain*
> *Contact*

Meetings:
> Annual Jewish Chaplains Training Conference
> Semi-annual plenary meeting of the Commission

812. JWB, Jewish Book Council

Jewish
Ruth Frank, Director
15 East 26th Street
New York, New York 10010
(212) 532-4949

The aim of the JWB Jewish Book Council is to stimulate interest in Jewish books through the dissemination of booklists: the promotion of Jewish Book Month; and the presentation of the National Jewish Book Awards annually in fiction, Jewish history, Holocaust, Israel, juvenile literature, poetry, Yiddish literature, and biennially in translation of a Jewish classic. It gives accreditation to libraries meeting its standards and serves as an informal clearing house and liaison with publishers in the Jewish field.

Founding Date: 1942

Staff: 2

Publications:

> *Jewish Book Annual,* contains articles in English, Hebrew and Yiddish on Jewish literary output, bibliographies and feature stories on Jewish literary figures
>
> *Jewish Books in Review,* bibliographies, program suggestions and library aids

813. JWB, Jewish Music Council

Jewish

Irene Heskes, Director
15 East 26th Street
New York, New York 10010
(212) 532-4949

The Jewish Music Council of JWB was founded to enrich American Jewish culture by highlighting its musical heritage. The Council annually sponsors and promotes the Jewish Music Festival. Over the years, by preparing and utilizing various types of resources and publications, and by stressing particular festival themes, the Council has made the annual music celebration into a significant Jewish calendar event. The objectives of the Jewish Music Council are: to coordinate Jewish musical activities nationally, and to help plan programs for the annual Jewish Music Festival and for year-round musical activities; to promote fine performances of Jewish music of high quality in concerts, radio, TV, and recordings; to encourage the composition of new musical works, additional publications, and academic research in the field of Jewish music; to offer information on Jewish music to individuals and groups in the United States and abroad; to serve the music cultural needs of the Jewish Community Centers and the national Jewish organizations, and to broaden the scope of general community participation in Jewish musical activities, program events, and special projects.

Founding Date: 1944

Staff: 1

Membership: 64 affiliated organizations

Publications:

> Music programs and program aids, resource materials, bibliographies of Jewish music, etc.

814. Kappa Gamma Pi

Roman Catholic
Marie Gedris Pokora, National President
2415 Hillcrest Drive
Stow, Ohio 44224
(216) 688-1407

Kappa Gamma Pi is a national Catholic college women's honor society for graduates, whose motto is "Faith and Service." Its purpose is to strive for a high standard of personal Christian excellence and scholarship among its members; to encourage individual and group initiative and participation in local and national church and secular affairs; and to awaken a spirit of Christian leadership among the undergraduates of Kappa affiliated colleges.

Founding Date: 1926
Membership: 22,000 lay; 900 clerical
Publications:
    Kappa Gamma Pi News, 5 times a year
Meetings:
    Biennial convention

815. Knights of Columbus

Roman Catholic
Virgil C. Dechant, Supreme Knight
Post Office Drawer 1670
New Haven, Connecticut 06507
(203) 772-2130

The Knights of Columbus was founded by Father Michael J. McGivney with the purpose of furthering the religious formation of individual members, assisting the work of the Church, improving community life, and promoting the welfare of the country. One of the Knights' religious activities is a Catholic information program which offers free booklets to anyone seeking information on the Catholic Church. Since 1948, the Knights have distributed literature to more than six million inquirers and conducted special courses in Catholic beliefs for 600,000 persons. The Catholic advertising project funds religious television and radio programs and conferences to spread religious idealism. Recently, the Knights have funded TV programs from the Vatican to bring the Pope to audiences throughout the world via satellite. The junior organization of the Knights of Columbus is Columbian Squires. The Squires are Catholic boys between the ages of 12 and 18 who are members of a unit called a circle. A boy may join the organization by invitation from a Squire or a Knight.

Founding Date: 1882
Membership: 1,300,000 lay; 50,000 clerical
Publications:
    Columbia Magazine, monthly
    Squires
    Campus Knight

816. Knights of Peter Claver*

Roman Catholic
Ernest Granger, Sr., Supreme Knight
1825 Orleans Avenue
New Orleans, Louisiana 70116
(504) 821-4225

The Knights of Peter Claver is a Catholic lay organization which provides social and intellectual fellowship for its members, as well as proper guidance and participation in the everchanging structure of social and economic life. The objectives of the Knights are to participate collectively in various parish activities; to promote civic improvements; to encourage lay apostolic and Catholic action; to provide financial assistance to sick members and benefits at very low cost; to make contributions to worthwhile causes; to award scholarships; to foster recreational assemblies and facilities; and to develop youth. The Knights also have a Ladies Auxiliary and sponsor the Junior Knights and Junior Daughters of Peter Claver, which strive to build good character and leadership qualities.

Membership: 15,000

Publications:

The Claverite, trimonthly

Meetings:

1 annually

817. Knights of St. John

Roman Catholic

John T. Schneider, Supreme President
6517 Charles Avenue
Parma, Ohio 44129
(216) 845-0570

Members of the Knights of St. John serve as an escort to the hierarchy of the Catholic Church. The organization is semi-military in nature, and is engaged in the promotion of charitable causes. It sponsors and participates in sports activities, and provides social functions for family participation. In addition to its cadet group, it also has a women's organization. The Knights maintain a death benefit fund for the membership.

Founding Date: 1878

Staff: 3

Membership: 7,500 lay; 300 clerical

Publications:

Knights of St. John Journal, quarterly

818. Koinonia Foundation

Nondenominational

Dorothy T. Samuel, Executive Director
1400 Greenspring Valley Road
Stevenson, Maryland 21153
(301) 486-6262

Koinonia is a residential facility dedicated to building health through the fullest development of spirit. Its basic objectives are: to cultivate a spot where the healing powers of the Spirit emanate from the grounds, the residents, the disciplines, the conversation, and the teachings, and to offer prayer, meditation, study, physical development, spiritualized work, and natural food as ways to a total realization of one's own responsibility, under God, for the life and wellness one demonstrates; to draw to that spot persons in the healing and helping professions, as well as those who wish to become individual "each-one-teach-one" centers of radiating spiritual energy and power, and to provide for them a period of training and experience in spiritual, mental, and spiritually-infused physical disciplines and practices; to send such people back into the world imbued with a sense of harmony with God, power in the Spirit, vigor of body, and the practices by which to help and heal those around them; to arm them with the spiritual resources to handle stress and deflect crippling emotions and illnesses in themselves and in others; to contribute, through Koinonia graduates, to renewing of the world in a sense of human family within the circle of God's love; and to release humanity from the sense of aloneness and powerlessness which has alienated our lives and societies from God and a sense of God's purpose.

Founding Date: 1951

Staff: 20 resident staff

Membership:

No membership as such; mailing list of about 7,000

Publications:

Newsletter, quarterly
Class and workshop brochure 4 times a year
Residential Term booklet annually
Epistle (a sustaining letter to former Koinonians) 6 times a year
Special materials as necessary to promote the program

Meetings:

3-month residential programs
1 and 2-week residential programs
Weekend workshops, and evening classes, all held on premises

819. Korea International Mission, Inc. (KIM)*

David J. Cho, President
3423 East Chapman
Orange, California 92669

Mailing Address
Post Office Box 2070
Orange, California 92669
(714) 997-3920

Korean International Mission sponsors Korean missionaries working in other countries of Asia. As an agent of the Asia Missions Association, it administers the East West Center for Mission Research and Training in Seoul, Korea.
Membership: 15

820. Koren Relief, Inc.

Roman Catholic
Rev. Al Schwartz, President
4815 Edmonston Road
Hyattsville, Maryland 20781
(301) 779-4141

Korean Relief, Inc., is a direct, people-to-people, non-sectarian, non-profit foundation dedicated to the relief of poverty in Korea. It was founded by Reverend Aloysius Schwartz, native of Washington, D.C., who has been engaged in relief work in Korea since 1957. Korean Relief is registered with the Social Welfare Department of the Republic of Korea and is fully accredited as a voluntary agency, and member of Korea Association of Voluntary Agencies (KAVA). The agency supports more than 30 hospitals, orphanages, and other charity institutions throughout Korea. It has many famous American sponsors, pays no commissions, and uses no paid agents or solicitors.
Founding Date: 1961
Staff:
> 6 staff members in the United States
> 150 staff members in Korea

821. Kregel Publications

Evangelical
Robert L. Kregel, President
525 Eastern Avenue, S.E.
Grand Rapids, Michigan 49501

Mailing Address
Post Office Box 2607
Grand Rapids, Michigan 49501
(616) 459-9444

Kregel Publications publishes and distributes Christian evangelical literature with subject matter including sermon outlines, missions, evangelism, Christian living, and commentaries. It presently carries 250 titles, mainly reprints of the classic religious and theological works that have been out of print for many years and for which there is a present demand.

822. Krishna-Gordon Press

Nondenominational
R. Gordon
Post Office Box 459
Bowling Green Station
New York, New York 10004

Krishna-Gordon Press publishes scholarly books on religious mysticism; Catholic, Protestant, Jewish and Islamic mysticism and doctoral dissertations.

823. Kuyper Institute (Christianity on Campus, Inc.)

Interdenominational
Jon Kennedy, Director/Senior Fellow
Room 16A, Old Union Clubhouse
Stanford, California 94305

Mailing Address
Post Office Box 5252
Stanford, California 94305
(415) 497-0574

Kuyper Institute is a Christian "think tank" developing and disseminating a biblical perspective on media, academics, society, and culture. The Institute takes up to six students per year in its graduate program in Media/Communication. It offers both church-oriented and secular seminars on writing, publishing, and public relations.
Founding Date: 1969
Staff: 3
Publications:
> *New Reformation,* monthly worldview review
> *Christian Studies,* long and short monographs, academics from a Christian perspective
> Books, and booklets

824. Lama Foundation

Eclectic

Jamil Kilbride, Co-ordinator
Post Office Box 444
San Cristobal, New Mexico 87564

The purpose of Lama, according to its bylaws, is to: "serve as an instrument for the awakening of consciousness, individual and collective, thereby aiding its membership and all sentient beings in achieving a more complete awareness of their position in the universal structure through integration of the threefold nature of man into one harmonious being operating to the fullest possible potential in all spheres of existence." The Lama Foundation operates a center for the pursuit of studies and disciplines leading to the fulfillment of these purposes and makes known by various and diverse means the way leading to this fulfillment.

Staff: 30

Meetings:
5 to 10 per year

825. Language Institute for Evangelism (LIFE)

Interdenominational

Kenneth P. Wendling, President
Jerry Hardy, Executive Vice President
32 North Curtis
Alhambra, California 91802

Mailing Address
Post Office Box 200
Alhambra, California 91802
(213) 289-5031

Language Institute for Evangelism is an interdenominational evangelical mission. LIFE is a member of the Interdenominational Foreign Mission Association and the Evangelical Counsel for Financial Accountability. LIFE uses the vehicle of teaching conversational English as a means of relating to the non-Christian Japanese community. Presently LIFE is involved in student ministries, church planting, and a summer ministry utilizing North American summer workers called "Scrum Dendo."

Founding Date: 1967

Membership:
23 missionaries serving in Japan
10 United States support missionaries
102 Scrum Dendo summer workers
4 student centers

Publications:
Lifelines, quarterly

Meetings:
Institute on Asian Evangelism held in June

826. LAOS, Inc.

Nondenominational

Morris H. Bratton, Executive Director
4920 Piney Branch Road, N.W.
Washington, D.C. 20011
(202) 723-8273

LAOS, Inc., is an ecumenical, nonprofit, Christian center and network of Christian people, committed to serving as a catalyst among church people for: the development of a new consciousness about the activity of God in personal and historical events which is bringing about the liberation and enrichment of the whole human family and the earth; the development of a new commitment among church people to participate in the liberating and enriching events which are happening; and the seeking of justice for all people. LAOS performs its catalyst role through theological education and the servant/-enablement lifestyle. Volunteers are placed in institutions, agencies, and programs concerned with the same liberating events and movements as LAOS, particularly as they relate to hunger, poverty, racism, sexism, peace, nuclear issues, and education. Evening workshops, weekend and week-long seminars are conducted to develop the new consciousness and commitment among church people to God's liberating and enriching activity and the ways they can participate in it. Actual development of gardening, solar energy, and other projects are undetaken to aid people in seeing alternative ways of living which are more sensitive to problems of hunger, etc. In addition, staff and network people are involved in local programs which are demonstrating alternative ways of liberating and enriching human life, and seeking justice for the whole human family.

Founding Date: 1962

Publications:

Conversations, Concerns, and Challenges, quarterly

Meetings:

20-30 per year at the LAOS Center and in churches

Former Names:

(1968) Laymen's Overseas Service
Laos Team, Inc.

827. Latin America Mission

Clayton L. Berg, Jr., President
1826 Ponce de Leon Boulevard
Coral Gables, Florida 33134

Mailing Address
Post Office Box 341368
Coral Gables, Florida 33114
(305) 444-6228

Latin America Mission is an interdenominational, evangelical mission. Its missionaries serve with Latin American organizations whose leaders and boards of directors are Latins and are engaged in evangelization, discipleship, education, and helping the needy. Missionaries serve under contract for specified periods, usually three years at a time, after which contracts are reviewed and may be renewed for another term of service.

Founding Date: 1921

Membership: 178

Publications:

Latin America Evangelist, bimonthly
Perspectives, newsletter for pastors, 3 times per year

Meetings:

Latin American Perspectives Seminars, overseas, twice yearly

828. Latin Liturgy Association (LLA)

Roman Catholic
James Hitchcock, Chairman
Office of the Secretary
5 Forestwood Court
Columbus, Georgia 31907

The Latin Liturgy Association exists to promote the use of the Latin language primarily in the liturgy and worship of the Roman Catholic Church, secondarily in schools and seminaries. The organization accepts the liturgical changes mandated by the Second Vatican Council and seeks to encourage and make known the validity of at least occasional Latin worship in as many parishes as possible. In addition, through its newsletter, the Association seeks to make its members aware of the availability of the Latin Mass, of official Church pronouncements bearing on the subject, of books and articles of interest to members.

Membership: 110

Publications:

Newsletter, quarterly

829. The Lay Mission-Helpers Association

Roman Catholic
Reverend Monsignor Lawrence O'Leary, Director
1531 West 9th Street
Los Angeles, California 90015
(213) 388-8101

The Lay Mission-Helpers Association supplies professional skills in Catholic missions throughout the world. It recruits and trains lay men and women, both married and single, to utilize their skills in mission areas of the church in Africa, Thailand, New Guinea, and Micronesia. People must be proficient in their profession since the purpose of the work is to ultimately prepare the indigenous people to take over the work. There is a broad range of professions and skills needed from teacher to mechanic, from nurse to secretary. The Association does not take on total projects but works in collaboration with similar people from other countries under the direction of the local Bishop.

Founding Date: 1955

Membership: 50 members in the field

830. The Laymen's National Bible Committee, Inc.

Nondenominational

John F. Fisler, Executive Director
815 Second Avenue, Suite 512
New York, New York 10017
(212) 687-0555

The Laymen's National Bible Committee promotes the reading and study of the Bible; sponsors National Bible Week to coincide with Thanksgiving each year; places ads in magazines and newspapers designed to motivate interest in the Bible; produces radio and TV material for the same purpose; promotes teaching of the Bible as a valid part of public education as defined by the Supreme Court; and gives recognition and awards to individuals and groups who further the goals of the interfaith lay committee.

Founding Date: 1940

Staff: 3

Membership: 5,000

Publications:
  Newsletter, 3 times a year

Radio/TV Programs:
  Radio and TV spots, one per year

Meetings:
  4 meetings of the Board of Directors per year
  5 Executive Committee meetings per year

Former Name: (1969) Laymen's National Committee

831. Leadership Conference of Women Religious (LCWR)

Roman Catholic

M. Theresa Kane, RSM, President
1302 18th Street, N.W., Suite 701
Washington, D.C. 20036
(202) 293-1483

The purpose of the Leadership Conference of Women Religious is to assist its members personally, collec-

tively, and corporately in developing creative and responsive leadership and in undertaking those forms of service consonant with the evolving Gospel mission of women religious in the world through the Church. The Conference possesses policy-making and executive authority sufficient for its own organization and the administration of its own affairs. In accord with its statement of purpose, the role of the Conference is to undertake through its membership and in collaboration with other sisters those services which develop the life and mission of women religious in responding to the Gospel message in the contemporary world by developing and undertaking programs among and for the benefit of its members on local, regional, and national levels, and ensuring good communications among its members; sponsoring, conducting, and coordinating study and research on trends and issues of concern to its members and other women religious; and developing and undertaking programs on behalf of its members in relation to and in collaboration with others in the Church and in society, and striving for good communication with them.

Founding Date: 1952

Staff: 7

Membership: 630

Publications:
  Newsletter, 3 times a year
  Update, monthly

Meetings:
  Annual Assembly for membership

832. League of St. Dymphna, (LOSD)

Roman Catholic

Rev. M.M. Herttna, Director
National Shrine of St. Dymphna
3000 Erie Street, S.W.
Massillon, Ohio 44646

Mailing Address
Post Office Box 4
Massillon, Ohio 44646
(216) 833-8478

The League of St. Dymphna is comprised of members from the United States, Canada, and overseas. Membership in the League costs $2.00 a year per person. Benefits include remembrance in daily Mass and novenas and votive candles lighted at the Outdoor Shrine. The Shrine is the Catholic Chapel located on the grounds of the Massillon State Hospital. The Shrine was built in 1937 and dedicated

May 15, 1938, on St. Dymphna's feast day. St. Dymphna is the patron saint of those afflicted with mental and nervous disorders. The Shrine is visited daily by many patients in the hospital and by visitors from all over the United States. Many groups also make pilgrimages to the Shrine.

Founding Date: 1937

833. Lend A Hand Society

Unitarian Universalist
Donald W. Moreland, President
34½ Beacon Street
Boston, Massachusetts 02108
(617) 523-2554

The Lend A Hand Society was founded by Edward Everett Hale. The Lend A Hand Society provides grants for the aged, and for needy children, and emergency relief.

Founding Date: 1870

834. Lester Sumrall Evangelistic Association

Evangelical
Post Office Box 12
South Bend, Indiana 46624
(219) 291-3292

The Lester Sumrall Evangelistic Association is involved in the following ministries: religious television and radio; childcare in 14 countries supporting nearly 1,000 children; support of missionaries and nationals in various countries; and overseas crusades, some as large as 50,000 people.

Founding Date: 1957
Membership: 55,000 people on the mailing list
Publications:
Monthly newsletters, bimonthly magazine
Radio/TV Programs:
One-hour daily program *Today with Lester Sumrall*
One-half hour program of special lectures on *How to Cope With Life's Problems*
A daily half-hour musical program *Sharing*
Meetings:
Leads a group to the Holy Land each year and conducts conferences in the evenings
Conferences in the Orient each year, usually in Korea, Hong Kong, and the Philippines

835. Letters of Interest*

Plymouth Brethren
Neil M. Glass
218 Willow Street
Wheaton, Illinois 60187
(312) 653-6550

Letters of Interest of the Brethren Church publishes a news and ministry magazine for Plymouth Brethren Churches; makes gifts supporting 500 home workers; conducts conferences; and maintains a military chaplain's commission.

Publications:
Interest
Meetings:
3 or 4 conferences per year

836. The Lewis and Harriet Lederer Foundation, Inc.

Nondenominational
Mrs. Henry Einspruch, Executive Secretary
6204 Park Heights Avenue
Baltimore, Maryland 21215
(301) 358-6471

The purpose of the Lederer Foundation is to publish and distribute Christian literature for Jews. The Foundation knows no geographic or denominational boundaries. Thousands of pieces of literature are sent out each year all over the world, wherever there are Jews. The literature is not sold, but is made available to inquirers and workers in the field of Jewish evangelism. The Foundation is supported by income from the endowment and from voluntary contributions of churches, organizations, and individuals.

Founding Date: 1920
Publications:
Quarterly newsletter for Christian supporters
literature for Jewish inquirers
Also Known As: The Lederer Foundation

837. Liberal Religious Education Directors Association (LREDA)*

Unitarian Universalist Association
Roberta Nelson, Director of Religious Education
25 Beacon Street
Boston, Massachusetts 02108
(617) 742-2100

The function of the Liberal Religious Education Directors Association is to further the interest of liberal religious education by maintaining high professional standards and working toward full professional recognition for religious educators; by providing experiences in continuing education, helping to disseminate program ideas, resources, and leadership training materials, and through its members, providing assistance and encouragement for all those who are responsible for Unitarian Universalist religious education programming; by serving in an advisory and consultative capacity to the Department of Education and Social Concern; and by articulating and interpreting the philosophy, curriculum, and methodology of liberal religious education.

Founding Date: 1949

Membership: 150

Meetings:
2 per year

Former Name:
(1954) Unitarian Educational Directors Association

838. Liberal Religious Peace Fellowship (LRPF)*

Unitarian Universalist Association

Miss Ruth Neuendorffer
15 Dixon Street
Tarrytown, New York 10591

The purposes of the Liberal Religious Peace Fellowship are: to witness opposition to war of any kind; to be guided by a personal commitment to a philosophy of personal conscience; to support conscientious objectors; to provide peace education services to the Unitarian Universalists and other liberal denominations and their churches, conferences and institutes, to deepen understanding of the peace heritage and witness of liberal religion; and to join in cooperative efforts with other organizations in bringing about the psychological, social, economic, and religious conditions for peace and to help create a foreign policy leading to a world of peace and justice. The Liberal Religious Peace Fellowship, founded originally as a division of the Fellowship of Reconciliation, hopes to become a growing force within the Unitarian Universalist Association. Annual business meetings are held at the time of the General Assembly of the UUA.

839. Liberal Religious Youth*

Unitarian Universalist Association

Board of Trustees
25 Beacon Street
Boston, Massachusetts 02108
(617) 742-2105

Liberal Religious Youth is a non-credal, autonomous youth organization associated with the Unitarian Universalist Association. The membership consists of people, generally high school age, who are members of local groups in Unitarian Universalist Societies across the continent. The local groups are members of federations which meet at a conference, generally three or more times yearly. They are fully governed, organized and staffed by people under the age of 21.

Founding Date: 1953

Staff: 4

Membership: 6,000 lay; 4 clerical

Publications:
People Soup, 8 times yearly

Meetings:
125 Federation Conferences per year
Continental Conference in August
Annual Board Meeting in August

840. Liebenzell Mission of USA, Inc.

Interdenominational

Rev. Norman Dietsch, Acting Director
26 Heath Lane
Schooley's Mountain, New Jersey 07870
(201) 852-3044 and 852-6012

The primary purpose of the Liebenzell Mission is to bring people to a saving knowledge of Jesus Christ by Village, Youth, and Radio Evangelism. Church planting and development, medical and educational ministries, translation work, and publishing Christian literature are some of the additional avenues of service. Mission personnel staff two high schools on Palau, Micronesia, and work with the youth on university and high school campuses. A centrally located Bible School for Micronesia was opened in 1975 to train young Christians for service. Theological Education by Extension is helping ministers become more effective witnesses for Jesus Christ. Liebenzell Mission works in Papua, New Guinea and the Micronesian Islands of Palau, Yap, Truk, and Guam. It operates two bookstores, one at the Mission Headquarters and one on the Island of Truk.

Founding Date: 1941

Staff: 13

Membership: 21 general members

Publications:

Currents, quarterly

Prayer Guide, monthly

Informative brochures on Mission work and locations

Radio/TV Programs:

Radio programming in Micronesia

Meetings:

Meetings conducted for 8 weeks during the summer, with special speakers

Retreats and conferences held mostly on weekends

841. Life Changers

Interdenominational

Bob Mumford, Chairman of the Board

6301 Pembroke Road

Hollywood, Florida 33023

(305) 987-6922

The activities of Life Changers concentrate on the distribution of teaching materials that present biblical teaching on personal Christian maturity, church government in growth, marriage, interpersonal relationships with the Church, the Church community, practical pastoral care and aspects of the charismatic renewal. These materials include books, audio tapes, pamphlets, and newsletters.

Membership: 10

Publications:

Newsletters, monthly

842. Life Messengers*

Nondenominational

Ray W. Johnson

Post Office Box 1967

Seattle, Washington 98111

(206) 632-8500

Life Messengers creates and publishes evangelistic literature. It sells booklets and tracts in the United States, and raises funds for overseas printing.

Publications:

Booklets, 30 in print (6-8 million per year)

843. Life Video Gospel Association

Seventh-day Adventist

Donald M. Vories, President

1435 Central Avenue

College Place, Washington 99324

Mailing Address

Post Office Box 395

College Place, Washington 99324

(509) 529-5093

Life Video Gospel Association markets video cassettes containing only religious material and gospel music. Currently the Association markets two series of Christ-oriented videotapes which were produced by dedicated laymen. These series are called *LifeSpirit* and *ComeAlive.* They both utilize music of the Heritage Singers. These tapes teach directly from the Bible. Written material is available to go along with the program topics to simulate a classroom setting. The tapes are marketed to churches, religious private schools, hospitals, and private individuals. Video hardware is also made available for those without equipment. The Association's goal is to produce further programs on health topics, children's stories, etc. All programs would be based from a spiritual point of view. Its general goal is to enhance the spiritual growth of all those who are interested in growing as Christians.

Founding Date: 1979

Staff: 3 plus numerous volunteers

Membership: 35

Publications:

Lifespirit News, quarterly

Meetings:

Approximately 50 per year

Most meetings are in the Pacific Northwest

Former Name: Life Video, Inc.

844. Lifegate, Inc.

Fundamental, Nondenominational

Robert F. Porter, President

6300 Berean Road

Martinsville, Indiana 46151

Mailing Address

Post Office Box 1771

Martinsville, Indiana 46151

(317) 528-2261

The purpose of Lifegate is to help evangelize the world through the spreading of the gospel of the Lord

Jesus Christ. The primary method of communicating the gospel is through the distribution of the tract entitled *God's Simple Plan of Salvation.* Gospel films are also available as a means of presenting the gospel. Many churches purchase *God's Simple Plan of Salvation* tracts with their personal information imprinted on the front. Such information as church name and address, pastor's name and picture, schedule of services, and quotations can be printed to promote the ministry of the church. This service is also available for individuals. Christian businessmen use the tract as a calling card with the information about their business or company printed on the front. Two gospel films are also available for rental or purchase. *Suicide Mountain* was filmed in Japan and is the dramatic, true story of how Hideya is delivered from suicide at Suicide Mountain through the message of *God's Simple Plan of Salvation* and later brought to Christ. *The Way Out* is the true story of Al Johnson, a bank robber who was converted to Christ through *God's Simple Plan of Salvation.* Both films were awarded the best film in their category for the year produced. A card record system for churches is also available. It includes such cards as the Invitation Response Card, Welcome Card, Prospect Card, Survey Card, and Membership Card.

Founding Date: 1947
Staff: 8
Publications:
    Crowns, irregularly
Former Name: Berean Gospel Distributors

845. Lifeliners International

Pentecostal Holiness

Rev. E. Terry Tripp, General Director
Post Office Box 12526
Oklahoma City, Oklahoma 73157
(405) 787-7110

Lifeliners International is the youth department of the Pentecostal Holiness Church. The many and varied activities of the group all reach toward four basic goals: to lead young people to a genuine, personal experience of God's saving grace; to lead them into deeper experiences and active church membership; to lead them to Christian maturity; and to train them for active service. Among the activities available to the youth of the Church are: Family Night, a program seeking to focus upon the real prob-

lems of teenage life; Truth on Wheels, a program challenging the youth to raise money to purchase motor vehicles and provide for the transportation needs of missionaries around the world; Impact Teams, a group of young people in each state who witness for Jesus Christ in their area and often help in building new churches, Teen Talent and Junior Talent, encouraging youth to develop their talents for service to Jesus Christ, Bible Quiz, a program designed to make Bible study intensely interesting; Rescue Squad, a select group of youth traveling across the United States carrying on a preaching and singing ministry; Ambassadors for Christ, a program providing outdoor activity with spiritual emphasis for boys from six to fifteen years of age; Youth Camps and Retreats, conference and area programs of training and inspiration for young people of all ages.

Publications:
    Reach, quarterly

846. Light and Life Press

Free Methodist Church of North America

Donald Chilcote, General Publisher
999 College Avenue
Winona Lake, Indiana 46590
(219) 267-7161

Light and Life Press, denominational publisher for the Free Methodist Church of North America, carries on a ministry of communicating the message of God to all age levels through a variety of publications. The Church and the people who work for the Press believe this to be an imperative and thrilling task. It strengthens every other ministry of the Church and assists ministers, missionaries, teachers, evangelists, and Christian workers everywhere. Since its beginning, the Press has had a two-fold objective — to serve its denominational constituency, and to meet the needs of others. It has always reflected complete loyalty to the Church without sectarian bias. Traditionally, its ministry has extended to all those who share its distinctives. The Press has a complete printing ministry that includes magazines, books, and curriculum materials.

Founding Date: 1886
Staff: 4 staff members; 65-75 employees
Publications:
    Light and Life, a denominational periodical

847. Light-for-the-Lost (LFTL)

Assemblies of God

Rev. Dwain Jones, National Secretary
Assemblies of God
1445 Boonville Avenue
Springfield, Missouri 65802
(417) 862-2781

Light for the Lost is the overseas evangelism literature ministry of the Assemblies of God, Men's Department. Sponsored by a National Council of dedicated laymen, the program provides evangelistic literature for foreign missionaries and national workers in over 100 nations. All appointed Assemblies of God missionaries are eligible to receive LFTL funds upon approval of their project applications. Projects are presented by each field secretary to a special Division of Foreign Missions/Light-for-the-Lost committee and after being approved are shared with laymen and churches across the country by the national LFTL team. Projects include Good News Crusades, literature saturation campaigns, evangelistic programs of International Correspondence Institute, house-to-house witnessing of Ambassadors in Mission teams, and other soul winning endeavors.

Membership:
   Approximately 3,200 members of the National Council of Laymen

Publications:
   Spotlight, bimonthly

Meetings:
   National Convention held yearly in April, location varies throughout the continental United States

848. Liguori Publications

Roman Catholic

Daniel Lowery, CSSR, Director
One Liguori Drive
Liguori, Missouri 63057
(314) 464-2500

Liquori Publications publishes the *Liguorian* magazine, a monthly publication having a circulation of over a half million subscribers. In addition to the monthly magazine, a wide selection of Sunday bulletins are circulated to many United States and Canadian parishes. An extensive book and pamphlet department publishes various small and large publications on a wide variety of pastoral and spiritual subjects. Many other smaller services are available for individual and parish use.

Publications:
   Liguorian, monthly
   Liguori Sunday Bulletins, monthly
   Books, booklets, and pamphlets
   St. Gerard Bulletin, monthly
   PH Bulletin, monthly
   Scrupulous Anonymous Bulletin, monthly

Meetings:
   Varying from year to year

849. Link Care Center

Nondenominational

Robert P. Heinrich, Executive Vice President
1734 West Shaw
Fresno, California 93711
(209) 439-5920

In response to numerous requests by missionaries and pastors, Link Care Center was established to apply information and principles from psychology and the behavioral sciences to increase the effectiveness of the church's ministry; to help translate the love of God into specific behavioral patterns, and enhance the helping skills and interpersonal relationships within the church and community. In accordance with these purposes, the Link Care staff is available to individuals, families, churches, mission boards, and other organizations. The staff is prepared to consult and assist in the development of programs, staff training, personal counseling services and other areas as needed.

Founding Date: 1969

Staff: 15

Radio/TV Programs:
   Interchange, radio program

Meetings:
   3 annual Mission Institutes, San Francisco and Fresno
   35 seminars, workshops, courses

Former Name: Link Care Foundation

850. Literacy and Evangelism, Inc.

United Presbyterian Church in the USA

Rev. Robert F. Rice, Director
1800 South Jackson Avenue
Tulsa, Oklahoma 74107
(918) 585-3826

Literacy and Evangleism, Inc., is a missionary training and sending organization. It has developed Bible content adult literacy primers in over 50 languages, primarily for use in Africa and South Asia. It is currently completing a revision of an adult literacy Bible content primer-reader series in the English language. It has also organized the Tulsa Literacy Center and plans to implement a literacy evangelism ministry in other cities of the United States. The organization assists missions and churches in any language area to set up their own adult literacy primers with Bible content to be printed and used by the respective denomination or mission. It trains Christians to teach both Christians and non-Christians to read Scripture, and it teaches the literate Christian to witness to his non-Christian neighbor while helping him learn to read. Consultants For Christian Witness, a Ministry of Literacy and Evangelism, Inc., assists smaller churches to realize and develop their potential for Christian witness and church renewal. Literacy and Evangelism, Inc., shares its ministry — a slide presentation, a message, or other desired information — with any church, session, or committee, without obligation. It is an ecumenical ministry, both inter-church and inter-mission, and is supported by concerned churches and individuals.

Founding Date: 1967

Staff:

    11 staff members; 12 missionaries
    7 Board of Trustees Members
    43 Members Trustees (Advisory)

Publications:

    Firm Foundations, literacy primers in English and over 50 overseas languages, bimonthly
    Prayer-newsletter to supporters

Radio/TV Programs:

    Occasional local literacy announcements

Meetings:

    12 local literacy tutor training workshops (5 hours each)
    1 missionary training seminar each year

851. Lithuanian American Catholic Services (LACS)

Roman Catholic

Rev. Casimir Pugevičius, Executive Director
351 Highland Boulevard
Brooklyn, New York 11207
(212) 647-2434

Lithuanian American Catholic Services is the service arm of the Lithuanian Catholic Priests' League of America. It attempts to foster mutual support and communication between Lithuanian parishes, institutions, and organization in the United States. It serves as a resource center, and helps provide entry-level contacts for those who are interested in strengthening their ethnic and spiritual roots. LACS provides a medium by which those who have new publications, services, special talents, funding, etc., can be brought together with those who have specific needs.

Founding Date: 1974

Staff: 2

Publications:

    351, newsletter, monthly
    Chronicle of the Catholic Church in Lithuania, in cooperation with the Lithuanian Roman Catholic Priests' League of America
    Other liturgical materials

Meetings:

    Annual Convention of the Lithuanian Roman Catholic Priests' League
    Annual retreat for priests
    Others, as needed in cooperation with co-sponsoring groups

852. Lithuanian Catholic Federation, Ateitis, Incorporated

Catholic

Mr. Joseph B. Laucka, President
9610 Singleton Drive
Bethesda, Maryland 20034

Mailing Address
2749 Ordway Street, N.W., #5
Washington, D.C. 20008
(301) 530-5631

The Lithuanian Catholic Federation, Ateitis, Incorporated, is an educational, religious, and cultural organization of Catholic youth, students, and graduates of Lithuanian origin or heritage. Founded to counteract anti-religious sentiment in academic life in Lithuania, it provides guidance to aid members in the development of intellectual, moral, and spiritual values and in preparation for civic leadership. It is comprised of four autonomous associations: Association of Lithuanian Catholic Children (Grades 1-4), Lithuanian Catholic Youth Association (Grades 5-12), Lithuanian Catholic Students Association, Ateitis, and Ateitis Association of Lithuanian Catholic Alumni. Chapters of these associations are found in the United States, Canada, Brazil, Australia, West Germany, and Italy.

Founding Date: 1910

Staff: 7

Publications:
>   *Ateitis*, monthly except July and August

Meetings:
>   Congresses of the Lithuanian Catholic Federation, Ateitis, Inc. are held every four years, the last one being in 1981

Former Name:
>   American Lithuanian Roman Catholic Federation Ateitis

853. Lithuanian Catholic Religious Aid (LCRA)

Roman Catholic

Rev. Casimir Pugevičius, Executive Director
351 Highland Boulevard
Brooklyn, New York 11207
(212) 647-2434

Lithuanian Catholic Religious Aid is the only agency in the free world working full-time to provide assistance to the Catholic Church in Lithuania and elsewhere in the USSR. It provides material, moral support, and other assistance to the fewer than 700 priests and 1500 underground sisters left in Lithuania. LCRA seeks to supply Scriptures, catechisms, prayer books and other religious literature whenever possible, as well as vessels and other items necessary for the celebration of Holy Mass. LCRA encourages world-wide prayer campaigns for the Church in Lithuania. LCRA runs a comprehensive information center which disseminates news from Lithuania to the media, legislators, and human rights agencies.

Founding Date: 1961

Staff: 4

Membership: 124

Radio/TV Programs:
>   Helps to support Lithuanian-language Vatican Radio broadcasts

Meetings:
>   Annual meeting—directors and members, each spring
>   Conferences are planned on an *ad hoc* basis with cooperating organizations

854. Little Brothers of the Poor—Friends of the Elderly

Nondenominational

Kathleen Premer, President
1658 West Belmont Avenue
Chicago, Illinois 60657
(312) 477-7702

The Little Brothers of the Poor is an independent, non-profit organization whose goal is to help low-income elderly regardless of race, color, or creed. Various services are provided which will help the elderly preserve their independence rather than be institutionalized. Along with these services friendship, concern, and love are offered. Services and programs vary from city to city but usually include home delivered meals, transportation to medical appointments and shopping centers, homemaking, moving assistance, friendly visiting, and referrals or advocacy with public or private agencies. In carrying out the philosophy of "Flowers before Bread" holiday dinner parties, birthday parties, summer vacations, and outings are offered.

Founding Date: 1959

Staff: 82

855. Little Flower Mission League

Roman Catholic

Brother Andre M. Lucia, FSE, Director
Post Office Box 25
Plaucheville, Louisiana 71362
(318) 922-3630

The Little Flower Mission League's purpose is to spread devotion to St. Therese of the Child Jesus for world peace and the increase of vocations to the priesthood, brotherhood and sisterhood, and to help the Brothers of the Holy Eucharist in training young men to become Brothers. Membership is open to all. Members receive a membership card and a medal of St. Therese and share explicitly in all the prayers and good works of the Brothers of the Holy Eucharist. The members of the Little Flower Mission League recite daily the Memorare of St. Therese, the prayer for the conversion of Russia, and the prayer for an increase of vocations. Each month they offer up one Mass and Holy Communion for the intention of the Living and Deceased Members of the League.

Founding Date: 1957

Membership: 500

856. The Liturgical Press

Roman Catholic

Rev. Daniel Durkin, OSB, Director
St. John's Abbey
Collegeville, Minnesota 56321
(612) 363-2213

The Liturgical Press is the center of the publishing apostolate of the Benedictines of St. John's Abbey, Collegeville, Minnesota. Founded by Father Virgil Michel, OSB. The Liturgical Press publishes and distributes books, pamphlets, periodicals, recordings, prints, posters, filmstrips, cassettes, cards, and other liturgical teaching aids to assist pastors, teachers, students, and lay people in general to better understand and participate in the public worship of the Catholic Church. In addition to publishing material directly related to the liturgy, The Liturgical Press also features publications on the Bible, sacred music, Christian spirituality, family life, and Benedictine/monastic literature.

Founding Date: 1926

Staff: 13

Membership: 18

Publications:
> *Worship,* a liturgical studies journal
> *Sisters Today,* for women religious of the Catholic church
> *The Bible Today,* promoting study of the Bible
> *Book Trade News,* periodic news to book dealers

857. Living Bibles International (LBI)

Nondenominational

Lars B. Dunberg, Executive Director
1809 C Mill Street
Naperville, Illinois 60540
(312) 369-0100

The objective of Living Bibles International is to create translations of the Bible which are accurate and which are readable, culturally relevant, comprehensible, and emotive to the person of average education. It is comparable in these respects to the English Living Bible. The purpose of LBI is to aid to the Church in world evangelization and to contribute to the spiritual growth of Christians and the revitalization of the Church. LBI is dedicated to these specific goals: to create in the major languages of the world, and in other selected languages, living translations of the Bible; to distribute these living

translations as widely as possible; to encourage by every possible means the use of these living translations, and to foster an awareness of their importance for the Church and for evangelization; and to gather the financial resources necessary to accomplish these goals and to maintain careful stewardship in all aspects of the program.

Founding Date: 1968

Staff:
> International administration and fundraising — 11
> Field work of translation, production, and distribution — 1,000

Publications:
> LBI publishes newsletters in connection with its fundraising efforts, and publishes Bibles as part of its overall program, but these are not available to the general public on a subscription basis. However, foreign language Bibles are kept in stock for public sale.

Former Name: (1973) Living Letters Overseas

858. Living Church Foundation, Inc.

Episcopal

Rev. H. Boone Porter, Editor
407 East Michigan
Milwaukee, Wisconsin 53202
(414) 276-5420

The Living Church Foundation, a non-profit corporation, publishes *The Living Church*. The purposes of this magazine are to serve the people of the Church, by bringing to them current news of Church life; and to provide both a vehicle and forum for the free exchange of views and opinions relevant to the life and work of the Church in the world today.

Membership: 30

859. Living Reality

General Association of Regular Baptist Churches
1300 North Meachan
Schaumburg, Illinois 60195
(312) 843-1600

Living Reality is the Missionary Radio Voice of the General Association of Regular Baptist Churches. It is a 30-minute worldwide radio ministry heard by 59 nations every Sunday; it heralds the gospel to the English speaking world.

Publications:
> *Living Reality,* newsletter

860. The Living Rosary of Our Lady and Saint Dominic

Episcopal
Miss D. R. Howard, Secretary-Treasurer
20 Kline Street
Hudson, New York 12534

The Living Rosary of Our Lady and Saint Dominic is a sodality of Anglo-Catholics dedicated to the furtherance of devotion to Our Lady by means of the Holy Rosary.

861. Llewellyn Publications*

Carl L. Weschcke, President
213 East 4th Street
St. Paul, Minnesota 55165

Mailing Address
Post Office Box 3383
St. Paul, Minnesota 55165
(612) 224-8811

Llewellyn Publications is a commercial publisher of books and periodicals dealing exclusively in the "esoteric," i.e. astrology, the occult, witchcraft, pagan religion, graphology, palmistry. It is the oldest such specialty publisher in North America. It feels that wisdom starts with knowledge of self, grows with understanding at the forces of nature and the inner worlds, and progresses with experience of relationship between the inner and outer dimensions of man.

Founding Date: 1900

Staff: 50

Publications:
> Text and reference books, 100 titles in print
> 3 monthly magazines, 1 dealing with the serious side of astrology, 1 with the occult, and 1 with the popular aspects of the occult
> 1 annual dealing with the practical applications of astrology and attunement of Nature's rhythms

Meetings:
> 3 per year, one week each devoted to Astrology, Parapsychology, and Nature Religions

862. Logoi, Inc.

Nondenominational
Les Thompson, President
4100 West Flagler
Miami, Florida 33134
(305) 446-8297

Logoi is a Protestant Spanish literature missionary agency publishing books for the Latin market. This literature ministry has nearly 100 titles ranging from books for children to helpful inspirational titles, to Bible commentaries. The distribution program successfully reaches every area of the Spanish world. Approximately half of the titles are original in the Spanish language, the rest are translated from English. Logoi's goal is to give pastors and lay preachers a continuing education program.

Founding Date: 1965

Staff: 32

Membership: 3,200

Publications:
> Books—100 inspirational titles
> Books—42 pastor training materials

Meetings:
> 27 annual retreats throughout Latin America, for pastors and lay preachers, with 108 follow-up workshops throughout the year

863. Logos International Fellowship, Inc. (LIF)*

Nondenominational
Daniel Malachuk, President
201 Church Street
Plainfield, New Jersey 07061
(201) 754-0745

Logos International Fellowship publishes *Logos Journal,* a bimonthly Christian teaching magazine. LIF also sponsors world conferences on the Holy Spirit, and offers modular education through the Logos Institute of Biblical Studies. It provides a ministry to prisons; supports overseas missions, and sends them teachers; and publishes books of charismatic and evangelical interest.

Staff: 170

Membership: 60,000 lay

Publications:
> *Logos Journal,* bi-monthly
> Newspaper, biweekly

150 books, charismatic by Protestant, Catholic, and Jewish authors
Radio/TV Programs:
1 documentary on the First World Conference on the Holy Spirit
Meetings:
1 major conference
10 mini-conferences

864. Logos Ministry for Orthodox Renewal, Inc.

Greek Orthodox
Rev. Eusebius Stephanou
2707 South Calhoun
Fort Wayne, Indiana 46807
(219) 477-1255 and 456-6603

The purpose of Logos Ministry for Orthodox Renewal is to promote the cause of Charismatic Renewal in the Orthodox Church here and abroad. Father Eusebius Stephanou, the founder and president, and editor of *The Logos*, proclaims the end-time message of salvation, healing and deliverance by means of the written and spoken word. He ministers to spiritual renewal in Orthodox Churches throughout North America. Father Stephanou's ministry is primarily evangelical. He preaches the Gospel of the Lord Jesus Christ and helps Orthodox Christians to make their Orthodox Faith meaningful, relevant and viable. He assists them toward a personal relationship with Christ, ministering the Word of God to them and leading them into the Baptism of the Holy Spirit.

Membership:
No general membership
Members are considered those who are either subscribers or donors or both
Publications:
The Logos, bi-monthly
Meetings:
Retreats conducted by Father Stephanou in various cities and periodically at the homebase in Fort Wayne

865. Loizeaux Brothers, Inc.

Nondenominational
Elie T. Loizeaux, President and General Manager
1238 Corlies Avenue
Neptune, New Jersey 07753

Mailing Address
Post Office Box 277
Neptune, New Jersey 07753
(201) 774-8144

Loizeaux Brothers, Inc. was founded by Paul and Timothy Loizeaux to publish evangelical, fundamental Christian literature. For more than a century it has specialized in Bible commentaries and devotional volumes. While its new books are limited to a select few annually, it has a large backlist, and considerable emphasis is given to keeping in print its older titles of continuing value and demand, such as the writings of C. H. Mackintosh, H. A. Ironside, F. W. Grant, and Samuel Ridout. Its current authors include such well-known names as Lehman Strauss, J. Allen Blair, Stephen Olford, T. Ernest Wilson, Herbert Lockyer, E. Schuyler English, Charles C. Ryrie, Renald Showers, Cyril J. Barber, and Woodrow Michael Kroll. Loizeaux Brothers books are sold in Christian bookstores around the world, and are also available by mail to readers who may not have convenient access to Christian bookstores. While Loizeaux Brothers does not solicit funds, it does transmit funds earmarked for missionaries and missionary projects.

Founding Date: 1876
Staff: 20
Membership: 19 lay members
Meetings:
Corporation meetings for membership

866. The Lord's Day Alliance of the United States

Interdenominational
Dr. James P. Wesberry, Executive Director and Editor
2930 Flowers Road South, Suite 107
Atlanta, Georgia 30341
(404) 451-7315

The Lord's Day Alliance of the United States is an interdenominational organization dedicated to supporting and strengthening the institution of the Lord's Day as a day of unique religious significance. The Alliance undergirds the entire program of the local church through continuing emphasis on the need for regular participation in worship, religious instruction, family culture, and service to others. It establishes a liaison with labor and management with two objectives: insuring employees of a day a week to pursue their religious practices; and maintaining the essential religious character of the Lord's Day in the community.

Founding Date: 1888

Membership:

23 denominations on the Board of Managers
Increasing millions of lay members

Publications:

Sunday, quarterly
Brochures, pamphlets, posters decals, cassettes, books

Radio/TV Programs:

Radio spots and a movie entitled *The Lord's Day* which will be televised over WSB-TV Atlanta

Meetings:

2 board meetings each year
Furnish speakers for all manner of occasions

867. Lord's Way Inn Ministries, Inc.*

Craig La Caille, President
1933 L Avenue, #6
National City, California 92050
(714) 474-1971

The Lord's Way Inn Ministries, Inc., was organized to bring the Gospel to the men and women in the Armed Services. It operates a Christian servicemen's center in the heart of downtown San Diego called The Lord's Way Inn, which is open seven days a week until midnight. It offers the servicemen and women an alternative to the bars, porno shops, and "massage parlors" that line the streets. The alternative is a personal relationship with Jesus Christ. Members serve home cooked meals every evening. After dinner they gather together for a Bible Study or Worship Service. They also have a library and recreation room. Campouts and afternoon activities in the community are a part of the "reach out" program.

868. Los PADRES Inc.

Roman Catholic

Rev. Ramon Gaitan, OAR, President
Mr. Mario Cepeda, Executive Assistant
3310 Garfield Avenue
Kansas City, Kansas 66104
(913) 342-9246 or 342-9247

Los PADRES (Padres Asociados para Derechos Religiosos Educativos y Sociales) is dedicated to the formation of grass roots Hispanic Community

Leadership Development Programs and basic Christian communities. Its objectives include: establishment of national and regional centers for preparing lay, religious, and clerical workers for the Hispanic ministry; adequate formation of Hispanic ministerial students (promotion of seminary restructure and reformation); promotion of native Hispanic leadership within the church and society, e.g., Hispanic bishops; and use of mass media as a tool for the formation and reflection of positive self-image of Hispano, and the fraternity of mutual support in Christ of liberation theology in practice.

Founding Date: 1970

Staff: 2

Membership: 900

Publications:

PADRES, quarterly

Meetings:

1 National Conference every two years
4-6 regional meetings per year

869. Lott Carey Baptist Foreign Mission Convention

Baptist

Dr. Wendell C. Somerville, Executive
Secretary/Treasurer
1501 11th Street, N.W.
Washington, D.C. 20001
(202) 667-8493

The Lott Carey Baptist Foreign Mission Convention consists of representatives from local Baptist congregations, associations and state organizations. The Parent Body and Auxiliaries meet jointly each year in various cities on the Tuesday before the first Sunday in September. The Convention's purpose is to exalt the name of the Lord Jesus Christ everywhere and to persuade all men to accept Him as Lord and Master. It works toward these goals through Evangelism, Education, the Ministry of Healing, and the training of Nationals of various lands to become leaders among their people.

Founding Date: 1897

Staff: 3 full-time staff members

Membership: 20 affiliates

Publications:

Lott Carey Herald, quarterly

Meetings:

Executive Committee Meeting every November

Mid-year Executive Committee and Board Meeting on the Wednesday following Easter Sunday each year

Publications:
Church Newsletter News
Stencil Illustration Service

870. The Louis Foundation

Spiritualist

J. Starr Farish, Vice President
Post Office Box 210
Eastsound, Washington 98245
(206) 376-2581

The Louis Foundation is a spiritual transformation organization composed of individuals from all religions who recognize that the main purpose in life is to grow by expanding their consciousness and acting accordingly. Service to mankind, in one form or another, is the key to this action. The organization teaches and trains people in this process so that it becomes an integral part of their lives.

Staff: Approximately 9, Core Group

Membership:
General membership, 3,500 on mailing list

Publications:
Newsletter, monthly
Words from the Source (1971)
Listen Listen Listen (1980)

Meetings:
Many—anything that helps to be a positive influence on peoples lives: i.e., nutrition, meditation, things of a holistic nature

871. Louis Neibauer Company, Inc.

Interdenominational

Nathan Neibauer, Vice President
20 Industrial Drive
Ivyland, Pennsylvania 18974
(215) 322-6200

The Louis Neibauer Corporation was established to publish stewardship, tithing, church enlargement, and family programs for churches and church-related institutions. The corporation customizes programs for larger institutions, and produces materials for church mimeographing and offset.

Membership: 25

872. The Love Project (LP)

Nondenominational

Arleen Lorrance, Executive Director
Diane K. Pike, Co-Director
Post Office Box 7601
San Diego, California 92107
(714) 225-0133

The Love Project is an organization with a New Age Consciousness-raising orientation. It is non-affiliated, interdenominational, and inter-religious, with the focus on learning how to live in universal love. It is a way of life available to persons who want to be more loving and who seek alternatives to passive, apathetic, negative, hostile, critical, and violent living. It is six simple principles which make love not an ideal to reach for, but specific attitudes and actions to be and to do. The Love Project is a way for seekers to link energies in a universal chain of caring; a chain forged with the strength of the uniqueness of each individual. It is person-to-person love. The Love Project offers practice sessions in applying its principles; it offers experiential seminars and open dialogue sharings, group travel experiences, and sharing between and among individuals. The services of the Love Project are available to individuals and families, community groups and organizations, schools and colleges, churches and synagogues, business and industry, governments, and the United Nations.

Founding Date: 1970

Membership:
Active sponsorship group of 600 persons
Mailing list of over 8,000 persons

Publications:
The Seeker Newsletter, quarterly
Articles and books

Meetings:
Sponsor week-long "Journeys Into Self" twice a year, usually in San Diego
Weekend, day-long and evening Practice Sessions held all over the country almost every weekend of the year

Supersedes:
Bishop Pike Foundation, founded 1969 and formerly Foundation for Religious Transition

873. Loyal Christian Benefit Association (LCBA)*

Nondenominational
Bertha M. Leavy, National President
305 West 6th Street
Erie, Pennsylvania 16512

Mailing Address
Post Office Box 6196
Erie, Pennsylvania 16512
(814) 453-4331

The Loyal Christian Benefit Association is a benevolent association dedicated to providing fraternal life insurance to Christian men, women, and children. Its business and financial affairs have been so successfully managed that it has attained the highest solvency rating of any insurance company in the nation. Many fraternal activities are currently sponsored by the LCBA, including aid and the deaf, college scholarships, orphan benefits, and various social and benevolent programs. LCBA publishes a bimonthly magazine which carries official pronouncements and general news about organization activities at all levels.

Founding Date: 1890
Publications:
The Fraternal Leader, bimonthly

874. Ludhiana Christian Medical College Board, USA, Inc.*

Charles Reynolds, Executive Director
475 Riverside Drive, Room 250
New York, New York 10115
(212) 870-2641

The Ludhiana Christian Medical College, Ludhiana, India, has maintained an unbroken medical ministry since 1894. The total number of patients served is over 270,000 each year in all programs of the institution. The college offers a primary degree in medicine (MBBS); a degree in nursing (BS Nursing); paramedical training for therapists and technicians; and post-graduate specialty training in 11 clinical areas. The 700-bed Brown Memorial Hospital is the clinical training hospital offering all areas of specialty service. The Ophthalmology Department maintains a mobile hospital unit for visiting remote villages with eye camps, and screens over 20,000 eye patients each year. The Community Health Department pro-

vides medical care to over 150,000 persons in a block of villages through two rural hospitals, one suburban residential clinic, an urban ghetto area clinic, and 14 sub-health centers in rural areas.

Founding Date: 1894
Staff: 1,600 on field
Radio/TV Programs:
    Radio programs are taped for local stations of Far Eastern Broadcasting Corporation
Meetings:
    Approximately 12 each year

875. Lutheran Academy for Scholarship

Lutheran
Richard Junghuntz, President
c/o Valpariso University
Valparaiso, Indiana 46383
(219) 464-5459

The Lutheran Academy for Scholarship seeks to encourage in the Lutheran community scholarly research and thoughtful, responsible discussion of the issues that confront church and society. The Academy exists to serve as a means whereby professionally-trained persons belonging to the Lutheran Church may jointly confront and discuss the major problems of church and society; as an instrument providing an opportunity for the individual member of the Academy to contribute at his/her level of accomplishment to the thought and life of the Lutheran Church; as an instrument helping to preserve and develop the distinctive accents of Lutheranism within our pluralistic society; and as a means of creating opportunities to discuss and to formulate the specific ethical concerns of the Lutheran Church in various academic disciplines and in particular professions. In short, the Academy seeks to encourage Lutherans in professions to profess what it means to ba a Christian scholar. Members of the Academy ordinarily must hold a Bachelor's degree, have pursued or be pursuing graduate study (or its equivalent), and show promise of productive scholarship.

Founding Date: 1942
Membership: 400
Publications:
Academy: Lutherans in Profession, biannually

876. Lutheran Bible Translators, Inc.

Lutheran-Independent

Rev. Roy Gesch, Executive Director
Post Office Box 5566
Orange, California 92667
(714) 639-2850

Messengers of Christ-Lutheran Bible Translators, Inc., is an independent, international missionary endeavor. Its ministry is to provide the Word of God in the heart languages of those people who have not had the opportunity to learn of Christ in their own tongues. It also assumes responsibility for training those people to read their own language. It does so through the skills of linguistics, literacy, and Bible translation. In its home countries the organization conducts a ministry of motivational information and education, using its periodicals, brochures, films and filmstrips, and rally presentations.

Founding Date: 1964

Membership:
    120 workers in 15 countries working in 39 languages

Publications:
    Messengers of Christ, quarterly

Former Names:
    (1964) Messengers of Christ
    Messengers of Christ-Lutheran Bible Translators, Inc.

877. Lutheran Braille Evangelism Association

Lutheran

Rev. Car. C. Sunwall, Executive Director
660 East Montana Avenue
Saint Paul, Minnesota 55106
(612) 776-8430

Lutheran Braille Evangelism Association provides and publishes Christian literature for the blind and others with impaired vision in Braille, large print, and Talking Book records and tape cassettes. It publishes a 20-page monthly devotional magazine in Braille sent to blind individuals in the United States and 20 foreign countries free of charge. It also publishes a 12-page monthly devotional magazine in large print (18 pt.) at a subscription rate of $2.00 per year, transcribes and provides Christian education lesson materials for blind pupils (children, youth, and adults), and teachers in Braille free of charge, and provides scriptures in Braille, large print and tape cassettes.

Founding Date: 1952

Staff: 2

Membership: 2,000

Publications:
    Two monthly devotional magazines

Meetings:
    Annual meetings in May each year

878. Lutheran Braille Workers, Inc.

Nondenominational

Helene Loewe Koehler, Executive Director
11735 Peach Tree Circle
Yucaipa, California 92399
(714) 797-3093

The purpose of the Lutheran Braille Workers is to share with the blind and the visually impaired God's word in a form which they can use. While the organization is Lutheran, the materials produced (devotional literature and Scripture portions) are used by all people. The LBW is not directly supported by any church organization. Its 14,000 volunteers make possible the free distribution of materials to all who request them. Expenses and supplies are paid for by contributions.

Founding Date: 1944

Staff: 15

Membership: 14,000 volunteers

Publications:
    75,000 braille books in 1976 and a total of 7,778,000 sheets of braille and sight saving in that year
    Newsletter, three time a year

879. Lutheran Brethren Publishing Company

Church of the Lutheran Brethren

Robert B. Wallin, Business Manager
704 Vernon Avenue, West
Fergus Falls, Minnesota 56537
(218) 736-5637

In addition to its publishing activities, Lutheran Brethren Publishing Company operates a bookstore and mail order service for its denomination. It carries a wide range of Christian literature, including materials pertaining to the Church of the Lutheran Brethren. Its personnel assist and counsel students and church librarians in their selection of books. In addition, they are available for setting up book displays and conducting workshops at Sunday School conferences.

Founding Date: 1900

Membership: 6

Publications:

Faith and Fellowship, twice monthly
The Alumnus, bulletin inserts
Scores of brochures, letterheads, and other graphic communications

880. Lutheran Brethren Schools, World Mission Society

Church of the Lutheran Brethren

Rollin J. Tonneson, President
Vernon Avenue, West
Fergus Falls, Minnesota 56537
(218) 739-3371

The Lutheran Brethren Schools World Mission Society, formerly called the LBS China Mission Society was organized by a group of Bible School students. The Mission Society is an organization of professing Christians who have been registered as students at the Lutheran Brethren Schools; who are interested in missions; and who are willing to contribute annually to the mission program. Through the years thousands of dollars have been raised by this society for the support of foreign missions. In addition to providing financial assistance, the Society also provides prayer support so vitally needed by its missionary staff.

Founding Date: 1907

Membership:

Anybody who has been affiliated with Lutheran Brethren Schools can be a member if they participate in some way
Regular mailing list of 2,300

Publications:

Newsletter 3 times per year to inform the membership of any news related to the organization

Meetings:

1 annual conference at Lutheran Brethren

Schools in Fergus Falls held first weekend in February

Former Name: LBS China Mission Society

881. Lutheran Brethren Youth Fellowship

Church of the Lutheran Brethren

Rev. Elroy J. Vesta, Director of Youth Ministries
1007 Westside Drive
Fergus Falls, Minnesota 56537

Mailing Address
Post Office Box 655
Fergus Falls, Minnesota 56537

The purpose of the Lutheran Brethren Youth Fellowship is to awaken in youth an interest in spiritual things so that their lives may become a reflection of Jesus. It supports the ministries of the Church of the Lutheran Brethren by contributing to its World Mission Department, Home Mission Department, and support of Lutheran Brethren Schools. Its purpose is to foster relationships between young people of member congregations and encourage them in service to the Church.

Membership:

Members are those who are involved in the local congregation youth program

Meetings:

Biennial Convention rotated among the member Districts
A Leadership Seminar conducted in the off-year

882. Lutheran Charismatic Renewal Service (LCRS)

Lutheran

Richard Denny, Executive Secretary
Post Office Box 14344, University Station
Minneapolis, Minnesota 55414
(612) 636-7032

Lutheran Charismatic Renewal Service was formed to serve as a non-profit organization to meet the needs of the Charismatic renewal among Lutherans. LCRS serves a three-fold function: first as a shepherding agent for Lutheran Charismatics; second as a necessary point of contact between church officials and the Renewal movement; and third as an organization that relates with people who are outside of the formal structure of the Lutheran Church. These functions are carried out through meetings, retreats, and mini-conferences, as well as one large annual conference.

Founding Date: 1974

Membership: 28,000 subscribers

Publications:
Monthly newsletter
Quarterly newsletter

Meetings:
25-27 conferences across the country with one main conference in Minneapolis annually, the first week in August
Retreat in Minneapolis

883. Lutheran Church in America, Board of Pensions

Lutheran Church in America

L. Edwin Wang, Administrator
608 Second Avenue South, Suite 280
Minneapolis, Minnesota 55402
(612) 333-7651

The purpose of the Board of Pensions, Lutheran Church in America, is to provide health, disability, retirement, and survivor benefit coverages for eligible ministers, missionaries, deaconesses, lay employees, seminarians, and, where applicable, for dependents of such persons. Objectives of the Board are: to design benefit coverage which, when coordinated with available social insurance, makes maximum use of the benefit-contribution dollar; to maintain the current, extremely high enrollment rate of recently-ordained persons, improve the enrollment rate of those previously-ordained, and greatly increase the enrollment rate of eligible lay employees; to aid participants, persons eligible for participation, congregations, benefit recipients, and other interested persons in understanding the benefit plans which apply to them; to improve "customer" service; to improve the satisfaction level of participants and other benefit recipients; to minimize operating expense rates while providing excellent service; and to maximize investment return while maintaining an acceptable degree of risk.

Founding Date: 1963

Staff: 45

Membership: 35,000 insured

Meetings:
Biennial Board of Directors meeting, Minneapolis, Minnesota

884. Lutheran Church in America, Board of Publication

Lutheran Church in America

Robert W. Endruschat, General Manager
2900 Queen Lane
Philadelphia, Pennsylvania 19129
(215) 848-6800

The Board of Publication is the publishing and supply agency of the Lutheran Church in America. Its purpose is the propagation of the Gospel and the edification of Christian believers through the printed word and allied activities. It publishes the materials prepared by the Division for Parish Services and issues 50 to 60 general religious books each year under its Fortress Press imprint. It owns and operates 17 Fortress Church Supply Stores. The Board reports on its property and financial condition and transactions to the Office for Administration and Finance at its request. It reports to the convention through the Office for Communications.

885. Lutheran Church in America, Department for Church in Society

Lutheran Church in America

Dr. William Lazareth, Director
231 Madison Avenue
New York, New York 10016
(212) 481-9705

The Department of Church in Society is involved with research and study of social issues, the socio-ethical imperatives viewed from the perspective of Lutheran theology, and the formulation of policy on social issues for program implementation throughout the church.

Publications:
75 books in print
Pamphlets analyzing social issues

Meetings:
Faith and Life Institutes — 6 annually
100 throughout networks

886. Lutheran Church in America, Division for Mission in North America*

Lutheran Church in America

Dr. Kenneth C. Senft, Executive Director
231 Madison Avenue
New York, New York 10016
(212) 481-9674

The activities of the Division for Mission in North America of the LCA include: mission extension in North America; social welfare agencies and institutional relationships; higher education; social concern in church and society; community action programs; community organization; church building and financing; program support of congregations; and Faith and Life Institute for the laity.

Publications:

45 books on social concern issues

Meetings:

95 per year—training, educational, social concern

887. Lutheran Church in America, Division for Parish Services

Lutheran Church in America

W. Kent Gilbert III, Executive Director
2900 Queen Lane
Philadelphia, Pennsylvania 19129
(215) 438-5600

The Division for Parish Services, Lutheran Church in America, supports congregations in the fulfillment of their common and unique ministries. It does this by initiating and producing program materials, resources, studies, and services which can be provided most effectively and efficiently on a churchwide and interchurch basis. It provides guidance and program resources for serving persons of all ages, situations, and life styles through a process of teamwork with congregations and synods which includes goal-setting, planning, and implementation in such areas as learning, witnessing, serving, worshipping, and administering the congregation. It challenges congregations with new ideas through periodicals and leadership training in cooperation with synods. The Division includes Departments for Parish Support, Research and Planning, and Program Resources.

Founding Date: 1963

Staff: 67

Publications:

The division prepares a broad range of many hundreds of publications used by LCA congregations and their members. Most are distributed by the LCA Board of Publication. Catalogues can be secured upon request.

888. Lutherqan Church in America, Division for Professional Leadership (DPL)

Lutheran Church in America

Dr. Lloyd E. Sheneman, Executive Director
2900 Queen Lane
Philadelphia, Pennsylvania 19129
(215) 849-5800

The Division for Professional Leadership oversees, guides, and supports the educational and professional development of LCA clergy and lay professional leaders. Through its regional workshops, interview training, and program grants, the Division helps the LCA's 33 synods and its nine seminaries work more effectively with church occupations candidates. It also makes scholarship funds available to synods for seminarians and candidates for certification as lay professionals. Continuing education opportunities for church leaders and their spouses are available through the Division's Growth in Ministry program, which offers seven workshops and trains synodical leaders for each workshop. The Division's PLACE (Professional Leaders' Aid to Continuing Education) program helps professional leaders plan a holistic program of continuing education in cooperation with their congregations. DPL also publishes a bimonthly magazine which explores issues related to both ordained and lay professional ministry. The Division encourages congregations to give full and equal consideration to women in church leadership and also to persons of diverse racial backgrounds and ages. Strategies for developing a racially inclusive ministry within the church include orientation days for high school students, financial support of ethnic minority students and seminarians, and on-the-job summer apprenticeships in a parish or church agency. DPL also maintains a liaison with the LCA Deaconess Community and encourages seminaries and synodical leaders to include deaconesses in their guidance programs for church occupations candidates. The Division is responsible for the guidance and oversight of the nine associated seminaries of the LCA.

Staff: Full time 11, support 11

Publications:

LCA Partners, bimonthly

Meetings:

Each department may conduct an unspecified number of conferences, meetings, workshops, and retreats according to its budgeted programming

889. Lutheran Church in America, Division for World Mission and Ecumenism

Lutheran Church in America

The Rev. Dr. David L. Vikner, Executive Director
231 Madison Avenue
New York, New York 10016
(212) 481-9628

The Division for World Mission and Ecumenism is the means through which the LCA carries out its mission outside North America. It communicates the Gospel in such a manner that persons and groups are confronted by Jesus Christ; assists individuals and groups to mature; serves people; promotes justice; fosters wise use of human and natural resources to advance human fulfillment; participates in efforts of Christians to work together at home and abroad and relates to agencies of other faiths and of secular good will; secures, develops, and supports personnel; and identifies, develops, and renews organizational supports that advance the church's mission abroad and that coordinate LCA ecumenical and interfaith activities at home and abroad.

Founding Date: 1842

Former Name: Board of World Missions

890. Lutheran Church in America, Office for Communications*

Lutheran Church in America

Howard E. Sandum, Executive Director
231 Madison Avenue
New York, New York 10010
(212) 481-9600

The Office for Communications, Lutheran Church in America, provides supporting communication services for the church and works with all churchwide agencies in designing, coordinating, and evaluating a communications program. It strives to improve the quality and effectiveness of the communications of churchwide agencies. Through the Department of Press, Radio and Television, it seeks to extend the Gospel by the effective use of mass media such as the public press, magazines, motion pictures, radio, and television. It acts as agent for the church in the publication of the periodical, *The Lutheran*, a magazine designed to appeal to the whole constituency of the church. It maintains liaison with the

Board of Publication which reports to the convention through this office.

Publications:
> *The Lutheran*

891. Lutheran Church Library Association (LCLA)*

Wilma W. Jensen, Executive Secretary
122 West Franklin Avenue
Minneapolis, Minnesota 55404
(612) 870-3623

The purpose of the Lutheran Church Library Association is to promote the growth of church libraries by publishing a journal; providing book lists of recommended books; assisting member libraries with technical problems of setting up and operating a library; providing meetings for mutual encouragement, assistance, and exchange of ideas; and establishing chapters of the association.

Founding Date: 1958

Membership: 1,450

Publications:
> 1 workbook for church libraries
> *Lutheran Libraries,* quarterly
> Service bulletins

Meetings:
> Approximately 25 workshops each year
> 1 three-day conference for church librarians every 2 or 3 years

892. The Lutheran Church — Missouri Synod, Armed Forces Commission

The Lutheran Church — Missouri Synod

Rev. Dr. M.S. Ernstmeyer
475 L'Enfant Plaza, S.W.
Suite 2720
Washington, D.C. 20024

Mailing Address
3558 South Jefferson Avenue
St. Louis, Missouri 63118
(202) 484-3957

The Armed Forces Commission of the Lutheran Church — Missouri Synod recruits seminarians and pastors for the chaplaincy; screens all applicants; endorses pastors for the military chaplaincy; calls pastors and reserve chaplains to active duty; supports and supplies chaplains in the reserves and on active duty; supervises and guides chaplains; publicizes chaplains' activities through synodical media; and assists chaplains returning to civilian life. It prepares and mails devotional materials; refers Lutherans in the military to Lutheran chaplains; directs Lutherans in uniform to the nearest Lutheran Communion services; and promotes lay leadership among Lutherans in uniform. In addition, the Commission receives, maintains, and transfers church records; endorses and calls Veterans Administration chaplains; and prepares and supplies suitable literature and materials for use in Veterans Hospitals.

Staff: 4

Membership:
> 5 clergy, 2 laymen

Publications:
> *Loyalty, Christ and Country,* monthly devotional brochure

Meetings:
> Participates in the Retreat program of the Division of Service to Military Personnel of The Lutheran Council in the United States
>
> 5 retreats conducted annually, 3 stateside and 2 overseas

893. The Lutheran Church — Missouri Synod, Board for Missions*

Lutheran Church — Missouri Synod

Rev. Edward A. Westcott, DD, Executive Secretary
500 North Broadway
St. Louis, Missouri 63102
(314) 231-6969

The Board for Missions formulates, recommends, reviews and supervises the mission policy of the Synod, directs and adopts planning in keeping therewith, establishes and supervises budgets, reviews organizational effectiveness, effects the correlation and coordination of the synodical mission endeavor with other boards, agencies, and auxiliaries of the Synod, and does all else necessary to provide for an agressive and united mission effort for the Synod. Work is done in many countries throughout the world.

Founding Date: 1847

Publications:
> 3 theological journals
> 10 general church papers
> *Lutheran Witness,* monthly
> *Lutheran Witness Reporter,* biweekly

Radio/TV Programs:
> 50 radio programs, evangelical, educational and cultural
> 10 evangelical TV programs

894. The Lutheran Church — Missouri Synod, Church Extension Board*

Lutheran Church — Missouri Synod

F. E. Lietz, Executive Secretary
500 North Broadway, Suite 1400
St. Louis, Missouri 63102
(314) 231-6969

The Church Extension Board of The Lutheran Church — Missouri Synod provides financing for member congregations for church sites and worship and educational facilities. Members are invited to invest their savings and investment funds. They receive a favorable return on their investments. The Board has available loan funds for congregations that cannot obtain commercial loans.

895. The Lutheran Church — Missouri Synod, Commission on Health and Healing

Lutheran Church — Missouri Synod

Florence Montz, Staff Administrator
500 North Broadway
St. Louis, Missouri 63102
(314) 231-6969 Ext. 308

The Commission on Health and Healing acts as a consultant to all boards and commissions of The Lutheran Church — Missouri Synod in matters relating to health and healing ministries throughout the world.

Staff: 1

Membership: 6

Publications:
> *Cross and Caduceus,* twice a year

896. Lutheran Church Women (LCW)

Lutheran Church in America

Dr. Kathryn E. Kopf, Executive Director
2900 Queen Lane
Philadelphia, Pennsylvania 19129
(215) 438-2200

Lutheran Church Women is the auxiliary of the Lutheran Church in America. It enables women to grow in their faith and use their abilities through their congregations, communities, synods, and the church-at-large. LCW makes a significant contribution through leadership development and through advocacy and action in a broad spectrum of social concerns. In addition, LCW produces educational and devotional resources, the award-winning *Lutheran Women* magazine, and organizational helps. The auxiliary encourages both inter-Lutheran and interdenominational cooperation among women. In addition to these programmatic contributions to the church, LCW also gives an annual gift of nearly $1 million to the Lutheran Church in America for its ministry in North America and around the world.

Founding Date: 1962

Staff: 20 staff and support staff

Membership:
    5,067 congregational organizations
    220,000 women

Publications:
    Lutheran Women, 10 times a year
    Newsletters for leadership in synodical units, congregational organizations, and for social concerns

Meetings:
    National conventions triennially
    Regional conferences annually or biennially

Merger:
    United Lutheran Church Women and the women's organizations of the American Evangelical Lutheran Church, Augustan Lutheran Church and Lutheran Church, Suomi Synod

897. Lutheran Deaconess Association, Inc. (LDA)

Lutheran

E. Louise Williams, Director of Deaconess Services
Deaconess Hall
Valparaiso, Indiana 46383
(219) 464-5033

The purpose of the Lutheran Deaconess Association is to recruit and educate women for service as deaconesses in congregations, agencies, and institutions of the Lutheran Church; to provide support services to deaconesses; and to encourage Christians in the diaconal task of the church. The Association owns and operates Deaconess Hall, a residence for deaconess students, on the campus of Valparaiso University. It employs staff to teach and counsel students; offers extra-curricular educational programs for deaconess students; provides scholarships and grants for undergraduate students; and conducts workshops for field workers, interns, and their supervisors. The Association provides resource staff for the Lutheran Deaconess Conference, the professional organization for deaconesses which meets annually on the national level and more frequently in local groups. It also provides interest-free loans to deaconesses for graduate study.

Founding Date: 1919

Staff: 3

Membership:
    250 deaconesses
    219 voting members

Publications:
    Newsletter 3-5 times a year

Meetings:
    3 board meetings per year
    Annual conference
    1-5 retreats/workshops per year at various locations

898. Lutheran Education Association (LEA)

Lutheran Church—Missouri Synod

Dr. Norman Young, President (July 1982-June 1984)
7400 Augusta
River Forest, Illinois 60305
(312) 771-8300

The guiding purpose of the Lutheran Education Association is to support Christian education in the mission of the Church and to serve Christian educators as instruments of God in the world. The priorities implied by this central purpose are detailed periodically in the program and projects approved by the Association and its affiliated departments. They are: the Department of TEAM Ministries (Theological Educators in Associated Ministries); the Department of Lutheran Elementary School Principals; the

Department of Early Childhood Education; the Department of Elementary Teachers; and the Department of Secondary Teachers.

Founding Date: 1942

Staff: 1

Membership: 3,000

Publications:
Yearbooks and newspapers, quarterly
LEA News

Meetings:
Departmental conferences, once a year
Organization convention once a year

899. Lutheran Educational Conference of North America (LECNA)

Lutheran

J. Victor Hahn, Secretary
475 L'Enfant Plaza, S.W.
Suite 2720 West Building
Washington, D.C. 20024
(202) 484-3950

The purpose of the Lutheran Educational Conference of North America is to encourage, assist, and promote cooperation among Lutheran colleges and universities, and to clarify and strengthen their sense of identity, educational mission, and fellowship as partners in Lutheran higher education.

Founding Date: 1910

Staff: 2

Membership:
45 Lutheran colleges and universities
3 Lutheran church body boards, divisions, departments

Publications:
Papers and Proceedings of annual meetings

Meetings:
Annual meetings, usually in Washington, D.C.

Former Name:
(1967) National Lutheran Educational Conference

900. Lutheran Gospel Hour

Lutheran Brethren

Pastor R. Norheim, Director & Speaker
Post Office Box 12
Pasadena, California 91102
(213) 798-2784

Lutheran Gospel Hour ministry has conducted radio broadcasts in Brooklyn, New York; Eau Claire, Wisconsin; and Pasadena-Fullerton, California, and the broadcasts have grown in response to requests from churches coast to coast. The purpose of the broadcasts is evangelistic—to clearly present the way of salvation and to build deeper faith in believers.

Staff: 4

Publications:
The Lamplighter, monthly

Radio/TV Programs:
Radio broadcasts on 50 stations

Meetings:
1 annual retreat and several weeks of evangelistic meetings in the United States and Canada

901. Lutheran Historical Conference (LHC)

Lutheran

James W. Albers, President
Concordia Historical Institute
801 DeMun Avenue
St. Louis, Missouri 63105
(314) 721-5934

The Lutheran Historical Conference is a professional organization for Lutheran archivists, librarians, and historians. It provides the means for effective cooperation among persons concerned with the research, documentation, and preservation of resources about Lutheranism in the Americas. The Conference helps coordinate the archival, microfilm, and historical activities of the Lutheran synods in North America; pools the interests and concerns of archivists, librarians, and historians in American Lutheran church history; and serves as a channel of communication for research and production of scholarly works dealing with the history of Lutheranism in the Americas.

Founding Date: 1962

Membership: 95

Publications:
Newsletters, approximately 3 times a year

Meetings:
Biennial conferences, location varies

902. Lutheran Human Relations Association of America (LHRAA)

Lutheran

Susan and Charles Ruehle, Co-directors
2703 North Sherman Boulevard
Milwaukee, Wisconsin 53210
(414) 871-7300

Lutheran Human Relations Association of America is a voluntary organization of lay and clergy, working exclusively in the area of human relations problems; enlisting and engaging people who are Christian in response to problems of racism, sexism, poverty, and injustice. In 24 cities, the Association works through a coordinator program using non-salaried, volunteer representatives of LHRAA in local areas. The State Council program sponsors annual state-wide meetings and occasional newsletters to encourage participation in human relations issues. It also offers resource and consultative service to church leaders, judicatories, groups, institutions, and individuals.

Founding Date: 1953

Staff: 3

Membership: Approximately 5,000

Publications:
The Vanguard, 10 times per year

Meetings:
Annual Institute on Human Relations
Workshops in local areas

903. Lutheran Resources Commission-Washington (LRC-W)

Lutheran-Ecumenical

Lloyd Foerster, Executive Director
1346 Connecticut Avenue, N.W., #823
Washington, D.C. 20036
(202) 872-0110

Lutheran Resources Commission-Washington (LRC-W) is a grants consultation agency serving units of the American Lutheran Church, the Lutheran Church in America, the Lutheran Church-Missouri Synod, the Presbyterian Church in the United States, the Roman Catholic Archdiocese of Washington, D.C., the United Presbyterian Church, and the United Methodist Church. Through a purchase of service agreement with Aid Association for Lutherans, LRC-W assists all Lutheran colleges, universities, and Bible institutes. LRC-W also handles grant requests referred to it by the Review Section of

Lutheran Brotherhood through a purchase of service agreement. LRC-W does not make grants. Rather, it consults with agencies on the development of competitive proposals and guides them to government, foundation, or corporate funding sources. Since it was established, LRC-W has serviced nearly 1,300 requests and has assisted client agencies in obtaining more than $25 million for their projects. The projects include the fields of aging, child care, drug abuse, education, rehabilitation, health, housing, nutrition, media, women's concerns, and youth employment. Agencies desiring to use the grant consultation services of LRC-W must first obtain authorization from one of the participating churches, unless the project comes under the purchase of service agreement with either of the Lutheran fraternal benefit societies. Agencies requesting such authorization should be duly established non-profit organizations with 501(c)(3) status assigned by the Internal Revenue Service. Proof of such status is usually required by government or private funding sources.

Founding Date: 1969

Staff: 8

Membership:
6 Church Bodies; 4 Service Organizations

Publications:
Newsbriefs, monthly

Meetings:
2 regional Resource Development Conferences annually

904. Lutheran Women's Missionary League (LWLM)

Lutheran Church—Missouri Synod

Mrs. Helen Gienapp, President
3558 South Jefferson
St. Louis, Missouri 63118
(314) 664-7000

The Lutheran Women's Missionary League is organized to equip the women of the Lutheran Church—Missouri Synod for mission service. Its program places strong emphasis on Bible study and prayer as tools. Each year one Bible booklet is published and a prayer service is distributed. The League also has a leadership training program and publishes a quarterly magazine. All funds are raised through voluntary offerings. Except for a small percentage for administration of the League, those monies go to the mission outreach of the Lutheran Church—Missouri Synod.

Founding Date: 1942
Staff: 3
Membership: 200,000 women
Publications:
The Lutheran Woman's Quarterly
Meetings:
Biennial convention
Many retreats and workshops
Also Known As:
International Lutheran Women's Missionary League

905. Lutheran World Ministries (USA National Committee of the Lutheran World Federation)

Lutheran
Rev. Dr. Paul A. Wee, General Secretary
360 Park Avenue South
New York, New York 10010
(212) 532-6350

Lutheran World Ministries serves as an agency of the American Lutheran Church, Association of Evangelical Lutheran Churches, and the Lutheran Church in America. In its capacity as the USA National Committee of the Lutheran World Federation (whose headquarters are in Geneva, Switzerland), Lutheran World Ministries serves as a liaison for member churches in the United States in cooperating with and supporting the program of the LWF, especially in its activities of theological study, inter-church aid, service to refugees, material relief, community development, world hunger programs, and international scholarship exchange. LWM also assists the churches in an understanding of world community and human rights, in programs of missionary orientation, and in coordinating volunteer services. It conducts ecumenical theological dialogues and cooperates with and supports ecumenical organizations.

Founding Date: 1918
Staff: 19
Membership:
Agency for 3 member church bodies with a total of almost 5½ million baptized persons
Publications:
Inside Lines, occasional newsletter directed to specific leadership audience
Namibia Update, 3 times per year newsletter to church staff and concerned laity

Volunteer, a newsletter sent approximately 4 times per year to a select leadership list
Meetings:
Commission and 6 standing committees each meet twice per year, usually in New York or Minneapolis
Roman Catholic/Lutheran Dialogues meetings twice yearly jointly with the Bishops Committee for Ecumenical and Interreligious Affairs of the Roman Catholic Church
Former Name: (1976) National Lutheran Council

906. Lutheran World Relief

Lutheran
Norman E. Barth, Executive Director
Robert J. Marshall, President, Board of Directors
360 Park Avenue South
New York, New York 10010
(212) 532-6350

While providing emergency relief in the form of food, medicine and clothing, Lutheran World Relief lays heavy emphasis on developing human potential. It helps people toward self-reliance and the determination of their own destiny as they work to increase their food production, control and try to prevent disease, and train for more productive vocations. LWR supports United States foreign aid legislation aimed at substantially increasing the scale of economic assistance, particularly for the rural poor; separating consideration of military and economic assistance; and making more use of multilateral channels, such as the United Nations.

Founding Date: 1945
Publications:
Annual Report, yearly
World Hunger Update, semiannually
Condensed Resource Guide on Hunger and Development, yearly

907. Lutherans Concerned, A Christian Ministry for Gay Understanding

Lutheran
Diane Fraser and Howard Erickson, Coordinators
Post Office Box 19114A
Los Angeles, California 90019
(213) 663-7816

Lutherans Concerned is an association of gay and non-gay women and men who are working to foster within the church a climate of understanding, justice and reconciliation among all people, regardless of affectional preference. Since the founding of the association in Minneapolis with financial assistance from the American missions division of the American Lutheran Church, it has drawn lay and clergy members from across the country and several lands abroad, including all major Lutheran synods in the United States. Through its 20 chapters around the country and in its central ministry, the association counsels and affirms gay Lutherans as women and men whom God surely loves and for whom Christ died. It seeks to encourage the church at all levels to understand gay people and their families, and to work to open the doors of the church to all who worship the Risen Lord.

Founding Date: 1974

Membership: 20 chapters

Publications:

    The Gay Lutheran, 10 times a year

Meetings:

    20 local chapters meet monthly or more often for worship, speakers, or Christian social evenings

    A national Assembly is held in even-numbered years (site moveable)

908. M A Religious Designs, Inc.

Nondenominational

Ralph D. Kuether, President
1917 Xerxes Avenue North
Minneapolis, Minnesota 55411
(612) 521-6561

M A Religious Designs, Inc., is a for-profit company publishing art for use in church newsletters and overhead transparency materials for teaching biblical stories, and custom-designing jewelry for churches. In addition a line of mimeograph supplies is carried.

909. Macalester Park Publishing Company

Nondenominational

Norman K. Elliott, President
1571 Grand Avenue
St. Paul, Minnesota 55105
(612) 698-8877

Macalester Park Publishing Company operates a mail-order bookstore of service to churches of all denominations; publishes devotional books and literature; and emphasizes books on prayer and healing. It operates in close association with Association of Camps Farthest Out (having the same founder) and supplies its camps and retreats with books and literature. Macalester promotes, when possible, speakers, leaders, and activities of such camps.

Founding Date: 1930

Staff: 6

Publications:
   50 books and pamphlets on the life of prayer, healing, and devotional life

911. MAP International (Medical Assistance Programs, Inc.)

Nondenominational

J. Raymond Knighton, President
327 Gundersen Drive
Carol Stream, Illinois 60187

Mailing Address
Post Office Box 50
Wheaton, Illinois 60187
(312) 653-6010

MAP International sends donated medical supplies to over 400 Christian medical institutions in 84 developing countries. MAP also responds to disasters by sending supplies. It is engaged in long-term development assistance in agricultural productivity, water resources, and other needs. In support of its supply of materials program, MAP also arranges for final-year medical students from the United States to work for short periods in developing countries.

Founding Date: 1954

Staff: 80

Publications:
   MAP International Report, quarterly

Radio/TV Programs:
   A fund-raising documentary in 1980

Meetings:
   International Convention on Missionary Medicine held in Wheaton, Illinois once every three years
   Workshops on community health and development held as needed, overseas and domestic

Former Name:
   (1976) Medical Assistance Programs

912. Maranatha Baptist Mission

Independent Baptist Faith Mission

Dr. James W. Crumpton, President and Director
808 Myrtle Avenue
Natchez, Mississippi 39120

Mailing Address
Post Office Drawer 1425
Natchez, Mississippi 39120
(601) 442-0141

Maranatha Baptist Mission, Incorporated, is an international faith missionary ministry. It is supported by the free-will offerings of churches and individuals who have a burden to help get missionaries to the mission fields of the world. Maranatha Baptist Mission seeks to provide a channel through which local churches can extend their missionary efforts around the world by direct support of separated, soul-winning missionaries. They believe that in conformity with the Scriptural example of Acts 13, it is the function of the local church to authorize and send forth its own missionaries. It is their policy to encourage and promote that principle. Therefore, every missionary candidate, to become eligible for appointment under this Mission, must be a member of and commissioned by a local New Testament church. Thus, there is established and maintained a vital relationship between the missionary on the field and his home church. Every authorizing and every supporting church, as well as every missionary, becomes an integral part of the Maranatha Baptist Mission family, and establishes a modern operation of the Scriptural method of missionary enterprise.

Founding Date: 1961
Staff: 16
Membership: 225
Publications:
   The Maranatha, monthly
Meetings:
   Annual mission school for all missionaries, Natchez, Mississippi held each summer for 27 days
   Semi-annual staff meeting held the last week of February each year

913. The Margaret Coffin Prayer Book Society

Episcopal

John M. Gallop, President
1 Joy Street
Boston, Massachusetts 02108

The Margaret Coffin Prayer Book Society, the only organization in New England for the free distribution of the Book of Common Prayer, seeks to provide Prayer Books and Hymnals in any place of genuine need. In recent years this has applied to missions, schools and summer camps, prisons and hospitals, and under special circumstances to parish churches. The funds of the Society are administered in Boston by a Board consisting of four officers, trustees, and other members. In the past 25 years the Society has distributed 25,965 Prayer Books and 17,401 Hymnals in all parts of the church at home and overseas. Distribution policies evolve as needs require.

Membership: 23
Meetings:
   1 annual meeting

914. Marianist Training Network (MTN)

Roman Catholic

Rev. Norbert Brockman, SM, Director
Post Office Box 1283
Dayton, Ohio 45401
(513) 222-4641

The Marianist Training Network offers training events such as workshops, study days, and seminars, and also offers consulting services, primarily to Catholic religious orders. The organization is concerned with assisting in the renewal efforts of communities in a great variety of ways: planning, retreats, lifework planning, decision-making, training of local superiors, among others.

Staff: 15 part-time
Meetings:
   Approximately 50 conferences per year

915. The Mariological Society of America (MSA)

Roman Catholic

Rev. Theodore A. Koehler, SM, Executive Secretary
Marian Library
University of Dayton
Dayton, Ohio 45469
(513) 229-4214

The Mariological Society of America was founded under the leadership of Rev. Juniper Carol, OFM, by a group of Catholic theologians intent on promoting a more theological knowledge of the Blessed Virgin and furthering scientific research in the field of Mariology. Not restricted to professional theologians, active membership is open to priests and scholars who wish to broaden their knowledge of Mary in keeping with the inspirations and ecclesial orientations expressed in the documents of Vatican Council II. Other persons who share the aims of the Society may join either as Supporting Members or as Associate Members. All members receive a copy of *Marian Studies,* the proceedings of the Annual Convention. After 31 such conventions (1950-80), the periodical constitutes a unique collection of scholarly articles comprising many themes of Mariology and related theological sciences, studying current problems of Marian doctrine and devotion; and updating Mariology with regard to scriptural exegesis, Patristics, Church history, pastoral approaches, moral implications, and ecumenical dialogue. A Cardinal Wright Award is granted each year to a member of the Mariological Society who has made some outstanding contribution to Marian scholarship.

Founding Date: 1949

Staff: 12

Membership: 276

Publications:
> *Marian Studies,* annually, proceedings of the national convention

Meetings:
> Annual National Convention in various locations held in January
> Local conferences sponsored in various locations throughout the year

916. Mark-Age, Inc.

Nondenominational
Charles B. Gentzel, Executive Director
5555 S.W. 64th Avenue
Fort Lauderdale, Florida 33314
(305) 583-5755

Mark-Age is one of hundreds of New Age organizations to herald a new evolutionary era of spiritual activities prophesied in all scriptures of various religions since time immemorial. It is commissioned by divine guidance to establish a prototype of a spiritual government on Earth (non-political and non-denominational). The organization is made up of five divisions: Mark-Age Inform-Nations (MAIN, media); Mark-Age Meditations (MAM network, broadcasting weekly via cassette tapes to membership and similar

organizations); Healing Haven; Centers of Light; and University of Life. The organization's primary teaching is the Second Coming which is two-fold: the second coming of Jesus and the second coming of each one's Christ or I Am Self.

Publications:
> *Main,* bimonthly

Radio/TV Programs:
> MAM network, 15-minute cassette tapes, for group and media use, weekly
> Life Production Company, a part of the University of Life division, is preparing to produce video and audio educational tools for churches, schools, and educational outlets

917. Marketplace of the Master, Inc.

Richard C. Krause, President
3727 North Kedzie Avenue
Chicago, Illinois 60618
(312) 539-4674

Marketplace of the Master is a church supplies dealer. It represents many book publishers and suppliers of non-book materials. The organization offers curricula for Sunday Schools and schools, audio-visual equipment, Vacation Bible School materials, church office supplies, Certificates of Marriage, Confirmation, Baptism, etc., and church furnishings including communion ware, offering plates, church furniture, paraments, hangings, candelabra, candles, pews and pew cushions. Also available are clergy garb and choir robes.

Founding Date: 1941

Staff: 14

Publications:
> Seasonal catalogues; specialty catalogues

Former Name:
> Lutheran Bible and Church Supplies, Inc.

918. Markham Prayer Card Apostolate*

Roman Catholic
Rev. Herman H. Kenning, Director
60 Compton Road
Cincinnati, Ohio 45215
(513) 761-9036

The Markham Prayer Card Apostolate reproduces and distributes prayer cards containing *My Daily Prayer,* for use by priests, sisters, nurses, social workers, and others. The cards are distributed to those who seek salvation, as well as to non-Catholics who are dying and are in need of spiritual comfort. The work of the Markham Prayer Card Apostolate is perpetuated by the Franciscan Sisters of the Poor.

Founding Date: 1931

Former Name:
Apostolate to Aid the Dying
Apostolate to Assist Dying Non-Catholics

919. Marston Memorial Historical Center of the Free Methodist Church

Free Methodist Church of North America
Evelyn L. Mottweiler, Executive Secretary
901 College Avenue
Winona Lake, Indiana 46590
(219) 267-7656

The Marston Memorial Historical Center brings together books, pictures, documents, memorabilia, and other valuable records relating to the early history of the church, as well as current publications of Free Methodist authors and material that tomorrow will be history. The cataloged research library of 5,000 volumes includes the Heritage Collection of books by Free Methodist authors; bound copies of church-related periodicals; a large section on John Wesley and early Methodism in England; and Methodism in America, particularly Francis Asbury and the circuit riders. Free Methodist history and distinctive teachings, such as entire sanctification, are thoroughly covered. Books on related religious movements are also included. A collection of hymnals, the earliest dated 1743 entitled *Hymns for the Use of the People Called Methodists* by John Wesley, and many other rare Wesley books and pamphlets, some first editions, make the center outstanding in Wesleyana. A large collection of diaries, journals, record books, publications from the field, memorabilia, and artifacts from the early days of Free Methodist Missions is also housed in the center. Voices of Free Methodism (bishops, general officers, etc.) and important historic events in the life of the church are preserved on cassette tapes and filed in the center for future generations. There are "open box" files in which are kept conference histories, issues of conference papers, biographical material on conference ministers, and other materials pertaining to the conferences and their local churches. Services of the center include doing research, by

request, in the complete set of conference Yearbooks and Books of Discipline from 1860. Speakers, writers, and students find the resources of the center valuable in their endeavors. The center welcomes gifts of historic value and invites the use of its research and study facilities.

Founding Date: 1964

Staff: 2

Membership: 5 on Advisory Committee

Former Name: Free Methodist Historical Center

920. Mary Productions Guild

Mary-Eunice, President (Founder)
58 Lenison Avenue
Belford, New Jersey 07718
(201) 787-6018

Mary Productions Guild is the organization through which Mary-Eunice, international monologist, presents her *Lives of Saints and Historical People* at shrines, theatres, societies, schools, and on TV and radio. Her monologues on the saints and historical people are original. She has sent over 50,000 playscripts to missionaries and societies all over the world. Mary Productions publishes *Better World Bulletin.* The organization hopes to make a better world through its work. It is their hope to make the lives of Saints better known through their work.

Founding Date: 1950

Staff: 2

Publications:
Better World, quarterly

Radio/TV Programs:
Numerous programs throughout the country

921. Maryknoll Priest-Associates*

Roman Catholic
Reverend Raymond A. Hill, MM
Maryknoll Fathers
Maryknoll, New York 10545
(914) 941-7590

The Maryknoll Priest-Associates are Diocesan Catholic Priests of the United States who offer their services to the Catholic Foreign Mission Society of

America (Maryknoll) for a period of five years, renewable, to assist in the fulfillment of the Society's Mission work in Africa, Asia and Latin America. The particular purpose of Maryknoll is the participation in the missionary activity of the Church, carried out by means of Christian witness, verbal proclamation of the Gospel, initiation into Christian community, and continuing formation of the Christian community.

Membership: 10 clerical

922. Mass Media Ministries, Inc.

Interdenominational
Clifford J. York, President
2116 North Charles Street
Baltimore, Maryland 21218
(301) 727-3270

Mass Media Ministries maintains a nation-wide, ecumenical 16mm film library (rental/sale) for use by religious, educational, and community service organizations. A new Film Catalogue (free on request) describes films on a wide variety of program themes: family life; television awareness; relationships; aging; death and dying; clown ministry; communication; stewardship; etc. Inspirational films and film parables are recommended in seasonal brochures: *Films for Christmas, Films for Lent,* and *Films for Summer Church Programs.*

Founding Date: 1974
Staff: 9

923. Massachusetts Convention of Congregational Ministers

Congregational
Rev. Daniel G. Higgins, Moderator
2 Elm Street
Malden, Massachusetts 02148
(617) 322-8250

Formed in the 17th century, two hundred years before the schism in New England Congregationalism which resulted in the formation of the American Unitarian Association, the Massachusetts Convention of Congregational Ministers, which meets annually, receives the income from special funds held by both the American Unitarian Association (now the Unitarian Universalist Association) and the Massachusetts Congregation Charitable Society. It disburses these funds in the form of small grants to

widows of Congregational or Unitarian Universalist ministers whose husbands at one time served Massachusetts parishes.

Membership:
All United Church of Christ and Unitarian Universalist Association ministers in Massachusetts

Meetings:
Two meetings a year, a fall meeting and the spring annual meeting

924. Maynard Listener Library (MLL)

Roman Catholic
Merrill A. Maynard, Director
171 Washington Street
Taunton, Massachusetts 02780
(617) 823-3783

Maynard Listener Library provides free loan of books on open reel and cassette tapes for the ink-print handicapped. Currently the Library has more than 7,000 tapes to lend. Distribution is limited to the area of free matter for the blind and physically handicapped, United States Postal Service. Requests may be submitted in type, tape, Braille, telephone, and personal visits by appointment.

Founding Date: 1959
Membership: 115
Publications:
Catalogues on tape, in Braille, and mimeographed, annually
Former Name: (1965) Catholic Listener Library

925. Mazdaznan

Spiritualist
Henry L. Sorge, PhD, Elector
1159 South Norton Avenue
Los Angeles, California 90019
(213) 734-4359

Mazdaznan is a religious corporation in the State of California, with international headquarters in Los Angeles. It was founded in New York. The teaching was founded by Dr. O.Z.A. Hanish, who brought Mazdaznan to the western world from the Himalayan Mountains in Tibet. It is the pure and simple teaching of the original Zarathustra who lived more than 8,000 years ago. The purpose of this teaching is to establish greater harmony between body, mind, and soul through breathing exercises and proper posture. Concentrating the power of our thought upon the breath we can unlock all the treasures of heaven and earth; through better health as a result of proper breathing and diet; and through song, exercise, and prayer on the breath resulting in greater harmony between body, mind and soul. By combining song and prayer we bring about perfect harmony. Through greater wisdom and health we learn to apply the divine laws of God by expressing only "Good Thought, Good Words, and Good Deeds."

Founding Date: 1902

Membership: 200,000

Publications:
Magazine, quarterly
The *Mazdazan Magazines,* Germany, France, Belgium, Holland, Denmark, England

Meetings:
2 per year, 1159 South Norton Avenue, Los Angeles, California, during the last week in June and the last week in December

926. Men for Missions International (MFMI)

OMS International; Wesleyan

Harry Burr, Executive Director
Post Office Box A
Greenwood, Indiana 46142
(317) 881-6751

Men for Missions International is a movement of men rolling up their sleeves and utilizing their muscles and means to put the Message where the multitudes are. It began with a burning conviction that for too long the man-sized job of missions had been left to the ladies. From multiple church affiliations and every walk of life, thousands of men are finding in MFMI a channel for harnessing and releasing personal skills and abilities in practical, direct missionary involvement. Without dues, gimmicks, or organizational trappings, MFMI is calling men to action for the priority task of the church—winning the lost across the world to Jesus Christ. Any man, regardless of age or wage, can become involved.

Founding Date: 1954

Staff: 100

Membership: 15,000

Publications:
Action, quarterly

Meetings:
Meetings throughout the year, location and number vary

927. Mennonite Brethren Missions Services

Mennonite Brethren

Vernon R. Wiebe, General Secretary
315 South Lincoln
Hillsboro, Kansas 67063

Mailing Address
Post Office Box V
Hillsboro, Kansas 67063
(316) 947-3151

Mennonite Brethren Missions/Services is a denominational sending agency of evangelical Mennonite tradition, serving national churches and unevangelized areas of the world in evangelism, church planting, theological education, leadership training, community development, and medicine.

Founding Date: 1878

Membership:
150 missionaries; 6 executive secretaries

Publications:
Christian Leader
Tell, monthly newsletter

Radio/TV Programs:
German radio programs in Quito, Ecuador
Four radio programs aired regularly in Hyderabad, India
Russian programs developed in Canada, aired in the USSR

Meetings:
Meetings twice a year in Winnipeg, Manitoba, or Hillsboro, Kansas
Orientation for new workers and worker retreat annually
Missions conferences in local churches throughout the year

928. Mennonite Brethren Publishing House

United States Conference of Mennonite Brethren Churches

Wilmer Thiessen, General Manager
135 North Main Street, Box L
Hillsboro, Kansas 67063
(316) 947-3966

The Mennonite Brethren Publishing House is the publishing arm of the United States Conference of Mennonite Brethren Churches, a branch of the international General Conference of Mennonite Brethren Churches with congregations in various parts of the world, and active mission programs in 12 countries. It publishes adult Sunday school materials in English and German, a quarterly devotional guide, and a limited number of religious and historical books, particularly concerning Mennonite Brethren. A considerable number of informational and promotional materials are also published for both the United States Conference and the General Conference.

Publications:
   The Christian Leader

929. Mennonite Central Committee (MCC)

Mennonite and Brethren in Christ Churches

William T. Snyder, Executive Secretary
21 South 12th Street
Akron, Pennsylvania 17501
(717) 859-1151

Mennonite Central Committee is the cooperative relief and service agency of 17 North American Mennonite and Brethren in Christ churches. MCC was begun in response to hunger and related human needs brought on by war and revolution. MCC has over 700 personnel serving one to three-year assignments in 46 countries. In North America volunteers are involved in economic development, education, and social service programs in cities and rural areas. Volunteers outside North America are concentrated in Third World countries. Teachers, engineers, nurses, agriculturalists, social workers, and others work to promote a better life for local families, communities, and churches. Three million dollars of MCC's over 11-million-dollar budget goes for material aid. Departments such as Mennonite Disaster Service, Peace Section United States, Men-

nonite Mental Health Services, and Food and Hunger Concerns show some of the variety included in the MCC program.

Founding Date: 1920

Membership: 38

Publications:
   Washington Memo, bimonthly
   Peace Section Newsletter, bimonthly
   Women's Task Force Report, bimonthly
   Intercom, montly
   Contact, monthly
   News Service, weekly

Meetings:
   Annual meeting, usually held in a Mennonite community

930. Mennonite Church, Board of Education (MBE)

Mennonite Church

Albert J. Meyer, Executive Secretary
Post Office Box 1142
Elkhart, Indiana 46515
(219) 294-7531

The Mennonite Board of Education is responsible for coordinating the financial and personnel resources of the denomination in order to best fulfill the educational goals and expectations of congregations of the church. The Board operates two colleges and a seminary, and works in a coordinating and consulting relationship with several other colleges and with ten high schools operated by Mennonite Church bodies.

Founding Date: 1905

Membership: 12

Publications:
   Mennonite Educator, irregular

Meetings:
   Annual convention

931. Mennonite Church, Board of Missions

Mennonite Church

Paul M. Gingrich, President
500 South Main Street
Elkhart, Indiana 46515

Mailing Address
Post Office Box 370
Elkhart, Indiana 46515
(219) 294-7523

Mennonite Board of Missions is charged by the Mennonite Church to develop, administer, and promote missions and service through programs in overseas missions; missions in the United States and Canada; health and welfare institutional management and consultation services; public media ministries in North America and overseas; group serving experiences in voluntary service in North America; Christian group biking opportunities; and ministry with Mennonite students on non-church university and college campuses and urban young adults. The Board conducts the following programs: *Overseas Missions* in 20 areas with 125 missionaries and overseas mission associates; *Home Missions,* facilitating 22 Mennonite Church conferences and 5 regions in church extension and providing resources for Latino, native American, black, and other congregations in North America; *Voluntary Service* units in 40 communities with 200 workers in one- or two-year assignments; *Out-Spokin'* offering biking opportunities for Christian community on the move; *Student and Young Adult Services,* working with 5,000 Mennonites on 500 Canadian and United States non-Mennonite campuses/communities for church extension; *Media Ministries* offering English language radio programs and spots and TV spots for public media use, paperback book evangelism, correspondence Bible courses, and media materials in seven languages; and *Hospitals, Retirement Homes, Child Welfare Services* — institutions are administered in 20 communities in the United States, with operations supported financially by the service areas. Consultation services are available for local community efforts.

Founding Date: 1906

Staff: 100

Publications:

> *Alive,* quarterly (Media Ministries)
> *Agape,* 14 issues a year (Voluntary Service)
> *Branches,* quarterly (Associate in Mission) Partners
> *Feedback,* 9 isues per year (Student and Young Adult Services)
> *Mission Focus,* quarterly, for mission leaders
> *SENT, Stories of People in Mission,* bimonthly
> *Signing,* bimonthly (Deaf Ministries)

Radio/TV Programs:

> *In Touch,* 3½-minute daily radio program for the general listening audience

Your Time, daily 5-minute program especially for women
Choice, spots for public service radio time

Meetings:

> Annual Overseas Missions Seminar
> Annual Home Ministries Consultation

932. Mennonite Church, Board of Missions, Division of Media Ministries

Mennonite

Kenneth J. Weaver
Post Office Box 1252
Harrisonburg, Virginia 22801
(703) 434-6701

The objective of this organization is to provide leadership, resources, and assistance for the congregations and agencies of the Mennonite Church in the use of public media in calling persons to commitment and life in Jesus Christ, and in influencing, in accordance with Christian principles, the values and ethics of individuals in society. Its immediate program focus is on personal growth and development with an emphasis on the need for persons to relate to a caring community. It further seeks to challenge persons to think about their own potentials and growth possibilities in relationship to other persons, social groups, and to the Christian faith. Its responsibility and activity includes the full range of public media: radio, TV, print, space, and display advertising.

Founding Date: 1951

Publications:

> Inspirational and Christian-nurture paperback books
> Home Bible Studies courses
> Printed leaflets of radio messages
> *Alive* newsletter

Radio/TV Programs:

> Radio and TV spots
> 2½ and 5-minute daily programs
> Multimedia campaigns

Meetings:

> Friendship Evangelism Seminars to begin in 1980, offered to local congregations and groups for their local communities

Former Name: (1979) Mennonite Broadcasts, Inc.

933. Mennonite Church, Eastern Mennonite Board of Missions and Charities

Lancaster Conference of the Mennonite Church

Paul G. Landis, President
Oak Lane and Brandt Boulevard
Salunga, Pennsylvania 17538
(717) 898-2251

Since its beginning, the Eastern Mennonite Board of Missions and Charities has attempted to serve as the mission outreach of the Lancaster Conference of the Mennonite Church. This mission outreach now extends into 20 countries in Europe, Asia, Africa, and Latin America, as well as 12 eastern seaboard states of the United States. The objectives of the Board are as follows: to develop, support, and direct mission and evangelism at home and overseas; to promote the establishment and growth of the church and to work in partnership and coordination with developing churches; to support and provide relief and services at home and overseas; to provide education, literature, institutional care for the needy, and other services among all peoples as an integral part of the mission and evangelical activities when means and opportunity afford; and to promote mission and relief interests within the brotherhood.

Founding Date: 1914

Staff: 40

Membership:
150 persons serving in overseas mission program
100 persons serving in Voluntary Service Program

Publications:
Missionary Messenger, monthly
Newsletter, biweekly

Radio/TV Programs:
Focus, a 5-minute weekly newscast of activities, aired on two FM stations in South Central Pennsylvania

Meetings:
Annual mission meeting

934. Mennonite Economic Development Associates (MEDA)

Mennonite

Lloyd J. Fisher, Executive Director
21 South 12th Street
Akron, Pennsylvania 17501
(717) 859-1151

The Mennonite Economic Development Associates raises funds to loan to potential small businesses and for agriculture, including production credit and processing in developing countries. The program is locally administered. MEDA trains the local committee and backstops them through periodic visits. Seminars for project managers are also sponsored by MEDA. Funds are re-invested within the country as long as there is interest and a need. Interest earnings are used to meet program expenses within the country.

Founding Date: 1953

Membership: 350

Publications:
Yearly report

Meetings:
1 annual meeting in Goshen, Indiana

935. Mennonite Publishing House

Mennonite

Ben Cutrell, Publisher
616 Walnut Avenue
Scottdale, Pennsylvania 15683
(412) 887-8500

The Mennonite Publishing House publishes Christian education curricula and other items for congregational use and books for the general religious market under the name Herald Press. It also operates a chain of general religious bookstores under the name Provident Bookstores. The Publishing House is the literature communication facility of the Mennonite Church and is dedicated to strengthening the faith and life of its members and their witness. It develops and maintains programs deemed essential for planning, editing, manufacturing, and distributing literature and related materials.

Staff: 300

Publications:
Gospel Herald, weekly
Christian Living and Builder, monthly
Rejoice!, quarterly
Purpose, With, On the Line, and *Story Friends,* monthly

936. Mennonite World Conference (MWC)

Mennonite
Paul N. Kraybill, Executive Secretary
528 East Madison Street
Lombard, Illinois 60148
(312) 620-7802

The purpose of Mennonite World Conference is to bring together in fellowship the Mennonites and Brethren in Christ of the world. By its activities, under the leadership of the Holy Spirit, it seeks to deepen faith and hope, to stimulate and aid the church in its ministry to the world, and to promote the Kingdom of God in greater obedience to the Lord Jesus Christ through fellowship, communication, and facilitation.

Staff:
85 General Council members
2 staff members

Publications:
MWC Newsletter, quarterly

Meetings:
Assembly held every 6 years
General Council every 3 years
Executive Committee every year

937. Message of Life, Inc.

Interdenominational
Joe Sanders, Director
58607 Road 601
Ahwahnee, California 93601
(209) 683-7028

Message of Life, Inc., publishes Christian education material in Spanish at a subsidized price for Daily Vacation Bible Schools, Sunday Schools, etc., for children through sixth grade.

Founding Date: 1961

Staff: 3

Membership: General membership varies annually

Meetings:
Annual meeting

938. Messenger Publishing House

Pentecostal Church of God, Inc.

221 Main Street
Joplin, Missouri 74801
(417) 624-7050

Messenger Publishing House has produced more than three million pieces of Pentecostal-oriented literature. Included in its regular publishing schedule are books, tracts, and Church school literature, among others.

939. Messengers of the New Covenant, Inc.

Protestant, Interdenominational

John Binns, President
Edward N. Cleveland, General Secretary
242 Shunpike Road
Springfield, New Jersey 07081
(201) 467-0311 and (201) 667-4214

Messengers of the New Covenant is a mission to the Jewish believers in Christ. It ministers to a particular group of about 100 Jewish people by keeping in touch with them, encouraging them in the things of Christ, and providing frequent get-togethers for fellowship, Bible teaching, and instruction. The mission also has workers in Israel and provides funds and literature for the Jewish believers in Christ in Jerusalem.

Founding Date: 1943

Staff: 3 in the United States

Membership: 2 families working in Israel

Publications:
My Heart's Desire, bimonthly
Numerous prayers

Meetings:
1-2 retreats and 1-2 conferences
4 special meetings
Weekly Bible classes and Hebrew classes held in New Jersey and Eastern Pennsylvania

940. Messianic Jewish Movement International (MJMI)

Messianic Judaism

Manuel Brotman, President
Post Office Box 30313
Washington, D.C. 20014
(301) 656-7575

The Messianic Jewish Movement International exists to bring the good news of Messiah Yeshua (Jesus) to every Jewish person in the world. To accomplish this, MJMI has over 130 messianic materials for the salvation, spiritual growth, and discipleship of Jewish people. MJMI conducts training seminars on how to share the Messiah for local organizations and in citywide sessions.

Publications:
Newsletter, monthly
Radio/TV Programs:
30-minute radio program, five days a week
Meetings:
20-30 per year

941. Metaphysical Science Association (MSA)

Christian Science and Metaphysics

Metropolitan Station 6454
Los Angeles, California 90055

The Metaphysical Science Association publishes *Teaching and Addresses* of Edward A. Kimball, CSD, who was Mary Baker Eddy's principal lecturer. The Association handles for re-sale many other books pertaining to Christian Science and related metaphysical subjects.

942. Methodist Federation for Social Action (MFSA)

United Methodist

Rev. George McClain, Executive Secretary
76 Clinton Avenue
Staten Island, New York 10301
(212) 273-4941

The Methodist Federation for Social Action stands for: the complete abolition of war; the rejection of the struggle-for-profit as the economic base for society; the socio-economic planning to develop a society without race, sex, or class discrimination; and the defense of civil liberties as set forth in the Bill of Rights. The Federation urges its members to work with parties and movements seeking to implement these aims and promote social change by the responsible use of power. Membership is open to all persons in sympathy with the objectives of the Federation. The MFSA program strives to support liberation-oriented United Methodists and others as they witness to the Gospel's social imperatives in local churches and communities and in denominational and public policy matters. To achieve this the Federation encourages the formation of conference MFSA chapters. They also strive to act as a national organization and through conference chapters deal with carefully selected issues concerning the church's social witness. Major attention in 1980 was given to struggles to resist corporate power, especially through the boycott of J. P. Stevens and Nestle products; to combat racism, sexism, and classism; to influence the 1980 General Conference; and to promote radical spirituality and wholistic evangelism.

Founding Date: 1907
Membership: 1,000
Publications:
Social Questions Bulletin, bimonthly
Meetings:
Frequent meetings using local church facilities
Former Name:
Methodist Federation for Social Service

943. Methodist Hour International (MHI)

Methodist

Herbert L. Bowdoin, President
Post Office Box 77
Orlando, Florida 32802
(305) 830-0255

The purpose of Methodist Hour International is to further spread the good news of Our Lord Jesus Christ to the unsaved via a weekly 30-minute radio program and area-wide crusade meetings. Both functions are carried out on an international level. The radio program is currently aired on 250 radio stations each week, including the Far East Broadcasting Network which is carried behind the Iron Curtain, India, Africa, etc. Each year the organization holds an Annual Victorious Life Conference in Central Florida. It is based on evangelical Methodist principles, as the total ministry, and features three or more key-note speakers along with six to eight seminar speakers. Themes range from Emphasis on Church Renewal to Personal Evangelism. All denominations are encouraged to take part in the ministry and promote the Church worldwide. Methodist Hour International is an approved ministry from the United Methodist Church, but is completely independent of it.

Staff: 8

Publications:
Newsletter, bimonthly
Affiliates, describing meetings/travelings, etc.

Radio/TV Programs:
A weekly 30-minute radio program consisting of musical selections, an interview, devotional readings, and an evangelical message

Meetings:
Annual Conference; frequent crusdade meetings

944. Mexican American Cultural Center (MACC)

Roman Catholic
Rev. Ricardo Ramirez, CSB, Executive Vice President
3019 West French Place
San Antonio, Texas 78228

Mailing Address
Post Office Box 28185
San Antonio, Texas 78228
(512) 732-2156

The Mexican American Cultural Center was founded as a center of research, education, leadership formation, and publications dedicated to the liberation and integral development of the Latino Americano. It seeks to offer services to everyone regardless of race, color, or creed who is sincerely interested in working with the Hispanic community in the United States. The United States bishops have named MACC as a center of liturgical research. The preparation of ministers and materials for the Hispanic community is accomplished through the Pastoral and Leadership Institute, the Language and Communications Institute, and the Publications Department. Special programs are conducted throughout the year; Spanish language, pastoral renewal in Spanish, short term pastoral courses in English and Spanish;

intensive theological study weeks; a 7-month language and theological course for seminarians; Christian leadership training, and others. By request, staff members serve dioceses through workshops and seminars.

Staff: 42

Publications:
Visión, 3 times a year
A weekly newsletter

Meetings:
Numerous conferences, workshops, meetings, and workshops conducted by facilitators throughout the United States, Canada, Mexico, South Pacific, and Europe

945. Mexican Mission Ministries, Inc.

Nondenominational
Rev. Walter Gomez, President
Post Office Box 636
Pharr, Texas 78577
(512) 787-3543

The main purpose of the Mexican Mission Ministries is to establish indigenous local churches pastored by Bible-believing men trained in the Ministries' seminary or through Theological Education by Extension. This is done by visitation, youth work, jail work, film work, Bible bookstore, Pioneer Girls, Boys' Brigade, medical work, etc. The work is basically evangelistic in nature.

Founding Date: 1954

Publications:
Prayer/newsletter, bimonthly

Radio/TV Programs:
A weekly one 5-minute program broadcast over six stations in the United States

Meetings:
One missionary workshop and retreat for the staff and missionaries annually

Former Name: (1971) Mexican Militant Mission

946. Midwest Hebrew Ministries

Nondenominational
Earl Werner, Director
Robert Peterson, Chairman of the Board
4600 West 77th Street
Minneapolis, Minnesota 55435
(612) 831-0284

The Midwest Hebrew Ministries was founded by Rev. V. L. Peterson, Julia Solverude-Knutson, and a Board with a concern for sharing Messiah with Jewish people. Its ministries include: the distribution of letters, literature, and *Witnessing Packets* to Jewish people, churches, and concerned Christians; a radio ministry broadcasting the *Jewish-Gentile Fellowship Program;* Bible studies in homes, office areas, and churches; a literature table at the University of Minnesota; and a staff outreach program ministering to individuals and churches.

Founding Date: 1942

Staff: 2

Membership: 16

Publications:
Herald of Zion, quarterly

Radio/TV Programs:
Radio, Sunday AM at 9:30 on KTCR in Minneapolis and St. Paul

Meetings:
Annual prophetic conference
Meetings in churches, home Bible studies, luncheons, etc., approximately 400 per year

Former Name: Midwest Hebrew Mission

947. Migrant/Field Ministry*

National Council of Churches

Rev. Lucius Walker, Jr., Northeast Director
475 Riverside Drive, Room 572
New York, New York 10027
(212) 870-2387

The Migrant/Field Ministry program coordinates local, state, and national group activities centered on the concerns of migratory/seasonal agricultural laborers, the rural poor, and persons victimized by urban crisis. Special attention is given to health problems, education, and employment needs. This office convenes regional meetings of church staff working on these and related issues. It is a program of the Division of Church and Society.

Meetings:
2 or 3 per year

948. Military Chaplains Association of the United States of America (MCA)

Interdenominational

Chaplain E. J. Kingsley, Col. USAF Ret., Executive Director
7758 Wisconsin Avenue
Blackwell Building, #401
Bethesda, Maryland 20014
(301) 657-4077

The Military Chaplains Association of the United States of America represents approximately 10,000 chaplains, including reserve, retired, and former chaplains. It is the professional association for military chaplains of all religious faiths, in all branches of the Armed Forces, the Veterans Administration, and Civil Air Patrol. It is a non-profit agency that facilitates professional growth and fellowship across ecumenical patterns and interdenominational participation. The Association sponsors an annual Institute that combines professional growth workshops and annual convention-type business, such as elections and reports. It serves as the medium for chaplain ministry-sharing across the military services and with the Veterans Administration. It coordinates the activities of some 20 local chapters with regional Area Vice Presidents in the United States and overseas.

Founding Date: 1925

Staff: 2

Membership: 1,950

Publications:
The Military Chaplain, bimonthly
Annual promotional brochures

Meetings:
One annual meeting known as Institute in April at various locations
Conferences of local chapters 4-9 times a year
Professional workshops occasionally

Former Name:
(1940) Chaplains' Association of the Army of the United States of America

949. Minnesota Bible Fellowship, Inc.*

Nondenominational

Executive Board
Post Office Box 8295
Minneapolis, Minnesota 55408
(612) 729-4133

The Minnesota Bible Fellowship distributes free Christian literature in 76 foreign countries. Its recipients include Bible schools, seminaries, libraries, hospitals, prisons, missionaries, military personnel, pastors, evangelists, and others engaged in Christian work. Members of the Fellowship gather used and out-of-date new stocks of Bibles, Christian books, and Sunday School material and prepare it for shipment. They send as many as 2,500 packages a month to countries around the world.

Founding Date: 1962

Membership: 112

Publications:
Members publish books
Newsletter, three times a year

Radio/TV Programs:
A 13-week radio program

Meetings:
Conduct pastors' and laymen's training seminars
Meetings in secondary and high schools, seminaries, Bible schools, prisons and military establishments, covering about three areas a year

950. Mission Doctors Association

Roman Catholic

Herbert Sorensen, President
Msgr. Lawrence O'Leary, Spiritual Director
1531 West 9th Street
Los Angeles, California 90015
(213) 388-8101

Mission Doctors Association is a non-profit, lay, Catholic organization incorporated in the State of California. The Honorary Chairman is Cardinal Timothy Manning. The organization was founded by Msgr. Anthony J. Brouwers, and is directed by volunteer doctors who serve on the Board of Directors and are advised by returnee Mission Doctors throughout the United States. The purpose of the organization is to recruit, screen, prepare, and send volunteer Catholic doctors to serve in mission lands for a period of two to three years.

951. Mission Services Association

Church of Christ—Christian Churches

Eddie Berndt, Executive Director
Post Office Box 177
Kempton, Indiana 46049
(317) 947-5127

Mission Services Association has provided printing and mailing needs for over 2,000 missionaries. It sponsors the Mid-America Missionary Conference each April; it also prints a magazine to keep its churches updated and informed about worldwide missions, including their program material, slide and tape programs, and available missionary speaker lists. The Association publishes an up-to-date missionary directory of church-sent missionaries, their forwarding agents, Bible colleges, Christian homes and institutions, worldwide maps, and Christian literature and supplies. Mission Services Association is an information center in the growing Christian mission work.

Founding Date: 1946

Staff: 14

Publications:
Horizons
Missionary-type books and newsletters

Meetings:
4 meetings each year

Former Name: (1957) Mission to Youth, Inc.

952. Missionaries of Our Lady of the Prairies

Roman Catholic

Rev. Dr. Frederic J. Nelson, Superior General
Powers Lake, North Dakota 58773
(701) 464-5458

The purpose of the Missionaries of Our Lady of the Prairies is to promote devotion to the Blessed Virgin Mary, particularly under the title of Our Lady of the Prairies; to protect and defend the doctrines and morals of the Holy Roman Catholic Church and to uphold the teaching Magisterium of the Church; to promote the authentic religious life as conceived by the religious orders of history, and approved, commanded, and promoted by the Holy See; to educate youth in these same ideals; to care for the aged; and to operate and staff a National Shrine where all may come to participate in these purposes and/or make retreats and pilgrimages.

Staff: 50

Membership: 10

Publications:

The Maryfaithful, bimonthly newspaper-magazine

Radio/TV Programs:

The Marian Hour Radio Rosary Broadcast, weekly for 28 years

Meetings:

International Pilgrimage at the National Shrine of Our Lady of the Prairies, Powers Lake, North Dakota on the Sunday closest to August 15th.

953. Missionary Association of Catholic Women, Inc.*

Roman Catholic

Mrs. Joseph Gockel, President
1425 North Prospect Avenue
Milwaukee, Wisconsin 53202
(414) 276-5957

The Missionary Association of Catholic Women, Inc., is a Pontifical Society. Its objectives are to lend financial support to home and foreign missions; to prepare altar linens, vestments, garments, quilts, and other mission needs; and to distribute all these mission supplies in missionary countries throughout the world, regardless of race, color, or creed. The work of the Association is carried on by branches established in the various parishes throughout the United States. These branches consist of members who aid the missions financially, sew for mission needs, collect clothing, etc. and ship these through the Association.

Founding Date: 1914

954. Missionary Aviation Fellowship (MAF)

Nondenominational

Charles T. Bennett, President
1849 Wabash Avenue
Redlands, California 92373

Mailing Address
Post Office Box 202
Redlands, California 92373
(714) 794-1151

Some 35 years ago, during World War II, several Christian missionary airmen saw the airplane as a possible tool for extending the Gospel to remote places. They tried it. It worked. Small airplanes were warmly received as they speeded Christian and humanitarian work into remote areas of the world. They took missionaries and national pastors off the mule and out of the dugout canoes, saving days, months, years of productive time. Church planting and growth took place more rapidly. Aerial ambulance services saved lives. Emergency relief flights following natural disasters relieved much suffering and spared the lives of many. Planes added a whole new dimension. MAF service centers around the transportation and communication needs of the church. The mission's primary function is to meet this need by providing aircraft and competent pilots to fly them. The Fellowship applies its resources basically in two ways. The first has to do with the building of the church of Jesus Christ, giving every person an opportunity — understandable in the light of his own culture — to accept Jesus Christ as Saviour and Lord. The second has to do with the relief of human suffering. Services are available to all without regard to denomination. At present there are over 150 mission and church agencies served by MAF. A staff of more than 170 families now operate some 85 aircraft in nearly a score of countries.

Founding Date: 1944

Staff: 173 staff families

Publications:

Mission Aviation, quarterly
The Intercessor, monthly
Briefings for Praise and Prayer, monthly

Radio/TV Programs:

One TV special shown in selected areas of the United States

Meetings:

Conferences for membership only

Also Known As: Mission Aviation Fellowship

Former Names:

(1947) Christian Airmen's Missionary Fellowship
(1973) Missionary Aviation Fellowship

955. Missionary Cenacle Apostolate (MCA)

Roman Catholic

Joan Stanton, General Custodian
3501 Solly Avenue
Philadelphia, Pennsylvania 19136

The Missionary Cenacle Apostolate is the lay branch of the Missionary Cenacle family, comprised of the Missionary Servants of the Most Blessed Trinity, and The Blessed Trinity Missionary Institute. It is a Christian community founded under the inspiration of Father Thomas A. Judge, CM, to help members aid one another in response to the invitation of the church to share more fully in the priestly and prophetic life of Christ, and to participate in the church's mission not only to preach Christ and His love and grace to men, but also to bring the secular order to perfection by permeating it with the spirit of the Gospel message. Apostolic endeavors include helping to meet the physical, spiritual, and social needs of all God's people, especially the poor and abandoned. Much of the apostolic work is done in the providence of the members' daily lives.

Membership: 500

Publications:

MCA Newsletter, quarterly

Meetings:

Quarterly retreats
National inter-regional meetings twice yearly
Local meetings monthly
Seminars and workshops as needed

956. The Missionary Church, Division of Home Ministries

The Missionary Church

Rev. William E. Hesse, Director of Home Ministries
3901 South Wayne Avenue
Fort Wayne, Indiana 46807
(219) 744-1291

The Division of Home Ministries is responsible for coordinating and promoting the interests of the Missionary Church throughout the church in North America in such areas as evangelism, church planting, Christian education, social concerns, use of the media, and other areas as approved by the General Board or General Conference. The Division functions through a Board of Home Ministries and an Executive Director. The Division oversees the work of the Department of Educational Ministries, which is comprised of three age levels—children, youth, and adult—each having its own part-time director.

Founding Date: 1969

Staff: 8

Meetings:

2 annual meetings of the Board

957. The Missionary Church, Division of Overseas Missions

The Missionary Church

Eugene Ponchot, Director of Overseas Missions
3901 South Wayne Avenue
Fort Wayne, Indiana 46807
(219) 744-1291

The Division of Overseas Missions of The Missionary Church is primarily concerned with the church's activities in Brazil and Ecuador in South America; Nigeria and Sierra Leone in West Africa; Dominican Republic, Haiti, and Jamaica in the Caribbean; France; and Eastern India. There are also several staff members serving under other mission agencies in other parts of the world. The Division has never considered itself an "institutional" mission but rather has given itself to the planting and growth of churches in the several areas of ministry.

Founding Date: 1969

Staff: 114 missionaries

Membership:

21,000 overseas, plus another 18,000 adherents

Publications:

Emphasis, denominational magazine which includes articles from overseas fields

Radio/TV Programs:

134 programs per week overseas

958. The Missionary Church, Publications Committee

The Missionary Church

Mr. Richard Bagshaw, Director of Publications
Bethel Publishing Company
1819 South Main Street
Elkhart, Indiana 46514
(219) 293-8585

It is the responsibility of the Publications Committee, Missionary Church, Inc., to establish policy, accomplish long-range planning, and to provide overall supervision of the publication interests of the Missionary Church. This includes the publication/distribution of the official denominational organ, *Emphasis on Faith and Living;* selection and approval of Sunday school literature; decisions concerning new publications; and the overall operation of the Bethel Publishing Company and its four retail outlets.

Founding Date: 1903

Staff: 49

Publications:

> *Amish Cook Book*
> NIV tapes
> *Merging Streams,* a history of the Missionary Church

959. The Missionary Church, Women's Missionary Society

The Missionary Church
Mrs. Hilda M. Brenneman, President
3901 South Wayne Street
Fort Wayne, Indiana 46807
(219) 744-1291

As an auxiliary of the Missionary Church, the purpose of the Women's Missionary Society is threefold: 1) to assist in the overseas program of the church; 2) to reach out in the community; 3) fellowship and edification of ladies in the Society. To reach these goals, district and local conventions and workshops are organized and conducted for the purpose of spiritual growth, a challenge to help others, and leadership training. The local church has a chapter which meets monthly for prayer, study, fellowship, and promotion of the denominational activities. The Society strongly supports the overseas work of the church by the many projects which are selected at an annual meeting of officers and district presidents. The projects include support of missionaries and specific needs from the overseas budget. Many of the districts and local chapters help finance needs in their own communities.

Membership: 5,000

Publications:

> *Tabloid,* monthly
> Project folder and directory, annually

Meetings:

> Annual Board Meeting at the headquarters
> Rallies annually in the various districts
> Retreats held annually in many states and Canada

960. The Missionary Dentist, Inc. (Worldwide Dental Health Service, Inc.)

Interdenominational
Dr. Ernest E. Easley, Chairman
Dr. Vaughn V. Chapman, Director
20065 10th, N.W.
Seattle, Washington 98133
Mailing Address
Post Office Box 7002
Seattle, Washington 98133
(206) 546-1200

The Missionary Dentist is an interdenominational recruiting and sending agency evangelizing, cooperating with evangelical missions, and providing various dental health services by licensed professional individuals. Overseas personnel are generally only partially supported by the agency.

Founding Date: 1950

Publications:

> *News Report*
> *Prayer Bulletin,* bimonthly
> *Prayer Focus*

Meetings:

> Annual Overseas Training Seminar, approximately 2 weeks, held in Seattle

961. Missionary Electronics, Inc.

Nondenominational
James R. Ford, President
1061 North Shepard, Unit D
Anaheim, California 92806
(714) 630-0600

The purpose of Missionary Electronics is to develop teaching aids for missionaries for use in developing nations. In India, the organization developed and assisted nationals to produce an inexpensive cassette player for cassette evangelism. This outreach ministry has now progressed to include a church planting program. Missionary Electronics has developed a battery-free cassette player for missions' use. The player is designed to be easily manufactured in developing nations. The organization desires to acquire mission groups as partners to join in the manufacture of this device and the development of a effective cassette ministry in Africa, South America, and Asia-Pacific. The Missionary Electronics' technology and the partners' existing work and funds would join to be an effective tool in many countries to reach many for Christ. Publications are available for interested groups for further information.

Founding Date: 1948

Publications:

News from Missionary Electronics, 6 times per year

Appeal letter 6 times per year

Various technology profiles

Meetings:

Meetings in Anaheim as needed

Developing a training seminar for the manufacture of the battery-free cassette player

962. Missionary Gospel Fellowship, Inc. (MGF)

Protestant (Interdenominational)

Rev. Alfred J. Pratt, General Director

200 West Main Street

Turlock, California 95380

Mailing Address

Drawer W

Turlock, California 95380

(209) 634-8575

The Missionary Gospel Fellowship was organized under the direction of Paul J. Pietsch as a faith home mission society for the purpose of giving the Gospel of Christ to the migrants in the Farm Labor Supply Centers, principally in California and adjacent areas. It is interdenominational in its organization, ministry, and fellowship and was incorporated in 1942 to become a mission with diversified fields of service in addition to the work among the migrant workers. The MGF missionaries can now be found in the fertile valleys of the West Coast, ministering to the migrant population; in the desert regions of the Southern States, working with American Indians and Braceros; in the North-Central States, carrying on a year-round camping program with others involved in inter-city ministries; in the sub-tropical area of the Southeast, working with American blacks, migrants, and men from the West Indies; as well as in Hawaii ministering to the Orientals and Polynesians. The MGF ministries include the following: church planting, Sunday schools, Bible clubs, youth work, release-time classes, recreation, summer camps,

Spanish radio broadcast, scripture and tract distribution, and hospital chaplaincy.

Founding Date: 1939

Staff: 10

Membership: 75 missionaries

Publications:

The Fellowship Bulletin

Radio/TV Programs:

A Spanish Gospel radio broadcast

Meetings:

Two annual conferences; two mid-year meetings

Former Name: Migrant Gospel Fellowship

963. Missionary Information Exchange

Nondenominational

Robert Byrum Hicks, Executive Director

23225 Berkley

Oak Park, Michigan 48237

(313) 541-3688

The purpose of Missionary Information Exchange is to gather information which is deemed useful for missionaries, mission stations, agencies, hospitals, and the like. Selected medical, scientific, technical, agricultural, and other pertinent information is published and mailed to interested recipients. The Exchange also maintains a Christian literature and tract distribution ministry.

Founding Date: 1966

Staff: 5

Publications:

The Beacon, semiannually

964. Missionary Internship, Inc.

Nondenominational

Charles J. Mellis, Director

Post Office Box 457

Farmington, Michigan 48024

(313) 474-9110 or (313) 474-9111

Missionary Internship is an educational organization which exists to facilitate the development and orientation of Christian men and women for cross-cultural service, and to apply its resources to the missionary task of the Church. Missionary Internship offers pre-field orientation programs, language acquisition technique preparation, and furloughing missionary programs which strengthen ministry and communication skills for cross-cultural service. An eight-month comprehensive developmental program combines ministry in a local church with periodic workshops to provide career service preparation. Other workshops have included Theological Education by Extension, Women in Missions, and annual personnel workshops for the member missions of the Evangelical Foreign Missions Association and the Interdenominational Foreign Missions Association. Approximately three hundred men and women receive orientation for service each year.

Founding Date: 1952

Staff: 14

Publications:
Focus, quarterly

Meetings:
4 conferences per year

965. Missionary Literature Distributors*

Grace Gospel Fellowship

Mr. Rollie Phipps, Director
7514 Humbert Road
Godfrey, Illinois 62305
(618) 466-3704

Missionary Literature Distributors was founded by Mr. Rollie Phipps of Alton, Illinois. Its objective is to collect good Christian literature to be shipped to Christians in many parts of the world where economic conditions make it difficult to obtain such material.

Founding Date: 1957

966. Missionary Men International

The Missionary Church

Larry L. Wagner, President
26271 CR 50
Nappanee, Indiana 46550
(219) 773-4564

The Missionary Men International is an auxiliary organization of The Missionary Church. Its purpose is to foster fellowship among the men of the denomination; to promote evangelism by personal soul-winning; and to give active support to the home and foreign work in keeping with the objectives and policies of the denomination, and in correlation with the respecitve divisions and departments.

Founding Date: 1969

Meetings:
A denomination-wide meeting every two years in conjunction with the General Conference of the Missionary Church
Occasional meetings and/or retreats are held by the men of a local church or district

967. Missionary Society of St. James the Apostle

Roman Catholic

Rev. George F. Emerson, Director
24 Clark Street
Boston, Massachusetts 02109
(617) 742-4715

The St. James Society was founded by Richard Cardinal Cushing of Boston at the request of Pope Pius XII to help provide diocesan priests for service in South America. In the past 20 years over 260 diocesan priest missionaries have served in the Society's 27 parishes and seven dioceses of the countries of Peru, Ecuador, and Bolivia. They have come from the United States, Great Britain, Ireland, Canada, Australia, and New Zealand. Each volunteer gives a minimum of five years to the Church of Latin America before returning to his home diocese, where, in many instances, he becomes involved in pastoral service to primarily Spanish-speaking parishioners. In South America, the diocesan priest missionary cooperates with the local bishop in pastoral service to the poor and in collaborative response to pressing human needs through cooperatives, clinics, schools, and leadership training, among others.

Founding Date: 1959

Membership: 77

Radio/TV Programs:
One member of the Society serves as director of PROSAN (Producciones Santiago Apostol) in Lima, Peru that provides regular church news and worship service programs for numerous radio stations throughout Peru

Meetings:
An annual meeting for all members at St. James Society Center House, in Lima, Peru

968. Missionary Tape and Equipment Supply

Nondenominational

James W. Gilley, President
2826 East Centerville Road
Garland, Texas 75040
(800) 527-3458

The purpose of this organization is to supply at the very best prices tapes, recorders, and duplicators to Christian ministries.

Membership: 31

Publications:
Catalogue

969. Missions Advanced Research and Communications Center (MARC)

World Vision

Samuel Wilson, PhD, Director
919 West Huntington Drive
Monrovia, California 91016
(213) 357-7979 or (213) 357-1111

Missions Advanced Research and Communications Center has as its principal purpose enabling the evangelization of the world. This is accomplished by enhancing strategy development through the gathering and dissemination of needed information and through preparation of training materials. It is related internally to the evangelism and leadership personnel of World Vision International and externally to agencies and individuals active for the proclamation of the Kingdom.

Founding Date: 1966

Staff: 9

Publications:
Newsletter, bimonthly
Papers, workbooks
Position papers and training aids

970. Missions, Inc.

Nondenominational

Richard L. Shope, President-Executive Director
Zion Road, R.D. 5
Bellefonte, Pennsylvania 16823
(814) 355-7419

Missions, Inc., publishes and distributes missionary newsletters. The letters are designed to provide necessary contact between missionaries and their supporters. While the letters are distributed primarily in the United States and Canada, they are also used throughout the world.

Founding Date: 1959

971. Moody Bible Institute (MBI)

Nondenominational

George Sweeting, President
820 North La Salle Street
Chicago, Illinois 60610
(312) 329-4000

Moody Bible Institute trains Christians for a broad spectrum of Christian service. MBI's Educational Division operates day, evening and summer schools with more than 3,500 students. MBI's Correspondence School provides instruction to more than 110,000 persons. MBI utilizes the printed word through a publishing house, Moody Press; a monthly magazine, *Moody Monthly;* and Moody Literature Mission, a funding and distribution channel. Through its Extension Department, MBI sponsors conferences, seminars, and other special meetings. Moody Institute of Science produces educational science films with a distinctive Christian flavor. The Moody Literature Mission produces and distributes millions of pieces of Christian literature in more than 100 languages for use in nearly 120 countries each year.

Founding Date: 1886

Staff: 710

Membership: 42,000

Publications:
Moody Monthly Magazine
Fellowship Report Newsletter
Moody Student Newspaper

Radio/TV Programs:
Moody Bible Institute owns 11 radio stations, and distributes 115 programs to 320 radio stations

Meetings:
4 per year on Chicago Campus
16 per year at Keswick Conference in St. Petersburg, Florida

972. Moody Institue of Science, A Division of Moody Bible Institute

Nondenominational

Dr. George Sweeting, President
Moody Bible Institute
12000 East Washington Boulevard
Whittier, California 90606
(213) 698-8256

The Moody Institute of Science produces and distributes audio-visual materials in various languages for the purposes of evangelism, church planting, and Christian education. These materials are currently available in 22 languages and are being used in over 120 countries around the world by both nationals and missionaries.

Founding Date: 1945

Staff: 40

Radio/TV Programs:
Produce 16mm motion pictures that have been used as television program material both in the United States and other parts of the world

973. Morality in Media

Interdenominational

Morton A. Hill, SJ, President
475 Riverside Drive
New York, New York 10115
(212) 870-3222

Morality in Media is working to stop the traffic in pornography constitutionally and effectively, and working for media based on love, truth and taste. It maintains the National Obscenity Law Center.

Founding Date: 1962

Staff: 13

Membership: 46,500

Publications:
Newsletter, 8 time a year
Obscenity Law Bulletin, 6 times a year

Former Name: (1968) Operation Yorkville

974. Moravian Church in America, Board of World Mission

Moravian

Theodore F. Hartmann, Executive Director
Post Office Box 1245
Bethlehem, Pennsylvania 18018
(215) 868-1732

The Board of World Mission is the agency of the Moravian Church in America responsible for its overseas ministry in Alaska, Honduras, Nicaragua, Guyana, American Virgin Islands, Antigua, St. Kitts, Barbados, Trinidad and Tobago, the Dominican Republic, and Tanzania. The board sends out American missionaries who serve directly under the national leaders of the Moravian churches in the areas mentioned above. These overseas churches are completely autonomous and set their own policies for ministry. Their ministries include preaching, teaching, healing, and social concern. Specialized personnel are sent from America and nationals are brought to America for special events and training. Most of the theological training is done in the area where these overseas churches are located and in their culture. Additional training is given in America for selected persons as recommended by their national boards. The church has been involved in overseas ministries since 1732. The board also cooperates with ecumenical groups to provide specialized help as requested and needed.

Founding Date: 1949

Staff: 4

Publications:
North American Moravian

Meetings:
Meetings are held in conjunction with other Moravian Church institutions

975. Morehouse-Barlow Company, Inc.

Episcopal

Ronald C. Barlow, President
78 Danbury Road
Wilton, Connecticut 06897
(203) 762-0721

Morehouse-Barlow publishes and sells curriculum materials for the Episcopal Church and other Christian denominations. In addition to Church School materials, the company also provides general books, church bulletins, gifts and awards, Bible story books for children, cassettes, church register books, record forms, and other church supplies.

Staff: 27

Publications:

> *The Readiness for Religion* series
> *The Episcopal Church Fellowship* series
> Many individual titles

976. Morris Cerullo World Evangelism

Nondenominational

Morris Cerullo, President
Post Office Box 700
San Diego, California 92138
(714) 232-0161

Morris Cerullo World Evangelism is a worldwide "ministry of caring" which expresses itself in a sevenfold outreach. Dr. Cerullo conducts overseas missionary evangelistic crusades which often draw as many as 200,000 people to a single service; he conducts ministers' training institutes both in North America and overseas; he sponsors national evangelists' crusades overseas; has an Israel outreach; he publishes a magazine and other periodicals as well as evangelical books; he produces television specials; and he is Founder-President of the Morris Cerullo School of Ministry in San Diego, California, which trains nationals from around the world in the keys of effective evangelism.

Founding Date: 1961

Publications:

> *Deeper Life Magazine,* 10 issues a year
> *It's Happening Now,* a prophetic newsletter published monthly
> Inspirational and motivational Christian books, approximately 40 titles in print

Radio/TV Programs:

> TV specials in the form of docu-dramas, an hour long, shown nationwide once a year

Meetings:

> Approximately 18 per year

977. Mott Media

Nondenominational

George Mott, President
1000 East Huron Street
Milford, Michigan 48042
(313) 685-8773

Mott Media is a Christian evangelical publishing house whose primary thrust is the development and production of educational materials for Christian schools — elementary, high school, and college — and teachers and professionals. The secondary thrust is the publication and distribution of religious trade books of general interest — biographies and skills books particularly — with an educational purpose. It is a member of the Evangelical Christian Publishers Association and associate member of the Christian Booksellers Association.

Staff: 12

Publications:

> *Teacher's Bookshelf*
> *Pastor's Bookshelf*
> 35 religious trade book titles
> Religious book titles
> *A Christian Approach to Literature Studies* (teacher and student guides)

978. Mount Carmel Center

Palmarian Catholic

James R. McDonald, Captain, White Army
Post Office 356
Santa Rosa, California 95402
(707) 795-4041

Mount Carmel Center disseminates literature on contemporary Marian apparitions from various worldwide locations and conducts or sponsors lectures on these subjects. Activities are project-oriented, with participants and other volunteers recruited according to the subject.

Meetings:

> Frequent meetings, no regular schedule

979. Mount Hermon Christian Conference Center

Nondenominational
Edward L. Hayes, PhD, Executive Director
Post Office Box 413
Mount Hermon, California 95041
(408) 335-4466

Mount Hermon Christian Conference Center is a non-profit, interdenominational, evangelical arm of the church. The staff is dedicated to serving families, individuals, and the church through year-round programming. Mount Hermon consists of three separate resident facilities: The Conference Center — adult and family ministries for 500-700; Ponderosa Lodge — Senior High, College, and Single Adult ministries for 200; and Redwood Camp — Junior and Junior High camping for 150. Sierra Treks, a backpacking, rock-climbing, wilderness program in the Sierra Nevada mountains and elsewhere, is a satellite ministry. In the summer, Mount Hermon operates as a Christian family resort with all camp and conference activities open to any interested person. September to June, facilities are available to evangelical groups wishing to do their own programming. In addition, Mount Hermon programs weekends and a few midweeks for couples, pastors, single adults, youth, and Christian writers.

Founding Date: 1906

Staff:
>50 full-time
>220 summer students
>80 plus part-time (mostly for winters)

Publications:
>*Mount Hermon Log*, bimonthly
>*Upfront*, quarterly

Radio/TV Programs:
>One weekly radio program in summer
>Tapes sent nationwide for radio use throughout the year

Meetings:
>73 camps and/or conferences of its own planning
>300 plus guest conferences and camps by others
>Meetings of the Board of Directors monthly
>Advisory Committee meetings biannually
>A Boards and Administrative Staff Retreat annually
>Full Time Staff Retreat semi-annually
>Full Time Staff meetings every other week

980. Movement for a Better World* (MBW)

Roman Catholic
Post Office Box H
Far Rockaway, New York 11691
(201) 871-1620

The Movement for a Better World seeks to bring together bishops, clergy, religious, and laity of all ages and vocations in living community to share in dialogue and prayer. It's a movement at the service of the entire Church, geared toward promoting a better understanding among all people concerning every aspect of life.

Membership: 7 lay; 9 sisters, 8 clergy

981. Movimiento Familiar Cristiano/USA (MFC/USA)*

Roman Catholic
6932 Thrush Street
Houston, Texas 77087
(713) 741-0658

Movimiento Familiar Cristiano/USA is a lay movement of Spanish speaking Catholic families (open to all Christian denominations) who join each other to promote the Christian values of family life. It fosters among its members: communication and dialogue betwen husband and wife and between parents and children; better understanding of the environment in which they find themselves; a realization of the problems of the community, and the will to bring about constructive change; and the development of a life style in accordance with the human and Christian values most appropriate for them in their particular circumstances.

Membership: 3,000 families; 80 clerical

Publications:
>3 formative books in Spanish and English
>2 in Spanish: *Encuentro Conyugal and Retorno Conyugal*
>2 in Spanish-English: *Family Encounter* and *Sons-Daughters Encounter*
>1 monthly Spanish bulletin

Meetings:
>1 National Convention every three years
>Regional: conventions, meetings, workshops as requested

982. Mu-ne-dowk Foundation, Inc.

Interdenominational

Carl Stoelting, President
13127 Lax Chapel Road
Kiel, Wisconsin 53042

Mailing Address
1311 Lax Chapel Road
Kiel, Wisconsin 53042
(414) 894-2339

Mu-ne-dowk Foundation, Inc., is non-profit and nondenominational. Its purpose is to promote spiritual and educational goals of seekers. It is governed by an active nine-member board of directors. The facilities are rented out to groups from churches, organizations or groups interested in furthering their growth. Mu-ne-dowk sponsors seminars on the average of eight times a year. They have guest speakers from all phases of life speaking on various subjects to help those of all beliefs.

Founding Date: 1967

Staff: 10

Membership: 47

Publications:
> *Crystal Light,* monthly

Meetings:
> Eight sponsored per year, weekends
> Rented out, 20 per year, weekends

983. The Mustard Seed, Inc.*

Nondenominational

Mrs. Lillian R. Dickson, Founder/President
1377 East Colorado Street
Glendale, California 91205
(213) 241-3811

The Mustard Seed, Inc., is a non-profit interdenominational organization, serving wherever there is need. Its vast and diversified ministries include: fifteen prison chaplains; fourteen children's homes; home for pre-wed mothers; adoption agency for placing unwanted babies; Christian Teacher's Training School in Kalimantan, South Borneo for the Dyak (Iban) people — (four tribes pastors from Taiwan serve as missionaries in Sarawak, working among the Dyaks in a tribes-to-tribes ministry); three vocational schools and four community centres in the highlands of Papua, New Guinea; 10 free clinics, three TB

sanitariums and two maternity wards in Taiwan, along with Christian hostels, reading rooms, and church kindergartens (about 2,270 in the mountain churches).

Publications:
> Has had translated and published in Chinese some books, all Christian
> Report letter send to donors once a month

984. Nalanda Foundation

Nondenominational
Vajracarya the Venerable
Chögyam Trungpa Rinpoche, President
1111 Pearl Street
Boulder, Colorado 80302
(303) 444-0202

Nalanda Foundation is a secular, non-profit educational corporation. It consists of a number of agencies: the Naropa Institute, Shambala Training, the Mudra Theatre Group, Alaya Pre-school, Vidya Elementary School, the Shambala School of Dressage, and societies for the study of Zen archery, the Japanese tea ceremony, Imperial Japanese Dance, and the art of flower arranging. Naropa Institute, based in Boulder, Colorado, offers university level courses in art, religion, psychology, and Buddhist studies. It provides an environment in which Eastern and Western traditions interact, and in which they are grounded in the personal experiences of staff and students. All staff members are involved in the practice of some discipline related to psychological and spiritual growth. This forms a sound basis for integrating the intellectual and intuitive approaches to life. Shambala Training is a nonsectarian program in meditation practice and meditation in every day life. The teachings of Shambala Training have been preserved by a number of lineages and particularly by the Buddhist teachers of Tibet. They are taught in a series of week-end intensives, Shambala Training levels I-V, and Shambala graduate program levels, A-F. The Mudra Theatre Group (with groups in Boulder, New York, San Francisco, and Berkeley) is a continuing ensemble dedicated to the development of theatre techniques based on Buddhist psychological principles. The Nalanda Foundation is affiliated with Vajradhatu. The purposes of the former are secular, of the latter, religious.

Founding Date: 1972
Staff: 50
Publications:
Naropa Bulletin
Nalanda Foundation Bulletin
Numerous catalogues
Meetings:
30 in Boulder, Colorado and across America

985. Narramore Christian Foundation

Nondenominational
Clyde M. Narramore, President
1409 North Walnut Grove Avenue
Rosemead, California 91770
Mailing Address
Post Office Box 5000
Rosemead, California 91770
(213) 288-7000

The motto of the Narramore Christian Foundation is "every person is worth understanding." The purposes of the Foundation are: introducing people to Jesus Christ; encouraging people to grow through God's Word; helping people gain insights and resolve problems; and offering training to laymen and to Christian leaders. These services are accomplished through the following ministries: national radio broadcast (reaching millions daily); literature and monthly magazine (lasting, helpful booklets or articles); personal correspondence and telephoning (Immediate help for specific problems); missionary counseling services (screening, evaluating, and counseling ministers, missionaries, chaplains, and deans to improve counseling skills); seminar for lay people (one week at Rosemead for business, professional, and lay people to increase effectiveness); personal enrichment seminars (one day in local areas on practical help in daily living); personal enrichment clubs and classes (year long study and sharing groups in local communities and in church Sunday Schools); casssette tape messages (lasting help to changing lives); church bulletin inserts (monthly insights for congregations); films on Christian Home (church showing for family needs); and family financial consultation (planning for the future and helping the Lord's work).

Founding Date: 1958

Staff: 55

Membership: 30,000

Publications:
> *Psychology for Living,* monthly helpful articles on effective Christian living
> Newsletter: *The Foundation,* short articles on effective Christian living
> Booklets and pamphlets dealing with human problems from a psychological and spiritual viewpoint

Radio/TV Programs:
> Daily 15-minute radio program furnished to 186 radio stations for public service broadcasts
> One-half hour program furnished to individual and network TV stations for public service broadcast

Meetings:
> Rosemead: Business and Professional Seminar, three times a year; Ministers and Missionaries Seminar twice yearly; one seminar for educators a year; two seminars for parents a year; one Missionary Kids Seminar yearly; one Family Conference at New Year's
> Florida: one family conference annually at Lake Yale, Florida

986. National Academy for Adult Jewish Studies of the United Synagogue of America

Conservative Judaism
Rabbi Marvin S. Wiener, Director
155 Fifth Avenue
New York, New York 10010
(212) 533-7800

The National Academy for Adult Jewish Studies is the adult education arm of the United Synagogue of America. Its purpose is to encourage and promote adult learning, both formal and informal, in the synagogue and in the general Jewish community. Programs and services include: preparation and publication of textbooks, pamphlets, tracts, and study guides for use in adult institutes, home study and discussion groups; sponsorship of the El-Am Talmud Series, published in Israel, featuring the full original text with translation and commentaries in Engiish, together with biographical notes and illustrations; publication of the National Academy *Bulletin,* a newsletter for adult education chairmen, rabbis, and educators; distribution of 30- and 60-minute 16mm films, color and black-and-white, of the Eternal Light television programs on Jewish themes produced by the Jewish Theological Seminary of America in cooperation with the National Broadcasting Company; guidance and information on resources, courses, classes, and overall programs in adult Jewish education through publications, correspondence, conferences, and field service; cooperation with regions of the United Synagogue of America in planning educational projects; stimulation and fostering of Laymen's Institutes, Torah study sessions, and other projects in adult Jewish education; and promotion of regional adult education commissions to assist congregations in meeting national adult education standards.

Publications:
> 46 popular and scholarly books, dealing with all aspects of Judaism
> Bulletin, intermittently

Meetings:
> 3 each year

987. National Alliance of Czech Catholics*

Roman Catholic
2657-59 South Lawnsdale Avenue
Chicago, Illinois 60623
(312) 522-7575

The purpose of the National Alliance of Czech Catholics is to coordinate the Czech (Bohemian) Roman Catholic organizations with individuals of Czech birth or descent professing the Roman Catholic Faith, so that by their united action they may be more effective in matters of religious, civic, charitable, and educational activities throughout the United States.

988. National Assembly of Religious Brothers (NARB)*

Roman Catholic
9001 New Hampshire Avenue
Silver Spring, Maryland 20910

The National Assembly of Religious Brothers is a voluntary membership organization of religious Brothers from all orders. Activities include an annual meeting; publishing of a *Brothers Newsletter* and a *Brothers Bulletin;* liaison with other church groups; communications center for Brothers; and establishment of a national office for Brothers.

Membership: 600 religious Brothers

Publications:
    Scholarly, 3 paperbacks on *vows* and *priesthood, Brothers*
    Newsletter, quarterly
    Brothers Bulletin, occasionally
    Power and Authority

Meetings:
    1 annual national meeting of Brothers

989. National Assembly of Women Religious (NAWR)

Roman Catholic
Marjorie Tuite, OP, National Coordinator
1307 South Wabash
Chicago, Illinois 60605
(312) 663-1980

NAWR, The National Assembly of Women Religious, is a forum for grass roots sisters and a resource for information, support and training to assist them in living out their religious commitment. They organize locally (Councils/Senates/Units), regionally, and around issues (Committees and Task Forces). Members of NAWR believe that religious life is a sign of special consecration to God, to the Church and its mission, and that prayer, simplicity of life and ministry are means of expressing this consecration. NAWR seriously attempts to mobilize dedicated women religious for Gospel-inspired service to their Church and their nation, believing that their resources are among the most powerful which the Church and nation possess. NAWR steadily addresses concerns which include the most important issues facing America as it enters its third centenary.

Founding Date: 1971
Staff: 2
Membership: 1,400
Publications:
    Probe, bimonthly newspaper
Meetings:
    National convention, yearly

990. National Association of Boards of Education (NABE)

Roman Catholic
Mary-Angela Harper, PhD, Executive Director
1077 30th Street, N.W.
Washington, D.C. 10007
(202) 293-5954

The National Association of Boards of Education is a service department of the National Catholic Educational Association. NABE provides leadership at the national level to individuals who are committed to participatory decision-making in Catholic education and who seek current information, resources and formal means for supporting its implementation. NABE aims to give practical assistance in organizing new boards and education committees and to improve the performance quality of already established policymaking bodies; and to assist educational policymakers to identify and address the educational issues of our times, and to provide them with a national forum for expressing their concerns and articulating their insights regarding these issues. NABE services include workshops; a policy clearinghouse; and in-service training kits for Chief Administrators.

Founding Date: 1970
Staff: 2
Membership: 1,267
Publications:
    Policymaker, quarterly
    Ascent to Excellence in Catholic Education, by Mary-Angela Harper, PhD, a basic board resource book for Catholic educators
    NABE Cassette Series, complete training program on topics of ongoing concern, etc.
Meetings:
    Yearly meeting during Easter Week in conjunction with convention of the National Catholic Educational Association

991. National Association of Catholic Chaplains (NACC)

Roman Catholic

Rev. Timothy J. Toohey, Executive Director
3257 South Lake Drive
Milwaukee, Wisconsin 53207
(414) 483-4898

The National Association of Catholic Chaplains membership includes those who minister to the sick, the aged, and the imprisoned. The fundamental purposes of the NACC are to promote professionalism and to support persons in these diverse ministries. To assist the members to attain the realization of progressively higher ideals and professional competency, the objectives of the NACC are: to promote careful selection of pastoral persons for ministry in these specialized fields; to promote and coordinate the special education and training of professionals in accredited centers and institutions, as well as through national, regional, and local continuing education workshops and conferences; to encourage members to become qualified for certification by fulfilling the requirements established by the Board of Examiners, United States Catholic Conference; and to provide members with current information and literature concerning the integration of medicine and religion.

Founding Date: 1966

Staff: 3

Membership: 2,642

Publications:
Camillian, monthly

Meetings:
Annual convention

992. National Association of Christian Singles (NACS)

Nondenominational

Donald Davidson, Executive Director
Post Office Box 11394
Kansas City, Missouri 64112
(816) 763-9401

The purpose of the National Association of Christian Singles is to be a central clearing house for information on what is happening with singles. The Association disseminates that information in two publica-tions. For 1980, there are two membership divisions: NACS for Singles and NACS: Leadership.

Membership:
Members in over 45 states, exact number unknown

Publications:
Single i, monthly, designed to help the leaders of Christian singles' groups
Today's Single, quarterly

993. National Association of Church Business Administrators (NACBA)

Interdenominational

Mr. Floy Barnes, Executive Director
Post Office Box 7181
Kansas City, Missouri 64113
(913) 26-9571

The National Association of Church Business Administrators provides education and professional services to its members. It supports the ministry of administration in the local church, the denomination, and other manifestations of the church. It provides continuing support and encouragement toward a deepening and strengthening of the spiritual growth that would bring about a growing Christian maturity.

Founding Date: 1956

Membership: 650 active; 90 emeritus

Publications:
The NACBA Ledger, three times per year

Meetings:
Annual convention

994. National Association of Church Personnel Administrators (NACPA)

Mary Ann Barnhorn, SND, Executive Director
100 East Eighth Street
Cincinnati, Ohio 45202
(513) 421-3134

The National Association of Church Personnel Administrators helps with the management of the responsibilities of personnel assignments, adminis-tration, or ministry evaluation. NACPA provides opportunities for professional development, as well as the support of other women and men in Church related work. NACPA was established through the sponsorship of the National Federation of Priest's Councils and has provided quality service to church personnel directors for over ten years. NACPA publishes a newsletter, offers regional workshops, consultative and resource services and an annual convocation.

Founding Date: 1973

Staff: 17

Membership: 350

Publications:

Newsnotes, every 6 weeks, organizational newsletter
Newsletter, quarterly
Personnel Policies and Procedures, manual
Evaluation Needs and Assessment, manual
Cassette tapes

995. National Association of Diocesan Ecumenical Officers (NADEO)

Roman Catholic

Rev. Alex J. Brunett, President
17500 Farmington Road
Livonia, Michigan 48152
(313) 425-5950

The objectives of the National Association of Diocesan Ecumenical officers are: to stimulate an exchange of ideas, experiences, and evaluations among the ecumenical officers of the arch/dioceses in union with Rome; to promote programs which further the work of Christian unity and of interreligious cooperation; and to cooperate with the Bishops' Committee for Ecumenical and Interreligious Affairs of the National Conference of Catholic Bishops, and with other ecumenical and interreligious agencies.

Founding Date: 1976

Staff: 13

Membership:

184, all the Roman Catholic Dioceses in the United States

Publications:

The Lived Experience: A Survey of United States ARC Convenants
A Detailed Survey of Three Special Areas in the United States ARC Covenants
Educating for Unity: A Survey Concerning Diocesan Ecumenical Leadership
ARC Marriages: A Study of United States Couples Living Episcopal-Roman Catholic Marriages

Educating for Unity: A Survey Concerning Roman Catholic Seminary Education in the United States
Newsletter, quarterly

996. National Association of Ecumenical Staff

Nondenominational

Dr. Donald G. Jacobs, Executive Officer
475 Riverside Drive, Room 870
New York, New York 10027
(212) 870-2157

The National Association of Ecumenical Staff was established to provide creative relationships among persons serving in professional positions in the ecumenical ministry of the church, by enriching their fellowship as committed Christian workers in this specialized field, encouraging mutual support, and promoting personal and professional growth. Accordingly, the Association: mobilizes the creative energies of ecumenical staff for reflecting on critical concerns; devises strategies for addressing those concerns, mobilizes resources for achieving results, and enriches fellowship; develops standards and guidelines for identifying and responding to these concerns; arranges an annual conference for exchange of information, discussion of common concerns, devising of strategies, celebration, and training; provides communication for these purposes; and recruits personnel.

Founding Date: 1940

Membership: 300

Meetings:

Annual Convention

Former Name:

(1971) Association of Council Secretaries

997. National Association of Episcopal Schools (NAES)

Episcopal

The Rev. John D. Verdery, Directory
Ms. Susie Bennett, Executive Coordinator
815 Second Avenue
New York, New York 10017
(212) 867-8400 Ext. 298

The National Association of Episcopal Schools exists to help Episcopal schools promote the educational ministry of the Episcopal Church; to help strengthen the programs of those schools; to help those schools build strong communities of shared life and learning in the Christian faith; and to aid communication between the national Episcopal Church and its schools. The NAES provides some worship materials and resources geared specifically to the needs of Episcopal schools, publishes a Self-Study Manual to help schools examine and strengthen their total religious program, distributes promotional and interpretative literature (such as Episcopal School Week posters) designed to tell the Episcopal school story to the wider community; it holds a Triennial Conference on a national level and various smaller conferences from time to time, and provides a Directory of Episcopal Schools every three years, just prior to the Triennial Conference.

Founding Date: 1954

Membership: 300 schools

Publications:
NAES Newsletter, 3 times a year

Meetings:
Triennial conference (next one in 1984)

Former Name:
(1965) Episcopal School Association

998. National Association of Evangelicals

Interdenominational — Evangelical Protestant
Dr. Arthur Gay
450 East Gundersen Drive
Wheaton, Illinois 60187
(312) 665-0500

The National Association of Evangelicals is a voluntary association of evangelical denominations, churches, schools, organizations and individuals. It provides a positive identification, a united witness, and an extended outreach for its members. NAE provides consultation, regular and periodic publications, and a purchasing service for member churches and organizations. Throughout the year, seminars and workshops are scheduled in various parts of the nation. A reading program "Scriptures to Live by" is sponsored annually, as well as World Day of Prayer, NAE Sunday, WRC's Thanksgiving offering, Washington Leadership Briefing, Washington Student Seminar, and the national Convention. As occasion demands, NAE conducts special campaigns and projects. NAE provides a wide range of ministries through its commissions and affiliates: The

Evangelical Foreign Mission Association, The National Association of Christian Schools, The National Religious Broadcasters, National Sunday School Association, Commission on Chaplains, Fellowship Commission, Evangelism and Home Missions Association, Evangelical Social Action Commission, Stewardship Commission, World Relief Commission.

Founding Date: 1942

Staff: 30

Membership:
3.5 million in member denominations, churches, schools; and as individuals

Publications:
NAE Washington Insight, monthly
United Evangelical Action, quarterly
Profile, quarterly newsreview
National Evangelical, biennial directory

Meetings:
State seminars (spring and fall) held across the country
Annual convention (once each spring)
Washington Insight Briefing (once each spring, Washington, D.C.)
Washington Federal Seminar (every other winter, Washington, D.C.)

999. National Association of Evangelicals, Commission on Chaplains

Interdenominational
450 East Gundersen Drive
Wheaton, Illinois 60187
(312) 665-0500

The National Association of Evangelicals Commission on Chaplains provides spiritual support and encouragement, plus ecclesiastical endorsement for evangelical chaplains.

1000. National Association of Evangelicals, Commission on Higher Education

Interdenominational
450 East Gundersen Drive
Wheaton, Illinois 60187
(312) 665-0500

The National Association of Evangelicals Commission on Higher Education serves as a medium for interaction and the probing of common problems such as financing, governmental regulation, etc. In addition, NAE's affiliated American Association of Evangelical Students is active in providing leadership, communication and resources to student governments in Christian colleges and individual membership to evangelical students in secular colleges.

1001. National Association of Evangelicals, Commission on Stewardship

Interdenominational

450 East Gundersen Drive
Wheaton, Illinois 60187
(312) 665-0500

The National Association of Evangelicals Stewardship Commission uses seminars, publications and special in-church activities in offering helps and guidelines for effective Christian stewardship. Also offering means for responsible stewardship, NAE's Universal Travel Service uses its commissions to support mission work, thus giving travelers opportunity to further the Lord's work with no extra charge. And the Evangelical Purchasing Service, also a service agency of NAE, makes the most of churches' and layworkers' limited resources by offering equipment and supplies at the lowest possible cost.

1002. National Association of Evangelicals, Evangelism and Home Missions Association (EHMA)

National Association of Evangelicals

450 East Gundersen Drive
Wheaton, Illinois 60187
(312) 665-0500

The purpose of the Evangelism and Home Missions Association is cooperative action to accelerate missions work in North America. EHMA interests include spiritual revival, evangelism/church growth, church planting and working among immigrants, underprivileged communities, prison inmates and foreign language groups.

1003. National Association of Evangelicals, Family Service

National Association of Evangelicals

450 East Gundersen Drive
Wheaton, Illinois 60187
(312) 665-0500

The Evangelical Child and Family Agency (ECFA) was formed when a group in Chicago tried to place children in worthy homes. It is part of the effort of the National Association of Evangelicals to support families. In 1956, an Evangelical Family Service was formed. Family Services. Cries for help from today's families and children have not gone unheeded. Through Evangelical Child and Family Agency, Evangelical Family Services, Inc., and Family Ministries, NAE offers family services and support systems with evangelical sensitivity. In 1981, the campaign "Save the Family" was designed to provide pastors and laypersons alike information and direction in meeting the spiritual needs of the American home today. Its aim was to counter the debilitating effects of secular humanism in the home by stating biblical positions regarding the family; by examining and exposing governmental legislation affecting the family; and by commissioning a special task force to speak out for biblical norms regarding marriage and the family.

1004. National Association of Evangelicals, National Christian Education Association (NCEA)

National Association of Evangelicals

450 East Gundersen Drive
Wheaton, Illinois 60187
(312) 665-0500

Through the National Christian Education Association evangelicals share in the coordination of ideas, programs and research that can improve the quality and effectiveness of "CE" efforts in Sunday Schools, youth programs, and Christian day schools. With an eye to Christian education and the church's role in strengthening individuals and families, NAE held its first National Congress on Christian Education in November 1978; and in 1981 announced a nationwide "Save the Family" campaign designed to provide pastors and laypersons alike information and direction in meeting the spiritual needs so apparent in the American home today.

Founding Date: 1946

Former Name:

Commission on a Christian Philosophy of Education

1005. National Association of Evangelicals, Social Action Commission

Interdenominational

450 East Gundersen Drive
Wheaton, Illinois 60187
(312) 665-0500

The ongoing task of the National Association of Evangelicals Social Action Commission is raising the awareness of evangelicals to the urgent social issues of our nation and the world. Research papers, seminars and examinations of workable models help bring meaningful responses by evangelical churches and organizations.

Founding Date: 1951

1006. National Association of Evangelicals, Washington Office of Public Affairs

Interdenominational

Bob Dugan, Director
1430 K Street, N.W., Suite 900
Washington, D.C. 20005
(202) 628-7911

The National Association of Evangelicals, Washington Office of Public Affairs is serving specifically as a liaison between its evangelical constituency and the lawmaking machinery on Capitol Hill, the office monitors pending legislation that may affect the ministry of local churches or touch some moral or spiritual issue. The office also endeavors to keep track of the volumes of federal regulations that have the potential of impacting evangelicals and upsetting the delicate balance of church and state. With its reliability and consistency proven over time, the Office of Public Affairs has positively produced individual participation in politics, rather than institutionalized participation. In addition to testifying before Congress, meeting with media people and speaking prophetically to evangelicals, the NAE

Washington office spends considerable time developing relationships and rapport with government officials.

Founding Date: 1942

Publications:

NAE Washington Insight, monthly

Radio/TV Programs:

Weekly radio program; TV slots

Meetings:

Washington Insight Briefing, annually
Washington Federal Seminar, every other year

1007. National Association of Free Will Baptists, Board of Home Missions*

National Association of Free Will Baptists

Rev. Robert L. Shockey, General Director
3328 Percy Priest Drive
Nashville, Tennessee 37214
(615) 361-1010

The Home Missions Board National Association of Free Will Baptists, is charged with the responsibility of promoting and maintaining home missionary work in accordance with the tenets and doctrines of the Free Will Baptists of the United States. It provides literature in the fields of home missions, evangelism, follow up, and the training of soul winners. Some of the materials available are: *Missions Grams* (a bimonthly report on all its missionaries and their activities), Home Missions Directories, prayer cards of missionaries, home mission maps, home missions survey or history, salvation tracts, survey information, follow up lessons, new convert packets, instructions for soul winners, and pastor's packets.

Publications:

Missions Grams, bimonthly

1008. National Association of Free Will Baptists, Foreign Missions Department

Free Will Baptist

Reverend Rolla D. Smith, General Director
1134 Murfreesboro Road
Nashville, Tennessee 37202

Mailing Address

Post Office Box 1088
Nashville, Tennessee 37202
(615) 361-1010

Free Will Baptist Foreign Missions is a denominational sending agency engaged in evangelism and training in strategic areas around the world. Missionaries are charged with the responsibility of evangelizing, establishing new converts in the faith, and then seeking to enlist them in a fellowship of indigenous Free Will Baptist Churches. They train pastors and evangelists to perpetuate this cycle until Christ returns.

Founding Date: 1935

Membership: 18 lay; 78 clerical

Publications:
> *Heartbeat,* bimonthly
> *Intercom,* quarterly
> Missionary newsletters

Radio/TV Programs:
> 3 radio programs

Meetings:
> 2 annual board meetings
> 1 annual retreat

1009. National Association of Free Will Baptists, Sunday School and Church Training Department

National Association of Free Will Baptists

Dr. Roger C. Reeds, General Director
114 Bush Road
Nashville, Tennessee 37217

Mailing Address
Post Office Box 17306
Nashville, Tennessee 37217
(615) 361-1221

The Sunday School and Church Training Department publishes a complete line of Sunday School and Church Training materials. They also have published approximately 90 books and booklets. The Department promotes growth in Sunday schools and training groups, and conducts training programs for teachers and prospective teachers.

1010. National Association of Free Will Baptists, Women's National Auxiliary Convention (WNAC)

Free Will Baptist

Mrs. Cleo Pursell
1134 Murfreesboro Road
Nashville, Tennessee 37202

Mailing Address
Post Office Box 1088
Nashville, Tennessee 37202
(615) 361-1010 Ext. 45

The purpose of the Women's National Auxiliary Convention is to assist the various bodies composing the WNAC in providing opportunities for women to understand and fulfill their responsibilities in the family, in the church, in the community, and around the world. The Convention provides literature and supplies; provides a program of work for local, district, and state groups; plans and coordinates the annual conventions, retreats, etc.; receives from state treasurers and other donors gifts to missions and/or missionary objectives, Bible Colleges, etc.; allocates the funds monthly to national missions boards; and maintains a student loan fund for Bible college students.

Membership: 9,000

Publications:
> *Co-Laborer,* quarterly
> *Communicator,* 3 times a year
> *The Minister's Wife,* an occasional publication

Meetings:
> Annual convention
> Annual retreat
> Assistance in numerous state conventions and retreats

1011. National Association of Jewish Homes for the Aged

Jewish

Dr. Herbert Shore, Executive Vice President
2525 Centerville Road
Dallas, Texas 75228
(214) 327-4503

The National Association of Jewish Homes for the Aged operates non-profit charitable Jewish homes, retirement or nursing homes, geriatric hospitals, and special facilities for Jewish aged and chronically ill; conducts institutes and conferences; undertakes legislative activities; and compiles statistics.

Founding Date: 1960

Membership: 105

Publications:
> Newsletter
> *Directory,* biennial

Meetings:
> Annual meetings in May or June
> Midyear Institute in January or February

1012. National Association of Laity (NAL)

Roman Catholic
Dr. Joseph T. Skehan, President
638 East Third Street
Bloomsburg, Pennsylvania 17815

National Association of Laity seeks to see implemented the mandates of the Second Vatican Council (1963-65) regarding the communal nature of the Church, the full role of the laity *(Actuositatem Apostolicam)* the end of discrimination based on race, sex, economic circumstance *(Gaudiam et Spes)* full financial accounting to the "people of God" by professional religious at all levels, and a reassessment of the role of human sexuality in the development of the person, and restudy of the handling on all directives on sexual and sexist matters.

Founding Date: 1967

Former Name: National Association of Laymen

1013. National Association of Lay Ministry Coordinators

Roman Catholic
Mr. Joseph Chamberlin, Chairperson of Executive Committee
320 Cathedral Street
Baltimore, Maryland 21218

Mailing Address
1031 Superior Avenue
7th Floor Balcony
Cleveland, Ohio 44114
(301) 547-5456

The National Association of Lay Ministry Coordinators is a membership organization formed to: promote the universal call to ministry; foster research and development within the field of lay ministry; support those involved in the work of lay ministry; and promote the profession of lay ministry within the church.

Founding Date: 1980

Membership: Approximately 125

Publications:
 Lay Ministry, 3 times a year

Meetings:
 Annual meeting in June of each year

1014. The National Association of Native Religious (NANR)*

Roman Catholic
Brother Lorenzo Martin, OFM, Coordinator
Post Office Box No. B
Fort Defiance, Arizona 86504
(602) 729-2684

The National Association of Native Religious was established by Brother Lorenzo Martin, OFM (Tribe: Navajo), Sr. Gloria Davis, SBS (Tribe: Navajo/Choctaw), Sr. Celestine Rivera, OSF (Tribe: Navajo/-Spanish), Sr. Mary Theresa Chato, SBS (Tribe: Navajo), Sr. Conchita Boyer, OSF (Tribe: Chippewa), Sr. Mary Rosita Shiosee, SBS (Tribe: Laguna/Jemez), and Sr. Juana Clare Jose, OSF (Tribe: Papago). It is a response to the need felt by native religious to know Jesus Christ, to give support and encouragement to each other spiritually, and to find ways of spreading the Gospel message of Jesus Christ more effectively.

Membership:
 54 clerical and religious
 30 associate members

Meetings:
 Annual meetings are conducted on Indian Reservations

1015. National Association of Parish Coordinators/Directors of Religious Education (NPCD)

Roman Catholic
Rev. Francis D. Kelly, Executive Director
Department of Religious Education,
National Catholic Educational Association
1077 30th Street, N.W.
Washington, D.C. 20007
(202) 293-5954

The National Association of Parish Coordinators/Directors of Religious Education, a service department of the National Catholic Educational Association, is composed of full-tiime, paid parish Directors of religious education programs who are approved as such by their diocesan office of religious education. It seeks to promote the development of this new role in Catholic parish structure and to further its professionalization. It seeks to keep its members abreast of new trends and ideas in religious education and engages in national advocacy for its members.

Founding Date: 1972

Staff: 2

Membership: 550

Publications:
Parish Coordinators/Directors of Religious Education Newsletter, four times year

Meetings:
An annual meeting, location varies

1016. National Association of Pastoral Musicians (NPM)

Roman Catholic

Rev. Virgil C. Funk, President and Executive Director
225 Sheridan Street, N.W.
Washington, D.C. 20011
(202) 723-5800

The National Association of Pastoral Musicians is a society of priests and musicians working together for the following purposes: to provide mutual support for practicing parish musicians through improved repertoire, increased knowledge of the role of music in the liturgy, and practical helps for effective participation in parish liturgical committee planning of music; to provide a forum for advocating musical excellence in liturgical celebrations; to provide a vehicle for disseminating evaluations of new and current musical selections; and to assist diocesan and parish-level efforts in improving the quality of, and interest in parish music. NPM addresses all forms of music: congregational, choir, cantor, hymns, chant, folk, and brass, organ, and guitar. It recognizes that parish musicians cover a wide spectrum, from volunteer and part-time to full-time, from beginner to experienced and well-trained. It acknowledges the tremendous variety of parishes: urban, rural, suburban; large and small; ethnic; affluent and impoverished. National Association of Pastoral Musicians was formerly the National Catholic Music Educators Association.

Founding Date: 1976

Staff: 6

Membership: 9,000

Publications:
Pastoral Music Magazine, 6 a year
Pastoral Musicians' Notebook
Newsletter, 6 a year; handbooks

Meetings:
12 regional conventions in even years
1 national convention in odd years

Workshops, seminars, frequent music study tours during the year

Supersedes:
National Catholic Music Educators Association (founded 1942)

1017. National Association of Synagogue Administrators

Jewish

Joseph Miller, President
c/o Ohr Kodesh Congregation
8402 Freyman Drive
Chevy Chase, Maryland 20015

The National Association of Synagogue Administrators is an affiliate of the United Synagogue of America. It is a professional society espousing conservative Judaism while furthering the development of its profession.

1018. National Association of Temple Administrators (NATA)

Reform Judaism/Union of American Hebrew Congregations

838 Fifth Avenue
New York, New York 10021
(212) 249-0100

The National Association of Temple Administrators is the organization of professional executives of Reform congregations and works closely with the Department of Synagogue Administration. In conjunction with the Commission on Synagogue Administration, a joint body with the Central Conference of American Rabbis, it undertakes nationwide research projects on all facets of synagogue management. The NATA Research Studies Committee publishes periodic surveys on finance, publicity, and public relations practices, board and committee structure, use of facilities, and other aspects of synagogue administration. Through its Congregational Survey Service, the NATA offers a unique evaluation service to UAHC congregations to assist them in improving their administrative procedures and fiscal stability. In addition, its members conduct workshops for the training of lay leaders at UAHC and regional meetings. A journal is also published quarterly, and NATA provides a placement service.

1019. National Association of Temple Educators (NATE)

Reform Judaism/Union of American Hebrew Congregations

838 Fifth Avenue
New York, New York 10021
(212) 249-0100

The National Association of Temple Educators is a professional organization composed of directors of education, principals, and rabbis involved in religious education for member congregations of the UAHC. It works closely with the UAHC's Department of Jewish Education. NATE collates and evaluates the latest developments in curricula, administration, teaching methods, audio-visual techniques, and the use of art forms in religious education. NATE also conducts a placement service to help congregations obtain qualified temple educators and a consultation service which reviews and evaluates educational programs of member congregational schools.

Founding Date: 1955
Membership: 420
Publications:
   NATE News, semiannually
   Compass, 3 times a year
Meetings:
   Annual conference

1020. The National Association of the Holy Name Society*

Roman Catholic

Jos. Lanaux Marston, Jr., President
516 North Front Street
Minersville, Pennsylvania 17954

The National Association of the Holy Name Society is an association of Archdiocesan and Diocesan Unions of the Holy Name Society in the United States, furnishing to Union cohesiveness, unity, assistance, motivation, and guidance. The Association's activities are an annual convention; a supply service for literature and awards; a monthly newsletter; programs for youth, including an essay contest annually; furnishing of national leaders as speakers for local meetings; public relations for Holy Name movement; contact with American Catholic hierarchy; committees involved in social action; ecumenism, religious vocations; public affairs, and more.

Membership: 35 Union members

Publications:
   Holy Name Society Newsletter, monthly except June and July
Meetings:
   2 or more Executive Board meetings per year
   1 national convention per year

1021. National Baptist Convention, USA Inc., Foreign Mission Board*

National Baptist Convention

Dr. William J. Harvey, III, Corresponding Secretary
701-03 South 19th Street
Philadelphia, Pennsylvania 19146
(215) 735-7868

The Foreign Mission Board, NBC, USA, Inc., has sent missionaries to preach the Gospel of Jesus Christ in foreign lands. In conjunction with preaching, it has been sending teachers and medical personnel for the purpose of secular education at the primary and secondary levels and clinical services in areas devoid of such services. Mission stations are maintained in West Africa (Sierra Leone, Liberia, Ghana); East Africa (Malawi); South Africa (Lesotho, Swaziland, Botswana, Republic of South Africa); and the Western Hemisphere (The Bahamas, Jamaica, Nicaragua).

Founding Date: 1880
Publications:
   Mission Herald, bimonthly

1022. National Black Catholic Clergy Caucus (NBCCC)

Roman Catholic

Rev. Edward B. Branch, President
101 South Main Street
Grambling, Louisiana 71245

Mailing Address

Brother Cyprian Rowe, FMS, Executive Director
1419 V Street, N.W.
Washington, D.C. 20009
(202) 328-0718

The National Black Catholic Clergy Caucus (NBCCC) is an alliance of black priests, brothers, deacons, and seminarians who come together for the development of fraternal relations among the members, and to develop strategies for the uplift of black Catholics at large. The Clergy Caucus strives to provide means of communication among all black Catholic religious professionals to enhance their personal and career growth. It seeks to function as a liaison between its constituency and other black organizations within and without the church community which seek to neutralize those forces which impact negatively upon the black community. The Caucus seeks to present a prophetic voice within the church to decry its injustices and celebrate its fidelity to the gospel of Jesus Christ.

Founding Date: 1967

Staff: 1

Membership: 700

Publications:
> *NBCCC Quarterly*
> Periodic topical mailings

Meetings:
> Annual convention in August

1023. National Catholic Bandmasters' Association (NCBA)

Roman Catholic
James S. Phillips, President
National Office
Post Office Box 523
Notre Dame, Indiana 46556
(219) 283-7136 or (219) 283-1086

The National Catholic Bandmasters' Association is a national organization of Catholic band teachers dedicated to the development, encouragement, and coordination of band programs in the Catholic schools. Its major concerns are the maintenance and raising of high musical and ethical standards, the development of all phases of music within the Catholic educational system, and the assistance in personal growth of its members as individuals, teachers, and Catholic educators. NCBA attempts to meet these goals through intensive committee activity confronting the prevalent problems, through the encouragement of instrumental liturgical music activities, through its newsletter and national conference, through its national music program evaluations, and through the activities and leadership of its dedicated officers.

Founding Date: 1952

Membership: 200 lay and religious

Publications:
> Monthly newsletter
> Annual Conference Proceeding

Official Page in *School Musician Magazine*
The NCBA Liturgical Music Sourcebook

Meetings:
> 1 National Conference annually

1024. National Catholic Cemetery Conference*

Roman Catholic
James R. Mulvaney, Executive Secretary
710 North River Road
Des Plaines, Illinois 60016
(312) 824-8131

The objectives of the National Catholic Cemetery Conference are aimed at the thousands of small Catholic cemeteries scattered all over the nation, as well as the Catholic cemeteries in large metropolitan areas. The Conference provides a forum for the discussion of all phases of Catholic cemetery development, operation, and maintenance; it fosters and promotes the religious, charitable, and educational interests of Catholic cemeteries in the United States and their beneficiaries in cemetery service; aids and solves their cemetery problems by the assembling of accurate information; and aids them in improving cemetery services in the respective archdioceses and dioceses served by them.

Publications:
> *National Catholic Cemetery,* monthly
> *Cemetery Care and Pre-Need*
> Conference journal; leaflets

Meetings:
> Annual conference

1025. National Catholic Coalition for Responsible Investment (NCCRI)

Roman Catholic
Michael H. Crosby, OFMCap, Project Coordinator
3900 North Third Street
Milwaukee, Wisconsin 53212
(414) 264-0800

In January, 1973, representatives from various national Catholic organizations formed the National Catholic Coalition for Responsible Investment (NCCRI) to help create a Gospel impact on the United States economic sector. Because of the Church's responsibility to proclaim justice to corporations which affect the lives of people and in which it holds stocks, the NCCRI offers those involved in Church investments a chance to understand the role and influence of corporate involvement in the contemporary world; to raise theological and ethical questions related to investment; to determine criteria for ethical church investment; to bring about change in corporation decisions, practices, and policies; to move toward a firm commitment for a practical local program of social responsibility; and to plug the local program into the national effort. As an ongoing service, NCCRI continues to provide one to two-day workshops to promote its goals for individuals or gatherings of Catholic institutions. Regional coalitions of investors from Catholic institutions have been established. Activities of these regions are coordinated through membership in the Interfaith Center on Corporate Responsibility in New York.

Founding Date: 1973

Membership: 10

Publications:
1 monthly newsletter and various pamphlets
Various audio-visual materials and guides for groups

Meetings:
Annual Convention

1026. National Catholic Committee on Scouting (NCCS)

Roman Catholic

Henry B. Murphy, Chairman
1325 Walnut Hill Lane
Dallas/Fort Worth Airport, Texas 75261

Mailing Address
Post Office Box 61030
Dallas/Fort Worth Airport, Texas 75261
(214) 659-2109

The National Catholic Committee on Scouting has the responsibility of promoting and guiding cooperative contracts between the proper authorities of the Catholic Church in the United States and the Boy Scouts of America.

Founding Date: 1934

Staff: 3

Membership: 410 lay; 430 clerical

Publications:
Newsletter, quarterly

Meetings:
Biennial conferences of entire membership

1027. National Catholic Development Conference (NCDC)

Roman Catholic

George T. Holloway, Executive Director
119 North Park Avenue
Rockville Centre, New York 11570
(516) 764-6700

The National Catholic Development Conference is an association whose membership includes representatives of religious orders, dioceses, charitable institutions, hospitals, and colleges. Its chief function is to assist its members in developing effective methods of raising funds for the activities they support. The Conference seeks to maintain and encourage the confidence of the general public in the integrity of fund raising by promoting an ethical code, *The Precepts of Stewardship*, to which every member agrees to adhere. It also provides a central office as a forum through which members can exchange information and discuss their problems.

Founding Date: 1968

Staff: 7

Membership: 250-275

Publications:
Dimensions, monthly
Fund Raising Forum, monthly
Monitor, quarterly

Meetings:
Annual convention each September, different locations
15-20 seminars and regional meetings annually

1028. National Catholic Educational Association (NCEA)

Roman Catholic

One Dupont Circle, Suite 350
Washington, D.C. 20036
(202) 293-5954

The National Catholic Educational Association is the world's largest private educational enterprise, serving its voluntary membership—composed of Catholic institutions, educators, administrators, and policymakers on all educational levels—by promoting the ideals of Christian education through workshops, publications, consultative services, and an annual national convention. The Association's goals include these: to encourage and provide means whereby Catholic educators and their institutions can work cooperatively and effectively for professional growth; to promote and interpret the Catholic educational endeavor in its contribution to the total national educational enterprise and to the general welfare of the nation; and to seek and foster cooperation nationally and internationally between Catholic educational institutions and agencies which promote the welfare of society. In addition, NCEA presents to organizations, government officials, and the general public, the views of Catholic education on current issues. Its service departments include the National Association of Boards of Education, the National Catholic Educational Exhibitors, the National Forum of Catholic Parent Organizations, the National Conference of Directors of Religious Education, and the National Association of Parish Coordinators/Directors of Religious Education (see separate listings).

Founding Date: 1904

Staff: 40

Membership: 14,400

Publications:
> 40 educational books
> 1 quarterly journal
> 7 newsletters geared to educational levels
> 1 general association newsletter

Meetings:
> 1 annual national convention and exposition
> Numerous workshops across the country

1029. National Catholic Educational Exhibitors (NCEE)

Roman Catholic
John N. Gibney, Executive Secretary
329 West Elm Street
Granville, Ohio 43023
(614) 587-1884

The purpose of National Catholic Educational Exhibitors, a service department of the National Catholic Educational Association, is to promote the mutual interests of exhibitor members and affiliated members and Catholic schools, administrators, principals, and teachers in Catholic schools, and institutions by providing ethical and acceptable materials for schools and teachers; by providing moral support for Catholic education in both the educational and national fields; and by establishing effective norms for exhibiting and calling these materials and services to the attention of Catholic teachers and educators.

Founding Date: 1955

Staff: 3

Membership: 450

Publications:
> Bulletins, monthly
> *Membership Directory*

Meetings:
> Annual Exhibit at the Annual Convention of the National Catholic Educational Association and participation in exhibits connected with regional, diocesan and local Catholic school systems. Annual exhibits area-wide in colleges during summer Curriculum Week.

Former Name:
> (1961) Catholic Educational Exhibitors Association

1030. National Catholic Forensic League (NCFL)*

Roman Catholic
Office of Secretary-Treasurer
44 Cherry Street
Plymouth, Pennsylvania 19651
(717) 779-3105

The National Catholic Forensic League sponsors: speech activities on both the diocesan and national level; the NCFL National Grand Tournament for high school debaters, speakers, and student Congress; and a scholarship program for students attending the NCFL National Grand Tournament. It publishes a quarterly NCFL Newsletter; promotes leadership in speech activities in secondary schools; and participates in the National University Extension Association Committee on Discussion and Debate.

Membership: 800 secondary schools

Publications:
> Newsletter, quarterly

Meetings:
> NCFL National Grand Tournament

1031. National Catholic News Service (NC News Service)

Roman Catholic
Richard W. Daw, Director and Editor-in-Chief
1312 Massachusetts Avenue, N.W.
Washington, D.C. 20005
(202) 659-6724

National Catholic News Service provides domestic and world news daily by wire and by mail to subscribers in the United States and 40 other countries. It serves both print and broadcast media. In addition to news, NC provides a picture service; weekly columns of commentary and opinion; and a weekly religious education package, *Know Your Faith,* which reaches millions each week through the Catholic newspapers in which it is published. NC publishes a weekly documentary service, *Origins,* and a fortnightly newsletter, *Catholic Trends.* NC also publishes *The American Catholic Who's Who,* a biennial book that is the authority in its field. NC News Service is an editorially independent news agency created by the Catholic bishops of the United States more than a half century ago. It is financially self-sustaining, earning its operating funds from the sale of its services to clients. It is not a part of the public relations structure of the church. NC is headquartered in Washington where it is staffed by news professionals. All eligible staff members belong to the Newspaper Guild, AFL-CIO, with which NC has a union contract. NC maintains a three-person news bureau in Rome and special correspondents throughout the world. Although its primary purpose is to serve Catholic media, its services are available to others on an ecumenical basis.

1032. National Catholic Pharmacists Guild of the United States (NCPG)

Roman Catholic

John Paul Winkelmann, President and Executive Director
1012 Surrey Hills Drive
St. Louis, Missouri 63117
(314) 645-0085

The aim of The National Catholic Pharmacists Guild is to help elevate the profession of pharmacy with ideals of Faith-Love and Charity in the spirit of Christian Ecumenism. The purposes of the Guild are: to uphold the principles of the Catholic Faith, and of all laws of our country and especially those pertaining to the profession in the practice of Pharmacy; to assist the ecclesiastical authorities in the diffusion of Catholic Pharmacy ethics; to oppose the sale of pornographic and indecent literature, especially that being sold in pharmacies; to promote donations of funds and supplies to Catholic charitable groups, especially those engaged in the care of the sick, regardless of race, color or creed; to actively participate in all possible projects in which a love of God

and neighbor policy is pursued through the profession of Pharmacy; and to foster brotherhood and good will among all Pharmacists.

Founding Date: 1962

Membership: 375

Publications:
   The Catholic Pharmacist, quarterly

Meetings:
   Biennial convention

1033. National Catholic Reading Distributors (NCRD)*

Roman Catholic

Stanley Truskowski, Director
545 Island Road
Ramsey, New Jersey 07446
(201) 825-7300

A division of Paulist Press, National Catholic Reading Distributors is the nation's leading Catholic distributor of cloth, paperback, and children's books, and bulk copies of the leading Catholic magazines and newspapers through churches and schools. Its "Guaranteed Paperback Service" program is a monthly shipment of pre-selected paperback and children's books. NCRD's "Unified Magazine" program offers 17 of the nation's leading Catholic newspapers and periodicals on a "No-Risk" bulk basis to churches. Its "Quality Pack" consists of pre-selection of the more expensive paperback books for church rack sales. NCRD's direct mail operation handles selected titles from over 65 publishers.

1034. National Catholic Reporter Publishing Company

Catholic

Jason Petosa, Publisher
115 East Armour
Kansas City, Missouri 64111

Mailing Address
Post Office Box 281
Kansas City, Missouri 64141
(816) 531-0538 or (800) 821-7926

National Catholic Reporter Publishing Company publishes a newsweekly that has international distribution. It also is the leading Catholic publisher of audio cassettes, and it publishes *Celebration,* "a creative worship service," the largest such service to help churches prepare Sunday liturgies.

Founding Date: 1964

Staff: 35

Publications:
> *National Catholic Reporter,* 45 times per year
> *National Catholic Reporter Cassettes,* audio cassettes
> *Celebration,* a monthly liturgical service

1035. National Cathoic Rural Life Conference (NCRLC)

Roman Catholic

William J. Schaefer, Jr., Executive Director
4625 N.W. Beaver Drive
Des Monies, Iowa 50322
(515) 270-2634

The National Catholic Rural Life Conference is an educational linkage system whose primary purposes are to promote stewardship of the earth's resources, that is, to encourage a sense of responsibility towards conserving and enhancing the earth's resources in the context of the global community and to promote rural community and economic development, and improved Church ministry in the rural community. The organization provides educational materials, workshops, and information sessions in natural resources and rural community development; advocacy with government agencies and officials; and research and resource assistance. Its rural focus is on natural resource policy — land use, energy development and soil conservation; food policy — farm programs, vertical integration and corporate agriculture; rural development — housing, health care, and employment; and rural ministry — expanding the concept of ministry in consultation with those working in the rural areas to include advocacy for land, water, air, energy, and rural communities.

Founding Date: 1923

Staff: 7

Membership:
> 2,900 (includes individuals and organizations)

Publications:
> *Catholic Rural Life,* monthly
> *Washington Memorandum,* monthly
> *Rural Life Page,* monthly
> *Rural Parish Service,* monthly

Meetings:
> National Consultation, annually

1036. National Catholic Society of Foresters (NCSF)

Roman Catholic

Mrs. Dolores M. Johnson, National President
35 East Wacker Drive
Chicago, Illinois 60601
(312) 346-0377

The National Catholic Society of Foresters is a fraternal benefit society with the purpose of promoting friendship, unity, and true Catholic charity among its members, fostering fraternal and benevolent activities, and furthering the progress of the Catholic Church. The Society fosters a fraternal scholarship program, Catholic Communications Foundation; matching funds for seminarians burse; financial aid for courts functions; anniversary parties; and active participation in the National Council of Catholic Women and local ACCW. The Society is a member of the National Fraternal Congress of America consisting of 93 fraternal societies.

Founding Date: 1891

Staff: 32

Membership: 77,250 lay; 100 clerical

Publications:
> *National Catholic Forester,* bimonthly
> *Junior Newsletter,* bimonthly

Meetings:
> National convention every four years

Former Name:
> (1966) Women's Catholic Order of Foresters

1037. National Catholic Stewardship Council, Inc., (NCSC)

Roman Catholic

Rev. James M. Mackey, Executive Director
1 Columbia Place
Albany, New York 12207
(518) 456-0233

The general activities of the National Catholic Stewardship Council are three: to alert the People of God 1) to esteem all things as gifts of God's loving creation and inspire them to use them wisely and respectfully; 2) to recognize profoundly that creation is in man's trust, and to respond by managing justly the bounty of our precious resources; and 3) to adopt a lifestyle free of excessive materialism in order to share love and self with our fellow men. More specifically, the NCSC is committed to promoting the right use of God's gifts of Time, Talent, and Treasure for the upbuilding of Christ's Mystical Body the Church by working closely with bishops and pastors, with diocesan pastoral and parish councils, Catholic educators at all levels, and fund raisers, with a view to helping them teach and motivate Christians to come to understand the biblical Stewardship concept and to live Stewardship principles. The NCSC is, therefore, a service center which assists dioceses, parishes, religious communities, and organizations to: encourage adoption of the total stewardship concept; foster the exchange of ideas among dioceses and other Church related groups; promote Vatican II's doctrine of accountability; alert Christians to needs of mission dioceses in the United States and the world; help pastors build an authentic parish council by furnishing guidelines for council formation, goal-setting and function, consultative service for conducting an parish analysis, a Parish Program of Stewardship of Time and Talent for Lay Ministries, and methods for building parish community; and diocesan and parish fund-raising.

Founding Date: 1962

Staff: 2

Membership: 125

Publications:
Stewardship of Money
Stewardship Information Service (SIS),
  quarterly
Stewardship of Time and Talent, also available in Spanish
Spiritual Meaning of Stewardship of Time, Talent, and Treasure
Stewardship Kit for Increased Offertory
Stewardship Kit for Time and Talent
Wills Awareness Kit, and others

Meetings:
One annual convention

1038. National Catholic Vocational Council (NCVC)

Roman Catholic
Brother James Gaffney, FSC, President
1307 South Wabash Avenue, Suite 350
Chicago, Illinois 60605
(312) 663-5453

The National Catholic Vocation Council is composed of national autonomous vocation organizations. These include the National Conference of Diocesan Vocation Directors (NCDVD), the National Con-

ference of Religious Vocation Directors of Men (NCRVDM), the National Sisters Vocation Conference (NSVC), and Serra International. The NCVC Executive Board includes representatives from the Conference of Major Superiors of Men (CMSM), the Leadership Conference of Women Religious (LCWR) and the National Conference of Catholic Bishops (NCCB). The National Catholic Vocation Council strives to give the Church in the United States visible witness of the mutual collaboration of national vocation organizations in their efforts to promote awareness and undersanding of dedication to the Church, especially through the ordained ministry and the vowed life. The Council also receives encouragement and support from many individuals, lay persons, priests, and religious for whom vocation education is a value.

Founding Date: 1976

Staff:
4 members of the Board serve as the Administrative Committee who carry on the activities of the Council with a full-time Administrative Secretary

Membership:
No general membership because NCVC is a Council of several vocational organizations

Publications:
Yearly materials for *Church Vocation Awareness Week Materials*
Yearly materials for *World Vocation Day of Prayer* in April or May

Meetings:
Biannual Orientation Program for men and women involved in Roman Catholic Vocation Ministry, generally in August

Supersedes: National Center for Church Vocations

1039. National Catholic Women's Union (NCWU)

Roman Catholic
H. J. Johnson, Director
3835 Westminster Place
St. Louis, Missouri 63108
(314) 371-1653

The National Catholic Women's Union sponsors Catholic social action which includes mission support, collecting Mass stipends, other charitable endeavors, such as support for St. Elizabeth Settlement and Day Nursery for children, ages 2-13, and educational activities.

Founding Date: 1916

Membership: 15,200 lay; 164 clerical

Publications:
1 magazine, 10 issues annually

Meetings:
1 nationally
State meetings, and city chapter meetings, vary from monthly to quarterly to annually

1040. National Catholic Youth Organization Federation (NCYOF)

Roman Catholic

Rev. Rudy Beranek, Director
United States Catholic Conference
1312 Massachusetts Avenue, N.W.
Washington, D.C. 20005
(202) 659-6680

The National Catholic Youth Organization Federation consists of affiliated diocesan Catholic youth organizations which receive designated benefits in return for annual affiliation dues. NCYOF has a five-fold thrust, involving youth in spiritual, cultural, recreational, social, and community service activities on the parish and diocesan levels. The NCYOF holds a biennial convention and publishes *Emmaus Letter* magazine as well as program materials on many aspects of youth ministry.

Membership:
Over 100 affiliated dioceses, representing over 2 million Catholic teenagers

Publications:
Emmaus Letter, quarterly
An annual booklet as part of the Parish Youth Series, specifically designed for assisting programs in parishes

Meetings:
Convention every 2 years

1041. National Center for Urban Ethnic Affairs

Roman Catholic

Dr. John A. Kromkowski, President
1521 16th Street, N.W.
Washington, D.C. 20036
(202) 232-3600

The National Center for Urban Ethnic Affairs, a non-profit organization founded to develop neighborhood policies and programs that support efforts toward building group identity and a pluralistic society, is building leadership and establishing networks of people working toward the same goals and objectives. The Center has extensive experience and knowledge of federal programs and public policy implications that refer to ethnic issues at the community level and it is involved with national, public, and private organizations working to promote ethnic concerns. Through its work in neighborhoods throughout the East and Midwest, the Center has helped community groups to raise more than $5.3 million in funds in support of programs which meet individual community needs. Center staff people work with neighborhood people and local public officials through their local community organizations to find solutions to their problems and to build for a better today and tomorrow in the areas of ethnicity, multicultural education, community development leadership training, neighborhood development corporations, neighborhood planning, commercial revitalization, credit unions, housing, drug abuse, and research.

Founding Date: 1970

Publications:
Newsletter, quarterly
Various publications

Radio/TV Programs:
2 video tape programs

Meetings:
3-4 regional conferences
1 annual national conference

1042. National Center for Young Adult Ministry, Inc.

Catholic

Rev. Angelo Fazio, CP, President, Director
Merrimack College
North Andover, Massachusetts 01845
(617) 683-7111 Ext. 445

National Center for Young Adult Ministry is organized and operates in response to the United States Catholic community's need to establish a ministry with young adults, to prepare young adult ministry leaders, and to provide a learning center for research and reflection to sustain this new ministry. Its purposes include: organizing and developing a sharing community among those engaged in work among young adults; raising the consciousness of the Church and its communities by educational ministry to the thinking, issues, and needs of young adults; sharing the results of research in areas of young adult ministry by publications and communications; developing and providing resources for national meetings, regional seminars, and leadership workshops; encouraging young adult ministry by responding to diocesan and parish needs; and doing all things necessary and reasonably incidental to the achievement of such religious purposes.

Founding Date: 1978

Staff: 11

Membership: 300

Publications:

The Omega Point, quarterly

Meetings:

National Conference for Young Adult Ministers, yearly, different parts of the country

1043. National Christ Child Society*

Roman Catholic

Mr. Alfred C. Walsh, President
692 Mull Avenue, Apt. ID
Akron, Ohio 44313

The National Christ Child Society is a non-profit association of lay Catholic volunteers dedicating their love of Christ by personal service to needy children regardless of race, creed, or national origin. Organized as a federation of branches of the Christ Child Society, the Society has a three-fold purpose: to preserve the founding spirit of the Society; to serve as a bond between chapters; and to promote the establishment of new chapters. The Society sponsors medical, dental, and baby clinics; informs prospective mothers of prenatal and postnatal care; supplies equipment for institutions and appliances for handicapped children; provides facilities for care and treatment of emotionally disturbed children; and provides volunteers in hospitals and institutions for children. Educationally, it instructs children in Christian doctrine; conducts schools and play groups for physically and mentally handicapped children; provides remedial instruction for children with learning problems; and furnishes books, supplies, scholarships, and transportation for Catholic children to attend Catholic schools. In the field of recreation, the Society maintains settlement houses and neighborhood centers; sponsors clubs, activities, parties, and day camps for children, especially the ill or disadvantaged; and organizes trips for children in child care facilities. The Society makes layettes and garments for children, maintains funds to purchase clothing for the young, collects and renovates used garments for local and foreign distribution, furnishes first communion and confirmation clothing, conducts day nurseries for working mothers, and operates homes for temporary care of abandoned or neglected children.

Founding Date: 1916

Membership: 33 chapters

1044. National Church Goods Association (NCGA)

Interdenominational

Mr. Don Latendresse, Executive Secretary
1114 Greenfield Lane
Mount Prospect, Illinois 60056
(312) 253-5513

Like other trade groups, the National Church Goods Association is a non-profit organization of legitimate dealers, manufacturers, importers, and publishers dealing in church, school and institutional supplies. It is the aim and purpose of the NCGA to serve and to promote the welfare of all its members through its industry leadership; the furnishing of timely information; suggestions and advice through a bulletin service; through specific services performed for individual members upon request; and through representation in official organization contacts.

Staff: 1

Membership: 282

Publications:

Membership Roster
Supplier Directory

Meetings:

6 per year

1045. National Church Growth Research Center

Christian Church

Paul Benjamin, Director
8301 Greensboro Drive, Suite 1070
McLean, Virginia 22102

Mailing Address

Post Office Box 17575
Washington, D.C. 20041
(703) 734-0573

The National Church Growth Research Center was born for one basic purpose—to help churches grow. Since the Center began, over 50 resources have become available to churches. Thousands of American congregations have used the American Church Growth Study Series. A new set of books for the American preaching minister entitled *The Vision Splendid* is ready. Many churches are following an evangelistic strategy designed for the local congregation called *Harvest Now!* Ten additional books designed to equip An-Every-Member-Ministry can be obtained. Tapes and videocassettes are being developed. The Center conducts "on-the-field" training classes in evangelism. Called Action-Evangelism Seminars, following the class sessions, the participants are sent out to conduct a Witness-Survey of their community. Thousands of Christians have made their first evangelistic calls in these Seminars. Other types of seminars are also available through the Center. Several graduate courses can be taken through the Center. In addition to the concentrated holdings of the Center are vast resources of the Library of Congress. Plans are being laid now to increase the course offerings in American Church Growth. The Center sponsors the Washington Writers' Conference, and also offers consultative services to congregations.

Founding Date: 1972

Staff: 19

Publications:
> *Harvest Fields,* quarterly

Meetings:
> Washington Writers' Conference, biannually

1046. National Coalition of American Nuns (NCAN)*

Roman Catholic
1305 South Wabash Avenue, Suite 202
Chicago, Illinois 60605
(312) 427-4351

The National Coalition of American Nuns (NCAN) is an organization studying, working, and speaking out on issues related to human rights and social justice. The Coalition concentrates on relevant issues, finding specific expression in the areas of human rights and social justice. Special emphasis is on the contribution of women on such issues in society. Legislative protection of working women, the rights of welfare recipients, the protest against the debased image of women in communication media, and the move for a guaranteed annual income are among NCAN's interests.

Membership: 2,000

Publications:
> *NCAN Newsletter*

1047. National Committee for a Human Life Amendment, Inc., (NCHLA)

Roman Catholic
Ernest L. Ohloff, Executive Director
1707 L Street, #400
Washington, D.C. 20036
(202) 788-8061

The National Committee for a Human Life Amendment was founded and is entirely supported by the United States' Catholic Bishops for the sole purpose of securing a human life amendment to the Constitution. The primary work of the committee is in education of the nation's Catholics to the need for a human life amendment. Lobbying is also a function and the committee is registered for this purpose. A lay Board of Directors and a staff of six persons are active in the committee's work.

Founding Date: 1974

Staff: 5

Publications:
> Newsletter to key contacts who are members of a Congressional District Action Committee or other pro-life organizations

1048. National Committee for Furtherance of Jewish Education (NCFJE)

Jewish
Rabbi Jacob J. Hecht, Executive Vice-President
824 Eastern Parkway
Brooklyn, New York 11213
(212) 735-0200

The National Committee for Furtherance of Jewish Education is dedicated to the re-establishment and strengthening of the Judiac faith, principles, identity, commitment, and pride through the activities of its various divisions and programs, such as the Released-Time Program, which has reached over a quarter-million Jewish children, giving them an opportunity to discover their Jewish Heritage. Other programs include Hadar Hatorah for young Jewish men and Machon Chana for young Jewish women, programs to study the way of life offered by the Torah. The Anti-Shmad division wages war against the destructiveness of brain-washing, anti-semitic fad religions, intermarriage and assimilation. Camp Emunah and Camp Emunah Tiny Tots for young Jewish girls provide the finest in summer camping for many poor and underprivileged children. Heroes Fund rekindles the spark of hope and joy, and restores meaning and purpose to the hundreds of husbandless, fatherless families left behind by the fallen heroes of Israel's wars for survival. Iranian Children's Fund provides for the hundreds of Iranian Jewish youngsters rescued from that country with the love, care, shelter, and proper Jewish and secular education they require. Poor and Sick Fund helps families with insufficient earnings, families stricken with sickness without recourse to welfare, families in need of special medical care. Toys for Hospitalized Children brings love and joy into the lives of hospitalized Jewish children as well as the elderly with a religious celebration of Chanukah and a gift.

Staff: 50

Membership: 2,500

Radio/TV Programs:
1 public service radio program

Meetings:
2-3 per year

1049. National Conference of Catholic Bishops, American Board of Catholic Missions*

Roman Catholic

Most Rev. John J. Sullivan
1312 Massachusetts Avenue, N.W.
Washington, D.C. 20005

The American Board of Catholic Missions is concerned with assisting and facilitating the missionary work of the Church throughout the world.

1050. National Conference of Catholic Bishops, The Bishops' Committee on the Liturgy (BCL)

Roman Catholic

Reverend Thomas A. Krosnicki, SVD,
Executive Director
1312 Massachusetts Avenue, N.W.
Washington, D.C. 20005
(202) 659-6850

The Bishops' Committee on the Liturgy was established as the Bishops' Commission on the Liturgical Apostolate. The area of its responsibility as a permanent committee of the National Conference of Catholic Bishops (NCBB) is outlined in the 1963 Constitution on the Sacred Liturgy and subsequent ecclesiastical documents. The Committee assists NCCB in fulfilling its task of moderating the pastoral-liturgical activities of the Church in the United States, working in close cooperation with the Congregation for the Sacraments and Divine Worship (Rome) and the Federation of Diocesan Liturgical Commissions of the United States.

Founding Date: 1958

Staff: 3 Secretariat staff members

Membership: 22

Publications:
Bishops' Committee on the Liturgy Newsletter, monthly
BCL Study Text Series, biannually
BCL Reader Series, occasionally

Meetings:
Upon request, number and location vary

Former Name:
(1968) Bishop's Commission on the Liturgical Apostolate

1051. National Conference of Catholic Bishops, Committee for Ecumenical and Interreligious Affairs

Roman Catholic

Rev. John F. Hotchkin, Executive Director
1312 Massachusetts Avenue, N.W.
Washington, D.C. 20005
(202) 659-6855

The Committee for Ecumenical and Interreligious Affairs is a standing committee of the United States

Episcopal Conference which advises the bishops and their diocesan agencies in ecumenical matters, putting into practice the ecumenical policies of the Roman Catholic Church and establishing dialogue, consultations, and cooperation with the leaders and the ecumenical councils of other religious bodies and churches at the national level.

Founding Date: 1966

Staff: 5

Membership: 13

Meetings:

The committee joins in sponsoring national programs open to the public: the National Workshop for Christian Unity (annually) and the National Workshop for Christian-Jewish Relations (every 18 months)

It sponsors the Institute for Ecumenical Leadership for diocesan ecumenical officers (annually) and is engaged in eight bilateral consultations with other Christian churches and regular meetings with national Jewish councils and agencies

1052. National Conference of Catholic Bishops, Committee for Pastoral Research and Practices

Roman Catholic

Monsignor Richard K. Malone, Executive Director
1312 Massachusetts Avenue, N.W.
Washington, D.C. 20005
(202) 659-6750

The major objective of the Committee for Pastoral Research and Practices is to assist the bishops in the pastoral aspects of the exercise of their office, to provide information from theologians and scholars to members of the Conference, and to do research and prepare statements for the Conference to state in a pastoral way the Church's position on pastoral issues and to indicate ways of implementing such positions on the level of the local Church.

Founding Date: 1965

Staff: 4

Membership: 10

1053. National Conference of Catholic Bishops, Committee for the Church in Latin America

Roman Catholic

Bishop Juan Arzube, Chairman
1312 Massachusetts Avenue, N.W.
Washington, D.C. 20005
(202) 659-6828

The Committee for the Church in Latin America is concerned with the relationship between the Church in this country and the Church in Latin America, both in regard to the annual national collection for the Church in Latin America and various other matters of common concern in the areas of justice and peace.

1054. National Conference of Catholic Bishops, Committee on Arbitration*

Roman Catholic

Most Rev. Roger Mahony
1312 Massachusetts Avenue, N.W.
Washington, D.C. 20005

The Committee on Arbitration, National Conference is concerned with facilitating structures for mediation where such structures do not already exist in the routine forums of the Church.

1055. National Conference of Catholic Bishops, Committee on Canonical Affairs

Roman Catholic

Archbishop Joseph Bernardin
1312 Massachusetts Avenue, N.W.
Washington, D.C. 20005
(202) 659-6769

The Bishops' Committee on Canonical Affairs is concerned with the rules and regulations which pertain to the government of the Church as a visible society in its universal aspect, and particularly to the life of the Church in this country.

1056. National Conference of Catholic Bishops, Committee on Conference of Major Superiors of Men*

Roman Catholic

Most Rev. John May
1312 Massachusetts Avenue, N.W.
Washington, D.C. 20005

The Committee on Conference of Major Superiors of Men of the National Conference of Catholic Bishops is concerned with working cooperatively with the superiors of men religious on matters of mutual concern.

1057. National Conference of Catholic Bishops, Committee on Doctrine

Roman Catholic

Monsignor Richard K. Malone, Executive Director
1312 Massachusetts Avenue, N.W.
Washington, D.C. 20005
(202) 659-6750

The primary and essential mission of the Committee on Doctrine is to assist the bishops in the doctrinal aspects of the exercise of their teaching office. The Committee has further defined this function with the following eight responsibilities: to prepare doctrinal statements; to develop continuing education programs for the bishops; to review materials for doctrinal implications; to maintain informational contact with corresponding bodies of other Episcopal Conferences; to foster collaboration between bishops and theologians; to prepare information for bishops; to foster theological reflection on current questions; and to provide doctrinal consultation services for the bishops of the NCCB/USCC.

Founding Date: 1965

Staff: 4

Membership: 18

Meetings:
> Colloquy on Scholarship, Washington, D.C. (1 per year)

1058. National Conference of Catholic Bishops, Committee on Human Values*

Roman Catholic

Most Rev. Mark J. Hurley
1312 Massachusetts Avenue, N.W.
Washington, D.C. 20005

The Committee on Human Values serves as a point of contact and dialogue between the NCCB and research and think-tank groups, both church-related and secular, particularly in the field of science and technology. It also functions as the United States Episcopal Conference's counterpart to the Vatican Secretariat for Non-Believers.

1059. National Conference of Catholic Bishops, Committee on Leadership Conference Women Religious

Roman Catholic

Most Rev. John McGann
1312 Massachusetts Avenue, N.W.
Washington, D.C. 20005

The Committee on Leadership Conference Women Religious, NCCB, is concerned with fostering collaboration on matters of mutual concern with the heads of orders of religious women in the United States.

1060. National Conference of Catholic Bishops, Committee on Permanent Diaconate*

Roman Catholic

Most Rev. Ernst Unterkeofler
1312 Massachusetts Avenue, N.W.
Washington, D.C. 20005

The Committee on Permanent Diaconate, NCCB, is concerned with promoting the restoration of the Permanent Diaconate in the United States. The Permanent Diaconate, restored as a proper and permanent rank of the hierarchy, was made possible by the Second Vatican Council. Deacons share certain functions in the liturgy while working in parishes and engaging in a wide variety of service ministries. As of December 31, 1976, there were 1,747 Permanent Deacons in the Catholic Church in the United States, with another 2,507 candidates in various stages of preparation.

1061. National Conference of Catholic Bishops, Committee on Priestly Formation*

Roman Catholic
Most Rev. John A. Marshall
1312 Massachusetts Avenue, N.W.
Washington, D.C. 20005

The National Conference of Catholic Bishops Committee on Priestly Formation is concerned with the training of future priests and with the studies and regulations governing their training in 325 United States seminaries.

Membership: 12 clerical
Publications:
2 scholarly books
Meetings:
6 per year

1062. National Conference of Catholic Bishops, Committee on Priestly Life and Ministry*

Roman Catholic
Most Rev. Raymond Gallagher
1312 Massachusetts Avenue, N.W.
Washington, D.C. 20005

The National Conference of Catholic Bishops Committee on Priestly Life and Ministry has sponsored research on a number of matters concerning the needs, problems, and aspirations of American Catholic Priests.

1063. National Conference of Catholic Bishops, Liaison Committee*

Roman Catholic
Most Rev. James W. Malone
1312 Massachusetts Avenue, N.W.
Washington, D.C. 20005

The National Conference of Catholic Bishops, Bishops' Liaison Committee, has responsibility for meeting with various groups concerned with presenting their views to the Catholic bishops, and with relaying those views fully and objectively back to the full body of bishops.

1064. National Conference of Catholic Bishops, Secretariat for Catholic-Jewish Relations

Roman Catholic
Dr. Eugene J. Fisher, Executive Secretary
1312 Massachusetts Avenue, N.W.
Washington, D.C. 20005
(202) 659-6857

The Secretariat for Catholic-Jewish Relations promotes better understanding between Catholics and Jews, organizes national Catholic-Jewish workshops, and promotes dialogues, lectures, and seminars designed to improve Catholic-Jewish relations. The Secretariat was founded in response to the second Vatican Council's declaration on the Jews. It strives particularly to implement the 1975 Vatican *Guidelines* for improving Catholic-Jewish relations, cooperating with Bishops in the formation of diocesan commissions to further a sympathetic understanding of Judaism and the Jewish people, and providing information for persons involved in Catholic-Jewish dialogue.

Founding Date: 1965
Staff: 3
Membership: 15 members of Advisory Committee
Publications:
Occasional issues of *Interface,* the newsletter of the BCEIA
Other materials published in *Origins,* NC News Documentary Service
Meetings:
National Workshops on Christian-Jewish relations, co-sponsored with Synagogue Council of America and National Council of Churches
Various meetings, and consultations with major Jewish agencies
Supersedes:
(1967) Subcommission of Catholic-Jewish Relations

1065. National Conference of Catholic Bishops, Secretariat for the Laity

Roman Catholic

Mrs. Dolores Leckey, Executive Director
1312 Massachusetts Avenue, N.W.
Washington, D.C. 20005
(202) 659-6730

The day-to-day work of the Bishops' Committee on the Laity is carried out by its Secretariat which is its staff office. In this capacity it is a center for resources and education to raise the awareness of the lay role in the Church and in society, and to provide consultation, information, and assistance to those involved in developing the lay role in the Church. It is a center for communication through which lay groups, individuals, and the NCCB may engage in ongoing dialogue.

Staff: 2

Publications:

   Gifts, quarterly
   Lay Ministry Resource Packet
   Directory of Diocesan Lay Programs and Resources

Meetings:

   Number and location vary

1066. National Conference of Catholic Bishops, Secretariat for the Spanish Speaking*

Roman Catholic

Pablo Sedillo, Jr., Director
1312 Massachusetts Avenue, N.W.
Washington, D.C. 20005
(202) 659-6876

The Secretariat for the Spanish Speaking of the National Conference of Catholic Bishops and the United States Catholic Conference is a consultation service for 110 Diocesan Directors and is operated by the Catholic Bishops of the United States "for the purpose of assisting those dioceses with significant Hispanic population in their efforts to develop far-reaching and effective programs that will substantially enhance the physical and spiritual growth of the Spanish speaking in this country." It acts as an information and idea center concentrating on areas of nutrition and health; housing; manpower development and training; employment; education and leadership training; communications and information;

and pastoral and liturgical activities. It provides liaison with other churches, institutions, and governmental and private agencies concerned with the Spanish speaking. It maintains a small library and also sponsors regional and national conferences and seminars on issues of importance to the Spanish speaking. In addition to the Director, the Secretariat has an Education Specialist, a Pastoralist and a Migrant Specialist.

Founding Date: 1945

Staff: 4

Meetings:

   Regional and national conferences
   Seminars

1067. National Conference of Catholic Charities (NCCC)*

Roman Catholic

Msgr. Lawrence J. Corcoran, Executive Director
1346 Connecticut Avenue, N.W., Suite 307
Washington, D.C. 20036
(202) 785-2757

The National Conference of Catholic Charities is a national, self-governing membership organization representing the Catholic Charities movement. It seeks to act in three roles: providing direct social services, transforming and humanizing the social order, and convening the community for social justice education and action. It is supported by membership dues and provides these basic services to its members: publications, government relations services, an annual convention and special workshops, consultation in selected areas of development, a social services program, government regulations and legislation, and representation of the interest of Catholic Charities affiliates with other national bodies.

Founding Date: 1910

Membership: 1,855 lay; 1,147 clerical

Publications:

   Charities, USA, monthly
   Social Thought, quarterly
   Annual Directory
   Congressional Comment, 3 times a year
   Occasional monographs on social issues

Meetings:

   1 annual convention
   Topical seminars, 3 or 4 times per year

1068. National Conference of Christians and Jews (NCCJ)

Nondenominational

Dr. David Hyatt, President
43 West 57th Street, Suite 307
New York, New York 10019
(212) 688-7530

The National Conference of Christians and Jews is a non-profit organization engaged in a nationwide program of intergroup education to eliminate prejudice and discrimination. The NCCJ works to build bridges of understanding among all groups, to bring the forces of enlightenment and education to bear upon racial and religious prejudice, and to achieve implementation of the moral law: giving to others the same rights and respect we desire for ourselves. It enlists all those who, without compromise of conscience or of their distinctive commitments, work to build better relationships among persons of all religions, races, and nationalities.

Founding Date: 1928

Membership: 3,500

Meetings:
Hundreds of conferences, workshops, and seminars each year
Annual convention

1069. National Conference of Diocesan Directors of Religious Education-CCD (NCDD)

Roman Catholic

Rev. David E. Beebe, Executive Director
1312 Massachusetts Avenue, N.W.
Washington, D.C. 20005
(202) 659-6868

The National Conference of Diocesan Directors of Religious Education is a volunteer conference of the directors and assistant or associate directors of religious education in diocesan offices around the United States. Its membership is limited to those in these official positions. It plans meetings on the provincial, regional, and national level for the members and carries out the wishes of the membership in regard to specific projects voted on by the members. It plays an informational and service role for its membership, keeping them informed of developments around the country and developing materials for their use. It also exercises an advocacy role, making known to people on the national level the needs and concerns of people working in the field.

Membership:
171 Diocesan Offices of Religious Education

Publications:
NCDD Resource Papers

Meetings:
1 national meeting
Many regional meetings

1070. National Conference of Diocesan Vocation Directors (NCDVD)

Roman Catholic

Reverend Timothy K. Johnson, Executive Director
1307 South Wabash, Suite 350
Chicago, Illinois 60605
(312) 663-5456

The National Conference of Diocesan Vocation Directors is a service organization to the vocation offices of the Roman Catholic Church's dioceses which are affiliated with the United States Catholic Conference-National Conference of Catholic Bishops. It serves these offices by aiding their ministry of promoting Church vocations, or preserving priestly and/or religious vocations, and of communicating their work to the USCC-NCCB and other appropriate bodies. The NCDVD represents the concerns of its members on a national level and fosters support and education for its members nationally, regionally, and locally.

Founding Date: 1962

Staff: 1

Membership:
169 diocesan offices with 320 personnel

Publications:
NCDVD News, five times per year
NCDVD Directory, a directory of member offices' personnel, annually

Meetings:
Annual convention
Regional meetings held annually

1071. National Conference of Directors of Religious Education (NCDRE)

Roman Catholic

Rev. Francis D. Kelly, Executive Director
Department of Religious Education
National Catholic Educational Association
1077 30th Street, N.W.
Washington, D.C. 20007
(202) 293-5954

The National Conference of Directors of Religious Education, a service department of the National Catholic Educational Association, is composed of Directors of diocesan offices of religious education whose reponsibility is to supervise and oversee all parish and school religion programs in all of the parishes and schools within the diocese. The Conference, through its Annual Meeting, newsletters, and programs, seeks to facilitate communication between its members, address common needs, and provide national religious education leadership and vision.

Founding Date: 1968

Staff: 2

Membership: 113

Publications:
> *The Director's Newsletter,* periodically

Meetings:
> One annual three day meeting, location varies

1072. National Conference of Religious Vocation Directors of Men (NCRVDM)

Roman Catholic

Rev. James A. Vedro, OSC, Executive Director
1307 South Wabash Avenue, Suite 350
Chicago, Illinois 60605
(312) 663-5454

National Conference of Religious Vocation Directors of Men provides a way for the leadership in the Church to further religious vocations among men and women. At the same time, it is a vehicle for the collective experience of vocation directors of religious communities of men and women to be made available to the Church. NCRVDM hears from and speaks to the Church. More than that, it implements specific programs to deal with the vocation crisis.

NCRVDM is concerned for the professional training and the personal growth and support of vocation directors. This concern is, ultimately, a concern for church vocations themselves. Especially important is the service NCRVDM provides in introducing newly appointed brothers, sisters, and priests to this ministry, and in helping to sustain them in it.

Founding Date: 1969

Staff: 3

Membership: 510

Publications:
> *NCRVDM Newsletter,* quarterly
> *Call to Growth/Ministry,* quarterly vocation/formation journal

Meetings:
> Biannual national convention
> Biannual membership regional conventions, in alternate years
> Workshops conducted throughout the country: Major Superior and Vocation Directors Workshop; Vocation/Formation Personnel Workshop

1073. National Conference on Soviet Jewry (NCSJ)

Jewish

Theodore R. Mann, Chairman
Jerry Goodman, Executive Director
New York Office
10 East 40th Street
New York, New York 10016
Washington Office
2027 Massachusetts Avenue, N.W.
Washington, D.C. 20036
New York (212) 679-6122/Washington (202) 265-8114

The National Conference on Soviet Jewry is the major nationwide coordinating agency in the United States for activity and policy on behalf of Soviet Jews. Thirty-nine member agencies and nearly 300 local, affiliated community relations councils, federations, and committees comprise the NCSJ's constituents. The NCSJ is an autonomous body working to develop programs designed to be helpful in relieving the problems of Soviet Jews. This is accomplished via public education and social action, stimulating all segments of the community to maintain an interest in the problems of Soviet Jews through reports, pamphlets, special programs, forums, and projects.

The execution of these responsibilities is accomplished via the collection and dissemination of information from the Soviet Union; development of basic planning and strategies to foster an intensive and dynamic program; and coordination of effort of constituent agencies.

Founding Date: 1971

Staff: 6 professional; 6 administrative

Membership:

39 agencies representing the organized American Jewish Community

Publications:

Press Service, weekly
The Soviet Jewry Monthly, monthly

Meetings:

Policy conference, held once a year

Former Name:

(1971) American Jewish Conference on Soviet Jewry

1074. National Conference of Vicars for Religious

Roman Catholic

Rev. Angelo M. Caligiuri, President
100 South Elmwood Avenue
Buffalo, New York 14202
(716) 856-5550

Within the context of the ministry of the Church, the Conference of Vicars for Religious sees itself as an enabling, supportive group to foster the education of Vicars for Religious in the service of stimulating the prophetic vocation of religious life. The National Conference, the NCVR, facilitates communication and disseminates information among its members located in each of the Dioceses of the United States. At the National level, it sponsors an annual National Assembly for all its members, as well as four regional meetings every year.

Founding Date: 1967

Membership: 165

Publications:

Newsletter

Meetings:

National assembly held annually during the month of March
East, West, Mid-west and Southern Regional meetings held during the fall of each year

1075. National Council for Jewish Education (NCJE)

Jewish

Dr. Philip Jaffe, Executive Secretary
114 Fifth Avenue
New York, New York 10011
(212) 675-5656

The National Council for Jewish Education was founded as a fellowship of individuals professionally engaged in Jewish education. It consists of directors, administrators, and supervisors of national and local Jewish educational institutions and agencies of all ideological groupings. It includes faculty members of Hebrew colleges, theological seminaries, Jewish teachers' institutions, and Hebrew high schools as well as faculty members of Judaica and Hebrew departments of universities and colleges who are concerned with Jewish education. It also includes authors and rabbis concerned with Jewish education. The Council is dedicated to improving and strengthening the quality of Jewish life in America by furthering the cause of Jewish education, raising professional standards and practices, and promoting the welfare and growth of Jewish educators.

Founding Date: 1926

Membership: 400

Publications:

Jewish Education, quarterly
Sheviley Hahinuch, quarterly

Meetings:

Annual conference in various places in the United States
Mid-winter conference in New York City

1076. National Council of Catholic Laity (NCCL)

Roman Catholic

Thomas Simmons, President
Post Office Box 14525
Cincinnati, Ohio 45214
(513) 381-8510

The National Council of Catholic Laity is a federation of Catholics who want to be in the mainstream of the life of the Church. Its members are dedicated to being more effective witnesses to Christ and the Catholic faith in today's world. NCCL is related to the National Conference of Catholic Bishops through the committee of the lay apostolate and is an affiliated organization of the United States Catholic Conference. There are three general goals: the renewal of Church life; the challenge of the social order; and the concern for the future of the world. The objectives of NCCL are to help intensify the efforts of the Catholic laity in the United States; to mobilize and coordinate efforts of the Catholic laity to bring full life and meaning to the role of the laity in the mission of the Church in the United States; to be a medium through which the Catholic laity of the United States may speak on matters of common concern; to cooperate with other national and international organizations in the solution of modern day problems; and to cooperate with the clergy, religious, and hierarchy in fulfilling the mission of the Church.

Founding Date: 1971

Publications:

NCCL News, quarterly

1077. National Council of Catholic Women (NCCW)

Roman Catholic

Winfred E. Coleman
1312 Massachusetts Avenue, N.W.
Washington, D.C. 20005
(202) 638-5060

The National Council of Catholic Women is the nationwide federation in the United States of Catholic women and their organizations. It was founded by 200 concerned women at the call of the Bishops of the United States. The activities of NCCW are conducted through five internal units: the Church Communities Commission; Community Affairs Commission; Family Affairs Commission; International Affairs Commission; and Organization Services Commission.

Founding Date: 1920

Staff: 10

Membership:

8,000 affiliated Catholic women's organizations
45 member Executive Committee

Publications:

Catholic Woman, bimonthly

Meetings:

Biennial convention
General assembly in non-convention years

1078. National Council of Jewish Women

Jewish

Dadie Perlov, Executive Director
15 East 26th Street
New York, New York 10010
(212) 532-1740

The National Council of Jewish Women operates programs in education, social and legislative action, and community service for children and youth, the aging, the disadvantaged in Jewish and general communities. Concerns include the juvenile justice system as a basis for legislative reform and community projects. The Council is deeply involved in women's issues; and promotes education in Israel through NCJW Research Institute for Innovation in Education at Hebrew University, Jerusalem.

Founding Date: 1893

Membership: 100,000

Publications:

NCJW Journal, bimonthly tabloid
From the Desk of the President
Washington newsletter
NACS newsletter

Meetings:

Biennial Convention (every 2 years)
Joint Program Institute, Washington, D.C. (every 2 years)

1079. National Council of Churches of Christ in the United States of America, Church World Service (CWS)*

National Council of the Churches of Christ

Dr. Paul F. McCleary, Executive Director
475 Riverside Drive
New York, New York 10027

Church World Service was set up by 17 United States Protestant denominations to act as a cooperative relief and rehabilitation agency on a global scale. To date, 31 denominations have joined in the international ecumenical effort, including Orthodox groups. Much of the early CWS activity centered on compassionate response to the effects of disasters on the human body, mind, and spirit. CWS still responds to cries for help from all quarters of the globe including the continental United States. The CWS task and mandate could be simply described during its early days: to meet acute human need. While that is still its basic task, the CWS role has broadened to include community and national developmental projects or programs under the guidance of its participating denominations. These programs include vital work in family planning, nutrition, various types of refugee assistance, educational job training, and general aid to the aged and thousands of children. Geographical areas covered include four major continents containing the emerging, and in some cases still crises-prone nations in Asia, Africa, Latin America, the Middle East, and parts of Europe.

Founding Date: 1947

Membership:
31 member denominations and related agencies

Publications:
Disaster Fact Sheets
CWS Reports
CROP

1080. Natonal Council of the Churches of Christ in the United States of America, Commission on Regional and Local Ecumenism (CORLE)

National Council of the Churches of Christ
The Reverend Joan B. Campbell,
Assistant General Secretary of
NCCC for regional and local ecumenism
475 Riverside Drive
New York, New York 10115
(212) 870-2157

The Commission on Regional and Local Ecumenism (CORLE) is one of eight major units in the National Council of Churches of Christ. CORLE was organized for two purposes: to enhance the development of ecumenical life across the nation; and to provide the means by which local and regional ecumenical experiences might become components in national decision-making processes. The roles which CORLE plays in the National Council of Churches and in ecumenical life across the nation include at least the following: Communication; Ecumenical Development; Consultation; Professional Services; Linkage; and Special Agendas/Targets; and Reflection. Thus, CORLE is a commission uniquely charged with a responsibility for developing "grass-roots" ecumenical life and for establishing links with other levels of ecumenical experience.

Founding Date: 1960

Staff: 4

Membership: 60

Publications:
Living Ecumenism, usually four a year, published jointly by CORLE and NAES

Meetings:
Two commission meetings per year, usually immediately prior to the National Council of Churches' Governing Board meetings

1081. National Council of the Churches of Christ in the United States of America, Commission on Stewardship

National Council of the Churches of Christ

Dr. Nordan C. Murphy, Assistant General Secretary for Stewardship
475 Riverside Drive, Room 830
New York, New York 10115
(212) 870-2284

The functions of the Commission on Stewardship shall be to stimulate and help develop understanding of Christian stewardship and to assist the Council and its member communions in establishing and maintaining effective stewardship programs. The responsibility of this Commission shall be: to plan and implement a continuing program of stewardship education and practice to be related to all interests of Commission members; to cooperate with the Units and Work Groups of the Council in representing the resources of stewardship applicable in their particular areas of responsibility; to assist the Executive Committee, the Program Units, and Governing Board of the Council, where desired, in exploration and development of opportunities for the promotion of stewardship emphases; and to provide liaison with stewardship offices of church bodies in other nations.

Membership:
31 Protestant denominations are members in the Commission on Stewardship

Publications:
Journal of Stewardship, annually
Church Financial Statistics and Related Data, annual collection of charts and figures (brochures)

Meetings:
Annual December meeting, San Antonio, Texas (this year)

North American Conference on Christian Philanthropy, biennial conference

1082. National Council of the Churches of Christ in the United States of America, Communication Commission

National Council of the Churches of Christ

Dr. William F. Fore
475 Riverside Drive
New York, New York 10027
(212) 870-2567

The Communication Commission of the National Council of the Churches of Christ provides consultation in the production of network radio and TV programs; produces films, film-strips, and other audio-visuals; distributes and promotes denominational and ecumenical media materials; provides news and information about NCCC, member groups, and other religious news; provides Ecumedia News Service for radio programming; provides Cable Information Service; relates to government and industry on media matters; testifies before appropriate governmental bodies on media issues; and provides a forum for denominational and interfaith cooperation and deliberation on media concerns

Membership:
18 denominational or related agency cognate units

Meetings:
2-6 per year

1083. National Council of the Churches of Christ in the United States of America, Division of Overseas Ministries

National Council of the Churches of Christ

Dr. Eugene Stockwell, Associate General Secretary
for Overseas Ministries
475 Riverside Drive
New York, New York 10115
(212) 870-2175

The Division of Overseas Ministries of the National Council of Churches of Christ serves as the arm through which member communions and participating non-member organizations cooperate to witness to Christ through mission and service outside the United States. Housed within the Division are: Church World Service, the relief and development arm of the Division which operates through five geographical area offices in Africa, East Asia and the Pacific, Latin America and the Caribbean, Middle East, and Southern Asia, and six functional offices, CWS in the United States, Family Life and Population Program, Immigration and Refugee Program, Interpretation and Promotion, Material Resources Program, and Overseas Personnel; Agricultural Missions, which seeks to aid selected persons, institutions, and agencies in any part of the world which are in agricultural improvement-related fields; Human Rights, which acts in advocacy and network-building in response to serious threats and violations of the human rights of individuals and groups, and engages in constituency education and public outreach to develop wider support for these efforts; Intermedia, an ecumenical agency through which North American mission boards and agencies assist Christian adult basic education and communications ministries; Leadership Development, which supports a theological exchange program in cooperation with the scholarship office of the World Council of Churches, and provides emergency assistance for refugee students; International Congregations and Lay Ministry, which provides services to international English-speaking congregations; and Associated Mission Medical Office, which supervises missionary health.

Founding Date: 1893

Membership:
32 constituent bodies comprising the National Council of Churches

Publications:
Tri Annual Report, Division of Overseas Ministries; Annual Report, Church World Service; *DOM Notes,* quarterly; *CWS Update,* quarterly; *World Hunger Fact Sheet,* quarterly; *Refugees and Human Rights Newsletter,* occasionally; *TNT,* bimonthly; *Newsbriefs,* periodically; *Intermedia,* quarterly; *IHC Occasional Bulletin; Human Rights Perspective,* periodically; *Southern Asia Update,* periodically; *Briefs,* periodically; Newspaper: *Service News,* bimonthly; *Friends from Abroad,* annually

Radio/TV Programs:
14 radio spots per year
2-4 TV spots per year

Meetings:
Conferences and consultations called on specific subjects at different locations

1084. National Council of the Churches of Christ in the United States of America, Leadership Development*

National Council of the Churches of Christ
James W. Gunn, Executive
475 Riverside Drive, Room 770
New York, New York 10027

The Program Committee on Professional Church Leadership has as its focus the concern of the Church for its professional leadership, both lay and ordained. Its purpose is to encourage and to implement ecumenical efforts in the areas of enlistment, theological and professional training, career-span education, career assessment and planning, placement and deployment, specialized ministries, bi-occupational careers, salary support, and retirement. The Committee is also an advocate for women and minorities in ministry and other areas where it feels the Church should give special attention to the support needs of its professional leadership. The Committee's functions are: to provide occasions for denominational persons to explore common issues and to share information; to encourage and facilitate research and data gathering; to provide consultative services to denominational agencies and committees; to encourage and facilitate common projects and the development of common resources; and to provide liaison with consortia groups and other agencies working in similar areas of concern.

Membership: 34

Publications:
> Information pieces about church occupations, 14 titles
> *Quarterly Mailing*

Meetings:
> Program Committee meets twice annually, other working groups as necessary

1085. National Council of Young Israel

Jewish
Rabbi Ephraim H. Sturm, Executive Vice President
3 West 16th Street
New York, New York 10011
(212) 929-1525

The aims and purposes of the National Council of Young Israel are to foster and maintain a program of spiritual, cultural, social, and communal activity towards the advancement and perpetuation of traditional, Torah-true Judaism; and to instill in American youth an understanding and appreciation of the high ethical and spiritual values of Judaism and demonstrate the compatability of the ancient faith of Israel with good Americanism. The organization seeks to promote cooperation among the constituent branches, establish a close bond of kinship to the end that their individual and common problems may more easily be solved, and act as the federated and central body for the Young Israel Movement so that its influence as a force in Jewry may be felt and recognized in America and the world over.

Membership: 200,000 lay; 150 clerical

Publications:
> *Young Israel Viewpoint,* monthly
> *Young Israel Newsletter,* weekly
> *Intercollegiate Cultural Hashkafa Series,* quarterly

Radio/TV Programs:
> Weekly 15-minute sermons on radio station WNEW, New York

Meetings:
> 20 seminars each year
> 8 conferences
> 40 meetings
> 2 retreats

1086. National Council of Religion and Public Education (NCRPE)

Nondenominational
Lynn Taylor, Executive Director
University of Kansas
1300 Oread
Lawrence, Kansas 66045
(913) 843-7257

The National Council on Religion and Public Education provides a forum and a means for cooperation among organizations and institutions concerned with those ways of studying religion which are educationally appropriate and constitutionally acceptable to a secular program of public education. It establishes liaison among professional and lay groups involved in education. It works to create awareness in both public and professional circles of the need for the academic study of religion as part of the education of the general public. It gathers and provides information about resource persons, programs, projects, curriculum materials, teacher education opportunities, and legal decisions related to religion and public education.

Membership: 30 national and local organizations
Publications:
  NCRPE Bulletin, quarterly
Meetings:
  1 national conference each year
  Participate in annual conventions of member societies as well as in locally arranged and sponsored programs

1087. National Educators Fellowship, Inc. (NEF)

Interdenominational
Benjamin S. Weiss, President
1410 West Colorado
Pasadena, California 91105

Mailing Address
Post Office Box 243
South Pasadena, California 91105
(213) 684-1881

National Educators Fellowship is the only national Christian educators professional organization. The members are committed Christians, career educators engaged in all phases of public and private school education. They are concerned about the need for a personal moral and spiritual influence in their teaching activities. The objectives of NEF are to: encourage Christian educators to present a positive Christian testimony in their personal and professional activities; include moral and spiritual ideas and ideals in teaching the regular school subjects; influence educators to achieve excellence in their teaching activities as a Christian testimony; inspire Christian educators to communicate a positive Christian life through prayer, witnessing, Bible study, and personal evangelism; provide Christian fellowship to educators for social and spiritual enrichment through prayer and professional interaction; assist pupils in solving personal problems through counseling and friendly helpfulness; recruit Christian high school and college students for the teaching profession; and publish helpful material and information for teaching moral and spiritual values.

Founding Date: 1953
Staff: 6
Membership: 1,800
Publications:
  Vision, monthly
  Communique-Interdepartmental-Bulletin, monthly

Meetings:
  One national convention
  Area conferences
  Chapter meetings

1088. National Enthronement Center*

Roman Catholic
Rev. Francis Larkin, SSCC, National Director
3 Adams Street
Fairhaven, Massachusetts 02719
(617) 999-2680

The Work of the National Enthronement Center was founded by Father Mateo Crawley Boevery, SSCC. It encourages families to set up Christ as the King and Center of their home, making it a domestic sanctuary linked with the sanctuary of the church. Some members make night adoration (one hour a month in their home) in reparation for sins. Others, through the Apostolate of Suffering, offer their sufferings with the Crucified Christ. Younger members join the League of St. Tarcisius, junior apostoles of the Sacred Heart.

Founding Date: 1906
Publications:
  15 books

1089. National Farm Worker Ministry (NFWM)

Catholic and Protestant
The Reverend Wayne "Chris" Hartmire
1430 West Olympic Boulevard
Los Angeles, California 90015
(213) 386-8130

The National Farm Worker Ministry is a ministry of the churches whose purpose is to be present with and supportive of farm workers as they organize themselves to achieve a measure of self-determination, justice, and dignity.

Founding Date: 1971
Membership: 36 member organizations
Publications:
  NFWM Newsletter, quarterly
Meetings:
  2 meetings per year in Florida
Supersedes: (1920) Migrant Ministry

1090. National Federation of Catholic Physicians' Guilds (NFCPG)

Roman Catholic
Robert H. Herzog, Executive Director
850 Elm Grove Road
Elm Grove, Wisconsin 53122
(414) 784-3435

The purpose of the National Federation of Catholic Physicians' Guilds is to coordinate the activities of the various guilds, to uphold the principles of Catholic faith and morality as related to the science and practice of medicine, to communicate Catholic medical ethics to the medical profession and the community-at-large, to uphold Catholic hospitals in the application of Catholic moral principles, and to enable Catholic physicians to work together with deeper mutual support and understanding. Each local guild is autonomous, and carries on various activities as its members decide. Local guilds vary in size from six members (the minimum number), to over 400 members in some of the larger metropolitan areas. Some cities have two or more guilds. And there is a trend to form independent guilds in each major hospital in some of the larger cities. Activities include retreats, health care of the religious, fostering Catholic medical student groups, cooperating with local charity organizations in the care of the sick and the poor, sponsoring and staffing medical missions in the United States and foreign countries, actively supporting right-to-life groups, and providing advice and counsel on medical-moral matters to the local ordinary.

Founding Date: 1932
Staff: 2
Membership: 6,000
Publications:
Linacre Quarterly
NFCPG Newsletter, quarterly
Meetings:
Annual fall meeting

1091. Natonal Federation of Christian Life Communities (NFCLC)*

Marie A. Schimelfening, Executive Director
3700 West Pine Boulevard
St. Louis, Missouri 63108
(314) 533-3185

Christian Life Communities aim to develop and sustain men and women, adults and youth, who commit themselves to the service of the Church and the world in every area of life. Its communities are for all who feel the urgent need to unite their human life in all its dimensions with the fullness of their Christian faith. The CLC seeks to work for the reform of structures of society, to participate actively in vital efforts to eliminate the causes of injustice, to win liberation for victims of discrimination of any kind, and to strive to overcome the widening differences between rich and poor within the Church and wherever they exist.

Membership: 2,000 lay; 200 clerical
Publications:
7 books on Christian Life Communities
Christian Life Communicator, monthly
Meetings:
4 conferences
6-8 meetings
4 seminars/workshops
25-30 retreats

1092. National Federation of Jewish Men's Clubs

Conservative Judaism
Rabbi David L. Blumenfeld, PhD, National Executive Director
475 Riverside Drive, Suite 244
New York, New York 10027
(212) 749-8100

The National Federation of Jewish Men's Clubs aim to weld affiliated men's clubs within synagogues into a strong, well-knit body; to guide them toward their highest social, cultural, and religious objectives; to promote among them a more thorough knowledge and appreciation of their Jewish heritage; to incorporate the teachings of Judaism as a vital force in their daily lives; to deepen their loyalty to the synagogue; and to train them for active and responsible leadership in the American Jewish community.

Founding Date: 1929
Membership: 40,000
Publications:
Torchlight, quarterly
Meetings:
1 national convention
14 regional conferences
Seminars and retreats held monthly

1093. The National Federation of Priests' Councils (NFPC)

Roman Catholic

Rev. Neil McCauley, President
1307 South Wabash Avenue
Chicago, Illinois 60605
(312) 427-0115

The National Federation of Priests' Councils was organized to promote priestly brotherhood by facilitating communication among priests' councils; to provide a forum for the discussion of pastoral matters; to enable priests' councils to speak with a common, representative voice; to promote and collaborate in programs of pastoral research and action; to implement norms for the renewal of priestly life; and to provide means for nationally united priests councils to cooperate with other Church groups to address the Church's needs.

Founding Date: 1968

Membership: 110 priests' councils

Publications:
Books, pamphlets and studies

1094. National Federation of Spiritual Directors

Roman Catholic

Reverend Robert B. Sidner, President
Saint Meinrad College
St. Meinrad, Indiana 47577
(812) 357-6635

National Federation of Spiritual Directors is an association of persons charged with the responsibility of priestly spiritual formation in high school seminaries, college seminaries, novitiates, theologates, and houses of formation in the United States.

Membership: 200

Publications:
A periodical published by the Midwest Association of Spiritual Directors

Meetings:
A biennial conference
Conferences held by the three member associations in their own regions each year

1095. National Federation of Temple Brotherhoods (NFTB)

Union of American Hebrew Congregations

A. Bondarin, Executive Director
838 Fifth Avenue
New York, New York 10021
(212) 249-0100

The National Federation of Temple Brotherhoods is the service organization of 450 Temple Brotherhoods for the advancement of Reform Judaism and for better interfaith understanding. The Chautauqua Society, which it sponsors, endows accredited courses in Judaic studies at colleges; provides rabbinic lecturers on college campuses; donates Jewish reference books to college libraries; assigns teacher-counselors to Christian Church and Boy Scout Camps; produces and distributes films for public service TV and group showings; and sponsors Institutes for Christian Clergy.

Founding Date: 1923

Staff: 10

Membership: 75,000 lay members

Publications:
Brotherhood, quarterly

Radio/TV Progams:
19 public service announcements for television
20 half-hour and quarter-hour motion pictures for TV and group showings

Meetings:
10-15 a year

1096. National Federation of Temple Sisterhoods (NFTS)

Reform Judaism/Union of American Hebrew Congregations

Eleanor R. Schwartz, Executive Director
838 Fifth Avenue
New York, New York 10021
(212) 249-0100

The National Federation of Temple Sisterhoods is the women's agency of Reform Judaism, the oldest affiliate of UAHC. It is the representative organization of some 630 Reform Temple Sisterhoods with more than 110,000 members throughout the world. Its ever-growing membership is dramatic proof of the increasingly important role that women play today in Jewish religious and communal life. NFTS is also the women's agency of the World Union for Progressive Judaism, works on behalf of the Hebrew Union College-Jewish Institute of Religion, and participates with many national Jewish and non-Jewish groups on subjects of common concern. Beneficiaries of its Youth, Education and Sisterhood (YES) Fund include the UAHC's youth affiliate, the National Federation of Temple Youth, rabbinic students at the Hebrew Union College-Jewish Institute of Religion, overseas rabbinic students of the World Union, and NFTS itself for the further development of Sisterhood programs. The YES Fund includes proceeds from Union-grams — the Jewish message blank for all occasions — and contributions. NFTS was the founder and is a patron of the Jewish Braille Institute of America, Inc., and operates a unique program on behalf of the Jewish and non-Jewish blind. Through Braille, talking books, and large type printing, NFTS serves the Institute's library which opens the door to the Jewish heritage for sightless or visually handicapped youths and adults. Through its member units, District Federations, departments, and committees, NFTS serves Jewish and humanitarian causes, including projects for peaceful world relations and social justice, interfaith activities, religious education, and efforts in Israel. It publishes program guides and materials relating to the Jewish woman's role in facing vital issues of the day in the home, congregation, and community, as well as providing a wealth of services to its constituents. Services include: Religious Education Aids, Advice on Sisterhood Problems, Leadership Training, Speakers Bureau, Family Education, Program Materials, and Study Guides.

Founding Date: 1913

Staff: 45

Membership: 110,000

Publications:
  Notes for Now, quarterly

Meetings:
  Biennial conventions
  Regional conferences, meetings and seminars

1097. National Federation of Temple Youth (NFTY)

Reform Judaism/Union of American Hebrew Congregations
838 Fifth Avenue
New York, New York 10021
(212) 249-0100

The National Federation of Temple Youth offers a varied program in the areas of worship, study, service to community and congregation, leadership training, and artistic endeavor for its approximately 30,000 Reform Jewish members between the ages of 15½ and 18. NFTY congregational youth groups may range in size from two to more than 350 members. Programs are planned and executed by the young people themselves. Their activities range from serious Jewish study to purely social events, from volunteer work with underprivileged children to Jewish art festivals, from creative worship services to projects to aid a variety of causes, both at home and abroad. Through their congregations and regions, members participate in nationally sponsored events such as MECHINA, the national leadership training institute; sermonette, song, and visual arts competitions; KAVOD Award Program for youth group excellence; pilgrimages to the UAHC House of Living Judaism; the UAHC Religious Action Center in Washington, D.C.; the campuses of HUC-JIR; and national and regional UAHC camp-institutes and overseas travel programs. An extensive summer program is sparked by national events at the UAHC Kutz Camp-Institute at Warwick, New York, and enhanced by the UAHC's regional camps. The NFTY Eisendrath-International-Exchange (E-I-E) program offers a limited number of high school students the opportunity to study and live abroad for one or two semesters in Israel. Students from Israel spend an equal period of time living with NFTY members and their families and attending school in North America. The Academy Year in Israel on a Kibbutz, offered in conjuction with the HUC-JIR and Kibbutz Ma'aleh HaChamishah, enables a student who has completed one year of college the opportunity to combine a year's academic work (39 credits) with the challenge of 11 mongths living and working on a kibbutz, as well as extensive travel in Israel. Each year NFTY sponsors several summer, six-month and one-year events abroad: The NFTY Israel Academy, featuring travel and study in Israel, including a 12-day kibbutz work period; the NFTY International Institute, which includes Israel and a number of European communities; the Mitzvah Corps in Israels, and all-Israel experience in physical work, travel, and international living; the Archeological Seminar, which includes work and study at archeological digs in Israel, plus two weeks of travel and kibbutz living; the NFTY Ulpan at Ben Shemen for those interested in learing Hebrew; and the Confirmation Class Study Tour in Israel for students of the same congregation to share the Israel experience together.

Publications:
  Visions

1098. National Forum of Catholic Parent Organizations (NFCPO)

Catholic

Phyllis Evans, Acting Director
1077 30th Street, N.W.
Washington, D.C. 10007
(202) 293-5954

The National Forum of Catholic Parent Organizations is a service department of the National Catholic Educational Association. NCEA has provided the National Forum of Catholic Parent Organizations (NFCPO) as a network of communication among all the parochial school/religious education center parent organizations around the country. Through this network it is hoped to consolidate the power, perceptions, actions, and ideas of hundreds of thousands of Catholic parents concerned with living out their God-given educational partnership role. In particular, NFCPO will channel to all its members information and suggested action steps on: the best ways to promote the religious development of children in the home, in the parish, and in the community; utilizing home activities in religious education and specific subject areas such as reading and mathematics with children from pre-school through junior high; how to promote individually and as an organization parental rights in education and equitable governmental support of nonpublic education; and ideas that have worked with individual parent organizations as they have attempted to achieve their triad of purposes.

Founding Date: 1976

Staff: 2

Publications:
> *Parentcator,* five times a year

Meetings:
> Yearly meeting Easter Week in conjunction with convention of the National Catholic Educational Association

1099. National Guild of Churchmen, Inc. (NGC)

Episcopalian (Anglican)

Rev. Canon Rene Bozarth, LTh, DD,
President and Editor
44-660 San Pablo Avenida
Palm Desert, California 92260

Mailing Address
Post Office Box 100
Sandy, Oregon 97055
(503) 668-4119

The National Guild of Churchmen was founded in New York City nearly 40 years ago. Its New York State Charter of Incorporation specified that the Guild was an evangelistic enterprise and an educational effort as well. In 1971 the Guild added missionary projects to its program—supplying vestments, altar ware, and books (as well as direct cash grants to overseas missionaries with special needs) to clergy in mission fields anywhere in the worldwide Anglican Communion. The Guild is a not-for-profit Corporation of Episcopalians which circulates tracts and supports mission work teaching the Faith of the Anglican Church at home and abroad, including the teaching of the Book of Common Prayer, the traditions of the Church, and understanding the Scripture.

Founding Date: 1945

Membership: 2,030

Publications:
> *St. Paul's Printer,* quarterly

Meeting:
> One yearly meeting at the California Monastery, generally in Lent

1100. The National Institute for Campus Ministries (NICM)

Interdenominational

Robert L. Johnson, Jr., President
885 Centre Street
Newton Centre, Massachusetts 02159
(617) 965-2484

The National Institute for Campus Ministries assists Jews and Christians involved in higher education to understand and interpret their spiritual purposes in a cohesive way. Further, it aids them in creating effective strategies for pursuing those purposes as well as demonstrating the skills and knowledge necesary to implement the strategies. The supportive community is Jewish, Catholic, and Protestant campus ministers, university-appointed chaplains, faculty and administration, and other interested persons. Through regional and national programming, NICM attempts to build communities of faith in academia through continuing education conferences, consultations, research and publications.

Membership: 1,400

Publications:

> *NICM Journal,* quarterly
>
> *NICM Associates Newsletter,* quarterly

Meetings:

> Number and location vary

1101. The National Institute for the Word of God

Roman Catholic

Reverend John Burke, OP, Executive Director

487 Michigan Avenue, N.E.

Washington, D.C. 20017

(202) 529-0001

The National Institute for the Word of God is an unaffiliated, nonprofit organization whose purpose is to promote, support, conduct and assist in any way, educational, liturgical, and remedial programs and activities, public and private, through the use of any and all media, to further the effective communication of the revealed word of God, which is the primary pastoral work of the Church. Ongoing efforts include the dissemination of inspirational training and discussion aids such as books, films, and such services as Parish Renewals, Biblical preaching and/or liturgical conferences or workshops, and priests' retreats.

Founding Date: 1972

Membership: 4 lay; 16 clerical

Publications:

> 2 scholarly books
>
> *Good News Letter,* quarterly newsletter for preachers

Radio/TV Programs:

> 3 one-hour radio series shows for NBC *Guidelines*

Meetings:

> 29 conferences
>
> 5 retreats per year
>
> National Congress every two years

1102. National Interfaith Coalition on Aging (NICA)

Interdenominational

Thomas C. Cook, Jr., Executive Director

298 South Hull Street

Athens, Georgia 30603

Mailing Address

Post Office Box 1924

Athens, Georgia 30603

(404) 353-1331

National Interfaith Coalition on Aging identifies, supports, and sponsors appropriate research and development efforts, educational programs, and services for the aging, which may be best implemented through the resources of the nation's religious sector. NICA disseminates information designed to vitalize and develop the role of the church and synagogue in improving the quality of life and the spiritual well-being of the aging; stimulates "networking" between the nation's religious sector and the national, secular, private and public organizations whose programs relate to aging; and encourages aging individuals to continue giving to society from the wealth of their experience and to remain active within community life. Recent activities have included a national training grant (Title IV-A), 1977-80, to promote gerontology in seminary training (GIST); and a project to provide religious sector input into the 1981 White House Conference on Aging.

Membership:

> 31 national religious and secular organizations with voting privileges
>
> 30 national and regional organizations (non-voting)
>
> Approximately 125 individual members

Publications:

> *NICA Inform,* bimonthly
>
> Books

Meetings:

> 2 conferences a year

1103. National Interreligious Service Board for Conscientious Objectors (NISBCO)

Interdenominational

Warren W. Hoover, Executive Director

550 Washington Building

15th and New York Avenue, N.W.

Washington, D.C. 20005

(202) 393-4868

National Interreligious Service Board for Conscientious Objectors is a non-profit service organization sponsored by a broad coalition of national religious groups. NISBCO is committed to spreading understanding of conscientious objection along with truth about military recruitment, and is opposed to any form of registration, the draft, or compulsory national service. The services of the staff are available to anyone at no charge. Forty-seven religious bodies constitute the consultative council. NISBCO responds to the needs of concerned persons by: providing information on truth in military recruitment and initiatives for redress or discharge from within the military; providing information on how to register and document one's convictions as a conscientious objector; providing professional counseling for those who are working through problems with military service and convictions of conscientious objection; providing training for religious CO counselors; alerting concerned persons to changes that take place or are under serious consideration regarding military conscription, compulsory national service, and/or provisions for filing CO claims from within the military; aiding COs in the armed forces who seek discharge or transfer to noncombatant status; maintaining an extensive referral service to local counseling agencies in all areas of the country, and to attorneys who can aid those in need of legal counsel; acting as a national resource center for those interested in the CO/peace witness of the major religious bodies in the United States; and encouraging citizens through articles, speaking engagements, and NISBCO publications to conscientiously decide for themselves what they believe about participation in war.

Founding Date: 1940

Staff: 9

Membership: 47 religious bodies

Publications:
NISBCO's Monthly Newsletter

Meetings:
2 meetings a year of the Board of Directors and the consultative council
Draft Counseling Seminars conducted by the staff regularly

Former Name:
National Service Board for Religious Objectors

1104. National Interreligious Task Force on Soviet Jewry

Nondenominational

Sister Ann Gillen, SHCJ, Executive Director
1307 South Wabash, Room 221
Chicago, Illinois 60605
(312) 922-1983

The National Interreligious Task Force on Soviet Jewry was founded in Chicago by the cooperation of

The American Jewish Committee and the National Catholic Conference on Interracial Justice. The Task Force includes among its leaders major personalities of the Roman Catholic, Protestant, Eastern Orthodox, Evangelical, and Jewish communities. The Task Force, a major expression of human rights concerns shared by Christians and Jews, works in many ways to achieve freedom for Soviet Jews and Christians and other oppressed people. It carries on an intensive program of education, interpretation, and action through area meetings. The Task Force has sent high-level interreligious delegations to the Belgrade and Madrid Conferences, called to review the Helsinki Accords. It sponsors Project Co-Adoption, whereby Church and Synagogue groups form combined committees to work for the relief and freedom of Prisoners of Conscience in the USSR. It also publishes *The Task,* and provides guidance and assistance for various interreligious groups throughout the United States and in other parts of the world.

Founding Date: 1972

Publications:
The Task, a weekly newsletter

1105. National Jewish Committee on Scouting (NJCS)

Jewish

Dr. Harry B. Lasker, Director
Boy Scouts of America National Office
Post Office Box 61030
Dallas-Fort Worth Airport, Texas 75261
(214) 659-2000

The National Jewish Committee on Scouting advises Boy Scouts of America on all matters of religious policy; provides for the religious needs of scouts and leaders of Jewish faith attending national and world jamborees and Philmont Scout Ranch and Explorer-base; promotes the Aleph Award for cub scouts, Ner Tamid Award for boy scouts and explorers and Shofar Award for adults; and encourages Jewish youth to belong to BSA.

Founding Date: 1926

Membership: 160

Publications:
Ner Tamid News Bulletin, annual

Meetings:
Meets every two years in conjunction with national council meeting of BSA in various cities
Executive Committee meets several times a year

1106. National Jewish Community Relations Advisory Council (NJCRAC)

Jewish

Albert D. Chernin, Executive Vice Chairman
55 West 42nd Street, Suite 1530
New York, New York 10036
(212) 564-3450

National Jewish Community Relations Advisory Council is the national coordinating body for the field of Jewish community relations. Its goals are to foster democratic pluralism; freedom of religion, thought, and expression; equal opportunity; and a social climate in which differences among groups are accepted and respected. Its function is to facilitate joint policy making and program planning among its 11 national and 108 community member agencies.

Founding Date: 1944

Staff: 16

Membership:
11 national Jewish organizations and 108 local Jewish community relations councils

Publications:
Annual Joint Program Plan for Jewish Community Relations, a comprehensive guide to program planning of the constituent organizations

Meetings:
Annually, NJCRAC holds its Plenary Session, its highest policy making body comprising delegates from all of its member organizations; meetings are held in different major cities each year
Quarterly, its Executive Committee and five Commissions meet — two of the meetings are held in New York and the third is held in a major city in another part of the United States

Former Name:
National Community Relations Advisory Council

1107. National Jewish Hospitality Committee and Information Centers (NJHC)*

Jewish

201 South 18th Street, Room 1519
Philadelphia, Pennsylvania 19103
(215) 925-1951

National Jewish Hospitality Committee and Information Centers provide information about Judaism to non-Jews and Jews, and assists persons interested in conversion. It makes the general public aware that more than 10,000 men and women of all ages and backgrounds convert to Judaism every year in the United States alone.

Membership: 2,600

Publications:
10 religious-education concerning Jewish theology, practices, beliefs, history of conversion to Judaism, etc.
One newsletter: *Our Choice* bulletin

Meetings:
Several each year

1108. National Jewish Information Service for the Propagation of Judaism, Inc. (NJIS)

Jewish

Rabbi Moshe M. Maggal, Founder and President
5174 West 8th Street
Los Angeles, California 90036
(213) 936-6033

The National Jewish Information Service converts non-Jews to Judaism; maintains a college for Jewish Ambassadors for the training of Jewish missionaries, and the Correspondence Academy of Judaism for instruction on Judaism through the mail. The NJIS also distributes literature among the media, college campuses, church groups, and to government leaders both here and abroad in order to combat teachings of hatred against Jews, Judaism, and Israel.

Founding Date: 1960

Membership: 2,000

Publications:
The Voice of Judaism, periodically
Miscellaneous pamphlets and brochures

Meetings:
Occasionally

1109. National Lutheran Campus Ministry (NLCM)

The American Lutheran Church

The Reverend James R. Carr, Director
35 East Wacker Drive, Suite 1847
Chicago, Illinois 60601
(312) 332-1387

The National Lutheran Campus Ministry is a national agency of The American Lutheran Church, the Association of Evangelical Lutheran Churches, and the Lutheran Church in America, that secures personnel, finances, and supervises local campus ministry agencies and staff at major colleges and universities in the United States of America. The first full-time Lutheran campus pastor was called in 1907. The first cooperative campus ministry agency work of several Lutheran churches, which began in 1937, has now evolved into NLCM.

Staff: 170

Publications:

Circle: printed resources

Meetings:

More than 50 conferences, meetings, and seminars per year

1110. National Network of Episcopal Clergy Associations (NNECA)

Episcopal

The Rev. Douglas M. Spence, Convenor
425 Laurel Avenue
Highland Park, Illinois 60035
(312) 432-6653

The National Network of Episcopal Clergy Associations (NNECA) is a federation of diocesan clergy associations. Some 25 associations make up the membership. These member organizations are professional associations concerned with those issues that effect the lives and work of the clergy in the Episcopal Church. The national organization serves as a communication switchboard for the local associations chiefly through its newsletter, *Leaven.* It also attempts to coordinate efforts to deal with issues affecting the clergy on a national level.

Membership: 25 member associations

Publications:

Leaven, 20 times a year
What Are Clergy Associations All About?
What NNECA Has Accomplished

Meetings:

An annual conference held the last week of May in a different location each year

1111. The National Office for Black Catholics

Roman Catholic

Mr. James R. Henderson, Executive Director
1234 Massachusetts Avenue, N.W., Suite 1004
Washington, D.C. 20005
(202) 347-4619

The National Office of Black Catholics is an organization representing the more than 1,000,000 Black Catholics across the country. Goals of the office include the development and more effective utilization of Black clergy, religious, and laity; revitalization of Black parishes; providing guidance to Catholic bishops in the fight against racism; and advocating on behalf of the total Black community.

Founding Date: 1970

Publications:

Freeing the Spirit; IMPACT
Soulfull Worship; This Far by Faith
Black Perspectives on Evangelization in the Modern World

Meetings:
Approximately 4 total

1112. National Organization for the Continuing Education of Roman Catholic Clergy, Inc.

Roman Catholic

Rev. Edward Mahoney, President
351 North Avenue
Burlington, Vermont 05401
(415) 825-1472

The National Organization for the Continuing Education of Roman Catholic Clergy is primarily a service organization to aid Directors of Clergy Education in their local dioceses and provinces with information, study programs, models, personal training, etc. It is a clearing house for information regarding clergy education in the United States. It acts as a stimulus to regional meetings of clergy education directors at least once a year. The Organization maintains liaison with the United States Bishops Committee on Priestly life and ministry. On occasion it recommends policy regarding time, money, sabbaticals, and types of programs to be offered locally. And it encourages Bishops and Senates that have not yet done so to begin to take the need for clergy education more seriously.

Founding Date: 1972

Staff: 3

Membership: 120 dioceses; 70 Religious Provinces

Publications:

Newsletter, bimonthly

Task Force Reports: e.g., Rural Ministry, Sexuality, Sabbaticals, Workshop Directory, Retreat Directory, etc.

Meetings:

Convention of pastors throughout the United States (average 5 or 6 per year)

One annual convention, week before Ash Wednesday

1113. National Reform Association (NRA)

Nondenominational

Rev. R. W. Caskey, DD, Administrative Secretary
45 South Bryant Avenue
Pittsburgh, Pennsylvania 15202
(412) 766-5259

The National Reform Association is an interdenominational organization founded for the purpose of maintaining and promoting in our National life the Christian principles of civil government by awakening our citizens to the moral and spiritual standards essential for the preservation of our Nation and its people. Its objective is to combat the following: atheistic ideology, which leads to the rejection of moral absolutes and results in lawlessness and social irresponsibility; the use of alcoholic beverages, which results in alcoholism, delinquency, broken homes, and crimes in society; pornography and related evils that foster sexual license and indecency; the use of narcotics with the exploitation of young people; and gambling, whether legal or illegal, which feeds upon people and supports the underworld.

Founding Date: 1864

Staff: 2

Publications:

Christian Statesman, bimonthly

Meetings:

An annual dinner meeting

1114. National Religious Broadcasters (NRB)

Nondenominational

Dr. Ben L. Armstrong, Executive Director
Post Office Box 2254-R
Morristown, New Jersey 07960
(201) 540-8500

National Religious Broadcasters unites 900 individual broadcasters, national and international, large and small, to preserve free and complete access to radio and television lanes for the broadcasting of the Gospel of the Lord Jesus Christ. The fairness doctrine license renewal and the copyright issues are of concern to religious broadcasters and to NRB. NRB strives for program excellence and the observance of high standards in the broadcasting of the Gospel by the establishment of the NRB Code of Ethics for program producers and Christian station owners and operators. NRB provides a continuing relationship with the broadcasting industry, keeping abreast of current trends and developments with various national and international organizations. NRB provides a continuing relationship with governmental departments such as the Federal Communications Commission, Washington, D.C. The FCC chairman and commissioners often participate in NRB conventions.

Founding Date: 1944

Membership: 900

Publications:

Directory of Religious Broadcasting, annually
Religious Broadcasting, bimonthly
Hotline, newsletter, monthly

Meetings:

1 annual national convention
5 regional conventions

1115. National Right to Life Committee, Inc. (NRLC)

Nondenominational

J. C. Willke, MD, President
529 14th Street, N.W., Suite 341
Washington, D.C. 20045
(202) 638-4396

The National Right to Life Committee is an association of state and local organizations dedicated to countering contemporary society's increasing disrespect for human life, as evidenced by the growing incidence of abortion, euthanasia, and infanticide in the United States. The national organization maintains a lobbying presence in the United States Congress to promote an end of taxpayer-financed abortion and to achieve passage of a human life amendment to the Constitution to reverse the 1973 Supreme Court decisions in Roe v. Wade and Doe v. Bottom. The national committee also maintains an education foundation to educate the American people concerning the issues of abortion/euthanasia and to provide a credible source for research information on the medical, moral, and ethical implications of the "life issues." The National Right to Life Committee provides its associated chapters with information on legislation and legislative proposals, with speakers and speaking materials, and with information on the conduct of voter identification projects in local communities.

Founding Date: 1973
Staff: 10
Membership: 1,800 chapters nationwide
Publications:
  National Right to Life News, monthly
Meetings:
  Annual convention
  Legislative conferences, triannually

1116. National Service Committee of the Catholic Charismatic Renewal of the United States

Roman Catholic
Kevin M. Ranaghan, Director
National Communications Office
237 North Michigan Street
South Bend, Indiana 46601
(219) 234-6021

The National Service Committee of the Catholic Charismatic Renewal of the United States was formed by the common agreement of the people who had been responsible for the main services of the Catholic charismatic renewal up to that time. The NSC exercises pastoral concern for the Catholic charismatic renewal in the United States. It meets regularly with a 50-member group of advisors and consultants. The National Communications Office is the action agency of the NSC of the Catholic Charismatic

Renewal of the United States. Some of the principal NCO programs are: the NCO Newsletter, sent to about 7,500 leaders in the Church and the charismatic renewal; the National Service Committee Fund Appeal which raises about $200,000 annually to support renewal programs nationally and internationally, including the major support for the International Communication Office, Brussels, Belgium; the Charismatic Writers Association, which seeks to assist newsletter editors, free-lance writers, public relations people, and others active in the charismatic renewal who are concerned about writing and publishing; development and distribution of Catholic charismatic television programs for broadcast over Christian and secular stations; and an annual directory of prayer groups in the United States and Canada—including a list of world-wide renewal centers.

Founding Date: 1970
Staff:
  10 members of the National Service Committee
  7 members of the National Communications office
Publications:
  New Covenant, monthly
  National Communications Office Newsletter, about 8 times a year
  Charismatic Writers Association Bulletin, bimonthly
Radio/TV Programs:
  Pastoral Training Weekends—videotape workshops, 2 series
  Send Forth Your Spirit—10-part half-hour TV programs now being shown nationwide
Meetings:
  National Conference on the Catholic Charismatic Renewal annually
  Assists in planning some half-dozen regional conferences annually

1117. National Sisters Communications Service (NSCS)

Roman Catholic
Sister Elizabeth Thoman, CHM, Executive Director
1962 South Shenandoah Street
Los Angeles, California 90034
(213) 559-2944

The National Sisters Communications Service is a national non-profit agency providing mass communications consultation services and educational resources for religious orders of women and men in the Catholic Church. The NSCS is not a membership organization, but rather provides services on a subscription basis to congregations and individuals interested or involved in developing the ministry of communications, both in their own local order and nationally for all religious orders. In addition, the NSCS serves as a clearinghouse for the exchange of information about communications and public relations programs undertaken by religious orders, about jobs available for religious in the ministry of communications, and about justice issues in the media, particularly current legislative and regulatory issues. The NSCS also offers seminars and workshops to train communications personnel and religious leaders in contemporary mass communications programs and practices.

Founding Date: 1975

Staff: 5

Publications:
> *Media and Values,* quarterly
> *MediaKits,* a resource package of reprints and original materials (papers, books, audiotapes)

Meetings:
> An annual summer seminar

1118. National Sisters Vocation Conference (NSVC)

Roman Catholic
Sister Gertrude Wemhoff, OSB, Executive Director
1307 South Wabash, Suite 350
Chicago, Illinois 60605
(312) 939-6180

The National Sisters Vocation Conference is a service organization which is dedicated to deepening the understanding of the role of women, especially women religious in the Church, through service in the vocation apostolate. Its underlying philosophy is a pastoral approach to vocation—an ongoing, educative, informative process based on dynamic, existential concept of the baptized person, in the risen Lord Jesus, who is called to witness to His enduring presence. The objective of NSVC is to focus on the expertise, experiences, and current research in the approach to membership in religious communities. It provides a concerted effort on the part of women religious in the United States to encourage other women to total service in the Church and it provides support to those already ministering to the Christian commu-

nity, so that they may gain a fuller realization of their place in the Church and the world today.

Founding Date: 1967

Staff: 3

Membership: 1,000

Publications:
> *News/Views,* bimonthly
> *Directory*

Meetings:
> 1 annual national symposium
> 1 workshop in each of 15 regions annually
> On-going workshops

1119. The National Society of the Volunteers of America (VOA)

Nondenominational
General Ray C. Tremont, National Director
Volunteers of America
3939 North Causeway Boulevard, Suite 202
Metairie, Louisiana 70002
(504) 837-2652

The National Society of the Volunteers of America is a national Christian human service organization founded to provide material and spiritual assistance to those in need. Historically, the VOA has sought to establish programs which are responsive to community need, characterized by programmatic and managerial integrity, and consistent with its Christian commitment. Today the VOA is operating in approximately 150 communities across the nation. A wide range of community-based services, including day care, group homes, and foster care for children and youth; senior center and nutrition programs for the elderly; treatment, residential programs, and sheltered workshops for substance abusers; pre-release programs, half-way houses, and community programs for offenders and ex-offenders; residential treatment centers and employment assistance for the handicapped; and maternity and adoption programs and counseling and emergency shelters for families reflect the concerns of the organization and those of the communities it serves. The VOA develops and manages housing for the elderly and handicapped and for low and moderate income families. The organization also owns and operates nursing homes, primarily in the Midwest and the South, which provide both skilled and intermediate nursing care. Financial support derives from private contributions and government contracts.

Founding Date: 1896
Staff: 3,800
Membership: 500
Publications:
Volunteer Gazette, monthly
VOAgape, quarterly
Radio/TV Programs:
Assignment People
Meetings:
Grand Field Council — Annual meeting of the National Society
Various regional annual meetings and workshops

1120. National Women's Christian Temperance Union (WCTU)

Nondenominational
Mrs. Kermit Edgar, President
1730 Chicago Avenue
Evanston, Illinois 60201
(312) 864-1396

Major objectives of the National Woman's Christian Temperance Union are: protection of the home and community; building public sentiment for sobriety and promoting good citizenship involvement; building Christian temperance principles into the character of our children; informing society regarding the value of total abstinence by providing scientific facts concerning the nature and effects of alcohol and other narcotics; and promoting just laws and proper law enforcement. The program of the Union includes education through children and youth organizations teaching the scientific facts about the effects of alcohol, other narcotics, and tobacco on the body and in society, legislative support for women and children on moral social issues such as prostitution, abortion, gambling, and crime; providing for the needy in the neighborhood; and promoting the "Hour of Social Freedom" with recipes and information about entertaining without the use of alcoholic beverages.

Founding Date: 1874
Staff: 34
Membership: 250,000
Publications:
The Union Signal, monthly
The Young Crusader, children's monthly

Radio/TV Programs:
Films and filmstrips cleared for television use
15-, 20-, 30-, and 60-second spot announcements for public service broadcasting
Meetings:
1 national convention
2 narcotic education summer seminars for teachers
1 Leadership Training School
Annual conventions and mid-year conferences in separate states, as well as workshops, rallies, Youth Temperance Council camps and Loyal Temperance Legion Day camps

1121. National Yokefellow Prison Ministry, Inc. (NYPM)

Nondenominational
Newman R. Gaugler, President
112 Old Trail North
Shamokin Dam, Pennsylvania 17876
Mailing Address
Post Office Box 207
Shamokin Dam, Pennsylvania 17876
(717) 743-7832

The Yokefellow Prison Ministry began with the formation of a Yokefellow Group at the United States Penitentiary, McNeil Island, near Tacoma, Washington. The experience of this pioneering effort has been duplicated in federal, state, and county prisons nationwide. To provide support and central direction to this rapidly growing program, the National Yokefellow Prison Ministry was incorporated in 1969 as a non-profit organization with headquarters at Shamokin Dam, Pennsylvania. A Board of Directors, elected by the contributing membership, gives direction on a national level. The board is legally responsible for all monies contributed and holds title to property. For more than 20 years the original small spiritual growth group concept has remained central in the Yokefellow movement. The ministry's objectives are: to help serve the spiritual needs of residents in correctional institutions; to bridge the gap between those confined in prison and the outside community; to demonstrate continuing concern for offenders in the process of reintegration; to promote and cooperate in the establishment of community-operated Halfway Houses; to participate in programs designed to improve correctional methods; and to bear concern for the decisions made by those responsible for policies and procedures of rehabilitation efforts. These activities are pursued on a strictly voluntary basis by Regional Directors, Regional Advisors, and Local Area Councils scattered across the nation. The small gold Yoke Pin worn by a NYPM member symbolizes the love and concern of one human being for another.

Founding Date: 1969

Membership:
>   6 Regional Directors
>   26 Area Coordinators
>   200 Contributing Members

Publications:
>   *Yoke News,* semiannually
>   *Newsletter,* quarterly
>   *Annual Christmas Letter*

Meetings:
>   Annual National Yokefellow Prison Ministry
>   Conference and Workshop
>   Renewal Weekends (Lay Witness Missions)
>   Leadership Training Seminars
>   Volunteer Counselor Training Seminars

1122. Native Preacher Company

Interdenominational
G. L. Gremmels, Secretary
888 Seventh Avenue, Suite 400
New York, New York 10019
(212) 265-4300

Native Preacher Company, a non-profit organization, supports native missionaries in Asia, Africa, and South America. The organization sent 100% of the contributions it received directly to the missions.

1123. The Navigators

Nondenominational
Dr. Lorne C. Sanny, International President
Post Office Box 20
Colorado Springs, Colorado 80901
(303) 598-1212

The Navigators is an international, interdenominational, Christian service organization. Its primary aim is to multiply spiritual laborers in every nation, thus helping to fulfill Christ's Great Commission. The organization's staff of some 1,600 persons of 26 nationalities minister in more than 34 countries. The main thrust is among educated young adults, collegians, military, and business/professional persons in the community. The Navigators preach and teach the scriptural challenge of discipleship and spiritual multiplication.

Founding Date: 1933

Staff: 1,618

Publications:
>   *Navlog,* quarterly
>   *Daily Walk,* a monthly devotional guide

Meetings:
>   Many meetings a year

1124. Nazarene Theological Seminary Board

Church of the Nazarene
Terrell C. (Jack) Sanders
Nazarene Theological Seminary President
6401 The Paseo
Kansas City, Missouri 64131

The object of Nazarene Theological Seminary Board is to establish a seminary; to provide courses of study of graduate level preparatory for pastors, missionaries, religious educators, song evangelists, childrens workers, and teachers; and any other fields for the carrying out of the Great Commission of Jesus Christ. The Board is authorized to conduct institutes, lectureships, and any other courses of study which will better equip Christian workers. The primary purpose of the institution is to conserve, maintain, advocate, and promulgate the great Bible doctrine of "Entire Sanctification" as a second distinct work of divine grace wrought in the heart of the believer subsequent to regeneration.

1125. Near East Archaeological Society (NEAS)

Interdenominational
Dr. W. Harold Mare, President
12330 Conway Road
St. Louis, Missouri 63141
(314) 434-4044

The Near East Archaeological Society is a living society made up of evangelical Christians and institutions who are interested in encouraging, advancing, and participating in archaeological and scholarly research that will help illuminate the Biblical record. The NEAS was organized in 1960, principally to advance archaeological and Biblical work, particularly in Palestine. Late in the 1960's, the organization's scope was expanded to include such work and research in any of the areas of the Mediterranean and Near East Region. Goals of the NEAS are the encouragement and advancement of archaeological meetings and conferences, excavations, and all kinds of Biblical research in all the Mediterranean area and Near East Region where Bible history and church history have taken place.

Founding Date: 1960

Membership: 180 general members

Publications:

Newsletter, periodically

The Bulletin, annually, containing articles and conference reports

The Research Series, irregularly, containing reports of archaeological research

Meetings:

Annual meeting and conference with a program in conjunction with the Evangelical Theological Society Meetings

1126. Neturei Karta of USA (NKUSA)

Jewish

M.Z. Weberman
Government Post Office Box 2143
Brooklyn, New York 11202
(212) 384-4541

Neturei Karta of USA is an orthodox Jewish anti-Zionist organization devoted to spreading true Judaism among Jews and to publicizing the true Jewish stand among non-Jews concerning Zionism, the Zionist state, and Zionists, as well as all other psuedo-Jewish movements.

Founding Date: 1969

Staff: 5

Publications:

The Jewish Guardian, quarterly

Meetings:

1 meeting per year

Also Known As: Guardians of The Holy City

1127. NETWORK

Roman Catholic

Nancy Sylvester, IHM
806 Rhode Island Avenue, N.E.
Washington, D.C. 20018
(202) 526-4070

NETWORK, a registered lobby, focuses on the relationship of national legislation to social justice and provides a vehicle of communication and action for persons interested in social justice to make legislation more responsive to the concerns of all people, particularly those now oppressed. A resource staff in Washington, D.C., provides: publications on current legislation and social issues; workshops throughout the country; intern and volunteer programs; assistance for regional communication and organizing for political action; phone alerts; and skill training seminars.

Founding Date: 1971

Staff: 9

Membership: 6,500

Publications:

NETWORK, bimonthly

Action Alerts, timed to congressional activity on NETWORK's issues

Meetings:

Legislative seminar, June, Washington, D.C.

Skills training seminar, March and September, Washington, D.C.

Workshops, upon request, across the country

Political Action Practicums, April and October, Washington, D.C.

1128. New City Press (NCP)

Roman Catholic

Claude H. Blanc, General Manager
206 Skillman Avenue
Brooklyn, New York 11211
(212) 782-2844

New City Press is the publishing house of the Focolare Movement. It publishes and distributes books in 12 languages. The first books printed were collections of meditations written by Chiara Lubich, the foundress of the Focolare Movement. Since then a number of her further works dealing with a variety of important aspects of the spiritual life have also been published by NCP. They have also published the biographies of a few prominent spiritual leaders of our time, and recently have launched a series of books on family education. These are the aims of NCP: to share with everyone the rich and practical spirituality of the Focolare Movement which has grown out of 37 years of intense Christian life in the midst of today's world; and to seek out and offer to readers all that is positive in the various areas of human interest.

Staff: 18

Publications:

> *Living City,* monthly
> *Gen 2,* a newsletter for teenagers
> *Gen 3,* a newsletter for grammar school children

Meetings:

> 3 main gatherings called Mariapolises each summer at different locations

1129. The New Directions Evangelistic Association

Interdenominational
Reverend J. L. Williams, President
323 West Harden Street
Graham, North Carolina 27253
Mailing Address
Post Office Box 2347
Burlington, North Carolina 27215
(919) 227-1273

In 1968, a group of young people from Alamance County, North Carolina, began to meet together to study the Scriptures, to experience the reality of prayer, and to share with one another in their daily trails and triumphs of walking with Jesus Christ. Although no one projected it, it was out of this group of young believers that the New Directions were born. It seemed to be a natural progression that their longing for the life of Christ would find its fulfillment in looking at the Person of Christ and overflow into lauding the Name of Christ. What originally began as a group of brothers and sisters fellowshipping together by singing "psalms and hymns and spiritual songs" grew over the years into an internationally-known, multifaceted outreach of discipleship and evangelism. Travels have taken the New Directions into almost every part of the Western Hemisphere for concerts in schools, churches, shopping centers, beaches, prisons, stadiums, and campgrounds. In addition to the musical outreach, a variety of other ministries are incorporated in this Association. Video production plays a primary role in their outreach. Special video-taped teaching series by J. L.

Williams and other noted Christian speakers are distributed to home study groups, Sunday School classes, and church meetings. Publications cover a wide range of subjects, from practical helps for new converts through serious Bible study and apologetics, to skillful and sensible approaches to current cultism. Puppets have especially strong appeal for children. Recognizing the impact and potential that medium has for Christian education and evangelism, the New Directions use puppetry in a variety of presentations. Cassettes and recordings are other facets of this ministry. Inspirational music and teaching tapes are available in the home office and through the mail. Additionally, an extensive counseling ministry is provided by the full-time staff.

Founding Date: 1968

Staff: 14 singing team members and 10 staff

Publications:

> *New Directions,* monthly
> *The Director's Report,* monthly

Meetings:

> Six per year at Headquarters: 323 West Hardin Street, Graham, North Carolina 27253

1130. New Life Foundation (NLF)

Mennonite
Martin Weber, Administrator
Star Route A
Atmore, Alabama 36502
(205) 368-5457

New Life Foundation started as an assistance to the chaplain at the Atmore Prison Farm, now called G. K. Fountain Correctional Institution. At the present time, there are services at the Chapel and Trustee Barracks and five full-time counselors who help the chaplain. They spend time with the prisoners answering questions and helping them find meaning to life with the ultimate goal of leading them to Christ. The counselors also help with Bible Correspondence Courses and run a book ministry that both loans and gives books to the prisoners. Several days a week are spent working with the inmates of death row and segregation lock-up. There are two Bible teachers who work with prisoners. Class attendance is voluntary. New Life Foundation is also starting a warning type of teaching in high schools and county jails. This program includes a prisoner who discusses what happens to a person's freedom when they are put in the state prison system.

Staff: 11 staff members
Publications:
Newsletter, monthly

1131. New Life International

Pentecostal Assemblies of God
Rev. Larry Southwick, President
Post Office Box 11511
Fresno, California 93773

New Life International cooperates with the Pentecostal Assemblies of God which itself has missionary outreaches in more than 180 countries through nearly 50 national missionary-sending fellowships. The purposes of New Life International are: to assist in providing communication-media tools and publications; to share and expand information; to promote home and foreign missions' outreaches and local church growth of the Assemblies; to help pioneer new churches, especially among largely unreached ethnic and special interest groups; to research and write on church growth and world missions; and to maintain a lending and research book and tape library.

Founding Date: 1975
Staff: 6 staff members; 9 approved missionaries
Publications:
New Life International Total Ministry
Radio/TV Programs:
Under development
Meetings:
Meetings will be held through New Life International Bible College

1132. New Life Mission, Inc.

Nondenominational
Neil Macaulay, President
345 West Palmetto Park Road
Boca Raton, Florida 33432
(305) 395-1106

New Life Mission, Inc., is an international mass media ministry propagating the Christian Gospel to the far corners of the earth. Its main emphasis is on training overseas nationals to be national broadcasters of the Christian faith in the native tongue. Studios and headquarters located in Boca Raton,

Florida serve as recording headquarters for sacred and inspirational Christian music. Literature is printed and distributed, as is a house magazine entitled New Life News and World Report. There are also English language broadcasts by Neil Macaulay heard in the United States as well as on stations with international coverage such as Trans World Radio on Bonaire in the Dutch Antilles and Guam Island, and also Far East Broadcasting Co., in the Philippines.

Publications:
Newsletter, monthly
Magazines, quarterly
Radio/TV Programs:
Radio: *New Life,* ½-hour weekly (music, poems, speaking)
Great Hymns and Their Stories, organ melodies and meditations (15:00)
Great Moments in History, (5 min. daily)
Television: *New Life,* (music, guest, speaking)
Missionary Adventure, travelogue
Meetings:
Approximately 30 meetings and conferences per year in East and Southeast

1133. New Testament Missionary Union (NTMU)

Nondenominational
Mr. George A. Rice, Coordinating Secretary
U.S. Office
514 Banner Avenue
Winston-Salem, North Carolina 27107
(919) 722-0932

New Testament Missionary Union (headquarters in Buenos Aires, Argentina) is a company of missionaries called together by the Holy Spirit and taking as a pattern for the mission organization the New Testament missionary group of which Paul was leader. The mission's spiritual fellowship is with all those who love the Lord in truth. The Union seeks to fulfill the commission which the Lord gave, to urgently proclaim His saving grace, and to witness to His teaching concerning "the Church, which is His Body, the fullness of Him that filleth each one with Himself." Its message is "Christ in You." The NTMU's purpose is evangelism in the full New Testament sense — the bringing of men and women to a saving knowledge of Jesus Christ, the gathering of them into churches which function according to the pattern that Christ gave, and the giving to them of the whole counsel of

God that they may enter fully into the life manifested by the indwelling Christ.

Founding Date: 1902

Membership: 43

Publications:

Field News, quarterly, in English

Noticiero, monthly, in Spanish

Meetings:

Annual retreats in Posadas, Argentina and Villarica, Paraguay, usually held in January

Former Name:

(1932) South American Missionary Union

1134. New York International Bible Society

Interdenominational

The Reverend Y. R. Kindberg, President

144 Tices Lane

East Brunswick, New Jersey 08816

(201) 238-5454

The New York International Bible Society is engaged in translation, production, and distribution of the Bible in many parts, editions, and formats. It is also an evangelistic, missionary organization employing full-time missionaries and chaplains in special evangelistic outreach concerns.

Founding Date: 1809

Staff: 45

Publications:

Bible World, quarterly

Former Names:

New York Bible Society

New York Bible Society International

1135. New York Training School for Deaconesses

Episcopal

The Rt. Rev. Paul Moore, Jr., President

117 Chestnut Drive

Barnegat, New Jersey 08005

(609) 698-1866

The New York Training School for Deaconesses is not operated as an institution but offers financial aid to women who qualify. It assists only women attending seminary who are postulants or candidates for ordination in the Episcopal Church.

Staff:

4 lay; 7 clerical members of the Board of Trustees

1136. Next Towns Crusade

Nondenominational

John M. Bell, Director

3015 Gainesborough

San Antonio, Texas 78230

(512) 344-7467

Next Towns Crusade is a foreign missionary program to cover missionaries in Japan, Mexico, South America, and other countries who are working primarily in areas where there is no Gospel witness.

Founding Date: 1957

Staff:

5 Board members

3 missionaries in Japan, 4 in Mexico, and 2 in South America

Publications:

Prayer letters of associated missionaries

1137. Nocturnal Adoration Society in the United States*

Roman Catholic

Rev. Hector C. Lemieux, SSS

194 East 76th Street

New York, New York 10021

(212) 737-9373

The purpose of the Noctural Adoration Society is to bring Catholic men together in witness to Christ's sacrificial action in the Holy Eucharist, by sharing in His night prayer (Matt. 14:23, 26: 36-46; Mark 6:46, 14:32, Luke 6:12, 9:28). The members spend one hour a month before the Blessed Sacrament between 10 p.m. and 6 a.m.

Membership: 121,000 lay; 575 clerical

Publications:

Monthly newsletter

1138. North American Academy of Ecumenists*

Nondenominational

Dr. Joseph C. Weber, President
c/o COCU
228 Alexander Street
Princeton, New Jersey 08540

The North American Academy of Ecumenists holds an annual conference; it encourages special projects of research in the area of ecumenics. The purpose of the Academy is "to inform, relate, and encourage men and women professionally engaged in the study, teaching, and other practice of ecumenism."

Membership: 120

Publications:
Affiliated with the *Journal of Ecumenical Studies*

Meetings:
Annual meeting

1139. North American Baptist Fellowship (NABF)

Baptist

Charles F. Wills, Secretary
1628 Sixteenth Street, N.W.
Washington, D.C. 20009
(202) 265-5027

The members of the North American Baptist Fellowship are: American Baptist Churches in the United States of America; Baptist Federation of Canada; General Association of General Baptists; National Baptist Convention of America; Convencion Nacional Bautista de Mexico; North American Baptist Conference; Progressive National Baptist Convention; Seventh Day Baptist General Conference; and the Southern Baptist Convention. Its purpose is to provide a means of fellowship across convention lines and to share strategies and insights for mission.

Founding Date: 1965

Staff: 2

Membership:
9 Baptist conventions, federations, and conferences

Publications:
Insert to *The Baptist World,* quarterly

Meetings:
1 national meeting each year somewhere in North America
1 conference on church extension each year
Participate in 2 dialogues each year with the member bodies of the Lutheran Council

1140. North American Committee for IME, Institut Medical Evangelique Kimpese, Zaire*

Interdenominational

Glen W. Tuttle, MD, Secretary-Treasurer
3063 Virginia Avenue, South, Apt. 6
Minneapolis, Minnesota 55426
(612) 933-5436

The North American Committee for IME (Institut Medical Evangelique or Evangelical Medical Institute) is a supporting committee for the Evangelical Medical Institute located in Kimpese, Zaire. It raises funds and seeks staff for a 425-bed hospital which is international and interdenominational with supporting Mission Boards located in Britain, Canada, Sweden, and the United States. It has its own Board of Management located in Zaire.

1141. North American Jewish Students' Appeal (NAJSA)

Jewish

Roberta Shiffman, Executive Director
15 East 26th Street, Suite 1350
New York, New York 10010
(212) 679-2293

The North American Jewish Students' Appeal is the administrative, coordinating, and fund raising agency for a group of national, independent Jewish student organizations. Current constituents are: the Jewish Student Press Service, North American Jewish Students Network, Response Magazine, Student Struggle for Soviet Jewry, and Yugntruf-Youth for Yiddish. In addition, the NAJSA awards small beneficiary grants to local and regional student projects throughout the country and assists Jewish students in areas of budget formulation and proposal writing.

Founding Date: 1971

Staff: 2

1142. North American Jewish Students' Network

Jewish

David Makovsky, President
One Park Avenue, Suite 418
New York, New York 10016
(212) 689-0790

The North American Jewish Students' Network was created in 1970 by Jewish students who sought to develop an independent student-run organization that would respond to the needs of American and Canadian Jewish students. The students differed widely in the nature and style of their Jewish commitment, in their political orientation, in their cultural background and in the extent of their Jewish education. However, they shared a commitment to fulfilling a vital need for Jewish students across North America to Cultivate a feeling of solidarity and a sense of common purpose, and to stimulate outreach to unaffiliated, uninvolved Jewish students. Network is the independent union for Jewish students and Jewish student organizations. Network serves as a means of communication between Jewish student groups and a catalyst for turning ideas and aspirations of Jewish students into actual projects and events. Network sponsors and helps organize seminars, speaking tours, conferences and regional projects which concern Jewish cultural, educational and organizational activities. Network is one of the six members of the World Union of Jewish Students. Network is governed directly by its constituents, according to democratic principles and procedures, and in response to directives that are set at Network's biennial North American Jewish Students' Convention. The Convention brings together approximately 500 representatives from Jewish student groups throughout North America. Convention participants elect a North American President, United States Chairperson, Canadian Chairperson and regional coordinators.

Founding Date: 1970

Staff: 6

Publications:
   Guide to Jewish Student Groups
   Network Newspaper
   Network Pocket Calendar

Meetings:
   Monthly

1143. North American Jewish Students' Network, New Jewish Media Project*

Jewish

Terry Sutton, Director
15 East 26th Street
New York City, New York 10010
(212) 689-0790

The New Jewish Media Project is dedicated to the cause of increasing the Jewish community's awareness of the importance of media as an effective tool in strengthening Jewish identity and commitment. Therefore, it seeks: to create an atmosphere through film festivals, exhibits, personal contacts, and workshops in which experiments in Jewish media are encouraged and fostered; to secure funding that will enable them to create and assist in production of new Jewish media; to build a resource center for Jewish media materials, and to make available technical advice and other assistance to anyone in any place who wants to produce or employ Jewish media; to function as a clearing house where media producers can advertise and lend, rent, or sell their products and services; and to create a vehicle through which the many and scattered producers of media, both in the Diaspora and in Israel, can communicate with one another.

Membership: 55

Radio/TV Programs:
   Film, slide/tape presentations, radio tapes 30 already produced

1144. North American Jewish Youth Council (NAJYC)

Jewish

Stuart Fund, Chairman
515 Park Avenue
New York, New York 10022
(212) 751-6070

The North American Jewish Youth Council is the umbrella organization which services its constituent national Jewish Youth Organizations, its affiliated local Youth Councils, and other National Jewish Youth service organizations. It was founded in response to the need for closer cooperation among Jewish, youth groups serving Jewish community interests. NAJYC strives to aid its members in planning cooperative activities and in servicing its member organizations. The purpose of NAJYC is to provide the opportunity for cooperative endeavors by youth that express the spirit of the Jewish people. These include: national assemblies and demonstrations, regional educational conferences, workshops, and special reports. NAJYC seeks to assist national organizations and local youth councils in planning their own programs and activities.

Founding Date: 1964

Staff: 21

Membership: 25 Jewish youth organizations

1145. North American Liturgy Resources (NALR)

Nondenominational

Raymond P. Bruno, President
10802 North 23rd Avenue
Phoenix, Arizona 85029
(602) 864-1980

North American Liturgy Resources is a publishing house specializing in resources for worship and religious education, particularly the medium of contemporary music. It is characterized by the deep involvement of many of its composers and authors in the educational efforts of the company. While the major market is Roman Catholic, most NALR materials are considered ecumenical.

Membership:
65 including active composers and lecturers

Publications:
Over 200 titles in records, tapes, books, music.

1146. North American Patristic Society (NAPS)

Nondenominational

William R. Schoedel, President
Department of Religious Studies
John Carroll University
University Heights, Ohio 44118
(216) 491-4708

The purpose of the North American Patristic Society is to promote the study of Patristics, the study of the Fathers of the Church. The Society does this by organizing learned meetings; by participating in meetings of other organizations; by printing book reviews in its newsletter, and by keeping members abreast of activities in the field.

Founding Date: 1970

Membership: 285

Publications:
Patristics, semiannually
Directory of Patristic Scholars in North America

Meetings:
1 annual meeting
Occasional participation at meetings of other learned groups

1147. Northeast Catholic Pastoral Center for Hispanics

Roman Catholic

Mr. Mario J. Paredes
1011 First Avenue
New York, New York 10022
(212) 751-7045

Northeast Catholic Pastoral Center for Hispanics provides educational services in the areas of religion, culture, leadership, language, and social issues to Hispanics of the Northeast Region of the United States of America. It provides a resource library with printed materials in Spanish; publishes books and provides printed matter from Latin America and Europe. It trains Hispanic and non- Hispanic personnel interested in the Hispanic community; and has a Pastoral, a Vocation, a Communications, an Evangelization and a Leadership Department. The Center works closely with Hispanic youth on a regional level and has excellent working and collaborative relationships with the Hispanic National Office.

Founding Date: 1976

Staff: 12

Membership: 28

Publications:
Presencia, quarterly
Numerous books

Radio/TV Programs:
El Pueblo En Marcha, TV
El Mensaje Cristiano, Radio

Meetings:
Retreats, ten a year; conferences, 10-15

Meetings, 10-15; Summer Pastoral Courses, six weeks; Intensive English Language, eight weeks; Hispanic Ministry, one week; Youth Institutes, one week July/one week August; Catechetical Institute, one week

1148. North East India General Mission, Inc.

Evangelical

Rev. Duane M. Ray, General Secretary
100 West Park Avenue
Myerstown, Pennsylvania 17067

Mailing Address
Post Office Box 186
Myerstown, Pennsylvania 17067
(717) 866-2181

The North East India General Mission was established in Manipur State. A bible school was started with a white missionary in charge. The Christians were trained to minister to their own people. This type of ministry was very effective, as many were won to the Lord. In the 1950's, because of political problems in Nagaland to the north, the government closed the area to white people. Since that time the work has been carried on by the nationals. They are responsible to the home Board and receive directives from them. In the census of 1979, they reported 500 Chapels with 64,000 Christians.

Founding Date: 1910
Staff:
2 home office staff members; 10 Board members
Membership:
516 pastors, teachers, and evangelists in India
Publications:
Tidings, bimonthly
Meetings:
Annual Board meetings
Leaders' Conference and youth retreats in India annually

1149. Northwestern Publishing House

Wisconsin Evangelical Lutheran Synod
Walter R. Bunge, Manager
3624 West North Avenue
Milwaukee, Wisconsin 53208
(414) 442-1810

The Northwest Publishing House is organized exclu-

sively for religious charitable and educational pur poses consistent with the tenets of the Lutheran faith. This includes, but is not limited to, the carrying on and conducting of a general book selling publishing, and printing business, and particular the printing, publication, and dissemination of a such books, periodicals, and literature which ar beneficial to the Evangelical Lutheran faith.

Publications:
1 general religious biweekly
1 professional religious quarterly
1 daily meditation quarterly
1 children's religious monthly

1150. Notre Dame Center for Pastoral Liturgy

Roman Catholic
Rev. John Allyn Melloh, Director
Post Office Box 81
Notre Dame, Indiana 46556
(219) 283-8801

The Notre Dame Center for Pastoral Liturgy is liturgical pastoral institute, so designated by the American Catholic bishops in accordance with the recommendation of Vatican II. Its purpose is to promote the liturgical life of the Roman Catholic community in North America at national, diocesan, an parochial levels through research, publication, advis ory services, conferences, workshops, and lectures To this end it draws chiefly, but not exclusively, upon the academic resources of the University of Notre Dame and thus represents part of that University's effort to serve the welfare of the larger community. I also maintains a network of contacts throughout the Catholic community in the United States and Canada, especially by associating with its programs those who have been graduated in the liturgy pro gram of the university's theology department and have since assumed responsibility for the liturgy in diocesan and parish appointments.

Staff: 5 full-time; 2 part-time
Membership: 75 associates
Publications:
Assembly, 5 times a year
Meetings:
National Conference on Pastoral Liturgy annually
Week-long workshops on liturgical and pastoral practice held at Notre Dame and, by special

arrangement, in other parts of the country, 6-8 times a year

Former Name: Murphy Center for Liturgical Research

1151. Nyingma Community

Buddhist

Tarthang Tulku, Rinpoche, President-Founder
1815 Highland Place
Berkeley, California 94709
(415) 843-6812

The goal of the Nyingma Community is to apply to the West the teachings of Buddha. The Community includes meditation and study centers in Boulder, Colorado, and Tucson and Mesa in Arizona, as well as the Institute and Meditation Center in Berkeley. Professional training is available at these centers for those with an interest in developing counseling and therapeutic skills. Spring and summer sessions are offered. Dharma press in Oakland offers training in the many skills connected with the production and distribution of books. Nyingma bakeries in Berkeley, San Diego, Tucson, and Mesa provide work possibilities for those interested in baking, marketing and business administration. Odiyan, the country center located in eastern Sonoma county, has opportunities for those who would like to learn construction skills and gardening while living in a rural environment. Stained glass windows for the Odiyan temple are currently being created at a studio in Berkeley, where both beginner artisans and skilled crafts-people are welcome. Other activities and businesses are planned for the coming year, including the development of a graphic arts center.

Founding Date: 1973

Staff: 6

Publications:
> *Gesar,* quarterly

Meetings:
> Weekend retreats
> Spring and summer sessions
> Summer program for children

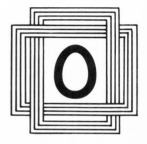

1152. Oblate Missionaries of Mary Immaculate

Roman Catholic
Murielle Valois, District Director
91 Brookfield Street
Lawrence, Massachusetts 01843
(617) 682-1564

The Oblate Missionaries of Mary Immaculate are members of a Secular Institute, a new form of dedication in the Church since 1947. Its membership is international and the Church officially recognized the group as a Secular Institute on February 2, 1962. Members profess the Gospel Counsels and live a life of apostolic commitment without practicing life in common, as religious are called to do. In most instances the members do not live together, but rely upon the solidarity of the Institute for fraternal and spiritual support. They strive to cooperate with the Church in the building up and strengthening of the Kingdom of God in the world and by bearing witness to the charity of Christ wherever they live and work. Persons who pursue this form of vocation accept the challenge of transforming the world from within.

Founding Date: 1952

Membership: 613

1153. OC Ministries, Inc.

Nondenominational
Dr. Clyde Cook, President
3033 Scott Boulevard
Santa Clara, California 95052

Mailing Address
Post Office Box 66
Santa Clara, California 95052
(408) 727-7111

The official statement of purpose of OC Ministries is: "In obedience to the Lord of the Harvest, the task of OC Ministries is to assist the Body of Christ to make disciples of all peoples. God has led us to do this by motivating, training, and mobilizing the Body of Christ to make obedient disciples and to establish churches among all peoples." In each country of ministry, teams of spiritually gifted men and women work with the whole Body of Christ in such ministries as pastors' conferences, church growth seminars, church growth bulletins, evangelistic crusades and rallies, Bible correspondence courses, mass media, youth and Christian education emphases, athletics, music, drama ministries, and many others. The ministries are selected and forged together in an overall strategy designed to make the maximum impact on the church of a given nation towards the discipling of that nation.

Founding Date: 1950

Staff: 35

Membership: 112 missionaries

Publications:
Global Church Growth Bulletin, bimonthly
World Spotlight, bimonthly
Individual newsletters from missionaries, monthly

Meetings:
Mount Hermon Family Conference, Mount Hermon, California, annually
OC Ministries Adult Conference, Forest Home, California, annually
OC Ministries Family Conference, George Fox College, Newberg, Oregon, annually
OC Ministries Family Conference, Taylor University, Upland, Indiana, annually

Former Name: (1979) Overseas Crusades, Inc.

1154. Odysseus

Nondenominational

Telemachos A. Greanias, Ph.D., Executive Director
401-C Alberto Way
Los Gatos, California 95030

Mailing Address
Post Office Box 394
Los Gatos, California 95031
(408) 356-3232

Odysseus is a spiritually-based consciousness research organization which disseminates information between other researchers as well as offering classes, lectures, seminars, and workshops to the public. Its purpose is to research and develop information and practical methods of application of new modes of determining what human existence and processes are. Research and application have developed the organization into a Growth Center where individuals and groups make contact with the farthest reaches of Transpersonal, Humanistic and Holistic Realities in action. Although the organization is spiritually based, the hard data from Consciousness Research and other fields are used as accompanying premises. The programs offered assist in developing the Self-knowledge, skills, and attitudes, as well as the preventative measures, to provide Holistic Health Concepts to guide the individual. Most of the mondalities offered are Psychic, Spiritual, Mental, Emotional, or Educational. They do produce changes in the inappropriate personal habits and effect physical changes as well.

Founding Date: 1970

Meetings:
12-15 annually at various locations

1155. The Officers' Christian Fellowship of the USA

Interdenominational

Mr. Paul C. Pettijohn, Executive Director
Post Office Box 36200
Denver, Colorado 80236
(303) 761-1984

The objectives of the Officers' Christian Fellowship of the USA are: to build up the individual member to spiritual maturity in his walk with God, his family, and his associates; and to be an instrument through which the individual member is helped to lead men and women in the military society to commit their lives to Jesus Christ, to grow to spiritual maturity in Him, and to use their individual spiritual gifts toward these same ends in the lives of others. These objectives are carried out primarily through local Bible studies in military officers' homes.

Staff: 21

Membership:
4,248 regular members
1,975 prayer partners

Publications:
Command Magazine
Monthly Newsletter

Meetings:
25 meetings annually at White Sulphur Springs, Colorado
20 meetings annually at Spring Canyon, Colorado
100 weekend conferences worldwide

1156. The Old Catholic Church in North America (the Catholicate of the West)

Old Catholic

Most Rev. Charles V. Hearn, Patriarch and Primate
1248 Eleventh Street "D"
Santa Monica, California 90401
(213) 395-0553

The Old Catholic Church in North America stresses both its ecumenicity and its similarity to the Roman Catholic Church in workship and doctrine. It accepts the primacy but denies the infallibility of the Pope, considers the apostolic succession vital in a valid Christian ministry, acknowledges seven sacraments, teaches trans-substantiation, prays for the departed, and venerates and invokes the glorious and immaculate Mother of God, the saints, and the angels. Its worship is in the vernacular. Its expressed aim is neither division nor reformation, but reconstruction or restructure on canonical lines.

Founding Date: 1950

Staff: 10

Membership: 12,000

Publications:
Monthly newsletter to the denominations clergy

Meetings:
Annual convention always in Santa Monica

1157. OLOGOS Publishing Mission (Orthodox Lore of the Gospel of Our Savior)

Greek Orthodox Eastern Church
Rev. George Mastrantonis, Founder-Editor
Post Office Box 5333
St. Louis, Missouri 63115
(314) 533-7755 or 721-4342

The OLOGOS Publishing Mission is a non-profit missionary organization which publishes and distributes pamphlets, booklets, and books on the Eastern Orthodox Church through churches and individuals. Free publications are sent to Eastern Orthodox Chaplains for distribution to members of the Orthodox Faith.

1158. Omni Communications International, Inc.

Interdenominational
Gary C. Wharton, Director
3040 Charlevoix Drive S.E.
Grand Rapids, Michigan 49506
(616) 949-2250

Omni Communications International provides total communications and marketing-sales services that include: marketing and management consultation; trade sales representation; media (advertising space) sales representation; the National Religious Bestsellers charts; retail promotional aids, catalogs, etc.; advertising and promotional services; and direct mail and catalog sales. Omni also cosponsors the annual National Religious Book Awards with Religious Book Review.

Publications:
    National Religious Bestsellers, monthly (under Christian News Service)
    Special charts for books, Bibles, music, records, including the Millionaires Club, 100,000 Club, etc.

Former Name: Christian News Service

1159. OMS International, Inc.

Nondenominational
Wesley L. Duewel, President
1200 Fry Road
Greenwood, Indiana 46142

Mailing Address
Post Office Box A
Greenwood, Indiana 46142
(317) 881-6751

The objectives of OMS International are: to promote missionary interests and work in the United States and foreign lands, including church-planting evangelism, the establishment and maintenance of schools for the training of missionaries, pastors, evangelists, Bible women, and teachers, and for the education of children; the establishment of gospel missions and churches, and dispensaries; the printing, distribution, and circulation of Bibles, religious books, papers, pamphlets, tracts, and similar publications relating to, or appropriate for, missionary work, radio ministry, social welfare and relief, and other missionary work and activities. OMS International today carries on its missionary work in twelve nations.

Founding Date: 1901

Staff: 456

Publications:
    OMS Outreach, 10 issues yearly
    Action, quarterly
    Intercesso-Gram, monthly

Radio/TV Programs:
    1 radio station in Cap Haitien, Haiti plus daily programs over 26 stations

Meetings:
    Annual convention in Greenwood, Indiana
    5,230 other meetings

Former Name: (1973) Oriental Missionary Society

1160. Open Air Campaigners

Nondenominational
Urban Meyer, Chairman, Field Executive Committee
Post Office Box 469
Wheaton, Illinois 60187
(312) 665-0313

The main thrust of Open Air Campaigners is to conduct evangelistic meetings in public places such as parks, beaches, bus stops, and street corners as weather permits. Indoor meetings are held in churches, jails, nursing homes, etc. Gospel messages, with visual aids, are carried from vans (outdoors) or other adequate stages (indoors). Bible correspondence courses are provided for follow-up where requested by inquirers. In addition to serving in the United States, evangelists are serving in Canada, England, Germany, Italy and Australia.

Founding Date: 1956

Staff: 2 office staff; 26 field evangelists

Publications:

Newsletter, quarterly

Meetings:

3-week seminar on open air evangelism held at Moody Bible Institute Summer School

Seminars conducted at various schools upon request

1161. Open Bible Standard Missions, Inc.

Open Bible Standard Churches

Rev. Paul V. Canfield, Director of World Missions
2020 Bell Avenue
Des Moines, Iowa 50315
(515) 288-6761

Open Bible Standard Missions, Inc., is a fundamental, evangelical, mission agency with the specific purpose of church planting in foreign countries. Closely aligned with the principle objective of church planting is the preaching and teaching of the Gospel of Jesus Christ. Open Bible Standard Missions is a department of the Open Bible Standard Churches, Inc., with headquarters at 2020 Bell Avenue, Des Moines, Iowa 50315. Open Bible Standard Missions maintains missionary personnel and/or national pastors along with corresponding church structure in the following countries: Liberia, Ghana and Guinea, West Africa, Spain, Trinidad, Grenada, Jamaica, Haiti, West Indies, Puerto Rico, Cuba, Mexico, Guatemala, El Salvador, Bolivia, Japan, the Philippines, and Papua New Guinea.

Founding Date: 1935

Staff; 9 office staff; 27 missionary staff

Publications:

World Vision, monthly

Prayer and Praise, monthly

1162. Open Doors International

Nondenominational

Edward Neteland, Executive Vice President
Post Office Box 2020
Orange, California 92669
(714) 639-6802

The aims of Open Doors International are: provision and personalized delivery of Bibles, materials, training, and other aids to build the Church, which is the Body of Christ, in the restricted countries of the world; motivation and training of the Church in threatened countries to be prepared to cope with persecution and suffering which may be imminent; and motivation, mobilization, and training of the Church in the free world to identify with and become involved in assisting the Suffering Church, believing that their burden will be lifted in the same measure in which we share in their suffering. The work is carried out by trained, mature Christians who travel as teams to almost every restricted country. They bring in Christian materials for church leaders and believers after carefully identifying both the need and the proper recipient.

Founding Date: 1955

Publications:

A bimonthly magazine

Arabic newsletter

Radio/TV Programs:

3 current TV specials on Africa, Eastern Europe, and China syndicated to markets throughout North America

Meetings:

Dinner meetings held in spring and fall each year throughout North America

Also Known As:

Open Doors with Brother Andrew

1163. Operation Mobilization (Send the Light, Inc.)

Interdenominational

David Hicks & Paul Troper, Co-Directors
121 Rea Avenue
Hawthorne, New Jersey 07506

Mailing Address
Post Office Box 148
Midland Park, New Jersey 07432
(201) 423-4551

Operation Mobilization (Send the Light, Inc.) is the interdenominational and interracial United States affiliate of Operation Mobilization worldwide. OM conducts short term (10 day, summer, 1 and 2 year) training programs for commited Christian young people in discipleship and cross-cultural evangelism. OM works in international teams in thirty nations of Europe, Middle East, South Asia, and Mexico. OM also operates for the same purpose two ocean-going ships, the MV Logos and Doulos which visit ports of the world conducting educational and Christian book exhibitions, conferences, training seminars, and various forms of evangelistic outreach.

Founding Date: 1957

Staff: 1,600 (year)

Membership: 3,000 (summer)

Publications:
International Monthly Report
Reports and prayer letters on OM work in India, Turkey, the Arab World, Europe, Pakistan

Meetings:
Conferences: Operation World in various cities
Summer Crusade Preparation each year in June in a major North American city

1164. Opus Dei (OD)

Roman Catholic
Raphael Caamano, Counselor
99 Overlook Circle
New Rochelle, New York 10804
(914) 235-0198

Opus Dei (the work of God) is an international association of lay men and women and secular priests. The objective of its members is to practice Christian virtues while pursuing secular occupations, thus making the doctrine of Christ known to society by their example and word.

Founding Date: 1928

Membership: 70,000

Also Known As: The Work of God, Inc.

1165. Orbis Books

Roman Catholic
Philip Scharper, Editor-in-chief
The Maryknoll Fathers and Brothers
Maryknoll, New York 10545
(914) 941-7590

Orbis Books, as the publishing department of The Maryknoll Fathers and Brothers, publishes books concerning the religious, economic, political, and social thought and problems of the third world. Its goal is to help provide a voice for the oppressed and powerless of the world who cry out for justice. It provides a channel for books from and about the Chris-

tian churches in the third world. Typical examples are books dealing with the theology of liberation from Latin America, African religious beliefs, the most recent contributions of Asian theologians, the Catholic Church's teaching on social justice, and Christian life-style in the global village.

Publications:
170 books dealing with the church in Asia, Africa, Latin America, social justice, contemporary spirituality

1166. Order of St. Andrew the Apostle

Greek Orthodox Church in the Americas
Dr. Anthony G. Borden, Commander
8 East 79 Street
New York, New York 10021
(212) 570-3500

The Order of St. Andrew the Apostle is a body of laymen of the Greek Orthodox Church in the Americas whose members have been honored with the title, "Archon of the Ecumenical Patriarchate." This historic title, "Archon" has its roots in ancient Greek and Byzantine history. It was a title bestowed by the Emperor or Patriarch upon the most able and trusted citizens of the Byzantine Empire (330-1054) who assumed such major responsibilities as foreign affairs, charitable and humanitarian services, the armed forces, ecclesiastical duties, etc. The chief functions of the Order of St. Andrew are in assisting the needs of the Patriarchate located in Istanbul. These include the 600-bed Greek Orthodox, nonsectarian hospital of Balukli, the childrens' camp, and general charitable and humanitarian needs. The Order also publishes educational materials, supports Archdiocese Institutions in America, and aids such causes as Hellenic college and the St. Photios Shrine, which are extensions and symbols of the Patriarchate on this continent. Is never-ending concern is supporting the cause of religious freedom and human rights in the ancient homeland of the Ecumenical Patriarchate. Over the centuries these basic rights have been, and are still being denied in Turkey to Christians and other minorities, and it is to this basic and fundamental grievance of a denial of human rights that the Order of St. Andrew addresses itself.

Staff: 2

Membership: 500

Publications:
Newsletter

Archon Album
Miscellaneous pamphlets and papers
Meetings:
Annual meeting on first Sunday of Great Lent, "The Sunday of Orthodoxy," usually in early March
Former Name: Knights of St. Andrew

1167. Order of Saint Luke the Physician

Interdenominational
Most Rev. Charles Virgil Hearn, PhD, DMin, Supreme Grand Commander
2210 Wilshire Boulevard, Suite 582
Santa Monica, California 90403
(213) 394-0553

The Order of Saint Luke the Physician is a band of Protestant Christian men and women bound together for the promotion of healing, good fellowship, mutual aid, and the preservation of a sound Christian moral fiber which will preserve for us and for our children the blessings of the Christian way of life, as well as spiritual, psychological, and physical good health.

Founding Date: 1842
Staff: 3
Membership: 500
Publications:
The Order, monthly
Meetings:
Convention, annually

1168. Order of the Thousandfold*

Episcopal
Rev. Dennis Whittle, Director
1242 Barracks Road
Charlottesville, Virginia 22901
(804) 293-6864

Members of the Order of the Thousandfold pray earnestly every day to be made a thousandfold more useful to God than ever before. This does not necessarily mean an increase in outward activities, for the time of some may already be fully occupied. It does mean, however, an increase in spiritual power and energy, so that what is done and said may exert an influence of such power and far-reaching effect as

to really amount to a thousandfold increase in spiritual efficiency.

1169. Oregon Catholic Press

Roman Catholic
Most Rev. Cornelius Power, President
2816 East Burnside
Portland, Oregon 97214
Mailing Address
Post Office Box 14809
Portland, Oregon 97214
(503) 234-5381

Oregon Catholic Press publishes a weekly newspaper of information relating to Cathoic Church activities and religion in a broad sense, and also publishes music and other material used in Catholic liturgy.

Founding Date: 1923
Staff: 26
Publications:
Catholic Sentinel
Today's Missal, missalette used in Catholic liturgy
Canticos, hymn book in Spanish language
Choir Book
Various collections of organ and choir music for religious use
Former Name:
(1981) Catholic Truth Society of Oregon

1170. Orthodox and Anglican Fellowship*

The Orthodox Church and the Anglican Communion
Rev. George H. MacMurray
8005 Ridge Boulevard
Brooklyn, New York 11209
(212) 745-8481

The Orthodox and Anglican Fellowship sponsors joint study by representatives of the two churches; maintains local chapters; and publishes a bulletin.

Membership: 350
Publications:
Anglicana
Meetings:
10 to 12 per year

1171. The Orthodox Brotherhood

Orthodox

Virginia E. Martin, National Chairman
3256 Warren Road
Cleveland, Ohio 44111
(216) 941-5550

This is a lay organization that functions as an auxiliary organization of the Orthodox Episcopate in America. Its purpose is to further the aims of the Episcopate and its parishes, and to cooperate with other Eastern Orthodox Churches in order to consolidate Orthodoxy in America. It also promotes and sponsors charitable works and works to strengthen the bonds of brotherhood among its members. A current project is to help integrate newcomers (refugees) into church life and American ways. Another project was to start golden-agers clubs in parishes.

Membership: 125

Publications:
Newspaper
Almanac

Meetings:
Participate in Orthodox retreats

1172. Orthodox Christian Educational Society

Greek Orthodox, Russian Orthodox, Eastern Orthodox

Constantine Andronis, President
1916 West Warner Avenue
Chicago, Illinois 60613

Branch Office
c/o Ralph Masterjohn
120-50 Fifth Avenue
College Point, New York 11356
(312) 549-0584

The Orthodox Christian Educational Society is primarily involved in translating the works of eminent theologians, ancient and contemporary, from Greek into English. The works are then published and circulated to public libraries in the United States and elsewhere and offered for sale through various means. All proceeds are for the perpetuation of the purpose of the organization, which is to enable Orthodox Christians to learn more about their faith and to enable other Christians and non-Christians to learn of the "one holy Catholic and Apostolic Church" founded through Holy Tradition commencing with the Day of the Pentecost.

Membership: 7

Publications:
Leaflets, pamphlets, soft cover books, hard cover books

Meetings:
Monthly informal meetings

1173. Orthodox Church in America, Department of History and Archives

Orthodox Church in America

John Erickson, Chairman
Route 25 A
Syosset, New York 11791

Mailing Address
Post Office Box 675
Syosset, New York 11791
(516) 922-0550

The Department of History and Archives of the Orthodox Church in America is engaged in researching the origins of the Orthodox mission in America. It has published, for the Orthodox Church in America, a Bicentennial Commemorative Book called *Orthodox America, 1794-1975,* which is the primary source book for the history of American Orthodoxy at the present time. It also has the duty of overseeing the archives located at the offices of the church administration at Syosset, New York. A Historical Society has been formed to promote and sponsor research and publications in the area of the history of Orthodoxy in America.

1174. Orthodox Church in America, Department of Religious Education (DRE)*

Orthodox Church in America

Bishop Theodosius, Chairman
Route 25A
Syosset, New York 11791

Mailing Address
Post Office Box 675
Syosset, New York 11791
(516) 922-0550

The Department of Religious Education, Orthodox Church in America, is responsible for the development of religious education programs and materials. The religious training of adults, young people and children falls within the scope of its activities. The DRE coordinates its programs with those of the Orthodox Christian Education Commission. At the same time, the DRE produces supplementary materials in the form of books and pamphlets for the use of adults and children alike.

1175. Orthodox Theological Society in America

The Standing Conference of Canonical Orthodox Bishops in the Americas
Rev. George C. Papademetriou
575 Scarsdale Road
Crestwood, New York 10707
(914) 961-8037

The Orthodox Theological Society in America was founded under the auspices of the Standing Conference of Canonical Orthodox Bishops in the Americas. Its purpose is to promote Orthodox theology; to cultivate fellowship and cooperation among Orthodox Christians; and to coordinate the work of Orthodox theologians in America. Membership is open to Orthodox Christians who are involved in theological work.

Founding Date: 1966
Publications:
    1 bulletin, monthly (10 times, Sept.-June)
Meetings:
    One major conference each year

1176. Osterhus Publishing House Inc.

Interdenominational
Ruth I. Osterhus, President
4500 West Broadway
Minneapolis, Minnesota 55422
(612) 537-8335

Osterhus Publishing House prints gospel tracts in about 45 different languages and each month sends hundreds of packages of tracts and *The Bible Friend* without cost to many countries of the world. Missionaries, evangelists, and national Christians distribute them. Every three months, 60,000 people on the mailing list receive samples of new tracts, a copy of *Gospel Tract Tidings,* and other inspirational

material. The specific ministry is to win souls to the Lord Jesus Christ and to encourage and "build up the faith" of Christians who may have become discouraged. Many letters tell of the blessings received, of souls saved, and prayers answered. Many requests are received for prayer and counseling; all are answered personally.

Founding Date: 1903
Staff: 12 in tract department
Publications:
    The Bible Friend, magazine, monthly
    About 1,000 different gospel tracts, booklets, books, pamphlets

1177. Our Lady of Angels Association

Roman Catholic
Rev. Joseph P. Ganley CM, Director
Niagara University Post Office
Niagara, New York 14109
(716) 285-1212

The purpose of Our Lady of Angels Association, formerly Our Lady of Angels Novenas, is to spread devotion to Our Lady of Angels, and to solicit her intercession on behalf of those who, by their prayers and donation, assist in the education of young men preparing for the Priesthood in the Vincentian Fathers. Members of the Association are specially remembered during the seven Novenas of Masses celebrated each year: Presentation of the Lord, Annunciation, Easter, Visitation, Assumption, Holy Rosary, and Immaculate Conception.

Founding Date: 1918
Membership: 85,000
Publications:
    Within the Sanctuary The Mass
Former Name:
    Our Lady of Angels Novenas

1178. Our Sunday Visitor, Inc. (OSV)

Roman Catholic
John F. Fink, President
200 Noll Plaza
Huntington, Indiana 46750
(219) 356-8400

Our Sunday Visitor is the largest Catholic publisher and printer in the United States. For 68 years it has devoted itself to serving the Church. Its publications include periodicals such as *Our Sunday Visitor*, with the highest circulation of all national Catholic Weeklies, plus other specialized magazines. OSV is also expanding rapidly in religious trade books, text books, audio-visuals, catechetics, and offertory envelopes. Revenue above operating expenses is donated to charitable organizations on national and international levels.

Founding Date: 1912

Publications:

OSV publishes newspapers, magazines, books, textbooks, education audio visual products. Periodicals include: *Our Sunday Visitor, The Harmonizer, Western New York Catholic Visitor, The Priest, My Daily Visitor, The Pope Speaks, Visions, Venture.*

1179. Outreach, Inc.

Nondenominational
Dave Adams, Area Director
Post Office Box 6
Salem, Oregon 97308

The purpose of Outreach, Inc., is to develop lay ministers among youth and provide programs for offenders in jails and prisons.

Membership: 10

Meetings:

3 or 4 seminars or retreats each year

1180. Overseas Christian Servicemen's Center (OCSC)

Dave Meschke, General Director
Post Office Box 10308
Denver, Colorado 80210
(303) 762-1400

The objectives of the Overseas Servicemen's Center are: to proclaim the Gospel to members of the Armed Forces and their families; to help establish Christians by instructing them in their responsibility to the local church and its mission; to serve as an agency of the church through which it may minister to the spiritual needs of military personnel, especially those overseas; to establish facilities accessible to military personnel where they may gather for fellowship and instruction in spiritual matters during their off-duty hours; and to provide a ministry that endeavors to complement and support the local military chapel program.

Founding Date: 1954

Publications:

OCSC Focus, small news magazine — 3 times a year
OCSC Lifeline, monthly prayer calendar
Each of 55 families publish a newsletter

Meetings:

8 each year

1181. Overseas Ministries Study Center (OMSC)

Nondenominational
The Rev. Gerald H. Anderson, PhD, Director
6315 Ocean Avenue
Ventnor, New Jersey 08406

Mailing Address
Post Office Box 2057
Ventnor, New Jersey 08406
(609) 823-6671

OMSC is a residential center for continuing education of persons engaged in the Christian world mission. Its programs and residential facilities (38 furnished apartments) are open to missionaries of all boards, societies, and denominations. It is primarily intended for missionaries and their families on furlough and overseas church persons who have come to North America on special missionary assignment or to study. All persons admitted into residence are expected to spend at least half their time in study and to respect any differing opinions held by others. Since 1970 missionary personnel and overseas nationals from more than 200 mission boards and agencies have been in residence. The Study Center is located in Ventnor, New Jersey, immediately west of Atlantic City, a few hundred feet from the Boardwalk and beach.

Founding Date: 1923

Publications:

Occasional Bulletin of Missionary Research, a scholarly quarterly journal

Meetings:

Offer 30 five-day intensive seminars each year, from Sept. to May, for intellectual and spiritual renewal of missionaries

1182. Overseas Missionary Fellowship (OMF)

Interdenominational

Rev. Daniel W. Bacon, Home Director (United States)
404 South Church Street
Robesonia, Pennsylvania 19551
(215) 693-5881

The Overseas Missionary Fellowship was founded by Reverend J. Hudson Taylor as China Inland Mission. The mission currently works in nine countries: Thailand, Malaysia, Singapore, Indonesia, Philippines, Taiwan, Hong Kong, Japan, and Korea. The Fellowship is evangelical in that it accepts the full inspiration and authority of the old and new testament scriptures; evangelistic in that it is concerned with propagating the gospel of the grace of God revealed in them; international in that it is open to people of any race or nationality; and interdenominational in that its members are from many different denominations and churches, and recognize that the points on which they may differ are less important then those which unite them. The Fellowship believes that God's primary instrument for evangelization is the local Church. The policy of the Fellowship is therefore to stimulate churches in the urgent prosecution of their task and to assist them in it. In order to ensure that the work of the Fellowship is church-centered, the ministry of its members is integrated into the life of local churches with which it has vital oneness in faith and conduct. The Fellowship aims at active and creative cooperation with these churches by lending qualified personnel to assist in evangelism, Christian education, leadership training, and other specialized work. The Fellowship believes in the spiritual oneness of all members of the body of Christ, and is concerned with fostering unity among Christians. It is, however, unwilling to share responsibility in Christian work with those who question or deny the basic tenets of the faith which God has entrusted to His people once for all. In areas where no church accepts responsibility, the Fellowship will, wherever possible, engage in pioneer evangelism with a view to establishing churches. The Fellowship encourages the indigenous development of these churches and avoids anything that would foster a spirit of dependence upon the missionary or the Fellowship rather than upon God.

Founding Date: 1865

Membership: 878

Publications:
East Asia Millions, bimonthly

Meetings:
Annual weekend prayer conferences throughout the United States and many one-day type meetings

Former Name: (1951) China Inland Mission

1183. P J Kennedy and Sons

Roman Catholic
866 Third Avenue
New York, New York 10022
(212) 935-5640

P.J. Kennedy and Sons publishes *The Official Catholic Directory.*

1184. Pacific Broadcasting Association

Interdenominational
Rev. Bernard E. Holritz, Executive Director
106 North Dorchester
Wheaton, Illinois 60187

Mailing Address
Post Office Box 941
Wheaton, Illinois 60187
(312) 653-6967

Pacific Broadcasting Association's purpose is to proclaim the gospel in Japanese, by Japanese, for Japanese. Thus it produces radio and television broadcasts which are aired domestically in Japan on 26 network stations. Pacific Broadcasting Association also uses the facilities of the Far East Broadcasting Company in Manila, Trans World Radio in Guam, and the Voice of the Andes in Quito, Ecuador to proclaim the gospel in Japanese by shortwave radio. Japanese programs are aired in the United States for Japanese-speaking Americans.

Founding Date: 1951
Membership: 30
Publications:
> *Dayori,* monthly, in Japanese
> *Announcer,* quarterly

Radio/TV Programs:
> 7 radio programs
> 1 television program

Meetings:
> 2 mission conferences per month

1185. Pacific Lutheran University Press* (PLU)

American Lutheran Church
Dr. William O. Rieke, President
Tacoma, Washington 98447
(206) 531-6900

Pacific Lutheran University Press is a communications arm of Pacific Lutheran University, a coeducational, independent liberal arts institution serving approximately 3,400 students. The book publishing function is presently inactive.

Publications:
> *Scene,* 5 times a year
> *Campus Scene,* weekly

Radio/TV Programs:
> Regular daytime fine music, news, interviews, campus events on its radio station, KPLU-FM

Meetings:
> 50 per year

1186. Parameter Press, Incorporated

Nondenominational
Jane L. Keddy, President
705 Main Street
Wakefield, Massachusetts 01880
(617) 245-9290

Parameter Press publishes books and journals. It specializes in publishing books which have particular significance for the conditions that are emerging in these times—books which standard publishers may hesitate to tackle. Parameter takes special care on two points: its books are beautifully designed; and its authors are scholars who write simply so that their books are helpful for the non-scholarly reader as well as for students. Parameter's religious books are by theologians who are respected by all communions and denominations. Its nonreligious books are by experts in their fields who are also competent Christian theologians.

Founding Date: 1972

Staff: 1

Membership: 1

Publications:
    4 titles in print

1187. Parchment Press

Nondenominational
Earnest Clevenger, Jr., President
8617 Clearwood Road
Chattanooga, Tennessee 37421

Mailing Address
Post Office Box 8534
Chattanooga, Tennessee 37411
(615) 899-0351

Parchment Press publishes material for use mainly by nondenominational churches of Christ. Tracts, sermon outline books, and psychology books make up its major trade list. It also produces flash cards and Bible—centered study materials for class use.

Founding Date: 1963

Staff: 2

Publications:
    30 titles, religious, Bible class, sermon books, scholarly, tracts

1188. Parish Evaluation Project (PEP)

Roman Catholic
Rev. Thomas P. Sweetser, SJ, Director
1307 South Wabash Avenue
Chicago, Illinois 60605
(312) 427-4392

The Parish Evaluation Project (PEP) is a consultative service offered to parishes (primarily Catholic parishes) anywhere in the United States and Canada who wish to learn the needs and expectations of the parishioners and to seek ways of responding to these needs. The PEP program provides parishes with the tools for assessing needs through scientific sampling and surveying, and works with the parish staffs and leaders over two years' time to help them plan effective programs in light of the survey results. The PEP approach is both sociological in providing an accurate picture of the parish and theological in offering possible models and objectives for the parish in response to Gospel imperatives.

1189. Partners in Mission*

Episcopal
Rev. David Birney
815 Second Avenue
New York, New York 10017
(212) 867-8400

Partners in Mission is an agency of the National and World Mission program of the Episcopal Church. Its purpose is to enable the Church to support and participate in the "Partners-in-Mission" process with other parts of the Anglican Communion for the achievement of coordination of mission strategy and program. Although still in the transition stage, when this process becomes a reality, the Episcopal Church will participate as a partner within the Anglican Communion in a mutual mission effort, rather than in separate relationship with individual Anglican dioceses.

1190. Pathways Foundation

Nondenominational
S'Open Wilson, Founder
Wrightwood, California 92397

The purpose of the Pathways Foundation is to open the eyes of individuals to the light of truth which is that: we are one; we are free; we were created to be happy. The foundation sets up Houses of Prayer which act as community focal points where physical and spiritual needs are met. Each House of Prayer has Praise Practice in which all present participate. There is no minister, as all are recognized as teachers and students. Praise Practice itself teaches the attitude necessary to live truth.

Publications:
> *Source,* irregularly
> *P.S.,* irregularly

1191. Paulist Communications

Catholic
Rev. John W. Mulhall, C.S.P., Director
2257 Barry Avenue
Los Angeles, California 90064
(213) 477-2559

Paulist Communications offers quality religious public service and public affairs radio programming. Programs are available in the following areas: General Audience; Contemporary; Country; Devotional; and Current Affairs. Seasonal specials are also offered, as is Spanish language programming.
Founding Date: 1970
Staff: 12

1192. Paulist Leadership and Renewal Project

Roman Catholic
Patricia Dunn, Coordinator
5 Park Street
Boston, Massachusetts 02108
(617) 742-7046

The Paulist Leadership and Renewal Project is an independent, non-profit agency funded by fees paid for services, by the Paulist Fathers, and by foundation and government grants. The Project uses facilities at the Paulist Center in Boston, at Weston School of Theology in Cambridge, and at local retreat houses — but the majority of the services and programs are designed for use in local parish settings. The services offered by the Project aim to promote a new understanding of the roles of clergy and laity in the life of the Church; and to provide new skills necessary to put such an understanding into practice. The Project offers a variety of parish renewal services, retreat programs, and leadership training programs. The programs are custom-tailored, in collaboration with each client, for use in their particular pastoral setting. In addition, the Project offers the

Lay Ministry Training Institute, a centrally located nine-month curriculum.

Founding Date: 1974
Membership: 4
Meetings:
> Numerous meetings according to needs

1193. Paulist League*

Roman Catholic
Rev. Robert A. O'Donnell, C.S.P., Director
415 West 59th Street
New York, New York 10019
(212) 246-3976

The Paulist League is an association of laity and clergy who are friends of the Paulist Fathers. Members of the League are the extended Paulist family. They aid the Paulist Fathers by their friendship, their voluntary services, their prayers and sacrifices, and their financial contributions. They are especially concerned about supporting the education and training of Paulist seminarians. In return, the members of the League participate in the spiritual benefits obtained through the daily prayers, Masses, and missionary work of every Paulist. They and their intentions are remembered in a special League Mass offered daily at the Paulist Seminary. They are a vital part of the Paulist mission.
Membership: 20,000 lay; 400 clerical

1194. Paulist Press

Roman Catholic
Kevin A. Lynch, C.S.P.
1865 Broadway
New York, New York 10023
(212) 265-4028

Paulist Press is a publisher of books and magazines. It publishes a variety of hardback and paperback books on theological and pastoral subjects, as well as religious education program materials. The Paulist Fathers began Paulist Press more than a century ago, and today it continues as the nation's leading Catholic publisher and distributor. Paulist Press is a non-profit apostolic enterprise. Each year its resources are used to contribute to the growth of the Press apostolate itself. While many Paulist Press books are broadly popular, others are published simply because of their inherent religious, academic value. Since Vatican Council II, Paulist Press has been noted for the publication of its "Come to the Father" elementary religious education series.

Staff: 50

Publications:
Religious books
New Catholic World
The Catholic Charismatic
The Ecumenist
Parish Ministry, newsletter

1195. Paulist Productions

Roman Catholic

Ellwood E. Kieser, C.S.P., President
17575 Pacific Coast Highway
Pacific Palisades, California 90272

Mailing Address
Post Office Box 1057
Pacific Palisades, California 90272
(213) 454-0688

The primary purpose of Paulist Productions is the sharing of the Good News of God's loving concern for all His children in the human family. Media is their mode of sharing. The confused, the frightened, and the depressed are the object of their special concern. In addition to television programming, Paulist Productions produces educational films. They are also engaged in an effort to train public school teachers in values education and character formation in the classroom.

Founding Date: 1968

Staff: 25

Radio/TV Programs:
Insight
Holiday specials
Specials for teens

1196. Pendle Hill

Society of Friends (Quaker)

Edwin A. Sanders, Executive Director
338 Plush Mill Road
Wallingford, Pennsylvania 19086
(215) 566-4507

Pendle Hill is an adult center for religious and social study and cooperative living maintained by members of the Society of Friends. Pendle Hill Publications is one aspect of the life of Pendle Hill. Its principal output is pamphlets centered on spiritual and related concerns, and usually of contemporary relevance. Starting in the 1930's, its pamphlets emphasized social concern. It now presents less of this, largely because it receives fewer such manuscripts. Pendle Hill's present trend is toward the inward life. The average length of its pamphlets is 32 pages. Pendle Hill publishes only original materials; it pays no royalties. In addition to its pamphlets, it also publishes an occasional book, usually with special reference to Pendle Hill or its community.

Staff: 35

Membership: 35 resident students

Publications:
7 books in print
6 pamphlets annually

Meetings:
40 per year

1197. Pentecostal Church of God of America, Inc., Department of Christian Education*

Pentecostal Church of God

Kenneth K. Foreman, Director
221 Main Street
Joplin, Missouri 64801
(417) 624-7050

The goal of the Christian Education Department of the Pentecostal Church of God is to furnish Sunday school literature which is educationally sound, Bible-oriented, and entirely true to the historic distinctives of the Pentecostal revival. The Department of Christian Education also is charged with the responsibility for building and maintaining a growing program of Sunday school conventions, workshops, seminars, and schools. These are operated through Regional and District Directors of Christian Education, and are implemented through annual programs, such as Christian Worker Training Month (February, Loyalty Month (March) and Sunday School Enlargement Month (September).

1198. Pentecostal Church of God of America, Inc., PLA Department, Pentecostal Ladies Auxiliary

Pentecostal Church of God
Willie Mae Chappell, President
1313 West 17th Street
Joplin, Missouri 64801
(417) 623-2201

The Pentecostal Ladies Auxiliary (PLA) Department of the Pentecostal Church of God has maintained a consistent service to needy children, missions and the field of education.

Founding Date: 1953

1199. Pentecostal Church of God of America, Inc., Radio KPCG

Pentecostal Church of God
Post Office Box 212
Joplin, Missouri 64801
(417) 781-8800

The establishment of radio station KPCG in Joplin, Missouri, inaugurated a new phase of broadcast ministries for The Pentecostal Church of God. The radio station operates 24 hours a day.

Founding Date: 1974

1200. Pentecostal Church of God of America, Inc., World Missions Department*

Pentecostal Church of God
Robert W. Boyle, Director
221 Main Street
Joplin, Missouri 64801
(417) 624-7050

The World Missions Department of the Pentecostal Church of God is guided by twenty-five missionary families who are currently under appointment, serving in twenty-one countries of the world. More than six hundred national missionaries join with several hundred capable workers to minister in eight hundred churches and outstations, in which the congregations number from fifty to one thousand. Ten Bible schools serve over eight hundred students each week, and fifteen day schools expand the teaching ministry to include the children. Homes for the aged, orphanages, and similar institutions are maintained to provide shelter, food, clothing, and spiritual training for the underprivileged and forsaken.

1201. Pentecostal Conquerors

United Pentecostal Church International
C. Patton William, President
8855 Dunn Road
Hazelwood, Missouri 63042
(314) 837-7300

Pentecostal Conquerors is the youth division of the United Pentecostal Church. It sponsors all activities of those in the age group 12-35. Various activities include Bible Quizzing, Youth Camps, and International and National Youth Corps. Their fund raising project is called "Sheaves for CHRIST," and raises over two million dollars annually for the purpose of providing vehicles for missionaries and other designated projects.

Publications:
Conquerors Tread, monthly
Meetings:
General conference, annually

1202. Pentecostal Free Will Baptist Church, Inc., Church Ministries Department

Pentecostal Free Will Baptist Church, Inc.
Rev. Don Sauls, Church Ministries Director
Post Office Box 1568
Dunn, North Carolina 28334
(919) 892-4161 or (919) 894-4569

The goals of the Church Ministries Department of the Pentecostal Free Will Baptist Church are evangelism and edification of believers. The focus of the Department is on the individual and his needs in relationship to Jesus Christ. All of its programs must be Christ-centered in every phase; person-centered in focus; Bible-centered in curriculum; method-centered in the experience of each age group; church-centered in organization; and missionary-centered in vision.

Founding Date: 1959
Staff: 9
Membership: 12,641

Meetings:
Numerous throughout the year

1203. Pentecostal Free Will Baptist Church, Inc., Ladies Auxiliary

Pentecostal Free Will Baptist Church, Inc.

Mrs. Shirley Hardison, General Director of Ladies Auxiliary
Post Office Box 1568
Dunn, North Carolina 28334
(919) 892-4161 or (919) 965-6483

The purpose of the Ladies Auxiliary is to promote interest among the women in the work of Christ's Kingdom, and to assist in all phases of the work of the Pentecostal Free Will Baptist Church.

Founding Date: 1959

Staff: 1

Membership: 4,000

Meetings:
Ladies Auxiliary Convention
Ladies Auxiliary Retreat
Ladies Auxiliary Day at Heritage Bible College

1204. Pentecostal Free Will Baptist Church, Inc., World Witness Department

Pentecostal Free Will Baptist Church, Inc.

William L. Ellis, DMin
Post Office Box 1568
Dunn, North Carolina 28334
(919) 892-4161

The World Witness Department is divided into three divisions: the Foreign Missions Division. The Home missions Division; and the Evangelism Division. The purpose of this department is to carry out the Lord's great commission in cooperation with the Holy Spirit for the spread of the full gospel by establishing self-supporting, self-propagating churches in areas where the Gospel has not been declared.

Founding Date: 1959

Publications:
Mission News

1205. Pentecostal Free Will Baptist Church, Inc., Youth Organizations

Pentecostal Free Will Baptist Church, Inc.

Rev. Don Sauls, Crusaders for Christ Director
Post Office Box 1568
Dunn, North Carolina 28334
(919) 892-4161 or (919) 894-4569

The Pentecostal Free Will Baptist youth organization is known as the Crusaders for Christ. Crusaders for Christ is organized for the cultivation of Christian fellowship among young people; the expression of their Christian experience in prayer, testimony, and exhortation; their instruction and training in personal evangelism; their training in church life and teaching; their employment in works of charity and social service; their instruction in missionary ideals and principles; their training in Christian stewardship; their direction to lives of service at home and abroad; and the supplying of their normal requirements of recreation and social life under the safeguards of religion and by the aid of courses of reading and study. An important function of Crusaders for Christ is the operation of Crusader Youth Camp.

Founding Date: 1948

Staff: 3 — 10 months; 30 — 2 months

Membership: 2,221

Publications:
Crusader Youth Camp, brochure
Youth Alive

Meetings:
Crusaders for Christ Convention
Crusader Youth Camp, 6 weeks

1206. Pentecostal Publishing House

United Pentecostal Church, Inc.

D. A. Schroeder, Manager
8855 Dunn Road
Hazelwood, Missouri 63042

All activities at the Pentecostal Publishing House center around World Evangelism. It produces Sunday School curriculum, tracts, books, and booklets that are doctrinally sound. It distributes them through religious bookstores, churches, ministers, and laity. Pentecostal also produces and mails denominational periodicals, publications, and promotional material. The World Aflame Bookstores market a complete line of evangelical books, Bibles, music, and supplies to the general Christian community.

Publications:
40 study books
45 tracts
Bible with Church doctrine supplement
Three hymnals

1207. Petra International, Inc.

Interdenominational
Paul Shirley, President
Stan Archer, Executive Secretary
406 Heritage Place
Rockwall, Texas 75087
(214) 722-6697

Petra, International, Inc., is a faith missions group that promotes world missions and operates as a sending and servicing agency for missionaries. It is interdenominational in nature and Wesleyan in tradition. Its main purpose is to channel support to mission endeavors and provide information from the field for those who are interested in the ministry. The primary fund raising responsibility rests with the individual missionaries, but social service and education projects are supported. Petra International believes that all people have a need to hear the gospel and to personally know God. Its ultimate emphasis is on leading men, women, and children into a genuine experience of regeneration (the spiritual new birth) and learning how they may live a fulfilled and victorious life as a Christian. Thus, Petra International works through people who are involved in evangelism and discipleship, introducing people to God and His ways. In helping to reach others Petra International looks for opportunities to minister wherever possible, such as in support of missionaries, national evangelistic workers, and pastors. This is done through financial support for Biblical and ministerial training, assistance in getting to the field, provision for the building of churches, and acquisition of equipment and supplies. It also helps by invoking the power of prayer support from friends of the ministry. Petra International is able to promote world missions through speaking opportunities in public forums and churches and by distributing printed materials.

Founding Date: 1977
Staff: 2
Membership: 30
Publications:
Periodic newsletters

1208. P'Eylim-American Yeshiva Student Union*

Jewish
Rabbi Avraham Hirsch
3 West 16th Street
New York, New York 10011
(212) 989-2500

P'Eylim-American Yeshiva Student Union is an independent, nonpolitical and nonpartisan organization dedicated to the guidance of immigrant youth in Eretz, Israel, France, and elsewhere. It is engaged in organizing religious schools in the immigrant camps and new refugee communities and providing buildings, equipment, and supplies. It sponsors summer camps, youth clubs, special publications, etc., for the young immigrant. P'Eylim encourages pioneer work by American Yeshiva graduates overseas.

Membership: 10,000 lay; 1,500 clerical
Publications:
P'Eylim Reporter
Meetings:
12 conferences per year

1209. Philadelphia Task Force on Women in Religion

Ecumenical
Nancy E. Krody, Coordinator
Post Office Box 24003
Philadelphia, Pennsylvania 19139
(215) 724-1247

The Philadelphia Task Force on Women in Religion is a support group for women in religion, ordained and lay. The task force provides educational resources where possible, and is available for radio and television appearances, panels, and the like. The task force serves as an advocate for women in denominations which do not ordain women, or for hiring in those denominations which do ordain women.

Membership: 12
Meetings:
Occasional membership meetings and
conferences

1210. The Philosophical Research Society, Inc.* (PRS)

Nondenominational

Dr. John W. Ervin, Vice President
3910 Los Feliz Boulevard
Los Angeles, California 90027
(213) 663-2167

The Philosophical Research Society, Inc., is a non-profit organization dedicated to the dissemination of useful knowledge in the fields of philosophy, comparative religion, and psychology. The aims and purposes of the Society are to discover additional knowledge by intensively investigating the essential teachings of the world's greatest scientific, spiritual, and cultural leaders, and by further clarifying and integrating man's heritage of wisdom; to apply these discoveries to the present needs of mankind by means of modern skills and the cooperation of outstanding experts; to make available these vital concepts to persons in every walk of life by lectures, publications, and other media; and to create an increasing awareness in the public mind of the usefulness of these ideas and ideals in solving the personal and collective problems of modern man. The Society maintains a library which houses an important collection of source books and manuscripts relating to the deeper issues of human thinking. The strength of the library lies in its manuscript department and its collection of books printed prior to 1800.

Publications:
    PRS Journal, quarterly
    40 books, 60 brochures
    Pictures, cassettes, and recordings
Meetings:
    Lectures and seminars are held weekly by our staff and guest speakers

1211. Pilgrim Publications*

Baptist

Bob L. Ross, Director
Post Office Box 66
Pasadena, Texas 77501
(713) 477-2329

Pilgrim Publications publishes the complete works of Charles H. Spurgeon (1834-1892), famous Baptist minister of London, England, including the longest consecutive weekly sermon series in Christian history, the 62-volume *Metropolitan Tabernacle Pulpit.*

Publications:
    Sermon and devotional books; about 100 titles

1212. Pinecrest Bible Training Center

Nondenominational

Wade Taylor, President
Salisbury Center, New York 13454
(315) 429-8521

The purpose of the Pinecrest Training Center is to train young people in the knowledge of the Word of God and in Christian character. This is done through chapel services, Bible classes, practical work duty assignments, and making room for the work of the Holy Spirit.

Staff: 50
Publications:
    The Banner, quarterly
Meetings:
    4 special conventions, weekly meetings, and retreats at announced times each year
    Weekly retreats at Pinecrest Retreat Center in Setauket, Long Island

1213. Pioneer Ministries (PM)

Interdenominational

Dr. Virginia Patterson, President
Post Office Box 788
Wheaton, Illinois 60187
(312) 293-1600

Pioneer Ministries is dedicated to helping its members grow socially, emotionally, mentally, spiritually, and physically. It does this through its weekly club meetings and its summer camp programs. It conducts 25 camps in the United States and Canada during the summer months. During the school year, there are approximately 6,000 clubs in session. There are adapted clubs in 20 foreign countries. Pioneer Ministries also conducts leadership training programs for volunteers. It produces its own materials for use by club members and their leaders.

Founding Date: 1939

Membership:
100,000 girls and leaders in the United States and Canada

Publications:
5 handbooks; 30 leadership books
3 magazines; 1 newsletter
6 sets of training materials

Meetings:
150 leadership training conferences and seminars each year

Former Names:
(1941) Girls' Guild; (1980) Pioneer Girls

1214. Pioneer Women, The Women's Labor Zionist Organization of America, Inc.

Jewish

Shoshonna Ebstein, Executive Director
200 Madison Avenue
New York, New York 10016
(212) 725-8010

Pioneer Women, founded in the United States in 1925, now has a membership of 50,000 in this country, with an additional 750,000 members in its sister organizations in 12 other countries. In Israel, Pioneer Women, cooperating with Na'amat, its sister organization, provides more than half of the vocational training, and educational and social services for women, youth and children; aids in the absorption of newcomers; and works toward raising the status of women. In America, Pioneer Women promotes Jewish education, participates actively in the American Jewish community, sponsors Labor Zionist youth groups, and fosters the preservation of civic rights and liberties through an informed citizenry. Pioneer Women is an authorized agency of Youth Aliyah.

Founding Date: 1925

Staff: 25

Membership: 50,000

Publications:
Pioneer Woman, monthly

Meetings:
Biennial convention

1215. Pious Union in Honor of St. Joseph for the Dying*

Roman Catholic

Rev. Emmet Malone, OFM, Director
110 West Madison Street
Chicago, Illinois 60602
(312) 372-5118

The Pious Union in Honor of St. Joseph for the Dying, a crusade of prayer for the dying, was founded by Father Guanella in the Church of St. Joseph's Death at Rome and raised by Pope Pius X to an Archconfraternity. This branch was canonically erected at St. Peter's Church in Chicago on January 18, 1930, and affiliated with the Roman Archconfraternity. There are no meetings, dues, officers, etc. The members pledge themselves, in different degrees, to pray for the dying, especially sinners, and are bound together by their common devotion to St. Joseph, Patron of a Happy Death.

Founding Date: 1900 (circa)

1216. The Pocket Testament League (PTL)

Interdenominational

Kenneth T. Durman, International Director
117 Main Street
Lincoln Park, New Jersey 07035
Mailing Address
Post Office Box 368
Lincoln Park, New Jersey 07035
(201) 696-1900

The Pocket Testament League is a member of the Interdenominational Foreign Missions Association. PTL is an interdenominational and international evangelical missionary ministry dedicated to winning souls to Christ through extensive free Scripture distribution coupled with mass evangelism. One of the purposes of The Pocket Testament League is to encourage Christians to read the Bible daily and to carry a New Testament or portion of Scripture with them in an honest effort to win souls for Christ. The League makes possible the participation of Christians in its active missionary ministry abroad by printing Gospels of John in the languages of many countries on all continents. These Gospels are given out by missionaries and evangelists whose objective is to make known God's way of salvation. Preaching and personal witness accompany these free distributions.

Founding Date: 1908

Staff: Office staff 20; Field staff 85

Publications:

Worldwide News, newsletter

Radio/TV Programs:

News in a Different Dimension, a weekly 15-minute radio program featuring news of spiritual significance, on-the-scene action reports from various mission fields, plus periodic interviews with prominent Christian personalities

Meetings:

Approximately 4 banquets per year

1217. The Prayer House

Nondenominational

Peary Nichols, President, Board of Directors
2449 East 7th Street
Tucson, Arizona 85719
(602) 327-4555

The Prayer House is a place where Christ-centered groups can come together for bible studies, conferences, and seminars. It is always open for new groups and people are on duty to welcome strangers and everyone with open arms and a glass of iced tea. Trained spirit-filled counselors for marriage and home needs are available. There is a Chapel open 24 hours daily where people can go to meditate and pray. Deaf groups meet, Camps Furthest Out hold meetings and Christian Singles groups meet on a monthly basis. Friday nights are Christian Creatives Evenings . . . fun for the family nights.

Staff: 2 Resident Directors

Membership: 500

Publications:

Calendar of activities, monthly

Meetings:

Conduct meetings daily

1218. Presbyterian and Reformed Publishing Company

Presbyterian Church in the United States

Charles H. Craig, Director and Editor
Post Office Box 817
Phillipsburg, New Jersey 08865
(201) 454-0505

The Presbyterian and Reformed Publishing Company is an independent, non-profit publishing company founded for the purpose of publishing and distributing books in exposition and defense of Biblical Christianity. Throughout the years the company has been strong in its stand, publishing only those works in line with the Reformed Faith, in the tradition of Calvin, Warfield, Hodge, and VanTil. By so doing, it strives to defend God's Word from liberal elements in the church that seek to erode the belief in God's infallible Word.

Publications:

Over 250 scholarly theological and philosophical titles in the following categories: International Library of Philosophy and Theology; Modern Thinkers Series; Practical Theology; Missiological Studies; The New Testament Student Series; Apologetics; Old Testament Studies; Christian Counseling

1219. Presbyterian Charismatic Communion

Presbyterian

George C. (Brick) Bradford
2629 Northwest 39th Street, Suite 2B
Oklahoma City, Oklahoma 73112
(405) 946-1427

The purposes of the Presbyterian Charismatic Communion, as stated in the By-Laws, are: to work and pray for a continuing spiritual renewal throughout the Church of Jesus Christ, but particularly in the Presbyterian and Reformed tradition; to encourage Presbyterians and others in the Reformed tradition through praise, prayer, edification, and fellowship to claim the reality and the power of Pentecost through submission to the Lordship of Jesus Christ under the leadership of the Holy Spirit; to extend Christ's Kingdom on earth by proclaiming the Gospel to non-Christians and by promoting love, peace, unity, and purity not only among Presbyterians and others in the Reformed tradition but also among all Christians in a truly inclusive ecumenical spirit to the glory of God the Father, Son, and Holy Spirit.

Founding Date: 1966

Staff: 12

Membership: 6,082

Publications:

Renewal News, bimonthly

Meetings:

10-20 per year

Former Name:
   (1974) Charismatic Communion of Presbyterian Ministers

1220. Presbyterian Historical Society

United Presbyterian Church in the USA
William B. Miller, Manager and Secretary
425 Lombard Street
Philadelphia, Pennsylvania 19147
(215) 627-1852

The Presbyterian Historical Society seeks to collect, preserve, and make available materials which serve to illustrate the history of the churches of the Presbyterian and Reformed Order in the United States as well as the history of interdenominational organizations in which Presbyterians have played a role. The Presbyterian Historical Society is the official archives of the United Presbyterian Church, National Council of the Churches of Christ, American Sunday School Union, Scotch-Irish Foundation, American Foreign and Christian Union, Gray Panthers, and the American Society of Church History.

Founding Date: 1852
Staff: 12
Membership: 1,100
Publications:
   Journal of Presbyterian History, quarterly
Also Known As:
   Department of History of the United Presbyterian Church

1221. Priests Eucharistic League (PEL)

Roman Catholic
Paul J. Bernier, SS, National Director
194 East 76th Street
New York, New York 10021
(212) 861-1076

The Priests Eucharistic League exists especially to promote a greater sense of vocation and commitment to ministry among the ordained members of the Church. It does this by fostering regular eucharistic prayer and ongoing education, and inculcating a sense of solidarity among the members.

Staff: 3
Membership: 16,000

Publications:
   Emmanuel, monthly; 1 book per year
Meetings:
   Occasional

1222. Priests for Equality

Roman Catholic
Brother Joseph Izzo, CFX, National Secretary
Post Office Box 651
Hyattsville, Maryland 20782
(301) 699-0042

Priests for Equality is a national organization of over 1,800 Roman Catholic priests and 600 lay and religious supporters who take seriously the words of St. Paul in the letter to the Galatians: "In Christ there is no difference between Jews and Gentiles, between slaves and free persons, between women and men. You are all one in union with Christ Jesus." (Gal. 3:28) As the charter of the organizatin says: "We are strong in our belief that women and men are called to unity, solidarity and equality in sharing life on this earth. We are deeply hopeful that the attempt to live out this freedom and build it into the structures of our society and of our Church will bring new blessings to both men and women."

Founding Date: 1975
Staff: 2
Membership: 2,300
Publications:
   Priests for Equality, quarterly
   Are Catholics Ready?, an exploration of the views of "emerging Catholics" on women in ministry
   Called to Break Bread?, a psychological investigation of 100 women who feel called to priesthood in the Catholic Church

1223. Prison Mission Association, Inc. (PMA)

Nondenominational
Rev. Joe B. Mason, General Director
3711 Wallace Street
Riverside, California 92519
Mailing Address
Post Office Box 3397
Riverside, California 92519
(714) 686-2613

Prison Mission Association was founded by Rev. Joe B. Mason in Texas. The work reaches into jail and penitentiaries with evangelism and Bible correspondence courses, Christian books, and Gospel films. The mission has offices and workers in England, Latin America, Cameroon, and the United States. An additional outreach is included under the names Servicemen's Division (of PMA) and Bible Correspondence Fellowship (of PMA).

Founding Date: 1955

Staff: 19

Publications:
Prison Echoes, quarterly

Radio/TV Programs:
1 15-minute radio program

Meetings:
Annual banquet

1224. Prisoner Visitation and Support (PVS)

Interdenominational
Eric Corson, Program Secretary
1501 Cherry Street
Philadelphia, Pennsylvania 19102
(215) 241-7117

Prisoner Visitation and Support (PVS), sponsored by 34 national religious bodies and socially concerned agencies, is a nationwide ecumenical, alternative ministry to prisoners in the federal and military prison systems. PVS has volunteers across the United States who regularly visit prisoners and work to maintain ties with prisoners' families. The focus of PVS's visitors is on those prisoners with an acute need for human contact: those serving long sentences, those in solitary confinement, those without visits, and those frequently transferred from prison to prison. PVS visitors offer friendship and moral support to prisoners by helping to maintain family ties, obtaining study materials, writing letters to parole boards, etc. As an ecumenical ministry, PVS visitors do not impose a particular religion or philosophy on prisoners. PVS welcomes inquiries regarding becoming a PVS visitor or making a donation.

Membership:
PVS is sponsored by 34 churches and organizations

Meetings:
Annual training workshop for prison visitors

1225. Pro Ecclesia Foundation

Roman Catholic
Timothy A. Mitchell
663 Fifth Avenue
New York, New York 10022
(212) 355-5794

The Pro Ecclesia Foundation works closely with a number of other Catholic organizations toward the promotion of the teachings of the Church. It came into existence as a response to the Second Vatican Council's Exhortation to the Laity to become more involved in the social order. Some leaflets have been produced which aim to give a clearer picture of both the social order and the teachings. In addition, the Foundation has assisted other groups and organizations in their work of promoting the teachings of the Church. The Foundation was begun in response to a scurrilous article against Pope Paul.

Publications:
Pro Ecclesia
The Common Good
Talks of Pope John Paul II
The Pope Talks to Youth

Radio/TV Programs:
Twice weekly cable television program in New York City, hosted by Dr. Timothy A. Mitchell

1226. Pro Maria Committee (PMC)

Roman Catholic
Miss Doris M. Poisson, Secretary
22 Second Avenue
Lowell, Massachusetts 08154
(617) 453-5281

The Pro Maria Committee is an organization dedicated to the spread of devotion to our Blessed Mother and her special message at Beauraing, Belgium. The Marian Union of Beauraing, an association of prayers for the conversion of sinners, has been formed to gather the faithful who wish to answer Our Lady's plea for prayers and sacrifices.

Founding Date: 1952

Membership: 8,000

Meetings:
Participate in Marian Congresses, Eucharistic Congresses, etc.

1227. ProBuColls Association

Nondenominational
John M. Fisco, Jr., Chairman
915 West Wisconsin Avenue, #214
Milwaukee, Wisconsin 53233
(414) 271-6400

"ProBuColls" is a name which comes from three words — PROfessional, BUsiness, and COLLegiates. The organization was begun as an interdenominational group of college and career age people. Those active in the organization have a real purpose in life: introducing Jesus Christ as Lord and Savior. This purpose is carried out through conducting meetings which are open to the public and which are held throughout the metropolitan Milwaukee area, including the University of Wisconsin-Milwaukee, where there is a registered ProBuColls chapter. Speakers at meetings have included government officials, lawyers, doctors, engineers, and people representing nearly every walk of life. Small group discussions, concerts, sports events, social activities, weekly Bible studies, retreats, seminars, and prayer fellowships are all on the list of things ProBuColls has sponsored. Outdoor activities such as picnics, road rallies, and water and snow skiing are features throughout the year.

Staff: 5
Membership: Open membership
Publications:
Christian Courier, monthly
Meetings:
Various meetings throughout the year which vary in location and activity

1228. Protestant Episcopal Church, Office of Social Welfare

Episcopal
Dr. Woodrow W. Carter, Officer for Social Welfare
815 Second Avenue
New York, New York 10017
(212) 867-8400

The Office of Social Welfare is a unit of National Mission in Church and Society of the Episcopal Church. It exists to help the church develop and implement programs to respond to basic human needs, insure justice, affirm human dignity, and promote self-determination. It also provides support for programs for persons with special needs: the aging, the blind, and the deaf. The activities of this office are carried out by offering consultation, providing human and some financial resources, assisting in developing model programs, and convening regional and provincial conferences.

Founding Date: 1919
Former Name:
Department of Christian Social Relations

1229. Protestant Health and Welfare Assembly (PHWA)

Interdenominational
Charles D. Phillips, Executive Secretary
1701 East Woodfield Road, Suite 311
Schaumburg, Illinois 60195
(312) 843-2701

The Protestant Health and Welfare Assembly is an association of institutions and agencies involved in serving the health and welfare needs of people who have voluntarily allied themselves in the joint development of PHWA programs and have formally affiliated in the cooperative implementation of Protestant Health and Welfare Assembly activities. The PHWA exercises its influence and utilizes its resources, consistent with Christian healing and caring, to enhance the efforts and performance of affiliated members in providing a forum for timely discussions, and the opportunity for fellowship and worship across denominational and agency lines.

Founding Date: 1970
Staff: 2
Meetings:
Annual convention held throughout the United States each March

1230. Protestant Radio and Television Center* (PRTVC)

Nondenominational
Peter Kontos, President
1727 Clifton Road, N.E.
Atlanta, Georgia 30329
(404) 634-3324

The Protestant Radio and Television Center is a production house for religious and social documentary programs of both a traditional and an experimental nature. It also serves as a clearing house for the coordination of research and development in the areas of value definition, communications, ministry and the Gospel (traditional and social), and problem solving.

Membership: 10 lay; 1 clerical

Publications:
> Books on religion and communications
> *Ministry and Mission,* newsletter for Candler School of Theology at Emory University

Radio/TV Programs:
> *Protestant Hour,* weekly 30-minute worship service sent to over 500 radio stations
> *Be Still and Know,* daily devotional program
> *Banners of Faith,* devotional for American Forces Radio/TV services

Meetings:
> 2-3 per year

1231. The Providence Association for Ukrainian Catholics in America

Roman Catholic

Mgsr. Robert M. Moskal, Supreme President
817 North Franklin Street
Philadelphia, Pennsylvania 19123
(215) 627-4993

The Providence Association for Ukrainian Catholics in America is a fraternal-beneficial organization rendering aid and assisting all Americans of Ukrainian descent and members of the Ukrainian Catholic Church. The Association publishes books, magazines, and the only Ukrainian Catholic daily newspaper in the world, *America,* both in Ukrainian and English. It works within the frame of the lay apostolate and acts as a custodian, upholding the rite of the Ukrainian Catholic Church and traditions of the Ukrainian nation. The Association seeks to unite all Americans of Ukrainian descent who belong to the Ukrainian Catholic Church in the United States. It issues insurance certificates for its members and their families, protecting them in case of need or unexpected occurrences. It provides low-interest-rate mortgage loans for the erection of churches, parochial schools, and rectories.

Founding Date: 1912

Membership: 18,960

Publications:
> *America,* daily

1232. Providence Mission Homes, Inc.

Interdenominational

William Jacquet Gribble, President
1421 Glengarry Road
Pasadena, California 91105
(213) 254-4142 or (213) 255-4023

Providence Mission Homes offers fully furnished apartments and homes to missionaries on furlough. It also includes a few retirees and a few candidates for missionary work. Automobiles, when donated, are available for missionaries' short-term use.

Founding Date: 1973

1233. Public Health Association of Seventh-day Adventists

Seventh-day Adventists

Robert Stotz, President
6840 Eastern Avenue, N.W.
Washington, D.C. 20012
(202) 723-0800

The Public Health Association of Seventh-day Adventists is an independent organization affiliated with the Seventh-day Adventist Church and the American Public Health Association. Registered as an official California corporation in 1969, it now has chapters in several areas of the United States as well as three areas overseas. The objectives of the organization are: to provide contact between Seventh-day Adventist members active in public health programs; to foster scientific, educational, and cultural research in the field of health among the members of the Seventh-day Adventist Church and the public at large; and to support the School of Health of Loma Linda University, Loma Linda, California.

Founding Date: 1969

Membership: 500

Publications:
> *Access,* a monthly news and information service for the members

Meetings:
> *Update* with the Loma Linda University, School of Health Alumni
> 1 annual sectional workshop for health educators is held at the same time

Former Name:
> Seventh-day Adventists, Health Department

1234. Pueblo Publishing Company, Inc.

Nondenominational

Bernard C. Benziger, President
1860 Broadway
New York, New York 10023
(212) 541-7665

The Pueblo Publishing Company, Inc., was organized to solicit manuscripts from authors and to edit, typeset, and publish books and other printed materials for churches, seminaries, and theology schools. Pueblo publishes texts in English and Spanish, as well as bilingual texts. The major market geographic area serviced by the company is the United States and Canada. A majority of works published are Roman Catholic as a major part of the sales effort is to Catholic institutions.

1235. The Quiet Hour, Inc.

Seventh-day Adventist

J. L. Tucker, President and Director
630 Brookside
Redlands, California 92373
(714) 793-2588

The Quiet Hour is a radio, television, literature, and worldwide mission outreach. The Quiet Hour was founded by J. L. Tucker as a religious radio broadcast and has been a completely self-supporting continuous faith ministry. Its entire ministry is dependent upon the prayers and support of those who care. The Quiet Hour broadcast is now released on more than 480 stations in North America, West Indies, Central America, Philippines, and Southern Asia. The television program is released weekly in color on approximately 50 stations in North America. Thousands of pieces of literature are mailed daily from The Quiet Hour headquarters to people from various parts of North America and the world. All of these pieces are requested and paid for by donations. The worldwide mission outreach is a growing feature of the ministry of The Quiet Hour. The Quiet Hour sponsors provide funds for mission airplanes, trucks, tractors, jeeps, etc.

Founding Date: 1937

Staff: 25

Publications:
> *The Quiet Hour Echoes,* monthly
> *Book of the Month,* compilation of radio broadcast sermons

Radio/TV Programs:
> *The Quiet Hour* radio broadcast on more than 480 radio stations weekly
> *Search* TV program telecast on approximately 50 stations weekly

Meetings:
> Conduct many radio/TV rallies, seminars, evangelistic meetings and conferences in the United States and abroad

1236. R. E. Winsett Music Co.

Protestant
Ellis J. Crum, President
North Shores Road
Kendallville, Indiana 46755
(219) 347-3758

The R. E. Winsett Music Company is more than 80 years old. Its founder was an accomplished musician. He wrote hundreds of songs, including the Dove Award-winning song *Jesus is Coming Soon.* He also wrote *Living by Faith* and purchased many well-known copyrights such as *Where the Soul Never Dies, The Dearest Friend I Ever Had, Where We'll Never Grow Old,* and scores of other well-known songs in gospel music. He published over 100 books. The work of publishing song books continues. Winsett's book, *Pentecostal Power Complete,* has sold into the millions. *Best Loved Songs and Hymns* has sold into the millions also. Six other books are still in print, and plans are in the making for publication of additional books.

Staff: 2

1237. Rabbinical Alliance of America

Orthodox Jewish
Rabbi Abraham R. Hecht, President
156 Fifth Avenue, Suite 807
New York, New York 10010
(212) 242-6240 or (212) 255-8313

The Rabbinical Alliance of America seeks to promulgate the cause of Torah-true Judaism through an organized rabbinate that is consistently Orthodox; to elevate the position of Orthodox rabbis nationally; and to defend the welfare of Jews the world over. The Rabbinical Alliance of America maintains an internationally-recognized Beth Din (Rabbinical Court) for Jewish divorces (Gittin) and ajudication and arbitration of disputes of all kinds.

Founding Date: 1943
Membership: 500
Hebrew Name: Igud Harabonim D'America

1238. Rabbinical Assembly*

Jewish-Conservative
Rabbi Wolfe Kelman
3080 Broadway
New York, New York 10027
(212) 749-8000

The object of the Rabbinical Assembly is to promote Conservative Judaism; to cooperate with the Jewish Theological Seminary of America and with the United Synagogue of America; to advance the cause of Jewish learning; to promote the welfare of the members; and to foster the spirit of fellowship and cooperation among the rabbis and other Jewish scholars.

Membership: 1,150 clerical
Publications:
Prayer books, proceedings, etc.
Conservative Judaism, quarterly
Meetings:
Annual convention

1239. Radio Gospel Fellowship (RGF)

Protestant (Assemblies of Brethren)
Albert H. Salter, President
Post Office Box 72
Denver, Colorado 80201
(303) 934-5521

The Radio Gospel Fellowship was organized more than 40 years ago in Southern California under the name "Youth For Christ." In 1952 the organization moved its headquarters to Denver, Colorado under the new name. Its main ministry is to supply Bible-reading broadcasts to radio stations for broadcast as a public service feature. There are no appeals made for funds or mail on these broadcasts, which are used by radio stations throughout the Caribbean area, Government stations, and also across West Africa. Much of the organization's activity, in addition to preparing and producing broadcasts, is involved with answering mail and helping many who have spiritual and social problems. The Radio Gospel Fellowship also helps with missionary projects including regular personal missions throughout the Caribbean, meetings and conferences, and the like.

Publications:
Strength, monthly

Radio/TV Programs:
Strength for the Day, a daily public service quarter-hour
The Quiet Time, a daily public service quarter-hour
The Hour of Faith, an evangelistic half-hour once a week
Life!, a 25-minute once a week contemporary public service program

Former Name: (1952) Youth for Christ

1240. Railroad Evangelistic Association, Inc.

Assemblies of God
Herman R. Rose, Secretary-Treasurer
Phillips Road
Spencer, Indiana 47460

Mailing Address
Route #4, Box 36D
Spencer, Indiana 47460
(812) 829-4667

The Railroad Evangelistic Association is a group of Christian railroaders and associates who endeavor to do missionary work among the railroad employees in the United States and around the world. The Association strives to bring together members of all Christian denominations and presently includes members of some 58 different branches of Baptist and Methodist faiths, as well as Wesleyan, Nazarene, Pentecostal, and Catholic.

Founding Date: 1941

Staff: 2
Membership: 1,000
Publications:
The Railroad Evangelist, monthly
Railroad Christian Tracts
Meetings:
2 district conventions
1 national convention annually

1241. Randall House Publications

Free Will Baptist
Dr. Roger C. Reeds, General Director
114 Bush Road
Nashville, Tennessee 37217

Mailing Address
Post Office Box 17306
Nashville, Tennessee 37217
(615) 361-1221

Randall House Publications considers its primary mission to be the preparation and publication of Christian education materials of an inter- and intra-denominational nature for the permanent institutions of the home and the church. A secondary mission is to make available resource persons and materials for non-permanent institutions such as Bible institutes, Christian day schools, camps, youth conferences, and Bible Colleges.

Staff: 55
Publications:
Quarterly Curriculum Materials
Scope of Christian Education
Meetings:
3 meetings, location varies

1242. The Reapers

Reformed Episcopal Church
Mrs. Jean Mulvaney
11 Caldwell Avenue
Marlton, New Jersey 08053
(609) 596-0934

The purpose of The Reapers is to create, increase, and unify interest among the women of the Reformed Episcopal Church in spreading the Gospel of Jesus Christ under the auspices of the General Council of the Reformed Episcopal Church.

Founding Date: 1971

Staff: 5 officers
Meetings:
    Three times per year

1243. Red Sea Mission Team, Inc., USA

Nondenominational
Wolfgang Stumpf, Team Leader
944 Barnett Street
Kerrville, Texas 78028

Mailing Address
Post Office Box 990
Kerrville, Texas 78028
(512) 257-3534

The sole purpose of the work of the Red Sea Mission Team is to preach the Gospel of the Lord Jesus Christ to the Muslim. Red Sea Mission Team maintains clinics, does agricultural work and distributes literature.

Founding Date: 1953
Staff: 68
Publications:
    Islam Shall Hear, quarterly
    Prayer and Praise, monthly

1244. Reformation Translation Fellowship (RTF)

Nondenominational
Dr. Samuel E. Boyle, President of the
    American Board of Directors
3575 Midiron Drive
Winter Park, Florida 32789

Mailing Address
Post Office Drawer G
Winchester, Kansas 66097
(305) 898-2939

The purpose of the Reformation Translation Fellowship is the translation into the Chinese language of Christian literature, the provision of Chinese original Christian writings, and the publication and distribution of such translations and original writings among the Chinese Christian community. The aim is to form a para-ecclesiastical auxiliary arm of the Chinese Church to try to bridge the gap of Communist oppression of religion in China so that, in the absence of missionary work inside Red China, a working partnership between some Chinese and some Western theo-

logians might endure. The Fellowship is beginning to get a few books back to mainland China's Christians hoping that some day it will be possible to replace the RTF with a fully indigenous Chinese Christian publication and distribution center in mainland China.

Founding Date: 1950
Publications:
    Reformed Faith and Life, 6 times a year, in
        Chinese, printed and distributed from Taipei,
        Taiwan
    Theological books and pamphlets

1245. Reformed Church in America, Reformed Church Women

Reformed Church in America
Dr. Beth E. Marcus, Executive Director
475 Riverside Drive
New York, New York 10115
(212) 870-2844

The purpose of Reformed Church Women is to unite all women of the Reformed Church in America in Christian fellowship in order to make Christ known throughout the world, to deepen the spiritual life of each of its members, and to develop a sense of personal responsibility for the whole mission of the Church through a program of prayer, education, giving, and service.

Staff: 10
Membership: 40,000
Publications:
    Newsletter, national and regional
Meetings:
    Semi-annual education conferences
    6 leadership seminars a year
    Triennial assembly

1246. Reformed Church Men's Council*

Reformed Church in America
Harold M. Hakken, Director
421 North Brookhurst, Suite 218
Anaheim, California 92801
(714) 778-2861

The Reformed Church Men's Council organizes and sponsors an annual convention for the men of the denomination, and prepares and furnishes materials for laity Sunday presentations.

Meetings:
Annual convention

1247. Reformed Ecumenical Synod (RES)

Reformed and Presbyterian Churches

Dr. Paul G. Schrotenboer, General Secretary
1677 Gentian Drive, S.E.
Grand Rapids, Michigan 49508
(616) 455-1126

The purpose of the Reformed Ecumenical Synod is: to express the Church's oneness in Christ and to promote the unity of the churches which profess and maintain the Reformed faith; to give united testimony to the Reformed faith in the midst of the world living in error and groping in darkness, and to the churches which have departed from the truth of God's Holy Word; to confer together regarding missionary work of the churches at home and abroad; to advise one another regarding questions and problems of import pertaining to the spiritual welfare and the Scriptural government of the churches; and to strive to attain a common course of action with respect to common problems, likewise to issue joint resolutions regarding movements, practices, or dangers when joint statements are deemed necessary. Activities include: quadrennial meetings of Synod; a Mission and Theological Conference held in conjunction with Synod meetings; dissemination of RES publications; Study Committees to focus in depth on theological and moral issues; consultations with other ecumenical bodies; and Regional Conferences on race, etc.

Staff: 7

Membership: 5½ million

Publications:
Reformed Ecumenical Synod News Exchange, monthly
Theological Journal, quarterly
Diaconal Bulletin, quarterly
World Survey of Reformed Missions, once every four years
RES Handbook, once every four years
Acts of Synod, once every four years
Various conference papers and assorted articles

Meetings:
Quadrennial Synod Meeting
Quadrennial Theological Conference

Quadrennial Missions Conference
Annual or semi-annual consultations and conferences
Semi-annual Interim Committee Meetings, location varies

1248. Reformed Episcopal Church, Board of Foreign Mission

Reformed Episcopal Church

The Rev. Samuel M. Forster, Chairman
430 Indian Crest Drive
Harleysville, Pennsylvania 19438
(215) 256-9012

The Board of Foreign Mission conducts one denominational mission work centered in Lalitpur, U.P., India, which gives witness to the Christian Gospel, serves the educational needs of the area, and ministers to the health and medical needs of the people. The work includes a local church, a six-form school, a hospital and medical clinic, and village evangelism, along with public health clinics. The medical work is under the supervision of the indigenous Emmanuel Hospital Association. The Board also accepts missionaries to serve with various independent missions agencies contributing to the missionary's support, but not determining the policies of the agency.

Membership: 18

Meetings:
Committee meets six times per year

1249. Reformed Episcopal Church, Board of National Church Extension

Reformed Episcopal Church

The Rev. Robert N. McIntyre, Chairman
RD #1, Post Office Box 416
Smithtown Road
Pipersville, Pennsylvania 18947
(215) 294-9289

The purpose of the Board of National Church Extension is to promote the growth of the Reformed Episcopal Church outside the present Synods by publicity correspondence; the establishing of missions and extension efforts; employing and overseeing the work of one or more church extension ministers; and raising the necessary funds for these efforts.

Membership: 12 lay; 13 clerical

Meetings:

3 scheduled Board meetings per year
Special meetings as necessary

1250. Reformed Episcopal Church, Four Brooks Bible Conference

Reformed Episcopal

Miss Barbara West, Director
RD #1, Box 411,Smithtown Road
Pipersville, Pennsylvania 18947

Mailing Address
Four Brooks Bible Conference
Smithtown Road, RR #1, Box 410
Pipersville, Pennsylvania 18947
(215) 294-9269

Four Brooks Bible Conference is a conference center open all year to churches and other Christian organizations for weekend and week-long conferences. In addition to leasing the facility to groups to run their own programs of Christian instruction and recreation, Four Brooks sponsors the following programs which are open to all: a family camp, children's camps, a camp for teens and Mustard Seed Farm, which is a camp for handicapped children. Their aim is to present the claims of Christ as Saviour and Lord; to encourage believers in their spiritual growth; and to disciple future leaders of the church of Christ. They view themselves as helpers of the local church in the ministry of evangelism and nurturing Christian growth. The staff, the comfortable facilities, the quiet country setting, and exciting recreational opportunities are all dedicated to achieving these aims.

Founding Date: 1961

Staff:

2 full time
Approximately 35 during the summer months

Publications:

Four Brooks Bridge, camper newsletter, 3 times a year

1251. Reformed Episcopal Church, Publication Society

Reformed Episcopal Church

The Rev. Donald L. Reader, Chairman
901 Church Road
Oreland, Pennsylvania 19075
(215) 536-5432

The Publication Society is the only agency authorized to publish material in the name of, and for use by, the Reformed Episcopal Church. The Society is responsible for publishing hymnals, prayer books, and study manuals which are authorized by the General Council. It operates a bookstore at 4225 Chestnut Street in Philadelphia.

Membership: 3 lay; 3 clerical

Publications:

Several religious books

1252. Regions Beyond Missionary Union, USA (RBMU)

Nondenominational

Rev. Joseph F. Conley, Executive Director
U.S. Council
8102 Elberon Avenue
Philadelphia, Pennsylvania 19111
(215) 745-0680

The Regions Beyond Missionary Union is a faith mission agency committed to the task of world evangelization, with autonomous home councils in the United States, Canada, and Australia. RBMU's primary objectives are evangelism, church planting, and training national leadership with the goal of establishing autonomous national churches which shall be alive with Christ's life and in turn assume the initiative as centers of missionary witness. RBMU is currently working in Peru, South America; Kalimantan and Irian Jaya, Indonesia; Zaire; India; and Nepal; with plans to commence work in the Philippine Islands and Chile, South America. Ministries include rural and urban evangelism and church planting, training national leadership through Bible Institutes and TEE programs, language reduction and translation, literacy and literature production, medical services, youth programs, and a Christian bookstore.

Founding Date: 1873

Staff: 116

Membership: 184

Publications:

Regions Beyond, quarterly
Prayer Fellowship Bulletin, monthly

Radio/TV Programs:

Produce weekly radio broadcasts in Peru, South America in the Lowland Quechu dialect for the Lowland Quechua Indians of the Dept. of San Martin

Meetings:

Frequent meetings overseas

Former Names:
(1878) East London Institute for Home and Foreign Missions
(1900) Livingston Inland Mission

1253. Regis College Lay Apostolate*

Roman Catholic
Sister M. John Sullivan, CSJ
Regis College
Weston, Massachusetts 02193
(617) 893-1820

The Regis College Lay Apostolate is a group of young college graduates who give one or more years of service in needy areas in both foreign and home missions. A few retired teachers have also served. Areas served by some of the volunteers include: Peru, Ecuador, Chile, Bolivia, Jamaica, the Virgin Islands, Guam, Puerto Rico, Hawaii, and Alaska. Others serve in the South and Southwestern sections of the United States.

Membership: 850

1254. Regular Baptist Press

General Association of Regular Baptists
1300 North Meacham Road
Schaumburg, Illinois 60195
(312) 843-1600

The Regular Baptist Press provides a complete curriculum of Sunday School material. Its materials are true to the Word of God, and are evangelistic and missionary in emphasis, as well as thoroughly Baptist. In addition to the Sunday School materials, it also publishes vacation Bible school materials for all levels. These materials feature a five to ten-day Bible lesson plan with missionary emphasis, visual aids, and handcrafts projects.

Founding Date: 1954

Staff: 30

Publications:
50 religious books; 1 religious monthly

1255. Reiner Publications*

Nondenominational
Swengel, Pennsylvania 17880
(717) 922-3213

Reiner Publications publishes and distributes Christian literature.

Publications:
200 books; 16 pamphlets

1256. Release, Incorporated

Nondenominational
Norman K. Elliott, Executive Officer
1571 Grand Avenue
Saint Paul, Minnesota 55105
(613) 698-8877

Release, Incorporated holds retreats and conferences in churches of all denominations, preaches missions, and conducts small group activities in a Christian context. It also publishes a newsletter and offers counseling services.

Publications:
Teaching and newsletters, and projected publishing of other literature

Meetings:
50 per year

1257. Religion and Ethics Institute, Inc. (REI)

Nondenominational
Howard M. Teeple, Executive Director
Post Office Box 664
Evanston, Illinois 60204
(312) 328-4049

Religion and Ethics Institute is a non-profit, tax-exempt organization. As stated in its charter, the institute's purpose is "to promote the discovery and distribution of sound historical and scientific knowledge in the fields of religion and ethics." The distinctive characteristic of REI is its total commitment to the premise that society is in urgent need of the scientific approach to religion and the development of ethical principles and conduct. Special interests of the institute are religion in the ancient world, the historical approach to the Bible, and new directions for religion and ethics in the future. The institute's primary activities are research and the publication of books and slide lectures. The books vary from the popular level (*Truth in Religion* series) to the academic research level. The slide lectures are visual aids featuring archaeology and are designed for use in college and seminary courses. Locally REI give slide lectures to members, college students, and the public.

The organization maintains a library and a 35mm slide collection to support its work. Membership is open to the public. A list of publications is available upon request.

Founding Date: 1972

Staff: 2

Membership: 50

Publications:
> *REI Newsletter,* semiannually
> Publish the results of research conducted by the staff or commissioned by the institute

Meetings:
> Annual board meeting
> Annual local members meeting
> Occasional public lectures, all held in Evanston or in Chicago

1258. Religion in American Life, Inc. (RIAL)

Interdenominational
Dr. David W. Gockley, President
815 Second Avenue, Suite 200
New York, New York 10017
(212) 697-5033

Religion in American Life is a cooperative program of the religious community in America. Members work together to proclaim, by various means, a message about religion and its values to the American people. For 31 years RIAL has had the endorsement of The Advertising Council as it prepares and distributes material to all the various media encouraging participation in worship at the 330,000 houses of worship across America, and the living of one's faith in daily life. RIAL also operates the *Hotel Church Directory* which enables local churches and synagogues to advertise their location and times of services on boards placed in hotels and motels across America. It also conducts seminars for clergy and laity on the overall theme *Morality—Whose Responsibility?"*

Founding Date: 1949

Staff: 6

Publications:
> *The RIAL Bulletin,* 6 times a year

Radio/TV Programs:
> 30 second- and 60-second radio and TV ads urging people to attend their local houses of worship

Meetings:
> Clergy-laity seminars 3 times a year

1259. Religion Newswriters Association of the United States and Canada (RNA)

Nondenominational
Ben Kaufman, President
Cincinnati Enquirer
617 Vine Street
Cincinnati, Ohio 45202
(513) 721-2700

The Religion Newswriters Association is a professional organization of reporters who cover religion for secular newspapers, wire services, and news magazines. The RNA encourages quality reporting in the field through its annual awards contest, programs at its annual convention (held in conjunction with major religious events), and through a newsletter which provides a continuing forum for the discussion of pertinent issues as well as an exchange of information and ideas. It has conducted seminars for publishers and editors on religious news reporting and investigated professional disputes.

Founding Date: 1949

Membership: 125

Publications:
> *RNA Newsletter,* 6 times a year

Meetings:
> Annual convention

Former Name: Religious Newswriters Association

1260. The Religion Publishing Group* (RPG)

Nondenominational
Mr. Alex Liepa
c/o Eve F. Roshevsky
Doubleday and Company, Inc.
245 Park Avenue
New York, New York 10017
(212) 953-4651

The Religion Publishing Group holds five luncheons per year, each featuring a different program on a topic of concern to those involved in religious publishing.

Membership: 88 lay; 4 clerical

Meetings:
> 5 luncheons per year

1261. Religious Arts Guild (RAG)

Unitarian Universalist

Barbara M. Hutchins, Executive Secretary
25 Beacon Street
Boston, Massachusetts 02108
(617) 742-2100

The major goal of the Religious Arts Guild is to promote the use of all the arts in churches and fellowships. The RAG provides complete worship services, focused on drama, music, poetry, and celebrations of life—many of them integrating social issues. The Guild sponsors worship services, performing artists, workshops, and special programs at Unitarian Universalist District meetings and at its annual General Assemblies. A vigorous Awards program is administered by the Guild, along with a loan library of anthems for UU Societies.

Founding Date: 1923

Staff: 1

Membership: 150 sponsoring members

Publications:

Over 100 pamphlets, worship services, drama bibliographies, resource listings, and recordings

Meetings:

3-4 meetings per year

1262. Religious Coalition for Abortion Rights

Protestant and Jewish

Karen R. Gubman, Executive Director
3049 East Genesse Street, Room 221
Syracuse, New York 13224
(315) 446-6151

The Religious Coalition for Abortion Rights is comprised of 26 national religious organizations representing 13 Christian, Jewish, and other denominations. All support the right of every woman to choose legal abortion. From its office in Washington, D.C., the Coalition monitors Congress, the Administration, and the courts on abortion-related matters, and coordinates work on the state and local levels. Coalition affiliates, active in key states across the country, develop grassroots support to affect local, state, and national legislation and policies. The purpose of the Coalition is: to educate the American public about the diversity of views on abortion in the religious community, and about the threat to religious liberty that is posed by anti-abortion legislation; to encourage and facilitate support for safe-guarding the option of legal abortion; and to oppose a constitutional amendment that would make abortion illegal, and legislation that would make it inaccessible to any group of women.

Founding Date: 1974

Staff: 1

Membership: 2-4 million

Publications:

Voice for Choice, bimonthly newsletter
What Would You Do?, explanatory brochure
Legislative Alerts

Meetings:

Legislative Day in Albany, every March
Annual Public Information and Award Dinner, every October

1263. The Religious Committee for the ERA (RCERA)

Interdenominational

The Rev. Delores J. Moss, National Coordinator
475 Riverside Drive, Room 830-A
New York, New York 10115
(212) 870-2995

The Religious Committee for the ERA is a non-profit, interdenominational organization which works to educate and mobilize religious people to work for ratification of the ERA. Its goal is to enable people within an unratified state to develop their own religious strategy which is in turn supported by the national membership. At present, its strategy has been to help religious people build local action networks in key ratified states so that they might work more effectively in statewide ratification campaigns with other state and national groups. For example, RCERA worked to form an Illinois RCERA during that state's most recent campaign. The IL RCERA activities, supported by the National RCERA, included development of action networks, legislative advocacy days at the capitol, an inter-religious prayer service before the ERA March on Chicago, and an emergency visit by religious leaders to the governor of Illinois.

Membership: 38 organizations

Publications:

Member groups' newsletter
Action Alert

Meetings:

National membership meetings 3 times a year

1264. Religious Convention Managers Association (RCMA)

Nondenominational

L. G. Wymore, Corresponding Secretary
Post Office Box 39456
Cincinnati, Ohio 45239
(513) 385-2470

The Religious Convention Managers Association was organized to serve the purpose of providing a common meeting place for those persons who are charged with the responsibility of providing leadership in logistics and promotion of large gatherings or conventions within their respective religious bodies. Its annual meeting is open to persons from all religious backgrounds as well as those who have facilities and services to offer the participants.

Founding Date: 1972

Membership: 75

Meetings:
> Annual meeting during the week making up the last days of January and the first days of February

1265. The Religious Education Association (REA)

Interdenominational

Boardman W. Kathan, Executive Secretary
409 Prospect Street
New Haven, Connecticut 06510
(203) 865-6141

The Religious Education Association is an interfaith, interdisciplinary organization which was founded by William Rainey Harper, the first President of the University of Chicago. The Association's purpose is threefold: "to inspire the educational forces of our country with the religious ideal; to inspire the religious forces of our country with the educational ideal; and to keep before the public mind the ideal of Religious Education, and the sense of its need and value." In order to carry out its goals and objectives, the founders developed 17 departments, including: universities and colleges; seminaries; churches and Sunday schools; private and public schools; teacher training; community agencies; and homes and libraries.

Founding Date: 1903

Staff: 5

Membership: 4,937

Publications:
> *Religious Education,* bimonthly
> *REACH,* a newsletter
> *Annual Review of Research*

Meetings:
> International convention in a different location in North America every two years
> Workshops, conferences, and seminars held irregularly

1266. Religious Formation Conference

Roman Catholic

Sister Carol Ann Jokerst, CCVI, Executive Director
1234 Massachusetts Avenue, N.W., #917
Washington, D.C. 20005
(202) 737-1892

The main purpose of the Religious Formation Conference is to assist men and women who are engaged in or interested in the ministry of formation (initial and ongoing formation). The Conference serves its members directly by responding to requests for specific services which come to the office by mail/phone, and generally by developing and undertaking programs for the benefit of its members; sponsoring, conducting, and/or coordinating study and research on issues of concern to its members; disseminating information on relevant topics through publications; cooperating and collaborating with other national organizations; encouraging and promoting activities on the regional level; raising consciousness about justice issues and providing assistance in integrating these concerns into programs of formation; and serving as a means for exchange and support among members.

Founding Date: 1948

Staff: 2 plus a 16 member Board

Membership: 1,500

Publications:
> *In-formation,* eight times a year
> Monographs on various topics of interest to members (varied titles)

Meetings:
> Regional meetings at various times throughout the year
> National meeting every other year (last one in November, 1981), location varies

Former Name: (1976) Sister Formation Conference

1267. Religious News Service

Interdenominational

Mr. Gerald A. Renner, Editor and Director
43 West 57th Street
New York, New York 10019
(212) 688-7094

Religious News Service produces daily reports, both domestic and foreign, of news in the world of religion. It also issues weekly features, a radio script and a TV package, and offers a daily photo service. It has a network of more than 900 correspondents in the United States and at all strategic points abroad. The service goes to major dailies, the religious press of all denominations, radio and TV stations, and civic and religious agencies in both this country and abroad.

Publications:
Daily reports and releases

1268. The Religious Public Relations Council (RPRC)

Interdenominational

Dr. Marvin C. Wilbur, Executive Secretary
475 Riverside Drive, Room 1031
New York, New York 10027
(212) 870-2013

The Religious Public Relations Council, Inc., is an organization whose purposes are: to establish, raise, and maintain high standards of public relations and communications to the end that religious faith and life may be advanced; and to promote fellowship, counseling, and exchange of ideas among its members. Active membership consists of persons who devote a major portion of their service in professional public relations activities to any religious communion, organization, or related agency duly accredited by the Board of Governors. These activities include information, audio-visuals, radio, television, promotion, and public relations administration. Associate membership consists of persons demonstrating interest in the Council and its activities but not qualified for active membership. The Council was originally founded as the Religious Publicity Council in Washington, D.C. There were 29 charter members representing seven denominations, the Federal Council of Churches, and four church-related agencies. In 1967 the Council opened its membership to

qualified people of all Christian Communions. In 1970 its membership was opened to all religious faiths. Today, RPRC has over 800 members in 13 chapters, as well as over 100 members-at-large in 25 states and Canada and four nations overseas. There are no institutional memberships, but the membership of the Council represents one of the broadest religious cross sections in America.

Founding Date: 1929
Membership: 800
Publications:
The Counselor, quarterly
Meetings:
Annual convention
1 annual Continuing Education Program
Monthly meetings of each chapter
Former Name: National Religious Publicity Council

1269. Religious Research Association (RRA)

Nondenominational

Dean R. Hoge, President
Post Office Box 303
Manhattanville Station
New York, New York 10027
(212) 870-2565

The goals of the Religious Research Association are: to increase understanding of the function of religion in individuals and society through the application of the methods and knowledge of the sciences; to promote the availability, circulation, interpretation, and use of the findings of religious research among religious bodies and other interested groups; to cooperate with other professional societies, groups, and individuals interested in the study of religion; and to promote the professional development of religious researchers and of users of research findings.

Founding Date: 1959
Membership: 500
Publications:
The Review of Religious Research, quarterly
Meetings:
Annual meeting, location varies
Former Name: (1959) Religious Research Fellowship

1270. Renaissance Church/Community

Nondenominational
John R. Pollard
Post Office Box 281
Turners Falls, Massachusetts 01376
(413) 863-9711

The Renaissance Church/Community is a non-profit spiritual community. It is now in the process of building a self-sufficient community using alternative energy systems such as solar and wind. The community, which will consist of several houses, a community center, a nursery for children, a recording studio, a theater, a garage, a woodworking shop, and a healing center, is being built on 80 acres of land in Gill, Massachusetts. The community is being built not only to house its 70 members and 50 children, but to be a learning center for any who want to know "Why am I here?" "Who am I?" "Where am I going?"

Membership: Community 120; church 300

Radio/TV Programs:
60 public service radio shows aimed at youth audience

Meetings:
Public meetings, meditations, healing services

1271. Research Foundation for Jewish Immigration, Inc.

Nondenominational
Curt C. Silberman, President
570 Seventh Avenue
New York, New York 10018
(212) 921-3871

The Research Foundation for Jewish Immigration does research and publishes books on the immigration and acculturation both of Jewish and other Nazi persecutees. It is connected with the Council of Jews from Germany (London-Jerusalem-New York) and supports the Council's projects. Archives include 25,000 biographical files of outstanding émigrés of all kinds worldwide, and an oral history collection with Jewish immigrants from Central Europe of the Nazi period. The Foundation is publishing the series *Jewish Immigrants of the Nazi Period in the USA* (Volumes 1-3, 1979-1982) and the *International Biographical Dictionary of Central European Emigrés, 1943-1945* (Volumes 1-3, 1980-1982).

1272. Retreats International (RI)

Roman Catholic
Rev. Thomas W. Gedeon, SJ, Executive Director
1112 Memorial Library
Notre Dame, Indiana 46556
(219) 283-2764

Retreats International is a service organization to the retreat movement, functioning primarily in the United States and Canada. It is an organization of retreat houses and renewal centers, and holds retreats for men, women, and youth. It operates through a Board of Directors which is elected by the delegates of the retreat houses at a triennial convention. It is supported by dues from the member houses. RI is a clearing house of information and ideas about the content and format of retreats as well as the organization of retreat houses, including recruiting of retreatants and fund raising. It publishes a newsletter, a directory of retreat houses, and recruiting pamphlets. It conducts conferences and seminars in the form of training programs for priests, religious, and lay people involved in retreat work.

Founding Date: 1977

Staff: 4

Membership:
400 retreat houses in the USA and Canada

Publications:
Retreat World, quarterly
Directory of Retreat Houses, annually

Meetings:
Annual Summer Institute at Notre Dame
Other conferences and workshops in various locations throughout the year

Mergers:
Retreats International-Men's Division (founded 1927, formerly National Catholic Laymen's Retreat Conference) and Retreats International—Women's Division (founded 1936, formerly National Laywomen's Retreat Movement)

1273. Review and Herald Publishing Association

Seventh-day Adventist
Mr. Harold Otis, Jr., General Manager
6856 Eastern Avenue, N.W.
Washington, D.C. 20012
(202) 723-3700

The Review and Herald Publishing Association was established to serve the publishing needs of the Seventh-day Adventist Church. It is structured to produce and mail every product from the acceptance of the manuscript to the finishing of the job. More than 300 people are involved in this production, from editorial to art work, layout, printing, binding, and shipping.

Staff: 30

Membership: 370

Publications:
> 4 monthly magazines, 3 weekly magazines
> 3 weekly magazines, 2 missionary journals
> 1 health journal, 2 professional journals
> 5 study guides

Meetings:
> 1 retreat, 2 general conferences

1274. Roa Films

Nondenominational

Miss Jean M. Larson, Executive Vice President
1696 North Astor Street
Milwaukee, Wisconsin 53202
(414) 271-0861

Roa Films is one of the largest audio-visual libraries in the United States. The company produces and distributes sound filmstrips with records and tapes that are widely used in the educational programs of many religious denominations. The filmstrip productions deal with prominent themes in religious education today: moral values, liturgy and worship, scripture, sacraments, and church history, to name just a few. The company's film rental division provides entertainment feature films, short subjects, and general interest films, as well as films on contemporary topics of social and personal concern. Roa Films also distributes films to business and industry in the areas of sales training, personnel management, safety, and quality control.

Staff: 40

Publications:
> Catalogues

1275. Robert Forester Evangelistic Foundation, Inc.

Nondenominational

Robert C. Forester, Sr., President
2545 North Madera Avenue
Kerman, California 93630
(209) 846-5353 or (209) 222-9325

The Forester Foundation is evangelistic in nature and purpose. A variety of activities support Christian work such as schools, medical facilities, social endeavor, churches, mission stations, and Christian literature. Mr. Robert Forester is involved in missionary evangelism, education, and publishing.

Also Known As: Forester Foundation

1276. Robert Schuller Institute for Successful Church Leadership

Reformed Church in America

Wilbert B. Eichenberger, Executive Director
12141 Lewis Street
Garden Grove, California 92640
(714) 971-4133

The Robert H. Schuller Institute for Successful Church Leadership conducts seminars for ministers, their wives, and decision-making lay leaders on how to provide successful and creative leadership and make their respective churches more vital. Conferences are also held each year in special interest areas of church ministry such as laity training, single adult ministry, and personal development conferences for women, married couples, and single adults. Over 10,000 graduates from all over the world and representing every major denomination have attended the Institute.

Meetings:
> 2 Institute sessions each year
> 7 specialized conferences each year

1277. Rocky Mountain Dharma Center

Buddhist

Michael McLellan and Martha Espeset, Directors
Route 1
Livermore, Colorado 80536
(303) 881-2372

Rocky Mountain Dharma Center is a major buddhist contemplative center under the direction of Vajracarya the Venerable Chogyam Trungpa, Rinpoche. It provides a spacious environment for the intensive practice of buddhist meditation, and offers group practice programs, study sessions, and seminars. A residency program is also available.

Founding Date: 1971

Staff: 15

Membership: 3,500

Publications:
Newsletter, quarterly

1278. Rod and Staff Publishers, Inc.

Mennonite
Paul M. Landis
Crockett, Kentucky 41413
(606) 522-4348

The purpose of Rod and Staff Publishers, Inc., is to provide the Christian home, church, and school with sound Bible-based material.

Membership: 1 lay; 6 clerical

Publications:
Children's and youth storybooks (43)
Textbooks (more than 60), and Sunday School materials
The Christian Contender, adult-religious
The Christian Example, youth religious
The Christian School Builder for parents, teachers, and school board
The Christian Pathway and Wee Lambs children's story papers
Star of Hope, evangelistic
Newsletter mailed quarterly
Gospel Tracts, 95 titles

Meetings:
2 public meetings yearly

1279. Romanian Missionary Society

Interdenominational
Dr. Peter Trutra, President
801 South Ocean Drive
Hollywood, Florida 33019
(305) 920-5639

The Romanian Missionary Society broadcasts daily Gospel messages through Station HCJB Quito, Equador, and IBRA Lisbon, Portugal, in the Romanian language; prints and disseminates Christian literature; and provides relief and medical aid.

Founding Date: 1968

Staff: 7

Membership: 150

Publications:
The Voice of Truth, quarterly
18 books

Radio/TV Programs:
8 radio programs per week
7 daily programs through Quito, Equador, and one weekly through IBRA, Lisbon, Portugal

Meetings:
One anniversary program per year

1280. Rural Parish Workers of Christ the King, Inc.

Catholic
Miss LaDonna Hermann, General Directress
Post Office Box 300, Route 1
Cadet, Missouri 63630
(314) 516-5171

Rural Parish Workers of Christ the King are dedicated by vows of poverty, chastity, and obedience to serve their neighbors in rural areas for the extension of God's Kingdom on Earth. They are basing their life and work on the Gospel of Jesus Christ and the Rule of St. Benedict, and are now living and working in the St. Joachim Parish and surrounding areas of Washington County. Members visit and share with neighbors; assist with food, clothing and personal service; transport to clinics and church; bring God's word to neighbors through the Parish School of Religion, discussion groups, and private instruction; arrange vocational guidance and training for the youth, often in cooperation with juvenile authorities; sponsor a Boy's Work Program; obtain medical and legal advice for those in need; provide a home nursing apostolate; participate actively in civic and parochial affairs; and offer cultural, social and recreational activities.

Founding Date: 1942

Membership: 8

Publications:
Newsletter, several times a year

1281. Russia for Christ, Inc.

Interdenominational

David V. Benson, President, Board of Directors
Post Office Box 30,000
Santa Barbara, California 93105
(805) 687-7696

Russia for Christ is primarily a radio ministry to the Communist world. The emphasis of programs produced by the mission appeals to leadership or those who have had unusual educational opportunities in the Soviet Union. The mission also has a ministry aimed at getting Christian literature and Bibles to Communist countries and in funding aid to persecuted believers behind the Iron Curtain.

Founding Date: 1958

Publications:

Freedom, a monthly newsletter on activities of the mission and news of believers in Communist countries

Radio/TV Programs:

A 30-minute radio program *Christ Warrior* aired weekly over seven missionary radio stations

1282. Rusthoi Soul Winning Publications

Nondenominational

Ralph W. Rusthoi
Post Office Box 595
Montrose, California 91020
(213) 241-7244

Rusthoi Soul Winning Publications publishes and distributes religious books. The sole purpose of this organization is to promote the Gospel of the Lord Jesus Christ through the printed page. The company specializes in personal evangelism materials.

Publications:

20 religious publications

1283. Sacred Heart League, Inc. (SHL)

Roman Catholic

Father Gregory Bezy, President
Walls, Mississippi 38680
(601) 781-1360

The purpose for which the Sacred Heart League was formed is religious: to promote devotion to the most Sacred Heart of the Lord Jesus Christ within the doctrines of the Roman Catholic Church. The objectives of the corporation include the following: support of the Sacred Heart Auto League; support of all projects, services, endeavors, and objectives of the Sacred Heart Southern Missions, Inc.; promotion of vocations to the Roman Catholic Priesthood through support of the Seminary system of the Priests of the Sacred Heart, Inc.; and support of the Sacred Heart Spiritual Society, an unincorporated religious association with its principal place of business in Walls, Mississippi. The promotion of the stated objectives includes the use of all methods and media of communication, such as the printing, publishing, and distribution of books, pamphlets, newspapers, magazines, audio-visual material such as video discs, films, and video tapes; and broadcasting of radio and television programs.

Founding Date: 1954

Membership: 620,000

Publications:
Books, booklets, pamphlets, religious prints, and devotional materials published periodically

Former Name:
Father Gregory Sacred Heart Auto League

1284. Sacred Selections, Inc.

Ellis Crum, President
North Shores Road
Kendallville, Indiana 46755
(219) 347-3758

The general purpose of Sacred Selections, Inc., is to publish hymnals. When *Sacred Selections for the Church* was published in 1956, it was one of the largest hymnals on the market. Over one and one-half million copies have been sold. It is the aim of Sacred Selections to keep on publishing hymnals, and to offer the largest and widest variety of songs on the market today. They own several copyrights, and have recently purchased the R. E. Winsett Music Co.; however it is being operated as a separate company. Sacred Selections intends to keep on providing the largest and most unique hymnals on the market. The company also publishes records and cassettes and a limited amount of sheet music, and offers song T-shirts. They also provide worldwide tours for churches and groups, especially to the Bible Lands.

Staff: 8

1285. Saint Ansgar's Scandinavian Catholic League (SASCL)

Roman Catholic

Viggo F. E. Rambusch, President
40 West 13th Street
New York, New York 10011
(213) 675-0400

Saint Ansgar's Scandinavian Catholic League works for the re-establishment of the Roman Catholic Church in the Scandinavian countries.

Founding Date: 1910

Membership: 700

Publications:
> *St. Ansgar's Bulletin,* annually

1286. Saint Anthony Messenger Press

Roman Catholic

Jeremy Harrington, OFM, Editor/Publisher
1615 Republic Street
Cincinnati, Ohio 45210
(513) 241-5615

Saint Anthony Messenger Press publishes magazines and paperback books. The Press also produces and distributes cassettes featuring noted speakers discussing topics of religious and spiritual interest.

Membership: 315,000 subscribers

Publications:
> *Saint Anthony Messenger,* monthly
> *Catholic Update,* monthly
> *Homily Helps,* monthly
> 46 paperback books

1287. St. Anthony's Guild

Roman Catholic

Rev. Salvator Fink, OFM, Director
St. Anthony's Guild
Paterson, New Jersey 07509
(201) 777-3737

St. Anthony's Guild, incorporated under the laws of the State of New Jersey, is a religious association sustained by private membership and directed by the Franciscan Fathers of the Province of the Most Holy Name of Jesus. Its headquarters is in Paterson, New Jersey. It has three principal purposes: it aids the education of young men who have a vocation to the priesthood or the Brotherhood in the Franciscan Order, but no means to pursue it. It is the principal support in training all of its future priests and Brothers; it is the principal support of all retired Franciscans who have spent their lives serving Holy Name Province as priests and Brothers; it gathers alms known as "St. Anthony's Bread for The Poor." This money is entirely spent in the conducting of several Anthony Houses in different parts of the Eastern United States. Anthony House in Jersey City is the only institution of its kind to shelter mothers and their children who are temporarily homeless. There is an Anthony House in Philadelphia run by the Francicans that serves homeless men. There is in construction a shelter for migrants and their families in Apopka, Florida. There is an Anthony House in New York City in Harlem. An Anthony House is in the process of being founded on Long Island in the Catholic Diocese of Rockville Centre.

Founding Date: 1924

Staff: 30

Membership: 120,000

Publications:
> *The Anthonian,* quarterly

1288. Saint Benedict Center*

Roman Catholic

Sisters of St. Benedict
Post Office Box 5070, Fox Bluff
Madison, Wisconsin 53705
(608) 836-1631

St. Benedict Center is a mission of the Sisters of St. Benedict of Madison, Wisconsin. Its goal is to enable others to share in a community of love and concern through work, leisure, and prayer. The Center sponsors retreats and conferences and hosts events for other religious or non-profit groups that have a compatible philosophy.

Founding Date: 1966

Membership: 19

Publications:
> Newsletter, quarterly

1289. Saint Dominic Savio Club

Roman Catholic

Brother Gerard Harasym, SDB, National Director
Filors Lane
West Haverstraw, New York 10993
(914) 947-2200

Saint Dominic Savio Club is a nation-wide apostolate of youth character-building with an effective "Spiritual Fitness" program. The Club's activities are designed to teach responsibility and foster universal friendships. Entertainment Days, rallies, progress reports, contests, and Savio-of-the-Year Awards are all part of the Club's activity in building Christian leadership and fostering the Sacramental life, all in imitation of St. Dominic Savio, and intended to ultimately direct youth to Christ. During the year, there are retreat and encounter workshops, as well as days of recollection. The Club has spread from the classroom to higher grades, CCD units, and block or home units. A new dimension has been added with the growing interest in the Lay Savio Movement (past Savios). The Club is active in almost all states, Canada, and in 12 other countries.

Founding Date: 1950

Staff: 3

Membership: 10,000

Publications:
> *Savio Notes,* monthly
> Leaflets and material for the Spiritual Fitness Program

Meetings:
> Retreats for boys and girls
> Seminars
> *Cross Leadership Challenge* weekends

Former Name:
> (1976) St. Dominic Savio Classroom Club

1290. St. Jude League (SJL)

Roman Catholic
Rev. Mark J. Brummel, CMF, Director
221 West Madison Street
Chicago, Illinois 60606
(312) 236-7782

The purpose of St. Jude League is to promote and foster devotion to the Apostle St. Jude.

Founding Date: 1929

Publications:
> *St. Jude Journal*
> *Newsletter,* 5 times a year

Meetings:
> 5 Solemn Novenas to St. Jude annually
> Weekly devotions to St. Jude

1291. Saint Martin de Porres Guild

Roman Catholic
C. Theodore Breslin, OP, General Director
141 East 65th Street
New York, New York 10021
(212) 744-2410

The objectives of Saint Martin de Porres Guild are: to make Saint Martin de Porres known around the world; to inspire confidence in his intercession and to promote his apostolate; to help all men realize they are brothers created by God and redeemed by the Blood of Christ; to motivate men to work together for the temporal and spiritual good of all men; to prove that all men, no matter what their race, origin, or condition of life may be, can reach sanctity by means of prayer, penance and the proper use of the Sacraments; to erase from the mind of the colored races the impression that the Catholic Church is only for the Western whites; to promote a truly Catholic mentality among all members of the Church in all parts of the world; and to help Saint Martin's poor throughout the world, especially in its Dominican Missions in West Pakistan and Chimbote, Peru.

Founding Date: 1935

Staff: 5

Membership: 33,000

Publications:
> *The Saint Martin de Porres Guild Newsletter,* quarterly

Former Name: Blessed Martin Guild

1292. Saint Mary's Press

Roman Catholic
Brother Damian Steger, President
Terrace Heights
Winona, Minnesota 55987
(507) 452-9090

Saint Mary's Press is a publisher in education, with an emphasis on religious education textbooks and teaching materials. The Christian message is presented for high school students and adults in both the school and the parish market. It is not limited to teaching materials for the students, but also provides resources and training programs for teachers of youth and adults. In order to remain contemporary, Saint Mary's Press maintains an active publishing house, as well as a complete printing plant.

Staff: 22 lay; 4 clerical
Publications:
    93 titles in print
Former Name: St. Mary's College Press

1293. Saint Philip's Society for Teaching Missions

Episcopal
Rev. Frederic John Eastman, Secretary-Treasurer
Mrs. Alfreda Joslin, Manager
West Stockbridge, Massachusetts 02166
(413) 232-7733

Saint Philip's Society was founded to provide religious pictures for every home. Although it is now a commercial firm, hundreds of pictures are still being sent free of charge to home and foreign mission fields of the Episcopal Church. The members sell jewelry, religious books, pictures, and the like (wholesale) to religious gift shops and church bazaars.
Staff: 3

1294. The Saint Thomas Aquinas Foundation of the Dominican Fathers of the United States (STAF)

Roman Catholic
Very Reverend Thomas H. McBrien, OP
National Director
141 East 65th Street
New York, New York 10021

The purpose of Saint Thomas Aquinas Foundation is to assist in recruiting personnel and in raising funds to complete the authentic (critical) edition of the writings of Saint Thomas Aquinas, one of the foremost philosophers and theologians of the Church, and a man whose wisdom has been a guiding light for the Church for many centuries.
Founding Date: 1964
Membership: 10 clerical
Publications:
    Sancti Thomae De Aquino Opera Omnia Jussu Leonis XIII, P.M.

1295. Saint Vladimir's Press*

Eastern Orthodox
575 Scarsdale Road
Crestwood, New York 10707

Saint Vladimir's Press is the world's largest publisher of Orthodox literature in the English language. Publications include pamphlets, tracts and books for every age.

1296. Saint Willibrord's Press

Christ Catholic Church
Hugo R. Pruter, Editor
1638 Granville Avenue
Chicago, Illinois 60660
(312) 743-0984

St. Willibrord's Press is engaged in the publication of books, pamphlets, and church school materials for use in Catholic churches.
Staff: 5
Publications:
    5 book titles (history, devotional, theological)
    34 pamphlets and Sunday School booklets

1297. Salt Lake Mormon Tabernacle Choir

The Church of Jesus Christ of Latter-day Saints
Oakley S. Evans, Choir President
50 East North Temple, 20th Floor
Salt Lake City, Utah 84150

The Salt Lake Mormon Tabernacle Choir represents the Church of Jesus Christ of Latter-day Saints in television and radio broadcasts, at general conferences, and in world tours. They are a choir of 350, singing inspirational music.

1298. The Salvation Army

Nondenominational
John D. Needham, Commissioner
799 Bloomfield Avenue
Verona, New Jersey 07044
(201) 239-0606

The original and still paramount purpose of the Salvation Army is to lead men and women into a proper relationship with God. The Army's Founder, General William Booth, was a realist, however. He recognized that help towards physical regeneration must go hand in hand with spiritual rebirth. He therefore instituted a social service program that was and is today a manifestation and practical application of the dominating spiritual motivation of The Salvation Army. Aid is given wherever and whenever the need is apparent without distinction as to race or creed and without demand for adherence, simulated or real, to the principles of the Army. Some of The Salvation Army's national and local programs include: evangelism, services to the aging, youth clubs, camping programs for children and senior citizens, residences for young business women and senior citizens, adult rehabilitation centers (for alcoholics), drug rehabilitation, correctional services, day care, foster home and adoption services, missing persons bureaus, employment bureaus, hospital ministries, visitations to confined or institutionalized individuals, emergency and disaster services, group homes for the retarded, and many more.

Founding Date: 1865

Staff: 24,000 lay; 5,000 officers

Membership: 400,000

Publications:
> The War Cry
> Say
> The Young Soldier
> The Musician

Radio/TV Programs:
> Radio ahd television public service spot announcements
> One-half hour films for television broadcast

Meetings:
> Conferences, meetings and retreats are conducted by the Army across the country, but not on a set schedule

1299. Samuel Zwemer Institute

Nondenominational
Rev. Don M. McCurry, Executive Director
1539 East Howard Street
Pasadena, California 91104

Mailing Address
Post Office Box 365
Altadena, California 91001
(213) 794-1121

The Samuel Zwemer Institute, moved by love and respect for Muslim peoples, exists to help the Church of Jesus Christ fulfill its mission to them, in order that Muslim men, women and children, wherever found, may be given a valid opportunity to accept Jesus Christ as Lord and Savior and worship Him among a community of fellow-believers in a manner appropriate to their culture.

Founding Date: 1979

Staff: 7

Publications:
> *The Samuel Zwemer Institute Newsletter,* quarterly
> *Iranians in America. . . Handbook for Sharing the Gospel,* Zwemer Institute, 1982
> *Muslim/Christian Cross-cultural Dating and Marriage: Interviews with 5 American Women,* Samuel Zwemer Institute, 1981

Meetings:
> Muslim Awareness Seminar, held in churches and on college campuses nationwide

1300. Schambach Miracle Revivals, Inc.

Nondenominational
Dr. R. W. Schambach, President
1405 Woodside Avenue
Ellwood City, Pennsylvania 16117

Mailing Address
Post Office Box 1
Ellwood City, Pennsylvania 16117
(412) 758-8900

Schambach Miracle Revivals, Inc., a non-profit interdenominational religious organization, was founded by Rev. R. W. Schambach. Since its beginning and during its rapid growth, Rev. Schambach has preached on more than 250 radio stations daily and on Sundays with radio programs all across the country and in several foreign countries. Besides the radio programs, Rev. Schambach carried a full schedule of auditorium and tent campaigns across the country and into foreign countries. Rev. Schambach also founded four churches, an orphanage, and the East Texas Bible College.

Founding Date: 1959

Staff: 38

Membership: 1,300

Publications:
> *Power,* monthly

Radio/TV Programs:
Religious radio programs on approximately 250 stations

Meetings:
Frequent meetings held all over the country and abroad (approximately 200 in 1980)

1301. Schocken Books, Inc.*

Jewish

Eva Glaser, President
200 Madison Avenue
New York, New York 10016
(212) 685-6500

Shocken Books, Inc., is a publisher whose list includes a wide range of books in the area of Jewish studies. Among its distinguished authors are S. Y. Agnon, Gershom Scholem, Martin Buber, Leo Baeck, Nahum Glatzer, and Cecil Roth. Its large Judaica list includes more than 150 titles in hardcover and paperback. Schocken also publishes Christian writers, among them Kierkegaard, Andrew Greeley, and Daniel Maguire, as well as a number of works on Eastern religions and mysticism.

Publications:
Varied non-fiction books, 700 titles

1302. Schwenkfelder Church in the United States of America, Home and Foreign Board of Missions

Schwenkfelder Church

Arlan M. Bond
Main and Towamencin Avenue
Lansdale, Pennsylvania 19446
(215) 855-2863

The Schwenkfelder Mission Board is concerned with supporting individual missionaries and mission work through other denominational boards such as the United Church Boards, Mennonite Board of Missions, NCC, and other independent Mission Agencies. The Board is elected by five congregations of the Schwenkfelder Church and there is no paid staff. Funds are received from the five congregations for disbursement.

Membership: 2,600 lay; 6 clerical

1303. Scripture Press Ministries (SPM)

Nondenominational

David E. Hall, President
Wesley R. Willis, Executive Vice President
Post Office Box 513
Glen Ellyn, Illinois 60137
(312) 668-6000

The mission of Scripture Press Ministries is to assist the Church in discipling individuals by providing leadership training programs and support materials and by providing literature programs to win people to Christ and foster their spiritual growth.

Staff: 8

Publications:
Journal of Christian Education, 2 issues a year

Meetings:
Annual Christian Education Seminar, location varies

1304. Scripture Press Publications, Inc.

Nondenominational

David E. Hall, President
1825 College Avenue
Wheaton, Illinois 60187
(312) 668-6000

Scripture Press Publications, Inc., produces and distributes departmentally-graded All-Bible curricula for Sunday Schools, Vacation Bible Schools, children's church, and youth meetings. Included are teacher manuals, pupil manuals, departmental superintendent packets, teaching packets, pupil handwork packets, and teacher and music cassettes. It also produces Christian education teaching aids, including stories and lessons for the flannelboard, flannelgraph backgrounds, Christian educational books for children, a Sunday School record system, and more. Victor Books, a subsidiary of Scripture Press, publishes more than 200 titles. These are distributed through Scripture Press and include adult elective Bible studies with leader guides. Some guides include Multiuse Transparency Masters (MTMs) for making overhead projector transparencies, or to be used as flip charts, for making posters, etc. How-to-teach books, Christian biographies, gift editions, counseling titles, Christian guidance, and other titles for young people and adults are also included.

1305. SDA Kinship, International

Seventh-day Adventist
Vern Schlenker, Jr., President
Post Office Box 1233
Los Angeles, California 90028
(213) 933-3566

SDA Kinship, International, was organized to minister to the mental, emotional, social, and, most important, spiritual needs of lesbians and gay men who had experienced some contact with the Seventh-day Adventist church. The Kinship is a support group consisting of lesbians and gay men who either come from Adventist backgrounds or are still active members. There are also non-gay members who are sympathetic to the cause, as well as non-Adventist gay friends. In addition to ministering to gays, the SDA Kinship aims to lovingly educate the Seventh-day Adventist Church, and society in general, concerning the needs and feelings of lesbians and gay men. Activities include an annual "Kampmeeting," as well as vegetarian luncheons, guest speakers, discussion groups, camping retreats, and various social pursuits.

Membership: 300 plus general membership
Publications:
> Monthly newsletter

Meetings:
> Annual "Kampmeeting," location varies
> Monthly meetings of individual chapters

1306. The Seabury Press

Episcopalian
Werner Mark Linz, President
815 Second Avenue
New York, New York 10017
(212) 557-0500

The Seabury Press is the publisher of Crossroad Books. Continuing the Seabury Press/Herder and Herder religious publishing program, Crossroad Books offers an expanding list of ecumenical titles in theology and spirituality, religious education resource materials, and prayer books.

Staff: 90 lay; 1 clerical
Publications:
> *The New Review of Books and Religion,* monthly
> 100 new books annually
> Over 1,000 titles in print

1307. Seamen's Church Institute of New York and New Jersey

Episcopal
The Rev. James R. Whittemore
15 State Street
New York, New York 10004
(212) 269-2710

The Seamen's Church Institute of New York and New Jersey is a residential social service agency for merchant seamen of all nations when they are in the greater port of New York.

Founding Date: 1834
Staff: 165
Absorbed:
> (1975) Church Association for Seamen's Work (formerly Seamen's Church Institute of America

Supersedes:
> Young Men's Auxiliary Education and Missionary Society

1308. Security Church Finance, Inc.

Nondenominational
B. J. Barelay, President
5629 F. M. 1960 West, Suite 201
Houston, Texas 77069
(713) 893-1390

Security Church Finance, Inc., assists churches and other non-profit corporations to raise funds for purchasing land, erecting buildings, establishing missions and encampments, remodeling, or refinancing present debt by issuing and selling bonds.

Staff: 35

1309. Self Help Foundation (SHF)

Nondenominational
Ray C. Howland, Executive Director
Highway 3 East
Waverly, Iowa 50677
Mailing Address
Post Office Box 88
Waverly, Iowa 50677
(319) 352-4040

Self Help is a non-profit organization working to fight world hunger. The program is designed to facilitate development in rural areas of developing nations. A small, very simple tractor serves as the basis of the program—designed specifically for small acreages of poor farmers and the mechanical skill level of remote areas. In the program's first phase the tractors are introduced to rural communities so that small farmers can increase their agricultural productivity. Basic necessities become more affordable as farm incomes increase. The second phase involves vocational training in tractor mechanics and production. This basic education is oriented especially for rural students who are unable to continue in the formal education system or lack adequate finances. Actual production of the small simple tractor in the program's third phase provides a real sense of self-reliance to rural communities. Employment opportunities, trained workers, and more self-sufficient farmers are some of the results of this program of integrated rural development. The Self Help program, funded in large part by individuals and churches, attempts to help eliminate world hunger by providing opportunities for people to help themselves.

Founding Date: 1959

Staff: 15

Publications:

The Developer, 3 times a year

Meetings:

Meetings irregularly; attempt to have a yearly meeting for those interested in becoming more closely involved with the program

Former Name: Self Help Inc.

1310. Seraphic Society for Vocations

Roman Catholic

Father Frank Coens, OFM, Vocation Director
3320 Saint Paschal Drive
Oak Brook, Illinois 60521
(312) 654-4075

The Seraphic Society for Vocations encourages men and women to enter church-related vocations.

Publications:

Friar Action, bimonthly

1311. Serenity Spiritualist Association*

Spiritualism

Richard P. Goodwin, President
Post Office Box 137
Forest Knolls, California 94933
(707) 472-3633

The object and purpose of the Serenity Spiritualist Association is to share its Living Light philosophy, and religion of Spiritualism, through classes and seminars, books, periodicals, and cassette tapes. It also encourages the study of all related subjects which pertain to the nature of man, the universe, and God, and the relationship between them, leading to a sense of unity in peoples' consciousness promoting brotherhood among all races, creeds and persons.

Membership: 35

Publications:

The Living Light, spiritual awareness study book

The Serenity Sentinel, monthly magazine to promote The Living Light philosophy

Meetings:

Conducts 3 semesters (12 weeks each) spiritual awareness classes based on The Living Light philosophy

1312. Serra International

Roman Catholic

John A. Donahue, Executive Director
22 West Monroe
Chicago, Illinois 60603
(312) 782-2163

The purpose of Serra International is to foster and promote vocations to the ministerial priesthood of the Catholic Church, as well as to develop appreciation of the priesthood, and all religious vocations in the Catholic Church. Further, it seeks to advance Catholicism by encouraging its members, in fellowship through education, to fulfill their Christian vocations to service.

Founding Date: 1935

Staff: 7

Membership: 14,000

Publications:

Serran, bimonthly

Handbooks and vocation guides

Meetings:
75 regional and international conferences including 1 international annual convention

1313. Servant Publications

Nondenominational
George Martin, President
840 Airport Boulevard
Ann Arbor, Michigan 48104
Mailing Address
Post Office Box 8617
Ann Arbor, Michigan 48104
(313) 761-8505

Servant Publications' goal is to present solid Christian teaching in book and cassette form and to publish worship materials to serve the needs of Christians from a wide variety of backgrounds. Servant Books concentrates on works that deal with practical Christian teaching, bible study, scripture meditation, Christian community, prayer, the church in the world, and the charismatic renewal. Servant Music publishes songbooks and records to give Christians in prayer groups, communities, and churches the resources they need to worship the Lord with spiritual vitality and depth. Servant Cassettes provides teaching on living the Christian life.

Staff: 50
Publications:
New Covenant, monthly
Pastoral Renewal

1314. Seventh-day Adventists Church, Association of Privately Owned Seventh-day Adventists Services and Industries (ASI)

Seventh-day Adventist Church
Harold J. Lance, President
6840 Eastern Avenue, N.W.
Washington, D.C. 20012
(202) 722-6000

The Association of Privately Owned Seventh-day Adventist Services and Industries is a church-sponsored organization for the promotion of the interests of SDA privately owned and operated self-supporting enterprises in North America. The purpose of the ASI is: to foster and promote the interests of self--supporting missionary enterprises operated by Seventh-day Adventists throughout the North American Division; to encourage Seventh-day Adventist church members in privately owned enterprises of various types to unite their efforts with those of denominationally-operated enterprises in the furtherance and extension of the gospel to their immediate communities, and to the ends of the earth, according to their abilities and opportunities; and to encourage such enterprises to commit themselves to work in full and complete harmony with the standards and policies of the denomination in their relationships with conference and church administrations, ministers, church members, and with the people of their communities. The membership of ASI may be classified under the following types of institutions or enterprises: educational; industries and businesses; nursing homes; retirement centers; community and convalescent hospitals and sanitariums; homes for the handicapped and retarded; medical and dental clinics; foundations of various types; and personal members. Membership is limited to institutions and personal enterprises operated by SDA church members in harmony with denominational standards and principles, and according to professional and ethical standards, and recommended by local and union conference administrations and their ASI secretaries.

Founding Date: 1946
Publications:
ASI News, monthly
Former Names:
(1947) North American Commission for Self-Supporting Missionary Work
(1951) Association of Seventh-day Adventists Self-Supporting Institutions

1315. Seventh-day Adventists Church, Department of Communication

Seventh-day Adventist
James E. Chase, Director
6840 Eastern Avenue, N.W.
Washington, D.C. 20012
(202)723-0800

Because communication is the total church at work in witnessing, the Department of Communication, Seventh-day Adventists, is part and parcel of all programs, serving all departments and administrations with the communicative skills it possesses to further these programs. Department personnel aid administrators and other church leaders in communicating organizational policies to both internal and external publics, and conversely, interpret for administrators the attitudes of these publics toward the Church. Briefly stated, the objectives of the Department of Communication are to use and promote the use of all modern communication techniques and media in the most effective manner for the swiftest promulgation of the everlasting Gospel, and through a sound program of public relations to create a favorable climate for acceptance of the message of salvation through Christ.

Founding Date: 1973

Publications:
> *Tell Magazine,* monthly
> *Communique,* in-house, weekly

Radio/TV Progams:
> Adventist Radio Network programming: *Dialog, Bookshelf, Viewpoint*
> Affiliated with Adventist Media Center, production studio for *It Is Written* telecast, Voice of Prophecy radio broadcast, *Faith For Today* telecast, *Breath of Life* telecast
> A film: *To the Nations* (1974)
> *Dateline Religion,* weekly newscast

Meetings:
> Training seminars yearly, held at Andrews University, Berrien Springs, Michigan
> Advisories yearly (location varies)
> Workshops held four times per year (location varies)

Merger:
> Formed by the merger of the Bureau of Public Relations and The Radio Television Department

1316. Seventh-day Adventists Church, Department of Education

Seventh-day Adventist Church
Charles R. Taylor, Director
6840 Eastern Avenue, N.W.
Washington, D.C. 20012
(202) 722-6000

The Seventh-day Adventists Church, Department of Education fosters and directs the worldwide SDA educational system. The department counsels with the officers of the General Conference relative to educational matters and leads in formulating the major educational policies of the denomination; assists in finding and selecting teachers and other educational personnel; helps teachers find suitable employment; prepares textbooks for those academic subjects in which the denominational viewpoint is distinctive; prepares teachers' manuals and workbooks; issues promotional posters and leaflets; prepares analytical reports of the educational systems of SDA schools in various countries; encourages high standards of instruction; develops standards for teacher education, and issues teaching certificates; influences the standards and trends in secondary schools and schools of nursing, and accredits those that meet acceptable standards; conducts educational councils and workshops; maintains liaison with various governmental agencies; assists the schools and teachers in creating a strong spiritual atmosphere; visits and inspects schools; assists in educational planning; and helps with educational meetings and councils.

Publications:
> *The Journal of Adventist Education*

1317. Seventh-day Adventists Church, Department of Public Affairs and Religious Liberty

Seventh-day Adventist Church
Bert B. Beach, Director
6840 Eastern Avenue, N.W.
Washington, D.C. 20012
(202) 722-6000

The Department of Public Affairs and Religious Liberty is a department of the General Conference of the Seventh-day Adventists Church that represents the church in protecting and securing civil rights related to freedom of worship and belief: conducts public education with respect to the principles of religious liberty; coordinates the activities of unions and conferences in the field of religious liberty; and sponsors local, national, and international religious liberty associations. It is staffed by a secretary, associate secretaries, and office assistants, and has its headquarters at the General Conference offices. In the United States its staff concerns itself with matters such as Sunday legislation, municipal regulations restricting or prohibiting religious activities (for example, Green River ordinances, prohibitions of Ingathering solicitation), discrimination in employment and education arising out of the observance of the seventh-day Sabbath (for example, hiring, and discharge, unemployment compensation, and Saturday examinations), labor union relations, censorship of the religious press, calendar revisions that affect the continuity of the weekly cycle, family cases that involve religious freedom for parents or children (for example, adoption or religious training of children), tax exemption for churches and church schools, government subsidies to religious institutions (for example, free bus transportation for parochial school students, subsidies to teachers, free textbooks, grants for capital improvements), immigration and naturalization discrimination because of religious convictions, religious issues in public education, and religious involvements of the government (for example, the appointment of an envoy to the Vatican). Outside the United States the role of the department is largely consultative and educational.

The Ministerial/Stewardship Association combines those departments of the Seventh-day Adventists Church which implement a program for the total development and funding of spiritual and material objectives, and which, through a professional journal, *The Ministry,* conventions, institutes, and evangelistic field schools, endeavor to elevate the spiritual experience of, and increase the efficiency of, ministerial, evangelistic, and other gospel workers. In recent years there has been a new emphasis on including health professionals as part of the "blended ministry" team.

Founding Date: 1922

Merger:

Formed by merger of The Ministerial Association and the Department of Stewardship and Development

1318. Seventh-day Adventists Church, Lay Activities Department

Seventh-day Adventist Church
George E. Knowles, Director
6840 Eastern Avenue, N.W.
Washington, D.C. 20012
(202) 722-6000

The Lay Activities Department is that department of the General Conference, Seventh-day Adventists Church, that with its secretary, associate secretaries, and staff fosters the activities of laymen in any line of local missionary service anywhere in the world. By "missionary" service is meant personal or public evangelism or Community Services. Department activities include Bible correspondence school enrollment; community services including emergency provision of food and clothing, adult education classes in first aid, and summer camps for disadvantaged children; ingathering, lay Bible evangelism; and literature distribution.

Publications:

The Adventist Layman, quarterly

1319. Seventh-day Adventists Church, Ministerial/Stewardship Association

Seventh-day Adventist Church
J. Robert Spangler, Secretary
6840 Eastern Avenue, N.W.
Washington, D.C. 20012
(202) 722-6000

1320. Seventh-day Adventists Church, Radio, Television and Film Center

Seventh-day Adventist Church
Robert R. Frame, President
1100 Rancho Conejo Boulevard
Newbury Park, California 91320
(805) 498-4561

Following the request of Faith for Today to relocate in California, a study began in 1970 that resulted in the decision to create the Seventh-day Adventist Radio, Television, and Film Center. At the Annual Council in 1971 the proposals for the center were adopted. The center provides for certain services of Faith for Today, Voice of Prophecy, and other broadcasters to be merged under one management. Other units of the center include It Is Written, the Audio Visual Service, and Breath of Life. The department director serves as secretary of the board of the center.

Founding Date: 1971

1321. Seventh-day Adventists Church, Sabbath School Department

Seventh-day Adventist Church
Howard F. Rampton, Director
6840 Eastern Avenue, N.W.
Washington, D.C. 20012
(202) 722-6000

The Sabbath School Department is the branch of the Seventh-day Adventists Church that fosters and guides the operation of Sabbath schools, offers training and counsel to officers and teachers, and produces lessons and teaching aids. Sabbath School is the SDA equivalent, in general, of the Sunday school of other denominations, with certain distinctive features: (1) a regular part of the program is the fostering of interest in missions through reports of mission work in many lands, toward the support of which work the main regular offerings are devoted; and (2) the Sabbath school is intended to be not only a school for children and young people, but one for the whole church, including the adult members. Sabbath School Associations are formal regional groupings of local Sabbath schools formed with the object of fostering and promoting better Sabbath schools and helping the weaker schools.

1322. Seventh-day Adventists Church, Young People's Department

Seventh-day Adventist Church
Leo Ranzolin, Director
6840 Eastern Avenue, N.W.
Washington, D.C. 20012
(202) 722-6000

Evangelism has always been the basic purpose of the Young People's Department (Missionary Volunteers). In 1954 the MV Voice of Youth plan was developed and the MV Leadercraft Course (now Youth Ministry Training Course) for the training of youth leaders was put into operation. An annual Youth Ministry Seminar is also conducted at Andrews University by the department. The Voice of Youth program has been enlarged to include four sermon series plus visual aids. One to One evangelism was introduced in 1969, and the IN-Group plan was launched in 1970. Other programs of the Department include the Pathfinder Clubs and the Share Your Faith program. Youth congresses are conducted in the United States and abroad.
Founding Date: 1893

1323. Seventh-day Adventists Publishing Department

Seventh-day Adventist
L. A. Ramirez, Director
6840 Eastern Avenue, N.W.
Washington, D.C. 20012
(202) 723-0800

The Seventh-day Adventists Publishing Department gives guidance to the publishing work of the Church and promotes the sale of literature through a corps of literature evangelist and Adventist Book Centers operated by the Church.
Publications:
  300 magazines; 2,000 books

1324. Seventh-day Adventists World Service Inc., (SAWS)

Seventh-day Adventist Church
Richard W. O'Ffill, Secretary and Executive Director
6840 Eastern Avenue, N.W.
Washington, D.C. 20012
(202) 722-6000

Seventh-day Adventists World Service is an international relief organization established for the purpose of operating the church's inter-country disaster and famine relief program. SAWS is registerd with the U. S. AID of the United States Government and is eligible to receive surplus foods for distribution to needy people in developing countries. It also receives reimbursement for ocean freight for shipment of such foods and of normal supplies such as clothing, bedding, medicines, and hospital and vocational equipment. The board of trustees is composed of 15 members from the General Conference Committee. The relief program of SAWS is supported mainly by the Disaster and Famine Relief Offering received in all churches in the world field once each year. Each of the other world divisions remits one half of the offering received by them to SAWS, Washington. The remaining half is used for relief of disaster victims within the division. SAWS maintains cooperation with such other voluntary international relief organizations as CARE and Church World Service, but is independently controlled and operated.
Founding Date: 1956

1325. Seventh Day Baptist Board of Christian Education

Seventh Day Baptist
Mrs. Mary Clare, Executive Secretary
15 South Main Street
Alfred, New York 14802

The Board of Christian Education of the Seventh Day Baptist Church is involved in enabling a Loving Revolution aimed at strengthening personal and church spiritual growth. Publications for which the Board elects and advises editors, writers, and publishers are designed for this purpose. Publications from various sources are continuously being reviewed in order to have updated material in the Board's lending library. Board members are available to conduct Leader Labs for Camp, Youth Fellowship, and Church personnel.

Publications:
> *The Helping Hand*
> *The Sabbath Visitor*
> *The Beacon*
> Youth and children's pages in the *Sabbath Recorder*

Meetings:
> Conducts Leader Labs for Camp, Youth Fellowship and Church peronnel

1326. Seventh Day Baptist Council on Ministry

Seventh Day Baptist
Rev. Herbert E. Saunders, Dean, Center on Ministry
510 Watchung Avenue
Plainfield, New Jersey 07061

Seventh Day Baptist Council on Ministry operates the Center on Ministry. The Center coordinates and supplements theological training of candidates for the Seventh Day Baptist ministry. To this end the Center provides instruction in Seventh Day Baptist History, Policy, Beliefs, and Sabbath Philosophy. The Center, through its Dean, also provides pastor/-church relations services, maintains a theological book and cassette library, publishes a quarterly journal, and develops material for churches and pastors.

Founding Date: 1963
Publications:
> *Ministers' Quarterly*

1327. Seventh Day Baptist Historical Society

Seventh Day Baptist
Rev. C. Harmon Dickinson, Historian
510 Watchung Avenue
Plainfield, New Jersey 07061

Mailing Address
Post Office Box 868
Plainfield, New Jersey 07061
(201) 561-8700

The Seventh Day Baptist Historical Society, an independent agency of the Seventh Day Baptist General Conference, was founded for the preservation, interpretation, and communication of the history of Seventh Day Baptists, now covering a period of more than 300 years. In addition to performing the usual activities of an organizational archives, the Society maintains an extensive collection of early Sabbath literature and preserves older records of churches, associations, and other agencies within the denomination. The agency also holds complete files of denominational periodicals and maintains a person/churches/subjects index to that literature, now numbering about 80,000 entries. Its most significant manuscript collections are the Julius F. Sachse Collection of Ephrata Materials, and the materials relative to the Seventh Day Baptist missions in Shanghai, China, from 1847 to 1950, and in Nyasaland (Malawi) from 1899 to 1915.

Founding Date: 1961
Staff: 1
Membership: 100
Publications:
> Newsletters, occasionally
> Annual reports, brochures, books, infrequently

Meetings:
> Annual meeting in Plainfield, New Jersey in May

1328. The Seventh Day Baptist Missionary Society

Seventh Day Baptist
Rev. Leon R. Lawton, Executive Vice President
401 Washington Trust Building
Westerly, Rhode Island 02891
(401) 596-4326

The Seventh Day Baptist Missionary Society is a denominational sending agency which works on both the home and overseas fields. Its purpose is to carry out the command of Christ given in the great commission, and to build responsible disciples as members of local churches and of independent national bodies in overseas countries. In working toward these goals, its workers establish churches, offer support for national church organizations, and are engaged in evangelism, education, medicine, literature, and self-help projects. It is in fellowship with the 12 national member groups of the Seventh Day Baptist World Federation. The Society has missionaries, supports workers, and funds projects in seven of these groups.

Founding Date: 1818

Membership: 305

Publications:
> *Missionary Reporter,* quarterly
> *Sabbath Recorder,* monthly

Meetings:
> Quarterly and annual meetings in Westerly, Rhode Island
> 1-5 spiritual retreats in different locations

1329. Seventh Day Baptist Women's Society

Seventh Day Baptist
Ada J. Davis, President
1645 Miller Street
Lakewood, Colorado 80215

The purpose of the Women's Society of the Seventh Day Baptist Church is to encourage the women of the denomination in Christian Culture through worship, study, service, and sociability and to strengthen each woman to reach her highest potential as a Christian person. All women who are members of a recognized Seventh Day Baptist Church are by virtue of such membership members of this society.

Founding Date: 1884

1330. Shambhala Publications, Inc.

Spiritualism
Samuel Bercholz, President and Editor-in-Chief
1920 13th Street
Boulder, Colorado 80306
Mailing Address
Post Office Box 271
Boulder, Colorado 80306
(303) 449-6111

Shambhala Publications is a house dedicated to exploring and mapping the inner world of human beings, and to expressing creatively the potential of man's inner evolution, through the medium of books of quality. Shambhala publishes books in the fields of comparative religion, philosophy, and psychology,

and books dealing with man's relationship to his body and environment. The Great Eastern Book Co. and Prajna Press are divisions of Shambhala Publications, Inc.

Founding Date: 1968

Publications:
> 200 books on comparative religion, philosophy, and psychology

1331. Share the Care International

Interdenominational
Kenneth J. Stroman, President
Post Office Box 485
Pasadena, California 91102
(213) 258-3529

Share the Care International is an interdenominational evangelical missions agency providing child care, medical care, and relief in emergency areas, primarily in Mexico and India. Mexican activities include subsidies to orphanages and a training center for youth. In India the agency operates a medical outpatient clinic and supports three literacy workers and an evangelist. Emergency aid supported earthquake victims in Nicaragua and Guatemala and flood victims in Baja, Mexico.

Founding Date: 1960

Publications:
> Newsletter, bimonthly

Former Name: (1975) Mexican Fellowship

1332. The Shepherd's Center

Interdenominational
Elbert C. Cole, Executive Director
5200 Oak
Kansas City, Missouri 64112
(816) 444-1121

The Shepherd's Center is not a place or a piece of real estate. The Shepherd's Center is a concept of linking older people together so that identified needs can be met and life can be sustained with meaning and dignity. The purposes of the Shepherd's Center are defined as follows: to sustain older people who desire to live independently in their own homes and apartments in the community; to provide retired persons opportunity to use their experience, training, and skills in significant social roles; to enhance life-satisfaction in later maturity and enable self-realization through artistic expression, community service, caring relationships, life-long learning, and the discovery of inner resources; to demonstrate life at its best in later maturity, so as to provide attractive role models for successful aging; to advocate the right of older people to a fair share of society's goods, and to assist them in gaining access to services; and to contribute to knowledge about what is required for successful aging and to experiment with new approaches and programs for meeting the needs of older people. Twenty-five churches and synagogues in the Country Club-Waldo geographical area are involved in the support and operation of the Center.

Membership: 4,000

1333. "Shepherds" Tours and Cruises, Inc.

Nondenominational
Mr. George M. Lauer, Executive Vice President
1718 Peachtree Street, N.W., Suite 918
Atlanta, Georgia 30309
(404) 892-1996

"Shepherds" Tours and Cruises, Inc., organizes programs strictly for the Christian tourist interested in touring in similar companionship to areas throughout the world. The company also prepares special interest programs for members of the clergy only pursuing missionary works and the like.

Staff: 30
Publications:
Brochures and informative materials for the Christian traveler
Meetings:
Seminars throughout the United States of America for members of the clergy interested in knowing more about the company's Christian tour programs

1334. Sheriar Press

Nondenominational
Sheila Krynski, President
801 13th Avenue South
North Myrtle Beach, South Carolina 29582
(803) 272-5311

Sheriar Press is a commercial printer that, among its other activities, prints and publishes books by and about Meher Baba. Meher Baba is acknowledged by his many followers all over the world as the "Avatar of the Age." Although founded in the belief in the real and enduring value of Meher Baba's life and work, Sheriar Press has no direct affiliation with any religious organization.

Publications:
Meher News Exchange/East-West, a quarterly newsletter for followers of Meher Baba
Books — biographies, philosophy, religion, juvenile
Meetings:
Retreats at Meher Spiritual Center in Myrtle Beach, South Carolina

1335. Siddhartha Foundation*

Nondenominational
John Richard Turner, Director
91 Dobbins Street
Waltham, Massachusetts 02154
(617) 899-2356

The Siddhartha Foundation is dedicated to the exploration and balancing of the body, mind, and spirit as they apply to the rising evolutionary consciousness of all people. Workshops in Healing, as well as, lectures by noted speakers are offered. Open meetings, concluding with a Healing Service and Meditation, are held weekly in Boston.

Membership: 300 lay; 3 clerical
Publications:
Newsletter, monthly
Radio/TV Programs:
Weekly half-hour program
Meetings:
Workshops, lectures, and meetings are held continuously year round

1336. SIFAT (Servants in Faith and Technology)

United Methodist oriented
J. Kenneth Corson, Executive Secretary
402 Blake Ferry Road
Wedowee, Alabama 36278
(205) 357-4703

The purpose of SIFAT is to minister in the name of Christ to persons both in America and in the Third World at the point of their most acute needs by providing programs of self-help in social and economic areas and using this help as a tool for winning Christian converts and for church planting. Activities include: developing designs and testing models in "Appropriate Technology" suitable for use in Third World countries; through indigenous help, activating the tested technologies for local use in needy areas in Bolivia and Haiti; using social and economic help through technology as a tool for evangelism and church growth; and conducting inspirational and motivational seminars, retreats, and mission conferences in the United States to create concern over both the social and spiritual plights of underdeveloped peoples and to Christianize American lifestyles.

Publications:
   The Provoker, every two months
Meetings:
   Seminars, retreats, mission conferences and evangelistic series conducted regularly in various places across the East, South and Midwest
Also Known As: Servants in Faith and Technology

1337. The Singing News

Nondenominational
Jerry Kirksey, General Manager
Post Office Box 18010
Pensacola, Florida 32523
(904) 434-2773

The Singing News is a publisher of news and features pertaining to all fields of religious music.
Staff: 9 staff; 5 contributing editors/columnists
Publications:
   Monthly tabloid gospel music trade paper

1338. Sisters Uniting*

Roman Catholic
Sister Maria Iglesias, SC, Chairperson
2140 Homer Avenue
Bronx, New York 10473

Sisters Uniting is an enabling group composed of two official representatives from each of the nine national Sisters' organizations in the United States. The group meets annually to confer on issues of primary concern to each of the member conferences, to arrive at a broader understanding of movements among women religious in the Church, and to work toward greater mutual understanding and support. While respecting the individuality of the autonomous member conferences, Sisters Uniting serves as a vehicle for bringing together the broadest possible panorama of women religious by persons committed to the life and future of the Church. Membership is by organization, and individuals participate through the member organizations: The Association of Contemplative Sisters, Las Hermanas, the Leadership Conference of Women Religious, the National Assembly of Women Religious, the National Black Sisters' Conference, the National Coalition of American Nuns, the National Sisters Vocation Conference, the Religious Formation Conference, and Sisters for Christian Community.

Founding Date: 1971
Membership: 9 organizations
Meetings:
   Annual convention

1339. Slavic Gospel Association (SGA)

Interdenominational
Peter Deyneka, Jr., General Director
139 North Washington
Wheaton, Illinois 60187
Mailing Address
Post Office Box 1122
Wheaton, Illinois 60187
(312) 690-8900

The Slavic Gospel Association is a nondenominational, evangelical faith mission dedicated to reaching Russians and other Slavic peoples with the Gospel of Jesus Christ. Founded by the Rev. Peter Deyneka, it has grown to almost 200 missionaries and national workers in 20 countries. The mission establishes churches and missionary centers for preaching the Gospel; it prints and distributes Bibles and other Gospel literature in Slavic languages; it trains national Christian young people in Bible schools; it distributes relief to needy people; and it sponsors youth camps and short-term lay ministries. The mission prepares 700 monthly Christian broadcasts to the Soviet Union using 10 international shortwave stations located around the world. SGA also has important Russian emigré ministries in Rome, New York City, and Chicago.

Founding Date: 1934

Staff: 55

Membership: 87 missionaries; 80 national workers

Publications:

Breakthrough, 6 times a year, in English

Sparks, a quarterly news bulletin published as the official bulletin of the Institute of Slavic Studies operated by the SGA

Gospel Messenger, quarterly, in Russian

Russian-English New Testament, Russian Bible Concordance, Russian Bibles, etc.

Radio/TV Programs:

700 monthly Christian broadcasts to the Soviet Union over 10 radio stations in Asia, Europe, and South America

Meetings:

Annual conference at Gull Lake, Michigan

Annual conference at Warm Beach, Washington

Sponsors the Annual Russian Broadcasters Conference in the United States

3 annual Chicago area banquets for SGA friends

1340. Slavic Missionary Service

Russian-Ukrainian Evangelical Baptist Union of USA

Rev. Alex Leonovich, Executive Director

Post Office Box 131 (Route 44)

Ashford, Connecticut 06278

(201) 873-8981 or (201) 873-2173

The Slavic Missionary Service is a non-profit missionary organization dedicated to the reaching of the Slavic people, and others around the world, for Christ. The work is supported entirely through free will offerings, gifts, and contributions. It operates a home for the aged and has a printing department known as Slavic Missionary Publications.

Founding Date: 1933

Staff: 42 home staff; 65 overseas missionary staff

Publications:

Sower of Truth, monthly Gospel magazine in Russian

English Branch Herald, quarterly

Link, quarterly

Books and translations (Russian language)

Radio/TV Programs:

5 ½-hour Gospel programs weekly heard in major cities in the USA and by shortwave around the world

Meetings:

1 annual conference for constituency, Ashford, Connecticut, 4th of July week

Regional conferences, retreats, missionary and evangelistic conferences, camping programs, etc.

1341. Slovak Catholic Federation (SSK)*

Roman Catholic

Rev. Joseph V. Adamec, President

1515 Cass Avenue

Bay City, Michigan 48700

In its over 65 years of existence, the Slovak Catholic Federation has united organizations — creating necessary rapport with all other Catholic groups in the United States, providing literature and spiritual books, and in general, federating the Slovak people and priests in a bond of union that nurtured the faith of Slovak Catholics here and in Slovakia. Members of the Federation include the First Catholic Slovak Union, Cleveland, Ohio; The First Catholic Slovak Ladies Association, Beachwood, Ohio; The Slovak Catholic Sokol, Passaic, New Jersey; Pennsylvania Slovak Catholic Union, Wilkes Barre, Pennsylvania; the Ladies Pennsylvania Slovak Catholic Union, Wilkes Barre, Pennsylvania; and the Slovak Free Eagle, Trumbull, Connecticut.

Membership: 100,000 lay; 500 clerical

Publications:

Dobry Pastier (Good Shepherd), quarterly

1342. Society for Europe's Evanglization (SEE)

Baptist

Fathy Bakhach, Executive Director, USA

2910 Oakwood Avenue

Michigan City, Indiana 46360

Mailing Address

Post Office Box 176

Michigan City, Indiana 46360

(219) 874-4428

Society for Europe's Evangelization is an independent, fundamental Baptist missionary agency dedicated to planting local churches in Europe. This is done by means of permanent evangelistic and pastoral teams. The teams are composed of nationals and American missionaries. The nationals are trained in SEE's own Bible Institute on the field. The Americans are selected from like-faith local churches/or Bible Colleges. SEE carries a most unique program called Intensive Missionary Training allowing high-school graduates without Bible and/or language training to proceed directly to the field. They are trained on the field in both language and Bible while serving and acquiring the on-the-job experience of a missionary. SEE is aggressively evangelistic in its outreach, with the purpose of discipling new-born Christians and organizing them in local, New Testament Baptist churches. It strives to help the churches reach a self-supporting and self-perpetuating status in finances, outreach, and personnel. It stands for fundamentalism, teaches it, and represents it through conferences and meetings held in the SEE Bible Institutes, churches, or other grounds. SEE also has a Christian Camp Ministry and short-term missionary programs.

Founding Date: 1956

Staff: 5

Membership: 40 missionaries

1343. Society for Propagating the Gospel Among the Indians and Others in North America

Nondenominational

George R. Ursul, President
212 Dean Road
Brookline, Massachusetts 02146

The Society for Propagating the Gospel Among the Indians and Others in North America is the oldest missionary society in North America and continues to this day its work among American Indians. While it has traditionally carried on regional activities among urban and rural Indians in the Northeast, it has presently committed itself to scholarship assistance to students, with preference for those who hope to enter the ministry, studying in the Southeast.

Founding Date: 1787

Membership: 50

1344. Society for the Advancement of Continuing Education for Ministry (SACEM)

Nondenominational

Connolly C. Gamble, Jr., Executive Secretary
855 Locust Street
Collegeville, Pennsylvania 19426
(215) 489-6358

The Society for the Advancement of Continuing Education for Ministry is an international, ecumenical group of persons engaged in the work of continuing education for ministry who gather annually for a program and business, including program evaluation and sharing, examination of purposes and goals, and development and improvement of educational structures and methods. Its research committee reviews project proposals and identifies areas where study is needed.

Founding Date: 1967

Membership: 425

Publications:
> 4 books on continuing education for ministry
> Newsletter, bimonthly

Meetings:
> 1-2 specialized meetings per year, for members and others, on continuing education for ministry

1345. Society for the Arts, Religion, and Contemporary Culture (ARC)

Nondenominational

Howard E. Hunter, President
Saint Peter's Church
Citicorp Center
619 Lexington Avenue
New York City, New York 10022
(212) 832-3564

The Society for the Arts, Religion, and Contemporary Culture is a multi-disciplinary professional society which provides the occasion and the resources for bringing together persons from diverse professional backgrounds to consider basic issues of human conflict and community. ARC is committed to the radical clarification of those life-affirming values contributed to contemporary culture by the arts, philosophy, religion, technology, and the social sciences; and to the strengthening of vital interdisciplinary relationships. The Society disseminates the perspectives and insights derived from intimate conversational gatherings of its Fellows to a broader audience through a variety of ARC-sponsored public programs.

Founding Date: 1962

Membership: 300

Publications:
>Occasional books, journals, newsletters

Meetings:
>3 in New York City and others in regional locations

Former Name:
>(1968) Foundation for the Arts, Religion and Culture

1346. The Society for the Propagation of the Faith

Roman Catholic
Rev. Msgr. William J. McCormack, National Director
366 Fifth Avenue
New York, New York 10001
(212) 563-8700

The Society for the Propagation of the Faith is the Holy Father's channel for encouraging and gathering spiritual and financial support of the Missions. It provides the "daily bread" support for 883 dioceses around the world and makes one-time allocations to specific mission projects and emergency needs on as equitable a basis as possible. A director in every diocese helps coordinate the work of the Society on the local level. The National Director of the Society for the Propagation of the Faith is also the National Director of the Society of Saint Peter the Apostle for Native Clergy.

Founding Date: 1822

Publications:
>*Mission,* a fund-raising publication on behalf of the missionary efforts of the Church
>*Worldmission,* a quarterly journal of missiology and mission thought

1347. Society for the Scientific Study of Religion, Inc. (SSSR)

Nondenominational
W. Clark Roof, Executive Secretary
University of Connecticut
Storrs, Connecticut 06268
(203) 486-4424

The Society for the Scientific Study of Religion grew out of an exchange of views by students of religion and social science in 1949. Its purpose is to stimulate and communicate significant scientific research on religious institutions and religious experience. Membership is open to students and to mature scholars interested in the application of scientific methods to the study of religion. Present members represent a wide range of academic disciplines. The majority are college and university teachers of religion, philosophy, sociology, psychology, and anthropology. A smaller portion are administrators, parish clergymen, and practicing physicians. The members seek, through the association, to examine religion in a rigorous, fair-minded, and responsible way with no "hidden agenda" and with a minimum of constraints. Members are not asked to divest themselves of religion, nor to commit themselves to what they do not believe, but only to be willing to expose their thinking to diverse hypothesis and to various ideas and research findings. The Society members believe that in this way they will deepen their understanding of religion in their own and in other cultures.

Founding Date: 1949

Staff: 2

Membership: 1,600

Publications:
>*Journal for the Scientific Study of Religion,* quarterly

Meetings:
>Annual meeting held last weekend in October

1348. Society for the Study of Religion Under Communism (SSRC)

Interdenominational
Alan Scarfe, Executive Secretary
Post Office Box 2310
Orange, California 92669
(714) 639-2180

The Society for the Study of Religion Under Communism is the United States office of Keston College, England. SSRC monitors religious life in Communist countries, disseminating news and providing analysis and consultation services for organizations and individuals actively concerned for issues of religious freedom in Communist lands. The organization began in England as a direct request of Soviet Christians, who wished for a research center to relate their story in a responsible and reliable manner to the West. Activities include conferences; publications, including a journal *Religion in Communist Lands*; news service, *Keston News Service*; and a newsletter, *Right to Believe.* The Society offers membership to individuals and institutions. It provides a speakers' bureau for churches, religious organizations, and academic institutions, seeking to increase public awareness of needs of those persecuted for their religious beliefs, and works closely with a number of groups like Amnesty International, Helsinki Commission, CREED, and East European missionary groups.

Founding Date: 1971

Staff: 14

Membership: 360

Publications:

> *Religion in Communist Lands,* three times a year
> *Keston News Service,* 25 times a year
> *Right to Believe,* five times a year

Meetings:

> Four conference sessions sponsored per year, mainly ties in with meetings of other professional Societies, such as the American Association for the Advancement of Slavic Studies
>
> Annual meeting of the Society held in the spring, with special conference sessions. Planned for the Midwest and Washington, D.C. area on alternative years.

1349. Society for the Values in Higher Education (SVHE)

Nondenominational
David C. Smith, Executive Director
363 Saint Ronan Street
New Haven, Connecticut 06511
(203) 865-8839

The society for Values in Higher Education is a network of persons in the academic world and the professions who have a special concern for the ethical and religious dimensions of their work. Members engaged in a variety of programs expressive of their conviction that academic inquiry includes values questions and takes place within a framework of moral commitments. In seeking constructive answers to the problems that beset American colleges and universities, the Society conducts a variety of projects. A program committee of Fellows designs and guides projects with the assistance of the staff in New Haven. Foundations, corporations, and gov-

ernment agencies have generously supported these projects.

Founding Date: 1923

Staff: 3

Membership: Approximately 2,100

Publications:

> Quarterly newsletter for membership
> Biennial Directory of Fellows of the Society
> Reports on various activities of the Society's projects

Meetings:

> Annual Fellows' Meeting of the Society in August, location varies
> Sponsors summer institutes, regional conferences, area colloquies, and local meetings

Former Names:

> (1962) National Council on Religion in Higher Education
> (1976) Society for Religion in Higher Education

1350. Society of Biblical Literature (SBL)

Nondenominational
Paul J. Achtemeier, Executive Secretary
Union Theological Seminary
3401 Brook Road
Richmond, Virginia 23227
(804) 355-0671

The object of the Society of Biblical Literature is to stimulate the critical investigation of the classical biblical literatures, together with other related literature, by the exchange of scholarly research both in published form and in public forum. The Society endeavors to support those disciplines and sub-disciplines pertinent to the illumination of the literatures and religions of the ancient Near Eastern and Mediterranean regions, such as the study of ancient languages, textual criticism, history, and archaeology.

Founding Date: 1880

Membership: 4,800

Publications:

> *Journal of Biblical Literature,* quarterly
> *Semeia,* quarterly
> Monograph series and several other series of books

Meetings:

> 1 annual national meeting
> 12 annual regional meetings

Former Name:
(1964) Society of Biblical Literature and Exegesis

1351. The Society of Christian Ethics (SCE)

Nondenominational
Joseph L. Allen, Executive Secretary
Perkins School of Theology
Southern Methodist Unviversity
Dallas, Texas 75275
(214) 692-2222

The purpose of the Society is to promote scholarly work in the field of Christian ethics and in the relation of Christian ethics to other traditions of ethics and to social, economic, political, and cultural problems. The Society also seeks to encourage and improve the teaching of these fields in colleges, universities, and theological schools and to provide a fellowship of discourse and debate for those engaged professionally within these general fields.

Founding Date: 1959
Membership: 611
Publications:
SCE Selected Papers, annually
Meetings:
Annual meeting in January
Former Names:
American Society of Christian Social Ethics in the United States and Canada
(1980) American Society of Christian Ethics

1352. Society of Collectors of Religion on Stamps (COROS)

Nondenominational
Dr. Allan Hauck, President
Post Office Box 165
Somers, Wisconsin 53171
(414) 552-8740

The Society of Collectors of Religion on Stamps is devoted to the study of stamps and postmarks with religious themes. It publishes a journal six times a year and encourages the study and exchange of stamps with a religious theme.

Membership: 600 general members

Publications:
COROS, a journal devoted to the study of stamps and postmarks with a religious theme, six times a year
Meetings:
Occasional meetings scheduled at the same time as one of the larger philatelic meetings

1353. Society of Jewish Science

Jewish
Dr. Ethan Gologor, Executive Director
825 Round Swamp Road
Old Bethpage, New York 11804
Mailing Address
Post Office Box 114
Old Bethpage, New York 11804
(516) 249-6262

The Society of Jewish Science is dedicated to the concept of applying Judaism to everyday life. Based largely on the principles and methods of the Psalmists and later prophets, the Society offers counseling and healing programs designed to promote self-growth and to arrest emotional debilitation. Cognizant of the progress made by biology and medicine toward attaining better health, Jewish Science nevertheless believes that our mental faculties can assist us in attaining dominion over our own well-being.

Founding Date: 1922
Staff: 7
Membership: 80
Publications:
Interpreter, journal, 8 times a year
Several Jewish books

1354. The Society of Saint Peter the Apostle for Native Clergy

Roman Catholic
Rev. Msgr. William J. McCormack, National Director
366 Fifth Avenue
New York, New York 10001
(212) 563-8700

The Society of Saint Peter the Apostle for Native Clergy is the agency of the Holy Father and the Universal Church to maintain and educate seminarians in missionary countries. It is a companion society to the Society for the Propagation of the Faith with the further task of providing seminaries for Africa, Latin America, Oceania, and Asia. In every diocese, the Director of the Society for the Propagation of the Faith is also the Director of the Society of Saint Peter the Apostle for Native Clergy.

Founding Date: 1929

Membership:

98 major seminaries; 394 minor seminaries

1355. Society of Saint Stephen*

Episcopal

Joseph H. Smyth, OHC Director
Mount Calvary, Box 1296
Santa Barbara, California 93102

The purpose of the Society of Saint Stephen is to help and guide deaconesses to bind themselves to Christ and to one another in His service. This aim is achieved by the regular recitation of prayers and the exercise of spiritual readings as prescribed in the "Rule" of the Society.

Membership: 5

1356. Society of Saint Vincent De Paul (SVDP)*

Roman Catholic

Howard E. Halaska, President
4140 Lindell Boulevard
St. Louis, Missouri 63108
(314) 371-4980

The Society of Saint Vincent De Paul is an international Catholic organization of lay persons. No work of charity is foreign to the Society. Its work, through a person-to-person contact, encompasses every form of aid that alleviates suffering and promotes human dignity. A principal activity in the United States is emergency aid to needy families, extended by volunteer visitors. A variety of special works, dependent upon local needs and resources, are conducted; services to the institutionalized and home bound and sponsorship of summer camps for needy youngsters are typical undertakings.

Founding Date: 1833

Membership:

34,000 lay in the United States
700,000 men and women world-wide

Publications:

Ozanan News, 8 times a year

Meetings:

1 annual national meeting
8 regional meetings

1357. The Society of the Chronicle of Lithuania

The Lithuanian Roman Catholic Federation of America

Rev. Kazimieras Kuzminskas, President
6825 South Talman Avenue
Chicago, Illinois 60629

The Society of the Chronicle of Lithuania is the publisher of the books *The Chronicles of the Catholic Church in Lithuania, a journal of the human rights violations.* This multivolume book is translated and published in English, Spanish, French, and Lithuanian and has readers in at least 35 countries world over. New volumes are added as new Chronicles become available. The original material, an individual Chronicle, was written in the Lithuanian language in the underground of Soviet-occupied Lithuania and received into the Free World via a variety of routes. Each Chronicle is a documentary on the brutality of the Communist regime and its doctrines, directed and carried out against the civil and religious human rights: it is a documentary description of a true genesis of Communism in action against God, Man, and the common human decency.

Founding Date: 1972

Staff: 7

Membership: 7,500

Publications:

The Chronicles of the Catholic Church in Lithuania, a journal of the human rights violations

Former Name:

The Society for the Publication of the Chronicles of the Catholic Church in Lithuania, Inc.

1358. The Society of the Companions of the Holy Cross

Anglican

Helen B. Turnbull, Companion-in-Charge
Adelynrood
Byfield, Massachusetts 01922
(617) 462-6721

The Society of the Companions of the Holy Cross has a membership of about 650 women of the Anglican Communion who are bound together by a simple rule of life adapted to their various circumstances. Companions seek to walk in the Way of the Cross, sharing in intercession and thanksgiving, with special concern for social justice, Christian unity, and Christian mission. Adelynrood is the home and conference center of the Companions. Adelynrood offers Christian ministry through its retreats, conferences, and the sharing of its life with all interested persons and groups.

Membership: 650

Publications:

Newsletter, 3 times a year

Meetings:

2 conferences a year for members only (one at Adelynrood and one in a different location each year)

Approximately 10 retreats or conferences each summer for any interested persons at Adelynrood

1359. Sojourners

Interdenominational

James E. Wallis, Jr., President

1309 L Street, N.W.

Washington, D.C. 20005

(202) 737-2780

Sojourners is deeply committed to living out the Gospel in the current world context. The organization's members believe that the Gospel calls followers of Jesus to identify with the poor, seeking justice and equality for disenfranchised people. They also understand the Gospel as a call to peacemaking and reconciliation. They are committed to working for the rebuilding of the church, envisioning it as a community of faith that offers a visible alternative to the materialism and violence of Western culture. The Sojourners believe that a strong worship life and nurturing relationships must undergird this vision of incarnating a new order. The specific outworkings of these purposes take the form of several ministries issuing from Sojourners Fellowships, a church in inner-city Washington, D.C. The ministries include a monthly international magazine; a peace ministry; a speaking ministry; a wholesale food cooperative; a day care center; neighborhood children's programs; and tenant organizing. Members of the Fellowship submit their resources, gifts, and needs to God through the corporate body.

Founding Date: 1972

Staff: 25

Membership: No dues paying members

Publications:

Sojourners

Former Name: People's Christian Coalition

1360. Soldiers of Jesus Christ, Inc.

Nondenominational

Kenneth N. Sortedahl, School Supervisor

Post Office Box 40

Spring Valley, Wisconsin 54767

(715) 772-3171

The Soldiers of Jesus Christ, Inc., maintains a small Christian home and school for children. All of its services are provided to the children free of charge. The operation and organization is a work of faith. It is not affiliated with any particular church group or organization.

Staff: 1 clerical

Publications:

Occasional newsletter

Meetings:

3 tours each year to present work

Also Known As: Peniel Christian Home

1361. Solitaires

Interdenominational

Mary Brite, Advisor

321 Warbler Drive

Bedford, Texas 76021

(817) 498-6608

Solitaires is an organization of self-help groups formed to help widowed women through the initial stages of grief.

Founding Date: 1974

1362. Source of Light Ministries International

Nondenominational

Glenn E. Dix, General Director

Post Office Box 8

Madison, Georgia 30650

(404) 342-0397

The Source of Light Ministries International is engaged in a worldwide literature ministry. It is meeting the spiritual needs of untold thousands through Bible correspondence courses and other Christian literature. The Bible correspondence courses are supplied free of charge to students in over 72 countries through Source of Light Schools and associate schools. Bible courses, gospels, and tracts are also supplied to missionaries, missions, and other Christian organizations for use in their own areas.

Founding Date: 1953

Staff: 61

Publications:
Magazine, monthly

Radio/TV Programs:
Weekly broadcast giving a Gospel message

Former Name: Source of Light Mission, Inc.

1363. South America Mission, Inc. (SAM)

Interdenominational
Rev. G. Hunter Norwood, General Director
5217 South Military Trail
Lake Worth, Florida 33463

Mailing Address
Post Office Box 6560
Lake Worth, Florida 33461
(305) 965-1833

The South American Mission is an interdenominational foreign mission society seeking to obey Christ's commandment to "preach the gospel to every creature." SAM reaches Indians and Latins in South America with a corps of more than 140 missionaries. The goal of these workers is to evangelize and to establish churches.

Founding Date: 1914

Staff: 23

Membership:
119 missionaries; 11 retired missionaries

Publications:
Amazon Valley Indian, bimonthly

Radio/TV Programs:
15-20 religious radio programs

Meetings:
Number varies: young people's retreats, pastors' conferences, annual field conference for missionaries on each field of Columbia, Peru, Bolivia, and Brazil

Former Name: (1970) South America Indian Mission

1364. South American Crusades, Inc.

Interdenominational
Bruce Woodman, Executive Director
Post Office Box 2530
Boca Raton, Florida 33432
(305) 395-0880

South American Crusades, Inc., is an interdenominational missionary service organization chartered in the State of Illinois with headquarters in Boca Raton, Florida. Its goals are to reach the lost of the Spanish-speaking world and to promote spiritual growth in the "family" of Christ.

Founding Date: 1959

Staff: 41

Radio/TV Programs:
A daily 15-minute Spanish radio broadcast entitled *Impacto,* heard in every country of Latin America

Meetings:
Evangelistic Crusades and Pastors' Conferences

1365. Southern Baptist Convention, The Baptist Brotherhood Commission

Southern Baptist
James H. Smith, Executive Director
1548 Poplar Avenue
Memphis, Tennessee 38104
(901) 272-2461

The Baptist Brotherhood Commission is a Southern Baptist agency that helps 35,200 churches throughout the United States lead men, young men, and boys to deeper commitment to missions, to a more meaningful prayer life for missions, to a larger stewardship in behalf of missions, and to a personal involvement in missions. This missions' education and action effort is carried on in churches within a Brotherhood organization composed of units of Baptist Men and Royal Ambassadors (boys 6-17) using guidance materials prepared by the agency.

Membership: 469,315 enrollment

Publications:
Method books describing Brotherhood work
5 religious magazines
1 tabloid newspaper

Meetings:

National meetings of men and boys every five years

State and country-wide workshops as requested

1366. Southern Baptist Convention, Christian Life Commission

Southern Baptist

Dr. Foy D. Valentine, Executive Director
460 James Robertson Parkway
Nashville, Tennessee 37219
(615) 244-2495

The Christian Life Commission assists Southern Baptists to become more aware of the ethical imperatives of the Christian Gospel. Specific areas of concern are family life, human relations, moral issues, economic life, daily work, and Christian citizenship.

Staff: 6 lay; 6 ordained

Meetings:

1 annual seminar
2 summer conferences

1367. Southern Baptist Convention, Education Commission

Southern Baptist

Arthur L. Walker, Jr., Executive Director-Treasurer
460 James Robertson Parkway
Nashville, Tennessee 37219
(615) 244-2362

The purpose of the Education Commission is to promote cooperation among the educational institutions officially sponsored by the state Baptist conventions and/or Baptist district associations and the agencies of the Southern Baptist Convention. It provides specific service to Baptist colleges and schools, and maintains a liaison for them with regional accrediting associations, the United States Office of Education, state boards of higher education, boards of higher education in other religious bodies, and professional educational organizations and learned societies. The Commission reflects the Southern Baptist commitment to introduce Christian truth into every area of life and to be obedient to the clear intent of the Scriptures in carrying out a teaching ministry. This teaching ministry is accomplished through a system of seminaries, universities, col-

leges, academies, and Bible schools that constitute the Southern Baptist educational enterprise.

Staff: 5 lay; 12 clerical

Publications:

The Southern Baptist Educator, bimonthly

Meetings:

4 meetings per year, various locations

1368. Southern Baptist Convention, Foreign Mission Board

Southern Baptist

R. Keith Parks, Executive Director
3806 Monument Avenue
Richmond, Virginia 23230
(804) 353-0151

The Foreign Mission Board had 3,008 missionaries working in 95 countries at the end of 1979. During that year, 332 new missionaries were appointed. Of all Cooperative Program (undesignated) funds for Southern Baptist Convention causes, 48.69 percent went to foreign missions in 1979.

Founding Date: 1845

Membership: 3,340 missionaries

Publications:

The Commission, monthly

1369. Southern Baptist Convention, Historical Commission

Southern Baptist

Lynn E. May, Jr., Executive Director
127 Ninth Avenue North
Nashville, Tennessee 37234
(615) 251-2660

The Historical Commission of the Southern Baptist Convention serves the denomination in procuring, recording, preserving, and utilizing information of historical interest. Its work is implemented by a staff of eight persons in Nashville, Tennessee. The Commission publishes a quarterly journal, provides copy for *The Quarterly Review,* publishes an annual index to 46 Baptist periodicals, and produces technical leaflets. A professional staff of three conducts history conferences and workshops and provides consultation to churches and denominational organizations on preserving historical materials, writing

Baptist history, celebrating anniversaries, etc. The Commission operates a Baptist Research Center in Nashville in which it has placed more than 100,000 volumes of books, periodicals, denominational annuals (yearbooks), church histories, and other materials including manuscript collections, pamphlets, tape recordings, pictures, etc. In addition to these physical copies of materials, the Commission has placed in its Dargan-Carver Library 10,860,000 pages of Baptistiana on microfilm. The Commission conducts an oral history program and has developed a centralized computer system for information storage and retrieval known as the Baptist Information Retrieval System. The system currently stores 267,500 entries.

Founding Date: 1951

Staff: 8

Membership:
675 members of the Southern Baptist Historical Society, auxiliary to the Historical Commission

Publications:
Baptist History and Heritage, quarterly

Meetings:
1 annual meeting
Workshops and conferences

1370. Southern Baptist Convention, Home Mission Board

Southern Baptist

Dr. William G. Tanner, Executive Director-Treasurer
1350 Spring Street, N.W.
Atlanta, Georgia 30309
(404) 873-4041

The principle purpose of the Home Mission Board is to develop and promote a single uniform missions program to assist churches, associations, and state conventions in crossing barriers to make disciples for Christ of all people in the homeland.

Staff: 104 staff members

Membership: 2,922 missionaries

Publications:
Home Missions Magazine, monthly
21 books now in print including current *Home Missions Graded* series (4 books a year)
The Human Touch Series (10 books)

Meetings:
1 staff retreat
2 summer conferences

3 full board meetings
Several other conferences and retreats

1371. Southern Baptist Convention, Radio and Television Commission

Southern Baptist

Dr. Jimmy R. Allen, President
6350 West Freeway
Fort Worth, Texas 76150
(817) 737-4011

The Radio and Television Commission of the Southern Baptist Convention is the world's largest producer of radio and television programs to be aired on public service (free) broadcast time. Its four major television programs and seven major radio programs (all half-hour) are heard more than four thousand times weekly on more than 3,500 radio and TV stations in this country and abroad. The purpose of this organization is to tell people everywhere that, no matter what they have done, God loves them and has a better way for them to live their lives, and then to encourage listeners to join the nearest church of their choice, whatever denomination it may be.

Staff: 118

Publications:
Trio, quarterly
Beam International, 11 times a year
Share, quarterly

Radio/TV Programs:
4 TV programs: *The Human Dimension, JOT, Listen, The Athletes*
7 radio programs: *The Baptist Hour, Black Beat, Powerline, MasterControl, Country Crossroads, Streams in the Desert, Sounds of the Centurymen*

Meetings:
Conduct radio, television, and cable consultation annually to acquaint pastors and other church members with the best way to use the three media to spread the Gospel

1372. Southern Baptist Convention, Southern Baptist Foundation (SBF)

Southern Baptist

Hollis E. Johnson, III, Executive Secretary-Treasurer
460 James Robertson Parkway
Nashville, Tennessee 37219
(615) 254-8823

The Southern Baptist Foundation is a permanent agency established by the Southern Baptist Convention to serve any person who wishes to contribute to any Baptist institution, commission, or agency by gift, bequest, gift annuity, or otherwise for the advancement, promotion, extension, and maintenance of the various causes of the Southern Baptist Convention. All available funds, including endowments and reserves of the 20 agencies, are managed according to sound investment principles in order to effectively meet the many varied objectives.

Founding Date: 1947

Membership: Not a membership organization

1373. Southern Baptist Convention, Sunday School Board

Southern Baptist
Grady C. Cothen, President
127 Ninth Avenue, North
Nashville, Tennessee 37234
(615) 251-2000

The Sunday School Board supports the Southern Baptist Convention in its task of bringing men to God through Jesus Christ. This is accomplished by making available Bibles, lesson courses and materials, books, films and filmstrips, music and recordings, and church supplies. The Board fosters education and service programs to help churches establish, conduct, enlarge and improve their ministries of Bible teaching and Christian training. The Board owns and operates two conference centers equipped for year-round use by church and denominational groups.

Founding Date: 1891

Staff: 1,500

Publications:
> 150 monthly and quarterly periodicals and approximately 450 undated publications
> Broadman Press last year published 555 new books, audiovisuals, supplies and music items

Radio/TV Programs:
> *At Home with the Bible*

Meetings:
> National, regional, and state meetings, annually

1374. Southern Baptist Convention, Woman's Missionary Union (WMU)

Southern Baptist
Carolyn Weatherford, Executive Director
600 North 20th Street
Birmingham, Alabama 35203
(205) 322-6511

Woman's Missionary Union promotes missions among the 13 million constituents in 35,000 churches in the Southern Baptist Convention. The particular audience of WMU is women, girls, and preschoolers. Approximately 1.1 million persons are enrolled in the constituent age-level organizations of WMU: Baptist Women, Baptist Young Women, Acteens, Girls-in-Action, and Mission Friends. Women's Missionary Union seeks to involve these and other church members in the study of missions and in witnessing and ministering through mission action, in direct evangelism, in praying for missionaries and giving money for the support of missions, and in personal involvement on a career or volunteer basis in missions. Woman's Missionary Union is not a missionary-appointing body, but a missionary-supporting body, dedicated to the undergirding of programs of the Southern Baptist Convention Foreign Mission Board and Home Mission Board. Promotional literature and program design are provided nationally by headquarters in Birmingham, Alabama.

Staff: 114

Membership: 1,100,000

Publications:
> 3 quarterly magazines
> 9 monthly magazines
> 1 quarterly bulletin

Meetings:
> 1 national annual meeting held each June in connection with the Southern Baptist Convention
> 1 national training conference conducted at Glorieta Baptist Conference Center in New Mexico and another at Ridgecrest Baptist Conference Center in North Carolina
> Innumerable staff meetings and private consultations

1375. Southern California Council on Religion and the Homophile (SCCRH)

Interdenominational
2256 Venice Boulevard, Suite 203
Los Angeles, California 90006
(213) 735-4357

The Southern California Council on Religion and the Homophile, an independent offshoot of a similar organization started in 1964 in San Francisco, is made up of clergy and laymen from various denominations and persons associated with various local gay organizations. In its publications, programs, retreats, and counseling CRH seeks to bring a message that is redeeming rather than condemnatory to gays who have been condemned and rejected in un-Christlike fashion, based on a self-righteous misreading of scripture; and to enlighten churchmen as to both the spiritual and sexual sides of "being gay." The purpose of SCCRH are: to open the avenues of communication and understanding between churchmen and homophiles; to investigate and implement ways for meeting the spiritual needs and social responsibilities of homophiles; to encourage a more satisfactory climate of opinion within the community on broad matters of sex and morals; and to seek just social treatment of the homophile community.

Founding Date: 1964
Publications:
　　Occasional publications
Meetings:
　　Regular meetings

1376. Southwest Radio Church of the Air

Protestant
Dr. David F. Webber, President
Post Office Box 1144
Oklahoma City, Oklahoma 73101
(405) 235-5396

The Southwest Radio Church of the Air operates a daily half-hour radio broadcast heard in several hundred cities of the United States as well as in a growing number of foreign countries through international shortwave stations. The teaching ministry of the Church has been a consistent blessing across 47 years of daily broadcasting. It is one of the oldest daily religious programs on the air, and was founded by the late Dr. E. F. Webber. The organization is interdenominational and evangelical and shares the Word of God in a globe-circling strategy outlined by its founder. It is instructional, evangelistic, missionary, and prophetic in purpose. The Southwest Radio Church of the Air has been widely heralded for its thorough, comprehensive, and consistently scholarly presentation. Special emphasis is placed on the teaching of the prophetic Scriptures and on the area

of Christian apologetics. Verse by verse exposition of biblical passages are featured from time to time.

Founding Date: 1933
Staff: About 50 staff members
Publications:
　　Gospel Truth, monthly
　　Bible In The News, monthly
　　Books and literature published at the organization's own printing shop
Radio/TV Programs:
　　Daily half-hour radio broadcasts at home and abroad
Meetings:
　　Meetings held quarterly in the United States and abroad
　　Conduct tours to the Middle East and Bible Lands twice a year

1377. Spanish World Gospel Mission, Inc.

Nondenominational
Florent D. Toirac, Executive Director
Post Office Box 542
Winona Lake, Indiana 46590
(219) 267-8821

For over 25 years the Spanish World Gospel Mission has been reaching beyond the bounds of political and geographical barriers to touch the entire Spanish-speaking world with the Gospel message. Utilizing the airways, the "voice without barrier," the Mission's radio broadcast, *The Way of Life,* currently reaches an estimated 35 million people in 26 countries worldwide. Over 130 stations are now carrying the message of Jesus Christ. More will be added as funds become available. The goals of the Spanish Gospel Mission are: to evangelize and to establish offices in every country where broadcasts are carried for the purpose of evangelism, follow-up, and church planting; to carefully lead people being reached into spiritual growth and salvation by faith; to help people start local churches for the purpose of fellowship and service; and to promote the training of nationals as pastors, evangelists, missionaries and teachers.

Founding Date: 1959
Staff: 8
Membership:
　　19 workers
　　26 fields
　　135 radio stations carrying the broadcasts in Spanish

Publications:

Newsletters; brochures

The mission provides, as God makes it possible, Bibles, New Testaments, correspondence courses, booklets, tracts, etc., for those who write requesting them

Radio/TV Programs:

El Camino de la Vida (The Way of Life) is currently aired in 26 countries on approximately 125 radio stations. Almost 35 million people are reached every week

Meetings:

Participate in missionary conferences throughout the country

Former Name:

(1959) Spanish World Gospel Broadcasting

1378. Speak, Inc.

Episcopal

Rev. James B. Simpson, Rector
Hillspeak
Eureka Springs, Arkansas 72632
(501) 253-9701

HILLSPEAK is many things. Geographically, it consists at the present time of some 3,100 acres atop Grindstone Mountain in the Ozarks, four miles south of Eureka Springs, Arkansas. SPEAK, Society for Promoting and Encouraging the Arts and Knowledge (of the Church), is a non-profit, religious, educational, and charitable corporation doing business in the State of Arkansas. Hillspeak is the home of The Episcopal Book Club, The Anglican Digest, and Operation Pass-Along, all incorporated under SPEAK, Inc. The founder and guiding spirit was Father H. L. Foland (now retired and living in one of the nine residences on the property). The EBC began in Nevada, Missouri in 1953, and moved to Hillspeak on St. Mark's Day in 1960. EBC operates in much the same manner as any other book club except that it does NOT publish books, but acquires them from established publishers and issues only four books per year. In 1971, Operation Pass—Aalong (The Anglican Book Depot) came into being to distribute second-hand books about the Church to seminarians, new priests, new churches, and the like. Faithful visitors may also browse and take home books. More than 23,000 books have been passed along to date. Projects and dreams of SPEAK, Inc., are retreat facilities and a retirement center.

Founding Date: 1960

Publications:

The Anglican Digest, quarterly
The Episcopal Book Club

Also Known As:

Society for Promoting and Encouraging the Arts and Knowledge (of the Church), Inc.

1379. Spiritual Book Associates (SBA)

Roman Catholic

John Reedy, CSC, Publisher
Notre Dame, Indiana 46556

Mailing Address

Spiritual Book Associates
Notre Dame, Indiana 46556
(219) 287-2831

Spiritual Book Associates is America's leading spiritual book club. Operated by Ave Maria Press, SBA provides its members with a complete book service, a practical and convenient single source for obtaining the finest in spiritual reading. SBA's distinguished editorial board examines before publication all major spiritual and religious books, selecting those deemed most appropriate for quality, editorial excellence, and members' needs. Each member receives eight books per year, without any additional charges for postage or handling. They also receive the popular book club newsletter, *Spiritual Book News,* which reviews and evaluates not only the book club selections, but all the latest and most significant spiritual and religious books being published.

Founding Date: 1934

Staff: 7

Membership: 11,670

Publications:

Spiritual Book News, eight times per year

1380. Spiritual Counterfeits Project, Inc. (SCP)

Protestant

Bill Squires, Co-Director
Post Office Box 2418
Berkeley, California 94702
(415) 524-9534

The purposes of Spiritual Counterfeits Project, Inc., are: to research today's spiritual groups, gurus, and influences, and to critique them biblically; to equip

Christians with the knowledge, analysis, and discernment that will enable them to understand the significance of today's spiritual explosion. Current developments must be seen in the widest cultural context, which includes intellectual, moral, historical, political, and theological dimensions; to suggest a Christian response which engages the church with all levels of the situation. This response will involve issuing a strong prophetic warning to the secular society. The organization believes it will also involve calling much of the visible church to repent of its compromises with the world and follow the urgent call of its true Lord, Jesus Christ; to bring the good news of Jesus Christ and extend a hand of rescue (i.e., evangelism) to those who are in psychological and spiritual bondage. Christians need to carry the gospel to such people where they are. By caring enough to understand a person's belief system, one expresses the concern that motivates evangelism in the first place.

Staff: 18

Publications:
 SCP Journal, 2-3 times a year
 SCP Newsletter, 10 times a year

Meetings:
 Speaking engagements at churches and related conferences 20-30 times a year

1381.　Spiritual Frontiers Fellowship (SFF)

Nondenominational
Robert C. Walker, Executive Director
Executive Plaza
10819 Winner Road
Independence, Missouri 64052
(816) 254-8585

The Spiritual Frontiers Fellowship is a nondenominational organization founded in Chicago by laymen and clergymen active in the major Christian denominations of the United States. Its purpose is to sponsor, explore, and interpret the growing interest in psychic phenomena and mystical experience within the church wherever these experiences relate to effective prayer, spiritual healing, and personal survival. SFF organizes open meetings in communities throughout the United States and Canada; presenting lectures and discussions; organizes Study Groups; maintains a Research Committee; issues publications; operates a Bookshoppe; and maintains an extensive Lending Library for its members.

Founding Date: 1956
Staff: 7
Membership: 7,000
Publications:
 Spiritual Frontiers Newsletter, monthly
 Spiritual Frontiers Journal, quarterly
Meetings:
 Annual conference
 3 national retreats

1382.　Spiritual Life Institute

Roman Catholic
Father William McNamara, OCD
7126 Highway 179
Sedona, Arizona 86336
(602) 282-7668

The Spiritual Life Institute is a small Roman Catholic ecumenical monastic community of men and women who embrace a vowed life of solitude according to the primitive Carmelite ideal. Situated in the high desert of Sedona, Arizona and the woods of Kemptville, Nova Scotia, the Institute is characterized by earthly mysticism and steeped in a Christian humanism that lays the foundations for prayer in a vibrant natural life enhanced by the Carmelite spirit of the prophet Elijah, Teresa of Avila, and John of the Cross. The Institute does not offer a program of prayer but a lively human atmosphere of prayer. Guest-retreatants participate in the monastic rhythms of the contemplative community or choose solitude in their own hermitages. The Spiritual Life Institute fosters the contemplative spirit in America through occasional retreats "on the road"; a quarterly magazine entitled *Desert Call;* and a series of cassettes on contemplation in the modern world. Perhaps most importantly, however, is Nada Ranch, the Institute's desert center and motherhouse where men and women, young and old, Christian and non-Christian, clergy and lay, married and unmarried, may go "into the desert to pray." The Institute also maintains Nova Nada, a primitive wilderness heritage in Nova Scotia.

Founding Date: 1960

Membership: 7 lay; 4 clerical

Publications:
 Desert Call, quarterly
 Nada Network, newsletter
 4 religious books

1383. Standard Publishing

Nondenominational
Ralph M. Small, Publisher
8121 Hamilton Avenue
Cincinnati, Ohio 45231
(513) 931-4050

Standard Publishing produces nondenominational literature for church use. In addition to a weekly series of lesson literature for those age two through adult and an annual vacation Bible school course, it produces picture storybooks, Bible study guides, Christian gifts, games, puzzles, quiz books, jewelry, coloring books, pictures and plaques, postcards, membership and financial record supplies, sermon books, crafts, craft books and supplies, teacher training courses, teaching visual aids, class electives, program books, commentaries, music and hymnals, and classroom equipment.

Founding Date: 1866

Publications:
Juvenile, etc.—1,000 titles, approximately 80 each quarter

Meetings:
160 conferences and seminars

1384. Star Bible and Tract Corporation

Nondenominational
Alvin R. Jennings, President
7120 Burns Street
Fort Worth, Texas 76118
(817) 284-0521

The general purpose of Star Bible and Tract Corporation is to print and distribute Bibles and other related materials. It proclaims the message of Christ by publishing it in the permanent and powerful form of the printed page. Over five million copies of more than 350 different tracts have been distributed, and over 26 million copies of the *Star* magazine have been distributed by direct mail evangelism. The chief objective of all its publications is to reach people outside of Christ, wherever they are to be found—in this country and other countries. Star Bible and Tract Corporation serves principally churches of Christ.

Staff: 20

Publications:
Star, quarterly
A quarterly newspaper
20 books in print

1385. STEER, Inc.

Interdenominational
LaRue Goetz, Executive Director
Post Office Box 1236
Bismarck, North Dakota 58501
(701) 258-4911

STEER, Inc., is a non-profit, evangelical, interdenominational missionary enterprise with its office headquarters at Bismarck, North Dakota. It "steers" money to missions around the world by means of livestock and crop-sharing called "God's Acre." As a service arm to missions, STEER, Inc., is dedicated to helping strengthen and undergird all aspects of foreign missionary work. People who want to see their investment grow for the cause of Jesus Christ purchase a Steer or Cow Unit priced at $450 and $700. These funds are then used to provide interested farmers and ranchers with the capital to purchase livestock or to seed the crop of their choice. The gain is then sent to missions. Almost a million dollars has been sent to missionary work around the world since STEER's beginning in 1957. Eighty evangelical mission societies presently are members of STEER, Inc., and receive financial assistance.

Founding Date: 1957

Staff: 10 board members

Publications:
STEER Talk, twice a year
Flaming Brand Reporter, 6 times a year

Meetings:
World Mission Roundup Conference annually at Bismarck, North Dakota
Regional Mission Roundups in various areas (number varies)
STEER Banquet Rallies and Meetings in various churches (numerous)

1386. Stewards Foundation

Plymouth Brethren
J. W. McCracken
218 West Willow
Wheaton, Illinois 60187
(312) 653-6550

Stewards Foundation is a service organization incorporated to assist and support local Plymouth Brethren churches, camps, homes, and the like.

1387. Success With Youth Publications

Nondenominational

Arthur L. Miley, President
Post Office Box 82418
San Diego, California 92138
(714) 459-1150

The objective of Success With Youth Publications is to publish evangelical Christian education materials for churches on a non-denominational basis. The materials are graded for preschool, primary, junior, junior high, senior high, and adult.

Staff: 12

Publications:
Christian education materials for 10,000 churches: *Whirlybirds, Jet-Cadets, Alpha-Teens, Omega Plus, Can-Do Books, Rainbow Books*

Meetings:
Christian Education Training Conferences

1388. Successful Living, Inc.

Nondenominational

Ronald R. Rousar, President
5624 Lincoln Drive
Edina, Minnesota 55436
(612) 933-1717

Successful Living is a direct sales company distributing Christian books and other Christian items through an organization of franchises. The primary marketing methods are: Rack Jobbing — placing book racks in retail outlets such as supermarkets, department stores, discount stores, drug stores, hotels, hospital gift shops, and restaurants; Book Parties — demonstrating the products in homes through the use of samples and catalogs; Family Book Club — making Christian books available to school students and their parents by distributing the Family Book Club Catalog.

Membership:
Approximately 2,000 franchised distributors

Publications:
Only for use with the marketing organization: a magazine, 5 times a year; one newsletter, monthly; one newsletter, twice monthly

Meetings:
1 Annual Convention
8 Training Seminars a year
1 Manager Training a year, locations vary

1389. Sudan Interior Mission (SIM)

Interdenominational

Dr. Ian Hay, General Director
Rev. W. J. Trevor Ardill, U.S. Director
2 Woodstone Drive
Cedar Grove, New Jersey 07009

Mailing Address
Post Office Box C
Cedar Grove, New Jersey 07009
(201) 857-1100

The Sudan Interior Mission was formed by Messrs. Gowans, Kent, and Bingham. With a deep sense of the need in the areas across the broad expanse of Africa south of the Sahara Desert known as the Sudan, they sought to bring the gospel to the unreached. Constrained by the love of Christ and in the hope of His coming, the aim of the Mission is, by the help of God, to obey His command to preach the gospel to every creature; to bring men to a saving knowledge of the love of Christ; and to plant and build up evangelical churches. The Mission is evangelical, international, and interdenominational. The Mission serves in Benin, Ethiopia, Ghana, Ivory Coast, Liberia, Niger, Nigeria, Sudan, and Upper Volta. There are National Councils in Canada, the United States, United Kingdom, Europe, Australia, New Zealand, and South Africa. The purpose of the Mission is to develop and encourage interest in missions; to train and send forth missionaries to Africa and such other parts of the world as may be mutually agreed upon by the Mission; to preach the Gospel of our Lord Jesus Christ with the aim of establishing churches which are self-propagating; to receive and account for real and personal property and funds given it for the furtherance of the work; to receive and forward funds so received for the support of such missionaries as shall devote themselves to the work of the Mission; and to have charge of and direct missionary efforts in Africa and in any other area that may hereafter be mutually agreed upon by the Mission.

Founding Date: 1893

Staff: 1,113

Publications:
Africa Now Magazine, bimonthly

Radio/TV Programs:
Owns and operates a radio station in Monrovia, Liberia with daily broadcast in 47 languages
African Observer broadcast by approximately 70 radio stations in the United States

Meetings:

Church Missionary Conferences; Pastors Conferences; Bible Conferences, etc., throughout the United States

Also Known As: Society of International Missionaries

1390. Swedenborg Foundation, Inc. (SF)

Nondenominational

P. M. Alden, President of the Board of Directors
139 East 23rd Street
New York, New York 10010
(212) 673-7310

The Swedenborg Foundation was founded under the name of a American Swedenborg Printing and Publishing Society. An autonomous publishing body independent of any church organization, its activities are focused on maintaining a flow of the theological works of Emanuel Swedenborg into the mainstream of religious thought.

Founding Date: 1849

Staff: 6

Membership: 352

Publications:

Swedenborgiana: 200 hardback and paperback books
Tapes on Talking Books for the Blind
Newsletter, twice a year

Radio/TV Programs:

Occasional radio and TV spots
2 films for TV

Meetings:

Occasional seminars and lectures
Annual convention

Former Name:

(1928) American Swedenborg Printing and Publishing Company

1391. Tainan Evangelical Mission

Nondenominational

Mr. Frank Lin, Director
4606 Avenue H
Lubbock, Texas 79404
(806) 747-5417

The aim of the Tainan Evangelical Mission is to bring glory to God through the preaching of the Lord Jesus Christ to the unconverted; to have a Bible teaching ministry among the already established churches; to promote social welfare by the giving of physical and spiritual assistance to people suffering from leprosy and other afflictions; and to comfort and minister to the senior citizens.

1392. Teen Missions International, Inc.

Interdenominational

Robert M. Bland, Director and President
Post Office Box 1056
Merritt Island, Florida 32952
(305) 453-0350

Teen Missions International, Inc., was founded by a group of Christian people interested in youth becoming involved in missions around the world. Their goal was to instill a missionary concern and vision in teens so they might see the necessity of future training and the need for Christian workers. Since then thousands of young people have found it possible to serve the Lord and many are involved in missions today or are preparing to be involved in full-time Christian work in the future. There are two basic types of teams, work project teams and evangelistic teams. Work teams build orphanages, airstrips, churches, schools, clinics, or other similar projects. Evangelistic teams share the Gospel through open-air evangelism. Built into the cost of a teen par-

ticipating is a $100 fee which goes to the mission board with whom the Mission cooperates for purchase of building materials. Therefore a team of 30 teens invest $3,000 in building materials. In most cases, this pays for the entire project, as the teens do the work and are generally able to complete the project. During the summer of 1980 teams served in Australia, Israel, India, the Philippines, Mexico, the West Indies, England, southern Ireland, Scotland, Germany, France, Brazil, Chile, Colombia, Venezuela, and the United States.

Founding Date: 1970

Staff:
55 staff members
1,700 short-term summer missionaries
100 short-term winter missionaries

Publications:
Teen Missions Control, monthly except for the summer months

Radio/TV Programs:
The Dial-a-Teen Ministry uses TV, radio and newspaper advertising in major American and English-speaking foreign cities

Meetings:
6 Team Leader Seminars annually
Mission conferences
Church services, and retreats

1393. Teen Mission, USA, Inc.

Christian

Ken Henderson, Executive Director
Post Office Box 24336
Lexington, Kentucky 40524
(606) 887-2350

Teen Mission, USA, is a ministry directed toward young people in the public schools through assembly-type programs, the donation of books, and material produced on video cassettes. The ministry is also conducted in churches through evangelistic meetings which include adults. Various topics include: Creation-Evolution; Dating and Marriage; Spiritual Family; Holy Spirit; Discipline for Children; and Tips for Youth Sponsors.

Staff: 4

Publications:
Newsletter, 10 times a year

Radio/TV Programs:
Religious and educational TV programming

1394. Templegate Publishers*

Nondenominational

John Garvey
302 East Adams
Springfield, Illinois 62705
(217) 522-3353

Templegate is a religious publisher addressing itself principally to the Roman Catholic, Anglican, and Orthodox markets. The company has no church affiliation and is lay controlled. There are about 40 titles in its publications list. Although Templegate's list at this point is primarily Roman Catholic, Anglican, and Orthodox, it is open to any religious writing which is non-fundamentalist in nature. Templegate also operates a bookstore, which carries religious books, children's books, religious articles, and church goods.

Publications:
About 15 new books each year

1395. Teresian Institute

Roman Catholic

Aracelia M. Cantero
National Delegate for the United States
1540 Baracoa
Coral Gables, Florida 33146

Mailing Address
Post Office Box 34-3407
Coral Gables, Florida 33114
(305) 447-1135 (US Delegate)

The purpose of the Teresian Institute is to promote the integration of Christian faith and culture through the professional activity of its members. They live out their Christian call from within existing temporal structures, seeking to order and illuminate them, according to the plan of God, in the manner of leaven. The roots of the Teresian Institute are in the plan of its founder, Pedro Poveda, to organize Catholic educators in a movement to maintain and spread Christian values from within the secular world.

Founding Date: 1911

Staff: 5

Membership:
Over 3,000 world-wide; 40 core members in USA

Meetings:
In the USA there is an annual planning meeting

1396. The Theosophical Publishing House*

Theosophical Society

Dora Kunz, President
Post Office Box 270
Wheaton, Illinois 60187
(312) 665-0123

In pursuit of its first object, the formation of a nucleus of Brotherhood, the Theosophical Society and its affiliate, the Theosophical Publishing House, seek to disseminate the theosophical philosophy. This philosophy incorporates concepts from the major religions of the world, believing all religions have a valid basis. Such dissemination is implemented through their Department of Education, and principally through the publication of paperback books (Quest Books) on their philosophy.

Membership: 35,500 lay

Publications:
700 books
25 to 30 magazines

Radio/TV Programs:
5 to 15 minute broadcasts in four different cities on basic theosophy

Meetings:
Many conferences throughout the year

1397. The Theosophical Society in America

Theosophy

Mrs. Dora Kunz, President
1926 North Main
Wheaton, Illinois 60187

Mailing Address
Post Office Box 270
Wheaton, Illinois 60187
(312) 668-1571

The three objectives of the Theosophical Society are: to form a nucleus of the Universal Brotherhood of Humanity, without distinction of race, creed, sex, caste, or color; to encourage the study of comparative religion, philosophy, and science; and to investigate unexplained laws of nature and the powers latent in man. The Society is composed of individuals united by their approval of the above objectives and by their determination to promote brotherhood and to foster religious and racial tolerance. Their bond of union is a common search and aspiration for truth. They see every religion as an expression of the Divine Wisdom and prefer its study to its condemnation, its practice to proselytism. Peace is their watchword, as truth is their aim. Approximately 150 local branches and study centers in major cities of the country carry on active theosophical work. The Theosophical Society claims no monopoly on theosophy, maintaining that the Divine Wisdom cannot be limited, but its fellows seek to understand this Wisdom in ever-increasing measure. The Theosophical Society in America is the American branch of The Theosophical Society with international headquarters at Adyar, Madras, India. The Theosophical Publishing House is an affiliate of the Theosophical Society in America. Since the theosophical philosophy stresses the unity of mankind and the study of comparative religion, the Theosophical Publishing House publishes principally paperbacks (the Quest series), books on religion and the psychology of East and West to establish a bridge between cultures.

Founding Date: 1886

Staff: 49

Membership: 5,000

Publications:
  The American Theosophist, monthly
  The Light Within, a newsletter for prisoners
  Books

Radio/TV Programs:
  Quest radio series for college audiences
  Eternal Quest, radio series for religious/ spiritual audiences

Meetings:
  Summer sessions at Lake Geneva, Wisconsin
  6 seminars per year at National Headquarters in Wheaton, Illinois

1398. Thesis Theological Cassettes

Nondenominational
Frank C. Bates (Rev.)
300 Mount Lebanon Boulevard, Room 2217
Pittsburgh, Pennsylvania 15228
Mailing Address
Post Office Box 11724
Pittsburgh, Pennsylvania 15228
(412) 563-3056

Thesis Theological Cassettes publishes a variety of cassette resources for clergy continuing education and church school education programs. Most of these include printed materials which provide additional resources and discussion questions. Some examples of its own cassettes include: *Faith Alive,* a series of 14 60-minute cassettes containing Bible dramatizations for children and youth; *The Healing Ministry,* featuring Father Francis S. MacNutt, OP, and Dr. Morton Kelsey; and *Exorcism: The Devil, Demons and Possession;* and *God, Man and Archie Bunker,* a print and audio resource containing *excerpts from the All in the Family* show. They also record conferences and make these recordings available to participants.

Founding Date: 1978

Staff: 3

Membership: 1,000

Meetings:
  Pastors' Conference
  Ohio Pastors' Conference
  Partners in Ecumenism

1399. Things to Come Mission, Inc.

Nondenominational
Eldred Sidebottom, Director
Post Office Box 96
Cope, Colorado 80812
(303) 357-4291

The Things To Come Mission was organized to carry the Gospel of the Grace of God to the regions beyond, working through the national brethren. The Mission's main objective is to reach people for Christ and then train them to do the work of the ministry. It is carried out by establishing local churches, Training Centers, Bible Schools, Correspondence Schools, Radio Ministry, and Printing Ministry, all of which are turned over to trained nationals.

Founding Date: 1955

Publications:
> *International Harvest,* 1-2 issues a year
> Newsletter, 1-2 times a year
> Prayer letters bimonthly

Radio/TV Programs:
> 1 15-minute radio broadcasts daily in the Philippines (in the local dialects)

Meetings:
> 3 conferences a year in various churches across the country
> Missionary conferences in conjunction with a TCM Board meeting

1400. The Thomas More Association

Roman Catholic

Mr. Dan Herr, President
225 West Huron Street
Chicago, Illinois 60610
(312) 951-2100

The Thomas More Association is a not-for-profit organization dedicated to furthering Catholic thought through publication and distribution of books, newsletters, and cassettes. It operates the Thomas More Book Club and a national book service by mail and telephone orders. The Thomas More Press has approximately 60 books in print and issues about a dozen hard and soft-cover titles a year.

Publications:
> Books on religion, theology, religious sociology, scripture, spirituality
> Newsletters: *The Critic, Markings, You, Bottom Line, Overview, Mysterion*

1401. Thrust Communications Corporation (Easy-List)

Evangelical

Kanita Kanthavichai, President
117 West Wesley
Wheaton, Illinois 60187
(312) 668-8767

Thrust Communications Corporation provides mailing and donor list computer services to religious organizations, helping them to better maintain their mailing lists. It serves churches, missions, publishers, broadcasters, charities, fundraising groups, associations, schools, and others.

Membership:
> Over 225 religious organizations share time on the Corporation's computers

Publications:
> *Loveletter,* monthly

1402. Tokyo Gospel Mission, Inc.

Interdenominational

Dr. Hugh Moreton, Founder and Executive Director
1402 Magnolia
Norman, Oklahoma 73069
(405) 329-5931

The purpose of the Tokyo Gospel Mission, Inc., is to implant an active Christian ministry in the world's largest city, Tokyo, Japan, through trained Japanese Christians, following what is known as the Nevius method. It endeavors to exert its maximum influence throughout Japan by exposing young people to Christianity in the Protestant tradition, so that they in turn can bear witness to their nation. The Bible is read and applied daily to all aspects of life in the metropolis.

Founding Date: 1951

Staff: Approximately 50 staff members in Japan

Publications:
> Newsletter

Meetings:
> Quarterly conferences conducted at the field headquarters in Tokyo

1403. Tony and Susan Alamo Foundation, Inc.

Nondenominational

Tony Alamo, President
Post Office Box 398
Alma, Arkansas 72921
(501) 997-1811

The Tony and Susan Alamo Christian Foundation believes that Christ is alive and that he lives forevermore and is coming back to earth very soon. It believes, as the Bible says, that one must be born again. It is a commandment of God that people repent of their sins. The Tony and Susan Alamo Christian Foundation says that homosexuality, abortion, drugs, alcohol, and adultery are all sin and that God says He will send to hell those who commit these sins.

Meetings:
    Services

1404. Torah Umesorah, National Association of Hebrew Day School Parent-Teacher Associations

Orthodox Jewish
Mrs. Clarence Horwitz
Chairman, Executive Committee
229 Park Avenue South
New York, New York 10003
(212) 674-6700

The purpose of the National Association of Hebrew Day School Parent-Teacher Associations are: to fulfill our sacred duty to our children by inspiring in them abiding love of God, unswerving dedication to the study and discipline of Torah, and deep devotion to the Jewish people; to help the school maintain the highest possible standards in order that it may fulfil its responsibilities as the extension of the parent and the transmitter of our religious heritage; to make parents, teachers, and the community increasingly aware of their mutual responsibilities for the maximum development of every child; to foster programs of parent education as a means of harmonizing the cultural and religious values of the home with the Torah teachings of the Day School; to assist parents, teachers, and school administrators by providing a forum for the regular exchange of reliable information concerning the spiritual, psychological, educational, and physical development of our children; to work towards raising the social and economic status of the professional personnel of the Day School so that larger numbers of religiously observant men and women, well trained and talented, will be attracted to the teaching profession; and to stimulate the establishment and the support of Day Schools on the elementary and secondary levels and to project them to the community as the force which insures the perpetuity, the commitment, and the future leadership of our Jewish people.

Founding Date: 1948
Staff: 2
Membership: 500
Publications:
    National PTA Sidrah Series (Weekly Portion Reading), published 9 times during school year
    National PTA Bulletin, published 3 times during school year

Various parent education materials published periodically
    Fundraising with a Flair, National PTA publication

Meetings:
    Conference meetings with individual groups
    Workshops in specific PTA areas
    Periodic regional meetings

1405. Torah Umesorah, National Conference of Yeshiva Principals

Orthodox Jewish
Rabbi Joshua Fishman, Executive Vice-President
Rabbi Chaim Feuerman, EdD, President
229 Park Avenue South
New York, New York 10003
(212) 674-6700

The National Conference of Yeshiva Principals was established to meet the specific needs of principals, administrators, and all educators. Various projects such as an annual convention, teachers' conferences, teacher-training sessions, school visitations, and school evaluations are held.

Founding Date: 1956
Membership: Close to 1,000
Publications:
    Machberet Hamenahel, monthly, specifically geared for the principals and teachers in affiliate Hebrew Day Schools and Yeshivos
    Newsletters for principals
Meetings:
    Regional teachers conferences
    Annual Convention for principals, teachers, and administrators

1406. Torah Umesorah, National Society for Hebrew Day Schools

Orthodox Jewish
Rabbi Bernard Goldenberg, Chairman, Executive Committee
229 Park Avenue South
New York, New York 10003
(212) 674-6700

The activities of Torah Umesorah are carried out through seven departments. The School Organization Department is responsible for new schools, community surveys, public relations literature, and enrollment campaigns; Teacher Training Institutes handle recruitment and interviews; the Publications Department is responsible for curriculum aids, visual aid charts, records and film strips, and teachers' guides; Department of Education conducts surveys and consultations and educational research, and includes the Fryer Foundation for Ethics; the Association of Hebrew Day School PTA's is the department for parent education programs and programming material (see separate listing); the Hebrew Day School Administrators department conducts campaign counseling and surveys; and the National Conference of Yeshiva Principals conducts educational conferences and workshops. (See separate listing.)

Founding Date: 1944

Membership:
> 521 affiliated schools
> 1,200 members
> 1,500 donors

Publications:
> *Olomeinu (Our World),* a children's magazine, 10 times a year
> *Torah Umesorah Report,* quarterly
> *President's Report,* annually
> *Tempo,* semiannually
> *Educational News Letter,* 10 times a year

Radio/TV Programs:
> Radio and TV commercials for enrollment purposes

Meetings:
> Each of the affiliated organizations conducts conferences and meetings
> 4 parent retreats

1407. Totonac Bible Center, Inc.*

Nondenominational
Manvel Arenas, Director
Post Office Box 2050
Orange, California 92669
(714) 997-3920

Totonac Bible Center operates a center in LaUnion, Puebla, Mexico, for the purpose of meeting the educational, social, and religious needs of the Totonac Indians. The Center includes a secondary and Bible school, free clinic, experimental farm, multi-cultural congregation, and twice-weekly Totonac language radio broadcast.

Radio/TV Programs:
> 2 weekly programs, in the Totonac language

1408. Training Ecumenically to Advance Mission (TEAM)

Interdenominational
Barbara T. McNeel and William E. Ramsden, Executive Directors
1045 70th Avenue
Philadelphia, Pennsylvania 19126
(215) 424-8912

Training Ecumenically to Advance Mission operates in two divisions. Opportunity Associates provides training and consulting for religious organizations (congregations, denominational and ecumenical agencies, and special purpose groups). Management processes, planning, program development, and interpersonal relations have been major emphases in this service. Religious Opportunities Institute is devoted to research and development of management tools that can help religious organizations to plan, develop programs, etc., more effectively and more efficiently.

Founding Date: 1969

Staff: 2

Publications:
> *Datalert,* monthly newsletter interpreting events, trends and views for religious leaders

1409. Trans World Radio

Interdenominational
Dr. Paul E. Freed, President and Founder
560 Main Street
Chatham, New Jersey 07928
(201) 635-5775

Trans World Radio is a missionary radio organization that broadcasts the Gospel from six locations: Bonaire, Netherlands Antilles; Monte Carlo, Monaco; Island of Cyprus; Swaziland, Africa; Island of Guam; and Sri Lanka (formerly Ceylon). Trans World Radio utilizes 17 transmitters with a total power over five million watts and broadcasts in over 80 languages.

Founding Date: 1952

Staff: 841

Publications:
> *Towers to Eternity*
> *Reaching Arabs for Christ*
> *Let the Earth Hear*
> *The Daily Word,* a monthly devotional booklet

Radio/TV Programs:
> One hour TV special each year

1410. Transport for Christ International

Interdenominational

L. Latimer Brooker, Executive Director
409 Darrow Road
Akron, Ohio 44305

Mailing Address
Post Office Box 1562
Akron, Ohio 44309
(216) 794-0587

Transport for Christ International was established to meet the specialized spiritual, emotional, and social needs of those in the trucking industry. Its ministries include counseling and visitation, a number of mobile chapels, an audio/visual ministry, and a newsletter. A major emphasis of the organization's activities is safety.

Founding Date: 1951
Staff: 17
Membership: 600
Publications:

Highway Evangelist, monthly newspaper

Radio/TV Programs:
Just for Jammers, radio

Meetings:

Annual convention, alternates between the United States and Canada every other year

1411. Triniteam, Inc.

Nondenominational

Sister Claire Marie Wick, OSF, Director
Room 225, Physicians Building
Sacred Heart Hospital
Eau Claire, Wisconsin 54701

Triniteam is a private, non-profit organization dedicated to the building of relationships between persons with different needs for the mutual benefit of all. In reaching out to the aged, infirm, handicapped, and imprisoned in the Eau Claire-Chippewa Falls area, Triniteam is concerned first and foremost with the well-being of the individual and with the environment in which that person spends his/her days. Triniteam Released Prisoners is a grass-roots program of support for inmates and ex-offenders seeking a positive change in their lives and acceptance in society. Although Triniteam enjoys the direction of Sister Claire Marie Wick, OSF, the services of the organization are available to one and all, regardless of religious belief.

Founding Date: 1973
Staff: 6
Membership: 800 volunteers and leaders
Publications:

Trinitimes, monthly
Occasional newsletters

Radio/TV Programs:
Frequent radio programs

1412. Trinity Institute

Interdenominational

Bishop Whitlock, President
Drawer D
Lewiston, California 96052
(916) 778-3977

The purpose of Trinity Institute is to share with mankind the knowledge, gained through experience, that obedience to the teachings of Jesus Christ, the Son of God with power, produces a state of existence free of fear, hate, lust, sorrow, insecurity, disability, strife, iniquity, and all bondage to the power of Satan. The work of the Holy Spirit is to teach us all things, to guide into all truth. By asking, seeking, knocking, (Matt. 6:6; 7:7, 8), the Institute has attained a progress into the knowledge of what the fruit of the tree of good and evil consists of. They know who and what babylon is, and why God has judged her, and what will follow when He throws her down.

Founding Date: 1958
Staff: 12
Membership: 250
Radio/TV Programs:
Bible School of the Air, weekly

Meetings:

Lewiston, 4 retreats
Phoenix, 4 retreats
New York, 4 retreats

1413. Twyman Films, Inc.

Nondenominational

Alan P. Twyman, President
4700 Wadsworth Road
Dayton, Ohio 45401

Mailing Address
Post Office Box 605
Dayton, Ohio 45401
(800) 543-9594 in Ohio call (513) 276-5941

Twyman Films, Inc., is one of the oldest non-theatrical film distributors in the United States. The company distributes the feature length and short films of Walt Disney, Universal Pictures, Columbia Pictures, Warner Brothers, Pyramid Films, and other domestic and foreign film studios. All film distribution is on a rental basis. In 1980 Twyman became a distributor of home video cassettes for rent or sale. Twyman distributes video cassettes in VHS and Beta 2 formats of Warner Brothers, Disney, 20th Century Fox, RKO, Avco-Embassy, Paramount, and many others. Twyman's film catalog contains indices of movies suitable for religious inspiration and discussion use. From time to time, bulletins are published for the sole use of religious users.

Publications:

An annual catalogue of 16mm sound motion pictures for rent; quarterly listings of home video cassettes for rent or sale; other publications from time to time throughout the year

Radio/TV Programs:

Has exclusive distribution rights for some programs

1414. Unda-USA

Roman Catholic

Rev. John Geaney, CSP, President
3015 4th Street, N.E.
Washington, D.C. 20017
(202) 526-0750

Unda-USA is an autonomous, non-profit organization established primarily to serve the needs of Catholic broadcasters and allied communicators. Its membership is ecumenical. The organization meets annually for a General Assembly, publishes a bimonthly newsletter, maintains governmental and regulatory liason with the government and congress, and endeavors to keep its members up to date technically and through research.

Founding Date: 1972

Staff: 2

Membership: 300

Publications:
Newsletter, bimonthly

Meetings:
Annual General Assembly, location varies

Supersedes:
Catholic Broadcasters Association (founded 1948)

1415. Underground Christian Mission, Inc. (UCM)

Nondenominational

Jim Dimov, President
Post Office Box 1076
Los Angeles, California 90028
Office (213) 466-3453 Personal (213) 466-0678

The goal of the Underground Christian Missions is to bring the Word of God to all peoples under the iron fist of Communism. They hope to fulfill this mission by supplying Bibles, spiritual literature, and Sunday school hymn and song books, as well as clothing and financial assistance to the families of Christian martyrs and underground workers who are praying for the missions daily. The goal of UCM is fulfilled by participation of the general public through the giving of their finances as a result of hearing Jim Dimov speak at a meeting, reading a newsletter, or listening to the need on radio and responding.

Founding Date: 1973

Publications:
Newsletter, monthly

Radio/TV Programs:
We are broadcasting out of New Mexico for 15-minutes daily Monday through Friday. Jim Dimov tells the general public about the needs of the Christians behind the Iron Curtain.

1416. Unevangelized Fields Missions (UFM)

Nondenominational

Rev. Alfred Larson, General Director
306 Bala Avenue
Bala Cynwyd, Pennsylvania 19004

Mailing Address
Post Office Box 306
Bala Cynwyd, Pennsylvania 19004
(215) 667-7660

Unevangelized Fields Mission is a nondenominational sending agency of fundamentalist and evangelical traditions establishing national churches and emphasizing evangelism and training of national leadership. It is also engaged in education, literature production and distribution, linguistics, translation, radio, and medicine.

Founding Date: 1931
Staff: 25
Membership: 279 overseas personnel
Publications:
 Lifeline, quarterly

1417. Unevangelized Tribes Mission

Baptist
Dr. David W. Allen, President
Apartment F-23
Open Door Estates
Fort Washington, Pennsylvania 19034
(215) 646-4523

Unevangelized Tribes Mission is a forwarding organization for Baptist missionaries with the field in Zaire.
Founding Date: 1929
Membership: 6 members of the overseeing Council

1418. Union of American Hebrew Congregations, Aging Programs

Reform Judaism
838 Fifth Avenue
New York, New York 10021
(212) 249-0100

Aging Programs is a unique specialization of the Union of American Hebrew Congregations in programming for older people in the Jewish Community. Through seminars for synagogue leaders, workshops in conjunction with academic institutions such as the University of Southern California, the University of Chicago, the University of Miami, and Boston University, and a wide variety of publications, the UAHC aids congregations in programming effectively for their older members.

1419. Union of American Hebrew Congregations, Camps for Living Judaism

Reform Judaism
838 Fifth Avenue
New York, New York 10021
(212) 249-0100

The nine Union of American Hebrew Congregations, Camps for Living Judaism are engaged in creative

education. Tens of thousands of Reform Jewish youngsters experience Jewish living in summer and winter camp programs. The concept of total Jewish living includes study and recreational activities in a balanced program. The goal of the UAHC Camps for Living Judaism is the development of a knowledgeable and Jewishly literate community for the future. Camps have proven themselves, through the years, to be effective adjuncts to congregational life, the religious school, youth activities, and teacher education. Programs in UAHC camps are guided by the Commission on Jewish Education. The National Committee on Camp-Institutes is responsible for the development of new camp sites and the efficient use of facilities.

1420. Union of American Hebrew Congregations, College Education Department

Reform Judaism
838 Fifth Avenue
New York, New York 10021
(212) 249-0100

The Union of American Hebrew Congregations, College Education Department provides avenues through which college-age youth can establish and maintain their Jewish identity within the Reform movement. A network of *batim* (communal residences) and chavurot (fellowship groups) is maintained among active students on some 40 campuses. These campus groups hold regular Reform worship experiences for Shabbat and holidays, and plan programs involving Jewish study, social action on the local level, and social gatherings. The UAHC provides a number of important support services including leadership training and a special newsletter. In addition, a variety of programs are offered through the UAHC College Education Department that are available to all Jewish students, whether or not they are active in an ongoing campus Reform group. A series of weekend seminars is held to examine and discuss the meaning of Reform Judaism in students' lives. Summer programs are offered, both in the United States and in Israel. A mid-winter leadership trip to Israel is offered. Offerings range from three weeks to a full academic year on a kibbutz in Israel. The UAHC College Education Department encourages the students it serves to become involved in the emergence of a Reform Zionist movement. Moreover, encouragement is offered to congregations to develop locally based programs of service to college students.

Periodic research surveys
National curricular surveys

1421. Union of American Hebrew Congregations, Department of Education

Reform Judaism
838 Fifth Avenue
New York, New York 10021
(212) 249-0100

The Department of Education is at the core of UAHC programming and service to congregations. The department creates and maintains educational programs and materials in accordance with the broad policies outlined by UAHC-CCAR Joint Commission on Jewish Education. The department publishes a suggested curriculum for the congregational educational program, kindergarten to adult, and Experimental Education Editions, creative curricular units. Textual materials, audio-visual aids, and teaching aids are recommended. Summer teaching training institutes in all parts of the United States and Canada are sponsored by the department. One-day and weekend programs are conducted for rabbis, educators, teachers and school board personnel. Speakers for Teacher Education Program (STEP), in cooperation with the National Association of Temple Educators, is a program available to UAHC congregations. The director of the department and his staff are available for special regional and local teacher institutes, and to advise congregations on curriculum, educational policy, or publications. Curricular assistance and consultation services to existing Reform Day Schools are provided in addition to guidance materials for communities seeking to begin new schools. A National Teacher Certification program is available to teachers in Reform Religious Schools, as well as a National Principal Certification program. Study materials, discussion guides, and other Jewish learning materials for adult education are prepared by this department. The department also serves as an educational clearing house for ideas and programs in Jewish education.

Publications:
Keeping Posted, monthly
Compass, three times a year
Experimental Education Editions, ten times a year
What's Happening, four times a year
Idea Exchange Books, annually

1422. Union of American Hebrew Congregations, Department of Interreligious Affairs

Reform Judaism
838 Fifth Avenue
New York, New York 10021
(212) 249-0100

The national movement of Reform Judaism is alone among denominations of religious Jewry in America to maintain a program in Interreligious Affairs. Its purposes are two-fold: First, it works consultatively and programmatically with the national agencies of Protestantism and Roman Catholicism on matters of Jewish and interreligious concern. Second, it seeks to stimulate interreligous endeavor regionally and in Reform Jewish congregations in the areas of religious thought and action. As part of this effort, the department arranges interreligious institutes for educators and clergy as well as seminars for Christian and Jewish lay leaders. In addition, the department produces filmstrips on Judaism for Christian groups, and publishes articles on matters of Christian-Jewish interest. It also produces "Adventures in Judaism," a weekly half-hour, award-winning radio program carried by some 60 stations throughout the country. Cassettes of this series for purposes of youth and adult education are available at nominal cost. A complete catalog of interreligious programs and materials is available upon request.

1423. Union of American Hebrew Congregations, Department of Publications

Reform Judaism
838 Fifth Avenue
New York, New York 10021
(212) 249-0100

The Union of American Hebrew Congregations, Department of Publications is the largest publisher of Jewish textbooks in North America. As the publishing arm of the Commission on Jewish Education, curricular material for synagogue schools as well as audio-visual materials and teaching aids are regularly issued by the Union. The publication of high-quality educational materials is the core of the publishing program of the UAHC. In addition, the UAHC regularly publishes trade books of special interest to adults and young people outside the rubrics of the classroom. These are Jewish books with special attention paid to values, art, and design, and are available from Sisterhood Judaica Shops, in local Jewish bookstores, and frequently at general bookshops. The UAHC has been a pioneer in audio-visual education over the years. Its filmstrips, films, film loops, and other materials are widely used in Jewish schools of all denominations here and abroad. Transcontinental Music, a division of the UAHC, is the largest publisher of synagogue and other Jewish music in the world. Its materials are used in worship services in synagogues of all denominations as well as by high school and college choruses.

1424. Union of American Hebrew Congregations, Department of Social Action

Reform Judaism
838 Fifth Avenue
New York, New York 10021
(212) 249-0100

The Department of Social Action assists congregations in establishing social action committees which, in turn, can help their congregations to apply locally the ethical principles of Judaism to the problems of the world we live in. Hundreds of congregations have social action committees. The department directs the work of the Commission on Social Action of Reform Judaism, a joint body with the Central Conference of American Rabbis and the UAHC affiliates, and seeks to apply the insights of Jewish tradition to such urgent issues as world peace, civil liberties, religious freedom, juvenile delinquency, intergroup relations, and other major concerns of society. To help synagogue members become aware of social issues and stimulate them to appropriate action, the department provides a large selection of books, pamphlets, filmstrips, and other programmatic materials relevant to the whole range of contemporary social problems.

1425. Union of American Hebrew Congregations, Department of Synagogue Administration

Reform Judaism

838 Fifth Avenue
New York, New York 10021
(212) 249-0100

The Department of Synagogue Administration provides aid to congregations in the administration and financing of synagogues and has available a mass of information and literature in such areas as dues structures, fundraising, constitutions, membership campaigns, board and committee structure, insurance, cemetery operations, and the maintenance operation of buildings. In an attempt to cope with the ever-increasing mobility of American Jewish families, it is experimenting with computerized systems that will provide automatic referral of names of members who move from one community to another, as well as a means of locating unaffiliated Jews and providing their names to congregations. Since 1973 the department has been offering to our congregations the UAHC-Tru-Check Computer Systems. At little cost, congregations can convert their accounts receivable to electronic data processing which will improve cash flow, age accounts, and provide accurate and intelligible financial reports each month. There are also systems for the general ledger and the maintenance of membership and cemetery records. The department, in conjunction with the National Association of Temple-Administrators, has been collecting accurate and relevant data on all facets of synagogue activities and publishes periodic Synagogue Research Surveys. Periodically it arranges workshops in the regions of the UAHC and conducts Leadership Training Seminars for Board members. Congregations planning a new building, renovation or expansion of present facilities can take advantage of the UAHC's Architects Advisory Panel, the Accredited List of Synagogue Artists and Craftsmen, and the UAHC's Synagogue Art and Architectural Library at the House of Living Judaism. The library has numerous books and the largest collection in the world of slides on the synagogue building and its ceremonial objects and artistic embellishments. The department also has several traveling art exhibits and films about Jewish art and can assist in arranging Judaica programs with lecturers.

1426. Union of American Hebrew Congregations, Department of Worship

Reform Judaism
838 Fifth Avenue
New York, New York 10021
(212) 249-0100

The Department of Worship has designed a five-part program to serve the liturgical needs of its' congregations. The objectives of this program are: to engage in full-scale research on the content and form of worship services utilized in Reform congregations for the purpose of enhancing their beauty and their meaning; to explore and to analyze the theological problems implicit in prayer and religious belief; to assist congregations in making the most effective use of the new Union Prayer Books, *Shaarei Tefila* and *Shaarei Teshuvah,* published by the Central Conference of American Rabbis; to serve as a clearing house for the creative ideas of individual congregations so that they may be shared by other UAHC congregations; and to conduct workshops and seminars in cooperation with UAHC regions. The director of the department, as well as the UAHC-CCAR Commission on Worship, is readily available for on-going consultation with congregational Worship Committees.

1427. Union of American Hebrew Congregations, General Assembly

Reform Judaism
838 Fifth Avenue
New York, New York 10021
(212) 249-0100

The General Assembly is the Union of American Hebrew Congregations policy-making body. It is composed of accredited delegates who are selected members of UAHC congregations in proportion to the size of the congregation. The General Assembly meets biennially in accordance with the Constitution and By-Laws. The Board of Trustees, headed by its chairman and the president of the UAHC, is responsible to the General Assembly and meets twice each year. It numbers 180 men and women from all parts of the United States and Canada. The president of the UAHC is responsible for its guidance and for the recommendation and execution of its policies. He heads a staff of lay and rabbinic experts whose coordinated efforts have developed the extensive Jewish programs of the UAHC in response to the demands of its constituency. These programs are implemented by the professional staff in cooperation with the large and able UAHC corps of lay and rabbinic leaders in the Reform Jewish movement. The accumulated experience of the years, the specialized knowledge of the professional staff, the multitude of written materials available in the form of books, periodicals, audio-visual aids, recordings, as well as personal consultations, are all designed to enhance the viability of the synagogue. Most services of the UAHC are free to member congregations. Since its inception, the UAHC has persistently sought to safeguard and promote the rights of Jews and other minority groups throughout the world. Over the years its member congregations, through the UAHC General Assemblies, have spoken out forthrightly in behalf of Judaism's commitment to peace, to the elimination of discrimination against any segment of any society, to the abolition of poverty, and a host of other issues to which Judaism's moral teachings are relevant. A compilation of all of the resolutions adopted by the General Assemblies of the UAHC from its beginning, entitled "Where We Stand," is available on request.

1428. Union of American Hebrew Congregations, Program Outreach

Reform Judaism
838 Fifth Avenue
New York, New York 10021
(212) 249-0100

The Union of American Hebrew Congregations has established a three-part program of Outreach to aid in the development of Reform Judaism in the United States and Canada. This program involves: developing a sensitive program of welcoming and involving converts to Judaism, recognizing that those who choose Judaism in good faith are as authentic in their Jewish identity as those who are born Jewish; developing an effective outreach program by which the Reform synagogue can seek out mixed married couples in order to respond to the particular emotional and social stresses in their situations and to make the congregation, the rabbi, and Judaism itself available to them and their families; and planning a special program to bring the message of Judaism to any and all who wish to examine or embrace it. Judaism is not an exclusive club of born Jews; it is a universal faith with an ancient tradition which has deep resonance for people alive today.

1429. Union of American Hebrew Congregations, Rabbinical Pension Board

Reform Judaism
838 Fifth Avenue
New York, New York 10021
(212) 249-0100

The Union of American Hebrew Congregations and the Central Conference of American Rabbis, through the Rabbinical Pension Board, provide life insurance, pensions, long-term disability, and major medical coverage for rabbis, educators, and administrators of UAHC congregations and have organized the Temple Service Agency, Inc., to provide insurance coverage for other congregational and UAHC employees.

1430. Union of American Hebrew Congregations, Reform Jewish Appeal

Reform Judaism
838 Fifth Avenue
New York, New York 10021
(212) 249-0100

The Reform Jewish Appeal is the way in which members of congregations can express their individual commitment to the larger purposes of the Movement in all parts of the United States and Canada. The congregations' proportional dues are the foundation for broadbased support of our national institutions, but it is the gifts beyond basic dues which provide the supplementary financing for much of the UAHC's creative programming.

1431. Union of American Hebrew Congregations, Religious Action Center (RAC)

Reform Judaism
838 Fifth Avenue
New York, New York 10021
(212) 249-0100

The work of the Religious Action Center is supervised by the Commission on Social Action. The RAC maintains close liaison with government agencies and personnel. It follows pending legislation of concern to Reform Judaism, alerts the national Department of Social Action to such legislation, testifies as required before congressional committees, operates educational programs for youth and adult congregational groups, for students of the Hebrew Union College-Jewish Institute of Religion, and for clergy and theological students of other faiths, and cooperates with other religious organizations on matters of common concern.

1432. Union of American Hebrew Congregations and the Central Conference of American Rabbis, Board of Certification for Temple Administrators

Reform Judaism
Myron E. Schoen, FTA, Secretary
838 Fifth Avenue
New York, New York 10021
(212) 249-0100

The Board of Certification for Temple Administrators seeks to establish standards of qualifications for temple administrators and to further opportunities for their training; conducts examinations of candidates; and issues certificates of Fellow in Temple Administration.

Founding Date: 1963
Staff: 1
Membership: 50 FTA's
Publications:
   NATA Journal, quarterly
   Information bulletin
Meetings:
   Quarterly Board meetings

1433. Union of American Hebrew Congregations and the Central Conference of American Rabbis Commission on Jewish Education

Reform Judaism
Rabbi Daniel B. Syme, Director
838 Fifth Avenue
New York, New York 10021
(212) 249-0100

The Commission on Jewish Education sets national policy in pre-school through adult education; it develops the curriculum; publishes texts, magazines, and teacher aids; assists congregations in teacher training; and offers teacher certification and principal certification programs. The Commission offers consultative services, advising congregations on curriculum, educational policy, and publications. It also functions as an educational clearing house for ideas and programs in Jewish education.

Staff: 3
Membership: 35 Commission members

Publications:
   Compass, an educational periodical, 3 times per year
   E3, curricular units, 10 per year
   Idea Exchange Book I, II, classroom methods

Radio/TV Programs:
   TV-program for in-home use on a video cassette

Meetings:
   1 conference per year held in New York
   1 overseas seminar held in Israel
   100 teacher workshops held across the United States and Canada

1434. Union of American Hebrew Congregations and the Central Conference of American Rabbis, Commission on Social Action of Reform Judaism

Reform Judaism
Albert Vorspan, Director
838 Fifth Avenue
New York, New York 10021
(212) 249-0100

The Commission on Social Action of Reform Judaism helps organize social action committees in the congregations; prepares material on issues of concern; and works to make known the feelings of its members on international, national, and local issues. The primary objective of the Commission is the stimulation in Reform synagogues of a program of study and action on those contemporary issues about which Judaism has something to say. It is the Commission's hope that every Reform synagogue will conduct a program of social justice aimed at sensitizing its congregants to the relationship between Jewish ethical principles and modern problems. The Commission sends study materials on these subjects to every congregation. It has no authority to direct a congregation to study any specific problem or to take any particular action; it offers guidance and counsel. The Commission also cooperates with other groups in American life, Jewish and non-Jewish, in seeking to implement the positions on social issues taken by the Union at its biennial conventions. Examples of such issues are civil rights, civil liberties, United States immigration policy, separation of church and state, and strengthening the United Nations.

Membership:
   About 85 members; there are approximately

500 synagogue social action committees containing 5-100 members each

Publications:
   Newsletter, irregularly

Meetings:
   2 meetings a year in different locations
   Occasional conferences on specific issues, usually held in Washington, D.C.

1435. Union of American Hebrew Congregations and the Central Conference of American Rabbis, Joint Commission on Synagogue Administration

Reform Judaism
Myron E. Schoen, FTA, Director
838 Fifth Avenue
New York, New York 10021
(212) 249-0100

The Joint Commission on Synagogue Administration assists congregations in management, finance, building maintenance, design, construction, and art aspects of synagogues. It develops leadership training programs and provides EDP services. The Commission also maintains the Synagogue Architectural and Art Library consisting of slides and photos of contemporary and historical synagogue buildings.

Founding Date: 1962

Staff: 2

Membership: 25

Publications:
   Synagogue Service
   Temple Management Manual
   Successful Synagogue Administration

Meetings:
   Annual meeting, New York City

1436. Union of American Hebrew Congregations and the Central Conference of American Rabbis, National Commission on Rabbinic Congregation Relations (NCRCR)

Reform Judaism
838 Fifth Avenue
New York, New York 10021
(212) 249-0100

The National Commission on Rabbinic Congregation Relations seeks to promote harmonious relationships between rabbis and congregations. The commisson offers to the parties involved both conciliation and arbitration services, when necessary. The NCRCR also establishes guidelines for the proper and equitable basis of rabbinic-congregation relations. Its booklet "Suggestions for Procedures in Rabbinic-Congregation Relations" is available on request.

1437. Union of Orthodox Jewish Congregations of America, National Conference of Synagogue Youth

Orthodox Jewish

Rabbi Yitzchok Rosenberg, Director of National Affairs
Rabbi Raphael Butler, Director of National Programs and Regions
45 West 36th Street
New York, New York 10018
(212) 563-4000

The National Conference of Synagogue Youth is the youth arm of the Union of Orthodox Jewish Congregations of America. Functioning in 37 American states, five Canadian Provinces, and Israel, its organizational structure encompasses 465 chapters in 17 regions with a membership of over 20,000. Its aim is to strengthen and deepen the loyalty of Jewish youth to Torah, Mitzvot, the Jewish people, and the Orthodox Synagogue; to make youth part of the living congregation; and to insure Jewish continuity through a balanced, purposeful program of religious, recreational, educational, and social activities.

Membership: 20,000
Publications:
   Over 100 educational/religious; programming and organizational books
   Keeping Posted with NCSY, 8 times yearly
   Communications, newspaper
   Newsletter for youth leaders monthly
Meetings:
   Over 350 conventions, seminars, and shabbatons

1438. Union of Orthodox Jewish Congregations of America, Women's Branch

Orthodox Jewish

synagogal organizations; is the spokesman for these women on the national scene; participates in civic, educational and social welfare national organizations; is a non-governmental organization with accredited representation at the United Nations; sponsors scholarships for Stern College for Women of Yeshiva University and projects for the Jewish Braille Institute; prepares diversified educational and religious programming for sisterhood meetings; maintains a speakers bureau, sending qualified speakers across the country and Canada; services Jewish youth; and services Jewish men in the United States Army.

Membership: 150,350
Publications:
   21 religious titles
   Bimonthly newsletter
Meetings:
   Biannually

1439. Unitarian Sunday School Society*

Unitarian Universalist

Mrs. Barbara Marshman, President
19 Haskell Street
Lexington, Massachusetts 02173

The Unitarian Sunday School Society gives aid, advice, and encouragement to Sunday Schools through the denomination. The Society has a board of five directors elected at its annual meeting in May. Each Unitarian Universalist church may designate three persons to be members at the Society for one year with the privilege of voting at all meetings. The Society receives the income from special funds held by the UUA, from which it gives annual grants to the Department of Education and Social Concern, and contributes toward other religious education projects in line with its stated purpose "to promote moral and religious education in Sunday Schools." The directors encourage those with innovative ideas or research projects for Church Schools to submit these for consideration.

Founding Date: 1885

1440. Unitarian Universalist Association, Department of Communications and Development

Unitarian Universalist

25 Beacon Street
Boston, Massachusetts 02108

This department of the Unitarian Universalist Association has primary responsibility for all publishing of the Association (except Beacon Press), for information and public relations services, and for financial development programs.

Publications:

Unitarian Universalist World, 16 times a year

Merger:

Unitarian Universalist Association, Department of Publication

1441. Unitarian Universalist Association, The Laymen's League*

Unitarian Universalist

Kirk S. Giffen, Treasurer
25 Beacon Street
Boston, Massachusetts 02108

The Laymen's League of the Unitarian Universalist Association is a non-profit corporation which works for the extension of liberal religion in the United States. The League was originally the fund raising section of the Association. The League financed and directed the magazine advertising for several years and is credited with the addition of over 6,000 new members to the Unitarian Universalist churches and fellowships. It has existed under its present name since 1963, when it combined with Universalist Men. Since 1966, the membership has been open to women. Its principal function today is the funding of pilot projects in the area of extension for the UUA.

Founding Date: 1919

Former Name:

(1963) Unitarian Laymen's League

Merger:

With Universalist Men

1442. Unitarian Universalist Black Affairs Council (BAC)*

Unitarian Universalist

Louis J. Gothard
6503 Lincoln Drive
Philadelphia, Pennsylvania 19119

The Unitarian Universalist Black Affairs Council, Inc., is a non-profit program and funding agency whose programs are divided into three components: Community Organization, Economic Development, and Political Education. Three corporations govern each area of activity. BAC is designed to support and fund those programs within the black community which lead to its empowerment, unification, and self-determination. It seeks to promote the full participation of black Unitarian Universalists in carrying out this work. BAC policy is guided by a political movement of black Unitarian Universalists known as the Black Unitarian Universalist Caucus (BUUC).

1443. Unitarian Universalist Gay Caucus*

Unitarian Universalist

David Fanning, Co-coordinator
1187 Franklin Street
San Francisco, California 94109
(415) 861-1945

The Unitarian-Universalist Gay Caucus was founded in Washington, D.C., as the result of a concerned group at the UUA General Assembly. It exists to provide an opportunity for creating a self-affirming, self-determining, mutually-supportive community for gay people and bisexuals within the denomination. The caucus attempts to build local groups which meet the spiritual and social needs not presently being met in most of its congregations. To do this, worship materials have been assembled, and counseling services are being provided. The Caucus also exists to work with others towards creation of an open society where none need fear persecution or alienation.

Founding Date: 1971

Publications:

UU Gay World, bimonthly

1444. Unitarian Universalist Historical Society

Unitarian Universalist

Spencer Lavan, PhD, President
25 Beacon Street
Boston, Massachusetts 02108
(617) 742-2100 (ask for Office of Information)

The Unitarian Universalist Historical Society seeks to encourage the disciplined study of the history of liberal religion, especially Unitarianism and its antecedents. It publishes a scholarly journal, sponsors seminars and public meetings, and helps collect historical materials.

Founding Date: 1978

Membership: 150 lay; 70 clerical

Publications:
> *Proceedings of the Unitarian Historical Society,*
> biannually

Meetings:
> 1-2 seminars
> Annual convention

Merger:
> Unitarian Historical Society (founded 1901)
> Universalist Historical Society (founded 1834)

1445. Unitarian Universalist Ministers Association

Unitarian Universalist
Rev. Felix Danford Lion, President
6320 Main Street
Williamsville, New York 14221
(716) 634-3010

The Unitarian Universalist Ministers Association helps ministers to be more effective in their prophetic leadership and pastoral ministry. It promotes high standards in the ministry; the well-being of ministers and their families; professional conduct among colleagues; the profession of the ministry itself; and the Unitarian Universalist Association and its societies.

Membership: 800 members; 125 student members

Publications:
> Newsletter, quarterly

Meetings:
> Annual Institute of each of the 22 chapters
> in the United States and Canada
> Continent-wide Annual Meeting and Institute
> A major convocation every 5 years

1446. Unitarian Universalist Ministers' Mates Association*

Unitarian Universalist
Wynanda Helverson, President
25 Beacon Street
Boston, Massachusetts 02108
(617) 742-2100

The Unitarian Universalist Ministers' Mates Association was formed out of mutual interests of wives and widows of Unitarian and Universalist ministers.

Founding Date: 1961

1447. Unitarian Universalist Psi Symposium*

Unitarian Universalist
Rev. Richard Fewkes
644 Main Street
Norwell, Massachusetts 02061

The Unitarian Universalist Psi Symposium is an organization devoted to the study and discussion of psychic phenomena and related subjects and the drawing out of the implications of such study for a liberal religious and philosophical perspective. Psi Symposium works to promote interest in this field throughout the denomination and provides for individual and chapter membership in the Symposium. A board of directors meets regularly in Boston to coordinate the work of this continental organization that was started at the 1969 General Assembly in Boston. Members may vote at meetings of the Psi Symposium and receive a quarterly newsletter and annual journal that keep them informed of activities on both a national and chapter level, as well as the thinking of individual religious liberals on psychic phenomena. Psi Symposium sponsors a lecture at each General Assembly.

Founding Date: 1969

1448. Unitarian Universalist Service Committee*

Unitarian Universalist
Dr. Richard S. Scobie, Executive Director
78 Beacon Street
Boston, Massachusetts 02108

The Unitarian Universalist Service Committee strives to ensure justice, equality, liberty, and opportunity in the daily lives of all men, women, and children. The Committee was founded to help rescue Jews and liberals in Nazi-threatened Prague. Pressing for social reform and solution of social problems are the main goals of the Service Committee. Overseas projects include agricultural development for the Aymara Indians of Peru, adult literacy in Tanzania, education in El Salvador through a bimonthly newsletter, political and economic consciousness-raising in Guatemala, and health care, economic development, and population control in the Caribbean. Domestically, the Service Committee works for justice reform and more equitable distribution of the world's food resources.

Founding Date: 1939

Membership: 8,000
Publications:
Newsletters
Annual report
Resource materials on justice and hunger
Meetings:
Annual membership meeting

1449. Unitarian Universalist Society for Alcohol Education

Unitarian Universalist
Dwight S. Strong, President
223 West Springfield Street
Boston, Massachusetts 02118

Organized for the dissemination of literature relating to alcohol education, the Society is dedicated to the examination of the problems of alcoholism and seeks to prevent its adverse effects in human society.

Founding Date: 1886

1450. Unitarian Universalist United Nations Office, Inc., (UU-UN)

Unitarian Universalist
Dr. Walter D. Kring, President
777 United Nations Plaza, Room 7D
New York, New York 19917
(212) 986-5165

The Unitarian Universalist United Nations (UU-UN) Office is the major channel of the UUA to world affairs and the United Nations. It provides the denomination and its individual congregations with guides to programming on world issues; film and simulation game suggestions; posters; background publications from the United Nations, individual governments, and voluntary agencies; and news and analyses on the whole spectrum of world issues, from development through disarmament, peace-keeping, apartheid, religious freedom, food short-ages, population pressures, environmental concerns, multinational corporations, and the protection of the seabed. The UU-UN Office is dedicated to furthering the commitment of UUA to the world community, and to peace and social justice. It does this through stimulating action by individual societies, and by act-ing directly with the United States and Canadian governments, their missions at the UN, and with the United Nations bodies themselves. Accredited as a non-governmental organization in special consulta-tive status with the UN, the Office has reserved seats at meetings of the Security Council, General Assembly, ECOSOC and other UN meetings and con-ferences, both here and abroad. It has full access to UN documents, as well as to the personnel of the UN Secretariat, specialized agencies and the govern-ment missions. It is able to present UUA viewpoints both orally and in writing as official UN documents. It works closely with the entire community of some 300 non-governmental organizations to develop coali-tions and position papers furthering UUA values and goals. The UU-UN Office holds annual seminars at the United Nations which have been attended by Uni-tarian Universalists from virtually every state of the United States and province in Canada. It issues a regular newsletter on developments in the world community, detailed special reports on issues of cur-rent concern, worship services related to worldwide themes, program planning guidelines, and digests of UUA positions on world affairs. It arranges for group tours by congregation to the UN. It provides world-oriented programs at UUA General Assemblies. It answers requests for information and publications from its UN Envoys and other interested ministers and laymen, on all issues before the world commu-nity. The UU-UN Office is supported by individuals, churches, womens groups, and several grant-making organizations. The large majority of its funds comes from its hundreds of members throughout the conti-nent. Individual memberships, from $10.00 up per year, and group memberships at $25.00 and up per year, provide the members with the full range of UU-UN publications as well as the opportunity to become engaged in the challenge of helping to make possible a world community living in peace and pro-viding a decent life to all people of all nations.

Founding Date: 1961
Publications:
Newsletter
Meetings:
Annual seminars

1451. Unitarian Universalist Women's Federation (UUWF)*

Unitarian Universalist
25 Beacon Street
Boston, Massachusetts 02108
(617) 742-2100

The aim of the Unitarian Universalist Women's Federation is to encourage women to develop their full potential and to participate effectively in the church and denomination. It seeks to uphold and extend the philosophy of liberal religion through programs of education, service, and action.

Founding Date: 1963

Publications:
> *Federation Newsletter*
> *Kryiokos,* a literary magazine published in conjunction with *Unitarian Universalist World,* focusing on women's issues
> Brochure on printed materials for study and personal growth available from UUWF

1452. Unitarian Universalists for Black and White Action (BAWA)*

Unitarian Universalist Association
Ms. Betty Bobo Seiden, Co-Chairman
Post Office Box 347
Minneapolis, Minnesota 55440
(612) 338-2662

The purposes of Unitarian Universalists for Black and White Action are: to create a racially inclusive church and denomination in an open and just society, the benefits and privileges of which are available to all; to pursue a program of action and education within the Unitarian Universalist Association and within society at large; to foster cooperation among people of all races in the realization of their full human potential; and to oppose racial separatism.

Membership: 450 lay; 50 clerical

Publications:
> Newsletters

Radio/TV Programs:
> 30-second Public Service messages

Meetings:
> 2 per year

1453. The United Board for Christian Higher Education in Asia

Interdenominational
Dr. Paul T. Lauby, Executive Director
475 Riverside Drive, Room 1221
New York, New York 10027
(212) 870-2601

The United Board of Christian Higher Education in Asia is a cooperative agency through which the Christian community and others contribute to higher education and to the exchange of resources in and with Asia. It is concerned with the pursuit of truth and knowledge and the achievement of social justice and full human development understood from the perspective of Christian faith. To carry out this purpose, the Board: encourages experimentation in the areas of college curriculum, teaching methods, and materials; aids in faculty development, research, library development, and student aid programs; and stimulates a wide variety of outreach projects. It facilitates the appointment of overseas personnel and raises funds for capital projects.

Founding Date: 1932

Staff: 10

Publications:
> *New Horizons,* 3 times a year
> *Annual Report*
> Books

Meetings:
> 1 Asian Faculty Conference and 2 Board of Trustees Meetings, all at the Stony Point Conference Center, Stony Point, New York

1454. United Charity Institutions of Jerusalem

Hebrew
Sam Gabel, Executive Director
1141 Broadway
New York, New York 10001
(212) 683-3221

The purpose of United Charity Institutions of Jerusalem is to raise funds for educational and benevolent activities in Jerusalem. The organization maintains 18 institutions including schools, free kitchens, and a library.

Founding Date: 1903

1455. United Christian Ashrams

Interdenominational
Dr. Paul Wagner, General Secretary
Post Office Box 97
Damascus, Maryland 20750
(301) 253-2468

Ashrams have been known in India for centuries. Dr. E. Stanley Jones gave the Ashram a Christian connotation and established the United Christian Ashrams in India in 1930. He brought it to America in

1940. There are more than 50 residential United Christian Ashrams in North America, plus hundreds of week end Christian Ashrams. The purpose of United Christian Ashrams is to spread the Gospel of Jesus Christ and to deepen the spiritual lives of those who are willing to witness and serve as lay and ordained men and women. This endeavor is undertaken by conducting meetings in local geographic areas identified as Christian Ashrams under the direction of dedicated Christian leaders and teachers. The only qualification for membership in the fellowship is that "you come as you are, but that you want to be different, to be a person God intends you to be." United Christian Ashrams believes you will go away as He wants you to be. Someone has called the Ashram a 'healing of love for body, mind, spirit and relationships.' " All Ashrams are interdenominational, intercultural, and interracial. The Ashram movement is an international movement with national and local Ashrams in many countries in Europe, Asia, Africa, North and South America, and Australia.

Founding Date: 1930

Membership:
 Approximately 7,000 participants
 Over 1,000 Associates or supportive members

Publications:
 Transformation, quarterly

1456. United Church Coalition for Gay Concerns (UCCGC)

United Church of Christ
Rev. Loey Powell, Co-coordinator
Post Office Box 1926
San Francisco, California 94101
(415) 548-4172

The United Church Coalition for Gay Concerns is a special interest group of the United Church of Christ which seeks to address the needs of lesbians and gay persons within the UCC. It provides counseling and referrals; educational resources to clergy and laity; advocacy within the denomination for lesbian/-gay concerns; support for lesbians and gay persons of all ages and races and for families and friends of lesbians and gay persons; and an ecumenical link to other religious coalitions and caucuses and to the secular lesbian/gay world. Through the UCCGC the insights and experiences of lesbian and gay UCC members are shared with the whole church, and vitally needed networking is provided to members and their supporters. A newsletter provides news and

commentary on legislative concerns, denominational actions, Coalition plans, and available resources. Occasional national or regional meetings are held alongside of other denominational gatherings.

Membership: Several hundred

Publications:
 Newsletter, six times per year

Meetings:
 The UCCGC sponsors workshops on request for local churches or area groups; there are occasional membership meetings

1457. United Church Directories

Nondenominational
Delano E. Bellew, President
7916 Millsboro Road
Galion, Ohio 44833

Mailing Address
Post Office Box 507
Galion, Ohio 44833
(419) 468-4739

United Church Directories is the world's largest producer of promotional book and church directories. Since 1963 they have worked with over 80,000 churches and printed over 12 million church directories. They own *and* operate their own photographic laboratories, print shops, and creative layout departments. A well-planned promotional book and directory can be an invaluabe tool in helping members introduce their church to friends and newcomers. In addition to outreach, United books can be designed and used to serve as a "get acquainted" tool, to promote or recognize a specific department or activity of the church, as a recruiting tool, as a prayer list, as a means of preserving church memories, to re-activate members, or other specific objectives.

Founding Date: 1963
Staff: 400

1458. United Church of Christ, Ministers for Racial and Social Justice

United Church of Christ
Dr. Marvin Morgan, Chairman
First Congregational UCC
105 Courtland Street, N.E.
Atlanta, Georgia 30303
(404) 659-6255

The Ministers for Racial and Social Justice work toward increasing the effectiveness of the Black church members.

1459. United Church of Christ, Office for Church in Society

United Church of Christ

S. Garry Oniki, Executive Director
105 Madison Avenue
New York, New York 10016

110 Maryland Avenue, N.E.
Washington, D.C. 20002

New York (212) 683-5656 Washington (202) 543-1517

The Office for Church in Society was established by the Tenth General Synod as the successor to the Council for Christian Social Action and the Center for Social Action "to assume leadership function for social action concerns in the United Church of Christ, to provide resources to national, Conference, and local churches and to strengthen coordination of social action activities within the denomination." The Office for Church in Society seeks to: identify, analyze, and forecast national and international issues and recommend action; organize the resources of the UCC in Christian theology and social ethics for use in reflecting on contemporary society; maintain on behalf of the UCC an office in Washington, D.C., which will represent and help coordinate the denomination's ministry in the area of public policy advocacy; facilitate coordination of social action programs among the national agencies and Conferences; provide staff and consultative resources to Conference and local church requests; and develop selected programs of education and action.

Founding Date: 1976

Publications:
   UCC Network, monthly

Supersedes:
   Council for Christian Social Action of the United States

1460. United Church of Christ, Office of Communication

United Church of Christ

Dr. Everett C. Parker, Director
105 Madison Avenue, 9th Floor
New York, New York 10010
(212) 683-5656 or (212) 683-5740

The Office of Communication exercises leadership in establishing and maintaining public relations for the United Church of Christ and its Instrumentalities; in conducting the denomination's ministry in television and radio; in producing audio-visuals when requested to do so; in educational programming in the mass media for the benefit of the Instrumentalities, regional bodies, and local churches; and in research in mass communication. It cooperates with similarly responsible offices of other denominations in the planning, production, distribution, and utilization of mass media and audio-visual materials which seek to promote and interpret the witness of ecumenical Christianity.

Staff: 19

Publications:
   Keeping You Posted, twice monthly

Meetings:
   12-15 workshops per year

1461. United Church of Religious Science, Department of Education

Religious Science

3251 West Sixth Street
Los Angeles, California 90075

Mailing Address
Post Office Box 75127
Los Angeles, California 90075
(213) 388-2181

The Department of Education, United Church of Religious Science, writes, organizes, and markets all study material for the Church. It also keeps class records and correspondence files.

1462. United Church of Religious Science, Department of Member Churches

Religious Science

3251 West Sixth Street
Los Angeles, California 90075

Mailing Address
Post Office Box 75127
Los Angeles, California 90075
(213) 388-2181

The Department of Member Churches, United Church of Religious Science, services 150 member Churches and their ministers, and assists in the growth of the movement through 145 study groups.

1463. United Church of Religious Science, Ministry of Prayer

Religious Science

3251 West Sixth Street
Los Angeles, California 90075

Mailing Address
Post Office Box 75127
Los Angeles, California 90075
(213) 388-2181

The Ministry of Prayer, United Church of Religious Science, is a 24-hour ministry serving the needs of 40,000 persons per year. It has a staff of nine practitioners.

1464. United Church of Religious Science, Science of Mind Publications

Religious Science

3241 West Sixth Street
Los Angeles, California 90075

Mailing Address
Post Office Box 75127
Los Angeles, California 90075
(213) 388-2181

Science of Mind Publications is the department of the United Church of Religious Science that publishes the 53-year-old *Science of Mind* magazine. Over 100,000 copies are printed monthly. It is sold through subscription, on the newsstand, and in the field churches. The Department also publishes books.

Publications:
Science of Mind, monthly
Books

1465. United Hias Service*

Jewish

Carl Glick, President
200 Park Avenue South
New York, New York 10003
(212) 674-6800

The United Hias Service originated when three organizations of common purpose joined forces: the Hebrew Immigrant Aid Society, the United Service for New Americans, and the migration services of the American Joint Distribution Committee. The resulting United Hias Service, funded by the United Jewish

Appeal exists to rescue and resettle Jews from lands of oppression to Western nations outside Israel. Since its organization, the United Hias Service has assisted some 140,000 immigrants.

Founding Date: 1954
Publications:
Hias Newsletter
Radio/TV Programs:
The Voice of Hias

1466. United Indian Missions, Inc.

Nondenominational

Donald G. Fredericks, General Director
2920 North Third Street
Flagstaff, Arizona 86002

Mailing Address
Post Office Box U
Flagstaff, Arizona 86002
(602) 774-0651

The United Indian Missions is engaged in the basic ministries of evangelism and church planting. Its major goal is the establishment of self-governing and self-supporting churches on Indian reservations in the United States and Canada and in the villages of Mexico. Additionally, the Mission conducts summer camping ministries for young people.

Founding Date: 1936
Membership:
28 couples
9 singles
2 couples and 1 single in training
Publications:
United Indian, quarterly
Newsletters, quarterly
Meetings:
Periodic retreats and conferences for the immediate missionary force

1467. United Jewish Appeal, Inc.*

Jewish

Mr. Irving Bernstein, Executive Vice-Chairman
1290 Avenue of the Americas
New York, New York 10019
(212) 757-1500

United Jewish Appeal is a nationwide fund raising instrument for American Jewish Joint Distribution

Committee, United Israel Appeal, and New York Association for New Americans.

1468. United Lesbian and Gay Christian Scientists Inc.

Christian Science Faith
Mr. John W. VonDouris, Facilitator
256 South Robertson Boulevard
Beverly Hills, California 90211

Mailing Address
Post Office Box 7467
Beverly Hills, California 90211
(212) 656-9623

The purpose of United Lesbian and Gay Christian Scientists is: to develop and promote educational programs and activities designed to overcome the ignorance, fear, and bigotry that pertains to and surrounds human sexuality; to counsel and support Lesbian and Gay Christian Scientist's or persons and parents and families who are seeking to understand and to personally cope with the various aspects of human sexuality; to challenge and try to change prevailing society attitudes, misinformation, and distorted perspectives of human sexuality of the individual and families; to attain for homosexual persons the same basic human rights, liberties, and opportunities that are afforded to heterosexual persons; to conduct other appropriate activities that are lawful for a non-profit corporation; and to engage in the solicitation of funds by means of public and private appeals, special fund raising events, and any other means that are lawful persuant to the Non-Profit Corporation Act.

Founding Date: 1979

Staff: 10

Membership: Strictest confidentiality

Publications:
Faith and Understanding

Radio/TV Programs:
Upcoming television program in Boston, Massachusetts

Meetings:
One a year, various locations
Once a year in Los Angeles, California

Former Names:
Faith and Understanding
Emergence

1469. United Methodist Church, Board of Church and Society

United Methodist Church
Haviland C. Houston, General Secretary
100 Maryland Avenue, N.E.
Washington, D.C. 20002
(202) 546-1000

The Board of Church and Society, United Methodist Church, carries on a program of research, education, and action with its focus on the development of national social policy. Its work includes such aspects as communication, interpretation, mobilization, and training. It interprets and advocates United Methodist social policy to members of Congress, the federal administration, management, and church leadership and membership. It engages in efforts to arouse the constituency of the church to take action on specific social issues in relation to the social policies of the church. To carry out these objectives the board sponsors several departments: Human Welfare; Political and Human Rights; Peace and World Order; Social and Economic Justice; Environmental Justice and Survival; and Ethnic Minority local church.

Membership: 60 lay; 30 clerical

Publications:
1 monthly magazine
4 newsletters

Meetings:
Numerous study seminars annually

1470. United Methodist Church, Commission on the Status and Role of Women

United Methodist Church
Ms. Carolyn Oehler, President
1200 Davis Street
Evanston, Illinois 60201
(312) 869-7330

The Commission on the Status and Role of Women of the United Methodist Church seeks to raise consciousness on issues of sex discrimination; emphasizes concerns of Third World women; and seeks to increase leadership, employment, and participation of women in the annual conferences and in seminaries, colleges, agencies, and other areas throughout the church. The Commission carries on its work through three work units: Education and Advocacy,

Monitoring/Research; and Annual Conference Constituency Services.

Staff: 3

Membership: 48

1471. United Methodist Church, Committee on Family Life of the Board of Discipleship

United Methodist Church
Post Office Box 840
Nashville, Tennessee 37202
(625) 327-2700

The Committee on Family Life of the Board of Discipleship, United Methodist Church, serves as an advocate for family life within the Church and in the larger society. The responsibilities of the committee include the following: to identify the needs and concerns of families in a rapidly changing society and the various societal factors which impact families; to survey the Church's ministry with families and to identify and disseminate information on those models of experience that enhance Christian family life; to sponsor explorations of theological and philosophical meanings of Christian family living and the Church's ministry to Christian families, and to disseminate to the church appropriate reports of these explorations; to recommend programs and emphases to agencies of The United Methodist Church for development and implementation, either separately or cooperatively; to elect the representatives of The United Methodist Church to the North American Section of the World Methodist Committee on Family Life, and to nominate the United Methodist members of the World Methodist Committee on Family Life; and to advocate policies, activities, and services that would strengthen and enrich family life.

1472. United Methodist Church, Division of Chaplains and Related Ministreis of the Board of Higher Education and Ministry

United Methodist Church
Post Office Box 871
Nashville, Tennessee 37202
(615) 327-2700

The Division of Chaplains and Related Ministries, United Methodist Church, is responsible for clergy in extension ministries, such as: chaplaincy in the armed forces, Veterans Administration, industry, correctional and health care fields, and those other related ministries which conference Boards of Ordained Ministry and bishops may designate. Clergy to be appointed to any of the above extension ministries receive ecclesiastical endorsement through the Division of Chaplains and Related Ministries. Responsibilities of the Division include recruitment of persons for ministry; interpretation of the need for clergy to the Church at large; endorsement of ministers; general oversight of clergy; annual reappointment of clergy; advocacy for those serving in extension ministries; and the provision of a ministry for overseas United Methodist laity.

1473. United Methodist Church, General Board of Discipleship

United Methodist Church
Dr. Melvin G. Talbert, General Secretary
Post Office Box 840
Nashville, Tennessee 37202
(615) 327-2700

The Board of Discipleship, United Methodist Church, assists annual conferences, districts, and local churches in their efforts to win persons as disciples of Jesus Christ and to help them to live in the Spirit of God in every relationship and to fulfill their common discipleship in the world.

Membership: 50 lay; 44 clerical

Meetings:
  300

1474. United Methodist Church, General Board of Global Ministries

United Methodist Church
Dr. Tracy K. Jones, Jr., General Secretary
475 Riverside Drive
New York, New York 10027
(212) 678-6161

The United Methodist Church Board of Global Ministries works with colleague churches and ecumenical agencies in 112 countries through some 9,000 ministries. It carries out its program through seven divisions: Ecumenical and Interreligious Concerns;

Educational and Cultivation; Health and Welfare Ministries; National Division; United Methodist Committee on Relief; Women's Division; and World Division (see separate listing). There are also two Work Units, the Crusade Scholarship Committee and the Committee on Personnel in Mission. The program emphases of the Board are: evangelizing persons and systems; establishing and strengthening congregations and the development of mission leadership; recruitment, sending, and receiving personnel; engaging in mission through direct services; enabling the work for Christin unity, ecumenical cooperation, and interreligious dialogue to continue; and developing new forms of mission. The history of predecessor organizations for mission dates back over 150 years.

Staff:
> 169 Executive Staff
> 275 General Staff

Membership:
> 159 Voting Members of the Board
> 74 Division Members-at-Large

Publications:
> *New World Outlook,* monthly
> *response,* monthly
> Newsletters prepared for particular constituent groups

Radio/TV Programs:
> Limited radio programming

Meetings:
> One annual meeting in the fall and one in the spring
> Each Division holds a variety of meetings
> Meetings are held in ERA states

1475. United Methodist Church, General Board of Global Ministries, Committee on Relief

United Methodist Church

Dr. J. Harry Haines, Associate General Secretary
475 Riverside Drive, Room 1470
New York, New York 10115
(212) 678-6281

The United Methodist Committee on Relief administers on behalf of the denomination the emergency relief, refugee resettlement, and rehabilitation after a disaster programs, and carries out technological and leadership development programs in 62 countries including the United States. In 1980 it assisted some

5.5 million people. Its major efforts are directed at attacking technology and technology transfer; special programs for children; and efforts in support of human rights. Seventy percent of its programs are carried out ecumenically through Church World Service, the World Council of Churches, and regional and national councils of the Third World.

Publications:
> *Inasmuch,* 3 times a year

Meetings:
> Three times a year

1476. United Methodist Church, General Board of Global Ministries, Education and Cultivation

United Methodist Church

Ms. Betty Thompson
475 Riverside Drive
New York, New York 10027
(212) 678-6161

The Education and Cultivation Division of the Board of Global Ministries, United Methodist Church, exists to undergird the total program of the General Board of Global Ministries, affirming that relating persons to mission through communication, education, and cultivation is itself mission; and to initiate and develop programs and resources through which individuals and groups may understand the biblical background and theological basis of the Christian world mission, the involvement of The United Methodist Church in global ministries, the special concerns of women in mission, and the possibilities for personal and corporate witness involvement in and support of those ministries. The objectives of the Education and Cultivation Division are to strengthen local congregations in global outreach, and to enable persons to participate more actively in the mission of the church; to promote understanding, participation in, and support of the global ministries of The United Methodist Church through study and use of resources; and to cultivate through appropriate channels of the Church, financial support for global ministries.

1477. United Methodist Church, General Board of Global Ministries, Health and Welfare Ministries Division

United Methodist Church

John A. Murdock, Associate General Secretary
475 Riverside Drive, Suite 350
New York, New York 10115
(212) 678-6087

The Health and Welfare Ministries Division attempts to help United Methodists become interested in helping and healing ministries on local levels. As part of that work, the Division provides some limited services upon request to non-residential programs and residential institutions serving older people, providing health care services; serving children, youth and their families; and working with persons with handicapping conditions.

Publications:
   Newsletters, 2-3 per year

Meetings:
   12 to 15 meetings a year held in different parts of the United States and other nations

1478. United Methodist Church, General Board of Global Ministries, National Division

United Methodist Church
Dr. Randolph Nugent
475 Riverside Drive
New York, New York 10027
(212) 678-6161

The National Division of the Board of Global Ministries, United Methodist Church, exists to proclaim and witness to the saving grace of Jesus Christ through mission in the United States, Puerto Rico, and the Virgin Islands. The National Division is committed to an expression of faith which understands that God, through Jesus Christ, is active in all of life and works in church and secular society for dignity and justice among persons and communities. This faith directs the development of national mission strategies and programs. These require the development and strengthening of congregations as centers of Christian mission and the creation of ministries of compassion to persons and groups who suffer in body and spirit and to affect social patterns which continue such suffering. The responsibilities of the National Division include church growth and extension, development of strategies and mission programs, and funding and fund raising activities, as well as many other responsibilities.

1479. United Methodist Church, General Board of Global Ministries, Women's Division

United Methodist Church
Ms. Theresa Hoover
475 Riverside Drive
New York, New York 10027
(212) 678-6161

The Women's Division of the Board of Global Ministries, United Methodist Church, is actively engaged in fulfilling the mission of Christ and the Church and interpreting the purpose of United Methodist Women. With continuing awareness of the concerns and responsibilities of the Church in today's world, the Women's Division is an advocate for the oppressed and dispossessed, with special attention to the needs of women and children; works to build a supportive community among women; and engages in activities which foster growth in the Christian faith, mission education, and Christian social involvement throughout the organization. Among its responsibilities are: the provision of resources and opportunities for women to enrich their spiritual lives and increase their involvement in world needs; the securing of funds; the development of leadership in United Methodist women; and the enlistment of women as missionaries and deaconesses, and in other activities of moral and religious significance.

1480. United Methodist Church, General Board of Global Ministries, World Division

United Methodist Church
Ms. Lois Miller
475 Riverside Drive
New York, New York 10027
(212) 678-6161

The World Division of the Board of Global Ministries, United Methodist Church, exists to confess Jesus Christ as divine Lord and Savior to all people in every place, testifying to his redemptive and liberating power in every sphere of human existence and activity, and calling all people to Christian obedience and discipleship. The World Division seeks to fulfill its purpose by: coordination of relationships and administration of programs of The United Methodist Church as it relates to areas outside the United

States; and engaging mutually in mission with colleague churches and other bodies outside the United States, and facilitating their interaction with the Church and society in the United States so that all become more effective in Christian mission. The responsibilities of the World Division are: to develop and administer the missional relationships of The United Methodist Church with Central Conferences, autonomous Methodist and United General Churches, and ecumenical bodies outside the United States; and to formulate the objectives and strategies for the world mission of The United Methodist Church, within the context of the cultural and historical understandings out of which relationships have developed with the Christian communities in other nations.

1481. United Methodist Church, General Board of Higher Education and Ministry

United Methodist Church

F. Thomas Trotter, General Secretary
Post Office Box 871
Nashville, Tennessee 37202
(615) 327-2700

The purpose of the Board of Higher Education and Ministry, United Methodist Church, is to prepare and assist persons to fulfill their ministry in Christ in the several special ministries, ordained and lay, and to provide general oversight and care for institutions of higher education including schools, universities, and theological seminaries.

Staff: 30 professional staff; 44 support staff

Membership: 125 voting Members of the Board

Publications:
> *Colleague,* quarterly
> *Quarterly Review,* a scholarly journal for reflection on ministry
> *Orientation,* an annual tabloid for first-year college students

Meetings:
> Annual board meetings in October
> Annual meetings of the divisions
> Annual Institute of Higher Education held in Nashville each year

1482. United Methodist Church, General Commission on Communication

United Methodist Church

Curtis A. Chambers, General Secretary
601 West Riverview Avenue
Dayton, Ohio 45406
(513) 222-7068

United Methodist Communications serves the church as a central communications agency, seeking to develop a comprehensive system of communication. Its organizational structure consists of these departments: Division of Public Media, which communicates with the public through newspapers, magazines, radio, television, cable, film, etc.; Division of Production and Distribution, which produces and distributes print and audio-visual resources and handles publication circulation; Division of Program and Benevolence Interpretation, which brings about support for the church program and funds through media and persons; and Office of Communication Education, which relates communications training and education to churches, conferences, and districts. Major locations are Dayton, Ohio (headquarters and magazine editorial office); New York, New York (news service central desk, broadcast); Nashville, Tennessee (film studio, circulation and distribution center); and Evanston, Illinois (benevolence promotion).

Staff: 100

Publications:
> *Interpreter Magazine*
> *El Interprete* (in Spanish)
> *Communicator*

Radio/TV Programs:
> Radio series *Connection* and United Methodist Series of *The Protestant Hour*
> TV/film series *Begin with Goodbye* and *Learning to Live*

Meetings:
> Periodic meetings for training in communication skills and consultations

Also Known As: United Methodist Communications

1483. United Methodist Church, General Commission on Religion and Race

United Methodist Church

Dr. Woodie W. White, Executive Secretary
110 Maryland Avenue, N.E.
Washington, D.C. 20002

Mailing Address
Post Office Box 48-49
Washington, D.C. 20002
(202) 547-4270

The United Methodist Church General Commission on Religion and Race assumes general Church responsibility for such matters as coordinating the denominational concern and providing a channel of assistance so that ethnic and racial minority group members of The United Methodist Church will have equal opportunities for service, representation, and voice on every level of the Church's life and ministry. The Commission, with a membership of 48, is composed primarily of racial and ethnic minority representatives (Black, Native American, Hispanic, and Asian American) and meets twice a year. It evaluates the status of intergroup relations and ethnic participation in the church. It also makes financial grants to minority-directed projects.

Staff: 6

Publications:
　　Newsletter, quarterly

Meetings:
　　Numerous workshops and retreats annually in various locations

1484. United Methodist Church, General Council on Ministries

United Methodist Church

Norman E. Dewire, General Secretary
601 West Riverview Avenue
Dayton, Ohio 45406
(513) 222-6761

The General Council on Ministries has the responsibility of coordinating ministries and program emphases of the agencies of the Church. Activities of the Council include evaluating work of program agencies; working with annual conference Councils on Ministries; recommending funding of program agencies; coordinating research and planning; recommending a quadrennial theme or emphasis; electing chief executives of general program agencies; and assigning churchwide mission priorities.

1485. United Methodist Church, Standing Commission on Archives and History

United Methodist Church

Dr. John H. Ness, Jr., Executive Secretary
Post Office Box 488
Lake Junaluska, North Carolina 28745
(704) 456-9432

The United Methodist Church Commission on Archives and History is the official historical depository for the United Methodist Church and its predecessor denominations. Its library of 40,000 volumes and archives of nearly five million items houses the papers for most of the general church agencies. The guidance for the creation of archives and preservation of records at all levels of the Church require publication, training, and dissemination of information and material. The Commission also has responsibility for evaluating and designating national historic United Methodist shrines and landmarks which must be reported quadrennially to the General Conference for its approval. Its annual income is provided from the general church budget. The Commission has the final word in record disposition for any general church agency and is responsible for helping all agencies in their record management programs.

Founding Date: 1968

Staff: 7

Membership: 30

Publications:
　　Methodist History, quarterly
　　Historians Digest, bimonthly
　　3 scholarly books

Meetings:
　　Annual meeting

Merger:
　　Historical Society of the Evangelical United Brethren Church (founded 1885) and Association of Methodist Historical Societies (founded 1939)

1486. United Methodist Church, Standing General Commission on Christian Unity and Interreligious Concerns

United Methodist Church

475 Riverside Drive
New York, New York 10027

The Standing General Commission on Christian Unity and Interreligious Concerns has two major responsibilities; to advocate and work toward the full reception of the gift of Christian unity in every aspect of the church's life, and to foster approaches to ministry and mission which more fully reflect the oneness of Christ's Church in the human community; and to advocate and work for the establishment and strengthening of relationships with other living faith communities, to further dialogue with persons of other faiths, cultures, and ideologies, and to work toward the unity of humankind. In fulfilling these responsibilities, the Commission assists all United Methodist Agencies, provides counsel and resources, assists in the development of resources, develops and interprets relationships to other religious organizations, works with historical members of the Methodist denominational family, and coordinates and controls funding activities of all United Methodist agencies.

Membership: 30

Meetings:

    Annual convention

1487. United Methodist Church, World Service Fund

United Methodist Church

475 Riverside Drive
New York, New York 10027
(212) 678-6161

The World Service Fund of the United Methodist Church is the program through which World Service agencies are funded. The General Council on Finance and Administration and the General Council on Ministries formulate the World Service budget. The budget is reviewed at the quadrennial sessions of the General Conference, and, if approved, is disbursed as recommended to World Service Agencies. In addition to apportionment of general funds, the World Service Fund receives support funds through World Service Special Gifts and Advance Special Gifts.

1488. United Methodist National Youth Ministry Organization

United Methodist Church

475 Riverside Drive
New York, New York 10027
(212) 678-6161

The United National Youth Ministry Organization is composed of two basic units: the National Youth Ministry Organization Convocation and the National Youth Ministry Organization Steering Committee. The purposes of the Youth Ministry Organization are: to promote and administer the Youth Service Fund; to encourage and enable youth and adults to recognize and respond to the needs and concerns of

youth; and to encourage the inclusion of youth as full members and participants in United Methodist ministries and structures. The organization provides a setting in which youth can speak their concerns to the Church. The Steering Committee is charged with carrying out the directives set by the Convocation in its efforts to fulfill the stated goals.

Meetings:

    Biennial meeting

1489. The United Methodist Publishing House

United Methodist Church

John E. Proctor, President and Publisher
201 Eighth Avenue, South
Nashville, Tennessee 37202
(615) 749-6000

The United Methodist Publishing House is the official publisher, printer, and distributor for the United Methodist Church. It has as its principal objective the advancement of the cause of Christianity throughout the world by disseminating religious knowledge and useful literary, scientific, and educational information. Its publications include church school curriculum resources; general books; children's books; religious books; college texts; official publications for the church, such as the *Book of Hymns;* supplies for the church and church school; and church music.

Staff: 1,600

Publications:

    1,800 titles (publish 75-100 titles per year)
    48 church school curriculum periodicals
    1 general church newsletter, weekly
    1 scholarly journal, quarterly
    1 clergy magazine, monthly

1490. United Ministries in Education (UME)

Interdenominational

Harold H. Viehman, Executive Director
c/o Educational Ministries, ABC
Valley Forge, Pennsylvania 19481
(215) 768-2052

United Ministries in Education is the corporate mission of eight national denominational agencies. UME's purpose is to bring the whole church, at every level, into engagement with the institutions and processes of education in our learning society. Emphasis is placed on support of specialized ministries in education provided by churches and on educating and enabling congregations to identify issues and minister in their communities. A nationwide network of staff develops mutually supportive relationships with local and regional ministries in education and with professional education organizations in such program areas as community college ministry, parent education, human values in medical education, career development, and public schools. Through exploration UME is probing responsibilities in the areas of science and technology; aesthetics, theology, and education; and peace studies. An Office of Communication prepares and distributes resources for ministries in education.

Founding Date: 1980

Staff: 17

Membership: 8

Publications:

Connexion

Directory of Ministers in Higher Education, annually

Merger:

United Ministries in Higher Education and Ministries in Public Education

1491. United Order True Sisters, Inc. (UOTS)

Southern Baptist

Dr. Elias L. Golonka

236 West 72nd Street

New York, New York 10023

(212) 877-5120

United Nations and International Ministries is a joint program of the Home Mission Board of the Southern Baptist Convention and the Baptist Convention of New York to develop a ministry to the diplomatic community and internationals such as foreign businessmen, personnel of transnational companies, foreign students, visitors, tourists, and seamen coming to the New York metropolitan area. One of the unique goals is to develop a Christian-Marxist Dialogue with the diplomats and correspondents from the Socialist countries. The first Christian-Marxist Dialogue was developed with six Embassies representing the Soviety Union, Poland, Czechoslovakia, Rumania, Bulgaria, and Yugoslavia in Washington, D.C., in 1972/73. The organization's approach is building bridges of international friendship and understanding by establishing personal contacts with the leaders of the world. The basic goal is to share Christian love, faith, and the Gospel of Christ with all internationals who come to the United States on a temporary or diplomatic visa. In ministering to the United Nations personnel, they hope to bring Christ into the United Nations as a redeeming and unifying power for all nations.

Radio/TV Programs:

Good News, in Polish, weekly radio program

1492. United Order True Sisters, Inc. (UOTS)

Nondenominational

Nana Klein, National President

150 West 85th Street

New York, New York 10024

(212) 362-2520

United Order True Sisters, Inc., is a philanthropic fraternal organization concerned with community service. Its national projects include cancer service, aid to handicapped children, and aid to the deaf and blind.

Staff: 1

Membership: 12,000

Publications:

Echo, 5 times a year

Meetings:

5 national meetings annually

6 regional meetings annually

150 local meetings in New York City

1493. United Pentecostal Church International, Education Division

United Pentecostal Church International

Arless Glass, Superintendent

8855 Dunn Road

Hazelwood, Missouri 63042

(314) 837-7300

The Education Division of the United Pentecostal Church International supervises Bible Schools and promotes interest in Christian Education in other levels.

1494. United Pentecostal Church International, Foreign Missions Division

United Pentecostal Church International

Harry E. Scism, Director
8855 Dunn Road
Hazelwood, Missouri 63042
(314) 837-7300

The objectives of the Foreign Missions Division are as follows: to spend forth God-called missionaries into all the world to preach the gospel of the kingdom to every creature; to establish the United Pentecostal Church International in every nation in order to reach every creature or every nation with this gospel; to teach and train national workers and ministers that they might assist in the fulfillment of the Great Commission and be able to give leadership to the church among their own people, to produce under God a self-supporting, self-propagating, and self-governing church in every country in full fellowship with and as a part of the United Pentecostal Church International; and to create, by the power of the Word of God and the working of the Holy Spirit, a love for truth and holiness that will bind the church to the heart of God and produce the Bride of Christ from among every nation, tribe, and tongue in the whole world.

1495. United Pentecostal Church International, Harvestime

United Pentecostal Church International

J. Hugh Rose, Coordinator and Narrator
8855 Dunn Road
Hazelwood, Missouri 63042
(314) 837-7300

Harvestime is an international radio broadcast now in its 21st year. It is heard on over 200 stations in the United States and Canada, and on stations in foreign countries.

1496. United Pentecostal Church International, Home Mission Division

United Pentecostal Church International

Jack Yonts, Director
8855 Dunn Road
Hazelwood, Missouri 63042
(314) 837-7300

The Home Missions Division of the United Pentecostal Church International promotes the opening of new churches in the United States and Canada, and shelters the new ones until they are self-supporting.

1497. United Pentecostal Church International, Ladies Auxiliary

United Pentecostal Church International

Vera Kinzie, President
4840 Elm Place
Toledo, Ohio 43608

The Ladies Auxiliary of the United Pentecostal Church International serves the missionary cause worldwide and assists in many other special projects of the church.

Meetings:
General conference, annually

1498. United Pentecostal Church International, Pentecostal Publishing House

United Pentecostal Church International

J. O. Wallace, General Manager
8855 Dunn Road
Hazelwood, Missouri 63042
(314) 837-7300

Pentecostal Publishing House publishes and purchases literature for retailing to the public. It sends Sunday School literature, books, records, songbooks, Bibles, and church material of all sorts to Pentecostal and other denominational buyers.

Founding Date: 1945
Staff: 50 Publishing House employees alone
Membership: Approximately 7,000 preachers
Publications:
Pentecostal Herald
Outreach
Homelife
Conqueror
Meetings:
Each district has a spring district conference
Each district has a campmeeting in the summer
General Conference of the United Pentecostal Church, International, in the fall (different city each year)

1499. United Pentecostal Church International, Sunday School

United Pentecostal Church International
James Boatman, Director
8855 Dunn Road
Hazelwood, Missouri 63042
(314) 837-7300

The Sunday School Department of the United Pentecostal Church International directs and promotes Sunday Schools in all United Pentecostal Churches, including the providing of curriculum and subsequent literature.

1500. United Prayer Force (UPF)*

Nondenominational
John and Vera Durkovic, Executive Directors
Post Office Box 30289
Washington, D.C. 20014
(301) 593-7111

The purpose of the United Prayer Force is to encourage Christians to pause for a "prayer break" at 11 a.m. daily, praying in unity and one accord for our nation and for one another. To promote and facilitate this prayer plan, a Prayer Manual has been composed, setting forth a daily prayer theme along with selected Bible passages. A cassette tape ministry is further provided with inspirational messages to enrich each day's prayer theme. Its programs consist of a two-fold spiritual renewal movement: cooperating with existing prayer groups, bible classes and other church related groups, and individuals; and including those who are generally overlooked, the handicapped and those in nursing homes, hospitals, prisons and shut-ins.

Publications:
  UPF Prayer Manual
  UPF Prayer Reminder Card

1501. United Presbyterian Church in the USA, Advisory Council on Church and Society*

United Presbyterian
The Reverend Dean H. Lewis, Director
475 Riverside Drive, Room 1020
New York, New York 10027
(212) 870-2101

The Advisory Council conducts research on social issues and prepares background studies and draft policy statements for consideration by denominational legislative process. Special task forces are formed for these purposes and for studies published by the Advisory Council itself. The Advisory Council also recommends social witness program strategies to the national and regional agencies of the denomination and prepares occasional formal materials to guide implementation of social ministry objectives.

Membership: 10 lay, 8 clerical
Publications:
  Church and Society, 6 times a year
Meetings:
  20 each year

1502. United Presbyterian Church in the USA, Advisory Council on Discipleship and Worship

United Presbyterian
The Reverend James G. Kirk, Director
475 Riverside Drive, Room 1020
New York, New York 10027
(212) 870-2907

The United Presbyterian Church Advisory Council on Discipleship and Worship promotes the importance of liturgy and public worship within the church. It helps empower the Church for ministries of compassion, justice, and reconciliation—an authentic piety that motivates persons, groups, and structures within the Church toward disciplined commitment and action. Special Task Forces are formed for these purposes and for studies published by the Advisory Council itself or recommended for consideration by denominational legislative process.

Staff: 2
Membership: 24
Meetings:
  3 meetings each year in different parts of the country

1503. United Presbyterian Church in the USA, The Council of Theological Seminaries

United Presbyterian

Rev. John H. Galbreath, Director
475 Riverside Drive, Room 1060
New York, New York 10027
(212) 870-2825

The Council of Theological Seminaries is an agency of the General Assembly of the United Presbyterian Church in the United States of America. It is composed of twelve members elected by the General Assembly and five members from each of the seven seminaries of the Church. Included among the seminary representatives are the President, the Dean, a faculty member, a member of the governing board, and a student. The Council relates to the seminaries the needs and concerns of the Church; relates to the Church the needs and concerns of the seminaries; develops cooperative programs and standards among the seminaries of the Church; provides an arena for theological dialogue on issues of concern to the Church and to the seminaries; and allocates to the seminaries the resources made available by the General Assembly.

Membership: 47

Meetings:
Annual meeting
4 Executive Committee Meetings
Other conferences as the occasion calls for

1504. United Presbyterian Church in the USA, Council on Church and Race*

United Presbyterian

Rev. Gilbert Marrero, Program Director
475 Riverside Drive
New York, New York 10027

The Council on Church and Race defines issues and problems in the area of racial injustice and develops policies for the Church which promote racial, ethnic, and intercultural justice and harmony.

Membership: 26

1505. United Presbyterian Church in the USA, Council on Women and the Church*

United Presbyterian

475 Riverside Drive
New York, New York 10027

The Council on Women and the Church serves as the focal point for the definition of issues and policy on the status of women both within the United Presbyterian Church and in society at large.

1506. United Presbyterian Church in the USA, Office of Equal Employment Opportunity*

United Presbyterian

Rev. Robert W. Hoppe, Staff Executive
475 Riverside Drive
New York, New York 10027

The Office of Equal Employment Opportunity promotes the United Presbyterian Church's commitment to an affirmative action program to guarantee equal opportunity for employment.

1507. United Presbyterian Church in the USA, Program Agency

United Presbyterian

J. Oscar McCloud, General Director
475 Riverside Drive, Room 1108
New York, New York 10027
(212) 870-2687

The Program Agency of the United Presbyterian Church in the United States of America carries out a broad spectrum of ministries of direct action and enablement of others in mission, both in the United States and overseas. It deploys people and funds at the request and invitation of national churches throughout the world to enable their mission programs; provides money, consultation, and resources for nurture of individuals in congregations of the United States; aids people with special needs in cooperation with ecumenical agencies; and maintains relationships with national churches, national ecumenical bodies, and with Presbyterian institutions around the world.

Founding Date: 1837

Staff: 42 Board members

Publications:
1 publication on Evangelism
3 publications on Christian Education Materials
1 publication on Church and Society

Meetings:
Numerous training conferences

1508. United Presbyterian Church in the USA, Vocation Agency*

United Presbyterian

Rev. Donald P. Smith, General Director
475 Riverside Drive
New York, New York 10027

The Vocation Agency of the United Presbyterian Church in the United States of America is responsible for recruiting, preparing, and assisting lay persons and clergy for the fulfillment of the church's mission. It provides special links with the Council of Theological Seminaries and the Board of Pensions, and encompasses the work formerly done by the Department of Ministerial Relations.

Membership: 31

1509. United States Army Chaplain Board

Interdenominational

Chaplain (COL) Eugene E. Allen
Myer Hall
Fort Monmouth, New Jersey 07703
(201) 532-2401

The Mission of the United States Army Chaplain Board as field operating agency of the Chief of Chaplains is to execute programs in support of various religious and moral activities of the Army, focusing on meeting changing needs of the soldier; to collect and provide information regarding current needs of United States Army personnel and their dependents as they relate to chaplain activities; to provide consultant services to chaplains throughout the Army; and to assist the Chief of Chaplains in developing concepts of ministry and professional guidelines for chaplains and religious activities. This work is accomplished through the following branches: Religious Education; Journalism and Homiletics; Pastoral Planning; Parish Development; Marriage and Family Life Ministry; Audio Visual; and Management.

Staff: 4 lay; 7 clergy
Publications:
> *Military Chaplains' Review,* quarterly
> *Film Guide—Chaplain,* periodic updates of an annual publication

Radio/TV Programs:
> Numerous TV and 16mm film programs
> 10-15 30-minute programs per year

Meetings:
> Educational conferences, training seminars, and retreats in many areas of activity

1510. United States Catholic Conference, Department of Social Development and World Peace

Roman Catholic

Bishop Edward D. Head, Chairman
Msgr. Francis J. Lally, Secretary
1312 Massachusetts Avenue, N.W.
Washington, D.C. 20005
(202) 659-6820

The Department of Social Development and World Peace has two offices. The goals of the first office, the Domestic Social Development Office, are to bring the Gospel and Catholic social teaching to bear upon policies, programs, and concerns involving human need and social justice in the United States; to analyze and evaluate social and economic issues; to formulate and communicate positions on such matters; and to serve Church leadership and those active in the social ministry of the Church. The goals of the second office, International Justice and Peace Office, are to assist the Bishops of the United States in forming the consciences of American Catholics so that the message of the Gospel and the teachings of recent Popes, the Council, and the Synod of Bishops concerning peace and justice for all nations and peoples may be communicated more effectively and may be accepted more fully; and to represent the institutional Church vis-a-vis the Congress and the Executive, and the United Nations, under the direction of the General Secretary, on foreign policy questions judged to be of central concern to the Church's work for justice and peace.

Staff: 19
Publications:
> Pamphlets stating positions on domestic and international issues, serving as educational primers on various topics such as multinational corporations and pacifism, and providing studies on different issues of concern

Meetings:
> Advisory Committee Meetings biannually

1511. United States Catholic Conference, Division of Campus Ministry*

Roman Catholic
Rev. Dr. Patrick H. O'Neill, OSA
1312 Massachusetts Avenue, N.W.
Washington, D.C. 20005
(202) 659-6684

The activities of the Division of Campus Ministry encompass campus and young adult ministry.

Membership: 200 lay; 2,600 clerical

Publications:
Monthly newsletter
Quarterly scholarly journals

Meetings:
Regionally on a quarterly basis

1512. United States Catholic Conference, Education Department

Roman Catholic
Rev. Thomas G. Gallagher, Secretary
1312 Massachusetts Avenue, N.W.
Washington, D.C. 20005
(202) 659-6822

The Department of Education, United States Catholic Conference, serves the dioceses by implementing programs related to the catechetical/educational and other pastoral ministries of the Church. This mission is accomplished, within Conference policies, by facilitating communication, implementing pastoral action in programs, undertaking special projects, obtaining equitable benefits for Catholic schools from the government, sponsoring promotional and advocacy programs, gathering and disseminating information, and enabling structural development on the regional and national levels.

Publications:
Dimensions, every other month

Meetings:
Periodical meetings based on need

1513. United States Catholic Conference, Family Life Division

Roman Catholic
Rev. Donald B. Conroy, PhD, STL, USCC Representative for Family Life

1312 Massachusetts Avenue, N.W.
Washington, D.C. 20005
(202) 659-6672

The Family Life Division is the organizational liaison with the Family Life Directors and their offices throughout the United States. It acts as the Bishops' liaison with all national family life organizations and movements within the Catholic Church, such as Marriage Encounter, Christian Family Movement, and Teams of Our Lady; and keeps in contact with ecumenical and secular organizations and agencies dealing with marriage and family life. It also serves as a resource center for diocesan offices in connection with programs dealing with the Family Apostolate and provides services to the dioceses to assist them in the implementation of the Bishops' plan of pastoral action for family ministry. This aim is achieved by: facilitating communication; implementing programs of pastoral action; undertaking special projects; gathering and disseminating information; and by structural development at the national and regional levels.

Membership:
175 diocesan offices (general membership)

Publications:
Numerous publications intended to aid dioceses and parishes in on-going projects in family ministry or in the implementation of the Bishops' plan of pastoral action for family ministry

Radio/TV Programs:
4 TV spots: 2 30-second, 1 60-second, 1 20-second
10 30-second radio spots; all developed for the promotion of the Bishops' plan of pastoral action for family ministry

1514. United States Catholic Conference, Migration and Refugee Services

Roman Catholic
John E. McCarthy, Director
1312 Massachusetts Avenue, N.W.
Washington, D.C. 20005
(202) 659-6636

The purpose of the United States Catholic Conference, Migration and Refugee Services is to coordinate and provide for the Church's concern for migrants, immigrants, and refugees throughout the world. The agency operates one research center.

Staff: 125

Meetings:
> 8-10 meetings per year

1515. United States Catholic Conference, Office of Chaplain Services

Roman Catholic

Sister Anita Lapeyre, Coordinator of Chaplain Services
1312 Massachusetts Avenue, N.W.
Washington, D.C. 20005
(202) 659-6790

The Office of Chaplain Services is responsible for the certifying of Chaplains and Pastoral Associates in general health, mental health, geriatric care, corrections, and the seafarers. The Office certifies supervisors who sponsor training programs for those interested in certification, and accredits training programs.

Founding Date: 1965

Staff: 1

Membership: 3,000

Publications:
> *Boe Newsletter,* 6 per year
> *Policies and Procedures Manual,* every two years

Meetings:
> Annual Supervisors' Workshop, location changes every year
> Board of Examiners' Meeting, location changes (regional) 3 per year

1516. United States Catholic Conference, Youth Activities*

Roman Catholic

Rev. Rudy Beranek, Representative
1312 Massachusetts Avenue, N.W.
Washington, D.C. 20005
(202) 659-6664

The representative for Youth Activities of the United States Catholic Conference is responsible for coordination, communication, and policy leadership in the field of Catholic youth ministry. A part of the Department of Education, Youth Activities provides programming materials and periodic conferences to aid youth workers as they supplement the work of formal religious education. The representative for Youth Activities is also the Director of the National Catholic Youth Organization Federation, which, provides Catholic youth groups with social, cultural, spiritual, athletic, educational, and service-oriented programs. Other activities and services related to Youth Activities include youth ministry publications and representation to a variety of national organizations pertaining in some way to the interests of Catholic youth.

Publications:
> *Youth/Program Service,* 5 issues yearly
> Various youth ministry resources: booklets, manuals, multi-media, about 20 titles currently available

Meetings:
> 4-5 major meetings annually

1517. United States Catholic Historical Society*

Roman Catholic

Mr. Thomas A. Brennan, President
St. Joseph's Seminary
Dunwoodie
Yonkers, New York 10704
(914) 968-6200

The principal purposes of the Society are: presentation of lectures which relate to the history of the Catholic Church; publication of documents, books and papers; the development of Catholic culture; and encouragement and assistance to scholars in the field of American Church history. Two series of books, *Historical Records and Studies,* and the *Monograph Series,* are regularly published by the Society.

Membership: 275

Publications:
> Scholarly research works in Catholic Church history (about 25 titles in print)

Meetings:
> Annual meeting with "King" lecture in spring

1518. United States Conference of Secular Institutes (CSJ)

Roman Catholic

Barbara Ottinger, President
7007 Bradley Boulevard
Bethesda, Maryland 20034
(301) 365-0612

The purpose of the United States Conference of Secular Institutes is to seek ways and means to make better known, understood, and appreciated the call to consecrated secularity; to make known the Secular Institutes existing in the United States; to maintain an interchange of ideas and experiences among Secular Institutes in the United States; to do research in order to help the Church carry out her mission today; to make the resources of the Conference available to groups aspiring to the Canonical status of a Secular Institute; and to represent the Conference (CSI) officially in the World Conference of Secular Institutes and other national and international bodies.

Founding Date: 1972

Membership: 10 participating Institutes

Publications:

Communications, quarterly, a newsletter for participating Secular Institutes

Meetings:

1 annual meeting

Former Name:

(1969) Association of Secular Institutes

1519. United Synagogue Book Service

Jewish/Conservative

George L. Levine, Director
155 Fifth Avenue
New York, New York 10010
(212) 533-7800

The United Synagogue Book Service publishes text books, adult education materials, song books, and prayer books for 850 congregations affiliated with the United Synagogue of America.

Publications:

200 religious texts for schools and prayer books
United Synagogue Review, quarterly
Synagogue School, quarterly

Radio/TV Programs:

Eternal Light, NBC
Frontiers of Faith

Meetings:

30 per year

1520. United Synagogue Commission on Jewish Education

Jewish/Conservative

Dr. Morton K. Siegel, Director of Education
155 Fifth Avenue
New York, New York 10010
(212) 260-8450

The United Synagogue Commission on Jewish Education services the educational enterprises of the Conservative Movement in Judaism in North America, which include: conducting a publications program for the elementary, secondary, and adult family levels; servicing 64 all-day schools with an enrollment of some 12,000; servicing some 700 afternoon congregational schools with an enrollment of 150,000, publishing periodic bulletins; sponsoring a special education program; arranging field service to visit affiliate schools; and operating through a network of committees in various areas of specialization.

Founding Date: 1946

Staff: 3

Publications:

B'Kitzur, periodical for day schools
In Your Hands, a newsletter for Rabbis and Educators
Kol Bana'yikh, a newsletter for Parents of Jewish Special Children
Your Child, a quarterly newsletter for parents of Children in Day Schools or Congregational Schools

Meetings:

The location of the conferences varies in location. There are some 12 conferences (dealing with various areas of their work) in the course of a given year

1521. United Synagogue Youth/KADIMA (USY)

Jewish/Conservative

Rabbi Paul Freedman, Director
155 Fifth Avenue
New York, New York 10010
(212) 533-7800

United Synagogue Youth is an international Jewish youth organization sponsored by the United Synagogue of America. USY members range in age from 13 to 18. Members of USY meet on the chapter, regional, and international level through a variety of activities: regional encampments, international convention, kinnusim, USY on Wheels (a summer cross-country tour), and USY Israel Pilgrimage (a summer educational/religious trip to Israel). KADIMA is an international Jewish youth organization sponsored by the United Synagogue of America. KADIMA members are in 5th-8th grade. Members of KADIMA meet together on the chapter and regional level through a variety of activities: regional KADIMA days, encampments, and kinnusim.

Membership:
18,000 members of USY
9,000 members of KADIMA

Publications:
ACHSHAV FOR USY members
KADIMA magazine for KADIMA members

1522. United World Mission, Inc. (UWM)

Interdenominational
Rev. Gerald N. Boyer, General Director
Post Office Box 8000
St. Petersburg, Florida 33738
(813) 391-0195

United World Mission is basically a church planting/church developing agency ministering in 14 countries on four continents. The Mission is also engaged in sponsorship of orphans and needy children in Korea and a specialized ministry to the American-Korean mixed-blood children and the blind people of Korea. Priority is given to the founding of churches and the training of national workers to pastor these churches and train their own people. The Mission is deeply involved, both financially and with personnel, in the construction of overseas churches. Areas of Service include: Mali, Senegal, People's Republic of the Congo, India, Korea, the Philippines, Britain, Belgium, Spain, Bolivia, Brazil, Cuba, Guatemala, and Venezuela. UWM has established 300 organized overseas churches; one school for English-speaking children, three national elementary schools, and one national high school, as well as four resident Bible Schools and 14 extension centers. A Braille printing press produces Bible courses, song books, devotionals and children's stories. In addition, UWM operates two bookstores and four medical outposts. UWM is a member of EFMA and IFMA.

Founding Date: 1946

Staff: 16

Membership: 83 missionary personnel

Publications:
UWM Worldscan, 10 copies per year

Children's Ministries Newsletter, quarterly
Missionaries' newsletters

Radio/TV Programs:
Daily radio broadcast in Oviedo, Spain
2 weekly radio broadcast in Laoag City, Philippines
Weekly radio broadcasts in Senegal and Venezuela
Numerous broadcasts prepared in England for English-speaking Africa

Meetings:
Annual Missions Conference in St. Petersburg
30 Church Missions Conferences in Mid-west and Eastern states
Church conferences, youth retreats, and pastors' retreats in most fields

1523. Unity-in-Diversity Council (UDC)

Interdenominational
Leland P. Stewart, President
7433 Madora Avenue
Conoga Park, California 91306
(213) 998-7812

Unity-in-Diversity Council is a worldwide coordinating body of organizations and individuals fostering the emergence of a new universal person and civilization based on unity-in-diversity among all peoples. The activities of the Council include: an annual World Synergy Festival in January; a World Festival of Light (world-wide media outreach event); a monthly newsletter; regular programs and occasional programs featuring groups, one or more at a time; and projects.

Founding Date: 1965

Membership:
Approximately 100 groups
300 additional cooperating groups

Publications:
Spectrum, monthly
Newsprint, monthly
UDC Directory, annually

Meetings:
2 Council Festivals
Weekly meetings at headquarters
Monthly intergroup seminars in Los Angeles

Former Names:
(1965) Pageant for Peace
(1979) International Cooperation Council

1524. Unity of the Brethren, Sunday School Union

Unity of the Brethren
Stanley F. Mrnustik, President
205 North Shaw Street
Caldwell, Texas 77836

The Unity of the Brethren Sunday School Union has as its primary purposes: to unite the individual Sunday Schools within the Unity toward common and more effective work for the Lord; to counsel and encourage the Sunday Schools in their work and activities; to strengthen in their members the knowledge of mutual unity by arranging for convetions, carrying out of mutual affairs, and fostering of mutual interests; and to work so that the individual Sunday School members are brought into the best possible knowledge of the Word of God, using pure teaching of the Word of God, Christian songs, and prayer.

Staff: 6 Executive Committee Officers

Membership:
> 1,470 individual members in 21 member Sunday Schools

Publications:
> *The Brethren Journal*, co-published with the Unity of the Brethren, monthly

Meetings:
> Convention every 2 years
> 1 Rally (Spring) at Hus Encampment, Caldwell, Texas
> 1 Workshop (Fall)

1525. Unity School of Christianity

Nondenominational
Charles R. Fillmore, Chairman of the Board and President
Unity Village, Missouri 64065
(816) 524-3550
Prayer Ministry: (816) 251-2100

Unity School of Christianity is a nondenominational, religious education organization. Its primary purpose is to help people through prayer and religious education. The organization's work is centered in three major areas: prayer, publishing, and adult education. The Silent Unity Prayer Ministry, considered the largest in the world, is the heart of the Unity work. Approximately 200 workers answer thousands of prayer requests received daily by telephone and mail. A constant prayer vigil is maintained and telephones are answered 24 hours a day. One of the largest religious publishing houses in the Midwest is operated by Unity School. The publishing department produces a variety of literature including hardcover books and three periodicals. Unity literature is published in 12 languages and Grade 2 Braille. An active education department offers adult education programs through its Institute for Continuing Education. The programs, which offer Unity's approach to religion, are designed to help people who are seeking greater personal unfolding. They also serve to train interested lay people to become teachers in Unity ministries. Classes are open to all interested individuals and membership in a Unity church is not required to participate in the programs. Outreach activities include religious and non-religious radio broadcasts; cassette tape recordings; and distribution of free literature to hundreds of hospitals, prisons, orphanages, and other institutions, including Braille material for the blind.

Staff: 550 employees

Membership: 3 million subscribers

Publications:
> *Daily Word*, monthly
> *Unity Magazine*, a metaphysical journal
> *Wee Wisdom*, a children's magazine
> Hardcover books, pamphlets and brochures, an organizational newsletter

Radio/TV Programs:
> Non-religious public service radio and TV broadcasts entitled *The Word*
> A 30-minute religious radio broadcast

Meetings:
> 11 spiritual retreats conducted at Unity Village each year open to all interested individuals

1526. Universal Christian Movement (UCM)

Christian
Rev. B. I. Henson, Executive Director
Post Office Box 195
Glencoe, Illinois 60022

The purpose of the Universal Christian Movement is to gather people who are willing to obey the commandments of the Lord Jesus Christ.

Founding Date: 1970

Publications:
> *Christian Liberator*, irregularly
> *Be Healed*, booklet

1527. Universal Color Slide Company*

Sam Marcus, President
136 West 32nd Street
New York, New York 10001
(212) 564-8880

Universal Color Slide Company produces art and religious slides. Its catalogue list over 1,100 artists and 20,000 individual subjects.

1528. Universal Spiritual Center

Universal, Yoga, Divine Light, Theosophy, Comparitive Religion

Krsna Bhakti Vendanta Mishra Ghee, Richard Suraci
480 Watson Street
Monterey, California 93940
67 Maple Street
Newburgh, New York 12550
(408) 373-5218
(914) 561-5886

Universal Spiritual Center offers discussion relating to the comparitive examination of the Divine Light doctrines leading one to the experience of energy truth. They examine the personality structure in relation to growth in a spiritual manner, a mental understanding, and a physical well being. Active and inactive forms of meditation are practiced. Constructive community counseling is offered. Programs are designed for the needs of the people involved and participating. Spontaneity of exchange and program development is offered. Group discussion and musical inspirational teachings are offered. Flexibility of knowledge is offered for continued creative thought development.

Staff: 4

Membership: 7

1529. Universal Truth Foundation

Nondenominational

Norma J. Graham, President
Post Office Box 7663
Phoenix, Arizona 85011

Post Office Box 53
Martinsville, Missouri 64467
(602) 265-3054 (Arizona)
(816) 845-2271 (Missouri)

The purpose of the Universal Truth Foundation is to bring greater balance within individuals concerning their triune being — mental, physical, and spiritual; to bring greater understanding of the spiritual teachings given within their churches, going beyond the usual interpretations of scriptures and providing a deeper insight into them; and to bring spiritual healing to the public, as well as teaching the ability to channel God's healing energies.

Publications:
  Intermittent newsletter
  An annual magazine
  Metaphysical books
  Bulletins

Meetings:
  Conferences, meetings, and retreats intermittently
  Lecture series

1530. University of Notre Dame Press

Roman Catholic

James R. Langford, Director
Notre Dame, Indiana 46556
(219) 239-6346

The University of Notre Dame Press publishes scholarly books, serious nonfiction of a general interest, and paperback reprints in the areas of theology, philosophy, government and international relations, sociology (especially Mexican-American studies), English literature (especially Middle English period), history, and Mediaeval studies. Although its program is not restricted to religious books, the Press has a strong commitment to books which deal with subjects from a Judaeo-Christian and particularly a Roman Catholic perspective.

Membership: 13

Publications:
  Scholarly books and some books of general interest
  About 450 titles in print

1531. The Upper Room

Interdenominational

Maxie D. Dunnam, World Editor
1908 Grand Avenue
Nashville, Tennessee 37202
(615) 327-2700

The Upper Room is a publisher of religious magazines and resources with the purpose of enhancing the devotional/spiritual life of individuals and families through the media of its two periodicals and other devotional resources. *The Upper Room Daily Devotional Guide* is interdenominational, interracial, and international, and is read daily by more than eight million persons in 40 languages, 53 editions. This makes the magazine the world's most widely used devotional guide. The material used within this magazine is primarily freelance submissions. The magazine has been in publication since 1953. The publisher's devotional literature is formulated with a specific reading audience in mind, giving its spiritual resources wide acceptance in the religious marketplace. The Upper Room's companion magazine, *alive now!*, is a bi-monthly magazine developed for all ages. The magazine contains personal poetry, prose, and the use of graphics (sketches, photography). Each issue is based on a particular theme which can be used widely and metaphorically.

Staff:
> 12 professional staff members
> 20 support staff members

Publications:
> *The Upper Room Daily Devotional Guide,* bimonthly
> *alive now!,* bimonthly

Radio/TV Programs:
> Currently developing a series of 30-and 60-second TV spots that will be aired later in 1980

1532. Utah Missions, Inc.

Interdenominational
John L. Smith, Director
311 West Seminole
Marlow, Oklahoma 73055

Mailing Address
Post Office Box 348
Marlow, Oklahoma 73055
(405) 658-5631

Utah Missions, Inc., is a non-profit organization set up to foster and present the "Unique Ministries of John L. Smith." Smith, a Baptist minister, spent 17 years in Utah and has now spent almost 30 years in a ministry related to Mormonism. He feels that Mormonism is a dangerous cult and that its tremendous growth is a result of its militant and often misleading

missionary program. Its doctrine of God, the members' allegiance to their leader, and their current advertising campaign must be met with facts that are seldom known. Smith's speaking engagements, his six books, his cassette recordings, his film, and *The Utah Evangel* are being used to further that ministry.

Staff: 4

Publications:
> *The Utah Evangel,* monthly

Meetings:
> Speaking engagements 150-350 times a year in 15-25 states

1533. Vellore Christian Medical College Board (USA), Inc.* (CMC)

Nondenominational

The Rev. Herbert O. Muenstermann, Executive Director
475 Riverside Drive, Room 243
New York, New York 10027
(212) 264-2642

The Vellore Christian Medical College Board promotes Christian medical education of men and women in India by developing interest in, and securing support for, the Christian Medical College and Hospital in Vellore, South India, which is an international center of education, hospital care, research, rehabilitation, and rural service. The motivating force of the College and Hospital is the urge to meet the real health needs of the people in India.

Publications:
> Paperback edition of Dr. Ida — *Passing on the Torch of Life*
> Newsletters regarding the work of CMC, 3 times a year

1534. Vernacular Society

Roman Catholic

Reinhold Kissner, President
Post Office Box 207
Passaic, New Jersey 07055
(201) 773-2843

The Vernacular Society, members of which include Catholic clergy and laity, encourages and supports the use of English in the liturgy. To facilitate these purposes, they loan tapes, sell books, and maintain a speakers' bureau.

1535. Victory Mission of the Americas, Inc.

Nondenominational

Mr. William L. McCall, President
Post Office Box 14444
Fort Worth, Texas 76117
(817) 838-6342

Victory Mission of the Americas is a nondenominational sending agency of fundamental, evangelical tradition primarily involved in childcare programs, orphanage support, and international adoption. It is also engaged in evangelism, medicine, Bible distribution, education, and church construction. The agency supports Paraiso Infantil, an orphanage in Colombia placing children in Christian homes worldwide.

Founding Date: 1964

Staff: 12

Membership: 450 mailing list

Publications:
> A quarterly prayer letter
> An annual calender

Meetings:
> Annual Board Meeting
> Biannual youth retreats in Colombia
> Annual Missionary Orientation Program in Colombia

1536. Virginia Mennonite Board of Missions and Charities

Mennonite

Isaac Risser, President
901 Parkwood Drive
Harrisonburg, Virginia 22801
(703) 434-9727

The purposes of the Virginia Mennonite Board of Missions and Charities, under the guidance of the Holy Spirit, is to initiate, sponsor, supervise, assist, and promote the mission outreach of the Virginia Mennonite Conference at home and abroad. The Board carries on such charitable work as may be authorized in response to needs which present themselves. Virginia Mission Board has established and is helping support churches in Italy, Trinidad, Jamaica, Winston-Salem, North Carolina, Durham, North Carolina, and a ministry to seamen in Norfolk, Virginia.

Founding Date: 1919

Staff: 4

Publications:

Missionary Light, bimonthly

Radio/TV Programs:

A five minute weekly newscast of mission happenings, released on two local stations

Meetings:

A spring Missions Conference held in April at different Virginia Conference churches

A fall Missions Conference held in November at different churches

Former Name:

Virginia Mennonite Conference

1537. Vocation Central

Roman Catholic

Brother James Muller, SCJ, Director of Vocations

6889 South Lovers Lane Road

Franklin, Wisconsin 53132

Mailing Address

Post Office Box 206

Hales Corners, Wisconsin 53130-0206

(414) 425-8500, ext. 3222

Vocation Central is an organization of the Priests of the Sacred Heart. The Director of Vocation Central is responsible for the coordination and communication involved in Vocation Ministry with SCJ Regional Vocation Directors and local SCJ Community programs. Through a nationwide vocation awareness poster campaign one to two times annually, and other sources, Vocation Central communicates the names of men and women to those religious and diocesan vocation directors who desire new members in their communities. While this service is provided on alternating months, Vocation Central's primary function is to support the needs of each local SCJ community in their vocation awareness and orientation objectives.

Founding Date: 1962

Staff: 8

Membership: 230

Publications:

Brochures on religious life, the priest, the brother, the sister, the deacon

Brochures on SCJ programs and heritage, vocation prayer cards, all published each year

SCJ News, bimonthly

Meetings:

3-4 regional meetings annually

Popular Name:

Sacred Heart Fathers and Brothers; its religious initials are: SCJ

1538. Voice of Calvary Ministries

Nondenominational

Rev. John M. Perkins, President

1655 St. Charles Street

Jackson, Mississippi 39209

Mailing Address

Post Office Box 10562

Jackson, Mississippi 39209

(601) 353-1635

Voice of Calvary Ministries strives to communicate the gospel to poor and oppressed people in a wholistic way. This means both proclamation through evangelism and demonstration through social action, economic development, and justice. They seek to address the physical and economic needs of poor people through housing renovation and thrift stores and by bringing health care to underserved areas. The housing corporation and the thrift stores are set up as cooperative enterprises to provide an economic base for further development. They seek to develop young people as Christian leaders. The John M. Perkins International Study Center oversees a one-year program for leadership training in Christian community development work, and a volunteer program for work opportunities with Voice of Calvary Ministries. They seek to join together with other Christians in the local area to develop a strong church body that forms the center from which the ministries spring and which aims to be a local expression of the body of Christ in a poor community. They also seek lasting racial reconciliation by coming together as blacks and whites in work, worship, and shared lives in the body of Christ.

Founding Date: 1960

Staff: 15

Publications:

> *A Quiet Revolution,* quarterly
>
> *Walk Your Talk,* a syndicated weekly newspaper article oriented toward a black readership

Meetings:

> Periodic seminars in different parts of the country
>
> Biennial Jubilee conference in Jackson, Mississippi

1539. Voice of China and Asia Missionary Society, Inc.

Nondenominational

Robert B. Hammond, President

Post Office Box 15-M

Pasadena, California 91102

(213) 796-3117

The purposes of Voice of China and Asia Missionary Society are to promulgate the gospel of the Lord Jesus Christ by means of teaching the truths of the Bible through missionaries, teachers, faith missionary radio broadcasts, Christian literature, and world wide vision interdenominationally, with representatives in the larger cities of the United States, China, Canada, and other foreign countries; to render spiritual service and material aid to Chinese Christian workers and missionaries; to preach the Christian gospel to Chinese; and to administer relief and physical and medical care to orphans and the aged. The Society has a clinic in India; day care centers in India, Taiwan, Korea, and Hong Kong; kindergarten schools in Taiwan, Hong Kong, and Korea; a junior and senior high school in Korea; and a handicapped Children's Home in Korea. They also help the leprosariums in Korea and Taiwan and the Old People's Homes in Korea and Hong Kong, and help the people of India, Philippines, Korea, Taiwan, Hong Kong, and Mexico through relief work and national pastors.

Founding Date: 1946

Staff: 18

Publications:

> *Flashlight,* monthly
>
> Monthly Newsletter

Radio/TV Programs:

> 15 minute Missionary/Educational Broadcast

1540. The Voice of Prophecy

Seventh-day Adventist Church

H.M.S. Richards, Jr., Director-Speaker

1100 Rancho Conejo Boulevard

Newbury Park, California 91320

Mailing Address

Post Office Box 2525

Newbury Park, California 91320

Listener Mail

Post Office Box 55

Los Angeles, California 90053

(805) 499-1911

The Voice of Prophecy began as a radio ministry. Today the good news about Jesus is reaching millions around the world through the Voice of Prophecy radio, Bible correspondence school, and evangelistic crusade ministries. Around the world in 36 languages, God's Word is heard through the broadcast of the Voice of Prophecy. The Voice of Prophecy News reaches over 200,000 readers monthly with the good news that Jesus saves, and that He is coming again. In addition, The Voice of Prophecy operates the largest Bible correspondence school in the world. Courses are offered in 80 languages, in Braille, and in special English for the deaf.

Founding Date: 1930

Staff: 110

Publications:

> *Voice of Prophecy News* (general interest: donors and friends), monthly
>
> *Prime Time* (for senior citizens), quarterly
>
> Bible correspondence courses for adults, youth, children — basic courses offered at no charge; others at nominal charge

Radio/TV Programs:

> *Voice of Prophecy,* 30-minute Sunday broadcast on 521 stations in the U.S. and Canada
>
> *Voice of Prophecy,* 15-minute Mon-Fri broadcast on 165 stations in U.S. and Canada
>
> *Sunspots,* public service announcements (spots) 30-second and 60-second (4,090 stations)
>
> *La Voz de la Esperanza,* Spanish language religious program — 58 stations in the U.S., 30-minute Sunday
>
> *The Health File,* public service 5-minute broadcast (130 in series)
>
> *The Music Scrapbook,* public service 15-minute broadcasts (104 in series)
>
> Broadcasts in 36 languages worldwide — most produced by overseas affiliate offices — VOP programs aired by 1100 stations outside the U.S. and Canada

1541. W H Sadlier, Inc.,

Nondenominational
Ralph Fletcher, President
11 Park Place
New York, New York 10007
(212) 227-2120

W. H. Sadlier, Inc., publishes textbooks for religious teaching from kindergarten through adult, as well as audio-visual kits and supplementary materials. Sadlier also publishes textbooks for elementary, junior high and high school academic studies.

Founding Date: 1832

Publications:
Academic and religious texts

1542. Waikiki Beach Chaplaincy (WBC)

Interdenominational
Gene Ozbun, President
Post Office Box 15488
Honolulu, Hawaii 96815
(808) 923-3137

The Waikiki Beach Chaplaincy is an evangelistic outreach to over four million tourists who visit Hawaii annually. As an interdenominational faith ministry, the WBC is not supported financially by any one denomination, but works in cooperation with the local churches as an evangelistic arm of the church. The various aspects of the outreach include: street evangelism, radio broadcasts, hotel worship services, a unique Sunday morning beach worship service called "Sun and Soul Talk," phone counseling, and Bible Studies.

Membership: 10

Publications:
Occasional newsletter to supporters

Radio/TV Programs:
3 radio programs

1543. Wainwright House, Inc. (Center for Development of Human Resources)

Nondenominational
John W. Ballard, President
260 Stuyvesant Avenue
Rye, New York 10580
(914) 967-6080

Wainwright House is a center for spiritual growth, intellectually and intuitively, physically and emotionally. It aims to provide an atmosphere where people can find their own best path to spiritual growth. It helps members to develop inner resources for living their deepest convictions; to be enriched for meaningful contribution in the worlds around; and to find encouragement in their quest for love of God. Seminars, workshops, courses, lecture series, conferences, symposia, retreats, and informal gatherings are planned, developed, and carried out by and through nine learning centers at Wainwright House, which is a magnificent French chateau-style mansion on Long Island Sound. The nine learning centers emphasize Cross-Cultural Programs, Wholistic Health and Healing, Receptive Listening, Scope for retired and semi-retired persons, Religious and Philosophical Studies, Jungian Studies, Guild for Spiritual Guidance, Exploring New Dimensions in Consciousness, and Women's Studies and Creative Expression.

Founding Date: 1941

Staff: 18

Membership: 300

Publications:
A Program Calendar is published quarterly, along with brochures which describe individual seminars

Meetings:
24-36 per year

Former Name:
Laymen's Movement for a Christian World

1544. Warner Press, Inc.

Church of God

Donald A. Noffsinger, President
1200 East Fifth Street
Anderson, Indiana 46011

Mailing Address
Post Office Box 2499
Anderson, Indiana 46011
(317) 644-7721

Warner Press, Inc., is the publishing house owned and controlled by the Church of God. The editorial staff of Warner Press, Inc., under the leadership of Dr. Arlo F. Newell, Editor in Chief, helps the Church of God in its mission through *Vital Christianity* magazine, *Warner Press Bible-Based Curriculum, Reach, Action, Pathways to God,* the *Hymnal of the Church of God,* books, and other materials designed to help in the program of the local church. Beyond publishing for the Church of God, a large volume of Warner Press output goes into the general religious field. This includes "Christian Art," "Every Sunday Bulletins," "Sunshine Line" boxed greeting cards, "Christian Faith" Bible verse cards, "Egermeiers" Bible story books, "Christian Witness" distinctive religious gift items, and "Artwood" Christian plaques. The printing facilities of Warner Press are also used by the general church agencies. The Assembly elects twenty-five persons to serve as the Publication Board, which set the general policies of the company.

Publications:
Books, 120 titles in print
Church magazine, *Vital Christianity,* youth periodical *Reach,* and children's periodical *Action*

1545. Watch Tower Bible and Tract Society

Jehovah's Witnesses

F. W. Franz, President
25 Columbia Heights
Brooklyn, New York 11201
(212) 625-3600

The Watch Tower Bible and Tract Society warns humankind of the impending end of the present system by publishing Biblical proof of the "last days" and distributing it through hundreds of millions of books, tracts, pamphlets and magazines each year. During the past 100 years, they have circulated nearly eight billion pieces of such literature to promote Bible education. The 2.3 million workers donate their time in calling house-to-house and conducting free Bible studies with interested persons. Their adherence to the heavenly kingdom is reinforced by their non-participation in politics or national conflicts. They are not trinitarians but believe Jehovah is God, Jesus is his Son and the redeemer of believing mankind, and the Holy Spirit is God's active force for the accomplishing of His will.

Founding Date: 1884

Publications:
The Watchtower, semimonthly, a biblical journal that keeps watch on world events as they fulfill Bible prophecy
Awake!, semimonthly; its coverage includes news, religion, science, and numerous other matters of human interest; also millions of Bible study books, tracts, and pamphlets plus millions of Bibles in various translations and languages

Former Name: International Bible Students

1546. WE GO, Inc. (World Encounter Gospel Organization)

Interdenominational

Dr. Paul L. Morell, President
Paul Shirley, Executive Director
927 West Tenth
Dallas, Texas 75208
(214) 943-6365
(214) 946-8106

WE GO represents itself as a World Encounter Gospel Organization, sending forth into the mission fields at home and abroad those who believe, in accordance with Matthew 28:19,20, that "as the Lord commands, We Go." It is incorporated under the state laws of Texas as a non-profit faith Missions

Board. WE GO is independent and interdenominational with an historical linking to the Wesleyan perspective. WE GO missionaries are being supported in Asia, Latin America, Europe, and Africa. Believing that God sees world evangelization as the supreme task of the Church, WE GO was founded for evangelical missionary work in any and all countries and among any and all peoples. Primary activities include fund transmittal to the field and information exchange from the field. The missionaries are responsible for securing their support through the gifts of interested churches, friends, and family. WE GO helps as a service agency to assist them in raising and receiving funds, and in relaying news from the field to all persons interested in their ministry. WE GO works to raise missions consciousness through coordinating missionary conferences in churches; providing mission interpreters to speak to classes and study groups; and leading visits or voluntary work/ministry trips to foreign fields. WE GO acts as a missions Board for serious, evangelical Christians who are called by God to missionary endeavors. It also serves as a Board for foreign nationals called by God to work within their own countries and peoples. It is also the sponsoring agency for the Lanka Bible Institute in Kandy, Sri Lanka, which is the foremost training center for men and women seeking full-time Christian service in evangelism, pastoring, counseling, and Christian education in that nation.

Founding Date: 1974

Staff: 4

Membership: 25

Publications:
Periodic newsletters

Meetings:
Coordinate missionary conferences for local churches

1547. Weber Center

Roman Catholic
June Secor, O.P. Director
1257 East Siena Heights Drive
Adrian, Michigan 49221
(517) 265-5135

Weber Center, a retreat and conference center in Adrian, Michigan, offers retreats, workshops, and seminars for all men and women interested in their own formation and the formation of a human and just society. An additional program, the Institute in Human Growth and Development, is designed for on-going formation of men/women religious, clerics, and lay persons engaged in ministry. Set in a vibrant community atmosphere, the program enables participants to reflect on and to realize their own capabilities to grow spiritually, psychologically, and socially. A professionally competent and sensitive staff offers programs in theology, career development, human growth, and creative leisure skills. Community-centered prayer and liturgies are integrated in an affirming and growth-producing environment.

Staff: 10

Membership: 300

Publications:
Newsletter, quarterly
Brochures

Meetings:
Conferences, workshops, and retreats conducted at Weber Center all year long
Initiating a "Weber on Wheels" program for the states of Florida, South Carolina, Illinois, Arizona, and California

1548. WEFMinistries, Inc.

Nondenominational
Henry J. Hiejermans, General Director
Post Office Box 307
Langhorne, Pennsylvania 19047
(215) 752-1818

WEFMinistries is a church planting and developing organization with outreach in 18 countries. Though all of its personnel are actively engaged in this ministry, other contributing ministries are carried on as well. The agency seeks to organize believers into local congregations which do not maintain an organizational relationship with the mission but function independently as soon as possible.

Founding Date: 1959

Staff: 10

Membership: 170

Publications:
Bridge, for North American constituents
All manner of publications in the various fields

Radio/TV Programs:
Operate two FM Transmitters in Italy (in Trieste and Florence)
Broadcast at least 16 hours daily

Former Name:
(1979) Worldwide European Fellowship

1549. The Wesleyan Church, General Department of Education and the Ministry

The Wesleyan Church
Lee M. Haines, General Secretary
Post Office Box 2000
Marion, Indiana 46952
(317) 674-3301 ext. 155

The General Department of Education and the Ministry of The Wesleyan Church maintains liaison with the denomination's six colleges and coordinates their programs; administers general church financial aid programs for ministerial education; maintains relationships with five approved seminaries; represents the denomination in all matters related to military chaplaincies; and supervises the program of continuing education for ordained ministers in The Wesleyan Church.

Staff: 2

Meetings:
Biennial conferences in each institution

Former Name:
(1980) Department of Educational Institutions of The Wesleyan Church

1550. The Wesleyan Church, General Department of Extension and Evangelism

The Wesleyan Church
Joe C. Sawyer, General Secretary
Post Office Box 2000
Marion, Indiana 46952
(317) 674-3301

The ultimate objective of The Wesleyan Church is to fulfill the Great Commission of the Lord Jesus Christ by sharing with all mankind the good news and glorious experience of full salvation. To this end, The Wesleyan Church, through its General Department of Extension and Evangelism and General Department of World Missions, endeavors to: evangelize the nation of earth, seeking salvation of the individual and the entire sanctification of believers as the primary responsibility of all missionary work; gather the converts into churches and enlist them in the work of God's kingdom; place well-qualified and Spirit-filled pastors over the churches, giving special emphasis to the training of workers and leaders for the church; share the benefits of the gospel, and to facilitate evangelistic work through specialized ministries such as medical, educational, literary, and benevolent work; and promote, in accordance with Scriptural and indigenous principles, the growth and development of the churches in each field or area to a church body that is spiritually mature, well organized, financially responsible, and missionary minded, and that can assume its place in The Wesleyan Church.

Publications:
Home Missions Impact
The Herald
THe Broken Tomahawk

Radio/TV Programs:
The Wesleyan Hour, an international radio broadcast aired on about 160 stations around the world

Meetings:
4-5 conferences and seminars on Evangelism, Discipling, and Leadership at Marion, Indiana

1551. The Wesleyan Church, General Department of World Missions

The Wesleyan Church
Dr. Robert N. Lytle, General Secretary
Post Office Box 2000
Marion, Indiana 46952
(317) 674-3301

The General Department of World Missions of The Wesleyan Church exists for the purpose of opening and administering overseas mission units, recruiting and deploying missionaries, promoting said mission program among the homeland constituency of 1,812 churches, and raising adequate mission funds. To fulfill its purpose the department communicates through 18 duly-elected mission coordinators who are stationed overseas and who represent some two dozen countries and approximately 48 language groups. The home office maintains specialized operations for international travel, shipping, recruitment, bookkeeping and finance, communications, and local church ministries.

Founding Date: 1968
Staff: 17

Membership: 228 missionaries
Publications:
The Wesleyan World, monthly
Wesleyanagram, quarterly

1552. The Wesleyan Church, Local Church Education

The Wesleyan Church
David L. Keith, General Secretary
Post Office Box 2000
Marion, Indiana 46952
(317) 674-3301

The General Department of Local Church Education of The Wesleyan Church is responsible, on the general level, to carry out the objectives of The Wesleyan Church for Christian education in such phases as Sunday schools, vacation Bible schools, leadership training, membership training, children's church, weekday church schools and day care centers, released time classes, music ministries, and the promotion of Christian family life. The department is under the jurisdiction of the General Board of Administration and the supervision of the General Superintendent over the Commission on Christian Education, and is administered by the General Secretary of Local Church Education.

Staff: 13
Publications:
Sunday school curriculum and take home papers
Meetings:
BYF Chaparrals (one each at Houghton, New York; Marion, Indiana; Glorieta, New Mexico; St. Simons Island, Georgia)
Advance (annually, 1982 at Indianapolis)
Wesleyan Day (annual Sunday school rally — Cobo Hall, Detroit, Michigan)
Good News, (one in Texas and one in Pennsylvania)
ICEA (Detroit, Michigan)

1553. The Wesleyan Church, Youth Department

The Wesleyan Church
Keith W. Drury, General Secretary of Youth
1135 West 51st Street
Marion, Indiana 46952

Mailing Address
Post Office Box 2000
Marion, Indiana 46952
(317) 674-3301

The Youth Department of The Wesleyan Church organizes and leads the youth work ministry of The Wesleyan Church worldwide. It operates the International Wesleyan Youth Convention every four years, and produces materials, manuals, training, and programming resources for youth ministries, children's ministries, and ministries to singles, collegians, and young marrieds.

1554. Wesleyan Indian Ministries (WIM)

The Wesleyan Church
Mr. Leston Phipps, General Director
Drawer 891
Hot Springs, South Dakota 57747
(605) 745-4077

Wesleyan Indian Ministries operates 25-30 Indian chapels or preaching points on various reservations. Several Christian academies, along with Brainerd Indian School, are also operated by WIM, and all minister and serve the American Indian. This organization maintains a radio broadcast called *Decision Time Radio,* which is aired on more than 200 stations across North America.

Founding Date: 1948
Staff: 60
Publications:
Call of the American Red Man, quarterly
Radio/TV Programs:
Decision Time Radio
Meetings:
Annual meeting, Hot Springs, South Dakota, fourth week of June
Former Names:
Brainerd Indian School
Decision Time Ministries
Wesleyan Indian Missions

1555. West Shore Christian Fellowship

Nondenominational
Daniel S. Light and William A. McPhail, Co-Pastors
635 Lake Shore Boulevard
Muskegon, Michigan 49444
(616) 733-0342 or 739-8284

West Shore Christian Fellowship is a community of believers committed to New Testament Christianity, endeavoring to practice Christ's original formula for authentic discipleship, namely to "take up the cross"—which means "death" to one's self-will in preference to God's will—and "follow him," which involves explicit obedience to the directives of Jesus as presented in the New Testament. West Shore Christian Fellowship emphasizes a "body life" concept of the Christian congregation where mutual love and support among the members is essential. Services of worship are conducted in sensitivity to the direction of the Holy Spirit. The congregation is interracial. The Church sponsors a Christian school, grades K-12, as well as a nationwide television and publications ministry. The present membership includes individuals from approximately 30 denominational backgrounds.

Staff: 15
Publications:
Kerygma, a monthly inspirational magazine
Radio/TV Programs:
2 radio programs: *West Shore Perspectives,* daily, and *West Shore Sermon of the Week,* weekly
New Wine, TV program weekly on PTL satellite network
Meetings:
Irregular meetings

1556. Western Catholic Union (WCU)

Roman Catholic
John B. Heinz, Supreme President
906 WCU Building
Quincy, Illinois 62301
(217) 223-9721

The Western Catholic Union is a Fraternal Benefit Society founded in Quincy, Illinois. In addition to providing Life and Hospitalization Insurance for Catholic families, the Western Catholic Union also participates in fraternal and spiritual activities such as: Catholic Communications Foundation assistance; weekly Masses; pilgrimages; bus trips; distribution of auto decals; Communion Sundays; Memorial Services; and dances, picnics, and other social activities. The Western Catholic Union also sponsors the WCU Retirement Home, a 94-apartment retirement home for its members, Catholics, and others.

Founding Date: 1877

Staff: 25
Membership: 28,000
Publications:
8 monthly bulletin editions
4 quarterly publications
Radio/TV Programs:
Radio and TV programs about fraternal and spiritual activities
Meetings:
Meetings, spiritual, and fraternal activities
Former Name:
Supreme Council of the Western Catholic Union

1557. Westminster Biblical Missions (WBM)

Independent Presbyterian
Earl E. Pinckney, General Secretary
203 South Lincoln Avenue
Tampa, Florida 33609
Mailing Address
Post Office Box 18976
Tampa, Florida 33679
(813) 879-2209

Westminster Biblical Missions was born out of a Macedonian call from both Korea and Pakistan. Two groups in these countries needed aid at about the same time in 1973 to establish and maintain seminaries for the training of their young people. WBM is committed to use its influence for maintaining the purity of the church in its testimony both at home and on the foreign fields. It provides valuable information to churches and individuals who are desirous of being true to Christ, the head of the Church, in opposition to apostasy. At the same time the mission is committed to maintaining fellowship based on mutual love and confidence with national Christians through cooperation in establishing self-supporting, self-propagating and self-governing churches. This frees the nationals from the financial pressures and antagonisms which other methods often involve. The ultimate goal is for the nationals, free from paternalism, to develop sufficiently to carry on without the fellowship, should this become necessary.

Founding Date: 1973
Staff: 15
Membership: 12
Publications:
The WCC—A 1981 Update, Robert S. Rapp
Communism in South Korea, Robert S. Rapp

A Systematic Theology, Robert S. Rapp
Occasional publications

1558. The Westminster Press

United Presbyterian Church in the USA
Robert D. McIntyre, General Manager
925 Chestnut Street
Philadelphia, Pennsylvania 19107
(215) 928-2700

The Westminster Press, the publishing arm of the United Presbyterian Church in the USA, is mandated to publish and distribute a variety of books reflecting diverse and varied opinions and viewpoints. These include works that contribute to theological and Biblical scholarship, books for ministers and lay study, and books for children. The children's book program includes both fiction and non-fiction, and features team books, career books, and high interest/low reading level books. Major areas of importance in the religious book program are Biblical studies, theology, ethics, reference works, pastoral care, practical ministry, and Bible study and inspiration for laypeople.

Staff: 26 exempt; 60 non-exempt

1559. White Wing Publishing House and Press

Church of God of Prophecy
M. A. Tomlinson, General Overseer
North Keith Street
Cleveland, Tennessee 37311

Mailing Address
Post Office Box 1039
Cleveland, Tennessee 37311
(615) 476-8536

The White Wing Publishing House is the printing division of the Church of God of Prophecy and exists for the specific purpose of supplying literature for the organization and the merchandising of other general evangelical Christian literature.

Publications:

> *White Wing Messenger,* the official organ of the Church
> Sunday School Literature
> Tracts; various other publications

Radio/TV Programs:

> A weekly radio program, *The Voice of Salvation*
> Periodic TV specials

Meetings:

> Meetings in various locations, basically by districts and states

1560. William Carey Library Publishers

Nondenominational
Roger Schrage, General Manager
1705 North Sierra Bonita Avenue
Pasadena, California 91104
(213) 798-0819

The William Carey Library publishes books, pamphlets, and cassettes concerned with the Christian mission. Its books are of a technical and scholarly nature; they frequently explore cross-cultural communication and anthropological and social-scientific implications of spreading Christianity and provide the reader with careful case studies of foreign countries. The Library publishes about 25 books annually.

Publications:

> 125 books in print

1561. Wisconsin Evangelical Lutheran Synod, Board for Parish Education

Wisconsin Evangelical Lutheran Synod
Donald H. Zimmerman, Executive Secretary
3614 West North Avenue
Milwaukee, Wisconsin 53208
(414) 445-4030

The Board for Parish Education is responsible for encouraging, advising, and aiding congregations of the Wisconsin Synod in establishing and maintaining parish elementary schools and Lutheran high schools. The Board also supervises a system of Synod-wide school visitation. The Board is responsible for the production of religious curriculum materials for schools, Sunday schools, and Bible study classes.

Membership: 360 parish schools; 19 high schools
Publications:

> *The Lutheran Educator,* quarterly

Meetings:

> A variety of meetings per year

1562. Wisconsin Evangelical Lutheran Synod, Board for World Missions*

Wisconsin Evangelical Lutheran

Rev. Edgar Hoenecke, Executive Secretary
12367 Lomica Drive
San Diego, California 92128
(714) 487-7522

The Board for World Missions is the division of the Wisconsin Evangelical Lutheran Synod which is charged with the administration and expansion of the missionary activity of this body in all the world. At present, the Board is active on the five major continents, with mission staff now numbering about 75. Evangelistic work is conducted in 14 countries; medical dispensary work in three. It supports four Bible institutes and seminaries for training nationals for independent, indigenous missionary activity in their own cultures. These seminaries are in Zambia; Japan; Hong Kong; Medellin, Colombia; and El Paso, Texas.

Staff: 75

1563. Wisconsin Evangelical Lutheran Synod, Commission on Higher Education

Wisconsin Evangelical Lutheran Synod

Rev. Robert J. Voss, Executive Secretary
3512 West North Avenue
Milwaukee, Wisconsin 53208

The Commission on Higher Education of the Wisconsin Evangelical Lutheran Synod supervises the worker training institutions' educational programs to ensure that they make the maximum contribution to the Synod's objectives. The Commission is responsible for staffing the schools, planning and recommending additional physical facilities, administering a worker-training system, establishing policy, and approving programs for recruitment of and aid to students. Other activities include establishing policy, long-range planning, and consulting with the boards of control of the educational institutions.

1564. Wisconsin Evangelical Lutheran Synod, General Board for Home Missions

Wisconsin Evangelical Lutheran Synod

Rev. Norman W. Berg, Executive Secretary
3512 West North Avenue
Milwaukee, Wisconsin 53208
(414) 445-4030

The activities of the Wisconsin Evangelical Lutheran Synod General Board for Home Missions include coordination and administration of domestic mission activity of the Wisconsin Evangelical Lutheran Synod through its 14 district mission boards in the United States, Canada, and Antigua. These district boards supervise the mission outreach of 279 subsidized congregations in 48 states, three provinces of Canada, and in Antigua, as well as campus and institutional mission activity. The objectives of the Board for Home Missions are: to reach the unchurched with the Gospel of Jesus Christ primarily by the establishment of mission congregations; to conserve the membership of the Wisconsin Evangelical Lutheran Synod; and to extend spiritual service to those who share their confessional concerns.

Staff: 14 lay; 15 clerical

1565. Wisconsin Evangelical Lutheran Synod, Public Relations Committee

Wisconsin Evangelical Lutheran Synod

Rev. James P. Schaefer, Director of Public Information
3512 West North Avenue
Milwaukee, Wisconsin 53208
(414) 445-4030

The Public Relations Committee of the Wisconsin Evangelical Lutheran Synod is responsible for relating the Synod's activities to the general public and promoting public relations among the districts. The Committee keeps abreast of national legislation regarding the separation of church and state that would interfere with the preaching of the Gospel, and responds to such legislation if necessary.

Staff: 2 lay; 3 clerical

1566. Wisconsin Evangelical Lutheran Synod, Special Ministries Board*

Wisconsin Evangelical Lutheran Synod

Alfons Woldt, Executive Secretary
3512 West North Avenue
Milwaukee, Wisconsin 53208

The Special Ministries Board of the Wisconsin Evangelical Lutheran Synod has many varied activities consisting of: providing for the spiritual welfare of the Synod's members in the armed forces; maintaining a campus ministry, which gathers the names and addresses of students attending schools away from home and directs them to the nearest church of the Synod, supplies the local pastor with student's names, prepares and distributes suitable literature, and also counsels, assists, and serves as advisor in any matters relative to students' work; counseling and service to a ministry for the mentally retarded, to institutional ministries, and social service ministries.

Membership: 4 lay; 4 clerical

1567. Women's American ORT

Jewish

Mr. Nathan Gould, National Executive Director
1250 Broadway
New York, New York 10001
(212) 594-8500

Women's American ORT represents and advances the program and philosophy of ORT (Organization for Rehabilitation through Training) among the women of the American Jewish community through membership and educational activities. As the largest of voluntary groups in the 40-nation "ORT family," it supports materially the global vocational and technical education operations of ORT in some 800 schools on five continents; contributes to the American Jewish community through participation in its authorized campaigns and through general education to help raise the level of Jewish consciousness among American Jewish women; through its American Affairs program, works to achieve quality public education in the United States, to upgrade the image and performance of vocational schools and to promote the concepts of "career education" and the "comprehensive school"; and supports the innovative "breakthrough-in-education" Bramson ORT Technical Institute in New York City.

Founding Date: 1927
Staff: 50
Membership: 145,000
Publications:
REPORTER, quarterly

Radio/TV Programs:
So You Want To Be, monthly radio show on WHN (AM), New York City
Meetings:
Biennial conventions

1568. Women's League for Conservative Judaism (AWL)

Jewish/Conservative

Mrs. Murry Kweller, President
48 East 74th Street
New York, New York 10021
(212) 628-1600

Women's League for Conservative Judaism is the parent body of approximately 800 Sisterhoods of Conservative Synagogues in the United States, Canada, Puerto Rico, Mexico, and women's groups in Israel and other parts of the world, with a total membership of more than 200,000 women. The League is international in scope, giving guidance and service not only to its own Sisterhoods, but to lay and professional Jewish leaders throughout the world who are striving to enrich Jewish life in their communities. It is dedicated to the perpetuation of traditional Judaism in our modern society and the translation of its high ideals into practice through a living Judaism in the home, the Synagogue, and the community. The League believes that Judaism is an all-embracing way of life to guide our daily thoughts and actions. The League is associated with The Jewish Theological Seminary of America and works closely with the United Synagogue of America and the World Council of Synagogues.

Founding Date: 1917
Staff: 20
Membership: 200,000
Publications:
Women's League Outlook, quarterly
Ba O'lam-In the World, 6 times a year
Meetings:
Biennial convention
28 annual regional spring conferences
Interim conferences on special subjects
Former Names:
(1947) Women's League of the United Synagogue of America
(1973) National Women's League of the United Synagogue of America

1569. Women's League for Israel (WLI)

Jewish

Mrs. Harry M. Wiles, President
1860 Broadway
New York, New York 10023
(212) 245-8742

A voluntary women's service organization, the Women's League for Israel operates through 36 Chapters — 23 in the Metropolitan area of New York, including Connecticut and New Jersey, and 13 in the State of Florida. The League has built and maintains Y-Style Homes in the principal cities of Israel. They are designed to help young, disadvantaged girls secure the necessary training to become useful, contributing citizens of the society in which they live. More than 100,000 young people have been helped through these homes. At the Hebrew University of Jerusalem, the Women's League for Israel has built dormitories for women students on both the Givat Ram and Mt. Scopus Campus; the Students' Cafeteria; and the Student Center. WLI has endowed a teaching chair in Sociology, and has established the Women's League for Israel Scholarship Endowment Fund, with scholarships awarded to worthy and needy students, as well as the Book Endowment Fund in the School of Social Work Library.

Founding Date: 1928

Staff: 6

Membership: 5,000

Publications:
Newsletters

Meetings:
Monthly meetings of Chapters and the Executive Board

Former Name: Women's League for Palestine

1570. Women's Ordination Conference (WOC)

Roman Catholic

Office Ministerial Team
34 Monica Street
Rochester, New York 14619
(716) 436-6910

Women's Ordination Conference has been created to hasten the day when women will be ordained in the Roman Catholic Church within the context of a new ministry. WOC's tasks include the coordination of local and regional groups functioning as a clearing house for support services and the continuation of dialogue with Bishops. It is the hope of WOC to minister with individuals who believe in this issue, whether they aspire personally to the priesthood or not; to offer support, guidance, and resources; to strengthen the women's movement within the Church; and to support all women who thirst for justice and liberation.

Founding Date: 1975

Staff: 2

Membership: 1,600

Publications:
New Woman/New Church, bimonthly newspaper
Various feminist theological publication

Meetings:
Local meetings annually
Retreats, upon request

1571. Women's Theological Coalition of the Boston Theological Institute

Interdenominational

Carole R. Bohn, Coordinator
210 Herrick Road
Newton Centre, Massachusetts 02159
(617) 969-2946

The Women's Theological Coalition is a standing committee of the Boston Theological Institute. It is served by a half-time staff, led by the Women's Committee, and offers a variety of resources, programs, services, and opportunities. The Coalition is designed to promote the cause of women in theological education and works to serve the needs of the over 600 women students of the BTI, as well as women faculty and staff, and community women. The WTC maintains a syllabi/bibliography service that provides copies of material on women in religion from across the country. Over 55 syllabi and bibliographies from courses on women in religion are currently on file, with additional material constantly being added. In addition there are monographs, periodicals, newsletters, and other communications in the area of women in the church/theology/ministry, as well as limited job listings and financial aid information.

Membership:
Approximately 700 women students in the BTI member schools
50 women faculty

Publications:
    Affirmations, monthly
    Placement of Women in Religious Studies,
      bimonthly

Meetings:
    Monthly planning meetings at one of the member schools
    A variety of programs on women's issues

1572. WORD, Inc.

Nondenominational
Jarrell McCracken, President
Post Office Box 1790
Waco, Texas 76703
(817) 772-7650

WORD, Inc., began as a religious record company and has since grown into a diversified communications company, the largest of its kind in the United States. WORD releases albums on four labels of its own—WORD, MYRRH, DAYSPRING, and CANAAN, and distributes about a dozen other labels. The company publishes music with imprints of WORD, MYRRH, CANAANLAND, SACRED, and RODE-HEAVER, and books with imprints of Word Books, Key-Word Books, Thesis Books, and distributes Chosen Books. In its newest product line, WORD has Educational Products that include cassettes and study packages, other study materials, and the seven-film series "Focus on the Family" featuring Dr. James Dobson.

Founding Date: 1951

1573. The Word Foundation, Inc.

Nondenominational
Post Office Box 769
Forest Hills, New York 11375

The Word Foundation publishes, promotes, and distributes the four unique spiritual guidance books by Harold W. Percival: *Thinking and Destiny, Masonry and Its Symbols, Man and Woman and Child,* and *Democracy is Self Government.*

1574. Word of Life Fellowship, Inc.*

Nondenominational

Jack Wyrtzen, President
Schroon Lake, New York 12870
(518) 532-7111

The purpose of the Word of Life Fellowship is reaching youth with the Gospel of Jesus Christ.

Membership: 110 lay; 40 clerical

Publications:
    50 religious books
    5 informational newsletters

Radio/TV Programs:
    2 radio broadcasts, 1 daily and 1 weekly
    1 TV program, weekly

Meetings:
    Bible conferences
    Youth Seminars
    Evangelistic meetings year round on 5 continents

1575. Word of Truth Productions

Nondenominational
Bryant G. Wood, Business Manager
Post Office Box 288
Ballston Spa, New York 12020
(518) 885-7757

The purpose of Word of Truth Productions is to produce and distribute material on biblical archaeology. Word of Truth Productions publishes a quarterly journal, produces a weekly radio program, loans out slide-tape programs, and sells books and charts.

Staff: 3

Membership: 3,000 subscribers

Publications:
    Bible and Spade, a quarterly digest of biblical archaeology

Radio/TV Programs:
    Weekly 15-minute radio program, *The Stones Cry Out*

1576. Words of the Gospel

Mennonite Brethren
Donald F. MacNeill, Director of Media Ministries
4812 East Butler
Fresno, California 93727
(209) 251-8681

Words of the Gospel is the name of a weekly 30-minute radio program, but also represents the

Media Department of the Mennonite Brethren Conference (United States). Its ministries include Radio, Cassettes, Literature, Spiritual Counseling, and Musical Public Appearances. A subsidiary, M/B Media, is their production Department. They offer a 16-track recording studio, and cassette duplication and blank cassette services to churches and others. A full line of audio production equipment is available.

Founding Date: 1965

Staff: 12

Radio/TV Programs:
Radio, 30-minute weekly

Legal Name:
Mennonite Brethren Media Ministries, Inc.

1577. The Workers of Our Lady of Mount Carmel, Inc.

Roman Catholic

Joseph Lomangino, President
380 South 5th Street
Lindenhurst, New York 11757

Mailing Address
Post Office Box 606
Lindenhurst, New York 11757
(516) 226-4408

The Workers of Our Lady of Mount Carmel is a tax exempt, non-profit religious organization dedicated to the promotion of messages reportedly given by the Blessed Virgin Mary in her alleged apparitions to four young girls in the tiny mountain village of San Sebastian de Garabandal, Spain, from 1961 to 1965.

Founding Date: 1968

Staff: 2

Membership: 40

Publications:
Garabandal — The Message of Our Lady of Mount Carmel, quarterly

Former Name: Our Lady of Mount Carmel, Inc.

1578. World Challenge, Inc./David Wilkerson Crusades

Evangelical

David R. Wilkerson, President
Post Office Box 260
Lindale, Texas 75771
(214) 882-5591

World Challenge is a ministry dedicated to winning lost souls and ministering to those who are dominated by life-controlling problems. Crusades are held throughout the nation during the year by Mr. Wilkerson and the Crusade Team. Outreach Teams go into major cities to concentrate on reaching the street people and others whom the local churches usually do not succeed in reaching. World Challenge is also dedicated to producing Christian films dealing with today's problems.

Staff: 40

Publications:
Monthly newsletters

Meetings:
Approximately 80-100 crusades nationwide

Former Name: David Wilkerson Youth Crusades

1579. World Concern/Crista International

Interdenominational

Arthur Beals, Executive Director
19303 Fremont Avenue North
Seattle, Washington 98133

Mailing Address
Post Office Box 33000
Seattle, Washington 98133
(206) 546-7201

World Concern is a Christian humanitarian relief and development agency specializing in emergency relief and self-help projects in the Third World. These projects include agricultural development, water irrigation, public health, community organizing, cottage industry, and marketing assistance for craft items. World Concerns assigns both skilled and non-skilled personnel to projects around the world for terms ranging from three months to five years. The agency is heavily involved with the shipment of medicines, medical supplies, vegetable seeds, and clothing. WORLDCRAFT is a division of World Concern responsible for the import of Third World crafts and cottage industry products to the United States for marketing. World Concern is supported entirely by voluntary contributions from individuals and churches. Because of a heavy reliance on the use of volunteers in its programs, World Concern is able to maintain low overhead in operational costs. World Concern is a member of the Evangelical Council for Financial Accountability, the Evangelical Foreign Mission Association, and the Evangelical Press Association.

Founding Date: 1973
Staff: 90 overseas field workers
Publications:
>*World Concern Update,* monthly

Radio/TV Programs:
>One major TV documentary relating to world hunger, poverty, and injustice each year
>30-minute TV documentaries on specific issues or world trouble spots produced to assist with public education and fund raising

Meetings:
>"Futures Workshops" conducted on a request basis

1580. World Conference on Religion and Peace (WCRP)

Dr. Homer A. Jack, Secretary General
777 United Nations Plaza
New York, New York 10017
(212) 687-2163

The World Conference on Religion and Peace is an organization involved in multi-religious dialogue and action for world peace and justice.

Membership: 2,000
Publications:
>*Religion for Peace,* three times a year
>*WCRP Reports,* on UN issues

Meetings:
>World congress or assembly every 4-5 years
>Regional assemblies occasionally

1581. World Council of Churches

Interdenominational
Dr. Keith R. Bridston, Executive Director
475 Riverside Drive, Room 1062
New York, New York 10115
(212) 870-2533

The World Council of Churches is a fellowship of churches which confess the Lord Jesus Christ as God and Saviour according to the Scriptures, and therefore seek to fulfill together their common calling to the glory of the one God, Father, Son, and Holy Spirit. Programs and activities are carried out through units: on Faith and Witness—Faith and Order, World Mission and Evangelism, Church and

Society, and Dialogue with People of Living Faiths and Ideologies; on Justice and Service—Churches Participation in Development, International Affairs, Program to Combat Racism, and Interchurch Aid; and on Education and Renewal—Education, General and Church Youth, Lay, Women, and Renewal Groups.

Founding Date: 1948
Membership:
>301 member communions around the world

Publications:
>*One World,* monthly
>*The Ecumenical Review,* quarterly
>*International Review of Mission,* quarterly
>*Study Encounter,* quarterly
>*Risk,* quarterly
>*Ecumenical Press Service,* weekly
>*Ecumenical Courier,* quarterly

1582. World Evangelical Fellowship (WEF)

Evangelical
Waldron Scott, General Secretary
Post Office Box 670
Colorado Springs, Colorado 80901
(303) 635-1612

The purpose of the World Evangelical Fellowship is to promote identity, unity, and cooperation within the global evangelical community. WEF does this by developing national associations of evangelicals on all six continents and by organizing international commissions in areas of evangelical concern.

Founding Date: 1951
Membership: 44 national bodies
Publications:
>*Global Report,* bimonthly
>*Evangelical Review of Theology,* a scholarly journal, twice a year

Meetings:
>6-12 meetings a year in various parts of the world

Former Name: World's Evangelical Alliance

1583. World Evangelistic Enterprise Corporation

Nondenominational

Mike Maddex, President
2348 Troy Road
Springfield, Ohio 45504
(513) 399-7837

World Evangelistic Enterprise Corporation operates a nondenominational, non-profit, and non-commercial Christian radio station and an evening Bible Institute affiliated with the Evangelical Teacher Training Association; and supports a missionary couple in Sao Paolo, Brazil.

Staff: 11 lay; 2 clerical

Radio/TV Programs:
 1 TV program and several radio programs

Meetings:
 1 meeting a year

1584. World Gospel Crusades, Inc.

Nondenominational

Dr. Joe A. Rogers, President
Post Office Box 3
Upland, California 91786
(714) 982-1564

World Gospel Crusades has a threefold vision: to proclaim the message of Christ through the Word of God in printed form; to demonstrate the compassion of Christ by helping to provide the necessities of life for impoverished people of the world; and to challenge and train young people for the fulfillment of this vision. This vision is being fulfilled through the distribution of Scriptures, Bible correspondence courses, youth teams, and Mercy Airlift.

Founding Date: 1949

Staff: 25

Publications:
 Crusades, bimonthly
 Quarterly missionary prayer letters

Meetings:
 Lend assistance in conferences upon invitation

1585. World Gospel Mission (WGM)

Interdenominational

Dr. Thomas H. Hermiz, President
3783 State Road 18 East
Marion, Indiana 46952

Mailing Address
Post Office Box WGM
Marion, Indiana 46952
(317) 664-7331

The purpose of World Gospel Mission, in obedience to the Great Commission (Matthew 28:18-20) and in the power of the Holy Spirit (Acts 1:8), is to proclaim the good news of full salvation through faith in Jesus Christ. World Gospel Mission is an interdenominational missionary organization with 335 missionaries and homeland personnel serving in 15 countries of the world. International headquarters is in Marion, Indiana. Men With Vision work crusades offer an opportunity for men and women to work on a mission field with nationals and missionaries for one to three weeks. Volunteers In Action offers two weeks to six months of mission exposure to young people for the purpose of gaining knowledge and seeking guidance. The Prayer Ministries department has more than 1,000 prayer bands (children — Kids' Kadets, youth, and adult) and 5,000 prayer affiliates — individuals committed to prayer for missions. In addition, several hundred shut-ins carry a special burden for the health of the missionaries.

Founding Date: 1910

Staff: 717

Publications:
 Call to Prayer, official publication, 10 issues per year
 Memorial Supplement, sent to Stewardship Department constituency
 Direct Mail, bimonthly information sheet sharing particular projects of a financial nature

Radio/TV Programs:
 TV — Brazil, Kenya, Bolivia
 Radio — Brazil, Bolivia, Kenya, Haiti, Peniel Missions

Meetings:
 Many various crusades, seminars, retreats, celebrations, and meetings are held throughout the year

1586. World Home Bible League

Interdenominational

William Ackerman, International Director
16801 Van Dam Road
South Holland, Illinois 60473
(312) 331-2094

The World Home Bible League is an international and interdenominational Bible distribution agency. It distributes Scriptures through churches, missionaries, and lay workers in more than 70 different nations of the world and in more than 169 different languages. The World Home Bible League is a service organization. The World Home Bible League publishes a large number of tribal dialect Scriptures produced by leading missionary translators affiliated with Wycliffe Bible Translators, Lutheran Bible Translators, and others. The League also publishes Church Growth materials.

Founding Date: 1938

Staff: 100

Membership: 180,000 mailing list

Publications:
The Sower, bimonthly

Meetings:
Pastors' conferences

Former Name: American Home Bible League

1587. World Impact, Inc.

Nondenominational
Dr. Keith W. Philips, President
2001 South Vermont Avenue
Los Angeles, California 90007
(213) 735-1137

World Impact is a Christian missions organization dedicated to bringing God's love to the ghettos of America. The activities include children's and teenager's Bible clubs; adult Bible studies; tutoring and counseling; providing emergency food and clothing distribution; and ministering to the needs of the whole person. World Impact has as its purpose to know Christ and to make Him known, to share His love and to build disciples for Jesus Christ in the ghetto.

Staff: 106

Membership: 21,000 mailing list

Publications:
Bulletin, monthly
Monthly prayer letters

1588. World Library Publications, Inc.*

Nondenominational
Dorine Kaps, Manager
2145 Central Parkway
Cincinnati, Ohio 45214
(513) 421-1090

World Library Publications now publishes the *We Worship* seasonal missal; the *People's Mass Book;* a vast repertoire of choral music; organ music; choral Masses; descant books; a religious education program from grades 5-12; two programs for children's celebrations; and numerous folk collections and records. World Library has introduced to the folk field composers Joe Wise, Jack Miffleton, Sebastian Temple, Neil Blunt, Tom Parker, and others whose music is being sung in churches throughout the country. One of the best-known and loved composers World Library has introduced is Rev. Lucien Deiss, whose *Biblical Hymns and Psalms, Vols. I and II* have become an important part of the American Catholic liturgy. Father Deiss' *Spirit and Song of the New Liturgy* is an invaluable guide to the "how's and why's" of the post Vatican II changes in the Church. Other liturgical publications include ritual books (Baptism, Confirmation, Marriage, Christian Burial); cantor books; and themes, prayers, and intercessions. For Protestant worship, World Library provides *This Week* and *Models for Ministers.*

Publications:
Liturgy and music — approximately 480

Meetings:
12-15

1589. World Literature Crusade

Nondenominational
Dr. Jack McAlister
Post Office Box 1313
Studio City, California 91604
(213) 341-7870

World Literature Crusade sponsors Every Home Crusades, a systematic effort to place a printed witness of Christ in every home in a national and, ultimately, in every home in the world. It offers messages for children and adults and a follow-up Bible correspondence course. Distribution is carried out in cooperation with 415 different denominations and organizations.

Founding Date: 1946

Publications:
Everybody, monthly
30 books

Radio/TV Programs:
TV specials

1590. World Methodist Council (WMC)

Methodist
Joe Hale, General Secretary
39 Lake Shore Drive
Lake Junaluska, North Carolina 28745

Mailing Address
Post Office Box 518
Lake Junaluska, North Carolina 28745
(704) 456-9432

The World Methodist Council is a worldwide association of the churches in the Methodist tradition. Organized in London, it exists to give cohesion and unity to the witness of Methodist/Wesleyan people throughout the world. The 62 member churches are located in 90 countries, with a total constituency of 21,000,000 members. The Council is composed of 500 members, and the officers include a representative eight-member presidium. The headquarters of the Council is at Lake Junaluska, North Carolina, with an ancillary office in Geneva, Switzerland. One of the overarching purposes of the World Methodist Council is to "deepen the fellowship" of the Methodist people over the barriers of race, nationality, color, and language. The Council does its work through 15 standing world committees concerned with such matters as social and international affairs, bilateral ecumenical conversations, evangelism, and worship and liturgy.

Founding Date: 1881
Staff: 3
Membership: 62 Methodist Churches in 90 countries
Publications:
World Parish, 9 times a year
Meetings:
Major worldwide conference every 5 years
Annual Executive Committee Meetings

1591. World Methodist Historical Society

World Methodist Council
Dr. John H. Ness
Post Office Box 460
Mont Alto, Pennsylvania 17237
(717) 749-5132

The World Methodist Historical Society is an international agency organized to encourage the collecting, preservation, and dissemination of Methodist and Wesleyan history. The WMHS is an auxiliary of the World Methodist Council, an association of 60 Methodist-related denominations around the world. The WMHS encourages the publication and development of regional conferences for the study of history. Although it meets once in five years for business, its activities are supervised by an international executive committee. Regional conferences are generally held yearly. It counsels the World Methodist Council in its archival needs, and through that body to its constituent members. It is a volunteer organization with a non-paid staff. Its support comes from membership dues, grants from several organizations, and one foundation. Its purpose is to encourage the study and preservation of the Wesleyan tradition as it stems from its founder, John Wesley.

Founding Date: 1971
Membership: 215
Publications:
Historical Bulletin, quarterly
Meetings:
April, 1983, England Regional Conference
August 6-10, 1984, Regional Conference, Asbury Theological Seminary, Wilmore, Kentucky
Former Name:
International Methodist Historical Society

1592. World Mission Prayer League, Inc. (WWPL)

Independent Lutheran
Mr. Jonathan Lindell, General Director
232 Clifton Avenue
Minneapolis, Minnesota 55403
(612) 871-6843

The World Mission Prayer League is involved with hundreds of fellow Christians in forming a united witness and service for Christ in Mexico, Bolivia, Ecuador, Hong Kong, India, Pakistan, Nepal, Bangladesh, and Kenya; in forming and strengthening Christian churches in foreign lands by evangelism, Bible teaching, leadership training, radio and TV programs, and publishing and printing literature; and in many kinds of community service in the name of Jesus such as hospitals and medical care, schools and education, agricultural service, and training in industrial arts.

Founding Date: 1937
Membership:
117 lay missionaries
14 clerical missionaries

Publications:

Fellow Workers, monthly

Newsletter, a monthly letter to prayer partners

Radio/TV Programs:

7 45-minute radio programs

Meetings:

3-4 meetings per year overseas

1 missionary candidate Briefing Course per year at Home Office

Former Name:

(1940) South American Mission Prayer League

1593. World Missionary Assistance Plan (World MAP)

Interdenominational

Ralph Mahoney, President

900 North Glenoaks Boulevard

Burbank, California 91502

(213) 843-7233

The World Missionary Assistance Plan is an interdenominational missionary society seeking to extend and build up the body of Christ around the world, focusing on leadership training and support in Third World churches through Spiritual Seminars and *Acts* magazine. It further offers a full range of missionary support services for those who have committed themselves to spiritual renewal. It also supplies a free Tape-A-Month to any missionary who requests these cassettes of rich spiritual inspiration and Bible teaching. In the United States, the society sponsors the annual World MAP Camp Meetings and issues numerous renewal productions, both aimed at restoring the body of Christ to its potential spiritual vitality.

Founding Date: 1960

Staff: 35 staff members; 19 missionaries

Publications:

Acts

Digest

Praise and Prayer Bulletin, monthly

Faith Partners Report, monthly

Tape-A-Month, monthly

Meetings:

15 Spiritual Renewal Seminars in Third World nations in 1981

5 Summer Family Camps (Bible conferences) on the West Coast

1594. World Missionary Evangelism, Inc.*

Nondenominational

John E. Douglas, Sr.

2216 South Vernon

Dallas, Texas 75224

Mailing Address

Post Office Box 232813

Dallas, Texas 75222

World Missionary Evangelism supports native missionaries abroad, and assists schools and orphanages in foreign countries.

Publications:

World Evangelism

1595. World Missionary Press, Inc. (WMP)

Nondenominational

Watson Goodman, President

Post Office Box 120

New Paris, Indiana 46553

(219) 831-2111

World Missionary Press is an evangelical service mission established to publish free Scripture booklets in languages used around the world.

Founding Date: 1961

Staff: 23

Publications:

World Missionary Press News, 6 times per year

Booklets: *Help From Above, Satan vs CHRIST, Who Am I That a King Would Die in My Place?, The Power of God, Wings Over Zion, Let's Praise the Lord!, How To Know God, A Bible Study on Matthew, Meditations in the Psalms, A Bible Study on John, He Is Risen, The Night Before Christmas*

1596. World Missions Fellowship (WMF)

Interdenominational

Robert C. Minter, General Director

Post Office Box 1048

Grants Pass, Oregon 97526

(503) 479-3731

The purpose of World Missions Fellowship is to evangelize and establish all converts in the fellowship of the church of the living God. Children are the heritage of the Mission; hence the primary, though not exclusive, emphasis of the Mission is to reach children and youth with the Gospel of Christ and disciple them in the Holy Scriptures. To attain this purpose, the Mission places trained workers in the fields that God indicates and there they work out a comprehensive program in keeping with needs and opportunities in the following areas: ministries to the fatherless (including orphanages); camps and conferences; day schools and Bible schools; literature and radio (media); evangelism and church planting. The Mission has fields in Ireland (Erie), Japan, Austria, India, and Brazil, and a Christian day school in Grants Pass, Oregon, for grades Kindergarten through 12. The never-ending struggle of children in impoverished lands, the dreadful moral corruption of some societies, bringing blight and ruin to helpless children, is all a strident call to God's children to rise up and meet the task with dedication and dispatch. To such a call WMF has been dedicated for over 30 years.

Founding Date: 1946

Staff: 46

Publications:
Your Children, quarterly

Meetings:
Missions and Bible Conferences in Grants Pass, once a year

Former Name: (1978) World Missions to Children

1597. World Opportunities International

Nondenominational

Dr. Roy McKeown, President
1415 Cahuenga Boulevard
Hollywood, California 90028
(213) 466-7187

World Opportunities International is a non-profit Christian service agency meeting physical and spiritual needs of the desperately poor across America and around the world through four specific programs: Relief and Medical Assistance; Evangelism; Missionary and National Personnel; and Youth Guidance. World Opportunities International assists more than 3,000 missionaries and missionary agencies in more than 90 countries of the world.

Founding Date: 1961

Staff: 20; 40 missionaries overseas

Publications:
Through the Bible, monthly

Radio/TV Programs:
1 hour TV program weekly

1598. World Outreach (USA), Inc.

Interdenominational

Donald B. Crosbie, President
2501 Custer Road
Plano, Texas 75075
(214) 596-4515

World Outreach (USA) seeks to evangelize in two ways: by the direct evangelistic methods of literature distribution, radio follow-up, Bible Correspondence courses, evangelism campaigns, church planting, etc.; and by the training of nationals in residential training centers so that they can go and do the work of direct evangelism themselves. They also sponsor two orphanages.

Founding Date: 1967

Staff: 2

Publications:
The Evidence, bimonthly

1599. World Presbyterian Missions, Inc. *(WPM)

Reformed Presbyterian Church, Evangelical Synod

Rev. Nelson K. Malkus, General Secretary
901 North Broom Street
Wilmington, Delaware 19806
(302) 652-3204

World Presbyterian Missions operates small missions in 11 countries with a view to evangelism, training new believers for leadership, and establishing churches. Its special areas of service include translation, medicine, literacy, and radio broadcasting.

Founding Date: 1957

Staff: 5

Membership: 46 lay; 24 clerical

Radio/TV Programs:
India, Peru, Chile

1600. The World Radio Missionary Fellowship (WRMF)

Nondenominational
Dr. Abe Van Der Puy, President
20201 N.W. 37th Avenue
Miami, Florida 33055
(305) 624-4252

The World Radio Missionary Fellowship owns and operates Radio Station HCJB in Quito, Ecuador. This station includes local AM and FM outlets in Quito, a local FM station in Quayaquil, and an international short-wave station with close to half a million watts of power. Broadcasts in 14 of the world's major languages are beamed to all parts of the world at strategic listening times. The programs are religious and cultural in content. The WRMF also owns and operates two hospitals in Ecuador; a Bible Institute of the Air with more than 20,000 students studying the Bible by radio and correspondence; a print shop; and an evangelism department. In addition, HOXO-AM and FM in Panama and Kumvin, Texas, are affiliated stations.

Founding Date: 1931
Membership: 310
Publications:
   HCJB Radio Log, quarterly
   The President's Letter, quarterly
Radio/TV Programs:
   Thousands of radio programs annually

1601. World Relief Commission (WRC)*

National Association of Evangelicals
Jerry Bottard, President
Post Office Box WRC
Wheaton, Illinois 60187
(212) 783-0556

As a channel of Christian help and hope, World Relief Commission is the official overseas relief arm of the National Association of Evangelicals. WRC is also, by its Board action, the official but not exclusive relief arm of the Evangelical Foreign Missions Association (EFMA), the Interdenominational Foreign Missions Association (IFMA) and the World Evangelical Fellowship (WEF) This wide-ranging recognition represents an official relationship with 85% of all evangelical missionaries in the world and a majority of evangelical national Third World Christian leaders and their churches. The Commission's

outreach covers both emergency relief in times of war and natural disaster and long-range, self-help rehabilitative programs. This ministry of mercy includes: child welfare programs in daycare centers, hospitals, orphanages, blind schools, and nutrition clinics; the necessities of life for refugees, victims of national disaster, tuberculosis, and leprosy; educational opportunities in vocational schools where students become self-supporting through learning animal husbandry, improved agricultural methods, automotive mechanics, sewing, etc.; food-for-work civic improvement projects, such as land reclamation, building roads, community centers, churches, houses, etc.; and public health, teaching sanitation, giving inoculations, well-digging, and construction.

Founding Date: 1946

1602. The World Today Broadcasts*

Nondenominational
Kenneth H. Freeman
Friendly, West Virginia 26146
(304) 657-2916

The work of World Today Broadcasts is centered in broadcasting programs of prophecy and inspiration by radio, with a number of stations in the United States carrying the programs. Broadcasts from Radio Cyprus cover all of the Middle East and Israel. Swazi Music Radio in South Africa reaches most of South Africa, and Radio Sri Lanka is heard in all of India and surrounding countries.

Publications:
   Magazine, monthly
Radio/TV Programs:
   15-minute radio programs

1603. World Union for Progressive Judaism (WUPJ)

Jewish
Mr. Gerard Daniel, President
838 Fifth Avenue
New York, New York 10021
(212) 249-0100

The World Union for Progressive Judaism was founded by representatives from six countries who gathered in London to establish an organization that would maintain the highest ideals of Jewish tradition by fostering the growth of liberal Judaism throughout the world. The World Union now includes congregations in 25 countries and the combined membership of these congregations, known variously as Reform, Progressive, or Liberal, totals 1,300,000. The World Union works to assure the Jewish future. Its programs are shaped by the concrete needs of individuals and communities, and strive to resist Jewish indifference and assimilation. The World Union offers organizational and financial assistance to new congregations in many countries; organizes youth programs; publishes prayer books and religious texts in several languages; and assigns and employs rabbis wherever there are Jews in search of their religious heritage.

Founding Date: 1926

Staff: 6

Membership: 1,500,000

Meetings:
> An international conference every two years in a different location

1604. World University Roundtable (WUR)

Interdenominational
Howard John Zitko, D.D., President
711 East Blacklodge Drive
Tucson, Arizona 85719
(602) 622-2170

The World University Roundtable is a corporation that created the World University as a non-profit educational corporation in the State of Arizona to research the New Education and to discover new and more effective methods of academic practice. Both corporations are endeavoring: to fulfill the needs and aspirations of men and women of goodwill, who are preparing themselves for their part in building the world of the Planetary Age; to set before the student a broad overview of man's extant learning and to suggest the areas of research and study which will advance his comprehension of what lies within his immediate future; to lift education into a new spiritual dimension by shifting the learning process from mind training to soul cognition; to synthesize a group of world servers into a single cooperative coalition of spiritually motivated and responsible executives; to merge faculties of New Age learning and research centers across the world into a single, indivisible, autonomous educational commonwealth; to demonstrate to the vanguard of twentieth century man a twenty-second century learning in a twenty-

first century environment; and to evolve human consciousness and human character until the initiate stands free of all harm, suffering, and disintegration.

Founding Date: 1967

Staff:
> 2 staff members
> Volunteers

Membership: 300 general membership

Publications:
> *International Newsletter,* monthly
> Supplements, monthly
> Annual Reports

Meetings:
> One annual conference, location varies

1605. World Vision International

Interdenominational
W. Stanley Mooneyham, President
919 West Huntington Drive
Monrovia, California 91016
(213) 357-7979

The objectives of World Vision International are: ministering to children and families — assisting needy children through orphanage, school, and family aid programs by feeding, clothing, nurturing, healing, and spiritual ministries; providing emergency aid — providing food, medical aid, and immediate housing programs for people suffering as a result of war or natural disasters; developing self-reliance — helping people to produce adequate food, earn income, and create a community life resulting in long-term survival and growth; reaching the unreached — assisting indigenous evangelistic efforts to reach the lost for Jesus Christ; strengthening leadership — helping Christian leaders throughout the world to attain a more effective Christian ministry; and challenging to mission — calling Christians around the world to carry out the work of Christ where opportunity presents itself.

Founding Date: 1950

Staff: 150

Membership:
> Approximately 10,000 members at the project level

Publications:
> *MARC Newsletter,* monthly
> *Christian Leadership Letter,* monthly

Radio/TV Programs:
> *Come Love the Children,* 5 hour telethon TV

Hand to Hand, 1 hour special

Escape to No Where, half hour documentary on boat people

Meetings:

Approximately 6 Pastors' Conferences in developing nations each year

Former Name: (1978) World Vision Incorporated

1606. World's Christian Endeavor Union

Interdenominational

Charles W. Barner, General Secretary

1221 East Broad Street

Columbus, Ohio 43216

Mailing Address:

Post Office Box 1110

Columbus, Ohio 43216

(614) 258-9545

The World's Christian Endeavor Union seeks to unite in closer fellowship the Christian endeavorers of the world; to promote the interests of the Christian Endeavor Movement; to reinforce the Christian churches in every land; and to cement the spiritual union of Christians the world around. The Union is composed of two areas: Area I, composed of the Americas, the Caribbean, the Pacific Region, and Asia (with the exception of the countries named in Area II); and Area II, composed of Europe, Africa, India, Pakistan, and the Near East. The Union and its work are financed by annual contributions from national and international unions, personal gifts, and offerings. There are no full-time paid employees and most of the work is carried on by volunteer service. The World's Union has no power to legislate for any local society or local, state, provincial, national, or international union, but seeks to promote fellowship and understanding among Christians around the world based on the Christian Endeavor Pledge which begins: "Trusting in the Lord Jesus Christ for strength, I promise Him that I will strive to do whatever He would like to have me do . . ."

Founding Date: 1895

Publications:

The Christian Endeavor World

Meetings:

World Christian Endeavor Conventions every four years

Area Conferences between world conventions

1607. Worldteam*

Nondenominational

J. Allen Thompson, General Director

Post Office Box 343038

Coral Gables, Florida 33134

Worldteam is a nondenominational sending agency of independent tradition, establishing churches and serving national churches. The Mission is a member of IFMA, and is involved in education, medicine, child care, radio, and translation work. Areas of service are: Bahamas, Brazil, Cuba, Dominican Republic, Grenada, Guadeloupe, Haiti, Italy, Jamaica, Spain, St. Lucia, St. Vincent, Surinam, Trinidad and Tobago.

Membership: 81,165

Publications:

Religious study books — 12 titles

2 periodicals

Radio/TV Programs:

2 radio programs, religious

Meetings:

10 per year

Former Name: (1978) West Indies Mission

1608. World Wide Christian Chiropractors Association

Baptist

Cecil "Cec" Manewal, Executive Director

2224 South College Avenue

Fort Collins, Colorado 80525

The Christian Chiropractors Association offers the chiropractic profession a Christian fellowship in which believers of various denominational backgrounds can fellowship and serve the Lord Jesus Christ together. It seeks to gather and unify Christian Doctors of Chiropractic around the essentials of the Christian faith, leaving minor points of doctrine to the conscience of the individual believer. Personal faith in Jesus Christ and His Word is the basis of the fellowship. The Christian Chiropractors Association is conservative in theology, believing the Bible to be inspired, the only infallible, authoritative Word of God; believing in the deity of our Lord Jesus Christ, in His virgin birth, in His vicarious atoning death, and in His personal return in power and glory; believing that for the salvation of lost and sinful man, regeneration by the Holy Spirit is absolutely essential. The Christian Chiropractors Associaton places world missions at the heart of its program. Now contributing to several different mission fields, it looks forward to a constantly enlarging vision of missions that will assist in sending Christian Chiropractors out to many whitened harvest fields with the Gospel of Christ and Chiropractic before Christ comes.

Membership: 700

Publications:
Monthly newsletter

Meetings:
Approximately 10 a year across the United States

1609. Worldwide Evangelization Crusade (WEC)

Nondenominational

Rev. Elwin Palmer, General Director of the United States
Post Office Box A
Fort Washington, Pennsylvania 19034
(215) 646-2322

The Worldwide Evangelization Crusade is a foreign missionary sending organization founded by Charles T. Studd. The Crusade's aims are: to fulfill as speedily as possible the command of the Lord Jesus Christ to go and teach all nations by a definite attempt to evangelize the remaining unevangelized peoples of the Earth before His return; to plant local churches according to the pattern of the New Testament and establish them in the knowledge of the Word of God and spiritual power, and also to minister to existing churches when invited to do so; and to develop bases worldwide for the training and sending out of personnel to further the work of evangelization according to Acts 1:8, and to work together with other agencies of a similar vision. The following ministries are among those carried on in various fields: medical work including hospitals and clinics; literature work; radio; agricultural work in connection with Bible Schools; correspondence work; printing; teaching; student work among college and university students; translation projects; and the use of cassettes and films in a preaching and teaching ministry.

Founding Date: 1913

Staff:
104 overseas staff members
48 home staff or retired members

Publications:
Thrust, an official communique, monthly
Go, bimonthly, in English for Chinese Christians
OK, a bilingual (English-Chinese) bimonthly magazine for all Chinese
Youth, a quarterly youth paper for Third World students

Radio/TV Programs:
Broadcasts in several of the overseas fields

Meetings:
Monthly public conferences in the United States and Canada
Staff Conferences in the United States and Canada twice yearly
Missions Study Program in the United States twice yearly

Former Name: (1919) Heart of Africa Mission

1610. Worldwide Marriage Encounter

Interdenominational

Al and Barbara Regnier and Fr. Des Colleran, United States Executive Team
3711 Long Beach Boulevard, Suite 204
Long Beach, California 90807
(213) 595-5336

Worldwide Marriage Encounter is a program of Christian information to instruct married couples in the means to find God's plan in their lives, for their own spiritual development and the betterment of all humankind; and to develop, foster, and disseminate an adult catechesis supporting, furthering, and building upon such instruction. Worldwide Marriage Encounter offers the marriage encounter weekend experience in 150 dioceses in the United States as well as in 58 foreign countries. In the United States, over 1 million couples and 6,000 priests and bishops have experienced the Worldwide weekend.

Founding Date: 1969

Publications:
Worldwide Family Spirit, 10 issues per year

Radio/TV Programs:
Love Spots, co-produced with the Franciscan Communication Center, used as public service spots
INSIGHT, Paulist Productions
Decision To Love, 30-minute TV show

Meetings:
1 National Convention per year

1611. The World-Wide Missionary Crusader, Inc.

Nondenominational
Homer Duncan, Executive Director
4606 Avenue H
Lubbock, Texas 79404
(806) 747-5417

The World-Wide Missionary Crusader publishes a monthly 24-page magazine designed to create interest in and to inform about world missions. The Crusader also publishes a series of over 75 books and booklets dealing with various aspects of the Christian life; some are evangelistic, others are for new believers. The booklets are written primarily for overseas audiences. The Crusader is currently working in about 30 different foreign languages; however, it has published materials in over a hundred languages.

Founding Date: 1943
Publications:
  Missionary Crusader, monthly

1612. World-Wide Missions

Interdenominational
Esther M. Howard, President and Director
1593 East Colorado Boulevard
Pasadena, California 91106

Mailing Address
Post Office Box G
Pasadena, California 91109
(213) 449-4313

World-Wide Missions is a non-profit missionary organization. It now witnesses for Christ in 38 nations of the world. The organization has established churches, schools, hospitals, orphanages, and leper colonies. Its foreign staff consists of 2,500 missionaries, national pastors, evangelists, teachers, doctors, and nurses. The Missions' purpose is to minister to the whole person—body, mind, and soul. This extensive missionary soul-saving program is made possible through the prayers and gifts of devoted friends of all church groups.

Founding Date: 1950
Staff:
  25 home office staff
  2,500 overseas personnel
Publications:
  World-Wide Missions, monthly

1613. World Wide Pictures

Interdenominational
William F. Brown, President
1201 Hennepin Avenue
Minneapolis, Minnesota 55403
(612) 338-3335

World Wide Pictures was conceived in the early 1950's as an extended ministry of the Billy Graham Evangelistic Association. The film, *Mr. Texas,* starring Redd Harper, has been dubbed into several languages, and though over two decades old, is still shown around the world, particularly on mission fields. Since that first effort, World Wide Pictures has produced more than 100 films. Over 50 million viewers have attended showings of these films, and nearly one and half million persons have been individually counseled following the showings. Many of the films are available in foreign language editions—17 languages in all—and are shown on mission fields around the globe, as well as in churches, hospitals, prisons, schools, theatres, and civic auditoriums. Another facet of their ministry involves television presentations, both on local stations and on cable systems. The central purpose of all the organization's films, whether dramatic or documentary, is to show that Jesus Christ, and He alone, is the answer to mankind's problems and needs—that a personal, vital relationship with Him is not only possible, but necessary, if we are to fulfill the purpose for which we are created.

Founding Date: 1952
Staff: 75
Publications:
  World Wide Family
Former Name:
  Billy Graham Evangelistic Film Ministry, Inc.

1614. Wycliffe Associates, Inc. (WA)

Interdenominational
Alfred L. Ginty, Executive Vice President
202 South Prospect Street
Orange, California 92669

Mailing Address
Post Office Box 2000
Orange, California 92669
(714) 639-9950

Wycliffe Associates is the lay ministry of Wycliffe Bible Translators and has the same purpose as WBT—to make God's Word available in every language. Wycliffe Associates provides a channel through which lay people can have a part in Bible translation both at home and on the field. WA takes on special projects, providing funds through faith-promise banquets and the Newsletter and providing physical help on the fields through short-term work parties who do construction, maintenance, and installation of equipment. Personal services to Wycliffe missionaries include providing linens, a roster of hospitality homes where they can stay when traveling, cassette tapes of sermons, and a program called "Aunts and Uncles" for the missionaries' high school and college-age children going to school in the United States. Wycliffe Associates is a charter member of the Evangelical Council for Financial Accountability.

Founding Date: 1967

Staff: 21

Membership: 9,200

Publications:
　Wycliffe Associates Newsletter, 10 issues per year

Meetings:
　Annual Meeting once a year, various locations
　Quarterly Board Meetings
　200 banquets per year

1615. Wycliffe Bible Translators (WBT)

Nondenominational

Dr. Frank Robbins, Executive Vice President
19891 Beach Boulevard
Huntington Beach, California 92648
(714) 536-9346

Wycliffe Bible Translators, Inc., is dedicated to translating God's Word into the languages of the world that do not have it, and thus proclaiming and propagating the Gospel of the Lord Jesus Christ. There are still more than 3,000 languages of the world that have never been analyzed and written down. Before the speakers of such languages can have God's written Word, linguistic work must be done. Wycliffe does basic linguistic analysis and then follows through with translating the Bible into each of these languages. During this process many native speakers open their hearts to Christ as their Savior. Wycliffe translators are currently working in 680 minority languages in about 30 countries in North America, Latin America, Africa, Asia, and the Pacific. Of WBT's total membership, half are translators and half are support workers (pilots,

mechanics, teachers, administrators, medical personnel, agriculturists, etc.). Serving as a team, these members have completed 108 New Testaments. By 1985 it is anticipated that the number of printed New Testaments will be increased to 300.

Founding Date: 1935

Staff: 4,059

Publications:
　In Other Words, monthly

Radio/TV Programs:
　5-minute daily radio program *Translation Report*

1616. Xavier Society for the Blind (XSB)

Roman Catholic
Rev. A. F. LaBau, SJ, Director
154 East 23rd Street
New York, New York 10010
(212) 743-7800

Xavier Society for the Blind was founded by Rev. Joseph Stadelman, S.J., to serve the blind and visually handicapped. It operated for some time from the basement of Xavier High School; however, the name Xavier Society has a wider meaning these days, being known throughout the world as the largest private Braille library of any religious denomination, the largest single religious source of large print material in any language, and the largest producer of reading matter on cassettes for the visually impaired. Its specialities are textbooks for students at any level of education; a weekly spiritual newsletter in braille for the deafblind who have no other means of regular contact with developments in the church; and current periodicals on cassettes, a service it pioneered to bring to the visually impaired news and information in depth on religious matters.

Founding Date: 1900

Staff: 15

Membership: 4,000 blind people

Publications:
A weekly spiritual newsletter in Braille
Currently periodicals on cassettes

1617. Xaverian Brothers Auxiliary

Xaverian Brothers of Sacred Heart Province
Brother John Joseph, CFX, Director
10516 Summit Avenue
Kensington, Maryland 20895
(301) 946-5354

Xaverian Brothers Auxiliary is an organization of the Sacred Heart Province whose purpose is to publish the activities of the Brothers; news such as deaths, jubilees, elections, projects, and mission works.

Founding Date: 1929

Staff: 3

Membership: 5,000

Publications:
The Xaverian Brothers Auxiliary Newsletter, quarterly

1619. YWCA, National Board (Young Women's Christian Association)

Nondenominational
Mrs. Sara-Alyce P. Wright, Executive Director
600 Lexington Avenue
New York, New York 10022
(212) 753-4700

The YWCA of the United States is a multiservice organization serving women and girls of all ages; the mission of the YWCA is expressed in its Purpose, which calls on the organization to draw together women and girls of diverse experiences and faiths ". . . that their lives may be open to new understanding and deeper relationships and that together they may join in the struggles for peace and justice, freedom and dignity for all people." Out of the Purpose has grown an imperative to work toward the elimination of racism as an overriding thrust. Service programs include those in health, recreation, clubs and classes, and counseling and assistance to women and girls in the areas of employment, education, human sexuality, health, and juvenile justice. Advocacy programs address the conditions creating the need for services and include: passage of ERA; equal pay for work of comparable value; human rights/Southern Africa/political prisoners; development assistance to Third World countries; preservation of the legal option of abortion; prevention of teenage pregnancy; and support of the Fair Housing Amendments Act of 1979.

Founding Date: 1855

Staff: 23,653

Membership: 2,455,509

Publications:
> *YWCA Interchange,* 6 times yearly
> Manuals and pamphlets on YWCA history and purpose, program administration
> 5 newsletters
> Slides sets for program and recruitment
> Audiovisuals for use on radio and television

Radio/TV Programs:
> Public service announcements

Meetings:
> Training conferences 2-3 times a year at various locations
> Convention-related meetings yearly
> Special program plans sessions regionally and nationally
> National Convention every 3 years

1620. Yavneh, National Religious Jewish Students Association*

Orthodox Judaism

Naomi Terner, National President
156 Fifth Avenue
New York, New York 10010
(212) 929-5434

Yavneh is the National Religious Jewish Student Association which strives to unite both Orthodox Jewish youth and those Jews interested in Orthodoxy through a network of campus-based chapters throughout the United States and Canada. Yavneh is not affiliated with any parent body, but is completely student-run. The organization's chapters sponsor weekends for college and graduate students, lecture series, and other educational/social programs. Kol Yavneh, a magazine by and for Jewish students, is published and distributed nationally by the organization as are educational mailings and other publications. Yavneh believes in promoting Jewish education, facilitating full observance of Halachic Judaism, and following the ideals of religious Zionism. Yavneh is a member of the North American Jewish Student Appeal.

Publications:
> Books
> Yavneh newsletter
> *Kol Yavneh,* bimonthly

Meetings:
> 4 major conventions a year
> Professional seminar series – sponsored 4 times a year
> Weekends – sponsored by each chapter individually
> Annual National Labor Day Convention

1621. Yokefellows International Prison Ministry*

Nondenominational

230 College Avenue
Richmond, Indiana 47374

The Yokefellows International Prison Ministry is an interdenominational and interracial movement of volunteers. Its purpose is to bring the concern, compassion, and love of Jesus Christ to those in prisons and jails. Its pattern of operation is to establish small Yokefellow groups (usually 12 persons in each group) which meet each week to share in realistic discussions of how they can develop attitudes and skills which will enable them to live constructive lives. They examine their attitudes in the light of Christian concepts of living, seek to discover talents and skills they can use, and develop patterns of life which are meaningful and soul-satisfying. The inmates have a chance to talk about their lives and what they expect to do with them, to examine God's love and concern for them, and to show concern for fellow inmates and people beyond prison walls. While the Yokefellows Prison Ministry's primary purpose is to offer inmates an opportunity to meet in small groups with outside Yokefellows, other objectives include those of developing helpful relationships with families of inmates, the relating of former inmates to Yokefellow groups on the outside, the examination and possible adoption of alternatives to incarceration such as half-way houses, and working to eliminate the causes of crime.

1622. Young Adult League

Greek Orthodox

Rev. Constantine L. Sitaras, National Coordinator
8 East 79th Street
New York, New York 10021
(212) 628-2500

Young Adult League is the name of the youth program of the Greek Orthodox Archdiocese of America. It is directed towards serving the young people as they search to realize in themselves the living and resurrected Lord of Life. Through various programs, manuals, newspapers, and religious and social methods, they seek to develop Christ's icon in every man and woman. Activities vary on the local level, but the theme is the same: becoming God's best icon in the world.

Founding Date: 1951

Staff: 10

Membership: 193,000 young people

Publications:
>*Challenge,* a monthly youth newspaper
>*Be Ye Advised,* a newletter directed toward youth workers

Meetings:
>Annual meetings in various areas of the country

Former Name:
>Greek Orthodox Youth of America

1623. Young Calvinist Federation (YCF)*

Christian Reformed Church

Rev. James C. Lont, Director
1333 Alger S.E.
Grand Rapids, Michigan 49510

Mailing Address
Post Office Box 7244
Grand Rapids, Michigan 49510
(616) 241-5616

The Young Calvinist Federation is the youth ministry of the Christian Reformed Church and services more than 700 youth groups with leadership training, programming materials, reviews of films, books, songbooks, plays and drama, retreat programs, discussion materials and many of the other activities necessary for a ministry to youth. It also publishes two magazines, *Insight* and *Input*. *Insight* is a magazine for young people, and offers Bible study materials and discussion materials, as well as reviews on TV programs, movies, and books. *Input* is a magazine for youth leaders with ideas for leading groups and ideas for programming.

Membership: 15,000 lay; about 700 clerical

Publications:
>*Insight,* monthly
>*Input,* bimonthly

Meetings:
>Leadership Training in 16 different areas of the United States and Canada

1624. Young Life

Nondenominational

Robert Mitchell, President/Executive Director
720 West Monument Street
Colorado Springs, Colorado 80901

Mailing Address
Post Office Box 520
Colorado Springs, Colorado 80901
(303) 473-4262

Young Life's purpose is to present to adolescents the person of Jesus Christ and His relevance to modern life. It attempts to communicate these concepts in simple, understandable terms, and through meaningful personal relationships. Young Life welcomes young people of any race or faith. It believes everyone has a right to hear the truth and then to make his own choice, without coercion or highly emotional appeal.

Founding Date: 1941

Membership: 900 lay members

Publications:
>*Outlook,* 3 times a year

Former Name: Young Life Campaign

1625. Your Worship Hour

Nondenominational

Rev. Quinton J. Everest, Pastor-Director
3501 East Jefferson Boulevard
South Bend, Indiana 46615

Mailing Address
Post Office Box 6366
South Bend, Indiana 46660
(219) 233-1414

The purpose of Your Worship Hour is to present the Gospel to the multitudes around the world via radio and the printed page.

Founding Date: 1933

Staff: 7

Publications:
Sermon books

1626. Youth for Christ/USA, Inc. (YFC/USA)

Nondenominational
Jay Kesler, President
360 South Main Place
Carol Stream, Illinois 60187

Mailing Address
Post Office Box 419
Wheaton, Illinois 60187
(312) 668-6600

The purpose of Youth for Christ/USA is to participate within the body of Christ in the responsible evangelism of youth, presenting them with the teachings of Christ and discipling them into the church. It is the intention of YFC/USA, through every legitimate means, to encourage young people to witness to their peers and to live out their faith in their community. The 4,800 staff members of YFC, through the Campus Life program for mainstream teenagers, and Youth Guidance program for troubled teenagers, have regular contact with approximately 35,000 teenagers in club meetings, weekend camping trips, court referrals, group homes, neighborhood ministries, services in juvenile institutions, and large social and instructional events. Evangelism is viewed as both confrontational (explicitly explaining one's need for a personal relationship with Christ) and relational (sharing God's love through an accepting compassionate relationship with others). The "whole person" emphasis of YFC attempts an integration or balance of all areas of life—physical, mental, social, and spiritual. Family ministry through seminars, resource materials, and research of family concern complements the work with young people.

Founding Date: 1944

Staff:
1,000 full-time staff
3,800 part-time and volunteer staff

Publications:
Homemade, monthly
Campus Life, monthly

Radio/TV Programs:
The Youth for Christ, Johnny Cash TV Special, 3-4 hour special aired in selected television markets
Family Forum, a 5-minute daily radio program

Meetings:
Holiday Teen Conventions between Christmas and New Year's in 9 regions
Training Institute annually for new staff
Annual staff conference
Summer conferences in 9 regions for teenagers
Weekly meetings of Campus Life Clubs and Youth Guidance small groups
Family Affair Seminars for adults and church leaders

Former Name: (1913) Youth for Christ International

1627. Yugntruf Youth for Yiddish

Jewish
William Rosenfeld, Chairperson
3328 Bainbridge Avenue
Bronx, New York 10467
(212) 654-8540

Yugntruf was founded to give young people an opportunity to come together to speak Yiddish; read and study Yiddish works; and write, sing, dance, act, and create in Yiddish. It is affiliated with no political movement. Its members are of all ideological persuasions. Although all activities are conducted in Yiddish, only minimal fluency is required for membership. For Yugntruf, Yiddish is more than just a mode of linguistic expression in which one can take an academic interest. It is one of the symbols of the Jewish identity. It is an integral part of Jewish culture which connects Jews around the world with Jewish life during the last thousand years. Yugntruf is interested in ensuring the survival of Yiddish as a *living* language and culture. The fact that there was a Sholem Aleichem or Peretz is not enough to sustain a living culture. Culture cannot remain static, there must be new creativity and growth. Yugntruf aims to add the youthful vitality and creativity so seriously needed.

Founding Date: 1964

Staff: 3

Membership: 2,000

Publications:
Yugntruf, a quarterly magazine written and edited entirely by high school, college, and graduate students in Yiddish

Meetings:
Regular meetings to plan activities
Yearly winter conference
Yearly retreat of immersion in Yiddish in summer

1628. The Zondervan Corporation

Nondenominational

Peter Kladder, Jr., President
1415 Lake Drive, S.E.
Grand Rapids, Michigan 49506
(616) 459-6900

The Zondervan Corporation is a publisher of religious books, Bibles, and music, and a producer of religious records on a wholesale basis for sale to religious and general book stores, record stores, music stores, and college, seminary, and school book stores. They also publish religious textbooks and operate 56 religious book stores through the Zondervan Family Bookstore Division in the United States. Their products are sold throughout the United States, Canada, and around the world. The corporation's main purpose is to publish and produce materials that will lead men, women and children around the world to a knowledge of Jesus Christ as their Savior and Lord. They are nondenominational in character. They operate their own printing plant and shipping facilities. An additional operation is the publication of a 24-volume Book of Life, sold house-to-house through the Zondervan Book of Life Division.

Staff: 600

Meetings:

> Three sales meetings per year for book, Bible, and music salesmen, two of which are in Grand Rapids and one in conjunction with the Christian Booksellers Convention in July wherever it is held.
>
> Retreats for the Zondervan Book of Life division in various areas.